Medicinal Mandates

Nan Xia

Medicinal Mandates

The Intersection of Chinese Traditional Medical Knowledge and Modern Law

Springer

Nan Xia
Law School
China Jiliang University
Hangzhou, Zhejiang, China

ISBN 978-981-96-4107-9 ISBN 978-981-96-4108-6 (eBook)
https://doi.org/10.1007/978-981-96-4108-6

This Springer imprint is published by the registered company Springer Nature Singapore Pte Ltd.
The registered company address is: 152 Beach Road, #21-01/04 Gateway East, Singapore 189721, Singapore

Contents

Chapter 1
Introduction

1.1 Introduction

China, a civilisation that proudly stands among the world's oldest, possesses a wealth of unique and varied traditions.[1] These traditions paint a vibrant picture of contrasting histories and remarkable diversity, in terms of historical experiences and social and cultural aspects.[2] Emerging prominently from the traditions is traditional medical knowledge ('TMK'). This wisdom, rooted deeply in China's cultural soil for thousands of years, continues to retain its dynamism, adaptability, and relevance today.[3]

Despite the immense value of this knowledge, there are significant challenges and concerns associated with ensuring its adequate protection, proper utilisation, and suitable dissemination. Deeply intertwined with the history, culture, and identities of Chinese national and local communities, as well as of individual knowledge bearers, this wisdom is vulnerable to misinterpretation and misuse if extracted from its original context and employed by external entities without obtaining proper consent or providing due recognition.[4] Furthermore, the widespread commercialisation of traditional medical practices and remedies frequently marginalises the original guardians of this wisdom, depriving them of just financial rewards. Such disregard for equitable profit sharing only intensifies the prevailing economic disparities, signalling an urgent need for increased awareness and more stringent regulations. Given these considerations, it is crucial to maintain and protect this valuable storehouse of wisdom, to foster respectful use, adequate protection, and informed, thoughtful dissemination.

---

[1] David Curtis Wright, The History of China (ABC-CLIO, LLC, 2020) 11.

[2] Ibid.

[3] Anita Chen Marshall, 'Traditional Chinese Medicine and Clinical Pharmacology' in FJ Hock and MR Gralinski (eds), Drug Discovery and Evalu*ation: Methods in Clinical Pharmacology* (Springer Nature Switzerland AG, 2020) 463.

[4] Hallen Korn, 'Patenting Culture: The Cultural Conflict of Intellectual Property' (2012) 8 *The Morningside Review* 11, 13–14.

N. Xia, *Medicinal Mandates*, https://doi.org/10.1007/978-981-96-4108-6_1

This study explores China's unique historical and cultural nuances, and their influence on the interaction with, and shaping of, Chinese TMK. It also critically examines how these factors harmonise with globally recognised mechanisms dedicated to the protection, application, and dissemination of this knowledge. The book primarily focuses on three key mechanisms: the Intellectual Property ('IP') framework, the access and benefit-sharing ('ABS') system, and TMK information systems. Each of these systems plays a significant role in the protection, utilisation, and dissemination of TMK, together forming a robust strategy that contributes uniquely to the overall regulatory landscape in China. The implications of these systems, as viewed through the lens of China's unique sociocultural and historical landscape, are of immense significance.

Firstly, the IP framework is a universally established mechanism for the protection of knowledge and inventions.[5] This framework, when expertly applied to scientific knowledge and technological innovations, can significantly stimulate progress and innovation.[6] By providing robust legal protection, it serves as a strong incentive for thorough documentation, comprehensive research, and meticulous refinement of various areas of knowledge.[7] This encouragement not only aids in advancing the understanding of science and technology but also drives improvements in various sectors, including healthcare.[8] In this way, the treatments and solutions derived from cutting-edge scientific knowledge and technological innovation can continually evolve, improving lives and meeting the demands of the changing world.[9]

However, applying the IP framework, grounded in Western constructs of individual ownership and innovation, to Chinese TMK, introduces certain complexities. This body of knowledge is innately collective, dynamic, and passed down through generations.[10] This contrasts with the typical Western IP paradigms, presenting unique challenges to the integration of TMK with the existing IP framework.

Given these considerations, the current IP framework may not offer adequate protection for Chinese TMK. Its imposition could inadvertently result in misinterpretations and misappropriations of this body of knowledge.[11] It is therefore necessary to critically analyse the issues through a cultural-historical lens, which allows for a

---

[5] Shoaib Ali and Heng Tang, 'Is Intellectual Property Beneficial to Knowledge Management? Literature Review on Organizational Knowledge Protection' (2022) *Journal of the Knowledge Economy* 1, 1–15.

[6] Y Karanja and RL Murphy, 'Intellectual Property Protection and Commercialisation' in T.S. Douglas et al (eds), *Biomedical Engineering for Africa* (University of Cape Town Libraries, 2019) 161–162.

[7] Ibid.

[8] Shruti Dwivedi et al, 'Intellectual Property Rights in Healthcare: An Overview' in Debmalya Barh (eds), *Biotechnology in Healthcare* (Academic Press, 2022) 259–266.

[9] Ibid.

[10] 邓明峰 [Deng Mingfeng],《我国民族中医药传统知识专利保护研究》[Research on Patent Protection for TMK of China's Ethnic Groups] (2018) 12 贵州民族研究 *Guizhou Ethnic Studies* 96, 98.

[11] 彭丁带 [Peng Dingdai],《专利海盗"的危害及其法律应对》[The Harm of 'Patent Piracy' and Its Legal Response] (2017) 5 江西社会科学 *Jiangxi Social Science* 195, 197.

deeper understanding of the unique context surrounding Chinese TMK and helps to identify potential gaps in the current IP system.

Additionally, it is imperative to investigate prospective improvements, adaptations, or even alternative approaches that can effectively close the gap between the distinctive cultural and historical complexities of Chinese TMK and the globally recognised doctrines of IP mechanisms. The adoption of a cultural-historical lens in this exploration allows for a nuanced understanding of these complexities. This perspective facilitates an understanding of the context in which Chinese TMK has evolved, the cultural beliefs that inform it, and the historical factors that have shaped its development. This approach recognises that the mismatch between the current IP system and Chinese TMK is not simply a technical issue but one that is deeply embedded within broader cultural and historical contexts. Therefore, any proposed modifications or alternative strategies must be mindful of these aspects to ensure effective, respectful, and appropriate protection and utilisation of Chinese TMK.

Secondly, ABS is another pivotal mechanism that acknowledges and protects traditional knowledge, with TMK being a prime example.[12] This concept is deeply rooted in the principles of equity and fairness and is embedded in international law through the United Nations ('UN') *Convention on Biological Diversity* ('CBD') and its supplementary agreement, the *Nagoya Protocol*. ABS frameworks provide a structured approach for the effective protection and respectful usage of traditional knowledge.[13] In the specific context of China's TMK, these frameworks serve a crucial role in preventing misappropriation and unauthorised exploitation.[14] They ensure that appropriate recognition and compensation are extended to TMK holders and communities, and provide mechanisms to address potential misuse or misappropriation by external parties.[15] Moreover, these frameworks guarantee that the commercial exploitation of traditional medical practices does not marginalise the original guardians of this knowledge.[16]

While the ABS standards are designed to have global applicability, it is essential to consider the potential cultural disparities when implementing them in diverse sociocultural environments such as China. The unique historical and sociocultural subtleties of China's approach to the protection, utilisation, and dissemination of TMK may not align entirely with the fundamental beliefs and designs of international ABS standards, mostly shaped by Western values and ideologies.

---

[12] Gulzar S Sanghera, Dharminder Bhatia and KS Thind, 'Access and Benefit Sharing on the Use of Indigenous Traditional Knowledge' in Romesh Kumar Salgotra and Bharat Bhushan Gupta (eds), *Plant Genetic Resources and Traditional Knowledge for Food Security* (Springer, 2016) 163, 171–179.

[13] Ibid.

[14] 王华[Wang Hua],《中医药传统知识利益分享权研究》[Research on the Right to Share Benefits of Traditional Chinese Medicine Knowledge] [2017], 南京中医药大学学报 *Journal of Nanjing University of Traditional Chinese Medicine* 165, 167–168.

[15] Ibid.

[16] Ibid.

This study adopts a cultural-historical perspective to critically examine the potential discrepancies that may arise when implementing universally accepted ABS principles in a Chinese context. This investigation offers a deeper understanding of the nuanced interplay between global ABS norms and local Chinese realities.

It highlights the limitations of applying a one-size-fits-all approach and highlights the necessity for a more culturally sensitive implementation of ABS principles within China. It also calls attention to the pressing need for a comprehensive review and possible recalibration of ABS norms in order to harmonise them with China's unique historical and sociocultural landscape. Ultimately, the book contributes to the broader discourse on the reconciliation of universal principles with Chinese TMK in the unique local contexts of China.

Lastly, TMK information systems are also an internationally recognised system, taking on a myriad of roles in protecting, documenting, and disseminating TMK.[17] Far from being mere repositories, these information systems play a dynamic and composite role in preserving and promoting traditional medical practices across the world.[18]

When TMK is converted into a digitised format, these information systems provide a stable and durable platform that not only preserves but also protects this knowledge from unauthorised exploitation amidst rapid societal changes, such as urbanisation, generational transitions, and cultural shifts.[19] The digitisation process also enhances the accessibility of TMK, making it available to a broader audience, while still upholding the intent to respect and protect the rights of the original knowledge holders.[20] In addition, TMK information systems play a pivotal role in the dissemination of knowledge. They serve as platforms for the exchange of valuable medical insights, facilitating cross-cultural learning and promoting understanding among diverse communities.

While TMK information systems provide significant benefits, it is critical to acknowledge that such a mechanism could inadvertently superimpose Western values on this knowledge.[21] This stems from the fact that Western systems of categorisation and organisation underpin these technological constructs.[22] In effect, the risk of decontextualisation is high, as TMK, particularly from China, is deeply embedded within the nation's unique history and culture, which might not align with the epistemological foundations of current technological designs. The creation of these information systems, despite their well-intentioned goals of preserving and promoting TMK, may inadvertently marginalise specific forms of TMK held by local and ethnic

[17] Evana Wright, Protecting Traditional Knowledge: Lessons from Global Case Studies (Edward Elgar Publishing, 2020) 168–195.

[18] Ibid.

[19] Thomas J Krumenacher, 'Protection for Indigenous Peoples and their Traditional Knowledge: Would a Registry System Reduce the Misappropriation of Traditional Knowledge?' (2004) 8(1) *Marquette Intellectual Property Law Review* 143, 155–156.

[20] Wright (n 17) 68.

[21] Martin Fredriksson, 'India's Traditional Knowledge Digital Library and the Politics of Patent Classifications' (2023) 34 *Law and Critique* 1, 10.

[22] Ibid.

communities. This may occur as dominant, State-endorsed practices are prioritised, potentially overshadowing the valuable knowledge and contributions of these diverse communities.

This is where a cultural-historical lens becomes crucial in this book. To implement and develop TMK information systems in China effectively, it is paramount to consider the cultural, social, and historical contexts from which Chinese TMK originates. It is essential to understand that Chinese TMK is more than just a compendium of medical practices, but rather is a dynamic, evolving embodiment of a community's relationship with nature and its holistic health approach.

Thus, employing a cultural-historical perspective encourages a more nuanced understanding of TMK information systems. It highlights the need to not just focus on the technicalities of digitisation, but also to safeguard the inherent cultural values, historical continuity, and societal importance of the knowledge they aim to capture. This critical analysis paves the way for a more balanced, inclusive, and culturally sensitive approach to preserving TMK in the digital age.

The implications of failing to reconcile China's unique bottom-up cultural-historical context with the top-down imposition of Western assumptions underlying IP framework, ABS system, and TMK information systems could be substantial and multifaceted for China's TMK.

Firstly, there is an increased risk of misappropriation and misuse of TMK if the distinct cultural-historical context is overlooked. This misunderstanding or misapplication could lead to unauthorised exploitation, potentially causing harm to both users of TMK and its original custodians. TMK, being more than just a collection of medical practices, represents a significant facet of cultural heritage and communal identity. Therefore, the imposition of an unfamiliar legal and policy framework could lead to the erosion of cultural diversity and identity. There is a risk that the unique characteristics inherent to Chinese TMK could be diminished or completely overshadowed by the imposition of homogenised, standardised frameworks that are primarily shaped by Western-centric perspectives.

Furthermore, a significant concern lies in the potential for escalated conflicts and tensions if a bridge cannot be built between the cultural and historical intricacies of China's approach to protecting, utilising, and disseminating TMK, and the Western assumptions underlying IP framework, ABS system, and TMK information systems. This discord could give rise to legal disputes and conflicts on multiple levels. These could include international disputes between China and other countries, as well as domestic disputes within China itself, particularly between local communities and industrial or corporate actors.

This book aims to fill a gap in current literature by blending both Western and Chinese perspectives on Traditional Medical Knowledge (TMK). While much has been written about the frameworks for protecting and disseminating TMK, few studies have focused specifically on the Chinese context.[23] Even fewer have drawn

[23] ANM Alamgir, *Therapeutic Use of Medicinal Plants and Their Extracts* (Springer, 2017); Jackson Owiti and Ashah Owano, 'Use of Mobile Technologies in Dissemination of Traditional Medical Knowledge in Kenya: Case Study of Kenya Resource Centre for Indigenous Knowledge' in Jackson

on both Chinese and English sources to offer a holistic view.[24] This book addresses that gap, offering an innovative approach that combines China's cultural, historical, and legal realities. It critically examines the challenges of applying Western frameworks—such as intellectual property (IP), access and benefit-sharing (ABS), and TMK information systems—to Chinese TMK, highlighting the unique complexities that arise from China's distinct sociocultural and historical context. The result is a more comprehensive understanding of TMK in China, offering valuable insights for both scholars and practitioners looking for a more nuanced perspective on this important issue.

1.2 Research Questions

The overarching research question in this book is: How can the cultural and historical nuances inherent in China's approach to protecting, utilising, and disseminating TMK be effectively reconciled with the internationally established frameworks for Intellectual Property, access, and benefit-sharing, and TMK information systems?

To guide the research, the following subsidiary questions are explored:

1. What are the historical and cultural factors contributing to the tension between the protection of TMK and the growing unauthorised use of TMK in China, and what are possible strategies to resolve this issue?
2. How have China's unique historical and sociocultural factors shaped the ways Chinese TMK is protected and utilised at the national and local levels within IP frameworks?
3. What insights do other tools, namely ABS systems and TMK information systems, offer policymakers for balancing the protection, utilisation, and dissemination of TMK in China's historical and sociocultural contexts?
4. What are the priority areas for reform in China's IP framework, ABS system, and TMK information systems that could bolster protection and ensure the culturally appropriate utilisation of its TMK?

Owiti and Ashah Owano (eds), *Digital Technologies for Information and Knowledge Management* (2019) 433, 433–437.

[24] Ibid.

1.3 Background to the Study

1.3.1 Defining TMK

The definition of traditional knowledge ('TK') has been a focal point of extensive debates in many international forums. This is especially evident in discussions related to biodiversity, human rights, and health-centric issues.[25] Despite its widespread use, there is no universally agreed definition of TK. The *Convention on Biological Diversity* ('CBD')[26] refrains from providing a definition, instead opting to use the

[25] The *Convention on Biological Diversity* ('CBD')—1992: The CBD promotes the conservation of biological diversity, the sustainable use of its components, and the fair and equitable sharing of benefits arising from the use of genetic resources, including TK associated with such resources; the *Nagoya Protocol on Access and Benefit-sharing* ('ABS')—2010: This protocol is a supplementary agreement to the CBD that provides a legal framework for the fair and equitable sharing of benefits arising from the utilisation of genetic resources and traditional knowledge associated with them; the World Intellectual Property Organization ('WIPO') Intergovernmental Committee on Intellectual Property and Genetic Resources, Traditional Knowledge and Folklore ('IGC'): Established in 2000, the IGC aims to develop international legal instruments to protect TK, traditional cultural expressions ('TCEs'), and genetic resources; the *United Nations Declaration on the Rights of Indigenous Peoples* ('UNDRIP')—2007: UNDRIP acknowledges the rights of Indigenous peoples, including the protection of their cultural heritage, traditional knowledge and traditional cultural expressions; the *International Treaty on Plant Genetic Resources for Food and Agriculture* ('ITPGRFA')—2001: also known as the Plant Treaty, it focuses on conserving and sustainable use of plant genetic resources for food and agriculture, and the fair and equitable sharing of benefits derived from their use; the *United Nations Convention to Combat Desertification* ('UNCCD')—1994: This convention recognises the role of traditional knowledge in addressing desertification and land degradation and encourages the involvement of local communities in conservation efforts; the *United Nations Framework Convention on Climate Change* ('UNFCCC')—1992, and its *Paris Agreement*—2015: Both recognise the importance of traditional knowledge in addressing climate change and encourage the involvement of Indigenous peoples and local communities in climate change-related actions; the *Convention for the Safeguarding of Intangible Cultural Heritage*—2003: This UNESCO treaty aims to safeguard intangible cultural heritage, which includes traditional knowledge and practices, and promotes the respect and awareness of the importance of such heritage; the *Biodiversity Beyond National Jurisdiction* ('BBNJ')—ongoing negotiations: The BBNJ process is aimed at developing a legally binding instrument under the *United Nations Convention on the Law of the Sea* ('UNCLOS') for the conservation and sustainable use of marine biodiversity in areas beyond national jurisdiction. Traditional knowledge is expected to be an important aspect of the negotiations, particularly in terms of access to and sharing benefits from marine genetic resources; *Pandemic Influenza Preparedness (PIP) Framework*—2011: The PIP Framework is a global initiative under the World Health Organization ('WHO') that aims to improve and strengthen the sharing of influenza viruses with human pandemic potential and increase access to vaccines and other benefits. Traditional knowledge related to health and medicine is relevant in this context, as the framework recognises the importance of local and Indigenous knowledge in pandemic preparedness and response.

[26] *United Nations Convention on Biological Diversity*, opened for signature 5 June 1992, 1760 UNTS 79 (entered into force 29 December 1993).

phrase 'knowledge, innovations and practices of Indigenous and local communities embodying traditional lifestyles'.[27]

The World Intellectual Property Organization ('WIPO') adopts a working definition that aligns with other international frameworks. It describes TK as 'tradition-based literary, artistic or scientific works; performances; inventions; scientific discoveries; designs; marks and symbols; undisclosed information; and all other tradition-based innovations and creations resulting from intellectual activity in the industrial, scientific, literary or artistic fields'.[28]

However, this definition has been met with criticism as it is predominantly framed by those with a primary interest in IP rights.[29] This perspective potentially overlooks the fact that Indigenous peoples and local communities might not wish to contribute their knowledge to a framework that does not fully respect or understand the cultural significance and value of that knowledge.[30]

This critique underscores an important aspect often emphasised in international law and discourse: the intimate relationship between TK and its custodians—specifically, Indigenous peoples and local communities.[31] A notable reflection of this emphasis is enshrined in Article 31 of the *United Nations Declaration on the Rights of Indigenous Peoples* ('UNDRIP'), which advocates for the rights of Indigenous peoples to maintain, control, protect, and develop their cultural heritage, traditional knowledge, and traditional cultural expressions.[32] Nevertheless, this declaration, while broad, lacks enforceability and does not adequately address the intricate layers involved in defining and ensuring the protection of TK. When interpreted on its own, it merely serves as a general acknowledgement of the necessity for TK protection rather than offering specific measures or mechanisms.

---

[27] CBD (n 24) art 8(j); Article 8(j) states: 'Each contracting Party shall, as far as possible and as appropriate: Subject to national legislation, respect, preserve and maintain knowledge, innovations and practices of Indigenous and local communities embodying traditional lifestyles relevant for the conservation and sustainable use of biological diversity and promote their wider application with the approval and involvement of the holders of such knowledge, innovations and practices and encourage the equitable sharing of the benefits arising from the utilisation of such knowledge innovations and practices'. For further details on traditional knowledge and Article 8(j), see https://www.cbd.int/traditional/ (last accessed 22 July 2015).

[28] Secretariat of the World Intellectual Property Organization, *Traditional Knowledge and Folklore, Traditional Knowledge: Operational Terms and Definitions*, World Intellectual Property Organization Intergovernmental Committee on Intellectual Property and Genetic Resources, 13th Sess, WIPO Doc WIPO/GRTKF/IC/13/9 (June 2002).

[29] Saskia Vermeylen, 'Comparative Environmental Law and Orientalism: Reading beyond the 'Text' of Traditional Knowledge Protection' (2015) 24(3) *Review of European Community & International Environmental Law* 304, 311.

[30] Ibid.

[31] Clement Yow Mulalap et al, 'Traditional knowledge and the BBNJ instrument' (2020) 122 *Marine Policy* 1, 2.

[32] United Nations Declaration on the Rights of Indigenous Peoples, GA Res 61/295, UN GAOR, 61st session, 107th plen mtg, Agenda Item 68, UN Doc A/RES/61/295 (13 September 2007) ('UNDRIP') art 31.

The ambiguity that has resulted from the lack of a universal definition of TK has spurred numerous efforts to classify it into distinct categories. Broadly, the prevailing literature recognises three primary categories: traditional medical knowledge ('TMK'), traditional agricultural knowledge ('TAK') and traditional ecological knowledge ('TEK').[33] In light of these categories, this study deliberately narrows its focus to primarily concentrate on TMK. This concentrated approach allows for a more in-depth exploration and critical analysis of this particular facet of TK, instead of attempting to discuss the broader, more complex concept of TK in its entirety.

This approach is justified for two reasons. Firstly, there is no internationally agreed definition and scope for TK. As a result, any attempt to analyse it in a comprehensive manner, including all of its subsets such as TAK and TEK, would necessitate the use of broad generalisations. Such a wide-ranging approach may inadvertently introduce complications and dilute the depth of analysis when examining specific subsets. Focusing on a single subset, such as TMK, enables a deeper and more consistent analysis relevant to that specific field. This approach promotes a more nuanced understanding of its intricacies and complexities. Secondly, TMK has become the focal point of discussions and debates, at both the national and international levels, concerning the protection of TK. Its prominence has surged due to issues such as biopiracy, especially in relation to the application of TMK in the processes of drug discovery and development.[34] Such circumstances have sparked an extensive debate on the urgency of protecting TMK, especially in developing nations where it serves as a fundamental pillar for the health and wellness of economically disadvantaged households.[35] The significance of TMK is immense, as its implications extend to the health outcomes of populations globally. For billions of individuals around the world, TMK provides accessible and economical healthcare solutions.[36] Moreover, it fosters the development of innovative treatments and promotes holistic and culturally sensitive approaches to health and well-being.[37] The relevance and impact of TMK, therefore, cannot be overstated.

However, the emphasis on TMK in this study does not necessarily indicate that the analysis conducted focuses exclusively on TMK. At various junctures, TK is utilised as a broader concept for critical analysis. For example, Chapter 5 of this book which presents an analysis of the current international legal ABS framework refers to TK in

[33] GV Overwalle, 'Protecting and Sharing Biodiversity and Traditional Knowledge: Holder and User Tools' (2005) 53 *Ecological Economics* 585, 585–607.

[34] 顾怡 [Gu Yi],《"贵州苗药"向"生物海盗"说不》[Guizhou Miao Medicine Says No to 'Biopirates'] (2004) 贵州政协报 *Guizhou Political Consultative Conference News* 1, 1–2; Ikechi Mgbeoji, 'Patent Regime and Biopiracy', *Global Biopiracy: Patents, Plants, and Indigenous Knowledge* (University of British Columbia Press, 2006) 119, 119–178.

[35] 王家博 [Wang Jiabo]《传统中医药知识产权保护的难题与破解思路》[Challenges and Solutions for Intellectual Property Protection of Traditional Medical Knowledge] (2009) 4(9)中国实用医药 *Chinese Practical Medicine* 259, 259; Ren Hu, 'Protection of Cross Border Ethnic Groups' Traditional Medicine under International Law' (2013) 8(1) *Frontiers of Law in China* 186, 187–210.

[36] A Xu, 'Traditional Medicine Is the Valuable Resource for Global Health' (2021) 8(1) *Journal of Traditional Chinese Medical Sciences* 2, 2–3.

[37] Ibid.

a wide-ranging sense rather than specifically to TMK. However, in instances where the analysis is directly relevant to TMK, the discourse remains expressly within its boundaries.

Despite being a subcategory of TK, TMK is no less difficult to define. This complexity arises primarily due to the variations in the understanding of TMK across diverse cultures, languages, and geographic regions globally. For instance, in China, the *Law of the People's Republic of China on Traditional Chinese Medicine* provides a definition for TMK as follows:

> The total body of medical knowledge of the various ethnic groups in China, including the Han ethnic group and other ethnic minority groups, reflects China's various ethnic groups' understanding of life, health and illness, and is based on China's long historic tradition, unique theory and technical method.[38]

This definition specifically highlights the medical knowledge employed by various knowledge-holder communities, such as the Han ethnic group and other ethnic minority groups. These communities utilise their distinct yet interconnected systems of traditional medical practices to address a wide range of health conditions.[39] While these systems are independent in their historical and cultural origins, they collectively contribute to the rich tapestry of Chinese TMK as a whole.[40]

The definition encapsulates the essence of Chinese TMK by acknowledging its key characteristics. Firstly, it underscores its longstanding historical tradition, highlighting the fact that TMK has been passed down through generations. Secondly, it specifies the custodians of TMK by explicitly referring to the Han ethnic group and other ethnic minority groups within China. This defined understanding is particularly pertinent to the analysis presented in this book. Its value lies in its context-specific creation, crafted within China's unique cultural and societal framework, and it incorporates elements that are distinctly Chinese. As such, it provides an invaluable lens through which TMK can be understood within a specific cultural context.

Uniquely, this definition distinguishes between the dominant Han ethnic group, and other ethnic minority groups. This differentiation paves the way for an analysis of how China's regulatory framework and policies accommodate TMK from these diverse groups. Central to the analysis in this book is the intriguing distinction between how the TMK of the Han ethnic group is managed and regulated, compared to the practices of other ethnic minority groups.

This difference potentially leads to a situation where the Chinese government might prioritise providing additional protection and support to the TMK of ethnic minority groups. This could be seen as a strategic effort to promote medical and

---

38 《中华人民共和国中医药法》 [Law of the People's Republic of China on Traditional Chinese Medicine] (People's Republic of China) Standing Committee of the National People's Congress, December 25, 2016.

39 段莉敏 [Duan Limin] 《我国少数民族医药文化保护与传承政策发展现状分析》[Analysis of the Current Status of the Protection and Inheritance of Ethnic Minority Medical Culture in China] (2019) 39(10) 中国农村卫生事业管理 Rural Health Care Management in China 709, 709.

40 王平 [Wang Ping],《维吾尔医药学概述》[Uyghur Medicine Overview] (2010) 中国穆斯林 Chinese Muslims 12, 12.

cultural diversity within the nation. The support mechanisms might include dedicated institutions, specific legal provisions, or practical measures that are primarily aimed at preserving and promoting the TMK of these minorities.

Conversely, the TMK of the Han ethnic group, being ingrained within the dominant culture, may not necessitate the same degree of specific support or protection, considering it's less vulnerable to marginalisation or disappearance. However, this does not imply that the Han TMK is overlooked. In fact, the government likely maintains and upholds its importance through a broader spectrum of laws and policies. This nuanced strategy, therefore, offers intriguing insights into how the country preserves and promotes its diverse medical traditions.

The World Health Organization ('WHO') provides a definition for TMK in a broad sense. According to the WHO, TMK is defined as including 'diverse health practices, approaches, knowledge and beliefs incorporating plant, animal and/or mineral-based medicines, spiritual therapies, manual techniques and exercises applied singularly or in combination to maintain well-being, as well as to treat, diagnose or prevent illness'.[41]

Such a definition provided by the WHO encapsulates the holistic essence of TMK, integrating diverse traditional medical practices with the cultural beliefs, values, and spiritual aspects associated with the perception of illness, healing, and health. China's TMK system also embodies these holistic traits, fostering the belief that nature, society, and humans are interconnected by a bond that transcends observable limits.[42] While the WHO's definition does not overtly incorporate elements unique to China, its comprehensive nature facilitates the incorporation of holistic medical practices and diverse methods of preparation that are intrinsic to Chinese TMK. Therefore, these two definitions provide a substantial framework for the subsequent discussions and critical analyses presented in this book. This framework is particularly useful due to its flexible and all-encompassing nature, facilitating nuanced analysis without compromising the uniqueness and complexity of Chinese TMK.

Moreover, these definitions recognise that China's TMK is dynamic and evolving rather than static and fixed. By acknowledging the fluid nature of TMK, this book emphasises the importance of fostering innovation and development within traditional cultures. Consequently, the preservation and protection of TMK should not be seen as merely a means to prevent the public disclosure of outdated knowledge, but rather as a driving force for sustained cultural development and growth. This emphasis on continuous development and forward-thinking is fundamental to this study, as it channels wisdom from the past to illuminate the present and, in doing so, maps out a trajectory for future transformations.

---

[41] *WHO Traditional Medicine Strategy 2002–2005*, WHO Doc WHO/EDM/TRM/2002.1. http://whqlibdoc.who.int/hq/2002/who_edm_trm_2002.1.pdf.

[42] Alma Barbaso Schwartz, 'Traditional Chinese Medicine: Ancient Holistic Healing' (2004) 16(6) *Home Health Care Management & Practice* 494, 494–498.

In contrast to scientific knowledge which is often regulated by formal laws and systems, TMK is deeply rooted in the customs and practices of communities.[43] As a result, there is a complex network of relationships that govern who can access and utilise TMK, when it can be used, the appropriate applications, and the specific words or customary practices that must accompany its use.[44] This study's definition of TMK acknowledges the origins of TMK within complex and dynamic knowledge systems, intimately intertwined with the cultures, lives, and places they arise from. TMK is not a stagnant body of knowledge. Instead, it has evolved over centuries, nurtured by Indigenous populations and local communities. This understanding of TMK serves as the fundamental premise of this study.

Lastly, the study makes a distinction between two concepts: the use of TMK in China and the use of Chinese TMK. The use of TMK in China refers to the application and practice of TMK within China's borders, which includes not only Chinese TMK but also TMK originating from other countries. This encompasses the ways in which China adopts and integrates foreign TMK into its healthcare systems and practices.

On the other hand, Chinese TMK signifies the distinctive, Indigenous knowledge and traditions that have been shaped and honed through the ages by China's diverse populace. This utilisation of Chinese TMK refers explicitly to the application of wisdom and practices that stem from the various ethnic groups within China, encompassing the majority Han community as well as numerous ethnic minorities. This perspective foregrounds the profound depth of China's cultural heritage, highlighting the richness of knowledge accumulated through centuries of interaction between these diverse ethnic communities. Furthermore, the concept extends beyond the domestic sphere to include the global proliferation and adoption of Chinese TMK. This aspect highlights the extent of Chinese TMK's global reach, revealing its significant impact and important role in moulding international knowledge structures, therapeutic modalities, and cross-cultural interactions. It casts a spotlight on the resonating influence of Chinese TMK across the globe, reflecting its power to both shape and enrich worldwide perspectives on traditional wisdom, healing, and cultural exchange.

Throughout this book, although there may be occasional variations in wording, the principal emphasis is on the use of Chinese TMK within China's domestic contexts. By focusing on this, it seeks to offer a comprehensive and detailed understanding of the unique historical, cultural, and social settings that have shaped Chinese TMK's development and evolution. Additionally, it presents an examination of the legal, policy, and practical frameworks that are responsible for regulating the protection and utilisation of Chinese TMK, taking into account the interplay between national and international laws and their influence on this regulation. It also discusses the potential challenges and opportunities that arise from protecting and leveraging Chinese TMK

---

[43] 左岫仙 [Zuo Xiuxian],《民族医药的知识产权保护》[Protection of Intellectual Property Rights in Traditional Ethnic Medicine] (2010) 中南民族大学学报 *Journal of South-Central University for Nationalities* 76, 76.

[44] Brian Thom and Do Bain, Aboriginal Intangible Property in Canada: An Ethnographic Review (Discussion Paper, 2013) 1–45.

in the domestic context, with the aim of providing well-informed recommendations for its effective management.

1.3.2 *Significance of TMK*

According to the WHO, TMK has been recognised across the world as a vital healthcare resource.[45] Over 80% of the healthcare needs in developing countries are met through its use.[46] Among various types of traditional medical remedies in the world, traditional Chinese medicine is generally recognised as having major success in realising the society's goals of harnessing TMK at an affordable cost for favourable public health outcomes.[47] For centuries, China's national and local communities have developed and maintained a unique approach to their TMK.[48] This system incorporates a variety of traditional practices, such as acupuncture, diet therapy, cupping, and the use of herbal remedies.[49] Even today, TMK remains widely employed in China to prevent and treat a wide range of health conditions, including diabetes and high blood pressure.[50] However, despite the significance of TMK to the world's healthcare, there is still no generally agreed definition of TMK. In the Western worldview, such medical knowledge is usually defined under the banner of 'ethnomedicine',[51] considered as either an alternative to Western biomedicine or as complementary healing knowledge alongside Western medical science.[52] These views that merely focus on the complementary or alternative function of TMK undervalue its great potential for not only ensuring people's health and wellness but also for benefiting and subsidising industries such as healthcare and pharmaceutical.

[45] World Health Organization, 'New WHO Guidelines to Promote Proper Use of Alternative Medicines', (Media Release, 22 June 2004).

[46] Ibid.

[47] 管贞 [Guan Zhen], 中医药为世界贡献"中国处方"》[Traditional Chinese Medicine Contributes "Chinese Prescription" to the World] [2010] 国际人才交流 *International Talent Exchange* 30, 30–33; V Sujatha, 'Globalisation of South Asian Medicines: Knowledge, Power, Structure and Sustainability' (2020) 6(1) *Society and Culture in South Asia* 1, 8.

[48] 石雪芹 [Shi Xueqin], 《从中医药源流看中医药传统知识保护价值》[Examining the Value of Protecting Traditional Chinese Medicine Knowledge from the Perspective of the Origins and Development of Chinese Medicine] (2022) 19(21) 中国医药导报 *China Medical Herald* 30, 30–33; Elaine Yu and Hakima Amri, 'China's Other Medical Systems: Recognizing Uyghur, Tibetan, and Mongolian Traditional Medicines' (2016) 5(1) *Global Advances in Health and Medicine* 79, 79–86; Lili Lai and Judith Farquhar, Nationality Medicines in China: Institutional Rationality and Healing Charisma' (2015) 57(2) *Comparative Studies in Society and History* 381, 381–406.

[49] Josephine Agu, 'Traditional Medicines Must Be Integrated into Health Care for Culturally Diverse Groups', *The Conversation (*Web Page, 2019*)* < https://theconversation.com/traditional-medicines-must-be-integrated-into-health-care-for-culturally-diverse-groups-114980 > .

[50] Ibid.

[51] KG Ramawat, Herbal Drugs: Ethnomedicine to Modern Medicine (Springer, 2009) 34.

[52] Ibid.

Despite the modern commercial pharmaceutical industry's hesitation to admit the value of TMK, it has indisputably and systematically relied on it as a significant source for the identification of bioactive substances that can be used in the drug discovery process.[53] Such knowledge of the traditional harvest, medicinal preparation, traits, storage, and toxins of plants provides valuable insights into the pharmaceutical value of the flora and fauna.[54] Some top-selling medications that have revolutionised modern healthcare systems were discovered and produced from the plant species and animal breeds used in traditional or Indigenous societies.[55] For instance, Tamiflu, widely utilised in the treatment of a variety of influenza infections, is derived from shikimic acid.[56] This compound is extracted from star anise, a culinary spice extensively used in traditional Chinese medicine.[57]

Moreover, to identify novel bioactive compounds with specific medicinal characteristics, the pharmaceutical industries tend to rely on the reverse pharmacology approach based on past discoveries.[58] Some of these will certainly have TMK origins. For instance, in China, *Artemisia (Qinghao)* plants were documented over 1,600 years ago for the treatment of malaria.[59] China's abundant TMK later proved instrumental in the discovery and development of *artemisinin*. Extracted from the leaves of the *Artemisia annua* (wormwood) plant, it is used in combination with other products and is considered the most effective antimalarial medication available today.[60] This situation gives pharmaceutical firms the chemical blueprints to decode the TMK of substances that have been used in traditional forms for generations by local communities, and to develop industrial uses, pursue patents, and commercialise the specific products under a corporate brand.[61]

---

[53] Lan Qiu et al, 'Public Funding and Private Investment for R&D: a Survey in China's Pharmaceutical Industry' (2014) 12(27) *Health Research Policy and Systems* 1, 1–11.

[54] P Sheng-Ji, 'Ethnobotanical Approaches of Traditional Medicine Studies: Some Experiences from Asia' (2001) 39 *Pharmaceutical Biology* 74, 77.

[55] WR Strohl, 'The Role of Natural Products in a Modern Drug Discovery Program.' (2000) 5 *Drug Discovery Today* 39, 39–41.

[56] Roberta Lee and Michael J. Balick, 'Flu for You? The Common Cold, Influenza, and Traditional Medicine' (2006) 2(3) *Explore* 252, 253.

[57] Ibid.

[58] Young-Joon Surh, 'Reverse Pharmacology Applicable for Botanical Drug Development—Inspiration from the Legacy of Traditional Wisdom' (2011) 1(1) *Journal of Traditional and Complementary Medicine* 5, 5–7.

[59] 吴致远 [Wu Zhiyuan],《从知识的地方性到技术的民族性》[From the locality of knowledge to the nationality of technology] (2022) 3 广西大学学报 *Journal of Guangxi University* 44, 48; Colin W Wright et al, 'Ancient Chinese Methods Are Remarkably Effective for the Preparation of Artemisinin-Rich Extracts of Qing Hao with Potent Antimalarial Activity' (2010) 15(2) *Molecules* 804, 805.

[60] Louis H Miller and Xinzhuan Su, 'Artemisinin: Discovery from the Chinese Herbal Garden' (2011) 146(6) *Cell* 855, 855–858.

[61] Devinder Sharma, 'Corporate Theft of "Traditional Knowledge": Biopiracy by Another Name', *HIMAL SOUTHASIAN* (online, 1 August 2002) < https://www.himalmag.com/corporate-theft-of-traditional-knowledge-biopiracy-by-another-name/ >.

1.3.3 The Need for Effective Frameworks for Regulating and Governing TMK

Despite the great significance and value of TMK, in China, TMK is subject to threats posed by outsiders, economic globalisation, and commodification of knowledge.[62] For instance, bioprospecting activities, and the commercialisation and unauthorised use of TMK contribute to a complex web of ethical, legal, and social concerns.[63] These issues often disproportionately affect the communities that hold such knowledge, leading to potential imbalances and disruptions within their traditional knowledge systems.[64] Moreover, the increasing prevalence of IP rights has made it more challenging to define TMK as communal resources because these rights emphasise individual ownership, which conflicts with the collective nature of TMK.[65] As a result, in situations where the outsiders who utilised TMK to develop the patented innovation seek to enforce their IP rights, TMK holders might be compelled to purchase the technology from the patentee, or at least to pay a commission for its utilisation.[66] Eventually, not only would TMK holders be barely compensated for their roles in creating and safeguarding the TMK but also would need to spend financial resources to utilise the TMK that they themselves possessed for centuries.

The absence of applicable approaches to safeguard TMK in China presents significant challenges.[67] To adequately protect and recognise TMK-holding communities, it is essential to develop tailored policies, and legal and practical frameworks. Without such measures, these communities may face difficulties in asserting their rights and preventing misappropriation by external entities. Moreover, the lack of effective protection systems may hinder the legitimate utilisation of TMK in research, innovation, and international partnerships, particularly within the pharmaceutical industry.[68]

---

[62] Dongguo Chen, 'Chinese Traditional Medicine Encountering Biopiracy Is Not Alarmist' (2006) 35 *Pharmaceutical Economics* 1, 1; Li Wang, 'Guizhou: Protecting Traditional Medicine and Rejecting "Biological Pirates"' (2006) 7 *China Reform* 1, 1.

[63] 赵阳 [Zhao Yang],《名古屋议定书履约挑战与对策:以植物制剂行业为例》[Challenges and Countermeasures in Implementing the Nagoya Protocol: A Case Study of the Plant-based Formulation Industry] [2021] 中国土地资源经济*Natural Resource Economics of China* 57, 60–61.

[64] Javier Garcia, 'Fighting Biopiracy: The Legislative Protection of Traditional Knowledge' (2007) 18 *Berkerley La Raza Law Journal* 5, 11.

[65] Thomas Cottier and Marion Panizzon, 'Legal Perspectives on Traditional Knowledge: The Case for Intellectual Property Protection' (2004) 7(2) *Journal of International Economic Law* 371, 371–399.

[66] R Manley, 'Developmental Perspectives on the TRIPS and Traditional Knowledge Debate' (2006) 3(1) *The Macquarie Journal of International and Comparative Environmental Law* 113, 113–133.

[67] 吕文清 [Lv Wenqing],《非洲传统医药知识的立法保护及其对我国的启示》[Legislative Protection of African Traditional Medical Knowledge and Its Implications for Our Country] (2018) 19(2) 南京中医药大学学报 *Journal of Nanjing University of TCM* 111, 116.

[68] Ad Hoc Open-ended Informal Working Group, Letter Dated 30 June 2011 from the Co-Chairs of the Ad Hoc Open-ended Informal Working Group to the President of the General Assembly, UN Doc A/66/119 (30 June 2011), para 6; Implementation of paragraph 6 of the Doha Declaration on the TRIPS Agreement and Public Health (World Trade Organization General Council Decision, 30 August 2003).

This may ultimately hinder the development of valuable medicines and therapies that could benefit a global population. In response to these challenges, this book argues that adopting a culturally sensitive strategy is crucial for ensuring proper protection, responsible use, and suitable dissemination within the distinct legal, policy, and practical frameworks of China.

In China, the framework regulating TMK is a series of complex patchworks of national laws, regulations, and international agreements that it has acceded to.[69] However, this complex framework only partially addresses imminent threats to Chinese TMK, falling short of ensuring adequate protection, responsible utilisation, and suitable dissemination. This study probes these deficiencies within China's current TMK legal, policy, and practical infrastructure, with a particular emphasis on its IP framework, ABS system, and TMK information systems. The objective is to develop contextually relevant recommendations, deeply rooted in China's historical and cultural fabric, for creating a more proficient system dedicated to the comprehensive protection, responsible utilisation, and appropriate dissemination of TMK.

1.3.4 TK and International Frameworks

In order to conduct a comprehensive and critical analysis of the protection and utilisation of TMK within China's legal, policy, and practical frameworks, it is essential to examine the interplay between these concepts and the international frameworks governing them. This not only provides the necessary context for understanding the China's TMK frameworks but also highlights the significance of international frameworks such as IP and ABS in shaping the research topic.

International frameworks hold significant relevance for this study, given their direct impacts on ensuring the comprehensive protection, responsible utilisation, and appropriate dissemination of Chinese TMK. This study critically examines them to

[69] National Laws and Regulations: *The Law of the People's Republic of China on Traditional Chinese Medicine* (2016): This law provides a legal framework for the development, management and promotion of traditional Chinese medicine ('TCM') in China; *The Regulations on the Protection of Traditional Chinese Medicine* (2003): These regulations aim to protect and develop TCM resources, ensure their sustainable use, and promote the development of TCM in China; *The Patent Law of the People's Republic of China* (1984, last amended in 2020): This law provides intellectual property protection, including for traditional medical knowledge, through patent rights. International Agreements: World Trade Organization ('WTO') *Agreement on Trade-Related Aspects of Intellectual Property Rights* ('TRIPS'): As a member of the WTO, China is obligated to protect intellectual property rights, including traditional medical knowledge, in accordance with the TRIPS agreement. *Convention on Biological Diversity* ('CBD'): China is a party to the CBD, which promotes the conservation of biological diversity, the sustainable use of its components, and the fair and equitable sharing of benefits arising from the use of genetic resources; the *Nagoya Protocol on Access to Genetic Resources and the Fair and Equitable Sharing of Benefits Arising from their Utilization* (2010): This international agreement, which China has ratified, aims to ensure that the benefits derived from genetic resources and traditional knowledge are shared fairly and equitably.

gain a clearer understanding of the legal, policy, and practical milieu that impacts China's TMK governance. Such a rigorous analysis is vital to pinpoint potential deficiencies or restrictions in their implementations. These insights are instrumental in shaping nuanced recommendations aimed at enabling China to enhance its regulatory measures for TMK, respecting its unique historical and sociocultural contexts.

1.3.4.1 International IP Frameworks

The protection of Traditional Knowledge (TK) has been a subject of intense scrutiny across various international forums, employing both existing Intellectual Property (IP) frameworks and alternative approaches. The World Trade Organization ('WTO') has been particularly influential in this area since TK was introduced as a subject for work on IP in the Doha Round of WTO negotiations in 2001.[70] At the WTO, numerous proposals have advocated for the mandatory disclosure of the origin of TK in patent applications.[71] However, progress within the WTO has been hindered by a stalemate in the Doha Round negotiations, leading to limited advancements in incorporating TK protection within its framework.

In contrast, the World Intellectual Property Organization (WIPO) played a foundational role in elevating the issue of TK protection on the global stage, particularly through the work of its Global Issues Division. In the late 1990s, WIPO's Fact-Finding Missions were instrumental in identifying TK as a significant global IP issue.[72] These missions emerged in response to the shortcomings of the TRIPS Agreement in recognising and protecting TK. By gathering extensive information on the utilisation and protection of TK across various cultural contexts, these missions highlighted the unique challenges and considerations surrounding TK.[73] The insights garnered from these missions were pivotal in establishing the WIPO Intergovernmental Committee (IGC) on Intellectual Property and Genetic Resources, Traditional Knowledge, and Folklore. The IGC, which held its first meeting in 2001,[74]

---

[70] *Doha Ministerial Declaration*, World Intellectual Property Organization, WTO Doc WT/MIN(01)/DEC/1 (20 November 2001) Para 19: 'We instruct the Council for TRIPS, in pursuing its work program including under the review of Article 27.3(b), the review of the implementation of the TRIPS Agreement under Article 71.1 and the work foreseen pursuant to paragraph 12 of this declaration, to examine, inter alia, the relationship between the TRIPS Agreement and the Convention on Biological Diversity, the protection of traditional knowledge and folklore'.

[71] Joshua D Sarnoff and Glushko Samuelson, *Analysis of Options for Implementing Disclosure of Origin Requirements in Intellectual Property Applications,* United Nations Conference on Trade and Development (UNCTAD), UN DocUNCTAD/DITC/TED/2004114 (2006).

[72] World Intellectual Property Organization, '*Intellectual Property Needs and Expectations of Traditional Knowledge Holders: WIPO Report on Fact-Finding Missions on Intellectual Property and Traditional Knowledge (1998-1999)*' (2001).

[73] Ibid.

[74] *Revised Draft Agenda*, World Intellectual Property Organization (WIPO) Intergovernmental Committee on Intellectual Property and Genetic Resources, Traditional Knowledge and Folklore, 1st Sess, WIPO Doc GRTKF/IC/1/1 REV (2010).

was expressly created to provide a dedicated forum for negotiations concerning the interface between IP and TK.[75]

Further advancing its commitment, in 2005, WIPO established the Voluntary Fund to support and promote the participation of Indigenous Peoples and Local Communities ('IPLCs') in the IGC negotiation.[76] By 2009, the IGC was tasked with the mandate to formulate an international legal instrument for IP protection of TK, cultural expressions, and genetic resources.[77] Following widespread consultations with various stakeholders, the work of the IGC has resulted in the development of a series of draft provisions related to the legal protection of TK, including a gap analysis commissioned by the IGC to examine how conventional IP rights can best meet the needs of TK holders and to identify any gaps related to the protection of TK.

Amid these developments, TK, despite its integral role in diverse cultural and societal contexts, continues to present significant definitional challenges for organisations such as WIPO. WIPO's struggle to formulate a universally accepted definition highlights the task's complexity.[78] The primary issue is the diffuse and diverse nature of TK, held and used by a wide variety of groups, from Indigenous peoples, communities, and nations to non-Indigenous entities.[79] Although Indigenous entities often serve as traditional knowledge holders, it is crucial to acknowledge that they are not the sole knowledge possessors. The presence of such a broad range of stakeholders complicates the formulation of a comprehensive definition.

Additionally, the diversity of TK further complicates efforts towards a singular, comprehensive definition.[80] Such knowledge is influenced by a multitude of factors such as culture, geography, history, and local environment, varying considerably from one community or nation to another.[81] Consequently, any attempt to confine it within a uniform definition risks oversimplification or, worse, misrepresentation of its inherent richness and diversity.

---

[75] *Report*, World Intellectual Property Organization (WIPO) General Assembly, 26th Sess, WIPO Doc WO/GA/26/10 (2000).

[76] *Experts' Study on Exclusions from Patentable Subject Matter and Exceptions and Limitations to the Rights*, World Intellectual Property Organization General Assembly, 39th Sess, WIPO Doc WO/GA/39/14 (2010) 218.

[77] *The Protection of Traditional Knowledge: Draft Articles (Rev. 2)*, World Intellectual Property Organization General Assembly, WIPO Doc WIPO/GRTKF/IC/24 (2013). < http://www.wipo.int/meetings/en/doc_details.jsp?doc_id=238182 > .

[78] J Janewa OseiTutu, 'Emerging Scholars Series: A Sui Generis Regime for Traditional Knowledge: The Cultural Divide in Intellectual Property Law' (2011) 15(1) *Marqueette Intellectual Property Law Review* 147, 161.

[79] Ibid.

[80] Graham Dutfield, 'TRIPS-Related Aspects of Traditional Knowledge' (2001) 33(2) *Case Western Reserve Journal of International Law* 233, 240.

[81] Ibid.

The complexity of defining TK is further compounded by the absence of global consensus.[82] Interpretations of what it constitutes varies greatly among nations, shaped by their unique cultural, historical, and societal perspectives.[83] This difference creates substantial challenges when attempts are made to harmonise a definition on an international stage, such as WIPO.

The case of China serves as a compelling example of the complexities involved in defining TK. Despite its profound cultural diversity and rich history, China lacks a nationally accepted definition. This absence, however, is not a result of inaction; instead, it is due to the intricate nature of this issue that warrants a culturally sensitive approach.

China, as a nation, is home to a myriad of distinct ethnic groups and communities, each bringing their own unique interpretation of what constitutes TK. These stakeholders, given the cultural, regional, and historical diversity they embody, further complicate the quest for a nationally accepted definition.

Thus, the endeavour of defining TK is an intricate one. It must meticulously reflect the varied nuances and interpretations prevalent across China's extensive geographical boundaries. This challenge transcends basic generalisations and calls for a profound comprehension and respectful recognition of the unique cultural intricacies inherent within the nation.

1.3.4.2 United Nations Frameworks for ABS

The global debate on access to TK (including TMK) and genetic resources, along with the associated sharing of benefits, emerged out of increasing dissatisfaction with the prevalent practice of unrestricted access to such resources and knowledge. The necessity to tackle issues of fairness and equity became a core focus during negotiations leading up to the adoption of the *Convention on Biodiversity* ('CBD') in 1992. This supports the idea of international cooperation to protect States' rights to regulate access to TK and genetic resources and promote conservation, sustainable use, and benefit-sharing.[84] The ABS approach was advanced through the adoption of the *Nagoya Protocol* and subsequent initiatives, such as the *International Treaty on Plant Genetic Resources for Food and Agriculture* (Plant Treaty or 'ITPGRFA') and the *Pandemic Influenza Preparedness (PIP) Framework*.[85] These frameworks, operating under the United Nations, provide guidelines for the regulation of access

[82] Saskia Vermeylen, 'Comparative Environmental Law and Orientalism: Reading beyond the 'Text' of Traditional Knowledge Protection' (2015) 24(3) *Review of European, Comparative and International Environmental Law* 304, 304.

[83] Ibid.

[84] DM McGraw, 'The CBD—Key Characteristics and Implications for Implementation' (2002) 11(1) *Review of European, Comparative & International Environmental Law* 17, 19; CBD (n 24) arts 5–6.

[85] Sixty-Fourth World Health Assembly, Resolutions and Decisions, WHA64/2011/REC/1, 8–9 and Annex 2 (WHA64.5) (PIP Framework) (2011).

to TK (including TMK), as well as the sharing of benefits that arise from their utilisation.[86] Examining these frameworks can inform the main research question of this study by providing a broader perspective on the issue of protecting and utilising TMK in China. This information is particularly relevant to Chapter 5 of this book which explores the potential of ABS regimes functioning independently of the IP framework for the governance of TMK, and focuses on the challenges and opportunities presented by China's historical and sociocultural context.

The CBD and the Nagoya Protocol

When the CBD was being adopted in Rio at the Earth Summit arranged by the United Nations Environment Programme in 1992, policymakers defined two objectives as conserving and sustainably using genetic resources.[87] The third objective introduces the concept of ABS, which refers to how genetic resources can be accessed and how the benefits resulting from their use are shared between the users and providers of the resources.[88]

The CBD not only governs the ABS of genetic resources but also extends to the protection and management of TK associated with genetic resources. It recognises the significance of TK, including the knowledge of IPLCs, in the conservation of biodiversity and the sustainable use of its components.[89] It requires State parties to 'respect, preserve, and maintain the knowledge, innovations and practices of IPLCs',[90] calls for the approval and involvement of TK holders, and emphasises the need for fair and equitable benefit-sharing of TK.[91] This is a recognition of the contribution that IPLCs make to the conservation of biological diversity and the significance of their TK in its sustainable use and management.

---

[86] The main UN CBD provision on TK is Article 8(j), which states: 'Each contracting Party shall, as far as possible and as appropriate: (j) Subject to national legislation, respect, preserve and maintain knowledge, innovations, and practices of Indigenous and local communities embodying traditional lifestyles relevant for the conservation and sustainable use of biological diversity and promote their wider application with the approval and involvement of the holders of such knowledge, innovations, and practices and encourage the equitable sharing of the benefits arising from the utilization of such knowledge innovations and practices.'; Under Article 9 of the Plant Treaty ('ITPGRFA'), 'farmers rights' are recognised, allowing for the preservation and protection of TK, and a 'multilateral system of access and benefit sharing' is established through Article 11.2; Under the *Nagoya Protocol*, the most prominent references to TK are found in the Preamble. Article 7 and Article 5(5) address access to TK and benefit-sharing, respectively, and Article 12 is more inclusive of broader issues relating to TK.

[87] CBD (n 24) art 1.

[88] Ibid.

[89] CBD (n 24) art 8(j).

[90] Ibid.

[91] Ibid.

The *Nagoya Protocol*[92] implements and further develops the CBD's ABS concept by establishing a global framework that complements the ABS regulations of the CBD.[93] Since coming into force, it has played a crucial role in addressing biodiversity conservation and ABS at the international level, complementing the CBD's existing framework.[94] It highlights the core principle of the ABS concept within the CBD. This principle stipulates that parties should provide access to genetic resources in exchange for a fair and equitable share of the benefits derived from their utilisation.[95] As an essential implementing agreement, the *Protocol* enhances the effectiveness of the CBD in achieving its objectives.

The four key elements that constitute the ABS concept include:

1. State Sovereignty: The principle that countries have sovereign rights over their own genetic resources, granting them the authority to regulate access and determine the terms and conditions under which these resources can be utilised.[96]
2. Prior Informed Consent ('PIC'): The requirement that access to genetic resources and/or traditional knowledge must be based on the PIC of the providing country or Indigenous/local community, ensuring that access is granted only after obtaining proper authorisation.[97]
3. Mutually Agreed Terms ('MAT'): The establishment of clear terms and conditions between the provider and user of genetic resources, defining the scope, duration, and purpose of access, as well as the benefits to be shared and any restrictions on the use of the resources.[98]
4. User Measures: The implementation of legal, practical, and policy measures by user countries to support compliance with the ABS concept, such as the development of national legislation or regulations governing access to genetic resources and benefit-sharing, and monitoring the utilisation of such resources.[99]

The *Protocol* offers greater clarity on ABS operations by outlining fundamental principles and processes for parties to integrate into their domestic legal systems.[100]

---

92 The United Nations' *Nagoya Protocol on Access to Genetic Resources and the Fair and Equitable Sharing of Benefits Arising from Their Utilization to the Convention on Biological Diversity*, opened for signature 29 October 2010, [2012] ATNIF 3 (entered into force 12 October 2014).

93 Kanchana Kariyawasam and Matthew Tsai, 'Access to Genetic Resources and Benefit-sharing: Implications of Nagoya Protocol on Providers and Users' (2018) 21(5–6) *The Journal of World Intellectual Property* 289, 290.

94 Evanson C Kamau, Bevis Fedder and Gerd Winter, 'The Nagoya Protocol on Access to Genetic Resources and Benefit Sharing. What Is New and What Are the Implications for Provider and User Countries and The Scientific Community' (2010) 6(3) *Law Environment and Development Journal* 248, 262.

95 Elisa Morgera, Elsa Tsioumani and Matthias Buck, Unravelling the Nagoya Protocol: A Commentary on the Nagoya Protocol on Access and Benefit-sharing to the Convention on Biological Diversity (Brill, 2014) 2–3.

96 *Nagoya Protocol* (n 89) art 6.

97 *Nagoya Protocol* (n 89) arts 5, 6.1, 7 and 12.

98 *Nagoya Protocol* (n 89) arts 5, 6.3, 7, 12.

99 *Nagoya Protocol* (n 89) arts 15.1, 15.2, 16, 17, 18.

100 Elisa Morgera et al (n 92) 2–3.

By building on and elaborating the interplay between the CBD's four main elements, it strengthens the ABS regimes' overall success and supports the CBD in achieving its objectives.[101]

These regimes not only regulate the international sharing of genetic resources but also provide a framework for the use of TK that is associated with these resources and owned by IPLCs.[102] The *Protocol* facilitates the creation of a TK ABS system, thereby enhancing the ability of IPLCs to benefit from their knowledge, innovations, and practices, as stated in its Introduction.

The Preamble to the *Nagoya Protocol* outlines the underlying assumptions on which its TK provisions rest.[103] It highlights: the interconnectedness between genetic resources and TK; the inseparable nature of TK and genetic resources; the diverse contexts in which IPLCs hold or own TK associated with genetic resources; the right of IPLCs to determine the legitimate holders of their TK; and the various forms that TK might encompass as part of a rich cultural heritage relevant to conserving and promoting the sustainable use of biological diversity.[104] In essence, the *Nagoya Protocol*'s definition of 'traditional knowledge' is intended to be comprehensive, encompassing all types and aspects of TK.[105] Moreover, although it derives its authority from Article 8(j) of the CBD, its scope is informed by the more comprehensive understanding of TK addressed by the entire CBD.[106]

The *Nagoya Protocol* distinguishes itself from the CBD by offering more concrete obligations for protecting TK, despite occasional ambiguities and soft commitments.[107] This is particularly evident when comparing the aspirational nature of Article 8(j) in the CBD to the provisions within the *Nagoya Protocol.*

The *Nagoya Protocol* requires countries to establish mechanisms that ensure access to TK associated with genetic resources is granted with PIC or approval from the relevant IPLC, and under MAT.[108] These mechanisms, which may be practical, legislative, or policy-based, should consider the customary laws and protocols of the community concerned.[109] Furthermore, the *Nagoya Protocol* obligates countries to support the development of community protocols and model contractual clauses, promoting fair and equitable sharing of benefits arising from TK use.[110]

---

[101] Ibid.

[102] *Nagoya Protocol* (n 89) art 7 and art 12.

[103] *Nagoya Protocol* (n 89) Preamble.

[104] Ibid.

[105] Michelle F Rourke, 'When Knowledge Goes Viral: Assessing the Possibility of Virus-related Traditional Knowledge for Access and Benefit-sharing' (2018) 21(5–6) *Journal of World Intellectual Property* 356, 360.

[106] Ibid.

[107] Elisa Morgera, Elsa Tsioumani and Matthias Buck, Unraveling the Nagoya Protocol: A Commentary on the Nagoya Protocol on Access and Benefit-sharing to the Convention on Biological Diversity (Brill, 2015) 2.

[108] *Nagoya Protocol* (n 89) art 7.

[109] *Nagoya Protocol* (n 89) art 12.

[110] *Nagoya Protocol* (n 89) art 5(5).

Article 21(1) of the *Nagoya Protocol* encourages parties to involve IPLCs as stakeholders in implementing TK-related ABS measures, with the extent of their involvement left to the State's discretion. Additionally, the *Protocol* introduces monitoring and compliance mechanisms surpassing those in the CBD.[111] Article 16 mandates that parties ensure TK access adheres to PIC and MAT, requires parties to address non-compliance, and calls for cooperation in cases of alleged violations. In summary, the *Nagoya Protocol* enhances the protection of TK by introducing more concrete obligations, increased stakeholder involvement, and monitoring and compliance mechanisms, thereby expanding upon the foundational principles of the CBD.

As noted by Richerzhagen, the concept of ABS is based on a market-based system that aims to regulate the conservation and use of TK and genetic resources.[112] It transforms TK and genetic resources from being freely accessible to being private or club goods, establishes a market for these resources, and creates a market for trading TK and genetic resources for compensation.[113] The market-based approach of ABS has faced criticism for encouraging the commodification of TK,[114] which can conflict with the core beliefs and cultural traditions of certain communities. These communities often view TK as a shared cultural heritage or collective wisdom that should not be commercialised.[115] To address these concerns, ABS implementation must be tailored to respect the diverse cultural perspectives and values at play, ensuring that TK, including TMK, is managed with consideration for its cultural significance, while also preventing potential negative consequences for knowledge holders and their communities.

In this context, investigating ABS mechanisms becomes crucial in analysing legal and policy approaches that effectively tackle the distinct challenges of regulating and safeguarding TMK within China's unique setting. Given the country's distinct sociocultural and historical circumstances, ABS mechanisms also provide opportunities that can work in tandem with IP protection. This facilitates innovation while ensuring the equitable distribution of benefits derived from the TMK and for humanity's short and long-term welfare.[116]

The CBD Secretariat's review of the impact of IP on the ABS framework emphasised that the identification and allocation of IP is an essential aspect of regulating access to TK and genetic resources and facilitating the fair and equitable sharing of

---

[111] *Nagoya Protocol* (n 89) arts 15–18.

[112] Carmen Richerzhagen, 'Effective Governance of Access and Benefit-sharing under the Convention on Biological Diversity' (2011) 20 *Biodiversity Conservation* 2243, 2244.

[113] Ibid.

[114] Abdul Haseeb Ansari and Lekha Laxman, 'A Review of the International Framework for Access and Benefit Sharing of Genetic Resources with Special Reference to the Nagoya Protocol' (2013) 16 *Asia Pacific Journal of Environmental Law* 105, 125.

[115] John Tustin, 'Traditional Knowledge and Intellectual Property in Brazilian Biodiversity Law' (2006) 14 *Texas Intellectual Property Law Journal* 131, 140.

[116] The *Convention on Biological Diversity and the Nagoya Protocol: Intellectual Property Implications—A Handbook on the Interface between Global Access and Benefit Sharing Rules and Intellectual Property*, UN Doc UNCTAD/DIAE/PCB/2014/3 (2014) 1, 1–7.

benefits.[117] Within the ABS framework, IP clauses may influence mutually agreed terms related to the utilisation of TK, including TMK and genetic resources.[118] In addition, IP rights not only contribute to stimulating and disseminating innovation but also play a vital role in generating more benefits that can be shared among stakeholders, providing a means to share benefits that are derived from TK.[119] This is particularly important in the Chinese context where the equitable distribution of benefits is essential for preserving TMK and promoting its sustainable development.

By delving into ABS mechanisms in China, it becomes possible to better understand the complex interactions between IP rights, TMK, and the diverse stakeholders involved. This exploration can lead to the development of more effective legal and policy strategies for regulating and protecting TMK. Chapter 5 of this book examines the intricacies surrounding TMK and ABS frameworks in China. The chapter highlights the importance of recognising China's unique cultural values and historical background for the successful implementation of international ABS agreements and the fulfilment of related obligations.

1.3.5 Westernised Values and Perspectives Embodied Within International Legal and Policy Instruments

This study is based on the premise that international legal and policy constructs, specifically those related to IP rights, ABS mechanisms, and TK information systems, are significantly influenced by Western paradigms. This trend, often implicit, reinforces a pervasive Western bias that permeates the global landscape, particularly under the banner of globalisation, with its impacts deeply resonating within low- and middle-income countries. A typical example of this trend can be observed in China, where Western philosophies and systems have been introduced, assimilated, and, to a certain degree, firmly institutionalised. This Western bias becomes particularly evident when these global legal and policy instruments are employed to govern areas such as TK and, more significantly, TMK. The failure to thoroughly comprehend and respect the philosophies and structures underpinning these traditional knowledge systems, instead approaching them through a Western-centric lens, can result in misunderstanding, improper use, and potentially, exploitation.

For instance, the adoption and internationalisation of treaty standards of IP are linked to the imposition of Western values and views, for instance, individualistic,

---

[117] *The Impact of Intellectual Property Rights Systems on the Conservation and Sustainable Use of Biological Diversity and on the Equitable Sharing of Benefits from Its Use*, UN Doc UNEP/CBD/CGP/3/22 (22 September 1996).

[118] A Ganashree, 'Who Owns Ocean Biodiversity? The Legal Status and Role of Patents as a Means to Achieve Equitable Distribution of Benefits' (2021) 53(1) *Case Western Reserve Journal of International Law* 197, 215.

[119] Ibid., 220–222.

monopolistic, materialistic, and capitalistic values, on all parts of the globe.[120] This is evident in the dominance of Western legal principles within international IP structures. These have the potential to facilitate the misappropriation of TMK, often proving incommensurable, irrelevant, or irreconcilable when transposed to different sociocultural contexts.[121]

This scenario is particularly prominent in China, where the Western IP model has not found solid ground due to the country's unique cultural, political, and historical fabric. As noted by Alford, the Western model of the IP system has never taken hold in China because of the realities of China's cultural, political, and historical experiences.[122] This reality underscores the challenges faced by nations like China when external pressure to adopt Western IP norms increases, primarily due to the complexity of integrating foreign legal values, structures, and practices into their deeply embedded social, cultural, and historical frameworks.

At the heart of the problem is an implicit bias ingrained within the primarily Western-focused IP system.[123] When applied to China's TMK, this model provokes a range of significant implications. This bias stems from the imposition of primarily Western legal ideologies onto a setting that differs markedly in cultural, historical, and political aspects.[124] These inherent disparities between the two paradigms may enable potential misuse, misappropriation, and exploitation of China's TMK. Not only does this pose a significant threat to the preservation of, and respect for, Chinese TMK, but it also calls into question the equity and universal suitability of these laws.

Moreover, the international ABS rules, established by the CBD, the *Nagoya Protocol*, and other agreements, are designed to be universally applicable. However, these rules also reflect Western perspectives that emphasise the exchange, profit, and capital accumulation inherent in capitalism, often overshadowing the interests of groups with limited financial resources.[125] Some scholars have noted that the ABS regime is established on the basis of 'asymmetrical patterns' of trade and exchange that favour the Western market-oriented approach.[126] Essentially, this structure is intended to advantage developed nations and large corporations at the expense of

---

[120] K Roisah et al, 'Trends of Global Values in Legal Political Formation of Intellectual Property Law in Indonesia' (2017) 8(9) *International Journal of Civil Engineering and Technology* 391, 393.

[121] Akalemwa Ngenda, 'The Nature of the International Intellectual Property System: Universal Norms and Values or Western Chauvinism?' (2005) 14(1) *Information & Communications Technology Law* 59, 73.

[122] William P Alford, To Steal a Book Is an Elegant Offense: Intellectual Property Law in Chinese Civilization (Stanford University Press, 1995) 9–29.

[123] Graham Dutfield, 'The Public and Private Domains: Intellectual Property Rights in Traditional Knowledge' (2000) 21(3) *Science Communication* 274, 288.

[124] Sunder, Madhavi, 'The Invention of Traditional Knowledge' (2007) 70(97) *Law and Contemporary Problems* 97, 107.

[125] DQ Hodnett, 'Legitimising Biopiracy? Fairness and Efficacy of the Nagoya Protocol' (2021) 2 *York Law Review* 75, 86.

[126] Hodnett (n 122) 92; Carmen Richerzhagen, 'Effective Governance of Access and Benefit-sharing under the Convention on Biological Diversity' (2011) 20 *Biodiversity Conservation* 2243, 2244.

developing countries and Indigenous communities.[127] A significant factor reinforcing this bias is the fact that developed nations and corporations command far greater resources and negotiation leverage compared to their developing counterparts and Indigenous groups.[128] This resource and power disparity substantially hampers these disadvantaged groups when negotiating fair and equitable terms for the usage of their TMK.

A clear manifestation of this problem can be seen when considering the application of the Western-centric ABS system to Chinese TMK. The Western orientation of the ABS rules imposes a structure that may not align with the ethos and traditions of Chinese TMK. This imposition can lead to unfair conditions that favour developed nations and corporations, potentially undermining the interests of Chinese TMK holders and communities reliant on this knowledge. As a result, it exacerbates the disparities and biases within the ABS framework, heightening the need for systemic changes to ensure equitable treatment for all involved parties.

As China has opened up its economy to international trade and investment, it has signed on to international agreements that promote the universal application of IP and ABS rules.[129] This has resulted in China incorporating Western models of legal, practical, and policy mechanisms for regulating Chinese TMK. However, when adopting these Western frameworks, the crucial influence of historical, social, and cultural factors in shaping the norms within them is often neglected.[130] The critical inquiry of this study is the fundamental reasoning behind forcing Western-oriented regulations on Chinese TMK.

The study accentuates the challenges presented by the adaptation of Western legal and policy mechanisms for regulating Chinese TMK. Specifically, it investigates how these instruments can undermine the essence of the TMK system within China and its local communities. Therefore, it is argued that the successful application of Western-style regulations on Chinese TMK requires these systems to be tailored to China's unique historical and sociocultural landscape. A failure to do so risks surface-level implementation, devoid of an understanding of China's distinct values, beliefs, and historical context.

---

[127] Hodnett (n 122) 76–77.

[128] G Kristin Rosendal, 'Balancing Access and Benefit Sharing and Legal Protection of Innovations from Bioprospecting' (2006) 15(4) *The Journal of Environment & Development* 428, 437.

[129] N Yacoub and H Souei, 'Is Drug Patent Protection a Determinant of the Location of Pharmaceutical FDI? China's Experience' in Andreas Pyka and Keun Lee (eds), *Innovation, Catch-up, and Sustainable Development: A Schumpeterian Perspective* (Springer, 2022) 209, 217; Xiaoou Zheng, 'Key Legal Challenges and Opportunities in the Implementation of the Nagoya Protocol: The Case of China (2019) 28(2) *Review of European, Comparative & International Environmental Law* 175, 175.

[130] Peter K Yu, 'The Transplant and Transformation of Intellectual Property Laws in China' in Niklas Bruun, Nari Lee and Mingde Li (eds), *Governance of Intellectual Property Rights in China and Europe* (Elgar Intellectual Property and Global Development series, 2016) 20, 36–38; Olufunmilayo B Arewa, 'TRIPs and Traditional Knowledge: Local Communities, Local Knowledge, and Global Intellectual Property Frameworks' (2006) 10(2) *Marquette Intellectual Property Law Review* 156, 156–159.

Thus, the study stresses the necessity of recognising the differences between Western and Chinese legal and policy frameworks. This recognition is critical to devising effective and culturally appropriate solutions for the protection, utilisation, and dissemination of Chinese TMK. By articulating the implicit Western bias of the system, it seeks to illuminate the complexities of imposing a one-size-fits-all approach onto a culture rich in unique traditional knowledge and practices. Such an approach necessitates a more nuanced understanding of the complexities of Chinese TMK, moving beyond a broad-brush application of a Western legal framework, towards a more tailored, context-specific approach.

1.3.6 National Initiatives and Debates

China's existing policy, legislative, and practical solutions for dealing with TMK are largely a patchwork of China's national laws, regulations, and international agreements that China has acceded to.[131] These legal instruments vary in their implementation and enforcement mechanisms which has sparked national debates in recent decades.[132]

The protection of TMK is the subject of a wide variety of studies on China's IP laws. As noted by Li and Li, China's TMK consists of largely intellectual creation and innovation passed from generation to generation.[133] Therefore, it could produce enormous economic advantages for the nation and alleviate the potential risks of biopiracy by developed countries if the protection of TMK could be secured by a regime of private property rights.[134] Jin shared a similar view but with added concerns about the lack of adequate IP protection of TMK in China and the resulting legal uncertainty. This may lead to a situation that fails to sufficiently tackle the misappropriation and exploitation of TMK by foreign countries.[135] A number of measures have been taken to squeeze TMK and associated innovations into the IP system. For instance, China's first modern Patent Law was promulgated in 1984[136] and was further revised three times in 1992, 2000, and 2008. As noted by Lo: 'The revised Patent Law expanded protection for patentees, as well as brought the Chinese standards more in line with

131 Tianbao Qin, 'Common Pools of Traditional Chinese Medical Knowledge in China' in Gerd Winter and Evanson Chege Kamau (eds), *Common Pools of Genetic Resources: Equity and Innovation in International Biodiversity Law* (2013) 150, 150–164.

132 Ibid.

133 MeiYing Li and XianYuan Li, 'Perspectives on Current Protection of Intellectual Property Rights for Traditional Chinese Medicine' (2015) 42(4) *Journal of International Pharmaceutical Research* 467, 467–472.

134 Ibid.

135 Zhi-Hai Jin, 'Intellectual Property Protection and Countermeasures in the Field of Traditional Chinese Medicine' (2005) 15(1) *Journal of Intellectual Property* 34, 34–36.

136《中华人民共和国专利法》[Patent Law of the People's Republic of China] (People's Republic of China) National People's Congress Standing Committee, Order No 11, March 1984.

international norms'.[137] For instance, after the revisions of China's Patent Law, a wide variety of pharmaceutical products became patentable in China. The establishment and improvement of China's patent system have led to a dramatic increase in TMK-related patent applications.[138] In 1993, China's State Council further promulgated Regulation on the Protection of Traditional Chinese Medicines to strengthen the protection of TMK.[139] In this regime, novelty is not a prerequisite. However, only the enterprises can apply for a protection certificate.[140] During the period of the protection, those enterprises possessing such a certificate are allowed to manufacture the respective traditional medicine and formula.[141]

China's existing Patent Law along with other administrative regulations have provided patentees with rights comparable to those of Western countries.[142] However, more and more limitations on using IP for TMK were found in practice.[143] As noted by Wang, China's IP system is incomplete and was established at a relatively late stage for a number of historical reasons.[144] This, combined with TMK's unique characteristics, presents major challenges in effectively protecting TMK. Wang and Wang shared a similar viewpoint and suggested that the inconsistencies between Eastern philosophies and IP doctrines could establish some limitations on the protection of TMK.[145] They advocate for a comprehensive reform of China's IP system that takes into account the country's traditional culture and TMK philosophies. This better aligns the legal framework with China's historical and sociocultural context, ensuring more effective protection and preservation of TMK.[146] This study contributes to this critical analysis by exploring ways to better align the IP framework with China's historical and sociocultural context.

---

[137] Vai Io Lo, 'The Developments of Intellectual Property Protection in China Since Deng's Southern Tour' in John Wong and Yongnian Zheng (eds), *The Nanxun Legacy And China's Development In The Post-deng Era* (2001) 271, 273.

[138] 张今 [Zhang Jin]《中药的专利保护: 现状、问题及对策》[Patent Protection of Chinese Traditional Medicines: Current Situation, Problems, and Countermeasures] (2004) 3 中国现代中药 *Modern Chinese Medicine* 94, 94.

[139]《中药品种保护条例》[Regulation on the Protection of Traditional Chinese Medicine] (People's Republic of China) State Council, Order No 106, 1992.

[140] Ibid.

[141] Ibid.

[142] Ibid.

[143] 刘燕玲 [Liu Yanling]《中医药知识产权保护迫在眉睫》[The Urgent Need for Intellectual Property Protection of Traditional Chinese Medicine Knowledge] (2010) 12(6) 中国现代中药 *Modern Chinese Medicine* 7, 8.

[144] Bing Wang et al, 'Establish a Legal System with Chinese Characteristics to Protect the Intellectual Property Rights of Traditional Chinese Medicines' (2002) 17(1) *Journal of Tsinghua University* 73, 73–77.

[145] Jin-Guo Wang and Na Wang, 'The Present Situation and the Improvement Measures of Intellectual Property Protection of Traditional Chinese Medicine in China' (Conference Paper, International Conference on Humanities and Social Science, 2017).

[146] Ibid.

After a complex negotiating process, China became a party to the *Nagoya Protocol* in September 2016.[147] China's Ministry of Ecology and Environment then developed the legislative approach, the *Draft Regulation* for the implementation of the *Nagoya Protocol*.[148] The *Draft Regulation* represents the first attempt by the Chinese government to establish overarching regulatory ABS mechanisms governing the entire use of TK (including TMK). This situation offers the Chinese government a distinctive opportunity to conduct a comprehensive assessment of the national ABS framework. Nevertheless, the legislative process for adopting the *Draft Regulation* has stalled for four years. It is not clear whether the government is still considering it. Moreover, China promulgated the *Law of the People's Republic of China on Traditional Chinese Medicine* in 2017,[149] which is also relevant to ABS and TMK. It provides that the holders of TMK should have the rights to inherit and use the TMK, and requests PIC for, and benefit-sharing from, the use of the TMK that they possess.[150] However, these ABS-related provisions are mainly advisory in practice and lack enforcement muscle.

Meanwhile, despite the significance of ABS in relation to TMK, only three pieces of literature from China study the relationships and interactions between ABS and TMK in the country. In 2009, Zeng for the first time suggested addressing the protection of TMK through ABS measures.[151] He provided a legal analysis of the existing challenges surrounding TMK protection and critically analyse the need for an ABS framework to address these challenges.[152] However, this analysis leads to merely tentative suggestions which are simplistic and limited. In the end, the author calls for the policymakers to consider how TMK could be protected more effectively in the context of ABS by introducing a more comprehensive ABS scheme.[153] In 2016, Wang discussed the possibilities of implementing the CBD obligations to regulate access to TMK, ensure fair and equitable benefit-sharing, and provide a robust framework for TMK protection.[154] They noted that despite the limitations of the CBD, implementing the CBD could provide alternative means for protection of TMK, and

147 Secretariat of the Convention on Biological Diversity, 'Parties to the *Nagoya Protocol*', (*Convention on Biological Diversity*) < https://www.cbd.int/abs/nagoya-protocol/signatories/ > .

148 Ibid.

149《中华人民共和国中医药法》[Law of the People's Republic of China on Traditional Chinese Medicine] (People's Republic of China) Standing Committee of the National People's Congress, 2016.

150 Law of the People's Republic of China on Traditional Chinese Medicine (n 146) art 43.

151 曾真 [Zeng Zhen],《获取与惠益分享制度及其在中药领域的运用》[Access and Benefit Sharing Regime and Its Application in the Field of Chinese Medicine] (2009) 20(30)中国药房 *China Pharmacy* 2321, 2321–2323.

152 Ibid.

153 Ibid.

154 怀永, 王艳 翚[Zeng Zhen] and [Wang Yanhui],《惠益分享视角下的中药炮制知识产权保护研究》[Study on the Protection of Intellectual Property Rights of Traditional Chinese Medicine Processing under the Perspective of Benefit Sharing] (2016) 13(11) 中国医药导报 *China Medical Herald* 172, 172–175.

strike a balance between the needs of users and providers of TMK.[155] In 2016, Wang and Huai proposed that ABS measures should play an integral role in supporting current IP legal strategies and act as an auxiliary enabler for improving situations of TMK protection in China.[156] However, neither of these articles offers a concrete or substantive legal analysis that takes into account the historical and sociocultural context of TMK in China. With China's accession to the *Nagoya Protocol* in 2016, and the development of the *Draft Regulation* for its implementation in 2017, there is an urgent need for such an analysis.

The establishment and implementation of TMK information systems in China have emerged as a critical subject in the discourse surrounding the protection, utilisation, and dissemination of TMK.[157] These information systems were first launched in the early 2000s, when the Chinese central government backed the broad application of information technology.[158] To date, the Traditional Chinese Medicine Patent Database ('CTCMPD'), with its foundation in IP rights—particularly patents—stands as China's most advanced TMK information system.[159]

These information systems are designed to serve as comprehensive repositories, documenting a wide array of traditional medicinal practices, herbal formulations, acupuncture techniques and other knowledge that have been refined and passed down through generations.[160] Standing at the intersection of tradition and modernity, TMK information systems endeavour to both safeguard and promote centuries-old wisdom in an accessible digital format.

While there is significant potential for the development and implementation of TMK information systems in China, there are also noteworthy limitations that could impede their full realisation and utilisation. Huang, in particular, pinpointed two critical issues with the existing TMK information systems[161]: their restricted openness and the narrow breadth of TMK inclusion. To tackle these issues, Huang proposed the creation of a semi-open database model. This model seeks to encourage active

155 Ibid.

156 Ibid.

157 吴弈天 [Wu Yitian],《中医药传统知识数据库构建思路初探》[A Preliminary Exploration of the Construction Ideas for Traditional Chinese Medicine Knowledge Database] (2022) 4中国卫生法制 *Chinese Journal of Health Law and Regulation* 6, 11; 刘琴 [Liu Qin],《活态中医药传统知识数据库的构建与应用意义》The Construction and Significance of a Dynamic Traditional Chinese Medicine Knowledge Database] (2022) 4 世界科学技术-中医药现代化 *Modernization of Traditional Chinese Medicine and Materia Medica-World Science and Technology* 1, 1–8.

158 Yanling Sun and Yanhuai Liu, 'China traditional Chinese Medicine (TCM) Patent Database' (2004) 26(1) *World Patent Information* 91, 91.

159 Ibid.

160 R. Lakshmi Poorna, M Mymoon and A Hariharan, 'Preservation and Protection of Traditional Knowledge—Diverse Documentation Initiatives Across the Globe' (2014) 107(8) *Current Science* 1240, 1243.

161 黄玉烨 [Huang Yuye],《我国传统知识数据库保护模式及其法律机制研究》[Research on the Protection Mode and Legal Mechanisms of Traditional Knowledge Databases in China.] (2022) 4 河南财经政法大学学报 *The Journal of Henan University of Economics and Law* 55, 55–56.

user engagement while simultaneously ensuring the protection and recognition of the interests of traditional knowledge holders.[162]

Wu identified another primary limitation of existing information systems.[163] They criticised the notable absence of exhaustive data collection.[164] This shortcoming stems from inconsistent or insufficient collection methods, leading to a dearth of comprehensive data within these information systems.[165] This gap not only restricts the quantity of available information but also threatens to marginalise important segments of TMK that may not be captured due to these flawed methodologies.[166]

While existing research provides insightful critiques, it often lacks substantial analysis that thoroughly considers China's historical and sociocultural context. This gap can be addressed by examining China's current TMK information system through the historical and cultural lens. This approach presents a novel understanding of TMK information systems, specifically tailored to facilitate the protection, utilisation, and dissemination of TMK while emphasising their cultural and historical significance. By incorporating these perspectives, scholars and policymakers can better understand and address the challenges and opportunities presented by the TMK information systems, ultimately fostering a more sustainable and culturally sensitive approach to their development and use. This book addresses this gap, offering a holistic, culturally sensitive approach to the development and implementation of TMK information systems that will better inform research and policy-making in this area.

The previous discussion underscores a significant gap in existing scholarship, specifically around the challenge of aligning China's distinct, bottom-up approach, deeply embedded in its cultural and historical milieu, with the top-down enforcement of Western-based assumptions inherent in international IP laws, ABS regulations, and TMK information systems. This analytical perspective paves the way for critical insights and debates that have predominantly been overlooked in the existing literature. A key component of this analysis involves a culturally historical exploration, examining the sociocultural contexts and historical influences shaping China's TMK. This involves acknowledging how the cultural and historical foundations of this knowledge inform its protection, dissemination, and its utilisation (by pharmaceutical sector) within China's legal and regulatory frameworks.

IP laws and other mechanisms such as the ABS regime and TMK information systems have been suggested as potential pathways for TMK protection.[167] However, their implementations in China have faced hurdles due to distinct factors rooted in

---

162 Ibid.

163 吴弈天 [Wu Yitian] (n 154) 10.

164 Ibid.

165 Ibid.

166 Ibid.

167 刘长秋 [Liu Changqiu],《我国中医药知识产权保护的问题与对策》[Research on the Main Problems and Countermeasures of Intellectual Property Protection of Chinese Medicine] (2019) 34(11) 中华中医药杂志 *China Journal of Traditional Chinese Medicine and Pharmacy* 5011, 5011–5013; 曾真 [Zeng Zhen],《获取与惠益分享制度及其在中药领域的运用》[Access and Benefit-sharing System and Its Application in the Field of Traditional Chinese Medicine] (2009) 20(30) 中国药房 *China Pharmacy* 2321, 2321–2323.

the country's history and culture. These challenges arise from aspects such as the collective nature of TMK, the diverse ethnic groups and their traditions, cultural diversity, and the complex interplay between traditional customs and modern legal frameworks. By addressing this issue, this study significantly contributes to bridging the research gap by critically examining how China can effectively utilise its IP frameworks and other mechanisms, such as the ABS regime and TMK information systems, to ensure adequate preservation, responsible utilisation, and proper dissemination of the country's valuable TMK.

By offering an in-depth analysis of the historical and sociocultural factors influencing TMK governance in China, the study illuminates the complexities and challenges that emerge in a rapidly evolving society that maintains deep connections to its cultural traditions. In addition, it presents practical suggestions for creating culturally and historically pertinent legal, policy, and practical frameworks that can ensure adequate preservation, responsible utilisation, and proper dissemination of the country's valuable TMK. By identifying the limitations and challenges within the current approaches to TMK governance, it not only fills a critical void in China's TMK protection literature but also serves as a valuable resource for policymakers, scholars, and practitioners seeking to develop effective strategies for TMK governance in China and beyond.

1.4 An Overview of the Book

This book provides a comprehensive analysis of the challenges and opportunities surrounding the preservation, utilisation, and dissemination of China's Traditional Medical Knowledge (TMK). By delving into the country's unique historical, cultural, and social context, it explores how TMK can be effectively governed through legal frameworks and alternative mechanisms, such as access and benefit-sharing (ABS) regimes and TMK information systems.

The discussion begins by introducing TMK as a dynamic heritage that reflects the diverse histories and practices of China's ethnic groups. This rich tradition has become a cornerstone of pharmaceutical innovation, yet its commercialisation raises ethical and legal complexities. The book highlights the escalating tensions surrounding the unauthorised use of TMK, particularly in patent applications, and advocates for frameworks that respect traditional ownership and treat TMK as a collective resource.

From this foundation, the analysis moves into the challenges posed by Western-centric intellectual property (IP) systems. The Western IP framework, designed to incentivise individual innovation, is often at odds with the communal and cultural nature of TMK. This tension is explored through a critical lens, revealing how Western legal norms can inadvertently erode TMK values and facilitate its exploitation. Drawing on China's historical and philosophical traditions, the book proposes a culturally sensitive governance model that better aligns with the collective ethos of TMK.

The discussion then shifts to the intersection of TMK and China's pharmaceutical industry. The rapid evolution of this sector has highlighted the systemic biases within the current IP framework, where corporate interests often overshadow the rights of traditional knowledge holders. The analysis underscores the need for reforms to ensure a balance between innovation and the equitable treatment of TMK custodians, with recommendations rooted in China's dialectical philosophy.

Building on this, the book examines the potential of international frameworks, such as ABS mechanisms, to protect TMK. It critiques the application of globally accepted ABS principles, such as prior informed consent and benefit-sharing, within China's unique sociocultural and legal context. The book argues for the adaptation of these frameworks to better reflect China's historical emphasis on communal knowledge and social harmony.

Finally, the book explores the complexities of digitising TMK through information systems. While these systems offer significant opportunities for preservation and innovation, they also risk decontextualising TMK from its origins and marginalising the knowledge of minority communities. By tracing the development of China's TMK information systems, the book highlights both their potential and their pitfalls. Reform suggestions focus on creating adaptive, inclusive, and culturally sensitive digital tools to safeguard the integrity of TMK.

The conclusion synthesises the key findings, reflecting on the interplay between international legal norms and China's historical and cultural landscape. It offers practical recommendations for future governance frameworks and highlights areas for further research. Through this analysis, the book provides valuable insights for policymakers, legal professionals, and scholars, aiming to bridge the gap between tradition and modernity in the regulation of Chinese TMK.

References

《中华人民共和国中医药法》[Law of the People's Republic of China on Traditional Chinese Medicine] (People's Republic of China) Standing Committee of the National People's Congress, December 25, 2016.

《中华人民共和国中医药法》[Law of the People's Republic of China on Traditional Chinese Medicine] (People's Republic of China) Standing Committee of the National People's Congress, 2016.

《中华人民共和国专利法》[Patent Law of the People's Republic of China] (People's Republic of China) National People's Congress Standing Committee, Order No 11, March 1984.

《中药品种保护条例》[Regulation on the Protection of Traditional Chinese Medicine] (People's Republic of China) State Council, Order No 106, 1992.

A Ganashree, 'Who Owns Ocean Biodiversity? The Legal Status and Role of Patents as a Means to Achieve Equitable Distribution of Benefits' (2021) 53(1) *Case Western Reserve Journal of International Law* 197.

A Xu, 'Traditional Medicine Is the Valuable Resource for Global Health' (2021) 8(1) *Journal of Traditional Chinese Medical Sciences* 2.

Abdul Haseeb Ansari and Lekha Laxman, 'A Review of the International Framework for Access and Benefit Sharing of Genetic Resources with Special Reference to the Nagoya Protocol' (2013) 16 *Asia Pacific Journal of Environmental Law* 105.

Akalemwa Ngenda, 'The Nature of the International Intellectual Property System: Universal Norms and Values or Western Chauvinism?' (2005) 14(1) *Information & Communications Technology Law* 59, 73.

Alma Barbaso Schwartz, 'Traditional Chinese Medicine: Ancient Holistic Healing' (2004) 16(6) *Home Health Care Management & Practice* 494.

Anita Chen Marshall, 'Traditional Chinese Medicine and Clinical Pharmacology' in FJ Hock and MR Gralinski (eds), Drug Discovery and Evalu*ation: Methods in Clinical Pharmacology* (Springer Nature Switzerland AG, 2020) 463.

ANM Alamgir, *Therapeutic Use of Medicinal Plants and Their Extracts* (Springer, 2017).

Bing Wang et al, 'Establish a Legal System with Chinese Characteristics to Protect the Intellectual Property Rights of Traditional Chinese Medicines' (2002) 17(1) *Journal of Tsinghua University* 73.

Brian Thom and Do Bain, Aboriginal Intangible Property in Canada: An Ethnographic Review (Discussion Paper, 2013) 1–45.

Carmen Richerzhagen, 'Effective Governance of Access and Benefit-sharing under the Convention on Biological Diversity' (2011) 20 *Biodiversity Conservation* 2243.

Clement Yow Mulalap et al, 'Traditional knowledge and the BBNJ instrument' (2020) 122 *Marine Policy* 1.

Colin W Wright et al, 'Ancient Chinese Methods Are Remarkably Effective for the Preparation of Artemisinin-Rich Extracts of Qing Hao with Potent Antimalarial Activity' (2010) 15(2) *Molecules* 804.

David Curtis Wright, The History of China (ABC-CLIO, LLC, 2020) 11.

Devinder Sharma, 'Corporate Theft of "Traditional Knowledge": Biopiracy by Another Name', *HIMAL SOUTHASIAN* (online, 1 August 2002) <https://www.himalmag.com/corporate-theft-of-traditional-knowledge-biopiracy-by-another-name/>.

DM McGraw, 'The CBD—Key Characteristics and Implications for Implementation' (2002) 11(1) *Review of European, Comparative & International Environmental Law* 17.

Dongguo Chen, 'Chinese Traditional Medicine Encountering Biopiracy Is Not Alarmist' (2006) 35 *Pharmaceutical Economics* 1.

DQ Hodnett, 'Legitimising Biopiracy? Fairness and Efficacy of the Nagoya Protocol' (2021) 2 *York Law Review* 75.

Elaine Yu and Hakima Amri, 'China's Other Medical Systems: Recognizing Uyghur, Tibetan, and Mongolian Traditional Medicines' (2016) 5(1) *Global Advances in Health and Medicine* 79.

Elisa Morgera, Elsa Tsioumani and Matthias Buck, Unravelling the Nagoya Protocol: A Commentary on the Nagoya Protocol on Access and Benefit-sharing to the Convention on Biological Diversity (Brill, 2014) 2–3.

Evana Wright, Protecting Traditional Knowledge: Lessons from Global Case Studies (Edward Elgar Publishing, 2020) 168–195.

Evanson C Kamau, Bevis Fedder and Gerd Winter, 'The Nagoya Protocol on Access to Genetic Resources and Benefit Sharing. What Is New and What Are the Implications for Provider and User Countries and The Scientific Community' (2010) 6(3) *Law Environment and Development Journal* 248.

Experts' Study on Exclusions from Patentable Subject Matter and Exceptions and Limitations to the Rights, World Intellectual Property Organization General Assembly, 39th Sess, WIPO Doc WO/GA/39/14 (2010) 218.

G Kristin Rosendal, 'Balancing Access and Benefit Sharing and Legal Protection of Innovations from Bioprospecting' (2006) 15(4) *The Journal of Environment & Development* 428.

Graham Dutfield, 'The Public and Private Domains: Intellectual Property Rights in Traditional Knowledge' (2000) 21(3) *Science Communication* 274.

Graham Dutfield, 'TRIPS-Related Aspects of Traditional Knowledge' (2001) 33(2) *Case Western Reserve Journal of International Law* 233.

Gulzar S Sanghera, Dharminder Bhatia and KS Thind, 'Access and Benefit Sharing on the Use of Indigenous Traditional Knowledge' in Romesh Kumar Salgotra and Bharat Bhushan Gupta (eds), *Plant Genetic Resources and Traditional Knowledge for Food Security* (Springer, 2016) 163.

GV Overwalle, 'Protecting and Sharing Biodiversity and Traditional Knowledge: Holder and User Tools' (2005) 53 *Ecological Economics* 585.

Hallen Korn, 'Patenting Culture: The Cultural Conflict of Intellectual Property' (2012) 8 *The Morningside Review* 11.

Ikechi Mgbeoji, 'Patent Regime and Biopiracy', *Global Biopiracy: Patents, Plants, and Indigenous Knowledge* (University of British Columbia Press, 2006) 119.

J Janewa OseiTutu, 'Emerging Scholars Series: A Sui Generis Regime for Traditional Knowledge: The Cultural Divide in Intellectual Property Law' (2011) 15(1) *Marqueette Intellectual Property Law Review* 147.

Jackson Owiti and Ashah Owano, 'Use of Mobile Technologies in Dissemination of Traditional Medical Knowledge in Kenya: Case Study of Kenya Resource Centre for Indigenous Knowledge' in Jackson Owiti and Ashah Owano (eds), *Digital Technologies for Information and Knowledge Management* (2019) 433.

Javier Garcia, 'Fighting Biopiracy: The Legislative Protection of Traditional Knowledge' (2007) 18 *Berkerley La Raza Law Journal* 5.

Jin-Guo Wang and Na Wang, 'The Present Situation and the Improvement Measures of Intellectual Property Protection of Traditional Chinese Medicine in China' (Conference Paper, International Conference on Humanities and Social Science, 2017).

John Tustin, 'Traditional Knowledge and Intellectual Property in Brazilian Biodiversity Law' (2006) 14 *Texas Intellectual Property Law Journal* 131.

Josephine Agu, 'Traditional Medicines Must Be Integrated into Health Care for Culturally Diverse Groups', *The Conversation* (Web Page, 2019) <https://theconversation.com/traditional-medicines-must-be-integrated-into-health-care-for-culturally-diverse-groups-114980>.

Joshua D Sarnoff and Glushko Samuelson, *Analysis of Options for Implementing Disclosure of Origin Requirements in Intellectual Property Applications,* United Nations Conference on Trade and Development (UNCTAD), UN DocUNCTAD/DITC/TED/2004114 (2006).

K Roisah et al, 'Trends of Global Values in Legal Political Formation of Intellectual Property Law in Indonesia' (2017) 8(9) *International Journal of Civil Engineering and Technology* 391.

Kanchana Kariyawasam and Matthew Tsai, 'Access to Genetic Resources and Benefit-sharing: Implications of Nagoya Protocol on Providers and Users' (2018) 21(5–6) *The Journal of World Intellectual Property* 289.

KG Ramawat, Herbal Drugs: Ethnomedicine to Modern Medicine (Springer, 2009) 34.

Lan Qiu et al, 'Public Funding and Private Investment for R&D: A Survey in China's Pharmaceutical Industry' (2014) 12(27) *Health Research Policy and Systems* 1.

Li Wang, 'Guizhou: Protecting Traditional Medicine and Rejecting "Biological Pirates"' (2006) 7 *China Reform* 1.

Lili Lai and Judith Farquhar, 'Nationality Medicines in China: Institutional Rationality and Healing Charisma' (2015) 57(2) *Comparative Studies in Society and History* 381.

Louis H Miller and Xinzhuan Su, 'Artemisinin: Discovery from the Chinese Herbal Garden' (2011) 146(6) *Cell* 855.

Martin Fredriksson, 'India's Traditional Knowledge Digital Library and the Politics of Patent Classifications' (2023) 34 *Law and Critique* 1.

MeiYing Li and XianYuan Li, 'Perspectives on Current Protection of Intellectual Property Rights for Traditional Chinese Medicine' (2015) 42(4) *Journal of International Pharmaceutical Research* 467.

Michelle F Rourke, 'When Knowledge Goes Viral: Assessing the Possibility of Virus-related Traditional Knowledge for Access and Benefit-sharing' (2018) 21(5–6) *Journal of World Intellectual Property* 356.

N Yacoub and H Souei, 'Is Drug Patent Protection a Determinant of the Location of Pharmaceutical FDI? China's Experience' in Andreas Pyka and Keun Lee (eds), *Innovation, Catch-up, and Sustainable Development: A Schumpeterian Perspective* (Springer, 2022) 209.

Olufunmilayo B Arewa, 'TRIPs and Traditional Knowledge: Local Communities, Local Knowledge, and Global Intellectual Property Frameworks' (2006) 10(2) *Marquette Intellectual Property Law Review* 156.

P Sheng-Ji, 'Ethnobotanical Approaches of Traditional Medicine Studies: Some Experiences from Asia' (2001) 39 *Pharmaceutical Biology* 74.

Peter K Yu, 'The Transplant and Transformation of Intellectual Property Laws in China' in Niklas Bruun, Nari Lee and Mingde Li (eds), *Governance of Intellectual Property Rights in China and Europe* (Elgar Intellectual Property and Global Development series, 2016) 20.

R Manley, 'Developmental Perspectives on the TRIPS and Traditional Knowledge Debate' (2006) 3(1) *The Macquarie Journal of International and Comparative Environmental Law* 113.

R Lakshmi Poorna, M Mymoon and A Hariharan, 'Preservation and Protection of Traditional Knowledge—Diverse Documentation Initiatives Across the Globe' (2014) 107(8) *Current Science* 1240.

Ren Hu, 'Protection of Cross Border Ethnic Groups' Traditional Medicine under International Law' (2013) 8(1) *Frontiers of Law in China* 186.

Report, World Intellectual Property Organization (WIPO) General Assembly, 26th Sess, WIPO Doc WO/GA/26/10 (2000).

Revised Draft Agenda, World Intellectual Property Organization (WIPO) Intergovernmental Committee on Intellectual Property and Genetic Resources, Traditional Knowledge and Folklore, 1st Sess, WIPO Doc GRTKF/IC/1/1 REV (2010).

Roberta Lee and Michael J. Balick, 'Flu for You? The Common Cold, Influenza, and Traditional Medicine' (2006) 2(3) *Explore* 252.

Saskia Vermeylen, 'Comparative Environmental Law and Orientalism: Reading beyond the 'Text' of Traditional Knowledge Protection' (2015) 24(3) *Review of European Community & International Environmental Law* 304.

Secretariat of the Convention on Biological Diversity, 'Parties to the *Nagoya Protocol*', (*Convention on Biological Diversity*) <https://www.cbd.int/abs/nagoya-protocol/signatories/>.

Secretariat of the World Intellectual Property Organization, *Traditional Knowledge and Folklore, Traditional Knowledge: Operational Terms and Definitions*, World Intellectual Property Organization Intergovernmental Committee on Intellectual Property and Genetic Resources, 13th Sess, WIPO Doc WIPO/GRTKF/IC/13/9 (June 2002).

Shoaib Ali and Heng Tang, 'Is Intellectual Property Beneficial to Knowledge Management? Literature Review on Organizational Knowledge Protection' (2022) *Journal of the Knowledge Economy* 1.

Shruti Dwivedi et al, 'Intellectual Property Rights in Healthcare: An Overview' in Debmalya Barh (eds), *Biotechnology in Healthcare* (Academic Press, 2022) 259–266.

Sixty-Fourth World Health Assembly, Resolutions and Decisions, WHA64/2011/REC/1, 8–9 and Annex 2 (WHA64.5) (PIP Framework) (2011).

Sunder, Madhavi, 'The Invention of Traditional Knowledge' (2007) 70(97) *Law and Contemporary Problems* 97.

The *Convention on Biological Diversity and the Nagoya Protocol: Intellectual Property Implications—A Handbook on the Interface between Global Access and Benefit Sharing Rules and Intellectual Property*, UN Doc UNCTAD/DIAE/PCB/2014/3 (2014) 1.

The Impact of Intellectual Property Rights Systems on the Conservation and Sustainable Use of Biological Diversity and on the Equitable Sharing of Benefits from Its Use, UN Doc UNEP/CBD/CGP/3/22 (22 September 1996).

The Protection of Traditional Knowledge: Draft Articles (Rev. 2), World Intellectual Property Organization General Assembly, WIPO Doc WIPO/GRTKF/IC/24 (2013) <http://www.wipo.int/meetings/en/doc_details.jsp?doc_id=238182>.

The United Nations' *Nagoya Protocol on Access to Genetic Resources and the Fair and Equitable Sharing of Benefits Arising from Their Utilization to the Convention on Biological Diversity*, opened for signature 29 October 2010, [2012] ATNIF 3 (entered into force 12 October 2014).

Thomas Cottier and Marion Panizzon, 'Legal Perspectives on Traditional Knowledge: The Case for Intellectual Property Protection' (2004) 7(2) *Journal of International Economic Law* 371.

Thomas J Krumenacher, 'Protection for Indigenous Peoples and their Traditional Knowledge: Would a Registry System Reduce the Misappropriation of Traditional Knowledge?' (2004) 8(1) *Marquette Intellectual Property Law Review* 143.

Tianbao Qin, 'Common Pools of Traditional Chinese Medical Knowledge in China' in Gerd Winter and Evanson Chege Kamau (eds), *Common Pools of Genetic Resources: Equity and Innovation in International Biodiversity Law* (2013) 150.

United Nations Convention on Biological Diversity, opened for signature 5 June 1992, 1760 UNTS 79 (entered into force 29 December 1993).

United Nations Declaration on the Rights of Indigenous Peoples, GA Res 61/295, UN GAOR, 61st session, 107th plen mtg, Agenda Item 68, UN Doc A/RES/61/295 (13 September 2007) ('UNDRIP') art 31.

V Sujatha, 'Globalisation of South Asian Medicines: Knowledge, Power, Structure and Sustainability' (2020) 6(1) *Society and Culture in South Asia* 1.

Vai Io Lo, 'The Developments of Intellectual Property Protection in China Since Deng's Southern Tour' in John Wong and Yongnian Zheng (eds), *The Nanxun Legacy And China's Development In The Post-deng Era* (2001) 271.

William P Alford, To Steal a Book Is an Elegant Offense: Intellectual Property Law in Chinese Civilization (Stanford University Press, 1995) 9–29.

World Health Organization, 'New WHO Guidelines to Promote Proper Use of Alternative Medicines', (Media Release, 22 June 2004).

World Intellectual Property Organization, '*Intellectual Property Needs and Expectations of Traditional Knowledge Holders: WIPO Report on Fact-Finding Missions on Intellectual Property and Traditional Knowledge (1998–1999)*' (2001).

WR Strohl, 'The Role of Natural Products in A Modern Drug Discovery Program' (2000) 5 *Drug Discovery Today* 39.

Xiaoou Zheng, 'Key legal challenges and opportunities in the implementation of the Nagoya Protocol: The case of China' (2019) 28(2) *Review of European, Comparative & International Environmental Law* 175.

Y Karanja and RL Murphy, 'Intellectual Property Protection and Commercialisation' in T.S. Douglas et al (eds), *Biomedical Engineering for Africa* (University of Cape Town Libraries, 2019) 161–162.

Yanling Sun and Yanhuai Liu, 'China Traditional Chinese Medicine (TCM) Patent Database' (2004) 26(1) *World Patent Information* 91.

Young-Joon Surh, 'Reverse Pharmacology Applicable for Botanical Drug Development—Inspiration from the Legacy of Traditional Wisdom' (2011) 1(1) *Journal of Traditional and Complementary Medicine* 5.

Zhi-Hai Jin, 'Intellectual Property Protection and Countermeasures in the Field of Traditional Chinese Medicine' (2005) 15(1) *Journal of Intellectual Property* 34.

曾真 [Zeng Zhen],《获取与惠益分享制度及其在中药领域的运用》[Access and Benefit Sharing Regime and Its Application in the Field of Chinese Medicine] (2009) 20(30)中国药房 *China Pharmacy* 2321.

邓明峰 [Deng Mingfeng],《我国民族中医药传统知识专利保护研究》[Research on Patent Protection for TMK of China's Ethnic Groups] (2018) 12 贵州民族研究 *Guizhou Ethnic Studies* 96.

段莉敏 [Duan Limin],《我国少数民族医药文化保护与传承政策发展现状分析》[Analysis of the Current Status of the Protection and Inheritance of Ethnic Minority Medical Culture in China] (2019) 39 (10) 中国农村卫生事业管理 Rural Health Care Management in China 709.

顾怡 [Gu Yi],《"贵州苗药"向"生物海盗"说不》[Guizhou Miao Medicine Says No to 'Biopirates'] (2004) 贵州政协报*Guizhou Political Consultative Conference News* 1.

管贞 [Guan Zhen], 中医药为世界贡献"中国处方"》[Traditional Chinese Medicine Contributes "Chinese Prescription" to the World] [2010] 国际人才交流 *International Talent Exchange* 30.

怀永, 王艳翚[Zeng Zhen] and [Wang Yanhui],《惠益分享视角下的中药炮制知识产权保护研究》[Study on the Protection of Intellectual Property Rights of Traditional Chinese Medicine Processing under the Perspective of Benefit Sharing] (2016) 13(11) 中国医药导报 *China Medical Herald* 172.
黄玉烨 [Huang Yuye],《我国传统知识数据库保护模式及其法律机制研究》[Research on the Protection Mode and Legal Mechanisms of Traditional Knowledge Databases in China.] (2022) 4 河南财经政法大学学报 *The Journal of Henan University of Economics and Law* 55.
刘琴 [Liu Qin],《活态中医药传统知识数据库的构建与应用意义》The Construction and Significance of a Dynamic Traditional Chinese Medicine Knowledge Database] (2022) 4 世界科学技术-中医药现代化 *Modernization of Traditional Chinese Medicine and Materia Medica-World Science and Technology* 1.
刘燕玲 [Liu Yanling],《中医药知识产权保护迫在眉睫》[The Urgent Need for Intellectual Property Protection of Traditional Chinese Medicine Knowledge] (2010) 12 (6) 中国现代中药 *Modern Chinese Medicine* 7.
刘长秋 [Liu Changqiu],《我国中医药知识产权保护的问题与对策》[Research on the Main Problems and Countermeasures of Intellectual Property Protection of Chinese Medicine] (2019) 34(11) 中华中医药杂志 *China Journal of Traditional Chinese Medicine and Pharmacy* 5011.
吕文清 [Lv Wenqing],《非洲传统医药知识的立法保护及其对我国的启示》[Legislative Protection of African Traditional Medical Knowledge and Its Implications for Our Country] (2018) 19(2) 南京中医药大学学报*Journal of Nanjing University of TCM* 111.
彭丁带 [Peng Dingdai],《"专利海盗"的危害及其法律应对》[The Harm of 'Patent Piracy' and Its Legal Response] (2017) 5 江西社会科学 *Jiangxi Social Science* 195.
石雪芹 [Shi Xueqin],《从中医药源流看中医药传统知识保护价值》[Examining the Value of Protecting Traditional Chinese Medicine Knowledge from the Perspective of the Origins and Development of Chinese Medicine] (2022) 19(21) 中国医药导报 *China Medical Herald* 30.
王华[Wang Hua],《中医药传统知识利益分享权研究》[Research on the Right to Share Benefits of Traditional Chinese Medicine Knowledge] [2017], 南京中医药大学学报 *Journal of Nanjing University of Traditional Chinese Medicine* 165.
王家博 [Wang Jiabo],《传统中医药知识产权保护的难题与破解思路》[Challenges and Solutions for Intellectual Property Protection of Traditional Medical Knowledge] (2009) 4(9)中国实用医药 *Chinese Practical Medicine* 259.
王平 [Wang Ping],《维吾尔医药学概述》[Uyghur Medicine Overview] (2010) 中国穆斯林 Chinese Muslims 12.
吴弈天 [Wu Yitian],《中医药传统知识数据库构建思路初探》[A Preliminary Exploration of the Construction Ideas for Traditional Chinese Medicine Knowledge Database] (2022) 4中国卫生法制 *Chinese Journal of Health Law and Regulation* 6.
吴致远 [Wu Zhiyuan],《从知识的地方性到技术的民族性》[From the Locality of Knowledge to the Nationality of Technology] (2022) 3 广西大学学报 *Journal of Guangxi University* 44.
张今 [Zhang Jin],《中药的专利保护:现状、问题及对策》[Patent Protection of Chinese Traditional Medicines: Current Situation, Problems, and Countermeasures] (2004) 3 中国现代中药 *Modern Chinese Medicine* 94.
赵阳 [Zhao Yang],《名古屋议定书履约挑战与对策 :以植物制剂行业为例》[Challenges and Countermeasures in Implementing the Nagoya Protocol: A Case Study of the Plant-based Formulation Industry] [2021] 中国土地资源经济*Natural Resource Economics of China* 57.
左岫仙 [Zuo Xiuxian],《民族医药的知识产权保护》[Protection of Intellectual Property Rights in Traditional Ethnic Medicine] (2010) 中南民族大学学报 *Journal of South-Central University for Nationalities* 76.

Chapter 2
Internal Conflicts Regarding Traditional Medical Knowledge in China

2.1 Introduction

The academic sphere is currently engrossed in a crucial discourse regarding the escalating trend of unauthorised use of traditional knowledge, specifically TMK, and the pressing need for its preservation.[1] Chapter One initiated the discussion on the elusive definition of traditional knowledge, with scholars from various disciplines contributing, albeit without achieving a consensus.

As this chapter progresses with exploring the intricacies of this multifaceted subject, it is essential to draw attention to a growing scholarly discourse: the inadequacy of IP systems to regulate traditional knowledge, including TMK.[2] Scholars argue that traditional knowledge, encompassing TMK, often hinges on communal ownership, is passed down through generations, and typically relies on oral transmission.[3] These characteristics clash with the prerequisites for IP protections such as patents which demand novelty, non-obviousness, and industrial applicability.[4] In light of these considerations, efforts to harness traditional knowledge under conventional IP rights have often been fraught with controversy. There have been instances where the application of traditional IP rights to traditional knowledge has led to corporations obtaining exclusive rights without adequately compensating or recognising

---

[1] Kamrul Hossain and Rosa Maria Ballardini, 'Protecting Indigenous Traditional Knowledge Through a Holistic Principle-Based Approach' (2021) 39(1) *Nordic Journal of Human Rights* 51, 53–54.

[2] Tesh Dagne, 'Protecting Traditional Knowledge in International Intellectual Property Law: Imperatives for Protection and Choice of Modalities' (2014) 14 The John Marshall Review of Intellectual Property Law 26, 26–49; 李 钰 [Li Jue]《中医药传统知识保护与知识产权制度的关系》[The Relationship Between the Protection of Traditional Chinese Medicine Knowledge and the Intellectual Property System] (2022) 19(27) 中国医药导报 China Medical Herald 119, 119–122.

[3] Xuan Li and Weiwei Li, 'Inadequacy of Patent Regime on Traditional Medicinal Knowledge—A Diagnosis of 13-year Traditional Medicinal Knowledge Patent Experience in China' (2007) 10(2) *The Journal of World Intellectual Property* 125, 125–148.

[4] Ibid, 132–144.

N. Xia, *Medicinal Mandates*, https://doi.org/10.1007/978-981-96-4108-6_2

the Indigenous communities that are the rightful guardians of this wisdom.[5] This phenomenon has sparked accusations of biopiracy, bringing to light ethical issues and inequities in the system.[6] It underscores profound questions about the suitability and ethics of using IP systems for traditional knowledge, thereby underlining the pressing need to address these challenges.

In response, the CBD[7] and its supplementary agreement the *Nagoya Protocol*[8] have introduced ABS, a set of principles and guidelines that govern how genetic resources and the associated traditional knowledge are accessed, and how the resulting benefits are shared.[9] However, there is growing concern that ABS may not sufficiently protect traditional knowledge due to several factors.

A primary concern stems from the unclear language of Article 8(j) of the CBD, related to traditional knowledge.[10] Despite alluding to the concept of traditional knowledge, this article does not clearly define any explicit obligations towards it.[11] Rather, it advocates for 'equitable sharing', a phrase open to broad interpretations due to the absence of comprehensive guidelines. Broad and subjective terminology used by the CBD, such as 'encourage', 'as far as possible and appropriate', and notably 'subject to its national legislation', creates room for significant interpretive flexibility. When combined with the aforementioned ambiguities, this gives contracting parties potential loopholes to sidestep ABS principles, which could result in inconsistent traditional knowledge protection and subsequently weaken the efficacy of ABS in preserving traditional knowledge.[12]

In the context of uncertainties surrounding Article 8(j), the *Nagoya Protocol* seeks to clarify some of these complexities. Nevertheless, it is not without its own issues and faces various challenges. Similar to the CBD, its language lacks the desired level

---

[5] LC Sahu and Aisha Amin, 'The Issue of Biopiracy & Protection of Traditional Knowledge' (2022) 5(1) *International Journal of Law) Management & Humanities* 2310, 2316–2320.

[6] Ibid.

[7] *Convention on Biological Diversity*, opened for signature on 5 June 1992, 1760 UNTS 79 (entered into force 29 December 1993) ('CBD').

[8] *Nagoya Protocol on Access to Genetic Resources and the Fair and Equitable Sharing of Benefits Arising from Their Utilization to the Convention on Biological Diversity*, opened for signature on 29 October 2010, [2012] ATNIF 3 (entered into force 12 October 2014) ('Nagoya Protocol').

[9] See Discussions in Chapter 5 of this thesis; Fran Humphries et al., 'A Systematic Quantitative Literature Review of Aquaculture Genetic Resource Access and Benefit Sharing' (2019) 11 Review in Aquaculture 1133, 1133–1134.

[10] Article 8(j) of the CBD provides that: 'Subject to its national legislation, Each party shall]respect, preserve and maintain knowledge, innovations and practices of Indigenous and local communities embodying traditional lifestyles relevant for the conservation and sustainable use of biological diversity and promote their wider application with the approval and involvement of the holders of such knowledge, innovations and practices and encourage the equitable sharing of the benefits arising from the utilization of such knowledge, innovations and practices'.

[11] Michelle F Rourke, 'Who Are "Indigenous and Local Communities" and What Is "Traditional Knowledge" for Virus Access and Benefit-sharing? A Textual Analysis of the Convention on Biological Diversity and Its Nagoya Protocol' (2018) 25(3) *Journal of Law and Medicine* 707, 711.

[12] Ibid, 712.

of clarity and precision, leading to a range of interpretations that could potentially be misused.[13]

Despite these issues, it has significantly changed the narratives surrounding traditional knowledge. While it forms an enforceable international framework that safeguards and enforces the rights of Indigenous peoples to their traditional knowledge and genetic resources,[14] it should be noted that this treaty runs in parallel to the principles of Article 31 of the United Nations Declaration on the Rights of Indigenous Peoples ('UNDRIP').[15] Article 31 acknowledges the rights of Indigenous peoples to maintain, control, protect, and develop their traditional knowledge.[16] The *Nagoya Protocol* reinforces this by embedding these principles in a legally binding agreement and extends them to 'local' communities—a term less defined in international law than 'Indigenous' communities'.[17] This inclusive approach is important for countries that assert they have no Indigenous populations within their borders.

While the *Nagoya Protocol* represents an important advancement in the protection of Indigenous and local communities' rights over their traditional knowledge, there is a scholarly consensus that it may not effectively address the full scope of traditional knowledge protection.[18] ABS mechanisms, largely based on a Western perspective, are less adaptable to the often complex and fluid nature of traditional knowledge, which is collectively held, inter-generational, and an integral part of cultural and spiritual identities.[19] This could lead to instances where traditional knowledge is commercialised without adequate compensation or where the spiritual or cultural significance of traditional knowledge is neglected in negotiations.[20] This neglect can exacerbate the tension between the need to protect traditional knowledge and the desire to capitalise on its potential benefits. Thus, while ABS mechanisms represent critical tools in the broader strategy for the regulation of traditional knowledge, they are not a universal solution for the complex issues involved in regulating it, thus

[13] Daniel Robinson et al., 'Legal geographies of kava, kastom and Indigenous knowledge: Next steps under the Nagoya Protocol' (2021) 118 *Geoforum* 169, 169.

[14] Elisa Morgera, Elsa Tsioumani and Matthias Buck, Unraveling the Nagoya Protocol: A Commentary on the Nagoya Protocol on Access and Benefit-sharing to the Convention on Biological Diversity (Brill, 2014) 171–172.

[15] *United Nations Declaration on the Rights of Indigenous Peoples*, GA Res 61/295, UN GAOR, 61st sess, 107th plen mtg, Agenda Item 68, UN Doc A/RES/61/295 (13 September 2007) ('*UNDRIP*').

[16] Article 31 of UNDRIP states: 'Indigenous peoples have the right to maintain, control, protect and develop their cultural heritage, traditional knowledge and traditional cultural expressions, as well as the manifestations of their sciences, technologies and cultures, including human and genetic resources, seeds, medicines, knowledge of the properties of fauna and flora, oral traditions, literatures, designs, sports and traditional games and visual and performing arts. They also have the right to maintain, control, protect and develop their intellectual property over such cultural heritage, traditional knowledge, and traditional cultural expressions'.

[17] *Nagoya Protocol* (n 8) art 12.

[18] DQ Hodnett, 'Legitimising Biopiracy? Fairness and Efficacy of the Nagoya Protocol' (2021) 2 *York Law Review* 75, 75–106.

[19] Ibid, 86.

[20] Ibid.

highlighting the necessity for more nuanced, culturally considerate, and context-specific strategies.

This discourse has found profound resonance in the context of China, given the nation's unique historical and sociocultural fabric, marked by a wealth of TMK in China and its rich TMK tradition.[21] The depth and breadth of China's rich TMK tradition, nurtured over centuries, present a complex interplay between the protection of this knowledge and the drive to exploit its potential benefits.

The dynamics of this scenario, necessitate a comprehensive inquiry. This investigation should not only seek to understand the current situation but also strive to uncover the root causes of these conflicts and tensions. Furthermore, it should analyse their effects and comprehend their wider ramifications within the national and international context. Such a thorough analysis has the potential to reveal the frequently understated complexities intrinsic to the regulation of Chinese TMK. Ultimately, the insights derived from this could lay the groundwork for establishing a more balanced and sustainable approach to the comprehensive protection, responsible utilisation, and suitable dissemination of TMK within the unique fabric of China's historical and sociocultural milieu.

The research presented in this chapter, therefore, situates itself at the intersection of these intricate dynamics. By critically examining the complexities and tensions inherent in the protection and utilisation of TMK within the Chinese context, the investigation seeks to contribute meaningfully to the academic discourse on the protection, utilisation, and dissemination of TMK in China. The findings have the potential has the potential to guide the formation and implementation of future policies and measures, thereby leading towards a more equitable and sustainable path for preserving and leveraging this invaluable resource.

In light of the aforementioned focus on the tensions surrounding TMK protection and utilisation, it is significant to recognise China's unique historical and sociocultural landscape that forms the backdrop of these challenges. China is unique in that it has been a multi-ethnic nation since ancient times.[22] This includes more than 50 diverse ethnic groups with a shared ethnic awareness, known as the Chinese nation (*zhonghua minzu* 中华民族).[23] Nevertheless, the local communities and various ethnic minorities still retained their cultural characteristics, customary rules, and

---

[21] 秦培洁 [Qin Peijie]《从中医药传统知识保护看民间中医药的传承发展》[Looking at the inheritance and development of folk traditional Chinese medicine from the perspective of the protection of traditional knowledge of Chinese medicine] (2023) 20(9) 中国医药导报 *China Pharmaceutical Guide* 127, 127–130; 张凤霞 [Zhang Fengxia]《中医药传统知识保护现状, 存在问题与对策研究》[Research on the current status, existing problems and countermeasures of Traditional Chinese Medicine (TCM) Knowledge Protection] (2023) 20(11) 中国医药导报 *China Medical Herald* 188, 188–192.

[22] 周平 [Zhou Ping]《中华民族的国家叙事》[The National Narrative of the Chinese Nation] (2022) 1 中华民族共同体研究 *Research on the Chinese National Community* 42, 46; Xiaotong Fei, 'The Formation and Development of the Chinese Nation with Multi-ethnic Groups' (2017) 1(1) *International Journal of Anthropology and Ethnology* 1, 1–31.

[23] 马小莉 [Ma Xiaoli]《互嵌交融: 论中华民族的同质性一体性结构》[Interlocking and Blending: On the Homogeneous and Integrated Structure of the Chinese Nation] (2022) 43(6) 贵州民族研究 *Guizhou Ethnic Studies* 42, 42–44.

community protocols within the Chinese nation.[24] Within their original communities, these local populations and ethnic minorities continue to hold, sustain, and enhance their TMK, innovations, and practices. These traditions and practices arise from complex and fluid systems of knowledge, which are intricately linked with the unique cultural and geographical characteristics of each community. The cumulative effect of these dynamic systems has fostered a robust reservoir of Chinese TMK, a precious resource with significant potential in various domains, most notably the pharmaceutical industry.[25] This highlights the significance of recognising this unique landscape in formulating policies or strategies for Chinese TMK protection and utilisation, as any approach that does not consider this context risks undermining the very essence of TMK and its associated community dynamics.

This chapter examines the multifaceted characteristics of Chinese TMK within the diverse and evolving sociocultural landscape of China. It highlights the historical significance, cultural plurality, customary rules, and the dynamic nature of TMK, shedding light on its importance across diverse ethnic communities, and the contemporary issues related to its use and potential misuse by corporate and industrial entities. This chapter has three main sections following this Introduction: Sect. 2.2 presents a critical analysis of the unique characteristics of TMK in China, including its historical background, cultural diversity, customary rules, and dynamism. The historical background highlights the rich and ancient heritage of TMK in China, with roots dating back thousands of years. The analysis of cultural diversity emphasises the contributions of the 56 ethnic groups in China, each with its own unique TMK system. Customary rules are critically analysed in terms of the collective heritage and patrimony of local communities and ethnic groups, where rules and practices have evolved to guide various aspects of life. Finally, the dynamism of TMK in China is explored, showing that it is not static but constantly evolving and adapting to social changes and external stimuli. The section also addresses the challenges faced by TMK when it is used by industrial and corporate powers, potentially leading to consequences such as its loss, devaluation, and unauthorised appropriation.

Section 2.3 examines the case of the Qinghao plant (*Artemisia annua*) and its development into the antimalarial drug artemisinin, illustrating the legal and ethical complexities associated with incorporating TMK into pharmaceutical advancements. The section also underscores the cultural and historical significance of Qinghao for multiple ethnic minority groups in China, emphasising the importance of respecting their collective interests, customs, and practices. It argues that commercialisation and IP activities pose challenges for the recognition and protection of TMK as collective assets. It also highlights the necessity for suitable legal, policy, and practical measures to accommodate the distinct attributes of TMK, as well as its historical and cultural significance.

---

[24] Lyu Zhennan and Siti Rohaya Yahaya, 'An Aesthetic Study on Traditional Batik Design of Miao Ethnicity in China' (2021) 9(2) *Jurnal Seni dan Pendidikan Seni* 12, 12–25; Ye Shu-xian and Liu Wan-er, 'Classic of Mountains and Seas and the Origin of White Jade Worship: On the Myths of the Yellow Emperor's Eating Jade and Queen Mother of the West's Presenting the White Jade Ring' (2016) 6(6) *Journal of Literature and Art Studies* 580, 622.

[25] Ibid.

Section 2.4 presents a patent landscape analysis to explore the rising use of TMK in innovation within China. The findings reveal a notable growth in patent applications involving active ingredients from Qinghao (*Artemisia annua*) in the past thirty years. Despite this, Indigenous contributions and community origins are often not acknowledged in the applications, indicating possible biopiracy in China's domestic sphere. This section highlights the importance of addressing this issue through the lens of IP laws and other governance frameworks, such as the ABS system, all the while considering China's unique historical and sociocultural context.

2.2 The Unique Characteristics of TMK in China

2.2.1 The Origin and Scope of TMK in China

Pinpointing the exact origins of the TMK in China is challenging. Nonetheless, historians believe that its origin might be traced back to the Stone Age when ancient Chinese were shifting from hunting and gathering to farming.[26] Shen-Nung (3737–2697 B.C.), revered as the 'Divine Farmer' and recognised as the founder of agriculture in ancient China, is said to have tasted hundreds of herbs to assess their medicinal properties.[27] He documented his findings in the *Pen-Tsao (Herbal Classics)* which became China's earliest TMK textbook.[28]

Throughout the Zhou dynasty (1046–221 BC), the foundation of native Chinese philosophy, including the most prominent (Confucianism, Daoism, and Legalism), was formed.[29] These philosophies contributed to the development of the medical theoretical basis for TMK in China, encompassing the study of health, diseases, and the nature of life.[30] Around the third century BC, the ancient medical professionals systematically analysed the existing medical theories and practices

---

[26] Francis F Hong, 'History of Medicine in China When Medicine Took an Alternative Pat' (2004) 8 *McGill Journal of Medicine* 79, 79; 程新法 [Cheng Xinfa]《略述中药的起源及其早期典籍》[A Brief Introduction to the Origin of Chinese Medicine and its Early Literature] (1998) 14(3) 药学教育 *Pharmaceutical Education* 61, 61.

[27] 郭静云 [Guo Jingyun]《神农神话源于中国的文化记》[Where Does the Cultural Memory of the Shennong Mythology Originate From?] (2020) 6 中国农史 *Chinese Agricultural History* 3, 10–11.

[28] Ralph C Croizier, Traditional Medicine in Modern China: Science, Nationalism, and the Tensions of Cultural Change (Harvard University Press, 1968) 13–36.

[29] 容中逵 [Rong Zhongkui]《当代中国传统文化传承的"中国"语境——中西关系维度下的中国文化历史演进视角》[The Chinese Context of Contemporary Chinese Traditional Culture Inheritance—The Perspective of Chinese Cultural Historical Evolution under the Dimension of Sino-Western Relations.] (2020) 6 教育科学研究 *Education Science Research* 24, 25–26; Francis F Hong, 'History of Medicine in China When Medicine Took an Alternative Path' (2004) 8 *McGill Journal of Medicine* 79, 79; Yuan Li, *Traditional Chinese Thinking on HRM Practices: Heritage and Transformation in China* (Palgrave Macmillan London, 2013) 85.

[30] Hong (n 26) 85.

of all the ethnic groups in China, compiling comprehensive records of the medical knowledge of their day and adding their observations.[31] These records remained in use for many thousands of years.[32]

The diverse ethnic makeup of China has significantly influenced the TMK landscape. China has been a multi-ethnic country for around two thousand years.[33] The largest ethnic group, the Han, currently accounts for over 90% of the Chinese population.[34] The other 55 ethnic minorities still maintain their unique traditions and customs.[35] Due to the differences in climatic conditions, geographical locations, and ethnic identities, the groups have distinctive lifestyles, customs, and disease spectrums.[36] These differences have led to the development of a broad range of traditional medicine practices.[37] Nevertheless, as expected from the frequent contacts among various ethnic groups and their shared and intertwined histories, the practices have drawn upon each other's strengths and gradually synergised as a whole.[38]

According to the *Law of the People's Republic of China on Traditional Chinese Medicine* in 2017, TMK in China is a general term that refers to the traditional medicine practices of all Chinese ethnic groups, regardless of whether they are Han or other ethnic minorities. TMK reflects the collective understanding of the entire Chinese nation regarding life, health, and disease.[39]

In summary, the examination of the multifaceted origins and scope of TMK in China reveals a complex web of challenges in regulating this knowledge. Recognising these intricacies enables a deeper understanding of the issues contributing to the tensions and complexities in the protection, responsible utilisation, and suitable dissemination of Chinese TMK. This understanding guides the development of nuanced and effective strategies. Furthermore, it helps stakeholders to appreciate the intricacies of China's TMK landscape and to devise well-informed approaches for addressing these tensions within current policy, legal, and practical frameworks,

---

[31] Hong (n 26) 80.

[32] Ibid.

[33] Rong Ma, 'Ethnic Relations in Contemporary China: Cultural Tradition and Ethnic Policies Since 1949' (2006) 25(1) *Policy and Society* 85, 85.

[34] Barry Sautman, 'Ethnic Law and Minority Rights in China: Progress and Constraints' (2002) 21(3) *Law & Policy* 283, 286.

[35] Ibid.

[36] Si-Yuan Pan et al., 'Historical Perspective of Traditional Indigenous Medical Practices: The Current Renaissance and Conservation of Herbal Resources' (2014) 2014 *Evid Based Complement Alternat Med* 1, 2–5.

[37] Ibid.

[38] 李志勇 [Li Zhiyong],《互鉴互融:论民族药的现代研究思路》[Mutual Learning and Integration -Discussing Modern Research Ideas of Ethnomedicine] (2017) 42(7) 中国中药杂志, *China Journal of Chinese Materia Medica* 71, 71–77; 任小巧 [Xiaoqiao Ren],《浅析民族医药学与中医药学的关系》[Discussing the Relationship between Ethnomedicine and Traditional Chinese Medicine] (2012)18 (3) 中国民族医药杂志 *Journal of Medicine & Pharmacy of Chinese Minorities* 60, 60–61.

[39]《中华人民共和国中医药法》[Law of the People's Republic of China on Traditional Chinese Medicine] (People's Republic of China) Standing Committee of the National People's Congress (2016), art 2.

ultimately promoting a harmonious and sustainable future for TMK in China and beyond.

2.2.2 *The Patterns in Which TMK is Held*

TMK in China exists in a complex web of interrelated patterns, influenced by various social ties and hierarchical relationships between individuals, families, local communities, ethnic minority groups, and the State[40] These interconnected dynamics require comprehensive examination to consider how TMK is held and shared at various levels, and to identify potential conflicts that could arise.

In China, a prevalent and characteristic pattern regarding the guardianship of traditional knowledge is that such wisdom is not held individually but is rather a collective asset, predominantly preserved by local communities or ethnic minority groups.[41] However, it is often only fully comprehended by a select group within the community. This group can include individuals like midwives, spiritualists, ecstatic and ritual specialists, bone setters, hereditary physicians, and barefoot doctors.[42]

A more nuanced examination may be afforded by considering the Naxi communities of southwest China. These communities have a profound spiritual belief system, known as the Dongba culture, which values harmonious and balanced relationships between humans and their natural surroundings.[43] This cultural belief system strongly influences their traditional medicinal practices, shaping a unique and rich TMK.[44] Specific roles within the Naxi community mirror those found across many ethnic groups in China. For instance, spiritualists, who are crucial figures in the Dongba culture, are often sought for treating mental illnesses like anxiety or nightmares.[45] Hereditary physicians, on the other hand, focus on treating physiological

---

[40] TJ Hinrichs, 'Healing and Medicine: Healing and Medicine in China' *Encyclopedia.com* (Web Page, 2005) <https://www.encyclopedia.com/environment/encyclopedias-almanacs-transcripts-and-maps/healing-and-medicine-healing-and-medicine> ; Tianbao Qin, 'Common Pools of Traditional Chinese Medical Knowledge in China' in Evanson Chege Kamau and Gerd Winter (eds), *Common Pools of Genetic Resources* (Routledge, 2013) 150, 151.

[41] 马得汶 [Ma Dewen],《西部民族地区患者择医的文化因素探析》[Analysis on Cultural Factors Concerning How Patients in China's Western Ethnic Minority Communities Seek Medical Treatment] (2017) 54(1) 西北师大学报 *Journal of Northwest Normal University* 71, 71–77.

[42] 'Xiaoping Fang, 'From Union Clinics to Barefoot Doctors: Healers, Medical Pluralism, and State Medicine in Chinese Villages, 1950–1970' (2010) 2(2) *Journal of Modern Chinese History* 221, 223.

[43] Bichang He, 'Contemporary Explanation of the Intangible Cultural Heritage of Naxi Dongba Culture' (Conference Paper, International Conference on Art Design, Music and Culture, 2019) 190–191.

[44] Ibid.

[45] Yanqiang Zhao et al., 'Skincare Plants of the Naxi of NW Yunnan, China' (2020) 42 *Plant Diversity* 473, 473–474.

diseases using complex and individually tailored herbal medicine, leaving external manifestations to the acupuncture specialists or chiropractors.[46]

One unique example of TMK maintained by the Naxi community is their specialised use of green thorn fruit oil.[47] Well known by a limited number of individuals in the community, it is used not only as a treatment for skin burns and scalds, but also as a means to ward off evil spirits.[48] This dual functionality embodies the harmony between practical medical applications and cultural spiritual beliefs, a reflection of the collective knowledge system upheld by the community. Despite the wide dissemination of these practices within the community, much of its TMK remains secret or protected, restricting access to traditional healing practices to the local population.[49] This is an excellent example of how the collective ownership of TMK operates within local Chinese communities, demonstrating the intricate interplay of culture, spirituality, and medicine.

TMK also forms an integral part of family heritage in certain regions of China, specifically among families with agricultural backgrounds.[50] These families and rural residents, often with limited financial resources, are more susceptible to healthcare risks and diseases.[51] Consequently, the affordability and accessibility of traditional health remedies make them the preferred choice.[52] Within many of these families, a unique collection of TMK remedies has been cultivated, each specifically adapted to the family's needs and experiences.[53] These remedies, embodying strategies for dietary management, massage therapy, herbal medicine, and contagion prevention, encapsulate the wisdom of generations.[54]

The sphere of herbal remedies is one area where the legacy of TMK is vividly portrayed. Over generations, Chinese families have learned to harness the therapeutic

---

[46] Ibid.

[47] Zhao (n 45) 474.

[48] Ibid.

[49] Elisabeth Hsu, *The Transmission of Chinese Medicine* (Cambridge University Press, 2009) 21–57; Louis Fu, 'Surgical History of Ancient China' (2010) 80(3) *ANZ Journal of Surgery* 133, 133–138.

[50] 麻勇恒 [Ma Yongheng],《少数民族传统医药知识的现代传承与创新—以苗族传统医药为例》[The Modern Inheritance and Innovation of Ethnic Minority Traditional Medical Knowledge — Taking Miao Ethnic Traditional Medicine as an Example] (2011) 3(1) 原生态民族文化学刊 *Journal of Original Ethnic Culture Studies* 104, 106.

[51] Mengtian Cao et al., 'The Influence Factors Analysis of Households' Poverty Vulnerability in Southwest Ethnic Areas of China Based on the Hierarchical Linear Model: A Case Study of Liangshan Yi Autonomous Prefecture' (2016) 66 *Applied Geography* 144, 144.

[52] Ibid.

[53] 翟华强 [Zhai Huaqiang], 基于师承与家传的古代中医药学人才培养模式 [The Training Model of Ancient Chinese Medicine Talents Based on the Inheritance of Master and Apprentice and Family Inheritance] (2014) 20(1) 中国中医基础医学杂志 *Chinese Journal of Basic Medicine in Traditional Chinese Medicine* 37, 37–39.

[54] Ibid.

properties of local plants.[55] Ginseng, a root highly valued for its medicinal properties, is commonly used to enhance overall well-being and vitality[56] Goji berries, which contain antioxidants, are traditionally consumed to safeguard and enhance visual health.[57] Even with evolving modern healthcare, these families remain deeply connected to their TMK remedies, often resorting to these time-honoured treatments prior to considering modern pharmaceutical alternatives.[58] This inclination underscores the pivotal role of familial heritage in the preservation and application of TMK, attesting to its enduring significance amidst changing times.

Another pattern of TMK ownership involves knowledge known and used by the general public in China and globally.[59] Much of China's TMK has been documented in ancient texts and, with the spread of literacy and the advent of commercial printing from the eleventh century, specialist medical works and ancient herbal pharmacopoeia began to circulate more widely.[60] This development significantly increased the accessibility of TMK in the public domain. In this context, TMK is considered part of the public domain, meaning that this widely accessible TMK is deemed public domain material and can be freely accessed. While some might argue that publicly available TMK should be considered public domain material, it is essential to recognise that TMK does not exist as ownerless goods.[61] Although some forms of TMK have been documented or otherwise recorded, others have not. However, they all reflect accumulated skills and ingenuity that generations of traditional communities and peoples have developed.[62] Therefore, these intangible intellectual creations should not be considered items without owners that can be freely acquired.

In 1992, *the CBD* upheld the principle of permanent sovereignty of nation-states over their natural resources, as emphasised in a 1962 UN Resolution, and recognised nations' authority over genetic resources within their territories.[63] *The Nagoya Protocol* later reinforced this stance, reaffirming the sovereign rights of

---

[55] 翟华强 (n 53) 37–39.

[56] 孔洋洋 [Kong Yangyang],《神农本草经与经方应用之人参篇》[The Classic of the Materia Medica of Shennong and the Application of Classical Prescriptions: The Chapter on Ginseng] (2023) 47(2) 山东中医药大学学报 *Journal of Shandong University of Traditional Chinese Medicine* 127, 127–131.

[57] 李静 [Li Jing],《药用枸杞本草考证》[Textual Research on Medicinal Goji Berries in Materia Medica] (2019) 14(10) 世界中医药 *World Traditional Chinese Medicine* 2593, 2593–2596.

[58] 翟华强 [Zhai Huaqiang] (n 53) 37–39.

[59] Tianbao Qin, 'Common Pools of Traditional Chinese Medical Knowledge in China' in Evanson Chege Kamau and Gerd Winter (eds), *Common Pools of Genetic Resources: Equity and Innovation in International Biodiversity Law* (Routledge, 2013) 151.

[60] Ibid.

[61] Ruth L Okediji, 'Traditional Knowledge and the Public Domain' (Conference Paper, Centre for International Governance Innovation, June 2018) 1, 11.

[62] Nan Xia, 'Access and benefit-sharing in China: Exploring the Extent to Which China Fulfils the Obligations of the Nagoya Protocol' (2023) 13(1) *Queen Mary Journal of Intellectual Property* 97, 97–120.

[63] CBD, art 3.

States over natural resources in line with the CBD's provisions.[64] One could reasonably argue that extending sovereignty rights to TMK does not represent a significant legal leap. Instead, this shift underscores the recognition of sovereignty over TMK within national boundaries, thereby reinforcing the protection and governance of this invaluable knowledge.

However, the notion of national sovereignty has been constantly debated, both in theory and in various political practices.[65] In any case, there is obviously a need to clarify the relationship between national sovereignty rights and those of local communities if States are seeking to increase their sovereignty over TMK and associated genetic resources, to avoid infringing on the communities' rights. In the Chinese context, all ethnic groups and local communities have been intertwined and have influenced each other culturally, collectively developing Chinese culture with Confucianism as its core.[66] They have created collective experiences, common heritage, and cultural memory together.[67] Therefore, all ethnic groups and local communities within Chinese territory form a unified national community.[68] This process includes the proposition, establishment, and universal consciousness and identity of the State among members of all ethnic groups.[69] Therefore, TMK known and used by the general public in China should still be considered as a collectively held, shared, and preserved resource. This distinction is rooted in China's unique culture and traditions, ensuring State sovereignty, not merely over the biological resources within its borders, but also over some TMK associated with these resources.

Therefore, despite various patterns in which TMK has been held by communities in China over time, it has remained part of the collective knowledge of local communities, ethnic minority groups, or a unified national community. This collective nature stems from the fact that no single individual within the communities possesses the knowledge to the exclusion or detriment of others.[70] Additionally, since TMK is

---

[64] The Preamble of the *Nagoya Protocol* reaffirms the principle of sovereign rights of States over their natural resources and recognises that such rights should be exercised in accordance with the provisions of the Convention.

[65] Paul Gepts, 'Who Owns Biodiversity, and How Should the Owners Be Compensated?' (2004) 134(4) *Plant Physiol* 1295, 1295.

[66] 霍维洮 [Huo Weitao],《中国近代民族认同的历史逻辑 ——兼论中华民族的形成》[China's Modern National Identity Historical Logic: On the Formation of the Chinese Nation] (2021) 3 回族研究 *HuiZu Yan Jiu* 5, 5–6.

[67] Ibid,; Dahua Zheng, 'Modern Chinese Nationalism and the Awakening of Self-Consciousness of the Chinese Nation' (2019) 3(11) *International Journal of Anthropology and Ethnology* 1, 6.

[68] 石硕 [Shi Shuo],《从汉族与少数民族的历史关系认识"中华民族共同体"的共同性》[Understanding the Commonality of the "Chinese National Community" from the Historical Relationship between the Han Ethnic Group and Minority Ethnic Groups] (2021) 3 中华民族共同体研究 *Research on the Chinese National Community* 73, 78–86.

[69] Shangli Lin, 'National Transformation: Modern Reconstruction of a Unified Society' (2016) 1 *Chinese Political Science Review* 113, 131; Dahua Zheng, 'Modern Chinese Nationalism and the Awakening of Self-Consciousness of the Chinese Nation' (2019) 3(11) *International Journal of Anthropology and Ethnology* 1, 2.

[70] Susy Frankel, 'The Mismatch of Geographical Indications and Innovative Traditional Knowledge' (Research Paper No.35/2011, Victoria University of Wellington, November 2011) 1, 8.

connected to the very identity, and intellectual and spiritual heritage of the communities, there is a collective interest in the occupation and utilisation of their TMK and associated genetic resources, as well as the right not to be deprived of this shared interest. As such, the recognition of this connection to communities, familial ties, group rights, and shared interests is vital when legitimising claims to TMK in China.

The same TMK can be shared among different communities and the State, a dynamic that calls for careful consideration of principles governing the relationships between individual community self-determination and State sovereignty. The Chinese government often perceives self-determination and rights advocacy from local communities as potential separatism and has repeatedly dismissed the idea that 'all peoples have the right to self-determination'.[71] Nevertheless, China has implemented viable alternatives to balance the extremes of State sovereignty and outright secession caused by self-determination. They have established 'self-autonomous province-level or sub-provincial-level jurisdictions to manage local concerns.[72] In Chinese, 'self-autonomous region' is 自治区(*zizhiqu*), which means 'self-rule region'. Despite the implication of self-rule, these autonomous regions are not entirely free from national government influence.[73]

These self-autonomous regions often offer the best of both worlds: they provide the advantages of being part of a large State, such as defence, foreign relations, and economic opportunities, while preserving local laws, customs, and culture, free from external interference.[74] If feasible, TMK shared by various communities (including national communities) should be utilised through the joint agreement of local communities and the central government, representing the Chinese people as a whole. This approach ensures local community interests are not automatically subordinate to State imperatives. Therefore, understanding the distribution of TMK requires a comprehensive study of the interconnected relationships between individuals, local communities, and the unified national community of China.

In summary, the preservation and utilisation of TMK in China is rooted in its unique pattern of collective ownership. This knowledge, amassed over centuries, is predominantly held and safeguarded by communities, ethnic minority groups, families, and, on a larger scale, the state, forming an integral part of their shared heritage.

---

[71] 黄一玲 [Huang Yiling],《论民族自决权的概念内涵与适用条件》[On the Conceptual Connotation and Applicable Conditions of the Right to National Self-Determination] (2017) 1 贵州民族研究 *Guizhou Ethnic Studies* 1, 3–4; President Xi Jinping pointed out at the Central Ethnic Working Conference held in 2014 that 'any form of self-determination must be firmly discarded'; Barry Sautman, 'Self-representation and Ethnic Minority Rights in China' (2014) 15(2) *Asian Ethnicity* 174, 179; Pan Zhiping, 'Correctly Understand 'National Self-Determination' and 'High Degree of Autonomy'' (2018) (1) *Theory and Reform* 43, 43–53.

[72] 玉凤 [Yu Feng],《论民族区域自治制度的法律保障》[Legal Guarantee of the System of Ethnic Regional Autonomy] (2017) 18 知识文库 Knowledge Library 235, 235; Colin Mackerras, *Ethnic Minorities in Modern China* (Routledge, 2011) 21–23.

[73] 张 彬 [Zhang Bin]《政府间纵向关系研究: 中央与民族区域自治地方关系的调整》[Research on Vertical Government Relations: Adjustment of the Relationship between the Central Government and Ethnic Regional Autonomous Areas] (2017) 18 改革研究 *Reform Research* 17, 17–23.

[74] Anonymous, 'China and the Principle of Self-Determination of Peoples' (2010) 1 *St Antony's International Review* 79, 92.

It is essential to appreciate these complexities of collective ownerships to truly understand the dynamics influencing the protection and utilisation of Chinese TMK. The key holders of this knowledge—communities, families, and at a broader level, the State—each play their distinct roles in preserving, perpetuating, and utilising this wealth of traditional wisdom. Addressing the challenges and tensions associated with protecting and using Chinese TMK requires an understanding of this collective ownership and the stakeholders involved. It is then possible to devise legal, policy, and practical frameworks that are well-suited to China's unique context. Such an approach ensures respect for the shared interests of all TMK holders and promotes a harmonious environment for the continued growth and preservation of TMK in China.

2.2.3 Customary Rules Relating to TMK in China

Given the aforementioned context, it is vital to understand that in China, TMK has predominantly been cultivated and passed down collectively by local communities, ethnic groups, and the unified national community. Therefore, TMK is a shared heritage that brings together various communities in China. It fosters links among diverse local communities and ethnic groups within the country, playing a significant role in strengthening the collective national identity.[75] Although certain forms of TMK may be linked to specific families or individuals with specialised expertise, it is essential to acknowledge these knowledge systems as part of the collective heritage. This is due to their role in promoting the overall well-being and welfare of, and benefit to, the wider community or ethnic groups. The abundant TMK that has been accumulated through centuries of close relationships with nature, such as medicinal plant remedies, has given rise to a variety of distinct customary rules and practices.[76] These reflect the unique worldviews, and conceptual and theoretical frameworks of the local communities, ethnic minorities, and unified national community of China and are intended to guide every aspect of their lives.[77] They define the obligations

---

[75] 景威栋 [Jing Weidong]《中华民族共同体意识视域下民族医药文化遗产保护探析》[Analysis on the Protection of Ethnic Medicine Cultural Heritage under the Vision of Chinese National Community Consciousness] (2023) 19(1) 亚太传统医药 *Asia Pacific Traditional Medicine* 4, 5; Pankaj Sharma Gupta, Kumar Vijay and Sushma Sharma, *Healing Traditions of the North-western Himalayas* (Springer New Delhi, 2014) 12.

[76] World Intellectual Property Organization (WIPO), 'Customary Law, Traditional Knowledge and Intellectual Property: An Outline of the Issues' (Report, WIPO, 2013) 1, 4–9.

[77] 宋佳美 [Song Jiamei],《侗族习俗文化中的民族医药保健探析》[Analysis of Ethnic Medicine and Healthcare in Dong Ethnic Customs and Culture] (2021) 30 (11) 中国民族民间医药 *Chinese Journal of Ethnomedicine and Ethnopharmacy* 1, 1–4; Cansong Li et al., 'Community Heritage Linking Place and Mobility: A Case Study of "Bangbei" in Ethnic Bai Villages of Yunnan Province, China' (2018) 10(7) *Sustainability* 2322, 2322–2334.

and rights related to TMK to satisfy the needs of the communities and ensure that TMK can be transmitted by tradition.[78]

Some types of TMK systems in China with a long and consistent history of use are well codified in monographs, ancient literature, and other texts.[79] Others, particularly those developed within smaller and more marginalised communities, are not well codified, rather they are orally transmitted over generations.[80] Nevertheless, despite these differences, all types adhere to the complicated community-based rules that serve to ensure ownership and cultural protection. In the TMK of the Han ethnic group, also known as Han medicine, the complex customary rules are deeply rooted in Confucian ideology.[81] One of the most significant aspects of these rules is the formation of exclusive bonds among the members of the community, particularly between master and disciple.[82] These relationships are built upon the foundation of filial piety, which is the most essential of the five cardinal relationships (五倫, *wǔlún*) in Confucianism.[83] This emphasises the importance of loyalty, respect, and reverence in the transmission of TMK.[84] A second aspect is that the customary rules also include the processes of transmission of TMK secrets within the families and communities. This process entails evaluating the potential successors' characters, merit, and capabilities to determine if they are fit to receive and subsequently pass on the TMK.[85] For instance, in typical families of TMK practitioners, TMK is merely transmitted to males in the family, who help their families from early childhood onwards, while females are normally excluded from this process.[86] In addition, families and communities as basic units for controlling the spread of contagious diseases are also bound by a series of customary rules and practices. Some local communities or ethnic minority groups have annual plague expulsion festivals influenced by their tradition.[87] The exorcistic activities are performed in the festivals to drive away plague demons.[88] For example, the famous Chinese Dragon Boat Festival

[78] Li et al. (n 77) 2330.

[79] Tianbao Qin, 'Common Pools of Traditional Chinese Medical Knowledge in China' in Gerd Winter and Evanson Chege Kamau (eds), *Common Pools of Genetic Resources: Equity and Innovation in International Biodiversity Law* (Routledge, 2013) 151–152.

[80] Ibid.

[81] 张红雷 [Zhang Honglei],《浅谈儒家思想与中医药发展》[A Brief Discussion on Confucian Thought and the Development of Traditional Chinese Medicine] (2023) 中国医学人文 *Chinese Medical Humanities* 19, 19–21.

[82] 李佳霏 [Li Jiafei]《观 "慈"在先秦儒家伦理下的安置及其现代内涵》[Observing "Benevolence" in Pre-Qin Confucian Ethics and Its Modern Connotations] (2020)23 青年与社会 *Youth and Society* 193, 193.

[83] TJ Hinrichs, 'New Geographies of Chinese Medicine' (1998) 13 Beyond Joseph Needham: Science, Technology, and Medicine in East and Southeast Asia 287, 300.

[84] Ibid.

[85] Ibid.

[86] Hsu (n 49) 474.

[87] PR Katz, 'The Pacification of Plagues: A Chinese Rite of Affliction' (1995) 9(1) *Journal of Ritual Studies* 55, 70–71.

[88] Ibid, 80.

is said to have protective functions against disease.[89] It is believed that plagues and contagious diseases spread within the community at the same time as the festival.[90] As a result, people follow the custom of making and wearing scented medicine bags around their necks to protect themselves from diseases and evil spirits.[91]

China recognises 55 ethnic minorities within its national boundaries, each with distinct customary rules and practices related to TMK that differ from the majority Han ethnicity.[92] Each ethnic minority community also has its own unique characteristics for customary rules and practices. These arise from their diverse religious beliefs, significant geographical variations, and distinctive historical and cultural factors.[93] Despite the differences among various ethnic minority communities, there are notable similarities in their fundamental customary principles or values.

Firstly, the customary rules and practices often share similar spiritual and holistic characteristics.[94] The communities perceive the natural world as being infused with spirit.[95] Mental, emotional, physical, and spiritual aspects of a person's life are perceived as an integrated system.[96]

Secondly, many ethnic minority communities in China strongly emphasise sharing and reciprocity.[97] Community members who benefit from the knowledge and resources of previous generations feel obligated to pass them on to the next generation or to other members in need. This ethic of sharing and reciprocity extends to their relationship with nature and Mother Earth.[98] As a result, community members often adopt proactive approaches to environmental protection and resource management,

---

89 Ibid, 62.

90 'Dragon Boat Festival Customs', *Beijing Tourism* (Web Page, 15 June 2012). <https://english.visitbeijing.com.cn/article/47OMfXjgCu0> .

91 Ibid.

92 Colin Mackerras, 'Ethnic Minorities' in Czeslaw Tubilewicz (ed), *Critical Issues in Contemporary China: Unity, Stability and Development* (Routledge, 2016) 1, 1–19.

93 Si-Yuan Pan et al., 'Historical Perspective of Traditional Indigenous Medical Practices: The Current Renaissance and Conservation of Herbal Resources' (2014) *Evidence-Based Complementary and Alternative Medicine* 1, 2–5.

94 滕建卓 [Teng Jianzhuo], 论土家族医药学的整体观 [Discussion On the Holistic Characters of Tujia Medicine] (2007) 2, 中国民族医药杂志 *Journal Of Medicine & Pharmacy Of Chinese Minorities* 6,7; 乌日图那顺 [Wuritu nashu], 蒙医学整体观及其应用价值 [The Holistic View of Mongolian Medicine and Its Application] (2014) 5 中国民族医药杂志 *Journal Of Medicine & Pharmacy Of Chinese Minorities* 58,59; 赵雅 [Zhao Ya], 基于藏族医学 "整体观"认识的防治糖尿病肾病新药发现思路 [The Discovery of New Drugs for the Treatment of Diabetic Based on the Understanding of the "Holistic View" of Tibetan Medicine] (2019) 25(3), 中国实验方剂学杂志 *Chinese Journal of Experimental Traditional Medical Formulae* 167, 167–171.

95 滕建卓 [Teng Jianzhuo] (n 94) 7.

96 赵雅 [Zhao Ya] (n 94) 167–171.

97 韩玉茹 [Zhang Yuru] et al., 苗族医药文化中的生态伦理思想概述 [An Overview of Ecological Ethics in the Medical Culture of Miao Nationality] (2017) 7, 中国民族医药杂志 Journal Of Medicine & Pharmacy Of Chinese Minorities 6,7; 张新和 [Zhang Xinhe], 藏医药学中的医学伦理思想研究 [Research on Medical Ethics in Tibetan Medicine] (2017) 10, 中国民族医药杂志 Journal Of Medicine & Pharmacy Of Chinese Minorities 1, 4.

98 张新和 [Zhang Xinhe] (n 97) 4.

driven by their cultural values and beliefs. This is because these values and beliefs are bonded with nature, and proposes that, as Mother Earth gave them medicine and food during a crisis, they must reciprocate by taking care of her.[99]

Thirdly, the customary worldviews of various ethnic minority groups in China acknowledge the importance of balance or equilibrium within the body and between the individual and their environment. They believe that when any element of a system changes, it disrupts the balance of the entire system.[100] This belief underscores the need for harmonious coexistence between humans and nature, as well as the importance of preserving TMK to maintain this delicate balance.

In summary, grasping the nuances of customary rules and practices linked to TMK is vital for developing culturally sensitive policies and frameworks that adeptly balance TMK protection, sustainable development, and utilisation, while simultaneously addressing the distinct needs of China's diverse communities. This understanding directly contributes to resolving tensions that arise from protecting TMK and its increasing use. It equips policymakers with the necessary insights to develop targeted interventions that not only actively safeguard TMK and its holders' unique cultural values and practices but also promote equitable access and benefits for all stakeholders involved, fostering a harmonious balance between knowledge protection and its modern applications.

2.2.4 Dynamism of TMK in China

Building on the importance of understanding customary rules and practices related to TMK in China, it is crucial to acknowledge another key characteristic: the inherent dynamism and constant evolution of TMK within communities. This aspect is driven by innovation, experimentation, fresh insights, and external factors, and should not be overlooked when addressing TMK governance.[101] TMK does not function in isolation. It is embedded in the sociocultural environment and local norms.[102] However, discussions and critical analysis surrounding its protection often

---

[99] Ibid.

[100] 宝龙 [Bao Long], 蒙医学与中医学传统思想观念的比较研究 [A Comparative Study of Traditional Ideas in Mongolian Medicine and Traditional Chinese Medicine](2008) 11 中国民族医药杂志 *Journal Of Medicine & Pharmacy Of Chinese Minorities* 1, 2; 韩玉茹 [Zhang Yuru] et al., 苗族医药文化中的生态伦理思想概述 [An Overview of Ecological Ethics in the Medical Culture of Miao Nationality] (2017) 7, 中国民族医药杂志 *Journal Of Medicine & Pharmacy Of Chinese Minorities* 1, 6; 洪宗国 [Hong Zongguo], 壮医药思想内核与理论框架思考 [Study of Zhuang Medicine Ideological Core and Theoretical Framework] (2008) 11 中南民族大学学报 *Journal of South-Central University for Nationalities* 46, 46–47.

[101] Stephen Mbae Muthamia, 'Effect of Traditional Knowledge Systems in Sustainable Development and Management of Natural Resources in Meru' (2021) 5(3) *Journal of Public Policy and Governance* 112, 120.

[102] Kumari Rajani et al., 'Traditional Knowledge and Its Promotion Through Proving Legal Rights' in Chandan Roy (ed), *The Role of Intellectual Property Rights in Agriculture and Allied Science* (Apple Academic Press, 2018) 130, 131.

insufficiently address its dynamic nature. It encompasses knowledge passed down through generations, continually refined, improved, and updated, in response to social needs.[103] Consequently, it should be viewed as the collective wisdom that has developed within China's various ethnic groups over numerous generations, adapting to societal and community advancements. It pertains to how medical knowledge is acquired and applied as an integral aspect of a community's traditional culture, involving a complex interplay of knowledge reproduction, loss, addition, and transformation.[104] This dynamic process simultaneously embraces continuity and change.[105]

Throughout generations, people in China have consistently engaged in trial-and-error approaches to discover innovative applications of local medicinal resources.[106] This ongoing process has contributed to the development and evolution of their TMK, showcasing its dynamic and adaptive nature.[107] One notable example is the evolving use of the Qinghao plant in Chinese history.[108] The plant's applications have changed over time in response to economic, environmental, and societal shifts, underscoring TMK's adaptability.[109]

The earliest recorded medicinal use of Qinghao in China dates back to 168 BC,[110] with archaeobotanical evidence found in the tombs of the Han Mawangdui dynasty,[111] indicating its initial use for treating haemorrhoids.[112] In the second century, amid a civil war that led to numerous casualties and wounds, *Shennong's Classic of Materia Medica*—a collection of TMK passed down orally for centuries—compiled around 220 AD, highlighted the effectiveness of Qinghao for treating ulcers and promoting

---

[103] Miriam Latorre Quinn, 'Protection for Indigenous Knowledge: An International Law Analysis' (2001) 14(2) *St. Thomas Law Review* 287, 292; SK Jain, 'Dynamism of Traditional Knowledge ' (2005) 4(2) *Indian Journal of Traditional Knowledge* 115, 115–117.

[104] Daniel J. Gervais, 'Spiritual but Not Intellectual? The Protection of Sacred Intangible Traditional Knowledge' (2003) 11 *Vanderbilt Law School Faculty Publications* 467, 472.

[105] Ibid.

[106] 邓大学 [Deng Daxue],《关于中医药现代化地认识》[Understanding the Modernization of Traditional Chinese Medicine] (2004) 16(1) 中医药临床杂志 *Journal of Traditional Chinese Medicine Clinical Practice* 1, 1.

[107] World Health Organization (WHO), *WHO International Standard Terminologies on Traditional Medicine in the Western Pacific Region* (Report, 2021)1, 1.

[108] 谭俊杰 [Tan Junjie],《青蒿药用食用历史考略》 [Review of the Medicinal and Edible History of Artemisia Annua (Qinghao)] (2020)16(8) 亚太传统医药 *Asia-Pacific Traditional Medicine* 75, 75–76.

[109] Ibid.

[110] Yahua, Niu, 'Artemisinin (Qing Hao Su)' in Jueming Hua and Lisheng Feng (eds), *Thirty Great Inventions of China:From Millet Agriculture to Artemisinin* (Springer, 2020) 815, 821.

[111] Elisabeth Hsu, 'Qing hao in the Chinese Materia Media' in Stephen Harris (ed), *Plants, Health and Healing: On the Interface of Ethnobotany and Medical Anthropology* (Berghahn Books, 2010) 83, 88–90.

[112] 王满元 [Wang Manyuan],《青蒿素类药物地发展历史》[Development History of Artemisinin-Based Drugs] (2012) 34(1) 自然杂志*Chinese Journal of Nature* 44, 45.

wound healing.[113] Qinghao was also employed during a devastating plague between 1551 and 1644, the second most severe in Chinese history.[114] To combat the outbreak, the *Compendium of Materia Medica*, completed in 1578, recommended Qinghao for treating intermittent fevers caused by infectious diseases.[115] This historical use aligns with Qinghao's contemporary applications as an antipyretic and antimalarial agent. These examples illuminate the dynamic quality of TMK in China, as it continuously evolves and adapts to societal changes. Its constant restructuring enables it to innovate from within and incorporate new knowledge to meet contemporary needs.[116]

The dynamic nature of TMK is also evident in its loss and devaluation.[117] Numerous factors contribute to this decline, with the most significant being the increasing influence of industrial and corporate powers.[118] These forces, along with the principles underlying industrial production, frequently undermine the sustainability of numerous local and traditional knowledge systems.[119] This occurs by subjecting them to competitive markets, and by supplanting local sociocultural practices and traditional reasoning with economic and industrial perspectives.[120]

As noted by Galindo, industrial factories' emphasis on mass production and large-scale prototyping has led to the massive displacement and devaluation of traditional knowledge systems.[121] In China, the industrial ecosystem is developing rapidly,[122] marked by the increased unauthorised use of genetic resources and TMK to create significant value in the pharmaceutical industry.[123] For instance, as noted

---

[113] 张衍箴 [Zhang Yanzhen],《青蒿地药用历史及品种调查》[Artemisia annua Medicinal History and Variety Investigation] (1981) 16(4) 中国药学杂志*Chinese Pharmaceutical Journal* 197, 200.

[114] Qiu-Hua Li et al., 'Overview of the Plague in the Late Ming Dynasty and Its Prevention and Control Measures' (2020) 5(3) *Talent of Medical Research Journal* 136, 136–143.

[115] Elisabeth Hsu, 'Reflections on the 'Discovery' of the Antimalarial Qinghao' (2006) 61(6) *British Journal of Clinical Pharmacology* 666, 666–670.

[116] Debasish Pattanaik and Munmun Jha, 'Knowledge of Identity among the Indigenous People' (2007) 7(2) *The Original Anthropologist* 199, 202; Ian S Mcintosh, 'Are There Indigenous People' (2000) 24(3) *Cultural Survival Quaterly* 1, 4–5.

[117] SK Jain, 'Dynamism of Traditional Knowledge' (2005) 4(2) *Indian Journal of Traditional Knowledge* 115, 116.

[118] Erik Gómez-Baggethun, 'Is there a Future for Indigenous and Local Knowledge?' (2021) 75 *The Journal of Peasant Studies* 6,7.

[119] Ibid.

[120] Ibid.

[121] De Sousa Santos, 'Epistemologies of the South: Justice Against Epistemicide' (Routledge, 2014)*;* Charles Z Levkoe. et al., 'People, Power, Change: Three Pillars of a Food Sovereignty Research Praxis' (2019) 46(7) *The Journal of Peasant Studies* 1389, 1391.

[122] 庞尧 [Pang Yao],《开放视角下的中国工业创新体系演进及未来展望》[The Evolution and Future Prospects of China's Industrial Innovation System under an Open Perspective] (2023) 2 天津社会科学 *Tianjin Social Science* 108, 108–116; Kiki Han, *The Dawn of China Biopharma Innovation* (McKinsey & Company, 2021) 1;. Kerong Zhang and Wuyi Liu, 'The Current Status, Trend, and Development Strategies of Chinese Biopharmaceutical Industry with a Challenging Perspective' [2020] *Sage Journals* 1, 1–2.

[123] Wenyuan Gao et al., 'In Vitro Culture and Cultivation of Chinese Medicinal Plants for Industrial Utilization and Genetic Resource Conservation' (2005) 3(2) *Plant Genetic Resources* 116, 116–126; Martin Saxer, *Manufacturing Tibetan Medicine: The Creation of an Industry and the Moral*

by Saxer, local communities in Chinese Tibet have faced the dilemma of having to buy medicines derived from their cultural practices and traditions at inflated prices from domestic corporations.[124] This situation has arisen due to a patent system that favours large industries, often sidelining local practitioners.[125]

Therefore, the rise of industrial and corporate power has inevitably led to the absorption of essential elements in economic activity, enabling these entities to reap significant benefits from the exploitation of TMK, while justifying their actions with IP law.[126] With their power and wealth, corporations can commodify TMK, transforming it from a collectively owned asset of local communities and ethnic minorities into a form recognised by scientific knowledge and industrial property systems, including patents.[127] This ongoing privilege allows corporations to quickly appropriate knowledge and maintain control, and to alter perceptions of TMK and associated genetic resources as commodities rather than community-owned assets. For instance, Saxer reported a case in China where the original TMK holders were denied the right to continue using their knowledge, which is now controlled by Chinese domestic corporations through patent exclusivity.[128] This situation conflicts with local and traditional philosophies, collective ownership of knowledge, and customary practices and beliefs. Over time, the commodification of TMK could erode the rights of local communities in China, potentially leading to domestic disputes regarding the ownership and use of, and access to, TMK.

In summary, the dynamic nature of TMK is multifaceted, with its adaptability and resilience reflecting its ability to evolve and survive through generations. However, this dynamism is also accompanied by TMK's vulnerability to loss and devaluation, primarily due to the increasing influence of industrial and corporate powers. These entities, driven by profit and market expansion, continue to exploit TMK, often disregarding the impact on the communities and the sustainability of TMK systems. As a result, it is crucial to confront these challenges and protect TMK from further erosion, ensuring that this invaluable resource remains a dynamic and living resource for generations to come.

Economy of Tibetanness (Berghahn Books, 2013) 95–136; Martin Saxer, *Manufacturing Tibetan Medicine: The Creation of an Industry and the Moral Economy of Tibetanness* (Berghahn Books, 2013) 137–163.

[124] Saxer (n 123) 137–163.

[125] Saxer (n 123) 137.

[126] Frédéric Thomas, 'Genetic Resources: A Way to Ensure Access to a Common Good, or to Compensate Its Commodification?' (2017) 88(3) *Entreprises et histoire* 103, 103–120; Erik Gómez-Baggethun, 'Is There a Future for Indigenous and Local Knowledge?' (2021) 75 *The Journal of Peasant Studies* 1, 5–6.

[127] Ibid.

[128] Saxer (n 123) 137–163.

2.2.5 Harnessing Chinese TMK for Pharmaceutical Innovation and Development

Pharmaceuticals encompass a wide range of medicinal products, including biopharmaceuticals, which are derived from biological resources.[129] The innovation in this field relies heavily on the availability of genetic resources and TMK for the discovery of new drugs, and research and development activities.[130] TMK, used for diagnosing, preventing, and treating diseases, plays a vital role in pharmaceutical innovation. Approximately 75% of modern pharmaceutical products derived from genetic resources are developed through research based on their traditional medicinal uses.[131] Utilising TMK in pharmaceutical innovation significantly increases the success rate of producing commercial drug products and streamlines the process of drug development at the lead discovery phase.[132]

As China's pharmaceutical sector experiences rapid growth,[133] it has become the second-largest market worldwide, valued at approximately US$130 billion.[134] This remarkable expansion is not merely a product of China's vast population and its rich biodiversity but is significantly propelled by the invaluable contribution of TMK. TMK, deeply rooted in centuries-old practices and wisdom, offers a rich reservoir of medical insights and natural compounds, many of which remain untapped and hold potential for novel pharmaceutical developments. The unique strength of TMK lies in its holistic approach to health and disease, emphasising prevention and the balance of bodily systems. This philosophy resonates with the global shift towards more natural and holistic healthcare practices, driving demand for TMK-based pharmaceutical products. Furthermore, the integration of TMK with modern scientific methods has

---

[129] Bhupinder Singh Sekhon, 'Biopharmaceuticals: an Overview' (2010) 34 *Thai Journal of Pharmaceutical Sciences* 1, 2.

[130] Ibid,; 'Disruptive Potential of Genomics Could Prompt Life Sciences Companies to Accelerate Deal-making', *Health Forward Blog* (Blog Post, 2018) < https://www2.deloitte.com/us/en/blog/health-care-blog/2018/disruptive-potential-genomics-prompt-companies-accelerate-deal.html> .

[131] Paul Kuruk, *Traditional Knowledge, Genetic Resources, Customary Law and Intellectual Property* (Edward Elgar Publishing, 2020) 17; Debra Harry Kanehe and Le'a Malia, 'Asserting Tribal Sovereignty over Cultural Property: Moving Towards Protection of Genetic Material and Indigenous Knowledge' (2006) 5(1) *Seattle Journal for Social Justice* 27, 33–34.

[132] Curtis M Horton, 'Protecting Biological Diversity and Cultural Diversity Under Intellectual Property Law' (1995) 10(1) *Journal of Environmental Law and Litigation* 1, 5.

[133] Kerong Zhang and Wuyi Liu, 'The Current Status, Trend, and Development Strategies of Chinese Biopharmaceutical Industry with a Challenging Perspective' [2020] *Sage Journals* 1, 1–16; Kiki Han, *The Dawn of China Biopharma Innovation* (McKinsey & Company, 2021) 1–9.

[134] 杨秀丽 [Yang Xiuli],《中医药产业创新生态系统构建》[Building an Innovative Ecosystem for the Traditional Chinese Medicine Industry] (2023) 40(4) 卫生经济研究*Health Economics Research* 34, 35; Bill Beeson, 'Weighing the Opportunities & Risks Within China's Biopharmaceutical Industry' *The China Guys* (Web Page, 22 July 2021).

<https://thechinaguys.com/opportunities-risks-china-biopharmaceuticals-industry/> ; Qian Xun Consultation, *2021 China Biopharmaceutical Market Analysis Report: Analysis of Market Scale, Status and Development Trend* (Report, 2021).

led to the discovery and development of new drugs that combine the best of both worlds—traditional wisdom and contemporary science.

Moreover, the Chinese government's support for TMK, including significant investments in research and development, and policies encouraging the modernisation and global integration of traditional medicine, have further catalysed the growth of the pharmaceutical sector. This strategic approach has not only led to domestic growth but also positioned China as a key player in the global market for traditional and herbal medicines.

At the core of pharmaceutical innovation, TMK serves as a critical starting point for pharmaceutical innovation, offering unique benefits that can streamline the research and development process. By providing original leads for potential drug candidates, TMK can significantly reduce the time and cost associated with pharmaceutical research.[135] Additionally, TMK enables the identification of new applications and undiscovered properties for existing drugs, a process referred to as 'renewing the old'.[136] This ability to repurpose and revitalise established medicines underscores the dynamic and evolving nature of TMK within the pharmaceutical industry.

The industry's reliance on bioresources such as genetic and biological samples, extractions, and compounds from natural sources further underscores the importance of TMK.[137] When pharmaceutical products are derived from plant or animal origins, TMK often plays a crucial and instrumental role in their development.

Several factors have contributed to the rise of China's domestic pharmaceutical sector. Firstly, China has introduced a series of national plans and policies aimed at improving market access and fostering pharmaceutical innovation.[138] These

---

[135] D Syiem and MB Syiem, 'Medicinal Plants and Conservation: Some Issues and Concerns' in P Tandon and YPASuman (eds), *Biodiversity and Its Significance* (I.K. International Publishing House, 2007) 150, 150.

[136] G Dutfield,'Why Traditional Knowledge Is Important in Drug Discovery'(2010) 2(9) *Future Medicinal Chemistry* 1407–1408.

[137] AF Jozala, DC Geraldes and LL Tundisi et al., 'Biopharmaceuticals from Microorganisms: from Production to Purification' (2016) 47 *Brazilian Journal of Microbiology* 51, 51–63; Surendra Sarsaiya et al., 'Bioengineering Tools for the Production of Pharmaceuticals: Current Perspective and Future Outlook' (2019) 10(1) *Bioengineering* 469, 469–470.

[138] 《中华人民共和国国民经济和社会发展第十三个五年规划纲要》[Outline of the 13th Five-Year Plan for the National Economic and Social Development of the People's Republic of China] (People's Republic of China) National People's Congress, March 2016; Mackenzie Mills, Anwen Zhang and Panos Kanavos(2019) 'Pharmaceutical Policy in China' *London School of Economics* 5, 24.

measures include the establishment of Good Clinical Practice international standards,[139] fast-track approval for new drugs,[140] and encouraging the innovation of Chinese domestic pharmaceuticals to reduce reliance on foreign imports.[141]

Secondly, increased access to capital flows has also provided a catalyst for the transformation and innovation of China's pharmaceutical sector.[142] Stock exchanges in Hong Kong, Shanghai, and Beijing have adapted their rules to allow early-stage pharmaceutical companies to access public capital.[143] Additionally, private investments through venture and private equity funds have increased, with government grants and institutional funding supporting biopharmaceutical innovation and development.[144]

In light of these factors, the unauthorised utilisation of Chinese TMK and genetic resources for pharmaceutical innovation and development is expected to rise in tandem with the growth of China's flourishing pharmaceutical industry. This ongoing expansion emphasises the crucial role that TMK plays in the research and development of modern pharmaceuticals. However, the rising unauthorised utilisation of TMK also brings to the forefront certain challenges, for instance sources of tension between the protection of TMK and the commercial interests of the pharmaceutical sector that must be carefully navigated.

---

[139] Mills et al. (n 138) 24.

[140] Ibid,;《中华人民共和国药品管理法》[The Drug Administration Law of the People's Republic of China] (People's Republic of China) National People's Congress, 2019. https://gkml.samr.gov.cn/nsjg/fgs/201909/t20190917_306828.html.

[141]《中国制造2025》[Made in China 2025] (People's Republic of China) State Council, May 2016; Robert D Atkinson, 'China's Biopharmaceutical Strategy: Challenge or Complement to U.S. Industry Competitiveness?' (Information Technology and Innovation Foundation, August 12, 2019).

[142] Robert D Atkinson, 'Healthy Funding: The Critical Role of Investing in NIH to Boost Health and Lower Costs' *Information Technology and Innovation Foundation* (2019) 1, 1–29; LEK Consulting, 'Innovation in China, Made in China 2025 and Implications for Healthcare MNCs', *GPS Healthcare Quarterly* (Web Page, 2018) 1, 1–8 <https://www.lek.com/insights/by/innovation-china-made-china-2025-and-implications-healthcare-mncs> .

[143] 吴致远 [Wu Zhiyuan],《上市融资渠道多元开放 生物制药企业哪里IPO最合适》[Diversified Financing Channels Open for Listed Companies: Which is the Most Suitable Place for IPOs of Biopharmaceutical Enterprises?] (2022) 3 21世纪经济报道*21st Century Economic Report* 1, 1–3. Shannon Ellis, 'Hong Kong Stock Exchange Opens to Biotechs' (2018) 36 *Nature Biotechnology* 482, 482; Lerong Lu 'Promoting High-Tech Innovations through Capital Markets Law Reform: Deciphering the Sci-Tech Innovation Board of the Shanghai Stock Exchange' (2020) 35 *Journal of International Banking and Financial Law* 140, 140–143.

[144]《VC/PE 纷纷持药》 [VC/PEs Are Actively Investing in Pharmaceuticals] [2012] 资本市场 *Capital Market* 109, 109–111; Lan Qiu et al., 'Public Funding and Private Investment for R&D: a Survey in China's Pharmaceutical Industry' (2014) 12(27) *Health Research Policy and Systems* 1, 1–11; Vicky Qing Xia, 'China Looks Inward and Outward: Investments in US and EU Biopharmaceutical Companies Are on the Rise', *Bioprocess International* (Web Page, 17 May 2019) <https://bioprocessintl.com/business/bioregions/china-looks-inward-and-outward-investments-in-us-and-eu-biopharmaceutical-companies-are-on-the-rise/> .

As the pharmaceutical sector becomes increasingly dependent on TMK and genetic resources, several critical issues emerge, including IP rights, cultural preservation, and ABS.[145] Such issues often arise when corporations or other entities seek to exploit TMK without adequately acknowledging or compensating the communities and the knowledge holders who have preserved and developed TMK over generations.[146] This prevailing situation highlights the significant tension between the imperative to safeguard TMK and the aspiration to leverage it for modern pharmaceutical advancements. Addressing these concerns necessitates a delicate balance that protects and preserves TMK while fostering its ethical and sustainable utilisation.

2.3 The Story of the Qinghao Plant (Artemisia Annua)

Building on the unique characteristics of TMK in China presented earlier, this section explores the legal and ethical intricacies that arise from employing TMK in diverse context. It also highlights the necessity of ensuring proper protection for TMK and related genetic resources in China, using Qinghao as an example.

Artemisia annua, a widely used species native to China, is commonly referred to as Qinghao.[147] It has been utilised for millennia in traditional Chinese medicine,[148] and is primarily employed to alleviate fever and fever-related ailments, some of which are now linked to malaria.[149]

During the tumultuous period of China's Cultural Revolution in the 1960s, a research team consisting of phytochemical, pharmacological, and ethnomedicinal experts was assembled to join a military project aimed at finding a cure for chloroquine-resistant malaria.[150] From a list of over 2,000 Chinese herb preparations

145 Graham Dutfield, 'Traditional Knowledge, Intellectual Property and Pharmaceutical Innovation: What's Left to Discuss?' in Matthew David and Debora Halbert (eds), *The Sage Handbook of Intellectual Property* (SAGE Publications Ltd, 2014) 649, 649–661; PG Sampath, *Regulating Bioprospecting: Institutions for Drug Research, Access, and Benefit-sharing* (United Nation University Press, 2005) 1–167.

146 Sushma Singh, 'Traditional Indian Medicine and Intellectual Property Rights: An Indian Perspective' (2021) 4(5) *International Journal of Law) Management & Humanities* 1405, 1406–1407.

147 严金海 [Yan Jinhai],《从青蒿素的发现看中药的发展方向》[Looking at the Development Direction of Traditional Chinese Medicine from the Discovery of Artemisinin] (2013) 34(4A) 医学与哲学*Medicine and Philosophy* 4, 7.

148 王晨飞 [Wang Chenfei],《黄蒿素：一本40年前的青蒿素研究报告汇编》[Artemisinin: A Compilation of Artemisinin Research Reports from 40 Years Ago] (2013) 32 (12) 赤峰学院学报*Journal of Chifeng University* 87, 92–93.

149 Pamela Weathers et al., 'Whole Plant Approaches to Therapeutic Use of Artemisia annua L. (Asteraceae)' in Tariq Aftab et al. (eds), *Artemisia annua -Pharmacology and Biotechnology* (Springer, 2014) 51, 51.

150 饶毅 [Rao Yi],《中药提取抗疟化学分子第一人》[The First Person to Extract Anti-Malarial Chemical Molecules from Traditional Chinese Medicine] [2015] 科技导报*Science and Technology Herald* 127,127; Guoqiao Li, Xingbo Guo and Linchun Fu, 'Persistent Pursuit in Research of

derived from China's TMK, 640 were identified as potentially having antimalarial effects.[151] Subsequently, over 380 extracts from various Chinese herbs were obtained and evaluated against a strain of malaria affecting mice.[152] Ultimately, the extract from Qinghao emerged as the most promising.[153]

However, as observed by Tu, its promising antimalarial effects could not be consistently replicated in subsequent experiments and appeared to conflict with findings in the existing literature.[154] Consequently, the research team re-examined every instance where Qinghao was mentioned in ancient pharmacopoeias and manuscripts.[155] After an extensive literature review, the researchers discovered a reference to the use of Qinghao plants for treating malaria symptoms in a fourth-century BC handbook written by Ge Hong (284–363).[156] His *A Handbook of Prescriptions for Emergencies* highlighted the potential antimalarial properties of Qinghao and provided instructions for its preparation and use. He highlighted its possible antimalaria effects and instructed: 'take a bunch of Qinghao and two sheng [2 × 0.2 L] of water for soaking it, wring it out to obtain the juice, and ingest it in its entirety'.[157]

Inspired by Ge Hong's instructions, the researchers hypobooked that the conventional extraction process' heat might have destroyed the active components and that a lower-temperature extraction method might be necessary to preserve the antimalarial activity.[158] Indeed, more consistent and effective antimalarial results were obtained after switching to a lower-temperature procedure. In 1972, the pure active ingredients from this extract were isolated and eventually named Qinghaosu, or artemisinin, as it became known in the West.[159] The development of artemisinin is regarded as one

---

Artemisinin: Fast Elimination of Malaria Commemoration for the 50th Anniversary of Project 523' (2017) 34(3) *Journal of Guangzhou University of Traditional Chinese Medicine* 303, 303–307.

151 朱安远 [Zhu Anyuan],《青蒿素之母: 2015年诺贝尔生理学或医学奖新科得主屠呦呦 (二)》[The First Person to Extract Anti-Malarial Chemical Molecules from Traditional Chinese Medicine] (2016) 14 中国市场*Chinese Market* 186, 186–187; Youyou Tu 'The Discovery of Artemisinin (qinghaosu) and Gifts from Chinese Medicine' (2011) 17 *Nature Medicine* 1217, 1217–1220.

152 Ibid.

153 Ibid.

154 Youyou Tu, 'Artemisinin- A Gift from Traditional Chinese Medicine to the World' (2016) 55(35) *Angewandte Chemie* 10,210, 10,210–10,226.

155 Ibid.

156 Elisabeth Hsu, 'Reflections on the ''Discovery'' of the Antimalarial Qinghao' (2006) 61(6) *British Journal of Clinical Pharmacology* 666, 667.

157 Ibid.

158 李巍 [Li Wei],《基于 "中华古籍保护计划"的古籍传承性保护利用》[Utilization and Inheritance Protection of Ancient Books Based on the "Chinese Ancient Books Protection Project"] (2021) 10 图书馆*Library* 90, 94.

159 Zengyi Chang, 'The Discovery of Qinghaosu (artemisinin) as an Effective Anti-malaria Drug: A Unique China Story' (2016) 59(1) *Science China Life Sciences* 81, 84; OS Michael, 'Artemisinin: The Journey from Natural Product to Nobel Prize' (2015) 13(2) *Annals of Ibadan Postgraduate Medicine* 113,114.

of the most significant success stories in utilising China's TMK for pharmaceutical innovation.[160]

In this success story, China's TMK-led scientist Youyou Tu, who does not have a doctorate, medical degree, or any Western biomedicine training, discovered artemisinin which has saved millions of lives. She received the Nobel Prize in 2015 for her work.[161] In her acceptance speech, Youyou Tu explicitly acknowledged China as the country of origin of TMK. She also acknowledged the source of the TMK (*A Handbook of Prescriptions for Emergencies*) in her research that led to the award.[162]

A lesser-known fact is that Youyou Tu's discovery was also strongly connected to the TMK of local communities and ethnic minority groups in China.[163] In the 1960s, a trainee doctor from the People's Liberation Army ('PLA') learned that some ethnic minorities in southwestern China had a tradition of making Qinghao decoction for malaria relief.[164] He reported his findings to the China Academy of Chinese Medical Sciences through various intermediaries, including the Kunming Institute of Botany.[165] This information received attention and ultimately inspired the groundbreaking work by Youyou Tu and her research team.[166] However, the community origins of the relevant TMK and their traditional and customary ownership were not consistently acknowledged.

The discovery of artemisinin showcases the wisdom of the Chinese nation and exemplifies the uniqueness of China's TMK as a national heritage. However, it is less well known that Qinghao has also long been used as a traditional remedy by various ethnic minority groups in China.[167] These minority groups make up

---

160 Youyou Tu (n 154) 10,218–10,219; Song-My Hoang, 'Alternative Medicine Could Treat Our Maladies, But We Have to Study It', *Massive Science* (Web Page, 2019) <https://massivesci.com/articles/eastern-alternative-traditional-medicine-scientific-basis-research-ginseng-st-john-wort> .

161 黄亚博 [Huang Yabo],《屠呦呦获诺贝尔奖与青蒿素研发对中医药发展的启示》[Tu Youyou's Nobel Prize Win and the Inspiration of Artemisinin Research and Development for the Development of Traditional Chinese Medicine] 江苏中医药 [2016] *Jiangsu Traditional Chinese Medicine* 6, 6–8; Wenxiu Liu and Yue Liu, 'Youyou Tu: significance of winning the 2015 Nobel Prize in Physiology or Medicine' (2016) 6(1) *Cardiovascular Diagnosis and Therapy* 1, 1–2; 'Women Who Changed Science', *The Nobel Prize* (Web Page, 2015). <https://www.nobelprize.org/womenwhochangedscience/stories/tu-youyou> .

162 Youyou Tu, 'Artemisinin- A Gift from Traditional Chinese Medicine to the World' (2016) 55(35) *Angewandte Chemie* 286, 286–290.

163 吴致远 [Wu Zhiyuan],《从知识的地方性到技术的民族性》[From Locality of Knowledge to Nationality of Technology] (2022) 3 广西大学学报 *Journal of Guangxi University* 44, 48.

164 抗瘧疾中藥—青蒿研究新知 [Anti-malarial Traditional Chinese Medicine: New Knowledge of Artemisia annua], 卫福部国家中医药研究所*National Research Institute of Chinese Medicine*. 'This was when a People's Liberation Army intern doctor in Yunnan learned about the local ethnic minority's practice of brewing Artemisia annua (sweet wormwood) soup to treat malaria. He then informed other doctors. After several referrals, the information was reported to the Yunnan Institute of Botany (a national-level institution), which subsequently initiated a research project on it, leading to a significant scientific breakthrough'.

165 Ibid.

166 Ibid.

167 刘雅 [Liu Ya],《民族本草 世界瑰宝 少数民族医药事业发展回顾与前瞻》[Ethnic Herbal Medicine: World Treasure—A Review and Prospective Look at the Development of Minority

around 8% of China's vast population, amounting to over 100 million people.[168] They inhabit 64% of Chinese territory, often residing in rural communities or remote areas along the borders.[169] Qinghao is predominantly found in these autonomous ethnic minority regions.[170]

Youyang Tujia and Miao Autonomous County, known as the 'hometown of Qinghao',[171] supplies 80% of raw materials for Qinghao-based medicine.[172] Historical records indicate that Indigenous Uyghurs have used Qinghao for herbal medicated bath therapy for centuries.[173] This therapy was traditionally employed to treat patients with asthenic fever, fatigue, and symptoms of malaria and jaundice.[174] Additionally, Qinghao was used by the Uyghurs for fumigation practices to treat cold symptoms and to bring down a fever.[175]

In 2007, a series of cemeteries were discovered in Xinjiang Uyghur autonomous region during a road construction project, in which the stems of Qinghao were found around the corners of tomb.[176] Comprehensive archaeobotanical studies were

---

Traditional Medicine] [2018] 中国民族*Chinese Ethnic Group* 22, 22; Jun-kui Bai, 'Analysis of Restricting Factors on Technological Innovation in the Exploitation of Nationality Culture and Civil Resources—Taking Nationality Culture and Civil Resources Exploitation of Flower-drum and Qinghao in Minority Nationality Areas of Chongqing, Hubei,Hunan,Guizhou and Sichuan as an example' (2008) 18(1) *Journal of Chongqing Technology and Business University* 43, 43–44; 'The Popularity Of the Folk Use of Qinghao to Treat Diseases in Xinjiang' (Web Page, 2015) <https://news.ifeng.com/a/20151009/44799115_0.shtml> ; Y Liu et al., 'Ethnomedicinal Plants Investigation in Hezhen nationality' (2015) 81(11) *Planta Medica* 552, 552–561; Borjigidai Almaz et al., 'Investigation and Application of Artemisia Plant Resources for Chinese Medicine and Mongolian Medicine in Inner Mongolia' (2013) 40(4) *Liaoning Journal of Traditional Chinese Medicine* 770, 770–774.

168 Reza Hasmath Reza and Margaret Maurer-fazio, 'The Contemporary Ethnic Minority in China: An Introduction' (2015) 56(1) *Eurasian Geography and Economics* 1,1.

169 June Teufel Dreyer, *China's Political System: Modernization and Tradition* (Palgrave Macmillan, 1993) 381.

170 Duan Xiao-Li, 'The Wide Distribution of Artemisia annua in Xinjiang and Its Popularity to Treat Disease', *City Consumption Morning Newspaper* (Web Page, 2015) <https://read01.com/zh-hk/0eaMRM.html#.YZSJeE5Bw2w> ; Xiaobo Zhang et al., 'The Influence of Guangxi Topography On the Level of Artemisinin in Artemisia Annua' (2009) 29(2) *ACTA ECOLOGICA SINICA* 688, 688–697.

171 罗钰坊 [Luo Yufang],《少数民族传统医药知识生产性保护研究》[Research on the Productive Protection of Traditional Medical Knowledge of Ethnic Minorities] (2018) 20 (4) 铜仁学院学报*Journal of Tongren University* 93, 96.

172 Linfang Huang et al., 'Mapping the Potential Distribution of High Artemisinin-yielding Artemisia annua L. (Qinghao) in China with a Geographic Information System' (2010) 5(18) *Chinese Medicine* 1, 1.

173 'The Popularity of the Folk Use of Qinghao to Treat Diseases in Xinjiang'(Web Page, 2015) <https://news.ifeng.com/a/20151009/44799115_0.shtml> ; Duan Xiao-Li'The Wide Distribution of Artemisia annua in Xinjiang and Its Popularity to Treat Disease', *City Consumption Morning Newspaper* (Web Page, 2015) <https://read01.com/zh-hk/0eaMRM.html#.YZSJeE5Bw2w> .

174 Ibid.

175 Ibid.

176 Huan Liu et al., 'The discovery of Artemisia annua L. in the Shengjindian cemetery, Xinjiang, China and its implications for early uses of traditional Chinese herbal medicine qinghao' (2013)

conducted on the plant remains, which were radiocarbon dated to around 2,400–2,000 BP, equivalent to 450–50 BC.[177] Although it remains unclear whether the plants were used for medical purposes, this discovery offers archaeobotanical evidence of Qinghao utilisations by the Indigenous Uyghur people.

Local communities and ethnic minorities, such as Uyghurs, view themselves as custodians or holders of the resource and knowledge. They believe TMK is important not only for its therapeutic value but also for its cultural significance, reflecting collective identities, heritage, livelihoods, and the ancient bond between people and nature.[178] These aspects should be protected, preserved, and promoted in a meaningful manner. Furthermore, being a caretaker of TMK entails various community responsibilities and customary rules that must be followed and respected. As such, protection measures should not overlook these customary practices and the collective interests of communities and future generations.

In 1985, when China's first Patent Law came into effect, the China Academy of Chinese Medical Sciences ('CACMS') filed its first patent in China, entitled 'The Production Process of Restoring Artemisinin'.[179] Following the first amendment of China's Patent Law in 1992, which allowed for the patenting of pharmaceutical compositions, Beijing Ketai Medical Technology Company, with the support and assistance of CACMS and the antimalarial research team, filed a product patent application for the antimalarial qualities of artemisinin compounds.[180]

After filing the patent application, Beijing Ketai Medical Technology Company invested millions of dollars in research and development for an antimalarial product named dihydroartemisinin.[181] The company and the researchers eventually made a good profit from this product, which was protected by patent monopolies.[182]

Subsequently, scientists from the Chinese PLA Academy of Military Medical Science ('AMMS') developed an artemisinin-based combination therapy ('ACT')

146(1) *Journal of ethnopharmacology* 278, 278–286; Hongen Jiang et al., 'Archaeobotanical Evidence of Plant Utilization in the Ancient Turpan of Xinjiang, China: A Case Study at the Shengjindian Cemetery' (2015) 24 *Vegetation History and Archaeobotany* 165, 165–177.

[177] Ibid.

[178] Zhen Gao et al., 'Emergence and Development of Uyghur Medicine from the Perspective of Chinese Traditional Medicine' (2019) 2(4) *Traditional Medicine and Modern Medicine* 139, 139–154; Yi Gou et al., 'Ethnobotanical Survey of Plants Traditionally Used against Hematophagous Invertebrates by Ethnic Groups in the Mountainous Area of Xishuangbanna, Southwest China' (2020) 42 *Plant Diversity* 415, 423; Lu Zhao et al., 'An Ethnopharmacological Study of Aromatic Uyghur Medicinal Plants in Xinjiang, China' (2017) 55(1) *Pharmaceutical Biology* 1,1.

[179] 李林 [Li Lin], 李国春 [Li Guochun] and 张溪 [Zhang Xi],《从青蒿素的专利历程和现状看医药科研成果的知识产权保护》[Examining Intellectual Property Protection of Medical Scientific Research Achievements from the Patent Process and Current Situation of Artemisinin] (2016)11(2) 中国医药生物技术*Chinese Pharmaceutical Biotechnology* 189, 189–190; CN Patent Application No 85100978, filed on 1 April,1985.

[180] Li et al. (n 179) 189–190; Only surnames for note references.CN Patent Application No 93103989, filed on 9th April,1993.

[181] Li et al. (n 179) 189–190.

[182] Ibid.

and filed a series of patent applications for this combination therapy in 1994.[183] After the patents were granted, AMMS signed a patent licence agreement with Ciba-Geigy, a Swiss pharmaceutical company that later merged with Novartis. In exchange, Ciba-Geigy agreed to source the antimalarial active pharmaceutical ingredients ('APIs') from China and pay AMMS a fixed royalty rate of 4% of its sales.[184] ACTs have now become the best treatment worldwide for uncomplicated falciparum malaria.[185]

This series of commercial and IP activities highlights the legal and ethical complexities that arise from employing TMK for diverse applications, as well as the necessity of ensuring proper protection for TMK and related genetic resources in China. There are concerns that local communities, ethnic minorities, and other knowledge holders may be short-changed or even harmed during these processes, where TMK might be appropriated without their consent and without sharing benefits with the knowledge holders.[186] As a result, these communities may face pressures to adapt their cultures away from traditional ways of life in order to protect their TMK and biological resources. This situation could weaken their cultural identities and community cohesion.

The story of the Qinghao plant (*Artemisia annua*) is a typical example that reveals the need for appropriate protection of TMK as a collective asset and demonstrates the legal and ethical complexities of utilising this knowledge for private pharmaceutical innovation. TMK's collective value in China stems from its transmission and application within the cultural traditions of communities.[187] The private value of TMK emerges through its commodification and commercialisation, which allows industries to profit and secure patents for products derived from TMK and related genetic resources.[188] However, the varied and occasionally conflicting interests of different stakeholders create challenges. This situation may lead to tensions between the utilisation and protection of TMK at China's national level. The far-reaching and

---

183 Li et al. (n 179) 190; Kathy Zhang et al., 'Science-Based Innovation in China: A Case Study of Artemisinin from Laboratory to the Market' (2018) 3(2) *Journal of Industrial Integration and Management* 1, 1–20; Richard J Maud, et al., 'Artemisinins: Preserving the "Magic Bullet"' (2010) 71(1) *Drug Development Research* 12, 15.

184 Ibid.

185 Fatoumata O Maiga et al., 'Artemisinin-based combination therapy for uncomplicated Plasmodium falciparum malaria in Mali: a systematic review and meta-analysis' (2021) 20 *Malaria Journal* 1, 1–13; MA Diallo et al., 'Efficacy and safety of artemisinin-based combination therapy and the implications of Pfkelch13 and Pfcoronin molecular markers in treatment failure in Senegal.' (2020) 10 *Scientific Reports* 1, 1–6.

186 Paul Kuruk, 'Regulating Access to Traditional Knowledge and Genetic Resources: The Disclosure Requirement as a Strategy to Combat Biopiracy' (2015) 17 *San Diego International Law Journal* 1, 70–73.

187 李自然 [Li Ziran],《民族传统文化地本质及特征刍议》[Discussion on the Essence and Characteristics of National Traditional Culture] (2008) 35 (5) 中央民族大学学报 *Journal of the Central University for Nationalities* 82, 86–87; Daniel J Gervais, 'Spiritual but Not Intellectual? The Protection of Sacred Intangible Traditional Knowledge' (2003) 11 *Vanderbilt Law School Faculty Publications* 467, 472.

188 Saskia AF Vermeylen, 'Between Law and Lore: The Tragedy of Traditional Knowledge (PhD Thesis, University of Surrey, 2007) 55–75.

interconnected implications of the tensions surrounding TMK in China cannot be overstated. These tensions can intensify power imbalances and perpetuate inequalities, as TMK-based innovations may disproportionately benefit large corporations and research institutions, leaving the knowledge holders at a disadvantage. Furthermore, the misappropriation and insufficient recognition of TMK could discourage its preservation and transmission, potentially leading to the loss of these invaluable practices and expertise.

As China's pharmaceutical sectors rapidly expand and TMK experiences revitalisation and modernisation within the national context,[189] a domestic solution to address these tensions becomes increasingly crucial. To effectively resolve these issues, it is essential to establish an inclusive legal and policy framework that acknowledges and respects the unique historical and cultural context that underpins China's TMK. This framework should accommodate TMK's distinctive characteristics while considering the various interests and rights of all stakeholders involved.

2.4 Patent Landscape Analysis for Qinghao Plants with Traditional Chinese Use

2.4.1 Introduction and Method

While the analysis in north–south terms remains relevant on a global scale, the tension between the use and protection of TMK within China demonstrates that the risk of misappropriation can also arise within a single country. Although there is a significant body of literature suggesting that developed countries have been exploiting TMK and associated genetic resources at the expense of developing nations,[190] Chinese domestic firms and researchers appear to be primarily focused on leveraging TMK and related genetic resources within their own country to maximise benefits. This creates a unique tension between the traditional custodians of TMK and the modern stakeholders seeking to capitalise on this knowledge for commercial and academic purposes.[191]

While it is impossible to determine the exact current domestic bioprospecting rate for TMK usage in China, monitoring and assessing the effectiveness of China's patent system, laws, and policies related to TMK and associated genetic resources

---

[189] See discussion in Sect. 2.2.5.

[190] YanJie Wang et al., 'Global Bio-piracy Cases and China's Countermeasures' (2014) 30(2) *Journal of Ecology and Rural Environment* 146, 146–154; Xiaodong Tou, 'Biopiracy in the Struggle for New Strategic Highlands of Genetic Resources and the Legal Governance Path' (2014) 5 *Law Science Magazine* 71, 71–83; Weilin Fu and Gong Cao, 'On Dealing with Bio-piracy under the System of Patent Law-Based on De'ang Acid Tea Traditional Knowledge' (2017) 2 *China Invention & Patent* 12, 12–16.

[191] Saxer (n 123) 137–163.

can provide a snapshot of the extent to which the TMK exploitation has expanded within the national context.

A purposive patent landscape analysis can help assist in measuring the extent of TMK exploitation and its associated genetic resources within China's domestic setting, shedding light on the nature of these tensions. This analysis focuses on the tension between traditional knowledge holders and contemporary stakeholders, resulting from the diverse interests surrounding TMK usage. By understanding these tensions, it becomes possible to inform the development of effective legal and policy frameworks that address these issues and strike a balance among the various parties involved.

The goal of this study's patent landscape analysis is to measure the exploitation of TMK and associated genetic resources for industrial development and pharmaceutical innovation in China, providing evidence that Chinese domestic companies and institutions predominantly use TMK and related genetic resources locally. These findings hold significance for examining the legal and ethical implications of collecting, researching, and enforcing patent monopolies on TMK and associated genetic resources in China under potential ABS systems, as well as for IP laws or reforms analysed in later chapters of this book.

Patent landscape analysis has long been employed to assess the use of TMK and associated genetic resources for innovation, and for identifying issues of misappropriation or biopiracy.[192] As Oldham et al. noted, this methodology offers a novel approach to examining innovation activities or discoveries concerning traditionally used foods and medicines with potential commercial value.[193] Patents, being the earliest sources of innovation disclosure, can help identify commercially valuable innovation activities,[194] major players in technological domains, and insights for forecasting and mapping trends in crucial technology areas.[195]

Robinson and Raven argued that, as modern industries become increasingly knowledge-intensive and invest more in patents related to medicines, cosmetics, and other areas, patent landscape analysis is being increasingly utilised to identify trends in science and technology.[196] In this study, the analysis tracks patent activities on TMK and associated genetic resources with concerns for misappropriation in China. Consequently, the analysis generates a 'map' or a range of results, quantifying TMK

---

[192] Daniel Robinson and Margaret Raven, 'Identifying and Preventing Biopiracy in Australia: Patent Landscapes and Legal Geographies for Plants with Indigenous Australian Uses' (2016) 48(3) *Australian Geographer* 311, 311–331; Daniel F Robinson et al., 'Patent landscaping for Vanuatu: Specific legal geographic methods for Indigenous knowledge protection and promotion' in Daniel F Robinson, Josephine Gillespie and Tayanah O'Donnell (eds), *Legal Geography* (2020) 74, 74–88; Paul Oldham et al., 'Biological Diversity in the Patent System' (2013) 8(11) *PLOS One* 1, 1–1.;

[193] Oldham et al. (n 192) 1–12.

[194] K Sastry et al., 'Research and Development Perspectives of Transgenic Cotton: Evidence from Patent Landscape Studies' (2011) 16(2) *Journal of Intellectual Property Rights* 139, 139–153.

[195] Sheetal Menon and Shishir Kumar Jha, 'Patent landscape analysis for crop biotechnology in India' (2015) 8(3) *Int. J. Intellectual Property Management* 111, 113.

[196] Robinson and Raven (n 192) 316.

and associated genetic resource usage within China's domestic context, identifying major actors in medical and pharmaceutical sciences, and offering insights to forecast and map trends of TMK usage for non-traditional purposes.

Bubela et al. highlighted the importance of patent landscape analysis, which involves examining the interactions among various indicators across temporal, technical, or spatial dimensions.[197] This type of analysis can range from in-depth assessments of specific patent statistics to comprehensive evaluations of entire technological fields.[198] By considering a whole body of related patent data rather than random samples, a more complete understanding of the field can be achieved. As such, defining the scale and scope of the patent landscape analysis is crucial.[199]

This study concentrates on analysing patent applications associated with the Qinghao Plant (*Artemisia annua*).[200] To develop a comprehensive search strategy, the title, abstract, and specifications of patent application documents are examined. In-depth reviews of the scientific literature are conducted in both English and Mandarin to identify subject-specific keywords related to Qinghao Plants, resulting in a list of pertinent keywords available in both languages to streamline the search process.

The search syntax includes a combination of keywords and International Patent Classification ('IPC') groups, which have been used to compile a comprehensive collection of patent application documents filed in China. Table 2.1 provides the patent retrieval strategies and parameters, including relevant keywords and IPC codes.

Furthermore, to determine how many patent applications have disclosed the country of origin and community of origin, another set of keywords is incorporated into the search syntax. Table 2.2 presents the parameters used to identify the disclosure of origin in patent applications.

According to WIPO, the IPC is a hierarchical system for the classifications of patent documents based on different technological fields, by using letters and numbers as codes.[201] As this study focuses on evaluating the exploitation of TMK for pharmaceutical innovation and development in China, the technological scope based on the IPC scheme is bound to 'medical and pharmaceutical science'. The searches and analyses of patent application documents in this study are limited to Chinese jurisdiction. Based on Smoch's 2009 report to WIPO concerning the IPC and Technology Concordance Table, the old IPC codes for medical and pharmaceutical science were A61K and A61P. WIPO's 2019 Concordance Table, further suggests A61K (excluding A61K-008/) and indicates that IPC codes related to organic fine chemistry (C07B, C07C, C07D, C07F, C07H, C07J, and C40B) and IPC codes

197 Tania Bubela et al., ' Patent Landscaping for Life Sciences Innovation: Toward Consistent and Transparent Practices' (2013) 31(3) *Nature Biotechnology* 202, 202.

198 Ibid.

199 Ibid.

200 Youyou Tu 'Artemisinin- A Gift from Traditional Chinese Medicine to the World' (2016) 55(35) *Angewandte Chemie* 286, 287.

201 World Intellectual Property Organization ('WIPO'), *International Patent Classification (IPC)* (Web Page, 2021) <https://www.wipo.int/classifications/ipc/en/> .

Table 2.1 Patent search strategies and parameters

Serial number	Original concept	Keywords and synonyms	IPC classification
1	Plant species (Qinghao)	'Artemisia annua L.' 'Artemisia annua Linn.' 'Herba Artemisiae' 'Herba Artemisiae Annuae' 'sweet wormwood herb' 'herb of sweet wormwood' OR 'Artemisia apiacea Hance' 'Artemisia apiacea' 'Artemisia capillaris Thunb' 'A. scoparia Waldst. Et Kitaib' 'Artemisia japonica Thunb.' OR 'Artemisia annua L.' 'QINGHAO' OR 'Qing Hao' 'Artemisia annua' southernwood 'sweet sagewort' 'sweet worm wood' 'Artemisia apiacea Hance' 'Artemisia apiacea' 'Artemisia capillaris Thunb' 'A. scoparia Waldst. Et Kitaib' 'Artemisia japonica Thunb.' 'Artemisia annua L.' 'QINGHAO' 'Qing Hao' 'Artemisia annua' southernwood 'sweet sagewort' 'sweet worm wood' 'Artemisiae Annuae Herba' 'Artemisia scoparia' 'Waldst. Et Kitaib' 'Artrmisia annual' 'A. apiacea' 'Artrmisia annua L.' 'Artemisia annuae' 'Artemisia annua Linn.' 'Artemisia annua L.' 'herba artemisiae annuae', 青蒿, 黄花蒿, 黄蒿, 草蒿, 三庚草, 白染艮, 香青蒿, 青蒿梗, 草青蒿, 草蒿子, 青蒿, 黄花蒿, 黄蒿, 草蒿, 三庚草, 白染艮, 香青蒿, 青蒿梗, 草青蒿, 草蒿子, 细叶蒿, 臭青蒿, 嫩青蒿, 鳖血青蒿, 香蒿, 黄花蒿, 卂蒿, 臭蒿, 蒿子, 菁蒿, 青藁, 青篙, 青篙草, 青嵩, 香青篙, 臭青藁	A61P, A61K (Not A61K-008/), C07B, C07C, C07D, C07F, C07H, C07J, C40B, C07G, C07K, C12M, C12N, C12P, C12Q, C12R, C12S
2	Traditional use in China (Treatment of fever, chills, fatigue, etc.)	'Fever', 'antipyretic', 'exhaustion', 'analgesic', fatigue', 'Jaundice', 'malaria', 'anti-infective', 'anti-inflammatory', 'dysentery', 'chills', 'night-sweat', 清热解暑, 除蒸, 发烧, 截疟,暑邪发热, 阴虚发热, 夜热早凉, 骨蒸劳热, 疟疾寒热, 湿热黄疸,清热,解暑, 避秽, 清湿热, 透骨蒸, 利湿退黄,湿热病, 暑热温病,黄疸	

Table 2.2 Parameters to identify the patent disclosure of origin

Serial number	Original concept	Keywords and synonyms
1	Country of Origin	'China' 'Materia Medica' 'Herbal Classic' ; 中华; 中国; 本草纲目, 神农本草经
2	Community of Origin	'minorit*' 'ethnic minorit*' 'communit*' 少数民族,民族,社区

concerning biotechnology (C07G, C07K, C12M, C12N, C12P, C12Q, C12R, and C12S) have considerable relevance to medical and pharmaceutical science.

The patent data for this study is collected and analysed using the Patsnap database, a global patent platform, covering the period between 1989 and 2017. This database offers a blend of machine and human-assisted translations from all major languages into English, Chinese, and Japanese. These translations are automatically connected, either directly or indirectly, to various foreign priority documents in different languages within a single patent family. Consequently, duplicate search results in different languages are avoided. Following the patent data collection, an iterative process is employed to refine and clean the search results.

It is important to note that the Chinese government has significantly tightened patent application procedures and considerably reduced financial incentives for Chinese patent filings since 2018.[202] This change aims to optimise application structures and foster a more robust, quality-based IP ecosystem.[203] As a result, there has been an atypical decline in Chinese patent applications since 2018. Thus, the cut-off date for this patent analysis is set at 31 December 2017.

2.4.2 Results and Analysis

In accordance with the search strategies, timeframe, and jurisdiction, the final dataset identifies 3,560 patent application records in Chinese jurisdiction between 1989 and 2017. Among these, the count of distinct patent families is identified as 894. Analysing the dataset comprising 3,560 patent applications, around 60% of these inventions, equating to approximately 2,136 patents, have been heavily reliant on TMK associated with the Qinghao Plant and its derivatives. This underscores the significant role that TMK has played in inspiring and guiding these inventions. Focusing specifically on combination therapies where artemisinin is a key ingredient, our analysis suggests that about 30% of these patents, which translates to roughly 1,068 patents, are likely to involve such therapies. This reflects the growing integration of artemisinin in modern pharmaceutical innovations, particularly in treatments that blend TMK with contemporary scientific approaches.

Moreover, our dataset reveals instances where advanced applications, such as synthetic biology, intersect with traditional knowledge. For example, the method used by Amyris for producing artemisinic acid, a synthetic derivative of artemisinin, signifies a fusion of traditional knowledge and modern scientific techniques. This highlights the evolution and adaptation of traditional remedies in contemporary medical and pharmaceutical innovations.

In our dataset, every patent application makes reference to the Qinghao Plant species or its derivatives in their claims, abstracts, or titles, emphasising their notable

---

202 Rouse Consultancy, *China: A Changing Focus on Patent Incentives*, (Web Page, 2019). <https://rouse.com/insights/news/2019/china-a-changing-focus-on-patent-incentives> .

203 Ibid.

antipyretic and antimalarial properties. A small but significant number of these patents acknowledge China as the Qinghao Plant's origin and detail the associated TMK for treating ailments like fever, chills, and fatigue. Examples include patent applications on methods for extracting artemisinin from Artemisia annua (CN. patent no 201410535519. X). The patent specification discloses that: 'the earliest written record of medical use of Qinghao was found in recipes for *Fifty-Two Ailments* — an ancient Chinese medical text that was unearthed from a Mawangdui tomb (around 168 BC)'.[204] 'The medical uses of Qinghao were subsequently recorded in other ancient Chinese medical texts such as *Compendium of Materia Medica* and Shennong's *Herbal Classic*'.[205] 'The country of origin of *Artemisia annua* is China despite its being widely planted in Australia, Argentina, Bulgaria, France, Hungary, Italy, Spain, and the United States'.[206] 'The Council of Scientific and Industrial Research of India, in patent application CN201980007346.5 (based on India priority application IN201811000290) also discloses that artemisinin is a component of the traditional Chinese medicinal herb Artemisia annua, which has been utilised for controlling symptoms of fever in China for over 1000 years'.[207] However, this review found that no patent has explicitly recognised the ownerships and contributions of the local people and communities or the specific community of origin of the TMK and associated species, despite their being the knowledge holders of Qinghao's antipyretic and antimalarial qualities to treat diseases for centuries.[208] This situation shows that China's existing frameworks for protecting TMK are incomplete.

Figure 2.2 indicates the distribution of Qinghao patent applications by the nationalities of patent applicants. Among these patent filing records, Chinese entities, including corporations and research institutions, have the most filings with 3,500 records. US' entities are a distant second with only 16 patent application records. Table 2.3 shows the top 15 assignees based on the number of Qinghao patent applications. It indicates that the only foreign entity in the top 15 applicants was Medicines for Malaria Venture ('MMV') with 13 patent applications. This situation indicates that China's domestic actors are much more likely to use the TMK and associated genetic resources that are in China's own backyard for patent monopoly, and the

[204] China Patent Application No 201410535519.X, filed on 23 October 2014, 1.

[205] Ibid.

[206] Ibid.

[207] India Patent Application No 201811000290, filed on 03 January 2018, 2; China Patent Application No 201980007346.5, filed on 03 January 2019, 2.

[208] 白俊奎 [Bai JunKui],《民族文化和民间资源开发中技术创新的阻碍因素——以渝鄂湘黔川民族地区花鼓和青蒿等民族文化和民间资源开发为例》[Obstacles to Technological Innovation in the Development of Ethnic Culture and Folk Resources - A Case Study of the Development of Flower Drum and Artemisia annua in the Chongqing-Hubei-Hunan-Guizhou-Sichuan Ethnic Regions] (2008) 18(1) 重庆工商大学学报 *Journal of Chongqing Technology and Business University* 43, 43–44; 'The Popularity Of the Folk Use of Qinghao to Treat Diseases in Xinjiang' (Web Page, 9 October 2015) <https://news.ifeng.com/a/20151009/44799115_0.shtml> ; Y Liu et al., 'Ethnomedicinal plants investigation in Hezhen nationality' (2015) 81(11) *Planta Medica* 552, 552–561; Almaz Borjigidai et al., 'Investigation and Application of Artemisia Plant Resources for Chinese Medicine and Mongolian Medicine in Inner Mongolia' (2013) 40(4) *Liaoning Journal of Traditional Chinese Medicine* 770, 770–774.

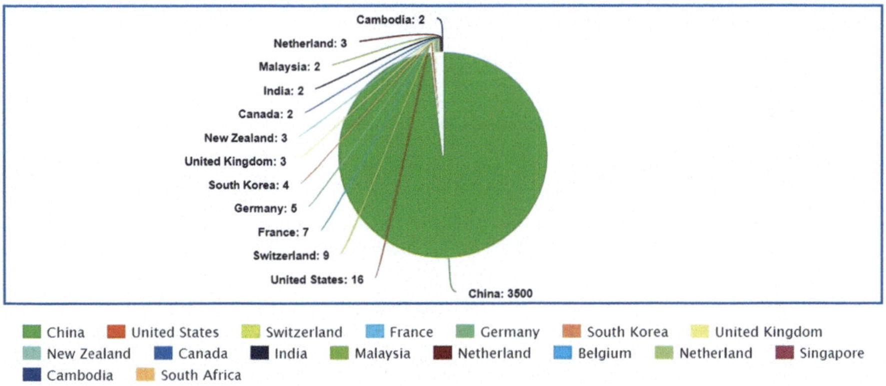

Fig. 2.2 Qing hao (*Artemisia annua*) Patent Application Landscape by Nationality

amount of these domestic activities is greater than one might think. Moreover, MMV is a Switzerland-based not-for-profit foundation established to discover, develop, and deliver new, effective, and affordable antimalarial pharmaceutical products. By analysing the claims and specifications of the patents filed by MMV against the information about traditional uses of Qinghao in the relevant literature, it is found that all of MMV's patents note an antimalarial and anti-infective lactone derived from Qinghao, namely artemisinin, in the claims (mainly dependent claims) or in the broader text of the patents. However, MMV did not disclose either the country of origin or the community of origin of Qinghao and TMK in the patent applications.

Figure 2.3 shows the trends of patent filings for Qinghao in China. In general, it demonstrates that patent applications related to Qinghao dramatically increased from 1989 to 2017, starting from the first-filed patents in 1989 to 472 in 2017. To be specific, after a modest increase for over a decade, patent applications related to Qinghao began to gain momentum around 2002, mainly prompted by the second revision of China's patent law and Chinese central government's initiatives of a new patent strategy in 2000. In the meantime, China launched generous patent subsidy programmes, which also contributed to the growth of domestic patent applications.[209] Around 2010, the trends started growing at a much faster rate. The number of patent filings concerning Qinghao had sharply increased in the six years up to 2016 despite the year 2017 seeing a decrease. Notably, a historical peak can be observed in 2016 when Youyou Tu was awarded the prestigious Lasker-DeBakey Clinical Medical Research Award and the Nobel Prize for the discovery and development of artemisinin with the assistance of China's TMK.[210] Therefore, based on the information from Fig. 2.3, it can be forecasted that, despite there being fluctuations around patent

---

[209] Lei Zhen et al., 'Are Chinese Patent Applications Politically Driven?' (Working Paper, Patent Statistics for Decision Makers Conference, 2012) 1, 8.

[210] 'Women Who Changed Science', *The Nobel Prize*, (Web Page, 2015). <https://www.nobelprize.org/womenwhochangedscience/stories/tu-youyou> .

Table 2.3 Top 15 assignees of Qinghao plants (*Artemisia annua*) patent applications

Rank	Number of patent documents	Assignees	Assignee type
1	19	Zhengzhou Houyi Pharmaceutical Co., Ltd	China's Domestic Corporation
2	18	Changsha Ruiduokang Biotechnology Co., Ltd	China's Domestic Corporation
3	18	Qingdao Lvman Bioengineering Co., Ltd	China's Domestic Corporation
4	19	ZhuZhou QianJin Pharmaceutical Co., Ltd	China's Domestic Corporation
5	17	Tianjin Shengji Group Co., Ltd	China's Domestic Corporation
6	15	Sichuan Jintang Haina Biomedical Technology Research Institute	China's Domestic Corporation
7	13	Medicines for Malaria Venture (MMV)	Foreign Corporation (Switzerland)
8	13	Jiangsu Kanion Pharmaceutical Co., Ltd	China's Domestic Corporation
9	12	Henan University of Chinese Medicine	China's Domestic University
10	15	Taizhou Xinwei Chemical Co., Ltd	China's Domestic Corporation
11	13	Shandong New Hope Liuhe Co., Ltd	China's Domestic Corporation
12	13	Chengdu fufosi Biotechnology Co., Ltd	China's Domestic Corporation
13	12	Beijing Yixintang Pharmaceutical Research Institute	China's Domestic Research Institute
14	13	Qingdao Tianrui Ecology Technology Co., Ltd	China's Domestic Corporation
15	8	Shanghai Jiao Tong University	China's Domestic University

trends due to policy reform or institutional changes, the increasing trend is likely to dominate in the future due to decades of continued upward trending growth.

To sum up, the patent landscape analysis provides a snapshot of how TMK in China has been used as an element of discovery and innovation for the patent. The analysis uses Qinghao as an example. This is because Qinghao has a worldwide reputation for its antipyretic and antimalarial properties. This reputation was reaffirmed in 2015 when the Nobel Prize for medicine was awarded to Youyou Tu for the findings of artemisinin in the traditional preparation of Qinghao.[211] In addition: 'China

[211] Xin-zhuan Su and Louis H Miller, 'The Discovery of Artemisinin and Nobel Prize in Physiology or Medicine' (2016) 58(11) *Science China Life Sciences* 1175, 1175–1179.

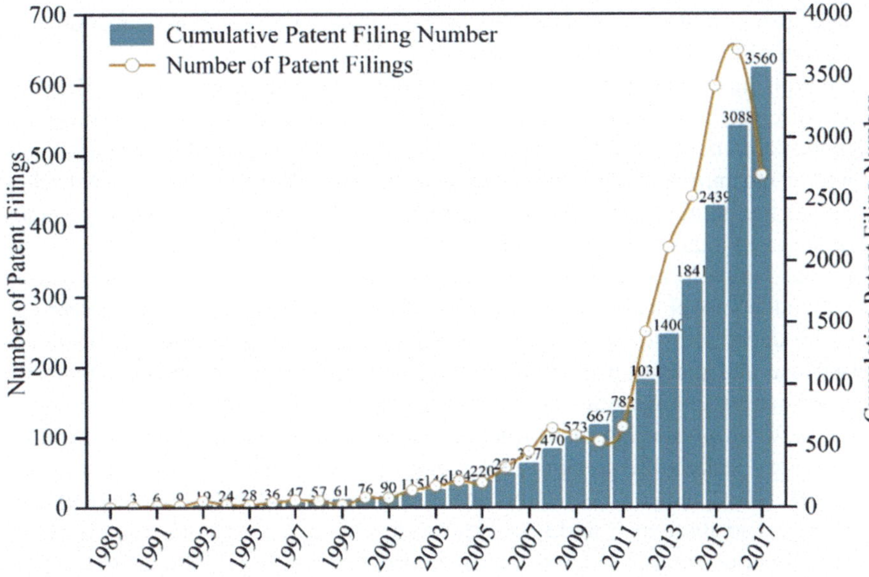

Fig. 2.3 Trends in Qinghao (*Artemisia annua*) Patent Filings in Chinese Jurisdiction, 1989–2017

is the place of origin of Qinghao (*Artemisia annua L.*), the largest supplier country of Qinghao (*Artemisia annua L.*) raw material on the global market, and the first country to extract artemisinin', according to a WHO document.[212] As a result, 3,560 patent filings of concern have been identified for the Qinghao Plant and associated TMK, which shows a dramatic increase over the past three decades. According to a document from the CBD's Third session of the Conference of the Parties, a number of commentators pointed out the regulatory options to encourage and propose a disclosure in patent applications of both the country of origin and the community of origin for genetic resources and informal knowledge used to create the invention.[213] On this basis, China's patent law has explicitly required the disclosure of both the 'direct source' and the 'original source' of genetic resources (including TMK-associated genetic resources) in the patent application, despite the vague nature of disclosure of origin rules.[214] The patentability or validity of any invention relying on genetic

---

[212] World Health Organization (WHO), 'WHO Monograph on Good Agricultural and Collection Practices (GACP) for Artemisia annua L' (Report, 2006) 1, 3.

[213] United Nations Environment Programme, 'The Convention on Biological Diversity and the Agreement on Trade-Related Intellectual Property Rights (TRIPS): Relationships and Synergies', UN Doc UNEP/CBD/COP/3/23, 3rd meeting (4–15 November 1996).

[214]《中华人民共和国专利法 (2020年修订)》[The Patent Law of the People's Republic of China (Revised in 2020)] (People's Republic of China) National People's Congress Standing Committee, Order No 55, August 2020, Art 26; Art 26 of China's patent law (2020) provides that: 'For inventions and creations that depend on genetic resources, the applicant should indicate the direct and original source of such genetic resources in the patent application documents; if the applicant cannot indicate the original source, they should state the reasons'.

resources can be denied if the access to, or the utilisation of, the genetic resources is in violation of the related laws and regulations.[215]

Although many patent filings refer to Qinghao and its associated TMK, they seldom disclose its country of origin, China. The patents do not recognise the Indigenous communities and ethnic minorities who have historically used Qinghao's antipyretic and antimalarial properties to treat illnesses. While not every patent relies directly on the input of these groups, their traditional knowledge frequently guides researchers and industrial actors in choosing Qinghao over other species.

In some complex cases, TMK may form the foundation for research or innovation but, with added novel technical contributions based on TMK, patentable inventions can be produced. However, even in such instances, issues may arise due to unauthorised use and patenting of TMK and associated genetic resources, especially when originating communities are not acknowledged. This highlights the ongoing tension between preserving and protecting TMK and its potential exploitation by contemporary stakeholders, signifying a gap in China's existing legal and policy framework. These tensions arise from the communities and ethnic minority groups being concerned about their traditional knowledge being misused or commercialised without proper consent or recognition. In contrast, researchers and industrial actors argue that incorporating TMK into their work is crucial for scientific advancement and innovation. Therefore, an urgent call arises for more fitting and inclusive policy, legal, and practical frameworks in China that encourage responsible TMK use while protecting it from unauthorised misuse.

While China's patent system mandates disclosure of source materials and associated knowledge to prevent improper patenting,[216] it also contributes to tensions between traditional knowledge holders and contemporary stakeholders due to the ambiguity of its origin disclosure rules. Specifically, the unclear definitions of terms like 'direct source' and 'original source' in Article 26 of Chinese patent law could enable patent applicants to bypass acknowledging the community origins of TMK and genetic resources.[217] This ambiguity serves as a pivot point, linking the inadequacy of existing legal tools to the broader conflict around TMK and modern exploitation, illustrating the urgent need for legal and policy reform.

Adding to this complexity, China's patent law does not necessitate the obligatory disclosure of origin. This loophole is highlighted by Chen's observation that 'if a patent applicant provides a false statement about the origin, the examiner will not find it because they only check whether the form is included'.[218] This absence of effective deterrence reinforces the demand for a more robust legal and policy structure, one that acknowledges and protects the rights and contributions of TMK holders, while simultaneously promoting innovation.

---

[215] Patent Law (n 11) Art 5.

[216] Patent Law (n 11) Art 26.

[217] Ibid.

[218] Wenting Cheng, 'The Protection of Genetic Resources in Chinese Patent Law' (2021) 43(4) *European Intellectual Property Review* 248, 251.

To address these tensions and establish a more equitable system, legislators and policy makers should:

1. Refine and clarify China's patent law's disclosure requirements by providing precise definitions for terms like 'direct source' and 'original source'.
2. Make the disclosure of origin mandatory to ensure that local communities and ethnic minority groups receive due recognition for their contributions to TMK.
3. Strengthen penalties and remedies for non-compliance to deter unauthorised exploitation and misappropriation, fostering a more balanced relationship between TMK preservation and its use for innovation.

In essence, by addressing ambiguous terms and concepts in China's patent law concerning the disclosure of origin requirements,[219] legislators can create deterrent effects that better protect traditional knowledge holders while facilitating responsible innovation. Such an approach aids in achieving a delicate balance, one that both safeguards Chinese TMK and promotes an environment conducive to responsible innovation and utilisation within the unique framework of China's legal and cultural landscape.

However, a significant challenge remains. The patent system, when used to secure monopolies and control over culturally significant TMK—a practice deeply rooted in various communities in China—often results in biopiracy.[220] This misuse typically undermines these communities, generating tensions between the knowledge bearers and contemporary stakeholders who exploit TMK for commercial or industrial benefits. This chapter's patent landscape analysis unveils a pervasive issue in China: the existence of erroneous patents based on Chinese TMK. Often referred to as 'biopiracy', this practice involves the unauthorised extraction and commercialisation of biological resources and Indigenous knowledge without providing equitable compensation to the originating communities.[221] This prevalent issue further amplifies the legal concerns and tensions stemming from the perceived shortcomings of existing laws, regulations, and policies in adequately protecting TMK and safeguarding the rights and interests of the communities.

Amidst these challenges, the *Nagoya Protocol* serves as a crucial international agreement that establishes a holistic legal framework to combat biopiracy, providing a roadmap to rectify such inequalities through its effective national implementation.[222] However, despite China being a signatory of the *Nagoya Protocol*, the absence of robust domestic legislation enforcing the necessary ABS obligations exacerbates

---

[219] For a more comprehensive discussion on the disclosure of origin requirements, which plays a crucial role in protecting Traditional Medical Knowledge ('TMK') from exploitation, please refer to Sect. 2.3.

[220] V Shiva, Protect or Plunder?:Understanding Intellectual Property Right (Zed Books, 2001) 49.

[221] Marcia Ellen DeGeer, 'Biopiracy: The Appropriation of Indigenous Peoples' Cultural Knowledge' (2003) 9 *New England Journal of International and Comparative Law* 179, 179.

[222] The ABS mechanism is discussed in more detail in Chapter 5.

tensions between TMK holders and modern stakeholders.[223] This legislative gap leaves room for unauthorised exploitation and use of TMK within China's borders.

Addressing these tensions necessitates that China construct an effective ABS framework in line with full implementation of the *Nagoya Protocol*.[224] This should include provisions that recognise the rights of local communities and uphold relevant obligations concerning traditional knowledge protection. While some studies suggest that individuals or corporations from developed nations have been appropriating TMK and associated genetic resources in China for years, securing patents under their names,[225] the findings from the patent landscape analysis paint a different picture. The analysis suggest that it is, in fact, domestic entities in China that are more likely to misappropriate TMK and claim patent ownership over related genetic resources, further intensifying the internal tensions within the Chinese context.

This scenario brings into sharp focus the controversy surrounding the domestic appropriation of TMK in China. This situation strains the relationships between local communities and domestic stakeholders, as establishing domestic patent monopolies over TMK can adversely affect the livelihoods of local communities. By potentially depriving these communities of their inherent rights to utilise TMK and nurture the genetic resources native to their regions, external entities can gain monopoly control. These actions disrupt traditional community control over these resources and forms of knowledge, fostering a sense of injustice and further escalating internal tensions.

The crux of the matter, therefore, is to find an approach that not only ensures robust protection of Chinese TMK but also encourages its responsible use and appropriate dissemination, respecting China's unique sociocultural milieu. Implementing a comprehensive ABS framework and refining domestic legislation are essential steps in achieving an equitable system. This will ease the tension between traditional knowledge holders and modern stakeholders, thereby promoting a harmonious coexistence of tradition and modernity.

Although the implications and complexities may not be thoroughly articulated in this chapter's patent landscape analysis, the significance of Chinese TMK in the

---

[223] Dayuan Xue and Lijie Cai, 'China's Legal and Policy Frameworks for Access to Genetic Resources and Benefit-Sharing from Their Use' (2009) 18(1) *Review of European Community & International Environmental Law* 91, 91–99; Xiaoou Zheng, 'Key legal challenges and opportunities in the implementation of the Nagoya Protocol: The case of China' (2019) 28(2) *Review of European, Comparative & International Environmental Law* 175, 175–184.

[224] A comprehensive discussion on creating an effective Access and Benefit Sharing (ABS) framework to govern the protection, utilisation, and dissemination of Chinese TMK is presented in Chapter 5.

[225] YanJie Wang et al., 'Global Bio-piracy Cases and China's Countermeasures' (2014) 30(2) *Journal of Ecology and Rural Environment* 146, 146–154; Xiaodong Tou, 'Biopiracy in the Struggle for New Strategic Highlands of Genetic Resources and the Legal Governance Path' (2014) 5 *Law Science Magazine* 71, 71–83; Weilin Fu and Gong Cao, 'On Dealing with Bio-piracy under the System of Patent Law: Based on De'ang Acid Tea Traditional Knowledge' (2017) 2 *China Invention & Patent* 12, 12–16.

global landscape cannot be understated. Its widespread dissemination and influence have transcended national boundaries, resonating across diverse regions worldwide.[226] This impact is particularly noticeable in neighbouring countries, such as Japan and Korea, where Chinese cultural practices and philosophies have been deeply embedded into their respective traditional medical knowledge systems.[227] The roots of many elements of their TMK can be traced back to China, demonstrating the depth of this influence.[228]

In Japan, the evolution of Kampo medicine provides an illustrative example.[229] Kampo medicine, while maintaining its unique Japanese characteristics, has incorporated many principles derived from Chinese TMK.[230] Similarly, Korean traditional medicine has also been significantly influenced by Chinese TMK.[231] It reflects a complex interplay of shared cultural heritage and knowledge exchange that has occurred over centuries, demonstrating how medical wisdom and techniques can cross borders and become integrated into different health paradigms.[232]

The exchange and blending of TMK across borders, while enriching, has sometimes given rise to international disputes and tensions.[233] These controversies often centre around IP rights, the ownership and control of TMK, with disagreements regarding its dissemination, commercialisation, and attribution.[234] To address the IP dimensions of these disputes, various solutions can be contemplated. Among these are defensive protection models, such as digital libraries and databases, cataloguing TMK.[235] These information systems can be synchronised with the IP offices of other nations to prevent the unwarranted granting of IP rights over shared TMK.[236]

---

226 薛益明 [Xue Yiming],《中医药传入日本与朝鲜》[The introduction of traditional Chinese medicine into Japan and Korea] [2009] 中医文献杂志*Journal of Traditional Chinese Medicine Literature* 47, 47–48.

227 Ibid.

228 Ibid.

229 袁钟瑜 [Yuan Zhongyu],《中日传统医学循证研究比较》[Comparison of evidence-based research in Chinese and Japanese traditional medicine] (2021) 36(4) 华西医学*Huaxi Medicine* 539, 539–543.

230 Ibid.

231 李士娟 [Li Shijuan],《中医古籍东传对朝(韩)医学理论的影响》[The influence of the eastward spread of ancient Chinese medical texts on Korean medical theory] (2015) 21(6) 中国中医基础医学杂志*Chinese Journal of Basic Medicine in Traditional Chinese Medicine* 677, 677–680.

232 Ibid.

233 Hu Ren, 'Protection of Cross Border Ethnic Groups' Traditional Medicine under International Law' (2013) 8(1) *Frontiers of Law in China* 186, 186–210.

234 Ibid.

235 Christoph Antons, 'Asian Borderlands and the Legal Protection of Traditional Knowledge and Traditional Cultural Expressions' (2013) 47(4) *Modern Asian Studies* 1403, 1432–1433.

236 Ibid.

In addition to the defensive protection models, another tool that can be utilised to address these disputes is the inventories and listings outlined in the UNESCO *Convention for the Safeguarding of the Intangible Cultural Heritage.*[237] These listings can be used to establish claims to culture and heritage, reinforcing the validity and recognition of TMK. Paying close attention to the *Convention's* international cooperation provisions is crucial in this context.[238] The *Convention* urges nations to cooperate at different levels: bilateral, subregional, regional, and international (Article 19).[239] This cooperation can help establish a consensus on the use and protection of shared TMK. Moreover, the *Convention* provides an opportunity for two or more State Parties to jointly request international assistance for the safeguarding of intangible cultural heritage (Article 23).[240] Such collaborations can enable the sharing of resources, expertise, and mechanisms to effectively protect and manage TMK across borders.

Therefore, it is vital for China to develop inclusive, comprehensive legal and policy structures, considering stakeholders' diverse interests. This would ease tensions and create harmonious relationships. Furthermore, this framework should reflect China's historical, cultural, and socioeconomic nuances, acknowledging the cultural legacy and contributions of communities and TMK custodians. This acknowledgement forms an essential part of a harmonious model for safeguarding Chinese TMK for future generations.

2.5 Conclusion

Rooted deeply in the unique historical, sociocultural, and economic landscape of China, TMK serves as the compendium of traditional knowledge, practices, and beliefs that have been in existence for thousands of years in China. The scope of TMK in China was found to be so broad that it revealed the understanding of the whole Chinese nation on life, health, and diseases. Although there are various patterns in which TMK is held in China, this chapter argued that TMK should still be recognised as a collective heritage of the communities, ethnic groups, or a unified national community of China. It also argued that, since the cultural and spiritual values and customary laws play an important and dynamic role in local communities in China, the protection and promotion of TMK should be based on the respect for, and understanding of, their customary laws and the cultural practices specific to the communities and related TMK holders. This chapter then pointed to the evolving nature of TMK in China and its ability to adapt and change in accordance with different contexts and times. On this basis, TMK in China should be regarded as a dynamic

[237] *Convention for the Safeguarding of the Intangible Cultural Heritage (The UNESCO Convention),* opened for signature 17 October 2003, 2368 UNTS 3 (entered into force 20 April 2006) Art 11 and Art 12.

[238] The UNESCO Convention (n 34) art 19 and art 23.

[239] The UNESCO Convention (n 34) art 19.

[240] The UNESCO Convention (n 34) art 23.

and flexible expression of knowledge, rather than as a static and unchanging one. In general, considering the complex nature of TMK in China as demonstrated in this chapter, it was argued that it should be protected and promoted in an appropriate way so that its collective and complex nature can be accommodated.

This chapter critically examined the legal, ethical, and cultural complexities that stem from the application of TMK in China's expanding pharmaceutical sector. Centring on the case of Qinghao (*Artemisia annua*), the analysis underscored how TMK, deeply entrenched in China's sociocultural fabric, has played a significant role in drug discovery and the country's pharmaceutical advancements. The narrative recounted the pivotal role of Qinghao in developing artemisinin, an antimalarial compound for which the discoverer won the Nobel Prize. It highlighted the important role of communities and ethnic groups, such as the Uyghurs, in the cultivation and traditional usage of Qinghao. This chapter then highlighted growing concerns about the misappropriation of TMK, inadequate recognition of TMK holders, and the potential disruption to community practices and livelihoods, despite the successful commercialisation and patenting of artemisinin-based products. The argument advanced in this chapter called for a balanced and comprehensive legal and policy framework dedicated to ensuring the comprehensive protection, responsible utilisation, and suitable dissemination of TMK within the unique context of China. This framework should thoughtfully take into account China's distinct historical and cultural context, respecting the customary laws, shared interests, and cultural traditions of the communities and knowledge holders. Moreover, the unique characteristics of Chinese TMK should be duly recognised and accommodated within this framework to maintain the integrity of this invaluable knowledge resource.

Lastly, this chapter embarked on an in-depth patent landscape analysis centred on TMK and associated genetic resources in China, with particular emphasis on the *Artemisia annua* plant, known locally as Qinghao. This plant, which has been widely used in traditional Chinese medicine for centuries, manifests a profound domestic discord within China between the traditional custodians of TMK and contemporary stakeholders seeking to commercially exploit this heritage. The analysis was conducted with the intention of critically examining the extent and evolution of TMK exploitation within the national confines of China.

The in-depth patent landscape analysis revealed a notable increase in patent applications associated with Qinghao over the past decades, highlighting a rampant surge in TMK appropriation and the monopolisation of associated genetic resources, mostly by domestic entities. Despite Qinghao's widespread use in traditional medicine for centuries and its deeply entrenched connection to local communities, many of these patent applications failed to acknowledge the origins of the TMK or the contributions of the local communities. While some did recognise China as the origin, the oversight in many applications has heightened tensions and could further stir domestic unrest.

The patent landscape analysis underscored the brewing tensions and potential conflict dynamics within China due to the escalating unauthorised use of Chinese TMK by corporations and industrial entities in their quest for novel drug discoveries. It also cast a spotlight on the urgent need to protect TMK and its custodians. The analysis revealed that domestic Chinese entities are most likely to exploit the

TMK and associated genetic resources found within their own nation, inadvertently fostering an environment of injustice. This act of patenting TMK encroaches upon the sovereignty of local communities, stripping them of their control over their knowledge and resources, and engendering both legal and ethical issues.

As this chapter concluded, it highlighted the imperative need for China to devise robust policy measures, legal infrastructures, and practical methods that facilitate the continued utilisations of TMK, while also safeguarding it from unauthorised exploitation. It emphasised that it is essential to approach this situation with consideration, acknowledging the origins of TMK, showing respect for the diverse stakeholders involved, and delicately balancing the intricate dynamics inherent in the safeguarding and proper utilisation of Chinese TMK. It recommended that this approach should reflect and resonate with China's distinctive cultural and historical backdrop, demonstrating a profound comprehension of its rich heritage and its complex contemporary realities.

References

AF Jozala, DC Geraldes and LL Tundisi et al, 'Biopharmaceuticals from Microorganisms: from Production to Purification' (2016) 47 *Brazilian Journal of Microbiology* 51.

Almaz Borjigidai et al, 'Investigation and Application of Artemisia Plant Resources for Chinese Medicine and Mongolian Medicine in Inner Mongolia' (2013) 40(4) *Liaoning Journal of Traditional Chinese Medicine* 770.

Anonymous, 'China and the Principle of Self-Determination of Peoples' (2010) 1 *St Antony's International Review* 79.

Barry Sautman, 'Ethnic Law and Minority Rights in China: Progress and Constraints' (2002) 21(3) *Law & Policy* 283.

Barry Sautman, 'Self-representation and Ethnic Minority Rights in China' (2014) 15(2) *Asian Ethnicity* 174.

Bhupinder Singh Sekhon, 'Biopharmaceuticals: an Overview' (2010) 34 *Thai Journal of Pharmaceutical Sciences*. 1.

Bichang He, 'Contemporary Explanation of the Intangible Cultural Heritage of Naxi Dongba Culture' (Conference Paper, International Conference on Art Design, Music and Culture, 2019) 190–191.

Bill Beeson, 'Weighing the Opportunities & Risks Within China's Biopharmaceutical Industry' *The China Guys* (Web Page, 22 July 2021). <https://thechinaguys.com/opportunities-risks-china-biopharmaceuticals-industry/>.

Borjigidai Almaz et al, 'Investigation and Application of Artemisia Plant Resources for Chinese Medicine and Mongolian Medicine in Inner Mongolia' (2013) 40(4) *Liaoning Journal of Traditional Chinese Medicine* 770.

Cansong Li et al, 'Community Heritage Linking Place and Mobility: A Case Study of "Bangbei" in Ethnic Bai Villages of Yunnan Province, China' (2018) 10(7) *Sustainability* 2322.

Charles Z Levkoe. et al, 'People, Power, Change: Three Pillars of a Food Sovereignty Research Praxis' (2019) 46(7) *The Journal of Peasant Studies* 1389.

Christoph Antons, 'Asian Borderlands and the Legal Protection of Traditional Knowledge and Traditional Cultural Expressions' (2013) 47(4) *Modern Asian Studies* 1403.

Colin Mackerras, 'Ethnic Minorities' in Czeslaw Tubilewicz (ed), *Critical Issues in Contemporary China: Unity, Stability and Development* (Routledge, 2016) 1.

Convention for the Safeguarding of the Intangible Cultural Heritage (The UNESCO Convention), opened for signature 17 October 2003, 2368 UNTS 3 (entered into force 20 April 2006) Art 11 and Art 12.

Convention on Biological Diversity, opened for signature on 5 June 1992, 1760 UNTS 79 (entered into force 29 December 1993) ('CBD').

Curtis M Horton, 'Protecting Biological Diversity and Cultural Diversity Under Intellectual Property Law' (1995) 10(1) *Journal of Environmental Law and Litigation* 1.

D Syiem and MB Syiem, 'Medicinal Plants and Conservation: Some Issues and Concerns' in P Tandon and YPASuman (eds), *Biodiversity and Its Significance* (I.K. International Publishing House, 2007) 150.

Dahua Zheng, 'Modern Chinese Nationalism and the Awakening of Self-Consciousness of the Chinese Nation' (2019) 3(11) *International Journal of Anthropology and Ethnology* 1.

Daniel F Robinson et al, 'Patent landscaping for Vanuatu: Specific legal geographic methods for Indigenous knowledge protection and promotion' in Daniel F Robinson , Josephine Gillespie and Tayanah O'Donnell (eds), *Legal Geography* (2020) 74.

Daniel J Gervais, 'Spiritual but Not Intellectual? The Protection of Sacred Intangible Traditional Knowledge' (2003) 11 *Vanderbilt Law School Faculty Publications* 467.

Daniel Robinson and Margaret Raven, 'Identifying and Preventing Biopiracy in Australia: Patent Landscapes and Legal Geographies for Plants with Indigenous Australian Uses' (2016) 48(3) *Australian Geographer* 311.

Daniel Robinson et al, 'Legal geographies of kava, kastom and Indigenous knowledge: Next steps under the Nagoya Protocol' (2021) 118 *Geoforum* 169.

Dayuan Xue and Lijie Cai, 'China's Legal and Policy Frameworks for Access to Genetic Resources and Benefit-Sharing from Their Use' (2009) 18(1) *Review of European Community & International Environmental Law* 91.

De Sousa Santos, 'Epistemologies of the South: Justice Against Epistemicide' (Routledge, 2014).

Debasish Pattanaik and Munmun Jha, 'Knowledge of Identity among the Indigenous People' (2007) 7(2) *The Original Anthropologist* 199.

Debra Harry Kanehe and Le'a Malia, 'Asserting Tribal Sovereignty over Cultural Property: Moving Towards Protection of Genetic Material and Indigenous Knowledge' (2006) 5(1) *Seattle Journal for Social Justice* 27.

'Disruptive Potential of Genomics Could Prompt Life Sciences Companies to Accelerate Deal-making', *Health Forward Blog* (Blog Post, 2018) <https://www2.deloitte.com/us/en/blog/health-care-blog/2018/disruptive-potential-genomics-prompt-companies-accelerate-deal.html>.

DQ Hodnett, 'Legitimising Biopiracy? Fairness and Efficacy of the Nagoya Protocol' (2021) 2 *York Law Review* 75.

'Dragon Boat Festival Customs', *Beijing Tourism* (Web Page, 15 June 2012).

Duan Xiao-Li, 'The Wide Distribution of Artemisia annua in Xinjiang and Its Popularity to Treat Disease', *City Consumption Morning Newspaper* (Web Page, 2015) <https://read01.com/zh-hk/0eaMRM.html#.YZSJeE5Bw2w>.

Elisa Morgera, Elsa Tsioumani and Matthias Buck, Unraveling the Nagoya Protocol: A Commentary on the Nagoya Protocol on Access and Benefit-sharing to the Convention on Biological Diversity (Brill, 2014) 171–172.

Elisabeth Hsu, 'Qing hao in the Chinese Materia Media' in Stephen Harris (ed), *Plants, Health and Healing: On the Interface of Ethnobotany and Medical Anthropology* (Berghahn Books, 2010) 83.

Elisabeth Hsu, 'Reflections on the 'Discovery' of the Antimalarial Qinghao' (2006) 61(6) *British Journal of Clinical Pharmacology* 666.

Elisabeth Hsu, *The Transmission of Chinese Medicine* (Cambridge University Press, 2009) 21–57.

Erik Gómez-Baggethun, 'Is there a Future for Indigenous and Local Knowledge?' (2021) 75 *The Journal of Peasant Studies* 6.

Fatoumata O Maiga et al, 'Artemisinin-based combination therapy for uncomplicated Plasmodium falciparum malaria in Mali: a systematic review and meta-analysis' (2021) 20 *Malaria Journal* 1.

Fran Humphries et al, 'A Systematic Quantitative Literature Review of Aquaculture Genetic Resource Access and Benefit Sharing' (2019) 11 Review in Aquaculture 1133.

Francis F Hong, 'History of Medicine in China When Medicine Took an Alternative Pat' (2004) 8 *McGill Journal of Medicine* 79.

Frédéric Thomas, 'Genetic Resources: A Way to Ensure Access to a Common Good, or to Compensate Its Commodification?' (2017) 88(3) *Entreprises et histoire* 103.

G Dutfield,'Why Traditional Knowledge Is Important in Drug Discovery'(2010) 2(9) *Future Medicinal Chemistry* 1407–1408.

Graham Dutfield, 'Traditional Knowledge, Intellectual Property and Pharmaceutical Innovation: What's Left to Discuss?' in Matthew David and Debora Halbert (eds), *The Sage Handbook of Intellectual Property* (SAGE Publications Ltd, 2014) 649.

Guoqiao Li, Xingbo Guo and Linchun Fu, 'Persistent Pursuit in Research of Artemisinin: Fast Elimination of Malaria Commemoration for the 50th Anniversary of Project 523' (2017) 34(3) *Journal of Guangzhou University of Traditional Chinese Medicine* 303.

Hongen Jiang et al, 'Archaeobotanical Evidence of Plant Utilization in the Ancient Turpan of Xinjiang, China: A Case Study at the Shengjindian Cemetery' (2015) 24 *Vegetation History and Archaeobotany* 165.

Hu Ren, 'Protection of Cross Border Ethnic Groups' Traditional Medicine under International Law' (2013) 8(1) *Frontiers of Law in China* 186.

Huan Liu et al, 'The discovery of Artemisia annua L. in the Shengjindian cemetery, Xinjiang, China and its implications for early uses of traditional Chinese herbal medicine qinghao' (2013) 146(1) *Journal of ethnopharmacology* 278.

Ian S Mcintosh, 'Are There Indigenous People' (2000) 24(3) *Cultural Survival Quaterly* 1.

June Teufel Dreyer, *China's Political System: Modernization and Tradition* (Palgrave Macmillan, 1993) 381.

Jun-kui Bai, 'Analysis of Restricting Factors on Technological Innovation in the Exploitation of Nationality Culture and Civil Resources—Taking Nationality Culture and Civil Resources Exploitation of Flower-drum and Qinghao in Minority Nationality Areas of Chongqing, Hubei,Hunan,Guizhou and Sichuan as an example' (2008) 18(1) *Journal of Chongqing Technology and Business University* 43;

K Sastry et al, 'Research and Development Perspectives of Transgenic Cotton: Evidence from Patent Landscape Studies' (2011) 16(2) *Journal of Intellectual Property Rights* 139.

Kamrul Hossain and Rosa Maria Ballardini, 'Protecting Indigenous Traditional Knowledge Through a Holistic Principle-Based Approach' (2021) 39(1) *Nordic Journal of Human Rights* 51.

Kathy Zhang et al, 'Science-Based Innovation in China: A Case Study of Artemisinin from Laboratory to the Market' (2018) 3(2) *Journal of Industrial Integration and Management* 1.

Kerong Zhang and Wuyi Liu, 'The Current Status, Trend, and Development Strategies of Chinese Biopharmaceutical Industry with a Challenging Perspective' [2020] *Sage Journals* 1.

Kiki Han, *The Dawn of China Biopharma Innovation* (McKinsey & Company, 2021) 1–9.

Kumari Rajani et al, 'Traditional Knowledge and Its Promotion Through Proving Legal Rights' in Chandan Roy (ed), *The Role of Intellectual Property Rights in Agriculture and Allied Science* (Apple Academic Press, 2018) 130.

Lan Qiu et al, 'Public Funding and Private Investment for R&D: a Survey in China's Pharmaceutical Industry' (2014) 12(27) *Health Research Policy and Systems* 1.

LC Sahu and Aisha Amin, 'The Issue of Biopiracy & Protection of Traditional Knowledge' (2022) 5(1) *International Journal of Law) Management & Humanities* 2310.

Lei Zhen et al, 'Are Chinese Patent Applications Politically Driven?' (Working Paper, Patent Statistics for Decision Makers Conference, 2012) 1.

LEK Consulting, 'Innovation in China, Made in China 2025 and Implications for Healthcare MNCs', *GPS Healthcare Quarterly* (Web Page, 2018) 1 <https://www.lek.com/insights/by/innovation-china-made-china-2025-and-implications-healthcare-mncs>.

Lerong Lu 'Promoting High-Tech Innovations through Capital Markets Law Reform: Deciphering the Sci-Tech Innovation Board of the Shanghai Stock Exchange' (2020) 35 *Journal of International Banking and Financial Law* 140.

Linfang Huang et al, 'Mapping the Potential Distribution of High Artemisinin-yielding Artemisia annua L. (Qinghao) in China with a Geographic Information System' (2010) 5(18) *Chinese Medicine* 1.

Louis Fu, 'Surgical History of Ancient China' (2010) 80(3) *ANZ Journal of Surgery* 133.

Lu Zhao et al, 'An Ethnopharmacological Study of Aromatic Uyghur Medicinal Plants in Xinjiang, China' (2017) 55(1) *Pharmaceutical Biology* 1.

Lyu Zhennan and Siti Rohaya Yahaya, 'An Aesthetic Study on Traditional Batik Design of Miao Ethnicity in China' (2021) 9(2) *Jurnal Seni dan Pendidikan Seni* 12.

MA Diallo et al, 'Efficacy and safety of artemisinin-based combination therapy and the implications of Pfkelch13 and Pfcoronin molecular markers in treatment failure in Senegal.' (2020) 10 *Scientific Reports* 1.

Mackenzie Mills, Anwen Zhang and Panos Kanavos(2019) 'Pharmaceutical Policy in China' *London School of Economics* 5.

Marcia Ellen DeGeer, 'Biopiracy: The Appropriation of Indigenous Peoples' Cultural Knowledge' (2003) 9 *New England Journal of International and Comparative Law* 179.

Martin Saxer, *Manufacturing Tibetan Medicine: The Creation of an Industry and the Moral Economy of Tibetanness* (Berghahn Books, 2013) 95–136.

Mengtian Cao et al,'The Influence Factors Analysis of Households' Poverty Vulnerability in Southwest Ethnic Areas of China Based on the Hierarchical Linear Model: A Case Study of Liangshan Yi Autonomous Prefecture' (2016) 66 *Applied Geography* 144.

Michelle F Rourke, 'Who Are "Indigenous and Local Communities" and What Is "Traditional Knowledge" for Virus Access and Benefit-sharing? A Textual Analysis of the Convention on Biological Diversity and Its Nagoya Protocol' (2018) 25(3) *Journal of Law and Medicine* 707.

Miriam Latorre Quinn, 'Protection for Indigenous Knowledge: An International Law Analysis' (2001) 14(2) *St. Thomas Law Review* 287.

Nagoya Protocol on Access to Genetic Resources and the Fair and Equitable Sharing of Benefits Arising from Their Utilization to the Convention on Biological Diversity, opened for signature on 29 October 2010, [2012] ATNIF 3 (entered into force 12 October 2014) ('Nagoya Protocol').

Nan Xia, 'Access and benefit-sharing in China: Exploring the Extent to Which China Fulfils the Obligations of the Nagoya Protocol' (2023) 13(1) *Queen Mary Journal of Intellectual Property* 97.

OS Michael, 'Artemisinin: The Journey from Natural Product to Nobel Prize' (2015) 13(2) *Annals of Ibadan Postgraduate Medicine* 113.

Pamela Weathers et al, 'Whole Plant Approaches to Therapeutic Use of Artemisia annua L. (Asteraceae)' in Tariq Aftab et al (eds), *Artemisia annua -Pharmacology and Biotechnology* (Springer, 2014) 51.

Pan Zhiping, 'Correctly Understand 'National Self-Determination' and 'High Degree of Autonomy'' (2018) (1) *Theory and Reform* 43.

Pankaj Sharma Gupta, Kumar Vijay and Sushma Sharma, *Healing Traditions of the North-western Himalayas* (Springer New Delhi, 2014) 12.

Paul Gepts, 'Who Owns Biodiversity, and How Should the Owners Be Compensated?' (2004) 134(4) *Plant Physiol* 1295.

Paul Kuruk, 'Regulating Access to Traditional Knowledge and Genetic Resources: The Disclosure Requirement as a Strategy to Combat Biopiracy' (2015) 17 *San Diego International Law Journal* 1.

Paul Kuruk, *Traditional Knowledge, Genetic Resources, Customary Law and Intellectual Property* (Edward Elgar Publishing, 2020) 17;

Paul Oldham et al, 'Biological Diversity in the Patent System' (2013) 8(11) *PLOS One* 1.
PG Sampath, *Regulating Bioprospecting: Institutions for Drug Research, Access, and Benefit-sharing* (United Nation University Press, 2005) 1–167.
PR Katz, 'The Pacification of Plagues: A Chinese Rite of Affliction' (1995) 9(1) *Journal of Ritual Studies* 55.
Qian Xun Consultation, *2021 China Biopharmaceutical Market Analysis Report: Analysis of Market Scale, Status and Development Trend* (Report, 2021).
Qiu-Hua Li et al, 'Overview of the Plague in the Late Ming Dynasty and Its Prevention and Control Measures' (2020) 5(3) *Talent of Medical Research Journal* 136.
Ralph C Croizier, Traditional Medicine in Modern China: Science, Nationalism, and the Tensions of Cultural Change (Harvard University Press, 1968) 13–36.
Reza Hasmath Reza and Margaret Maurer-fazio, 'The Contemporary Ethnic Minority in China: An Introduction' (2015) 56(1) *Eurasian Geography and Economics* 1.
Richard J Maud, et al, 'Artemisinins: Preserving the "Magic Bullet"' (2010) 71(1) *Drug Development Research* 12.
Robert D Atkinson, 'China's Biopharmaceutical Strategy: Challenge or Complement to U.S. Industry Competitiveness?' (Information Technology and Innovation Foundation, August 12, 2019).
Robert D Atkinson, 'Healthy Funding: The Critical Role of Investing in NIH to Boost Health and Lower Costs' *Information Technology and Innovation Foundation* (2019) 1.
Rong Ma , 'Ethnic Relations in Contemporary China: Cultural Tradition and Ethnic Policies Since 1949' (2006) 25(1) *Policy and Society* 85.
Rouse Consultancy, *China: A Changing Focus on Patent Incentives*, (Web Page, 2019). <https://rouse.com/insights/news/2019/china-a-changing-focus-on-patent-incentives>.
Ruth L Okediji, 'Traditional Knowledge and the Public Domain' (Conference Paper, Centre for International Governance Innovation, June 2018) 1.
Saskia AF Vermeylen, 'Between Law and Lore: The Tragedy of Traditional Knowledge (PhD Thesis, University of Surrey, 2007) 55–75.
Shangli Lin, 'National Transformation: Modern Reconstruction of a Unified Society' (2016) 1 *Chinese Political Science Review* 113.
Shannon Ellis, 'Hong Kong Stock Exchange Opens to Biotechs' (2018) 36 *Nature Biotechnology* 482.
Sheetal Menon and Shishir Kumar Jha, 'Patent landscape analysis for crop biotechnology in India' (2015) 8(3) *Int. J. Intellectual Property Management* 111.
Si-Yuan Pan et al, 'Historical Perspective of Traditional Indigenous Medical Practices: The Current Renaissance and Conservation of Herbal Resources' (2014) 2014 *Evid Based Complement Alternat Med* 1.
SK Jain, 'Dynamism of Traditional Knowledge' (2005) 4(2) *Indian Journal of Traditional Knowledge* 115.
Song-My Hoang, 'Alternative Medicine Could Treat Our Maladies, But We Have to Study It', *Massive Science* (Web Page, 2019) https://massivesci.com/articles/eastern-alternative-traditional-medicine-scientific-basis-research-ginseng-st-john-wort.
Stephen Mbae Muthamia, 'Effect of Traditional Knowledge Systems in Sustainable Development and Management of Natural Resources in Meru' (2021) 5(3) *Journal of Public Policy and Governance* 112.
Surendra Sarsaiya et al, 'Bioengineering Tools for the Production of Pharmaceuticals: Current Perspective and Future Outlook' (2019) 10(1) *Bioengineering* 469.
Sushma Singh, 'Traditional Indian Medicine and Intellectual Property Rights: An Indian Perspective' (2021) 4(5) *International Journal of Law) Management & Humanities* 1405.
Susy Frankel, 'The Mismatch of Geographical Indications and Innovative Traditional Knowledge' (Research Paper No.35/2011, Victoria University of Wellington, November 2011) 1.
Tania Bubela et al, ' Patent Landscaping for Life Sciences Innovation: Toward Consistent and Transparent Practices' (2013) 31(3) *Nature Biotechnology* 202.

Tesh Dagne, 'Protecting Traditional Knowledge in International Intellectual Property Law: Imperatives for Protection and Choice of Modalities' (2014) 14 The John Marshall Review of Intellectual Property Law 26.

'The Popularity Of the Folk Use of Qinghao to Treat Diseases in Xinjiang' (Web Page, 9 October 2015) <https://news.ifeng.com/a/20151009/44799115_0.shtml>.

Tianbao Qin, 'Common Pools of Traditional Chinese Medical Knowledge in China' in Gerd Winter and Evanson Chege Kamau (eds), *Common Pools of Genetic Resources : Equity and Innovation in International Biodiversity Law* (Routledge, 2013) 151–152.

TJ Hinrichs, 'Healing and Medicine: Healing and Medicine in China' *Encyclopedia.com* (Web Page, 2005) <https://www.encyclopedia.com/environment/encyclopedias-almanacs-transcripts-and-maps/healing-and-medicine-healing-and-medicine>.

TJ Hinrichs, 'New Geographies of Chinese Medicine' (1998) 13 Beyond Joseph Needham: Science, Technology, and Medicine in East and Southeast Asia 287.

United Nations Declaration on the Rights of Indigenous Peoples, GA Res 61/295, UN GAOR, 61st sess, 107th plen mtg, Agenda Item 68, UN Doc A/RES/61/295 (13 September 2007) ('*UNDRIP*').

United Nations Environment Programme, 'The Convention on Biological Diversity and the Agreement on Trade-Related Intellectual Property Rights (TRIPS): Relationships and Synergies', UN Doc UNEP/CBD/COP/3/23, 3rd meeting (4–15 November 1996).

V Shiva, Protect or Plunder?:Understanding Intellectual Property Right (Zed Books, 2001) 49.

Vicky Qing Xia, 'China Looks Inward and Outward: Investments in US and EU Biopharmaceutical Companies Are on the Rise', *Bioprocess International* (Web Page, 17 May 2019) <https://bioprocessintl.com/business/bioregions/china-looks-inward-and-outward-investments-in-us-and-eu-biopharmaceutical-companies-are-on-the-rise/>.

Weilin Fu and Gong Cao, 'On Dealing with Bio-piracy under the System of Patent Law: Based on De'ang Acid Tea Traditional Knowledge' (2017) 2 *China Invention & Patent* 12.

Wenting Cheng, 'The Protection of Genetic Resources in Chinese Patent Law' (2021) 43(4) *European Intellectual Property Review* 248.

Wenxiu Liu and Yue Liu, 'Youyou Tu: significance of winning the 2015 Nobel Prize in Physiology or Medicine' (2016) 6(1) *Cardiovascular Diagnosis and Therapy* 1.

Wenyuan Gao et al, 'In Vitro Culture and Cultivation of Chinese Medicinal Plants for Industrial Utilization and Genetic Resource Conservation' (2005) 3(2) *Plant Genetic Resources* 116.

World Health Organization (WHO), 'WHO Monograph on Good Agricultural and Collection Practices (GACP) for Artemisia annua L' (Report, 2006) 1.

World Health Organization (WHO), *WHO International Standard Terminologies on Traditional Medicine in the Western Pacific Region* (Report, 2021)1.

World Intellectual Property Organization ('WIPO'), *International Patent Classification (IPC)* (Web Page, 2021) <https://www.wipo.int/classifications/ipc/en/>.

World Intellectual Property Organization (WIPO), 'Customary Law, Traditional Knowledge and Intellectual Property: An Outline of the Issues' (Report, WIPO, 2013) 1.

Xiaobo Zhang et al, 'The Influence of Guangxi Topography On the Level of Artemisinin in Artemisia Annua' (2009) 29(2) *ACTA ECOLOGICA SINICA* 688.

Xiaodong Tou, 'Biopiracy in the Struggle for New Strategic Highlands of Genetic Resources and the Legal Governance Path' (2014) 5 *Law Science Magazine* 71.

Xiaoou Zheng, 'Key legal challenges and opportunities in the implementation of the Nagoya Protocol: The case of China' (2019) 28(2) *Review of European, Comparative & International Environmental Law* 175.

Xiaoping Fang, 'From Union Clinics to Barefoot Doctors: Healers, Medical Pluralism, and State Medicine in Chinese Villages, 1950–1970' (2010) 2(2) *Journal of Modern Chinese History* 221.

Xiaotong Fei, 'The Formation and Development of the Chinese Nation with Multi-ethnic Groups' (2017) 1(1) *International Journal of Anthropology and Ethnology* 1.

Xin-zhuan Su and Louis H Miller, 'The Discovery of Artemisinin and Nobel Prize in Physiology or Medicine' (2016) 58(11) *Science China Life Sciences* 1175.

Xuan Li and Weiwei Li, 'Inadequacy of Patent Regime on Traditional Medicinal Knowledge—A Diagnosis of 13-year Traditional Medicinal Knowledge Patent Experience in China' (2007) 10(2) *The Journal of World Intellectual Property* 125.

Y Liu et al, 'Ethnomedicinal Plants Investigation in Hezhen nationality' (2015) 81(11) *Planta Medica* 552.

Yahua, Niu, 'Artemisinin (Qing Hao Su)' in Jueming Hua and Lisheng Feng (eds), *Thirty Great Inventions of China:From Millet Agriculture to Artemisinin* (Springer, 2020) 815.

YanJie Wang et al, 'Global Bio-piracy Cases and China's Countermeasures' (2014) 30(2) *Journal of Ecology and Rural Environment* 146.

Yanqiang Zhao et al, 'Skincare Plants of the Naxi of NW Yunnan, China' (2020) 42 *Plant Diversity* 473.

Ye Shu-xian and Liu Wan-er, 'Classic of Mountains and Seas and the Origin of White Jade Worship: On the Myths of the Yellow Emperor's Eating Jade and Queen Mother of the West's Presenting the White Jade Ring' (2016) 6(6) *Journal of Literature and Art Studies* 580.

Yi Gou et al, 'Ethnobotanical Survey of Plants Traditionally Used against Hematophagous Invertebrates by Ethnic Groups in the Mountainous Area of Xishuangbanna, Southwest China' (2020) 42 *Plant Diversity* 415.

Youyou Tu 'The Discovery of Artemisinin (qinghaosu) and Gifts from Chinese Medicine' (2011) 17 *Nature Medicine* 1217.

Youyou Tu, 'Artemisinin- A Gift from Traditional Chinese Medicine to the World' (2016) 55(35) *Angewandte Chemie* 286;

Yuan Li, *Traditional Chinese Thinking on HRM Practices: Heritage and Transformation in China* (Palgrave Macmillan London, 2013) 85.

Zengyi Chang, 'The Discovery of Qinghaosu (artemisinin) as an Effective Anti-malaria Drug: A Unique China Story' (2016) 59(1) *Science China Life Sciences* 81.

Zhen Gao et al, 'Emergence and Development of Uyghur Medicine from the Perspective of Chinese Traditional Medicine' (2019) 2(4) *Traditional Medicine and Modern Medicine* 139;

白俊奎 [Bai JunKui],《民族文化和民间资源开发中技术创新的阻碍因素——以渝鄂湘黔川民族地区花鼓和青蒿等民族文化和民间资源开发为例》[Obstacles to Technological Innovation in the Development of Ethnic Culture and Folk Resources - A Case Study of the Development of Flower Drum and Artemisia annua in the Chongqing-Hubei-Hunan-Guizhou-Sichuan Ethnic Regions] (2008) 18(1) 重庆工商大学学报 *Journal of Chongqing Technology and Business University* 43.

宝龙 [Bao Long], 蒙医学与中医学传统思想观念的比较研究 [A Comparative Study of Traditional Ideas in Mongolian Medicine and Traditional Chinese Medicine] (2008) 11 中国民族医药杂志 *Journal Of Medicine & Pharmacy Of Chinese Minorities* 1.

程新法 [Cheng Xinfa]《略述中药的起源及其早期典籍》[A Brief Introduction to the Origin of Chinese Medicine and its Early Literature] (1998) 14(3) 药学教育 *Pharmaceutical Education* 61.

邓大学 [Deng Daxue],《关于中医药现代化地认识》[Understanding the Modernization of Traditional Chinese Medicine] (2004) 16(1) 中医药临床杂志 *Journal of Traditional Chinese Medicine Clinical Practice* 1.

翟华强 [Zhai Huaqiang], 基于师承与家传的古代中医药学人才培养模式 [The Training Model of Ancient Chinese Medicine Talents Based on the Inheritance of Master and Apprentice and Family Inheritance] (2014) 20(1) 中国中医基础医学杂志 *Chinese Journal of Basic Medicine in Traditional Chinese Medicine* 37.

郭静云 [Guo Jingyun]《神农神话源于中国的文化记》[Where Does the Cultural Memory of the Shennong Mythology Originate From?] (2020) 6 中国农史 *Chinese Agricultural History* 3.

韩玉茹 [Zhang Yuru] et al, 苗族医药文化中的生态伦理思想概述 [An Overview of Ecological Ethics in the Medical Culture of Miao Nationality] (2017) 7, 中国民族医药杂志 Journal Of Medicine & Pharmacy Of Chinese Minorities 6.

韩玉茹 [Zhang Yuru] et al, 苗族医药文化中的生态伦理思想概述 [An Overview of Ecological Ethics in the Medical Culture of Miao Nationality] (2017) 7, 中国民族医药杂志 *Journal Of Medicine & Pharmacy Of Chinese Minorities* 1.

洪宗国 [Hong Zongguo], 壮医药思想内核与理论框架思考 [Study of Zhuang Medicine Ideological Core and Theoretical Framework] (2008) 11 中南民族大学学报 *Journal of South-Central University for Nationalities* 46.

黄亚博 [Huang Yabo],《屠呦呦获诺贝尔奖与青蒿素研发对中医药发展的启示》[Tu Youyou's Nobel Prize Win and the Inspiration of Artemisinin Research and Development for the Development of Traditional Chinese Medicine] 江苏中医药 [2016] *Jiangsu Traditional Chinese Medicine* 6.

黄一玲 [Huang Yiling],《论民族自决权的概念内涵与适用条件》[On the Conceptual Connotation and Applicable Conditions of the Right to National Self-Determination] (2017) 1 贵州民族研究 *Guizhou Ethnic Studies* 1.

霍维洮 [Huo Weitao],《中国近代民族认同的历史逻辑 ——兼论中华民族的形成》[China's Modern National Identity Historical Logic: On the Formation of the Chinese Nation] (2021) 3 回族研究 *HuiZu Yan Jiu* 5.

景威栋 [Jing Weidong]《中华民族共同体意识视域下民族医药文化遗产保护探析》[Analysis on the Protection of Ethnic Medicine Cultural Heritage under the Vision of Chinese National Community Consciousness] (2023) 19(1) 亚太传统医药 *Asia Pacific Traditional Medicine* 4.

孔洋洋 [Kong Yangyang],《神农本草经与经方应用之人参篇》[The Classic of the Materia Medica of Shennong and the Application of Classical Prescriptions: The Chapter on Ginseng] (2023) 47(2) 山东中医药大学学报 *Journal of Shandong University of Traditional Chinese Medicine* 127.

李 钰 [Li Jue]《中医药传统知识保护与知识产权制度的关系》[The Relationship Between the Protection of Traditional Chinese Medicine Knowledge and the Intellectual Property System] (2022) 19(27) 中国医药导报 *China Medical Herald* 119.

李佳霏 [Li Jiafei]《观"慈"在先秦儒家伦理下的安置及其现代内涵》[Observing "Benevolence" in Pre-Qin Confucian Ethics and Its Modern Connotations] (2020)23 青年与社会 *Youth and Society* 193.

李静 [Li Jing],《药用枸杞本草考证》[Textual Research on Medicinal Goji Berries in Materia Medica] (2019) 14(10) 世界中医药 *World Traditional Chinese Medicine* 2593.

李林 [Li Lin], 李国春 [Li Guochun] and 张溪 [Zhang Xi],《从青蒿素的专利历程和现状看医药科研成果的知识产权保护》[Examining Intellectual Property Protection of Medical Scientific Research Achievements from the Patent Process and Current Situation of Artemisinin] (2016)11(2) 中国医药生物技术*Chinese Pharmaceutical Biotechnology* 189.

李士娟 [Li Shijuan],《中医古籍东传对朝(韩)医学理论的影响》[The influence of the eastward spread of ancient Chinese medical texts on Korean medical theory] (2015) 21(6) 中国中医基础医学杂志*Chinese Journal of Basic Medicine in Traditional Chinese Medicine* 677.

李巍 [Li Wei],《基于"中华古籍保护计划"的古籍传承性保护利用》[Utilization and Inheritance Protection of Ancient Books Based on the "Chinese Ancient Books Protection Project"] (2021) 10 图书馆*Library* 90.

李志勇 [Li Zhiyong],《互鉴互融:论民族药的现代研究思路》[Mutual Learning and Integration -Discussing Modern Research Ideas of Ethnomedicine] (2017) 42(7) 中国中药杂志, *China Journal of Chinese Materia Medica* 71.

李自然 [Li Ziran],《民族传统文化地本质及特征刍议》[Discussion on the Essence and Characteristics of National Traditional Culture] (2008) 35 (5) 中央民族大学学报*Journal of the Central University for Nationalities* 82.

刘雅 [Liu Ya],《民族本草 世界瑰宝 少数民族医药事业发展回顾与前瞻》 [Ethnic Herbal Medicine: World Treasure - A Review and Prospective Look at the Development of Minority Traditional Medicine] [2018] 中国民族*Chinese Ethnic Group* 22.

罗钰坊 [Luo Yufang],《少数民族传统医药知识生产性保护研究》[Research on the Productive Protection of Traditional Medical Knowledge of Ethnic Minorities] (2018) 20 (4) 铜仁学院学报*Journal of Tongren University* 93.

麻勇恒 [Ma Yongheng],《少数民族传统医药知识的现代传承与创新—以苗族传统医药为例》[The Modern Inheritance and Innovation of Ethnic Minority Traditional Medical Knowledge — Taking Miao Ethnic Traditional Medicine as an Example] (2011) 3(1) 原生态民族文化学刊 *Journal of Original Ethnic Culture Studies* 104.

马得汶 [Ma Dewen],《西部民族地区患者择医的文化因素探析》[Analysis on Cultural Factors Concerning How Patients in China's Western Ethnic Minority Communities Seek Medical Treatment] (2017) 54(1) 西北师大学报 *Journal of Northwest Normal University* 71.

马小莉 [Ma Xiaoli]《互嵌交融:论中华民族的同质性一体性结构》[Interlocking and Blending: On the Homogeneous and Integrated Structure of the Chinese Nation] (2022) 43(6) 贵州民族研究 *Guizhou Ethnic Studies* 42.

庞尧 [Pang Yao],《开放视角下的中国工业创新体系演进及未来展望》[The Evolution and Future Prospects of China's Industrial Innovation System under an Open Perspective] (2023) 2 天津社会科学 *Tianjin Social Science* 108.

秦培洁 [Qin Peijie]《从中医药传统知识保护看民间中医药的传承发展》[Looking at the inheritance and development of folk traditional Chinese medicine from the perspective of the protection of traditional knowledge of Chinese medicine] (2023) 20(9) 中国医药导报 *China Pharmaceutical Guide* 127.

饶毅 [Rao Yi],《中药提取抗疟化学分子第一人》[The First Person to Extract Anti-Malarial Chemical Molecules from Traditional Chinese Medicine] [2015]科技导报*Science and Technology Herald* 127.

任小巧 [Xiaoqiao Ren],《浅析民族医药学与中医药学的关系》[Discussing the Relationship between Ethnomedicine and Traditional Chinese Medicine] (2012)18 (3) 中国民族医药杂志 *Journal of Medicine & Pharmacy of Chinese Minorities* 60.

容中逵 [Rong Zhongkui]《当代中国传统文化传承的"中国"语境——中西关系维度下的中国文化历史演进视角》[The Chinese Context of Contemporary Chinese Traditional Culture Inheritance—The Perspective of Chinese Cultural Historical Evolution under the Dimension of Sino-Western Relations.] (2020) 6 教育科学研究 *Education Science Research* 24.

石硕 [Shi Shuo],《从汉族与少数民族的历史关系认识"中华民族共同体"的共同性》[Understanding the Commonality of the "Chinese National Community" from the Historical Relationship between the Han Ethnic Group and Minority Ethnic Groups] (2021) 3 中华民族共同体研究 *Research on the Chinese National Community* 73.

宋佳美 [Song Jiamei],《侗族习俗文化中的民族医药保健探析》[Analysis of Ethnic Medicine and Healthcare in Dong Ethnic Customs and Culture] (2021) 30 (11) 中国民族民间医药 *Chinese Journal of Ethnomedicine and Ethnopharmacy* 1.

谭俊杰 [Tan Junjie],《青蒿药用食用历史考略》[Review of the Medicinal and Edible History of Artemisia Annua (Qinghao)] (2020)16(8) 亚太传统医药*Asia-Pacific Traditional Medicine* 75.

滕建卓 [Teng Jianzhuo], 论土家族医药学的整体观 [Discussion On the Holistic Characters of Tujia Medicine] (2007) 2, 中国民族医药杂志 *Journal Of Medicine & Pharmacy Of Chinese Minorities* 6.

王晨飞 [Wang Chenfei],《黄蒿素:一本40年前的青蒿素研究报告汇编》[Artemisinin: A Compilation of Artemisinin Research Reports from 40 Years Ago] (2013) 32 (12) 赤峰学院学报*Journal of Chifeng University* 87.

王满元 [Wang Manyuan],《青蒿素类药物地发展历史》[Development History of Artemisinin-Based Drugs] (2012) 34(1) 自然杂志*Chinese Journal of Nature* 44.

乌日图那顺 [Wuritu nashu], 蒙医学整体观及其应用价值 [The Holistic View of Mongolian Medicine and Its Application] (2014) 5 中国民族医药杂志 *Journal Of Medicine & Pharmacy Of Chinese Minorities* 58.

吴致远 [Wu Zhiyuan],《从知识的地方性到技术的民族性》[From Locality of Knowledge to Nationality of Technology] (2022) 3 广西大学学报*Journal of Guangxi University* 44.

吴致远 [Wu Zhiyuan],《上市融资渠道多元开放 生物制药企业哪里IPO最合适》[Diversified Financing Channels Open for Listed Companies: Which is the Most Suitable Place for IPOs of Biopharmaceutical Enterprises?] (2022) 3 21世纪经济报道*21st Century Economic Report* 1.

薛益明 [Xue Yiming], 《中医药传入日本与朝鲜》 [The introduction of traditional Chinese medicine into Japan and Korea] [2009] 中医文献杂志*Journal of Traditional Chinese Medicine Literature* 47.

严金海 [Yan Jinhai],《从青蒿素的发现看中药的发展方向》[Looking at the Development Direction of Traditional Chinese Medicine from the Discovery of Artemisinin] (2013) 34(4A) 医学与哲学*Medicine and Philosophy* 4.

杨秀丽 [Yang Xiuli],《中医药产业创新生态系统构建》[Building an Innovative Ecosystem for the Traditional Chinese Medicine Industry] (2023) 40(4) 卫生经济研究*Health Economics Research* 34.

玉凤 [Yu Feng],《论民族区域自治制度的法律保障》[Legal Guarantee of the System of Ethnic Regional Autonomy] (2017) 18 知识文库 Knowledge Library 235, 235; Colin Mackerras, *Ethnic Minorities in Modern China* (Routledge, 2011) 21–23.

袁钟瑜 [Yuan Zhongyu],《中日传统医学循证研究比较》[Comparison of evidence-based research in Chinese and Japanese traditional medicine] (2021) 36(4) 华西医学*Huaxi Medicine* 539.

张 彬 [Zhang Bin]《政府间纵向关系研究: 中央与民族区域自治地方关系的调整》[Research on Vertical Government Relations: Adjustment of the Relationship between the Central Government and Ethnic Regional Autonomous Areas] (2017) 18 改革研究 *Reform Research* 17.

张凤霞 [Zhang Fengxia]《中医药传统知识保护现状, 存在问题与对策研究》[Research on the current status, existing problems and countermeasures of Traditional Chinese Medicine (TCM) Knowledge Protection] (2023) 20(11) 中国医药导报 *China Medical Herald* 188.

张红雷 [Zhang Honglei],《浅谈儒家思想与中医药发展》[A Brief Discussion on Confucian Thought and the Development of Traditional Chinese Medicine] (2023) 中国医学人文 *Chinese Medical Humanities* 19.

张新和 [Zhang Xinhe], 藏医药学中的医学伦理思想研究 [Research on Medical Ethics in Tibetan Medicine] (2017) 10, 中国民族医药杂志 Journal Of Medicine & Pharmacy Of Chinese Minorities 1.

张衍箴 [Zhang Yanzhen],《青蒿地药用历史及品种调查》[Artemisia annua Medicinal History and Variety Investigation] (1981) 16(4) 中国药学杂志*Chinese Pharmaceutical Journal* 197.

赵雅 [Zhao Ya], 基于藏族医学"整体观"认识的防治糖尿病肾病新药发现思路 [The Discovery of New Drugs for the Treatment of Diabetic Based on the Understanding of the "Holistic View" of Tibetan Medicine] (2019) 25(3), 中国实验方剂学杂志 *Chinese Journal of Experimental Traditional Medical Formulae* 167.

周平 [Zhou Ping]《中华民族的国家叙事》[The National Narrative of the Chinese Nation] (2022) 1 中华民族共同体研究 *Research on the Chinese National Community* 42;

朱安远 [Zhu Anyuan],《青蒿素之母:2015年诺贝尔生理学或医学奖新科得主屠呦呦 (二)》[The First Person to Extract Anti-Malarial Chemical Molecules from Traditional Chinese Medicine] (2016) 14 中国市场*Chinese Market* 186.

《VC/PE 纷纷持药》 [VC/PEs Are Actively Investing in Pharmaceuticals] [2012]资本市场 *Capital Market* 109;

《中国制造2025》[Made in China 2025] (People's Republic of China) State Council, May 2016.

《中华人民共和国国民经济和社会发展第十三个五年规划纲要》[Outline of the 13th Five-Year Plan for the National Economic and Social Development of the People's Republic of China] (People's Republic of China) National People's Congress, March 2016.

《中华人民共和国药品管理法》[The Drug Administration Law of the People's Republic of China] (People's Republic of China) National People's Congress, 2019.

《中华人民共和国中医药法》[Law of the People's Republic of China on Traditional Chinese Medicine] (People's Republic of China) Standing Committee of the National People's Congress (2016).

Chapter 3
Protecting China's Traditional Medical Knowledge: Intellectual Property as a Square Peg in a Round Hole?

3.1 Introduction

This chapter examines the multifaceted challenges and intricacies entailed in reconciliating China's unique historical and cultural landscapes, which fundamentally influence its TMK, with the prevailing international intellectual property ('IP') framework. Globally, the tension between traditional knowledge (TK) and IP frameworks has been a subject of significant debate, particularly due to the inherent conflict between IP systems designed to incentivise innovation and the communal nature of TK. Across various international platforms, such as WIPO, efforts have been made to address this conflict, yet these global approaches often fall short of addressing the specific socioeconomic, cultural, and political complexities in individual nations. This undertaking is not merely a legal exercise; it is also a cultural, historical, and philosophical exploration, probing the foundations and interactions of both TMK and IP rights. By providing a comprehensive analysis of China's historical and contemporary interactions with IP rights, this chapter seeks to evaluate the compatibility of TMK with the existing IP system. Ultimately, it aims to propose a culturally sensitive framework for the effective protection, responsible utilisation, and suitable dissemination of TMK within the context of the IP landscape.

The IP framework can serve as an effective instrument in catalysing progress and innovation, particularly when leveraged strategically in the areas of scientific knowledge and technological advancements.[1] It is designed to incentivise and protect the fruits of intellectual labour, thereby fostering an environment conducive to innovation and progress.[2] By offering exclusive rights to creators and inventors, the IP framework represents a strategic tool that can stimulate a broad spectrum of knowledge-based endeavours, from scientific research to technological innovations.

[1] CN Ciocoiu, 'Considerations about Intellectual Property Rights, Innovation and Economic Growth in the Digital Economy' (2011) 14(2) *Economia. Seria Management* 310, 310.

[2] Paul Kuruk, *Traditional Knowledge, Genetic Resources, Customary Law and Intellectual Property* (Edward Elgar Publishing, 2020) 33.

N. Xia, *Medicinal Mandates*, https://doi.org/10.1007/978-981-96-4108-6_3

While IP frameworks primarily function to safeguard the rights of creators and innovators, ensuring their intellectual contributions are duly recognised and benefited,[3] they can often be inadequate in accommodating TMK.[4] The international arena has long grappled with these challenges, as traditional knowledge systems—particularly in the context of Indigenous and cultural heritage—tend to operate under paradigms that differ significantly from the market-driven incentives of IP law. Many global initiatives, such as the WIPO Intergovernmental Committee on Intellectual Property and Genetic Resources, Traditional Knowledge and Folklore ('IGC'), have sought to bridge this gap by creating legal mechanisms tailored to TK. Despite these efforts, the global IP framework has struggled to adequately accommodate the diverse cultural and socio-political contexts that shape TK protection in countries like China. Since the 1980s, IP protection for traditional knowledge (including TMK) has been a subject of intense debates at various international forums.[5] Many international organisations and institutions have since explored various international methodologies for protecting traditional knowledge within and outside the conventional IP system. For instance, WIPO has established an Intergovernmental Committee on Intellectual Property and Genetic Resources, Traditional Knowledge and Folklore ('IGC'), as a forum for WIPO Member States to discuss IP matters concerning the protection of traditional knowledge.[6] The IGC has been active since 2000, based on a mandate to establish effective international legal instruments to protect traditional knowledge.[7] Its extensive efforts have resulted in a range of information, practical strategies, and policy resources. This includes a gap analysis conducted in 2018 which is constantly updated to identify the shortcomings of the existing IP regimes and explore the options to address those shortcomings for traditional knowledge (including TMK) protection.[8] These gap analyses have facilitated and supported the preparation of draft regulations for the protection of traditional cultural expressions/folklore and traditional knowledge against misappropriation.[9]

---

[3] Chidi Oguamanam, *International Law and Indigenous Knowledge* (University of Toronto Press, 2006) 58.

[4] Xuan Li and Weiwei Li, 'Inadequacy of Patent Regime on Traditional Medicinal Knowledge—A Diagnosis of 13-year Traditional Medicinal Knowledge Patent Experience in China' (2007) 10(2) *The Journal of World Intellectual Property* 125, 136–137.

[5] Krishna Ravi Srinivas, 'Traditional knowledge and Intellectual Property Rights: A Note on Issues, Some Solutions and Some Suggestions' (2008) 3 *Asian Journal of WTO & International Health Law and Policy* 81, 82.

[6] Daniel F Robinson, Pedro Roffe and Ahmed Abdel Latif, 'Introduction' in Ahmed Abdel-Latif, Pedro Roffe and Daniel F. Robinson (eds), *Protecting Traditional Knowledge: The WIPO Intergovernmental Committee on Intellectual Property and Genetic Resources, Traditional Knowledge and Folklore* (Routledge, 2017) 1, 3–8.

[7] Ibid.

[8] World Intellectual Property Organization (WIPO), *The Protection of Traditional Knowledge: Updated Draft Gap Analysis*, WIPO/GRTKF/IC/37/6 (20 July 2018).

[9] World Intellectual Property Organization (WIPO), *The Protection of Traditional Knowledge*, WIPO/GRTKF/IC/40 (19 June 2019); World Intellectual Property Organization (WIPO), *The Protection of Traditional Cultural Expression*, WIPO/GRTKF/IC/40 (19 June 2019).

Although literature on IP protection and TMK has surged since the early 2000s, a void persists in comprehending the distinct challenges and intricacies of TMK protection within China's unique milieu. Although existing research offers valuable insights, it does not thoroughly address the complex interplay of cultural, societal, and legal elements that emerge when reconciling these aspects with global IP frameworks, which are designed to safeguard, aptly utilise, and suitably disseminate Chinese TMK. China's socioeconomic, cultural, and political background adds additional layers of complexity to this issue. For instance, the central government's strong role in policy formation, the diversity of regional cultural practices, and the emphasis on Indigenous innovations significantly shape China's stance on IP and TK. The country's traditional knowledge, particularly in medicine, is deeply intertwined with its history, philosophy, and social fabric, which often complicates efforts to align it with Western-based IP systems.

This study aims to fill this gap and critically examines the historical, cultural, and socio-political factors that influence China's approach to protecting and regulating TMK within the framework of IP. It also explores potential solutions for a more culturally sensitive and effective approach to TMK protection in China. Moreover, this book notably seeks to expand upon the current body of literature on this subject by incorporating insights gleaned from both Chinese and English-speaking scholarly discourses. This comprehensive methodology guarantees a more balanced and holistic understanding of the complexities involved in TMK protection in China, thereby enriching the global discourse on this matter. It promotes an inclusive viewpoint, contributing to both the depth and breadth of the knowledge landscape surrounding China's IP law framework and its implications for the protection of TMK.

Local conditions, such as regional diversity and government-led initiatives, either exacerbate or mitigate TK-IP mismatches in China. Government policies, for instance, have sometimes created avenues for the commercialisation of traditional knowledge, though these efforts have been criticised for enabling the misappropriation of TMK by external actors. Additionally, Indigenous innovations, often spearheaded by local communities, further complicate the issue as they frequently resist commodification under traditional IP norms. By examining recent examples and case studies, such as government-led initiatives on the protection of TMK in specific regions, this chapter provides a detailed analysis of how these local conditions interact with broader IP norms.

This chapter argues that the existing IP rights system, primarily based on Western frameworks, struggles to effectively regulate TMK in China. The nation's unique cultural traits, distinctive national traditions, and the vast range and variation of Chinese TMK form a complex landscape that the existing IP infrastructure struggles to navigate. Although Western IP frameworks are primarily established to encourage innovation, their application within the realm of TMK can unintentionally erode the intrinsic values of TMK and its holders by facilitating the unauthorised appropriation and commercial exploitation of their knowledge. By critically examining the intricacies of this subject, this chapter aims to offer valuable insights and recommendations for the crafting of a culturally sensitive and more effective governance model for Chinese TMK under the IP framework. This chapter has three main sections:

Section 3.2 introduces the historical roots of IP rights and explores IP concerns in the legal history of imperial China and traditional Chinese culture. It identifies conflicts between Western IP concepts and Chinese cultural values, particularly those that favour collective over individual rights.

Section 3.3 introduces the development of modern IP agreements in China, particularly in relation to TMK. It explores China's engagement with international organisations and the challenges in adopting Western-style IP laws, particularly in the context of TMK's unique historical and sociocultural characteristics. The section also examines China's participation in international discussions on expanding the application of IP laws to other forms of subject matter, including traditional knowledge, and proposes the disclosure of the origin of traditional knowledge (including TMK) in patent applications as a way to accommodate China's unique historical and cultural landscape.

Section 3.4 introduces the challenges of protecting and regulating TMK in China using the Western-style IP system, particularly patent law, and proposes a new approach. The section identifies the cultural and philosophical differences between China's TMK system and Western IP, as well as the community-based nature of TMK, as significant barriers to IP protection. It also examines the limitations of using patent law to regulate TMK, such as evidentiary, substantive, and administrative obstacles. This section concludes by proposing a novel governance model for Chinese TMK under the IP framework.

3.2 The Early Growth of IP Rights and Their Influence on China: A Problematic Legal Transplant

3.2.1 Historical Origin and Development of the Modern IP Regime

It is widely acknowledged that the modern form of IP rights can be traced back to fifteenth-century Europe when early modern science was emerging as an approach to investigating the natural world.[10] The rise of capitalism and the development of new technologies, such as the printing press, contributed to the emergence of IP rights.[11] Yet, the origin of the early concept of IP can be traced back further. Indeed, during the twelfth and thirteenth centuries, medieval urban communities and free-market economies provided the impetus for the advent of a developed concept of IP, which

[10] Frank D Prager, 'A History of Intellectual Property from 1545 to 1787' (1944) 26 (11) *Journal of the Patent Office Society* 711, 711–749.

[11] Pablo Miguez, 'Intellectual Property and the Forced Commodification of Knowledge' (2018) 29 *Universitas, Revista de Ciencias Sociales* 42, 44.

was first present in the regulations of the guilds, where artisans and merchants were organised.[12]

Around that time, guilds were granted privileges to collect and transmit the particular knowledge inherited from the past and help protect the creations of others.[13] Although the guilds never used the term 'IP', their assertion that they possessed the collective knowledge of their members, shows recognition of the intangible values derived from the creation, accumulation, and dissemination of knowledge and skills.[14]

Over time, the collective knowledge curated by these guilds grew increasingly valuable. This value prompted a shift in the dynamics of knowledge ownership.[15] Some individuals began to break away from the collective structure of the guilds, carrying their unique perspectives on the guilds' knowledge into new arenas.[16] This shift marked the beginning of the clash between the communal monopolies of the guilds and an emerging, individualised form of IP rights.[17]

As these individuals embraced their own interpretations of the knowledge, they essentially laid the groundwork for the concept of individual IP rights. This ultimately led to the emancipation of individual knowledge holders and to the recognition of individual rights over intellectual creations.[18] Therefore, it can be argued that the contemporary concept of IP as an individual right emerged from the guild system of the Middle Ages. The term 'intellectual property' may not have existed then, but the ideas and practices surrounding it were already taking root, setting the stage for the more formalised systems of IP. The early development of IP rights has parallels to the way TMK was communally held and revered in China. This comparison becomes particularly fascinating as many scholarly studies illuminate how Chinese ethnic groups, perceive TMK to be an essential component of their spiritual and communal existence, rather than an entity of individual possession.[19]

The intricate tapestry of this Chinese cultural paradigm is richly woven with the contributions of both the dominant Han group and the plethora of ethnic minorities,

---

[12] Pamela O Long, 'Invention, Authorship, Intellectual Property, and the Origin of Patents: Notes Toward a Conceptual History' (1991) 32 *Technology and Culture* 846, 869.

[13] Ibid.

[14] Christopher May, 'The Venetian Moment: New Technologies, Legal Innovation and the Institutional Origins of Intellectual Property' (2002) 20 *Prometheus* 159, 167.

[15] Joanna Kostylo, 'From Gunpowder to Print: The Common Origins of Copyright and Patent' in Ronan Deazley et al (eds), *Privilege and Property Essays on the History of Copyright* (Cambridge OpenBook Publishers 2010) 1.

[16] Ibid.

[17] Ibid.

[18] Ibid.

[19] 苗丽 [Miao Li],《浅议云南民族医药文化的内涵及其特征》[A Brief Discussion on the Connotation and Characteristics of Yunnan Ethnic Medicine Culture] (2015) 24(16) 中国民族民间医药 *Chinese Journal of Ethnomedicine and Ethnopharmacy* 1, 1–2; 滕建卓 [Teng Jianzhuo]《论土家族医药学的整体观》[Discussion on the Holistic Characters of Tujia Medicine] (2015) 24(16)中国民族民间医药 *Chinese Journal of Ethnomedicine and Ethnopharmacy* 6, 6–7.

each group contributing its unique traditions and perspectives.[20] Within this broad spectrum, a consistent theme emerges: the profound emphasis on shared benefits and the reinforcement of familial and community bonds.[21] This ethos is mirrored in their perception of TMK, viewed not as individually held knowledge but as an ancestral legacy and communal asset.[22] This asset is woven into the very fabric of their social and spiritual existence, and it serves to benefit both their community and future generations,[23] akin to the collective benefit seen in the guild systems of Medieval Europe.

While this perspective offers a broad view, it is critical to underline that the conceptualisation of TMK ownership is not uniform, but rather varies substantially among different ethnic communities. Each of these communities embodies its unique cultural narratives, traditions, and belief systems.For certain communities, TMK represents an ancestral legacy.[24] This perspective sees ownership not just confined to the current generation but extending across time, creating a lineage of wisdom that links past, present, and future generations.[25] This temporally extended sense of stewardship underscores the continuity of knowledge and the enduring values of the community.

In the case of communities like the Naxi, the TMK is considered a sacred trust. It is revered, respected, and protected, akin to a sacred gift.[26] The use of this sacred knowledge is often bound by specific rituals or customs, reflecting a deep-seated respect for the sacredness of the knowledge and its role in maintaining cultural identity and communal harmony.[27] In the dominant Han groups, TMK is seen through

---

[20] 石硕 [Shi Shuo],《从汉族与少数民族的历史关系认识"中华民族共同体"的共同性》[Understanding the Commonality of the "Chinese National Community" from the Historical Relationship between the Han Ethnic Group and Minority Ethnic Groups] (2021) 3 中华民族共同体研究 Research on the Chinese National Community 73, 78–86.

[21] 曹 晟旻 [Cao Shengmin],《中西方视域下的群己权界论: 基于对儒家与社群主义的比较解读》[The Discussion of Collective and Individual Rights from Chinese and Western Perspectives: A Comparative Interpretation of Confucianism and Communitarianism] (2020) 26(3) 中南大学学报*Journal of Central South University* 50, 50–55; Linhua Zhang, 'China's Traditional Cultural Values and National Identity' (Carnegie Endowment for International Peace, 2013) < https://carnegieendowment.org/2013/11/21/china-s-traditional-cultural-values-and-national-identity-pub-53613 > accessed 9 October 2022.

[22] Tianbao Qin, 'Common Pools of Traditional Chinese Medical Knowledge in China' in Gerd Winter and Evanson Chege Kamau (eds), *Common Pools of Genetic Resources: Equity and Innovation in International Biodiversity Law* (2013) 150, 150–164.

[23] 王华 [Wang Hua],《中医药知识产权客体主体研究》[A Study on the Subject and Object of Intellectual Property in Traditional Chinese Medicine] (2020) 1 安徽广播电视大学学报 *Anhui Radio & Television University Journal* 19, 22.

[24] 邱冬 梅 [Qiu Dongmei],《多元一体民族观视阈下的清代满医药文化》[The Manchu Medical Culture in the Qing Dynasty from the Perspective of a 'Multi-element Integrated' Ethnic View] (2019) 6 黑龙江民族丛刊*Heilongjiang Ethnic Series* 101, 107.

[25] Ibid.

[26] Xi Yuhua, 'Shu: Naxi Nature Goddess Archetype' (2002) 6(3) *Gender, Technology and Development* 409, 414–422.

[27] Ibid.

the lens of hereditary transmission.[28] It represents an unbroken chain of knowledge, passed down from parent to child, signifying continuity and emphasising the role of the family as the guardian of traditional wisdom.[29]

These diverse cultural interpretations emphasise the importance of historical and cultural perspectives in understanding the concept of TMK ownership in China. In this context, 'ownership' is deeply ingrained in a sense of communal stewardship. The customs, traditions, and belief systems of each community shape this form of ownership, guiding the sharing, access, and transmission of TMK. Thus, much like the collective benefit upheld in the guild systems, this communal ownership underpins the continuity and preservation of TMK systems in China.

While the sense of communal stewardship in Chinese TMK ownership shares similarities with the practices of the guild systems, it is important to note how the evolution of IP rights diverged in these two cultural contexts. In Europe, the progression towards recognising individual rights over intellectual creations became a defining feature of IP rights' evolution. However, ancient China did not evolve a comparable framework recognising individual IP rights.[30] Therefore, the creative and innovative aspects of TMK were not linked to individual brilliance.[31] Instead, in China, these facets of TMK, deeply entrenched in the culture, continue to be seen as collective embodiments of a shared cultural legacy and communal wisdom.[32] These elements, fostered within communal environments, prosper through the ceaseless interchange and flow of ideas and information over time.[33] An unspoken understanding safeguards this practice, asserting that no individual should lay claim to exclusive rights over the shared TMK.

This distinctive dynamic has resulted in a complicated situation in modern China. The deeply entrenched model of communal ownership presents considerable challenges when attempting to shift towards an IP rights system that aligns more closely with the Western model. However, this intricacy is not only a challenge but also an opportunity. It offers a rich perspective on how different societies have traditionally managed and protected the collective wisdom of their communities.

Examining how historical events have shaped the evolution of IP rights is a worthy endeavour. The advent of the Industrial Revolution in the eighteenth-century marked an important turning point that significantly influenced the development of IP rights.[34]

---

28 马得汶 [Ma DeWen],《基于师承与家传的古代中医药学人才培养模式》[Ancient Chinese Medicine Talent Cultivation Model Based on Inheritance and Family Tradition] (2014) 20(1) 西北师大学报 *Journal of Northwest Normal University* 71, 71–77.

29 Ibid.

30 William P Alford, To Steal a Book Is an Elegant Offense: Intellectual Property Law in Chinese Civilization (Stanford University Press, 1995) 9–29.

31 王华 [Wang Hua] (n 23) 22.

32 Ibid.

33 Ibid.

34 D Greasley and L Oxley, 'Patenting, Intellectual Property Rights and Sectoral Outputs in Industrial Revolution Britain, 1780–1851' (2007) 139(2) *Journal of Econometrics* 340, 340–352.

This period marked an era of rapid technological advancements and industrial expansion in fields such as cotton, iron, and mining.[35] The associated surge in inventions and novel processes underscored the increased value and importance of IP protection, leading to a growing demand for more comprehensive and formalised IP systems.

This demand, in turn, triggered a substantial shift in the focus of rights holders. Rather than seeking protection solely for their unique inventions and creations, they began to emphasise safeguarding their domestic trades and industries from foreign competition.[36] This pivotal shift prompted the development and establishment of numerous bilateral treaties, conventions, and international agreements. These instruments were designed with a core objective: to provide robust international protection for IP rights.[37]

Nevertheless, the implementation of these agreements encountered challenges, particularly concerning disparities in domestic IP laws across different jurisdictions.[38] Legal frameworks for IP protection varied greatly from one country to another, resulting in uneven levels of protection for rights holders. While some countries implemented robust IP laws, others provided minimal safeguards.[39]

Moreover, there was significant disparity in the treatment of nationals versus foreigners in terms of IP rights protection.[40] Some jurisdictions extended full IP protection to their citizens while offering limited or no protection to foreign rights holders. This unequal treatment further complicated the international IP landscape, creating a convoluted system that often led to confusion and contention.[41]

These obstacles underscored the limitations inherent in the bilateral agreements and ignited the need for a more harmonised, global approach to IP protection. The collective call for more uniformity and cooperation culminated in the establishment of the *Paris Convention for the Protection of Industrial Property* in 1883, which stands as the first multinational treaty dedicated to IP protection.[42]

The path paved by the Paris Convention led to the emergence of other significant international agreements focusing on IP rights, such as those administered by WIPO and TRIPS, under the aegis of the WTO.[43] These international agreements

[35] Ibid.

[36] Brad Sherman et al, *The Making of Modern Intellectual Property Law: The British Experience, 1760–1911* (Cambridge University Press 1999) 161–162.

[37] Ibid.

[38] Catherine Seville, 'The Emergence and Development of Intellectual Property Law in Western Europe' in Rochelle Dreyfuss and Justine Pila (eds), *The Oxford Handbook of Intellectual Property Law* (Oxford University Press, 2017) 171, 192.

[39] Ibid.

[40] Ibid.

[41] Ibid.

[42] *Paris Convention for the Protection of Industrial Property*, opened for signature 14 July 1967, 828 UNTS 305 (entered into force 26 April 1970); Margrit Seckelmann, 'From the Paris Convention (1883) to the TRIPS Agreement (1994): The History of the International Patent Agreements as a History of Propertisation?' (2011) 21 *Jahrbuch der Juristischen Zeitgeschichte* 46, 54.

[43] Ibid.

and treaties introduced multilateral rules, aimed at promoting consistency across different jurisdictions.

Nevertheless, the development of IP protection in China did not follow the same path as it did in Western countries,[44] which can be attributed to several historical and cultural factors. For centuries, China was largely a self-sufficient, feudally based economy.[45] This structure limited the need for advanced science and technology as seen in the West during the Industrial Revolution and, as a result, did not foster an environment where IP protection was a significant concern.[46]

However, it is worth noting that this does not mean China lacked innovation or technological development. In fact, many technologies and inventions that laid the foundation for the West's Industrial Revolution originated in China. For example, papermaking, printing, the compass, and gunpowder, known as the 'Four Great Inventions', significantly contributed to global technological advancement.[47]

The discrepancy lies in how these innovations were perceived and treated. The value of individual invention and innovation, as opposed to collective knowledge or State-owned innovation, was not widely recognised in the traditional Chinese system.[48] As a result, the concept of IP protection, particularly in terms of individual rights to inventions or creations, did not evolve into a formalised system as it did in the West.

During the seventeenth and eighteenth centuries, Europe began to see a paradigm shift in the realm of IP. Inventors were increasingly recognised as having a property interest in their creations, as a means to safeguard against State exploitation.[49] This evolution positioned the individual creator at the centre, recognising the rights to control, profit from, and protect their creations.[50]

---

[44] Natalie Stoianoff, 'The Development of Intellectual Property Law in China' in Chan Lai-Ha et al (eds), *China At 60: Global–Local Interactions* (World Scientific, 2011) 183, 183–184; 黄渊琦 [Huang Yuanqi],《古代社会阻碍知识产权发展的负面因素》[Negative Factors that Hindered the Development of Intellectual Property Rights in Ancient Societies] (2016) 4, 大东方 *Great East* 1, 1–3.

[45] 盛辉 [Sheng Hui],《我国传统文化中知识产权产生与发展不利因素分析》[Analysis of Unfavorable Factors for the Emergence and Development of Intellectual Property Rights in Traditional Chinese Culture.] (2014) 9,科技管理研究 *Science and Technology Management Research* 240, 240–243; Jia Li, 'Intangible Assets are More Valuable than the Tangible: Study on the Innovation and Development of the Traditional Time-Honored Brands' (Conference Paper, International Conference on Social Science and Education Research, 2018) 242, 242; Liwei Wang, 'Chinese Traditions Inimical to the Patent Law, The Symposium: Doing business in China' (1993) 14(1) *Northwestern Journal of International Law & Business* 15, 40. See p112 AGLC4 Guide re conference papers.

[46] 盛辉 [Sheng Hui] (n 45) 240–243.

[47] Ning Xin and Jingjing Liao, 'History of the Silk Road' (2018) 36 *Chronos* 167, 189–190.

[48] Shi Wei, 'Cultural Perplexity in Intellectual Property: Is Stealing a Book an Elegant Offense?' (2006) 32(1) *North Carolina Journal of International Law* 1, 26.

[49] Alford (n 30) 19.

[50] Ibid.

By contrast, in China, the primary focus remained the preservation of State authority.[51] The State managed and controlled the outcomes of intellectual endeavours, rather than vesting the rights in individual creators.[52] This stance echoed the principles of the country's prevalent Confucian philosophy, which emphasised a collectivist orientation rather than individual property rights.

Confucian philosophy is grounded in the concept of hierarchical relationships, with an emphasis on familial piety, obedience, and respect for seniors.[53] As such, the responsibility of seniors for the nurturing of their juniors extends to intellectual pursuits. Innovation and knowledge are shared collectively rather than attributed to individuals. Hence, the results of intellectual creations are regarded as communal assets rather than private property.[54]

China's historical context reveals a lesser degree of industrial and technological advancement compared to Western nations. This fact is deemed to have influenced the progression of China's IP systems. Moreover, traditional Chinese culture held a Sinocentric perspective, perceiving China as the 'Celestial Empire' at the world's centre.[55] This worldview dictated a global hierarchy centred around the Chinese Emperor, the Son of Heaven,[56] thereby discounting the concept of legal equality and sovereignty among distinct States.[57] These longstanding cultural views appear incompatible with principles of equal international relations, territoriality, and national treatment as stipulated by international IP protection agreements.[58] Consequently, this historical backdrop poses challenges for China in adopting international IP agreements and fulfilling associated obligations.

---

[51] 孙羽 [Sun Yu],《我国知识产权法落后的文化原因》[The Cultural Reasons behind the Backwardness of Intellectual Property Laws in China] [2018]法制博览*Legality Vision*, 99, 99.

[52] Ibid.

[53] Andrew TW Hung, 'Atomism, Communitarianism, and Confucian Familism' (2022) 15 *Fudan Journal of the Humanities and Social Sciences* 259, 268.

[54] 崔立红 [Cui Lihong],《先秦儒家文化与知识产权法律》[Pre-Qin Confucian Culture and Intellectual Property Law] (2002) 15(1) 烟台大学学报 *Journal of Yantai University* 26, 26–31.

[55] 靳凤林 [Jin Fenglin],《先秦儒家文化与知识产权法律》[On the Ethical Parallax between China's Worldview and Western International Perspective] (2018) 4, 伦理学研究 *Studies in Ethics* 121, 121–125; Linyi Zheng and Xinying Hu, 'Inventing the Barbarians: The Changing Contexts of Yi in the Late Qing Dynasty' (2022) 12(4) *Psychology Research* 183, 186–188.

[56] 袁南生 [Yuan Nansheng],《中国千年外交与主流价值观念》[Chinese Millennium Diplomacy and Mainstream Values] [2018] 同舟共进 *Tóng Zhōu Gòng Jìn* 49, 49.

[57] Zewei Yang, 'Western International Law and China's Confucianism in the 19th Century: Collision and Integration' (2011) 13 *Journal of the History of International Law* 285, 287–294.

[58] Ibid.

3.2.2 IP Laws in Chinese Civilisation

There are no sustained Indigenous counterparts to IP law in Chinese history before the introduction of a Western standard of such a law in the early twentieth century.[59] As noted by many scholars, Chinese legal history has long been characterised as 'overwhelmingly penal in emphasis', while barely concerning itself with civil matters pertaining to private property.[60] For instance, prompted by the development of printing technology and a rise in literacy rates since the Song dynasty (960–1276), unauthorised reproduction and alteration of items in China increased over time.[61] This phenomenon reached its peak in the fifteenth century, including the reproduction and alteration of items that were exclusively controlled by the State and those deemed sensitive.[62] Concerned about the proliferation of unauthorised copying and piracy, the imperial Chinese State crafted various penalties to restrict such unauthorised reproductions.[63] Those who sought to make unauthorised use or reproduction of works (that were not under exclusive State control) were subject to 100 lashes with a heavy bamboo cane and the destruction of the reproduced items.[64] Persons who reproduced State-controlled items risked more severe punishment. According to the *Penal Conspectus*: 'Those who reproduce state-controlled items, spread the items …, and transmit them to stir up the multitude …, shall get a death sentence by strangulation'.[65] This high degree of State control and penalty over the unauthorised reproduction of items was established in order to sustain imperial power. This highlights the fact that, while the fifteenth century witnessed the emergence of a mechanism towards an individualised form of IP in Europe, no Indigenous counterparts were evolving in China. On the contrary, the State endeavoured to regulate this issue by predominantly focusing on how best to maintain its sovereign honour and authority.

---

59 刘钢 [Liu Gang],《对中国古代有无知识产权制度争议的思考》[A Reflection on the Controversy over the Existence of Intellectual Property Rights System in Ancient China] (2011) 24(6), 十堰职业技术学院学报 *Journal of Shiyan Technical Institute*, 36, 36–37.

60 Xiangyu Hu, 'Drawing the Line Between the Civil and the Criminal: A Study of Civil Cases Handled by the Board of Punishment in Qing China' (2014) 40 (1) *Modem China* 74, 75; Yang Xue, 'The Confucianization of Law and the Lenient Punishments in China' (2015) 10(1) *International Journal of Criminal Justice Sciences* 32, 35.

61 冯念华 [Feng Nianhua],《盗版对宋代版权保护现象的影响》[The Impact of Piracy on Copyright Protection in the Song Dynasty] (2006) 3(133) 图书馆工作与研究 *Library Work and Research* 63, 64–65.

62 Alford (n 30) 13.

63 祝尚书 [Zhu Shangshu],《论宋代的图书盗版与版权保护》[On Book Piracy and Copyright Protection in the Song Dynasty] (2000) 1(1) 文献季刊 *Wen Xian Quarterly* 77, 83–86; Sanqiang Qu, 'A Dilemma for Feudal China: To Launch a Copyright Scheme in the Late 19th Century' (2010) 5(3) *Frontiers of Law in China* 319, 328–329; Ye Dehui, *Quiet Talks among the Bookstacks* (Shanghai Classics Publishing House 1957) 143.

64 Sanqiang Qu (n 63) 75.

65 Chan Hok-Lam, *Control of Publication in China, Past and Present* (The Chinese University of Hong Kong Press, 1983) 5.

In imperial China (until 1912), there were no formal or informal sources of laws that provided individuals, communities, or families with enforceable 'rights' to protect their monopoly over intellectual creations against the imperial State or others.[66] The primary purpose of the few known cases of State support for what is now known as IP was to acquire and maintain imperial power. This included deciding which knowledge should be disseminated and which should be restricted, to serve the best interests of the imperial power.[67]

One of the most significant practices associated with China's imperial power was the Sinocentric approach developed by the imperial State towards Western ideas and knowledge.[68] The Chinese historically dismissed Western foreigners as 'outer barbarians' and were sceptical of Western ideas, including the concept of IP, science, and institutions.[69] The imperial leaders of China remained fixed in their belief in having superior wisdom and knowledge surpassing that of the outer barbarians.[70] The Emperor Qianlong of the Qing dynasty, for example, dismissed King George III of England's envoy with the famous words: 'We possess all things. I set no value on objects strange or ingenious, and have no use for your country's manufactures'.[71] China's long-closed door was forcibly opened by Western colonialists in the Opium War (1839–42) and the subsequent Arrow War (1856–60).[72] After this, and for the first time, the Western system of IP rights was imported into China 'with such inventions and novel ideas as the gunboat, opium, most favoured nation trading status, and the extraterritorial system'.[73]

Nevertheless, China's defeats in the Opium War and the humiliation it suffered under various unequal treaties made the Chinese comply selectively with, or resist, Western IP laws and other international instruments.[74] From a Chinese perspective,

66 李志明 [Li Zhiming],《中国知识产权文化发展中的文化冲突及解决方法: 以知识产权文化的历史演变为视角》[2013] [Cultural Conflicts and Solutions in the Development of Chinese Intellectual Property Culture: An Historical Perspective on the Evolution of Intellectual Property Culture] 江汉论坛 *The Yangtze-Han Forum*, 133, 133–134.

67 Alford (n 30) 16–17.

68 杜赫 [Du He],《从天下到国家: 近代中国国家观念在文明碰撞中的确立》[From Sinocentrism to Nationhood: The Formation of Modern Chinese National Consciousness in the Clash of Civilizations] [2022] 公关世界 *Public Relations World,*143, 143–144.

69 JK Fairbank, 'Tributary Trade and China's Relations with the West' (1942) 1(2) *The Far Eastern Quarterly* 129, 133.

70 许纪霖 [Xu Jilin],《天下主义/夷夏之辨及其在近代的变异》[Distinction between 'All Under Heaven' Ideology and 'Yi-Xia' Dichotomy and Their Transformations in Modern Times] (2012) 6 华东师范大学学报*Journal of East China Normal University* 66, 66–71.

71 Henrietta Harrison, 'The Qianlong Emperor's Letter to George III and the Early-twentieth-century Origins of Ideas about Traditional China's Foreign Relations' (2017) 122(3) *American Journal of Ophthalmology* 680, 680.

72 陈卫文 [Chen Weiwen],《鸦片战争对中国近代化的影响》[The Impact of the Opium War on Modernization in China] (2009) 20 大众文艺 *Popular Culture* 235, 235.

73 Peter Feng, *Intellectual Property in China* (Sweet & Maxwell Asia, 2003) 3.

74 Phil Chan, 'China's Approaches to International Law since the Opium War' (2014) 27 *Leiden Journal of International Law* 859, 860–861.

the Western IP system was viewed as representative of the expansion of Western powers and the rising foreign encroachments.[75]

Li Hongzhang, an influential government official during the period towards the close of imperial China (the 1850s-1890s), noted that, when China adopted international IP agreements and other international treaties, it did so under the threat of force, feeling threatened and deceived.[76] This historical experience and perception of international IP laws and other international treaties as hypocritical, deceptive, and threatening are crucial in understanding why the Western approach to IP has struggled to take root in China.

The legacy of these past experiences may contribute to the Chinese people's scepticism towards Western IP systems and result in businesses not fully embracing them, as evidenced by non-compliance or infringement cases. This context is essential for understanding the nuances of China's approach to IP and its relationship with Western IP systems.

Foreign pressure, coercive trade policies, and deceptive practices exerted by the Western powers have also contributed to China's cultural resistance to IP. In 1898, under foreign pressure and driven by 'sham' promises (by foreign imperialists) of ending the unequal treaties, in particular the extraterritoriality provisions, Emperor Guangxu formally issued the *Bylaws of Awarding Industrial Inventions*, which are considered to be 'the first modern experiment in intellectual property protection' in Chinese history.[77] However, once the government understood that the adoption of Western-style IP laws was not a solution to the lingering issues of unequal treaties from the late nineteenth century, or a means to change China's semi-colonial status, its enthusiasm for pursuing the reforms diminished.[78] China became sceptical of IP and regarded it as an extractive device that favoured Western 'knowledge monopolists'.[79] This resistant and sceptical attitude towards IP persisted until the 1970s.

Before 1978, there were no practical IP-related laws in China.[80] As noted by Bruun and Zhang, the socialist transformation of the economy in China essentially abolished all private and individual ownership so IP rights were not needed.[81] In 1963, China's central government established the *Regulation on Invention Reward*,

---

[75] Ibid.

[76] S Suzuki, 'China's Perceptions of International Society in the Nineteenth Century: Learning More about Power Politics?' (2004) 28 *Asian Perspectives* 115, 132.

[77] Jian Xu, 'The History of China's Patent System and Legislation', *China IP Blog* (Web Page, 2016) < https://niuyie.com/the-history-of-chinas-patent-system-and-legislation/ >.

[78] Ibid.

[79] 曲三强 [Qu Sanqiang],《被动立法的百年轮回：谈中国知识产权保护的发展历程》[A Century of Passive Legislation: Discussing the Development of Intellectual Property Protection in China] (1999) 2 中外法学*Peking University Law Journal* 119, 120; Servaas Storm, 'Why the West Grew Rich and the Rest did not, or How the Present Shapes Our Views of the Past' (2013) 44(5) *Development and Change* 1181, 1194.

[80] 曲三强 [Qu Sanqiang] (n 79) 120–122.

[81] Niklas Bruun and Liguo Zhang, 'Legal Transplant of Intellectual Property Rights in China: Norm Taker or Norm Maker?' in Niklas Bruun et al (eds), *Governance of Intellectual Property Rights in China and Europe* (Edward Elgar Publishing 2016) 43, 48.

under which inventors were not allowed to apply for IP rights but received a lump-sum bonus instead.[82] Article 23 of the Regulation provided that 'all the inventions belong to the State, no individuals and organisations are allowed to apply for a monopoly'.[83] 'All the organisations across the nation, including collectively owned corporations can use them'.[84] It thus appears that the Regulation merely sought to preserve as much discretion as possible for the State. It did not offer any ongoing property rights and interests to the inventors. Instead, the State could determine how the inventions could thereafter be used by other third parties, without the prior consent of inventors or the payment of a licensing fee.

With the radical economic and political reforms that occurred at the end of 1978, the legal system in China slowly began to converge with Western legal traditions.[85] This situation was important in the development of IP-related laws in China. It contrasts with China's different attitude to the Western notion of IP rights in the early decades of the twentieth century.[86] The IP regime which appeared in the early years of the new China was based mainly on the idea that individual achievements and accomplishments belonged to all of society.[87] However, since 1978, the Chinese leadership has understood that foreign investors might be more inclined to invest in China if the nation protected the individual rights of investors, particularly in the area of IP.[88] As a result, the country took the first steps towards establishing a comprehensive IP regime that often showed a striking resemblance to those in Western countries.[89] In particular, the Chinese government made great efforts to promulgate new patent, copyright, and trademark laws, as well as facilitate China's accession to international IP treaty regimes.[90] These efforts have encouraged overseas enterprises to part with their technology and investment, and channel the desired capital to stimulate China's socialist modernisation.[91] However, the enforcement of

---

[82] 孙丽伟 [Sun Liwei],《新中国专利制度的历史回顾和现实思考》[Review of the History of China's Patent System and Practical Considerations] [2016] 科技与法律 *Journal of Science, Technology and Law* 1032, 1033;《发明奖励条例》[Regulation on Invention Reward] (People's Republic of China) State Council, November 1963.

[83] Regulation on Invention Reward (n 82) art 23.

[84] Ibid.

[85] 孙丽伟 [Sun Liwei] (n 82) 1034; Natalie P Stoianoff, 'The Influence of the WTO over China's Intellectual Property Regime' (2012) 34 (1) *Sydney Law Review* 65, 69.

[86] Stoianoff (n 85) 69.

[87] Sunny Chang, 'Combating Trademark Squatting in China: New Developments in Chinese Trademark Law and Suggestions for the Future' (2014) 34(2) *Northwestern Journal of International Law & Business* 337, 342.

[88] Geoffrey T Willard, 'An Examination of China's Emerging Intellectual Property Regime: Historical Underpinnings, the Current System and Prospect for the Future' (1995) 6(2) *International and Comparative Law Review* 411, 421.

[89] PE Campbell and M Pecht, 'The Emperor's New Clothes: Intellectual Property Protections in China' (2012) 7(1) *Journal of Business and Technology Law* 69, 73.

[90] Scott J Palmer, 'An Identity Crisis: Regime Legitimacy and the Politics of Intellectual Property Rights in China' (2001) 8(2) *Indiana Journal of Global Legal Studies* 449, 449.

[91] Ibid.

IP rights was ineffective and a non-deterrent, which motivated Western countries to take actions targeting China's ineffective IP enforcement.[92]

Since the 1980s, exogenous pressure, particularly from the US, has contributed to the development of IP policies and laws in China.[93] It has taken a series of measures to bring its IP laws into greater alignment with the expectations of the US government.[94] These measures include the introduction of updated patent, copyright, and trademark legislation, along with efforts to join international IP treaty frameworks.[95] However, despite these developments, many criticisms persist concerning China's IP regime.[96] The crux of these criticisms now lies in the enforcement mechanisms designed to uphold the rights and obligations established by the legislation.[97] As a result, it is often asserted that IP protection in China remains more rhetorical than practical.[98] This can be attributed to the unique cultural characteristics and diverse historical experiences of China and its people, which make enforcing IP rights within the country a complex and potentially futile endeavour.[99] Therefore, adopting Western-centric IP laws without genuinely addressing the challenges of integrating these legal values into China's historical and sociocultural context could be seen as superficial or merely a symbolic gesture.

China's culture, traditional values, and historical background are arguably the main barriers to the growth of effective IP protection.[100] Its TMK, as explained in Sect. 3.1, can be seen as the embodiment of its culture, worldviews, and traditional

---

[92] Donald P Harris, 'The Honeymoon Is Over: the U.S.-China WTO Intellectual Property Complaint' in Perry Keller (ed), *Law and the Market Economy in China* (2011) 96, 97.

[93] 毛昊 [Mao Hao],《美国对华知识产权产权压力焦点变迁与趋势预见》[The focus and trend of US pressure on China's intellectual property rights and the outlook for the future] [2022] 科学学研究 *Studies in Science in Science* 1, 4–6; Dexin Tian 'The USTR Special 301 Reports: An Analysis of the US Hegemonic Pressure upon the Organizational Change in China's IPR Regime' (2008) 1 *Chinese Journal of Communication* 224, 225.

[94] 夏辰旭 [Xia Chenxu],《中国知识产权法律制度的历史发展与变革》[The Historical Development and Transformation of China's Intellectual Property Legal System] [2022] 法制视点 *The Rule of Law Perspectives* 128, 128–129; Peter K Yu, 'Intellectual Property, Economic Development, and the China Puzzle' in Daniel J. Gervais (ed), *Intellectual Property, Trade and Development: Strategies to Optimize Economic Development in a TRIPS Plus Era* (Oxford University Press 2007) 173, 185–188.

[95] Palmer (n 90) 449; 夏辰旭 [Xia Chenxu] (n 94) 128–129.

[96] Thomas Kristie, 'The Fight against Piracy: Working within the Administrative Enforcement System in China' in Hailing Shan, Johan Erauw and Paul Torremans (eds), *Intellectual Property and TRIPS Compliance in China* (2007) 85, 85–106.

[97] Ibid.

[98] Alexander Hendrie, 'China's Commitment to Intellectual Property Rights More Rhetoric than Reality' *Property Rights Alliance* (Web Page, October 2014) < http://www.propertyrightsalliance.org/news/china_s_commitment_to_intellectual_property_rights_ _more_rhetoric_than_reality_-2/ >.

[99] Liguo Zhang and Niklas Bruun, 'Legal Transplantation of Intellectual Property Rights in China: Resistance, Adaptation and Reconciliation' (2017) 48 *International Review of Intellectual Property and Competition Law* 4, 12–14; 李志明 [Li Zhiming] (n 66) 133–134.

[100] Ibid.

values. Thus, Western constructs of IP rights, particularly cultural identity and traditional values, are generally somewhat alien to TMK. Perhaps, more appropriately, they do not fit squarely into it.

A critical issue concerning the relationships between IP laws and TMK is their interactions with Western science. As Oguamanam has stated: 'Western IP rights legitimize a narrow view of science. Nevertheless, it does not acknowledge a different cultural account of knowledge formation'.[101] For example, Western IP laws do not recognise the collective rights over TMK which prevail within local communities and traditional societies. As argued by many Western scholars, Western IP laws are mainly based on Western scientific paradigms in which all other types of knowledge and theories of knowledge should be either delegitimised or assimilated to bring them into alignment with the episteme of Western culture.[102]

Upon their arrival in China, Westerners brought with them preconceived notions about IP, grounded in their cultural perspectives.[103] They assumed that China lacked systems for regulating and protecting IP. As they encountered China's TMK, their cultural background and understanding of IP led them to draw comparisons between Western scientific knowledge and TMK. From this comparison, they concluded that Chinese TMK was crude, inferior, and superstitious, making it unworthy of preservation.[104] In contrast, Western scientific knowledge was seen as the pinnacle of modernity and deserving of protection.[105] This viewpoint was influenced by a Eurocentric worldview that often diminished or undervalued non-Western knowledge systems.

This situation reflects what Anderson has contended: that the concept of IP merely promotes Western cultural interpretations of knowledge, ownership, individual property, and monopoly power.[106] As a result, Chinese methods of interpreting and understanding their TMK systems and knowledge practices are either delegitimised or marginalised.[107]

---

[101] Chidi Oguamanam, International Law and Indigenous Knowledge: Intellectual Property, Plant Biodiversity, and Traditional Medicine (University of Toronto Press 2006) 158.

[102] Ibid.

[103] Alford (n 30) 30–55.

[104] 吴立坤 钟赣生 [Wu Likun] and [Zhong Gansheng],《近代时期西方药学传入后对中药学发展的影响》(2009) 9(4) [The Impact of the Introduction of Western Pharmacology on the Development of Traditional Chinese Medicine during the Modern Dra] (2009) 9(4) 中药与临床 *Pharmacy and Clinics of Chinese Materia Medica* 235, 235. Yuet-Wah Cheung et al, 'Missionary doctors vs Chinese patients: Credibility of Missionary Health Care in Early Twentieth Century China' (1985) 21 *Social Science & Medicine* 309, 310–312.

[105] Yuet-Wah Cheung et al (n 104) 310–312.

[106] Jane Anderson, 'Indigenous/ Traditional Knowledge Intellectual Property' (Issue Paper, 2010) < https://web.law.duke.edu/cspd/pdf/ip_Indigenous-traditionalknowledge.pdf > accessed 11 October 2022.

[107] Ibid.

3.3 International IP Law and the Protection of TMK: The Chinese Approach

3.3.1 Overview of the International Framework for IP

The international IP system includes a variety of interactions and linkages among international treaties, international organisations, and plurilateral and bilateral negotiating venues.[108] As one of the most influential international IP law-making venues and treaty-based organisations, WIPO has hosted various IP conventions that form the cornerstones upon which almost all existing international IP regimes and instruments are built.[109] Two major treaties that WIPO administers are the *Paris Convention for the Protection of Industrial Property* and the *Berne Convention for the Protection of Literary and Artistic Works*.[110] These Conventions were based on two principles.[111] Firstly, Member States must provide in their national law certain minimum standards of IP protection, *substantive minima*.[112] Secondly, Member States were required to give the nationals of other Member States the same IP protection as their own nationals.[113] With this foundation, the Conventions provided for the protection of copyrights, patents, trademarks, industrial designs, utility models, service marks, trade names, geographical indications, and the repression of unfair competition. The *WIPO Convention*, adopted in Stockholm in 1967, was also important as it was WIPO's founding Convention. It represented the beginnings of the first international organisation focusing solely on IP.[114] According to Article 3(i), the main aim of WIPO was to 'promote the protection of IP throughout the world through cooperation among States and, where appropriate, in collaboration with any other international organization'. Its mission was 'to lead the development of a balanced and effective international IP system that enabled innovation and creativity for the benefit of all'. Despite this, over the past six decades, there had been little improvement in the norms of IP in WIPO.[115] Suggested reasons for this included WIPO's lack of cross-sectoral

---

108 Laurence R Helfer, 'Regime Shifting in the International Intellectual Property System' (2009) 7(1) *Perspectives on Politics* 39, 39.

109 S Bannerman, 'The World Intellectual Property Organization and the Sustainable Development Agenda' (2020) 122 *Futures* 3, 6.

110 *Berne Convention for the Protection of Literary and Artistic Works*, signed 9 September 1886, 828 UNTS 221 (entered into force 5 December 1887).

111 Dan Wielsch, 'Private Governance of Knowledge: Societally-crafted Intellectual Properties Regimes' (2013) 20(2) *Indian Journal of Global Legal Studies* 907, 911–912.

112 Ibid.

113 Ibid.

114 Alison Duxbury, 'The Role of WIPO as An International Organization' in Sam Ricketson (ed), *Research Handbook on the World Intellectual Property Organization: The First 50 Years and Beyond* (Edward Elgar Publishing, 2020) 1, 26.

115 Naomi A Bass, 'Implications of the TRIPs Agreement for Developing Countries: Pharmaceutical Patent Laws in Brazil and South Africa in the 21st Century' (2002) 34(1) *The George Washington International Law Review* 191, 195.

negotiating ability and its failure to provide effective protection and enforcement mechanisms for IP.[116] These factors led some technologically advanced countries to push for negotiations on IP by the WTO, leading to the adoption of the *TRIPS Agreement*.[117] This Agreement was a core component of WTO-administered agreements, which had incorporated a series of WIPO-administered treaties (including the Berne and Paris Conventions).

The *TRIPS Agreement* expanded the protection to all types of IP rights, including trademarks, patents, copyrights, industrial designs, trade secrets, geographical indicators, integrated circuit industrial designs, and other related IP rights.[118] The aims of TRIPS are to narrow the gaps between how IP rights are governed in different States and, in this way, to promote international trade.[119] It also establishes the universal minimum standards for all aspects of the protection and enforcement of IP rights, to fill the gaps that are not covered by national IP laws.[120] Most significantly, unlike WIPO-administered treaties, it has the power to sanction treaty violations through a dispute settlement body.[121] Consequently, it may be argued that it provides Member States of the WTO with the maximum possible security and predictability, and makes IP protection an integral part of the WTO trading regime.

TRIPS has established minimum standards for the regulations of various forms of IP. Although the WTO's Member States cannot provide a level of protection lower than the one established by these minimum standards, they are allowed to incorporate higher levels of IP protection, as long as the basic principles of the most favoured nation and national treatment under TRIPS are applied. However, if a country is forced to implement higher levels and more extensive standards of IP protection than those required by TRIPS, it can be said that 'TRIPS-plus' standards have been implemented by this country.[122] Thus, TRIPS is not the end of the story.

---

[116] Paul Salmon, 'Cooperation Between the World Intellectual Property Organization (WIPO) and the World Trade Organization (WTO)' (2003) 17 *Journal of Civil Rights and Economic Development* 429, 433.

[117] *Agreement on Trade-Related Aspects of Intellectual Property Rights*, April. 15, 1994, Marrakesh Agreement Establishing the World Trade Organization, Annex 1C, Legal Instrument Result of The Uruguay Round, 33 I.L.M. 81 (1994) ('*the TRIPS Agreement*').

[118] Ibid.

[119] Stefan Szymanski and Tommaso Valletti, 'Parallel Trade Price Discrimination, Investment and Price Caps' (2005) 20(44) *Economic Policy* 705, 714; Stephanie Peatman, 'Moving toward Uniform International Trademark Protection: How Amending the TRIPS Agreement will Make Parallel Importing of Gray Goods Less Gray' (2014) 20(2) *Southwestern Journal of International Law* 445, 458.

[120] Article 1.1 of the TRIPS Agreement provides that: 'Members shall give effect to the provisions of this Agreement. Members may, but shall not be obliged to, implement in their law more extensive protection than is required by this Agreement, provided that such protection does not contravene the provisions of this Agreement. Members shall be free to determine the appropriate method of implementing the provisions of this Agreement within their own legal system and practice'.

[121] Laurence R Heifer, 'Regime Shifting: The TRIPs Agreement and New Dynamics of International Intellectual Property Lawmaking' (2004) 29(1) *Yale Journal of International Law* 1, 2.

[122] Peter Drahos, 'Bits and Bips: Bilateralism in Intellectual Property' (2001) 4(6) *The Journal of World Intellectual Property* 791,791.

New developments have occurred at the regional and bilateral levels that build further on such standards.

Many technologically advanced countries have chosen to use their unequal bargaining power to reach bilateral or regional trade agreements with low- and middle-income countries, thus imposing TRIPS-plus obligations through a country-by-country approach.[123] For instance, the US' pursuit of TRIPS-plus protection for medicines in bilateral and regional trade agreements is well recognised.[124] Until 2021, the US had achieved bilateral or regional trade agreements with 20 countries, all of which included TRIPS-plus provisions.[125] The most prominent TRIPS-plus provisions comprise patent term extensions, data exclusivity, and patent linkages.[126] This effort is believed to be motivated by an intention to achieve the desired levels of protection expected from TRIPS but which TRIPS itself is unable to secure.[127] Consequently, stronger IP protection is considered more easily secured through bilateral or regional agreements than in the trade agreements within the WTO regime.[128]

3.3.2 *China's Engagement with the International, Regional, and Bilateral IP Agreements*

Since the second half of the twentieth century, technologically advanced nations have been working diligently to standardise and broaden IP rights worldwide.[129] China has frequently had to adapt its legislation and policies to meet the evolving standards established by various international, regional, and bilateral agreements concerning IP.[130] For instance it has enacted and amended its patent laws no fewer than five times in 36 years (in 1984, 1992, 2000, 2009, and 2020), in order to bring its

[123] Bryan Mercurio, 'TRIPS-Plus Provisions in FTAs: Recent Trends' in Lorand Bartels and Federico Ortino' (eds), *Regional Trade Agreement and the WTO Legal System* (Oxford University Press, 2006) 215.

[124] Ruth Lopert and Deborah Gleeson, 'The High Price of "Free" Trade: U.S. Trade Agreements and Access to Medicines' (2013) 41(1) *Journal of Law, Medicine & Ethics* 199, 199.

[125] 'Trade Agreement', *Office of United States Trade Representative* (Web Page) < https://ustr.gov/trade-agreements >.

[126] Matthew E Silverman, 'The Case for Flexible Intellectual Property Protections in the Trans-pacific Partnership' (2014) 27(2) *Journal of Law and Health* 215, 219.

[127] Silverman (n 126) 218.

[128] Jean-Frederic Morin, 'Multilateralizing TRIPs-Plus Agreements: Is the US Strategy a Failure?' (2009) 12(3) *The Journal of World Intellectual Property* 175, 176.

[129] 凌金铸 [Ling Jinzhu],《中美知识产权关系的发生、发展与影响》[The Emergence, Development, and Impact of Sino-American Intellectual Property Relations] (2007)14(5) 当代中国史研究 *Contemporary China History Studies* 108, 108–115.

[130] Kristie Thomas, Assessing Intellectual Property Compliance in Contemporary China (2017) 85, 89.

national legislation into closer compliance with international, regional, and bilateral IP agreements.[131]

China's initial engagement in international IP began with its accession to WIPO in the 1980s.[132] This important step aligned China with globally accepted IP protection standards and set the stage for the development of its contemporary IP system. The establishment of China's first patent law in 1984 serves as a prime example of this alignment.[133]

When China adopted this law in 1984, it integrated elements akin to those found in the patent laws of technologically advanced nations. To be specific, the internationally recognised criteria of 'novelty, non-obviousness and utility' were adopted to determine whether an invention is patent-eligible.[134] Similarly to the 'written description' and 'enablement' requirements of the US and other market economy countries' practice, this *Chinese Patent Law (1984)* provided that 'the claims shall be supported by the description' and 'the description shall set forth the invention in a manner sufficiently clear and complete so as to enable a person skilled in the relevant field of technology to carry it out'[135]; similarly to the systems of European countries and Japan, China's patent system was based on the first-to-file standard rather than the first-to-use standard.[136] To align with Article 27(2) and 27(3) of TRIPS, patent-eligible subject matter excludes scientific discoveries, methods for intellectual activities, diagnostic and therapeutic methods for the treatment of diseases, animal and plant varieties, and new materials created through a nuclear reaction.[137] Significantly, the *Chinese Patent Law (1984)* also defined the scope of the monopoly obtained as a result of the patent grant, which conferred upon a patent holder the exclusive right to make, use, or sell the patented invention.[138]

Nevertheless, despite its groundbreaking nature, the new patent law was criticised by Western scholars. Harrington, for example, described it as 'the emperor's new clothes' because of the structural defects and ambiguities embedded in it.[139] Major concerns were related to the patent subject matter limitations. The law

---

[131] 屈威, 鲁楠 [Qu Wei] and [Lu Nan],《从专利法修改看中国知识产权制度的发展》[Examining the Development of China's Intellectual Property System through Patent Law Revisions] (2022) 1 法制博览 Legal System Panorama 4, 4–6; Peter K Yu, 'Two Decades of TRIPS in China' (Research Paper, Texas A&M University School of Law Legal Studies Research, 2021) 1, 1–12.

[132] 沈浩蓝 [Shen Haolan],《从TRIPS到RCEP: 加入WTO以来中国参与和完善知识产权国际规则研究》[From TRIPS to RCEP: A Study of China's Participation and Improvement of International Intellectual Property Rules Since Joining WTO] (2022) 7 广西社会科学 *Guangxi Social Sciences* 79, 79–80.

[133]《中华人民共和国专利法》[Patent Law of the People's Republic of China] (People's Republic of China) National People's Congress Standing Committee, Order No 11, March 1984.

[134] Patent Law (n 133) art 22.

[135] Patent Law (n 133) art 26.

[136] Patent Law (n 133) art 9.

[137] Patent Law (n 133) art 25.

[138] Patent Law (n 133) art 11.

[139] Laurence P Harrington, 'Recent Amendments to China's Patent Law: The Emperor's New Clothes' (1994) 17(2) *Boston College International and Comparative Law Review* 337, 337–370.

limited the patentability of chemical products and pharmaceuticals because only processes, rather than products themselves, could receive patents.[140] Other defects included process problems, enormous powers retained by the State, and difficulties of enforcement.[141] Indeed, complaints by foreign patent holders of counterfeiting and infringement by the Chinese continued throughout the 1980s.[142]

This situation led the US Trade Representative to institute a Section 301 investigation (based on the *Trade Act of 1974*) against China's alleged insufficient protection of IP rights.[143] A Section 301 investigation is a mechanism designed to grant the US Executive a range of authorities to investigate the violation of trade practices and protect US economic interests abroad under trade agreements.[144] Prior to 1995 and the initiation of the WTO, the US extensively utilised Section 301 as a tool to pressure other countries to modify their laws and practices to provide more effective protection for IP rights and eliminate trade barriers to the US.[145] Initially, it seemed that the Sect. 301 investigation against China was successful.[146] Under foreign pressure and threats of sanctions, China reached a Memorandum of Understanding on the Protection of IP ('MOU') with the US, and promised to reform its weak IP rights enforcement system and eliminate its trade barriers to US products.[147] This MOU, which required China to tighten its patent law (1984), was the first bilateral IP agreement that China signed.[148] As a result, China adopted the 1992 amendment to this

140 William E Beaumont, 'The New Patent Law of the People's Republic of China (PRC): Evidence of a Second Chinese "Renaissance"?' (1988) 39 *IDEA* 1, 50; Janiece Marshall, 'Current Developments in the People's Republic of China: Has China Changed?' (1988) 1(2) *Global Business & Development Law Journal* 505, 521.

141 Harrington (n 139) 351.

142 Louis S Sorell, 'A Comparative Analysis of Selected Aspects of Patent Law in China and the United States' (2002) 11(2) *Washington International Law Journal* 319, 321.

143 胡键 [Hu Jian],《中美竞合关系：从零和博弈到正和博弈，何以可能?》[The China-US Competitive Cooperation Relationship: From Zero-Sum Game to Positive-Sum Game—How Is It Possible?] (2022) 1 国际观察 *International Observation* 54, 67; Trade Act of 1974, 19 USC § 2411 (1974), s301. Section 301 actions allow the US Trade Representative to impose severe sanctions in the form of greatly increased tariffs on countries found to violate trade practices.

144 Chris Noonan and Victoria Plekhanova, 'Digital Services Tax: Lessons from the Sect. 301 Investigation' (2021) *The British Tax Review* 83, 83–84.

145 Krzysztof J Pelc, 'Constraining Coercion? Legitimacy and Its Role in U.S. Trade Policy,1975–2000' (2010) 64 *International Organization* 65, 66.

146 Robert B Frost Jr, 'Intellectual Property Rights Disputes in the 1990s between the People's Republic of China and the United States' (1995) 4(1) *Tulane Journal of International and Comparative Law* 119, 134; 毛昊 [Mao Hao],《美国对华知识产权产权压力焦点变迁与趋势预见》[The Focus and Trend of US Pressure on China's Intellectual Property Rights and the Outlook for the Future] [2022] 科学学研究 *Studies in Science in Science* 1, 7.

147 Memorandum of Understanding Between the Government of the People's Republic of China and the Government of the United States of America on the Protection of Intellectual Property (MOU) (China—United States) (Jan 17, 1992) 34 ILM 676.

148 The provisions related to the proposed China's Patent Law revisions are included in Article 1 of the MOU.

law, with a possible exception for the revised provision for compulsory licences.[149] The amendment included:

- extending the duration of an invention patent to 20 years from 15 years,[150] the same term as in the US (consistent with Article 1(c) of the MOU);
- expanding the scope of patentable subject matter to all fields of technology, including pharmaceutical and chemical processes and products, for which only process patents were granted previously (consistent with Article 1(a) of the MOU).[151]
- allowing the patent holders the right to prevent the unauthorised sale or importation of patented products, which made the provision of China's patent law on 'rights conferred' consistent with Article 1(b) of the MOU.[152]

Furthermore, in 2000 as part of its accession package to the WTO, China undertook a significant overhaul of its patent laws.[153] These efforts were clearly made in direct response to the obligations required by TRIPS.[154] For instance, the amendments relating to the enforcement of patent rights, including allowing for criminal liabilities and injunctions, were introduced to comply with Article 50 of TRIPS.[155] This revision also extended the rights conferred to include the right to prohibit unauthorised 'offering for sale', consistent with Article 28.[156] More revisions regarding the judicial review of patent invalidations and stricter standards for issuing a compulsory licence were also added, in order to comply with Articles 32 and 31, respectively. The

149 《中华人民共和国专利法 (1992年修订)》 [The Patent Law of the People's Republic of China (Revised in 1992)] (People's Republic of China) National People's Congress Standing Committee, Order No 3, September 1992.

150 Patent Law (n 149) art 45.

151 The 1984 Patent Law, Article 25 contained a provision that explicitly excluded 'pharmaceutical products and substances obtained by means of a chemical process' from patent protection. This exclusion meant that inventors could not obtain patents for their innovations in these fields, which in turn limited the incentive for research and development in pharmaceuticals and chemical processes. In contrast, the 1992 Patent Law omitted this exclusion, allowing pharmaceutical products and substances obtained by means of a chemical process to be eligible for patent protection. This change in the law was significant as it provided inventors in these fields with the opportunity to secure patents for their innovations, promoting research and development in the pharmaceutical and chemical industries. The updated law aligned with international standards and encouraged investment in these sectors by granting inventors the exclusive rights to exploit their inventions for a certain period of time.

152 Patent Law (n 149) art 11.

153 《中华人民共和国专利法 (2000年修订)》 [The Patent Law of the People's Republic of China (Revised in 2000)] (People's Republic of China) National People's Congress Standing Committee, Order No 36, August 2000.

154 王兆丁 [Wang Zhaoding], 《加入WTO与我国的专利工作》(2003)17(3) [Joining the WTO and Its Impact on China's Patent Work] 软科学 *Soft Science* 32, 32; Guangzhou Hu and Gary H Jefferson, 'A Great Wall of Patents: What Is behind China's Recent Patent Explosion?' (2006) 90(1) *Journal of Development Economics* 1, 7.

155 Patent Law (n 153) art 61.

156 Patent Law (n 153) art 63.

amendment law established new standards to compute statutory damages,[157] which made the provision of China's patent law on statutory damages more consistent with Article 45. Nevertheless, despite this significant progress, concerns regarding the extent to which China's IP laws aligned with the international agreement still remained. For instance, the amended patent law disallowed the right to a granted patent that was contrary to social morality and public interest or violated China's laws.[158] Some argue that this situation could potentially enable China to justify the exclusion of an invention that might otherwise be eligible for patent rights under the TRIPS agreement.[159]

China's fear of losing foreign investment if it did not further improve its IP system led to the third amendment of the Chinese Patent Law, which was approved on December 27, 2008, and came into effect on October 1, 2009.[160] This provided detailed information about interim measures to prevent patent infringement, including pre-trial evidence preservation and property preservation measures consistent with Article 50 of TRIPS.[161] To comply with Article 62(5), the third amendment also permitted disappointed patent applicants to appeal against adverse administrative decisions in court.[162] The amendment raised the novelty criteria to an 'absolute novelty standard', which means that a patent application must be filed prior to any public disclosure.[163] Such recognition of any public disclosure for contesting the novelty of a subsequent application was consistent with the spirit of TRIPS in which Article 27 prevented discrimination as to the country of origin of the invention.

Since the *2001 Doha Declaration on the TRIPS Agreement and Public Health*, along with subsequent decisions, countries with insufficient pharmaceutical manufacturing capacities have been encouraged to make effective use of compulsory licensing under Article 31 of the *TRIPS Agreement*.[164] In response to these changes, China's third amendment to its patent law introduced provisions for compulsory licences in pharmaceutical manufacturing.[165] The extent and substance of these

---

157 Patent Law (n 153) art 60.

158 Patent Law (n 153) art 5.

159 Veronic Weinstein and Dennis Fernandez, 'Recent Development in China's Intellectual Property Laws' (2004) 3(1) *Chinese Journal of International Law* 227, 232.

160 《中华人民共和国专利法 (2008年修订)》 [The Patent Law of the People's Republic of China (Revised in 2008)] (People's Republic of China) National People's Congress Standing Committee, Order No 8, December 2008.

161 Patent Law (n 153) art 61.

162 Patent Law (n 153) art 63.

163 Patent Law (n 153) art 22; Shoukang Guo, 'Some Remarks on the Third Revision Draft of the Chinese Patent Law' in Martin J Adelman et al (eds), *Patents and Technological Progress in a Globalized World* (Springer Berlin 2009) 713, 716–717.

164 Matthew Kennedy, 'When Will the Protocol Amending the TRIPS Agreement Enter into Force?' (2010) 13(2) Journal of International Economic Law 1, 11; Thomas A Haag, 'TRIPS since Doha: How Far will the WTO Go toward Modifying the Terms for Compulsory Licensing' (2002) 84 (12) *Journal of the Patent and Trademark Office Society* 945, 947–981.

165 Patent Law (n 153) art 48–58.

amendments demonstrate China's considerable efforts to adhere to TRIPS and other related international agreements.[166]

Yet, despite this significant progress, China was still criticised for providing insufficient protection and enforcement of IP rights, and for the lack of a deterrent effect on infringement activity under the existing IP provisions.[167] The most intense criticism came from the US. As noted by the White House Office Trade and Manufacturing Policy, China's 'economic aggression', as the US understood it, led to many unsolved problems for the international IP system.[168] Moreover, the US Trade Representative Special 301 Report annually identifies countries that fail to adequately protect IP rights or provide market access to US companies and has highlighted China's non-compliance with TRIPS in the area of deterring IP infringement and enforcing IP rights.[169] Among the identified unsolved issues were forced technology transfer, discriminatory licensing practices, State-backed outbound acquisition of IP and technologies, and IP theft by computer hacking.[170] Based on the Special 301 Report, the US filed a complaint to the WTO against China for TRIPS non-compliance and imposed retaliatory trade tariffs on China's imports in 2018.[171] The complaint claimed that 'China deprived foreign IP rights holders of the ability to protect their IP rights in China'.[172] Under this pressure, China eventually agreed to the United States-China Economic and Trade Agreement in 2019, known as the Phase One Agreement.[173] The Phase One Agreement contained WTO-plus obligations in IP and other fields, which went beyond China's WTO accession commitments and the criteria of IP protection found in TRIPS.[174]

166 黄丽萍 [Huang Liping],《论我国现行药品专利强制许可立法的不足与完善》(2012) 5 [On the Shortcomings and Improvements of China's Current Pharmaceutical Patent Compulsory Licensing Legislation] 法学杂志 *Legal Studies Journal* 92, 92.

167 Konstantina K Athanasakou, 'China IPR Enforcement: Hard as Steel or Soft as TOFU—Bringing the Question to the WTO under TRIPS (2007) 39(1) *Georgetown Journal of International Law* 217, 222–223.

168 White House, 'How China's Economic Aggression Threatens the Technologies and Intellectual Property of the United States and the World', *White House Office of Trade and Manufacturing Policy* (Web Page, June 2018) < https://www.whitehouse.gov/wp-content/uploads/2018/06/FINAL-China-Technology-Report-6.18.18-PDF > .

169 Office of the United States Trade Representative, '2018 Special 301 Report' (Web Page, 2018) < https://ustr.gov/sites/default/files/files/Press/Reports/2018%20Special%20301.pdf > accessed 14 October 2022.

170 Jyh-An Lee, 'Shifting IP Battlegrounds in the U.S.–China Trade War' (2020) 43(2) *Columbia Journal of Law & the Arts* 147, 147–194.

171 *China—Certain Measures Concerning the Protection of Intellectual Property Rights*, WTO Doc WT/DS542/1, IP/D/38 (26 March 2018) (Request for Consultation by the United States).

172 Ibid.

173 许子昀 [Xu Ziyun],《中美第一阶段经贸协议: 推动知识产权保护全方位升级》[China-US Phase One Trade Agreement: Promoting a Comprehensive Upgrade in Intellectual Property Protection] (2023) 5中国外资 *Foreign Investment in China* 54, 54–57.

174 Wang Heng, 'How to Assess Regional Trade Agreements? Deep FTAs v. China's Trade Agreements' (2021) 54 *International Lawyer* 1, 9–10.

Following the signing of the Phase One Agreement, China swiftly enacted the fourth amendment to its patent law in 2020.[175] This move aimed to fulfil some of the commitments stipulated in the Agreement and to partially harmonise China's patent system with that of the US.[176] For instance, in accordance with Article 1.12 of the Phase One Agreement, China is required to permit patent term extensions to compensate for 'unreasonable delays' in the patent office and regulatory delays of pharmaceuticals. This commitment was implemented under Article 42 of the fourth and latest amendment to the patent law.

More notably, the fourth amendment established a patent linkage system for the early resolution of patent infringement disputes before competitor pharmaceuticals could potentially be launched in China.[177] This patent linkage system aligns with China's obligations under the Phase One Agreement and is inspired by the *US Hatch–Waxman Act* for resolving patent disputes related to generic drugs.[178] Thus, although some argue that external pressure may not lead to long-term outcomes in China,[179] it is essential to recognise that China made significant changes to its IP system in response to pressure from technologically advanced countries and the need to comply with international, regional, and bilateral IP agreements.

Nevertheless, in much of the existing literature, it is considered that the international, regional, and bilateral IP agreements were largely established to cater to the needs of the technologically advanced countries' economies.[180] It is further argued that such agreements largely ignored the extent to which China could affordably build stronger IP protection and, in return, gain greater access to the global value chain dominated by these technologically advanced countries. In this regard, as noted by some scholars, these agreements might be consistent with the interests of technologically advanced countries but might incur more costs than benefits when applied in

175 《中华人民共和国专利法 (2020年修订)》 [The Patent Law of the People's Republic of China (Revised in 2020)] (People's Republic of China) National People's Congress Standing Committee, Order No 55, August 2020.

176 伯雨鸿 [Bo Yuhong], 《我国专利法第四次修正之评析》 [An Analysis of the Fourth Amendment to China's Patent Law] (2021) 3 电子知识产权 Electronic Intellectual Property 39, 41–42.

177 Patent Law (n 175) art 76.

178 管荣齐 刘少华 [Guan Rongqi] and [Liu Shaohua], 《药品专利挑战的机制和策略》 [Mechanisms and Strategies for Pharmaceutical Patent Challenges] (2022) 15(2) 沈阳工业大学学报 *Journal of Shenyang University of Technology* 97, 98; Drug Price Competition and Patent Term Restoration Act of 1984, 21 USC §§ 355, 360 cc (1984).

179 郭晴 [Guo Qing], 《中美贸易摩擦对中国经济贸易的中长期影响研究》 [Study on the Medium and Long-Term Impact of China-US Trade Friction on China's Economy and Trade] (2019) 6 求索 *Quest* 55, 55–64.

180 Akalemwa Ngenda, 'The Nature of the International Intellectual Property System: Universal Norms and Values or Western Chauvinism?' (2005) 14(1) *Information & Communications Technology Law* 59, 59–79; Christopher May, 'The Hypocrisy of Forgetfulness: The Contemporary Significance of Early Innovations in Intellectual Property' (2007) 14 *Review of International Political Economy* 1, 1–25.

China.[181] Furthermore, bilateral agreements that compel China to adopt more stringent IP protection norms, like the US-China Phase One Agreement, might erode the 'policy space' and 'balance' allowed by TRIPS and other multilateral treaties.[182] Consequently, these agreements could limit the range and application of TRIPS flexibilities available to China.[183]

Therefore, it can be argued that the foreign efforts to bring China's IP practices up to international standards through pressure and resulting agreements may add symbolic value and normative rhetoric to the legal and policy changes, but run counter to the practical reality in China. This is because Chinese culture lacks acceptance of, and in many cases resists the notion of, IP rights.[184] External pressure does not necessarily result in the incorporation of IP rights concepts into the consciousness and culture of the Chinese people; instead, it may amplify their resistance and hostility towards IP rights. As Shao has described, the technologically advanced countries and many international organisations merely play a role akin to that of a Christian missionary, evangelising the Chinese with the Western IP perspective that is skewed towards the interests of powerful industries and companies.[185]

In doing so, this largely ignores China's political culture, the intellectual tradition developed through Confucianism, and many other non-legal factors that have shaped Chinese attitudes towards IP rights.[186] For instance, as Alford has argued, the concept of IP rights was historically and culturally unable to take root in China because of the tight political control over publication work, and Confucianism's focus on learning through imitation and reproduction.[187] This situation has led to the belief that the fundamental principles of democracy and the rules of law that influence

---

[181] 郭雪军 [Guo Xuejun],《我国知识产权法律移植的不适应, 原因及转型》[The Inadaptability of Transplanted Intellectual Property Laws in Our Country, Reasons and Transformation] (2014) 31(1) 山东农业工程学院学报*Journal of Shandong Agricultural Engineering College* 90, 90–92; Lisa Forman et al, 'Addressing Legal and Political Barriers to Global Pharmaceutical Access: Options for Remedying the Impact of the Agreement on Trade-Related Aspects of Intellectual Property Rights (TRIPS) and the Imposition of TRIPS-plus Standards' (2008) 3 *Health Economics, Policy and Law* 229, 244.

[182] Shao Ke, 'What May Validate Intellectual Property in the Traditional Chinese Mind? Examining the US-China IP Disputes through an Historical Inquiry' [2006] *Journal of Information, Law & Technology* 1, 3.

[183] Ibid.

[184] 盛辉 [Sheng Hui],《在我国传统文化中知识产权产生与发展的不利因素分析》[Analysis of the Adverse Factors in the Generation and Development of Intellectual Property Rights in China's Traditional Culture] (2014) 9 科技管理研究 *Science and Technology Management Research* 240, 240–243; Liwei Wang, 'The Chinese Traditions Inimical to the Patent Law' (1993) 14 *Northwestern Journal of International Law & Business* 15, 15–65; Peter K Yu, 'Intellectual Property and Confucianism' in Irene Calboli and Srividhya Ragavan (eds), *Diversity in Intellectual Property: Identities, Interests, and Intersections* (Cambridge University Press 2015) 1.

[185] Ke Shao, 'What May Validate Intellectual Property in a Traditional Chinese Mind? Examining the U.S.-China IP Disputes through An Historical Inquiry' (2006) 1 *Journal of Information, Law & Technology* 1, 1.

[186] Ibid.

[187] Alford (n 30) 222.

Western attitudes to IP rights have no Indigenous counterparts in Chinese culture and history.[188]

However, this does not mean that China is entirely unable to build a domestically suitable IP framework under the international, regional, and bilateral IP agreements. The point is that applying a Western-style IP system is not as simple as adhering to the standards established by international agreements. For the law to be effective, it must put specific emphasis on the understanding of the society and the distinctive culture, values, traditions, and customs which characterise the country in which the law is applied.[189] If this is the case, then Chinese people may change their attitudes and have incentives to utilise the law and require institutions to enforce it.

3.3.3 China's Approach to Protecting TMK Under International IP Agreements

In a variety of international forums, agreements, and policy networks, work has been done on the protection of traditional knowledge (including TMK) under IP laws. One typical proposal has been that the IP rights applicants should have an obligation of disclosure relating to the utilisation of traditional knowledge (including TMK) and associated genetic resources.[190] Some biodiversity-rich countries, such as the African Group and the Andean Community, have made submissions to the TRIPS Council to seek the implementation of this obligation, believing it to be a significant mechanism for reconciling TRIPS with the CBD.[191] This legal topic was expressly listed in the agenda of the TRIPS Council at the fourth Ministerial Conference of the WTO in Doha, Qatar, in 2001.[192] At the negotiations, at least two possible amendments to TRIPS were suggested, each with its own unique wording. The first proposal was an amendment to Article 27, to add an exception to patentability which provides that:

---

188 李强 [Li Qiang],《论知识产权制度的恶名》[On the Notoriety of the Intellectual Property System] (2007) 9(1) 西南政法大学学报*Journal of SWUPL* 42, 43; Alford (n 30) 9–29.

189 陈名涛 [Chen Mingtao],《中国知识产权移植问题探析》[An Analysis of Intellectual Property Transplant Issues in China] [2012] 社科纵横*Social Science Review* 113, 113; Setsuo Miyazawa, 'Legal Transplants in Contemporary Asia: Foreword' (2021) 8(2) *Asian Journal of Law and Society* 348, 349.

190 Martin A Girsberg, 'Transparency Measures under Patent Law regarding Genetic Resources and Traditional Knowledge: Disclosure of Source and Evidence of Prior Informed Consent and Benefit-sharing' (2004) 7(4) *The Journal of World Intellectual Property* 451, 454–456.

191 *Draft Modalities for TRIPS Related Issues*, WTO Doc TN/C/W/52 (19 July 2008); Daniel Robinson and Margraet Raven, 'Identifying and Preventing Biopiracy in Australia: Patent Landscapes and Legal Geographies for Plants with Indigenous Australian Uses' (2017) 48(3) *Australian Geographer* 311, 325.

192 Doha WTO Ministerial (2001) : Ministerial Declaration, WTO Doc WT/MIN (01)/DEC/1 (14 Nov 2001).

> Members may also exclude from patentability the products or processes which directly or indirectly include genetic resources or traditional knowledge obtained in the absence of compliance with international and national legislation on the subject.[193]

The second proposal was an amendment to Article 29 to include the following provision:

> Members shall require an applicant for a patent to disclose the country and area of origin of any biological resources and traditional knowledge used or involved in the invention, and to provide confirmation of compliance with all access regulations in the country of origin.[194]

However, many technologically advanced countries opposed this proposed amendment, arguing that adding the disclosure requirement to TRIPS would lead to 'legal uncertainty and other negative consequences'.[195] Consequently, the negotiation process was stuck because of these divergent views.

Developments in WIPO have contributed to the discussion about disclosure requirements in IP rights applications. The Conference of the Parties of the CBD invited it to explore the options for model provisions on disclosure requirements in IP rights applications.[196] The WIPO General Assembly decided that WIPO should respond positively to this invitation.[197] Diverse views were considered during debates of the WIPO-IGC, and some biodiversity-rich countries submitted proposals on disclosure of origin obligations, informed by their practical experience in implementing such an obligation in their domestic legislation. China had actively pushed for the incorporation of disclosure requirements in international IP agreements, regarding it as a way to adjust the Western-style IP framework to better align with the unique historical and sociocultural aspects of China's TMK. This move aimed to acknowledge and accommodate the distinct characteristics of TMK, creating a pathway for their protection and preservation.

In particular, the delegation from China was of the opinion that the introduction of disclosure requirements should be incorporated into the existing IP system, which could help to align it with the CBD, as well as to facilitate the implementation of PIC and benefit-sharing.[198] Given that China's national patent law had established the detailed principles for the disclosure requirements in a patent application,[199] the

---

[193] *Article 27.3(B), Relationship between the TRIPS Agreement and the CBD, and Protection of Traditional Knowledge and Folklore*', WTO Doc IP/C/W/447 (8 June 2005) (Communication from Peru).

[194] *Taking Forward the Review of Article 27.3(b) of the TRIPS Agreement* WTO Doc IP/C/W/404 (26 June 2003) (Joint Communication from the African Group).

[195] *Article 27.3(B), Relationship between the TRIPS Agreement and the CBD, and Protection of Traditional Knowledge and Folklore* WTO Doc IP/C/W/469 (13 March 2006) (Communication from the United States).

[196] *Certain Decision of the Seventh Conference of the Parties to the Convention on Biological Diversity*, WIPO/GRTKF/IC/6/13 (15 March 2004).

[197] Ibid.

[198] *Draft Report Prepa*red by the Secretariat, WIPO Doc WIPO/GRTKF/IC/23/8 (26 April 2013) < https://www.wipo.int/meetings/en/doc_details.jsp?doc_id=241343 > accessed 15 October 2022.

[199] 马海生 [Ma Haisheng],《遗传资源保护与专利申请中遗传资源披露: 兼评专利法修订草案中的相关条款》[Protection of Genetic Resources and Disclosure of Genetic Resources in Patent

Chinese delegation also supported the amendment of WIPO-administered treaties such as the *Patent Law Treaty* and *Patent Cooperation Treaty* to include relevant disclosure requirements.[200] This proposed amendment encourages other countries to follow suit and adopt similar measures to protect their own traditional knowledge, ultimately fostering a more inclusive and culturally sensitive IP system on a global scale. Nevertheless, a consensus was blocked by some technologically advanced countries, who considered the disclosure requirement as an innovation-deterring burden that introduced elements of legal uncertainty.[201] For instance, the following statements were made during the IGC Session:

> Any instrument would need to ensure that patent systems and related IP rights would not be threatened by any element of legal uncertainty ... A disclosure requirement that would create legal uncertainty in the patent system would not be in the interest of the Member States and patent users.[202]

Although there has been progress in the discussions and critical analysis of disclosure requirements regarding the utilisation of traditional knowledge (including TMK) in various international forums, no requirements have been put into effect globally because an agreement or consensus has not been reached among the participating nations.[203] At China's domestic level, its highest legislative body, the National People's Congress, promulgated the third amendment to the patent law in 2008, which took effect in 2009.[204] This amendment introduced a new provision that required patent applicants to declare the origin of genetic resources in a patent application despite the disclosure requirements for TMK not explicitly being mentioned.It provides that:

> Concerning an invention accomplished by relying on genetic resources, the applicant shall, in the patent application documents, indicate the origin and direct source of the genetic resources. If the applicant cannot indicate the origin, he/she shall state the reasons.[205]

Nevertheless, some scholars have argued that the disclosure requirement included in Article 26 of China's amended patent law and patent application procedure was

---

Applications: A Review of the Relevant Provisions in the Draft Amendment to the Patent Law] (2007) 17 知识产权Intellectual Property 37, 37–41.

200 Draft Report Prepared by the Secretariat, WIPO Doc WIPO/GRTKF/IC/23/8 (26 April 2013) < https://www.wipo.int/meetings/en/doc_details.jsp?doc_id=241343 > accessed 15 October 2022.

201 C Saez, 'WIPO Talks on Future of TK, Genetic Resources, Folklore Intensify', IP Watch (Web Page, 2013) < https://www.ip-watch.org/2013/07/24/wipo-talks-on-future-of-tk-genetic-resources-folklore-intensify/ > accessed 9 October 2022; Margo Bagley, 'Of Disclosure Straws and IP System Camels' in Daniel F Robinson et al (eds), Protecting Traditional Knowledge: The WIPO Intergovernmental Committee on Intellectual Property and Genetic Resources, Traditional Knowledge and Folklore (Routledge, 2017) 86, 89.

202 Report Adopted by the Committee, WIPO Doc WTO Doc IP/C/W/469 (13 March 2006).

203 Bagley (n 201) 117.

204 Bagley (n 201) 85.

205 Patent Law (n 175) art 26.

merely a formal requirement which did not require the patent office to check the credibility of the disclosed information.[206]

Such a standalone provision does not effectively prevent the misappropriation of related resources and knowledge. Therefore, China's amended Patent Law (2008) included another provision seeking to compensate for the insufficiencies of the weak disclosure mechanism established in Article 26. This provision stipulates that any invention reliant on genetic resources may be denied patentability if the use of the underlying genetic resources violates Chinese law or regulation.[207] Arguably, this provision creates a strong deterrent to non-compliance because failure to comply could lead to either the rejection or invalidation of a patent.

Against this backdrop, it is fair to say that China's national patent law has mandated disclosure requirements more extensively than was discussed at the international level, which many developing countries might wish to evaluate and draw upon. As China's State Intellectual Property Administration has noted, it is 'in the best interest of China to align with the same practice of developing countries in a field where international treaties have always focused on the interest of developed countries'.[208]

WIPO has also initiated efforts to explore forms of IP protection for TK by forming the WIPO Fact-finding Missions ('WIPO-FFMs') and the WIPO-IGC. As part of these efforts, the WIPO-IGC commissioned a gap analysis,[209] which identified four critical gaps in the existing legislation on the protection of traditional knowledge: (i) such knowledge is not an eligible subject matter for IP protection under existing IP law; (ii) existing IP systems do not recognise collective or community ownership, and so exclude IPLCs from the benefits of IP protection; (iii) some critical forms of protection, such as the specific disclosure requirement relating to TK, have not been provided under existing IP international standards; and (iv) the entitlement to remuneration from the use of traditional knowledge is absent.[210]

To address these gaps, certain options were suggested that either exist or might be developed.[211] A number of adjustments to the application of existing IP rights and potentially new sui generis adjuncts were then proposed.[212] The proposed adaptations are mainly characterised as 'defensive' or 'positive'.[213] Defensive protection aims to establish a mechanism that prevents third parties who are outside of the

---

[206] Cheng Wenting, 'The Protection of Genetic Resources in Chinese Patent Law' (2021) 43(4) *European Intellectual Property Review* 248, 251.

[207] Patent Law (n 175) art 5.

[208] The European Patent Office ('EPO') and The Ministry of Commerce ('MOFCOM'), *Third Revision of China's Patent Law: Legal Texts and Documents on the Drafting Process 2006–2008* (EU—China IPR2, 2009)1, 5.

[209] *The Protection of Traditional Cultural Expressions: Draft Gap Analysis*, WIPO Doc WIPO/GRTKF/IC/13/4(b) (26 March 2008); *The Protection of Traditional Cultural Expressions: Updated Draft Gap Analysis*, WIPO Doc WIPO/GRTKF/IC/37/6 (20 July 2018).

[210] Ibid.

[211] Ibid.

[212] Ibid.

[213] Ibid.

communities from obtaining IP rights over TK.[214] There are two options for defensive protection[215]: first, adopting the necessary legal, administrative, and judicial measures that recognise TK as prior art relating to patentability; second, creating an information system to make TK searchable by patent offices. Positive protection is oriented to grant exclusive IP rights in TK. It aims to empower communities to assert their Indigenous rights to ownership and control their TK, and allows them to take action against the misappropriation of their TK. The options of positive protection are usually reflected in two types of legal remedies: making effective use of conventional IP laws, and establishing sui generis or special laws to address the positive protection of TK.[216] These are complementary strategies that should be regarded as balancing elements, essential for the realisation of comprehensive protection of TK. As a longer-term approach, there have been many initiatives and calls from developing countries for a binding international sui generis system for providing comprehensive protection of TK.

At the national level, China did not choose between the two options. It followed the high-biodiversity countries' approaches to combine them flexibly to suit its own needs, priorities, and preferences. Firstly, a defensive protection measure has been implemented in China by establishing a series of TMK information systems such as databases and digital archives.[217] The largest TMK database (the Traditional Chinese Medicine Database) was set up by the Institute of Traditional Chinese Medicine Information. It includes 48 categories of sub-databases, possessing 120,000 items relating to China's TMK.[218] In addition, the China Traditional Chinese Medicine Patent Database was produced, and is maintained, by the State Intellectual Property Office and includes more than 22,000 of China's TMK-related patent records.[219]

---

214 Jay Erstling, 'Using Patent to Protect Traditional Knowledge' (2009) 15 *Texas Wesleyan Law Review* 295, 315.

215 Reto M Hilty et al, 'Traditional Knowledge, Databases and Prior Art—Options for an Effective Defensive Use of TK against Undue Patent Granting' in Irini Stamatoudi (ed), *Research Handbook on Intellectual Property and Cultural Heritage* (Elgaronline, 2022) 132, 132–133; MA Bagley, 'The Fallacy of Defensive Protection for Traditional Knowledge' (2019) 58(2) *Washburn L.J.* 323, 323–327.

216 陈染 [Chen Ran],《中医药传统知识特别权利保护模式探讨》[Discussion on the Protection Model of Special Rights for Traditional Chinese Medicine Knowledge] (2022) 36(4) 湖北第二师范学院学报 *Journal of Hubei University of Education* 51, 51–56.

217 要然 [Yao Ran],《浅析传统知识数据库及其应用》[Analyzing Traditional Knowledge Databases and Their Applications] (2013) 6中国发明与专利*China Invention and Patent* 50, 50–53; R Lakshmi Poorna and Others, 'Preservation and Protection of Traditional Knowledge—Diverse Documentation Initiatives across the Globe' (2014) 107(8) *Current Science* 1240, 1242–1244; MS Ansari, 'Evaluation of Role of Traditional Knowledge Digital Library and Traditional Chinese Medicine Database in Preservation of Traditional Medicinal Knowledge' (2016) 36(2) *Journal of Library & Information Technology* 73, 73–78; For more details, see Chapter 6 of this thesis.

218 Institute of Information on Traditional Chinese Medicine (IITCM), 'TCM Database System' (Website, 2014) < http://www.cintcm.ac.cn> accessed 14 October 2022.

219 Yanhuai Liu and Yanling Sun, 'China Traditional Chinese Medicine (TCM) Patent Database' (2004) 26(1) *World Patent Information* 91, 91–96.

Arguably, despite being non-legal mechanisms, these systems perform the significant function of safeguarding TMK in China. This is because the compilation of TMK in a digital format can be used as evidence of prior art by patent examiners and other authorities in China to prevent third parties from erroneously obtaining patents derived from TMK.[220] More importantly, this defensive protection measure is consistent with China's distinctive linguistic and cultural constructs. Unlike many other multi-ethnic States with a great variety of languages, China has successfully standardised and unified its language system to smooth out multiple discourses and the process of communication across the country.[221] On this basis, all official documents, deeds, and communications (including TMK documents and databases) in China recognise Mandarin as a common official language.[222] Therefore, while the TMK document's original language is still available in the system and represents the authentic text, the use of one single official language for standardised translation could make the databases, digital archives, and other information systems more accessible. It allows users to search for any information regarding TMK across the entire system, regardless of the original language. More significantly, the single language format eliminates the need for the patent office to recruit and train additional examiners with expertise in multiple ethnic languages. Ostensibly, it simplifies the patent application and examination process and significantly reduces the confusion over multi-ethnic filing practices.

Simultaneously, as China's policies are increasingly geared towards promoting the integration of its TMK into modern Western biomedical practices and facilitating innovation in TMK,[223] China has embraced its existing patent system as a viable positive protection mechanism.[224] This is because TMK incorporating Western scientific techniques makes the determination of patentability more straightforward and predictable. Meanwhile, the Chinese government is also pushing for proactive measures towards the recognition and maintenance of TMK's cultural philosophical roots and heritage. According to the Chinese State Council's Several Opinions on Supporting and Promoting the Development of TMK, the protection and

---

220 何俗非 [He Sufei],《中医药传统知识保护现状与思考》(2019) 21(6) [Current Situation and Considerations on the Protection of Traditional Chinese Medicine Knowledge] 世界科学技术 *World Science and Technology* 1147, 1149.

221 Xiulan Zuo, 'Transnational Curriculum Inquiry' (2007) 4(1) *Journal of the International Association for the Advancement of Curriculum Studies* 80, 84.

222 Wang Juan, 'National Language Movement—An Indispensable Perspective of Literary Revolution' (2018) 17(2) *Studies in Literature and Language* 114, 115.

223 李江涛 [Li Jiangtao],《西学东渐以来中医药自信的质疑与重塑》 [Since the Spread of Western Learning to the East: The Questioning and Reshaping of Confidence in Traditional Chinese Medicine] (2022) 1 中国高等医学教育 *Chinese Higher Medical Education* 6, 6–7.

224 Chidi Oguamanam, 'Patents and Traditional Medicine: Digital Capture, Creative Legal Interventions and the Dialectics of Knowledge Transformation' (2008) 15 *Indiana Journal of Global Legal Studies* 505, 505–511.

promotion of TMK should 'adhere to the unity of inheritance and innovation, maintain the characteristic advantages of TMK, and actively apply modern science and technology'.[225]

The Chinese State Council's emphasis on the unity of inheritance and innovation reflects China's dialectical attitudes towards the protection and promotion of its TMK. On one hand, it conveys messages of aggressively integrating its TMK system into the Western medical ontology and conventional IP system. On the other hand, it shows a determination to maintain TMK's natural philosophy and deep theoretical roots, which arise from its Indigenous practices, as alternatives to Western biomedicine. Such dialectical approaches are crucial in understanding China's TMK as a phenomenon emerging from contradictory social interactions in local communities and developing by consistently incorporating new knowledge and therapeutic ideas in response to changing needs in the local environment.[226]

In conclusion, China's push to mandate the disclosure of the origin of traditional knowledge (including TMK) at the international level can be seen as an effort to adjust the Western-style IP framework to better align with the unique historical and sociocultural aspects of China's TMK. By combining defensive and positive protection measures and advocating for the inclusion of disclosure requirements in international IP agreements, China seeks to acknowledge and accommodate the distinct characteristics of TMK, thereby creating a pathway for their protection and preservation. This approach offers valuable insights for other developing countries looking to protect their traditional knowledge within the global IP framework.

3.3.4 Impact of the 2024 WIPO Treaty on China's Approach to Genetic Resources and Traditional Medical Knowledge

The WIPO Treaty on Intellectual Property, Genetic Resources, and Associated Traditional Knowledge, adopted on May 24, 2024, marks a historic milestone after decades of negotiations.[227] This groundbreaking treaty establishes an international framework requiring patent applicants to disclose the origin of genetic resources and any associated traditional knowledge (TK) used in their inventions.[228] It is the first WIPO

[225] Chinese State Council, 'Several Opinions on Supporting and Promoting the Development of TMK' (2009).

[226] J Weeks, 'Chinese TCM Renaissance and the Global Movement for Integrative Health and Medicine' (2017) 23(2) *The Journal of Alternative and Complementary Medicine* 79, 79–81; Cai Jingfeng, 'Integration of Traditional Chinese Medicine with Western Medicine—Right or Wrong?' (1988) 27(5) *Social Science & Medicine* 521, 521–529.

[227] **WIPO Treaty on Intellectual Property, Genetic Resources and Associated Traditional Knowledge**, Diplomatic Conference to Conclude an International Legal Instrument Relating to Intellectual Property, Genetic Resources and Traditional Knowledge Associated with Genetic Resources, WIPO Doc GRATK/DC/7 (adopted 24 May 2024).

[228] Ibid.

treaty to specifically include provisions for the rights of Indigenous Peoples and local communities, reflecting a significant balance between intellectual property protection and the rights of those conserving and utilising these resources.

A central feature of the Treaty is the mandatory disclosure requirement, which obligates patent applicants to disclose the country of origin or source of the genetic resources (GR) or associated traditional knowledge (TK) used in their inventions.[229] This requirement addresses the need for greater transparency in the use of GR and TK, especially given the rapid advancements in biotechnology and the widespread availability of genetic information in databanks, such as gene banks. It also reflects the increasing reliance on TK 'shortcuts' in the development of new technologies. However, the decision to use 'based on' rather than 'utilization' as the trigger for disclosure has introduced ambiguity. While 'utilization' as a trigger provides a broader and more comprehensive scope, ensuring effective compliance with ABS regulations, 'based on' is narrower and may allow some parties to avoid disclosure obligations, leading to potential misappropriation.

In cases where the origin or source is unknown, applicants are required to submit a formal declaration. The Treaty provides sanctions and remedies, allowing applicants to correct failures to disclose unless there is fraudulent intent.[230] While sanctions may be imposed for non-disclosure, a patent cannot be revoked solely on this basis. Additionally, the Treaty promotes the creation of information systems, including databases of genetic resources and associated TK, to assist patent offices during examination processes.[231] It also includes provisions for periodic review and alignment with other international agreements, ensuring the Treaty remains relevant and effective in addressing emerging issues within the evolving global intellectual property landscape.[232]

For China, the implications of the WIPO Treaty are particularly relevant to Chinese TMK, which often relies on genetic resources. Currently, Chinese patent law requires the disclosure of the direct and original sources of genetic resources but does not extend similar protection to traditional knowledge. Given the importance of Chinese TMK and its connection to GR, the WIPO Treaty might necessitate amendments to Chinese patent regulations to include mandatory disclosure of TK (particularly TMK) used in inventions. This would align Chinese law with international standards while also providing protection against the exploitation of Chinese TMK without proper acknowledgement and benefit-sharing.

Furthermore, challenges related to Digital Sequence Information (DSI) add another layer of complexity, especially in the context of TMK. DSI refers to genetic information stored in digital formats, and it is increasingly being utilised in the

[229] Article 3 of WIPO Treaty on IP, GR & Associated TK.

[230] Article 5 of WIPO Treaty on IP, GR & Associated TK.

[231] Article 6 of WIPO Treaty on IP, GR & Associated TK.

[232] Article 7 and 8 of WIPO Treaty on IP, GR & Associated TK.

development and research of traditional medical formulations.[233] The WIPO Treaty acknowledges the role of DSI by including gene banks as potential sources of genetic resources. However, without clear and enforceable requirements for the disclosure of the origin of DSI associated with traditional medical knowledge, tracking compliance with ABS becomes challenging. For China, incorporating provisions for DSI related to TMK into its patent framework could ensure a more comprehensive approach to managing GR and TK, thus preventing the unauthorised use of genetic information derived from traditional medical resources.

Finally, the Treaty also highlights the burden of proving misappropriation or non-compliance, which poses a significant challenge for TK holders, especially in the context of traditional medicine. TMK is often informal and communal in nature, making it difficult to provide concrete evidence of fraudulent intent in cases of non-disclosure. This creates the risk that misappropriation could go unpunished, undermining the integrity of both international and national IP regimes. To protect TMK, China may need to ensure that its laws reduce the burden on the knowledge holders, thereby safeguarding the rights and interests of Indigenous and local communities that contribute to traditional medicine.

To effectively implement the 2024 WIPO Treaty, China must adopt a strategy that harmonises international obligations with domestic reforms while carefully considering its rich cultural and historical context. Chinese TMK is deeply embedded in the country's cultural heritage, and any policy shifts must reflect this unique aspect. A cultural-historical approach would prioritise the preservation and respectful use of TMK, recognising that such knowledge has been passed down through generations and forms part of the collective identity of local communities. Revising China's patent laws to explicitly require the mandatory disclosure of TMK, particularly when genetic resources (GR) are involved, would not only align with global standards but also honour the cultural significance of these practices. In doing so, China could also ensure that benefit-sharing mechanisms are culturally sensitive, compensating Indigenous and local communities in ways that respect their traditions and values.

In addition to legal reforms, China could establish a national registry or database for GR and TMK that reflects both historical and cultural aspects of the knowledge. Such a resource would not only support transparency in patent examinations but also serve as a tool for preserving the cultural narratives and origins associated with GR and TMK. The database could be developed in collaboration with local communities, ensuring that the knowledge is documented in a way that respects the communal and informal nature of its transmission, while simultaneously protecting against misappropriation or exploitation by external entities.

Addressing the challenges posed by DSI would require a culturally informed approach as well. China could introduce stricter regulations that mandate the disclosure of DSI sources linked to TMK, ensuring that any use of genetic information derived from traditional knowledge adheres to ABS principles. In doing so, China

233 Martin Brink and Theo van Hintum, 'Practical Consequences of Digital Sequence Information (DSI) Definitions and Access and Benefit-Sharing Scenarios from a Plant Genebank's Perspective' (2021) *Plants, People, Planet*, 23, 23–32.

could expand existing ABS frameworks to encompass DSI, ensuring the protection of traditional knowledge that may be digitised or extracted in non-physical forms, while still respecting the cultural roots of this knowledge.

Finally, China could take steps to ease the burden of proof on knowledge holders, particularly in Indigenous and local communities, by incorporating traditional governance models and culturally relevant legal structures. Shifting some compliance responsibility to patent applicants and third-party users of TMK, as well as supporting community-led initiatives for monitoring and enforcement, would align with the country's historical approach to communal knowledge. This would not only help safeguard TMK but also reflect a culturally respectful implementation of the WIPO Treaty, ensuring that China's policies protect its valuable heritage while fostering global cooperation on genetic resources and traditional knowledge.

3.4 The Mismatch Between the Western System of IP Rights and the TMK of China

3.4.1 Conflicts Between IP Rights and TMK: The Collision of Confucian Paradigm and Western IP Theory

Some scholars have attributed China's failure to achieve industrialisation and modern economic growth in the nineteenth century to a 'cultural problem'.[234] They argued that the Confucian worldview, which perceived China as 'central, superior, and self-sufficient', created long-term obstacles that hindered the country from adopting capitalism, individualism, and the global market economies exemplified by the Western philosophical tradition.[235] Similarly, it can be argued that the broader sociocultural context that shaped the concepts of IP rights, as opposed to TMK, also faced comparable challenges.

At the national level, China's TMK embodies its traditional beliefs, values, and practices and reflects Chinese thinking about illness and health.[236] According to a number of scholars, the Confucian philosophy forms the unique cultural and social

[234] 李建国 [Li Jianguo],《儒家文化对中国现代化发轫的负面影响》[The Negative Impact of Confucian Culture on the Modernization of China] [2006] 文化研究 *Cultural Research* 183, 183; A Eckstein, J K Fairbank and LS Yang, 'Economic Change in Early Modern China: An Analytical Framework' (1960) 9 *Economic Development and Cultural Change* 1, 1.

[235] Van Dongen, 'Confucianism, Community, Capitalism' in Tze-ki Hon and Kristin Stapleton (eds), *Confucianism for the Contemporary World: Global Order, Political Plurality, and Social Action* (SUNY Press, 2017) 19, 29.

[236] YC Chen, 'Chinese Values, Health and Nursing' (2001) 36 *Journal of Advanced Nursing* 270, 270–275; Joanna H Raven et al, 'Traditional Beliefs and Practices in the Postpartum Period in Fujian province, China: A Qualitative Study' (2007) 7 *BMC Pregnancy and Childbirth* 1, 2.

context in which TMK has developing in China.[237] For instance, *ren* (仁) (humaneness, benevolence, or human-heartedness) is one of the most fundamental concepts in Confucianism.[238] It arises from the complicated communal and familial system of ancient China.[239] According to Confucian philosophers, it reflects the ideal world of Confucianism which considers compassion and empathy as starting points and seeks to transform these moral qualities into virtues that prompt people to behave benevolently, constantly, and consistently.[240]

As noted by Pang-White, the ideas behind *ren* in Confucian terms have social meaning: seeking to make structural changes that benefit the less fortunate members of the population, including women, the elderly and the poor.[241] In this regard, Confucian principles such as *ren* are believed to have a strong influence on the development of TMK in China. In ancient China and other countries influenced by its culture, people pursued careers in medicine and became TMK practitioners, primarily motivated by the Confucian belief in fulfilling one's moral obligations to the community, family, and society as a whole.[242]According to influential Confucian classics (《朱子遗书》 'Posthumous Papers of Zhu Xi'), people should never leave their ailing parents or relatives in the hands of a quack doctor; this is considered a violation of Confucian principles. Therefore, it was considered to be the children's duty to learn medicine (病卧于床, 委之庸医, 比于不慈不孝。事亲者, 亦不可不知医).

Moreover, in an ancient treatise entitled 'On the Absolute Sincerity of Great Physicians' (also known as the Chinese Hippocratic Oath), physicians were required to develop a sense of compassion and empathy, commit to making every effort to save every living creature, treat every patient equally, and not seek wealth while treating

[237] Li, Chenyang, 'Confucian Perspectives on Science and Technology', *Ethics, Science, Technology, and Engineering: An International Resource* (2013) 1, 1–7; Anne D Birdwhistell, 'Medicine and History as Theoretical Tools in a Confucian Pragmatism' (1995) 45(1) *Philosophy East and West* 1, 1–28; 樊凯芳 [Fan Kaifang],《儒家思想对中医学的作用和影响》[The Influence and Impact of Confucianism on Traditional Chinese Medicine] (2011) 12(6) 山西中医学院学报 *Journal of Shanxi University of Traditional Chinese Medicine* 2, 2–3.

[238] 孙相娜 [Sun Xiangna],《儒家仁爱思想与中医药文化》[Confucian Benevolence Thought and Traditional Chinese Medicine Culture] (2015) 1林区教学 *Teaching of Forestry Region* 63, 63–64.

[239] D Gareth Jones and Jing-Bao Nie, 'Does Confucianism Allow for Body Donation?' (2018) 11(5) *Anatomical Sciences Education* 525, 527; Kwon Ivo, 'Confucianism Perspectives on Abortion' in Alireza Bagheri (ed), *Abortion: Global Positions and Practices, Religious and Legal Perspectives* (Springer, 2021) 217, 225.

[240] 孙相娜 [Sun Xiangna] (n 231) 63–64; A Pang-White, 'Caring in Confucian Philosophy (2011) 6 *Philosophy Compass* 374, 377–378.

[241] Ibid.

[242] 金春丽 [Jin Chunli],《中医药在日本传播与发展状况调查研究》[Investigating the Spread and Development of Traditional Chinese Medicine in Japan] (2022) 2 国际公关 *International Public Relations* 23, 24; Anwen Zheng, 'Ren (仁), the Benevolent Thought of Traditional Chinese Medicine' (2019) 2(3) *Chinese Medicine and Culture* 137, 138.

patients.[243] This situation is consistent with the theory of Confucianism. Therefore, just as many Confucian scholars noted, the principles of Confucianism and the TMK of China are inseparable.[244] Indeed, 'Medicine is nothing but the application of Confucianism in a healing field'.[245]

According to the Confucian worldview, a clan or family forms the fundamental unit of the human community.[246] TMK is considered as an accomplishment generated from that basic unit and is expected to be shared.[247] In China, creative and non-creative knowledge, including TMK, is influenced by Confucian thought, and is generally seen as belonging to the clan or family.[248] Ownership over that work or knowledge tends to reflect collective rather than individual needs. This is because, according to Confucian beliefs, collective or group rights should be placed above individual interests and all types of knowledge and innovation should be for the collective.[249]

In contrast, the concept of IP rights built by technologically advanced countries is considered to be more individualistic,[250] which is largely alien to Chinese culture and Confucian belief. According to Hamilton, Western-style IP law values individual creative endeavours, cherishes original innovation, and chooses the creative individual for recognition and rewards.[251] For instance, TRIPS is modelled on Western IP practices,[252] which rely heavily on notions of individuality, exclusive rights, and private reward, and imposes them on countries like China. The preamble of TRIPS explicitly recognises that IP rights are 'private rights'. These ideas are fundamentally

243 Simiao Sun, 'Prescriptions for Emergency Worth a Thousand Pieces of Gold (in Chinese)' in Chinese Medical Association (ed), *A Hundred Must Read Chinese Medicine Classics (in Chinese)* (Hua Xia Press 2008) 9–11.

244 Renzong Qiu, 'Confucianism, Traditional and Contemporary China' in Robert M Veatch (ed), *Cross-cultural Perspectives in Medical Ethics* (Jones & Bartlett Publishers, 2000) 292, 292–308.

245 Ibid.

246 Weiming Tu, 'Implications of the Rise of Confucian East Asia' in Shmuel N Eisenstadt (ed), *Multiple Modernities* (MIT Press 2019) 195; Laurence Jacobs et al, 'Confucian Roots in China: A Force for Today's Business' (1995) 33 *Management Decision* 29, 31–32.

247 翟华强 [Zhai Huaqing],《基于师承与家传的古代中医药学人才培养模式》[Ancient Chinese Medicine Talent Cultivation Model Based on Inheritance and Family Tradition] (2014) 20(1) 中国中医基础医学杂志 *Chinese Journal of Basic Medicine in Traditional Chinese Medicine* 37, 38–39.

248 Wei Shi, 'Cultural Perplexity in Intellectual Property: Is Stealing a Book an Elegant Offense?' (2006) 32(1) *North Carolina Journal of International Law* 1, 26.

249 Jonathan R Sills, 'China's Copyright Crisis: How the Internet Has Exacerbated China's Already Weak Copyright Laws and How the U.S. Can Combat the Pirating of Its Software' *Connecticut Intellectual Property Notes* (Web Page, 2006) < http://www.law.uconn.edu/journals/ cipn/ browse.html > .

250 R Keith Sawyer, 'The Western Cultural Model of Creativity: Its Influence on Intellectual Property Law' (2011) 86(5) *Notre Dame Law Review* 2029, 2042.

251 Marci Hamilton, 'The TRIPS Agreement: Imperialistic, Outdated, and Overprotective' (1996) *Vand. J. Transnat'l L* 613, 617.

252 J Sundaram, 'Brazil's Implementation of TRIPS Flexibilities: Ambitious Missions, Early Implementation, and the Plans for Reform' (2014) 23(2) *Information & Communications Technology Law* 81, 81.

at odds with China's deeply held Confucian cultural values and incompatible with the TMK arising from Chinese cultural and social underpinnings that value connection with the ancestors and collective identities.

One of the most prevailing justifications for IP rights, at least in Western countries and international treaties, is utilitarian theory.[253] This theory is rooted in the economic understanding of rights which provides that the grant of IP protection could create the commercial incentives of exclusive rights for a limited duration to inventors and help encourage them to create further inventions.[254] If IP rights were recognised, many inventors could recoup their investment in the creation of the invention which would have greater utility for, and financial effects on, the whole society.[255]

This traditional theoretical justification for IP rights cannot, however, justify the IP protection of TMK in China. This is because cultural tendencies have caused the Chinese to refrain from commercialising and commodifying TMK. These cultural tendencies primarily arise from the influence and impacts of Confucian values which stress social commitments rather than individual material gain.[256] To be precise, Chinese traditional culture has a strong disdain for commercial activity and repudiates the creation and use of knowledge (including TMK) for profit-making.[257] Confucius even expressed a negative attitude towards profit-making in his Analects: 'The noble-minded man comprehends righteousness while the inferior man comprehends profit'.[258] Therefore, it is no surprise that merchants who trade in commodities for personal profits are traditionally considered to be at the bottom

---

[253] Ishan Parashar, 'Philosophical Foundation of Intellectual Property' (2020) 21 *Supremo Amicus* 484, 484–490; Michael A Kanning, 'A Philosophical Analysis of Intellectual Property: In Defense of Instrumentalism' (2008) 8 *Scholars Commons University of Florida* 1, 16; Neil Wilkof, 'Theories of Intellectual Property: Is It Worth the Effort?' (2014) 9(4) *Journal of Intellectual Property Law & Practice* 257, 257.

[254] Jeanne C Fromer, 'Expressive Incentives in Intellectual Property' (2012) 98(8) *Virginia Law Review* 1745, 1751.

[255] Estelle Derclaye and Tim Taylor, 'Happy IP: Replacing the Law and Economics Justification for Intellectual Property Rights with a Well-being Approach' (2015) 37(4) *European Intellectual Property Review* 197, 199; Lisa P Ramsey, 'Intellectual Property Rights in Advertising' (2006) 12(2) *Michigan Telecommunications and Technology Law Review* 189, 190.

[256] 李立峰 [Li Lifeng],《儒家价值观与当代中国核心价值文化》[Confucian Values and Contemporary China's Core Value Culture] (2015) 1 江苏省社会主义学院学报*Journal of Jiangsu Provincial Academy of Socialism* 72, 72–74. Charles R Stone, 'What Plagiarism Was Not: Some Preliminary Observations on Classical Chinese Attitudes toward What the West Calls Intellectual Property' (2008) 92(1) *Marquette Law Review* 199, 223; Andrew Evans, 'Taming the Counterfeit Dragon: The WTO, TRIPS and Chinese Amendments to Intellectual Property Laws' (2003) 31(3) *Georgia Journal of International and Comparative Law* 587, 589.

[257] 喻小航 [Yu Xiaohang],《重农与轻商的中西比较》[Comparison of the Emphasis on Agriculture and the Neglect of Commerce in China and the West] (2012) 38(4) 西南大学学报*Journal of Southwest University* 162,169. Peter K Yu, 'Intellectual Property and Confucianism' in Irene Calboli and Srividhya Ragavan (eds), *Diversity in Intellectual Property: Identities, Interests, and Intersections* (Cambridge University Press, 2015) 1, 5.

[258] Liangnian Jin, *Annotated Translation of the Analects of Confucius* (Shanghai Ancient Books Publishing House 2004) 36.

of the social status scale in China.[259] Arguably, these deep-rooted cultural values and traditions are incomprehensible for those who regard the attaining of personal rewards and benefits as a critical prerequisite to the development of IP rights. Western IP rights, which focus on promoting the commodification and marketisation of knowledge, are in conflict with TMK that has evolved from China's unique cultural and historical context.

Recognising and protecting innovation and creativity (through IP rights) can largely be seen as a contemporary phenomenon, and as a result of urbanisation and industrialisation.[260] In the West, it is common to dismiss knowledge embedded in tradition as being unrelated to the contemporary situation by portraying it as traditional knowledge.[261] Such knowledge, obtained through tradition or anecdote, may be assumed to play no role in shaping and impacting the contemporary world. More significantly, as noted by Ford, Westerners tend to believe that real progress can only be achieved by breaking free of the ancient restraints of tradition.[262] Whether this is true or not, there are significant differences between Western and Chinese attitudes towards the knowledge gained through tradition. In Chinese civilisation, knowledge (including TMK) was traditionally considered as coming from divine inspiration or the past. Alford emphasised the enduring impact of 'the power of the past and its consequences for possession of the fruits of intellectual endeavour' throughout Chinese history.[263] 'The power of the past' can be reflected in Confucius' famous dictums, as quoted by Alford, such as 'I transmit rather than create; I believe in and love the ancients' and 'only through encountering the past would unique insight be provided into the essence of one's own character'.[264] These dictums have often been quoted to justify the appropriation of pre-existing knowledge with no need for consent or consultation. In China, knowledge is usually considered as something to be recovered or mimicked rather than discovered or created, thus disparaging the role of creativity and innovation in the advancement of society. The Chinese literary anecdote 'Luoyang zhi gui' (洛阳纸贵) reflects these cultural beliefs and values. The story is that in ancient China, as pre-existing knowledge or works became popular

259 Shaohua Hu, 'Confucianism and Contemporary Chinese Politics' (2007) 35(1) *Politics & Policy* 136, 145.

260 Joan Trullén and Rafael Boix, 'Knowledge Externalities and Networks of Cities in the Creative Metropolis' in Philip Cooke and Luciana Lazzeretti (eds), *Knowledge Externalities and Networks of Cities in the Creative Metropolis* (Edward Elgar Publishing, 2007) 211; Luciana Lazzeretti et al, 'Do Creative Industries Cluster? Mapping Creative Local Production Systems in Italy and Spain' (2008)15(5) *Industry and Innovation* 549, 549–567.

261 Christopher Ford, The Mind of Empire: China's History and Modern Foreign Relations (University Press of Kentucky, 2010) 11.

262 Ibid.

263 Alford (n 30) 25.

264 Ibid.

and famous, scholars competed to copy them so as to express admiration and appreciation for the author. This practice rendered paper as expensive as jade.[265] Consequently, the traditional knowledge (including TMK) embedded in Chinese cultural and ethical traditions stands in stark contrast to Western legal regimes, where laws have been created for the protection of novel knowledge rather than keeping the age-old knowledge alive.

3.4.2 Clashes Between IP Rights and TMK as a Community, Intellectual, and Cultural Asset

What sets TMK apart is not just its grounding in longstanding traditions while simultaneously maintaining dynamism and evolution, but also the community-oriented context of its transmission and creation process. This distinguishes it from other forms of general knowledge.[266] At the community level in China, ethnic and local communities, with their diverse cultures, represent a critical component of Chinese civilisation.[267] The ethnic and local medical knowledge of these communities forms an integral part of their culture, as it is created and shared within a communal setting.[268] This knowledge incorporates spiritual and cultural aspects that reflect the identity of the respective community.[269] Each ethnic group has developed its unique own system of medical knowledge systems, such as Tibetan medicine, Uyghur medicine, or Mongolian medicine, and these represent special branches of China's TMK.[270]

265 'Paper becomes expensive in Luoyang—Good Writings Make People Copy Them' *Chinlingo* (Web Page, 2016) < https://www.chinlingo.com/articles/800106/ > .

266 Margo A Bagley, 'The Fallacy of Defensive Protection for Traditional Knowledge' (2019) 58 *Washburn Law Journal* 323, 328; Antony Taubman and Matthias Leister, 'Analysis of Different Areas of Indigenous Resources: Traditional Knowledge' in Silke von Lewinski (ed), *Indigenous heritage and intellectual property: Genetic Resources, Traditional Knowledge and Folklore* (Kluwer Lae International, 2008) 59, 59–60.

267 Xiaotong Fei, 'The Formation and Development of the Chinese Nation with Multi-ethnic Groups' (2017) 1(1) *International Journal of Anthropology and Ethnology* 1, 1–31; 张甜甜[Zhang Tiantian],《论少数民族文化在中华文化形成与发展中的贡献》[On the Contributions of Ethnic Minority Cultures to the Formation and Development of Chinese Culture] (2018) 38(1) 中南民族大学学报 *Journal of South-Central University for Nationalities* 74, 74–78.

268 景威栋 [Jiang Weidong], 《中华民族共同体意识视域下民族医药文化遗产保护探析》[Analysis on the Protection of Ethnic Medical Cultural Heritage in the Perspective of Chinese National Community Consciousness] (2023) 19(1) 亚太传统医药 *Asian Pacific Traditional Medicine* 4, 5.

269 苗丽 [Miao Li],《浅议云南民族医药文化的内涵及其特征》[A Brief Discussion on the Connotation and Characteristics of Yunnan Ethnic Medicine Culture] (2015) 24(16) 中国民族民间医药 *Chinese Journal of Ethnomedicine and Ethnopharmacy* 1, 1–2; 滕建卓 [Teng Jianzhuo],《论土家族医药学的整体观》[Discussion on the Holistic Characters of Tujia Medicine] (2007) 2中国民族民间医药 *Chinese Journal of Ethnomedicine and Ethnopharmacy* 6, 6–7.

270 王居 [Wang Ju],《中国民族医药的保护与发展》[Protection and Development of Chinese Ethnic Medicine] [2006] 中国民族 *China's Ethnic Group* 52, 53.

In recent years, there has been a growing trend of commercial exploitation of TMK and customary herbal remedies from local communities. To be specific, since China's Tenth Five-Year Plan (2001–2005) was instituted, it has approved and funded many bioprospecting and ethnobotany research projects.[271] On this basis, until 2016, around 154 pharmaceutical corporations were established (mainly in the territorial area of ethnic and local communities) for the development and production of what has become known as 'ethnomedicine'. This resulted in a total of seven categories and 906 varieties of ethnomedical products.[272] These products were based on many nationally reputable TMK and customary herbal remedies from local communities, such as Yunnan Baiyao (Yi medicine), Mengwang (Mongolian ethnomedicine), and Chee zheng (Tibetan medicine).[273] These situations and others have resulted in increased awareness and efforts to protect the TMK of ethnic and local communities, which has extended to the realm of IP law.[274] Nevertheless, the TMK of these communities presents many challenges for IP protection and the existing Western system of IP rights may be ill-suited for the protection of TMK in China.

The TMK of the local communities is not only concerned with skills and technology for the treatment and prevention of diseases. It also represents the integration of physical, mental, social, and spiritual practices as holistic exercises to maintain health and prevent disease in local peoples.[275] For instance, as noted by Samuel, TMK used in the Tibetan community is typically viewed as a 'holistic health system grounded in a deeply spiritual approach to life'.[276] Unlike the Western biomedical tradition that usually disregards the religious, moral, and spiritual dimensions of illness and healing, Tibetan medical practitioners hope to treat the patient 'as a whole person, within a wider spiritual framework, rather than as a mere body with a physical problem'.[277] Nevertheless, when the amorphous character of the TMK of such communities is managed, the TMK has frequently been transformed and deployed in a narrow sense to comply with IP models. In this process, the communities are usually discounted as a 'generalised collective origin of tradition'.[278]

In order to adapt TMK to fit within the existing IP laws, such as the patent system, TMK is often limited to pharmaceutical and scientific discursive aspects.[279]

---

[271] Zhaoyun Zhu et al, 'Innovative Development Path of Ehnomedicines: An Overview of Ethnomedicines in China' (2016) 10 *Front Med* 166, 173.

[272] Ibid.

[273] Ibid 174.

[274] Fuming Lee, 'The Legal Protection of Tibetan Intangible Cultural Heritage in China: From the Perspective of Tibetan Customary Law and Intellectual Property Law' (2019) 7(1) *China Legal Science* 91, 106–107; Mohammd Ushur, 'On Restructuring the Chinese IPR Regime from Ethnic Group Prospect' (2015) 10(4) *Frontiers of Law in China* 732, 742–744.

[275] 苗丽 [Miao Li] (n 262) 1–2.

[276] GB Samuel, 'Tibetan Medicine and Biomedicine: Epistemological Conflicts, Practical Solutions' (2006) 2(1) *Asian Medicine* 72, 73.

[277] Ibid.

[278] Jane E Anderson, *Law, Knowledge, Culture: The Production of Indigenous Knowledge in Intellectual Property Law* (Edward Elgar Publishing, 2009) 181.

[279] Ibid.

This approach neglects the religious, cultural, and spiritual dimensions that are also integral to traditional medical practices.[280] By focusing primarily on the scientific components, the broader context and holistic nature of TMK may be overlooked, potentially diminishing the richness and complexity of these practices.

IP protection of Chinese TMK often separates its technical components from the cultural and traditional values that establish its collective ownership. This separation can be detrimental to the ethnic and local communities, as it undermines the cultural and spiritual aspects of their TMK. These communities' TMK is dynamic, evolving, and usually transmitted orally through generations, possessing specific cultural traits not intended for general public access.[281]

Nevertheless, in modern IP laws, novel knowledge must be disclosed in some way to the public,[282] and 'fixed' in a tangible form such as in a written transcription in order for rights to be acknowledged.[283] For instance, the 'enablement' and 'sufficiency of disclosure' requirements introduced in patent law demand that a novel idea is disclosed in sufficient detail and in material forms so that the person skilled in the art could implement that idea.[284]

As Scassa and Taylor have argued, the main reason for these requirements is that they could serve an evidentiary purpose to facilitate the assessment of possible infringements, in order to enforce and protect the rights vested in the inventor.[285] However, the oral nature of ethnic and local communities' TMK conflicts with these enablement and fixation requirements. As a result, the current IP system may not adequately accommodate the unique characteristics of TMK, potentially hindering its protection and preservation for future generations.

More significantly, according to Bell and Schier, IP laws recognise those who have committed the act of disclosure and fixation as the IP rights holders, rather than those who have actually created the knowledge.[286] Therefore, while IP rights may be suitable for the societies in which written transcriptions and documentation are privileged, they are not suitable for the ethnic and local communities of China where knowledge has been developed and preserved through an oral tradition.

The traditional development of TMK in China's ethnic and local communities poses a significant challenge to the compatibility and applicability of IP rights. TMK

---

[280] Ibid.

[281] 鄢良 [Yan Liang],《世界传统医药体系及其在当代的法律地位形态》[World Traditional Medical Systems and Their Contemporary Legal Status and Forms] (2013) 9(5) 亚太传统医药 *Asia–Pacific Traditional Medicine* 7, 7–9.

[282] Jeanne C Fromer, 'Patent Disclosure' (2009) 94 *Iowa Law Review* 539, 541.

[283] Johanna Gibson, *Community Resources: Intellectual Property, International Trade and Protection of Traditional Knowledge* (Routledge, 2005) 115.

[284] MS Gupta, 'Sufficiency of Disclosure in Patent Specification' (2009) 14 *Journal of Intellectual Property Rights* 307, 307–316; Jason Rantanen, 'The Doctrinal Structure of Patent Law's Enablement Requirement' (2016) 69(6) *Vanderbilt Law Review* 1679, 1679–1714.

[285] T Scassa and F Taylor, 'Legal and Ethical Issues around Traditional Knowledge in Polar Data Infrastructures' (2017) 16(3) *Data Science Journal* 1, 7.

[286] C Bell and C Schier 'Control of Information Originating from Aboriginal Communities: Legal and Ethical Contexts' (2011) 35 *Études Inuit Studies* 36, 36–49.

in these communities typically develops through a collective and incremental trial-and-error process to address local needs for living and treatment.[287] As Madhavan suggested, TMK innovation in some Chinese ethnic communities involves cumulative improvements to existing medical knowledge or discovering new processes for knowledge production and transmission, primarily developed through empirical experience and reinforced by trial and error.[288]

This communal and incremental nature of TMK presents a major obstacle to the Western IP system's compatibility. IP frameworks, particularly patent law, often emphasise substantial and notable technical advances rather than gradual and incremental innovation.[289] Furthermore, IP law generally requires the identification of the actual inventor or inventors behind the innovation when applying for IP rights.[290]

The gradual and incremental development of Chinese TMK, however, makes it challenging or even impossible to pinpoint the actual inventors within the community. Consequently, applying standard IP protection requirements, such as originality, entitlement, inventive steps, and novelty, to TMK could exclude the majority of its innovation from IP protection. As Gibson argued, the criteria of novelty and non-obviousness are 'unsuitable and artificial when applied to traditional knowledge in order to assimilate it within IP law'.[291]

The Chinese patent law (2020) aligns with the core tenets of Western IP systems by instituting finite protection durations. This approach exemplifies a crucial paradigm of Western capitalism—employing competition and temporary monopolies as drivers for constant innovation and evolution.[292] Under this framework, irrespective of the intrinsic value of the protected knowledge, the law safeguards invention patents for a period of up to 20 years, design patents for 15 years, and utility models for a duration

[287] 邓明峰 [Deng Mingfeng],《我国民族中医药传统知识专利保护研究》[Research on Patent Protection for TMK of China's Ethnic Groups] (2018) 12 贵州民族研究 *Guizhou Ethnic Studies* 96, 98; Geoffroy Fauchet, 'Dai Medicine: Preservation of and Changes in Ancient Healing Practices' (2006) 621 *Independent Study Project (ISP) Collection* 1, 5; Zhiyong Li et al, 'Policies and Problems of Modernizing Ethnomedicine in China: A Focus on the Yi and Dai Traditional Medicines of Yunnan Province' [2020] *Evidence-Based Complementary and Alternative Medicine* 1, 1; EJ Buenz, 'The Ethno-pharmacologic Contribution to Bioprospecting Natural Products' (2018) 58 *Annual Review of Pharmacology and Toxicology* 509, 509–530.

[288] Harilal Madhavan, 'Below the Radar Innovations and Emerging Property Right Approaches in Tibetan Medicine' (2017) 20 *The Journal of World Intellectual Property* 239, 252.

[289] Patent Law (n 175) art 22: 'Inventiveness means that, as compared with the technology existing before the date of filing, the invention has prominent substantive features and represents a notable progress'; Xuan Li and Weiwei Li, 'Inadequacy of Patent Regime on Traditional Medicinal Knowledge—A Diagnosis of 13-year Traditional Medicinal Knowledge Patent Experience in China' (2007) 10(2) *The Journal of World Intellectual Property* 125, 136–137.

[290] Deepa Varadarajan, 'A Trade Secret Approach to Protecting Traditional Knowledge' (2011) 36 *The Yale Journal of International Law* 371, 384.

[291] Gibson (n 276) 118.

[292] Mohammed Rafiquzzaman, 'The Optimal Patent Term under Uncertainty' (1987) 5 *International Journal of Industrial Organization* 233, 233.

of 10 years.[293] This model, while effective for most forms of intangible property, may fall short when applied to the realm of TMK.

For China's ethnic and local communities, TMK holds a pivotal and intricate role, extending beyond the temporal bounds associated with Western IP systems. Unlike these Western models, the importance of TMK to these communities transcends time: It is deeply woven into their identities and enduring cultures, and its significance is passed down through generations.[294] This fact highlights the inherent complexities and potential limitations of applying Western IP systems to Chinese TMK. Such systems, which typically endorse finite protections, may not sufficiently accommodate the unique, enduring nature of TMK in these communities, as it cannot be confined to fixed durations.

WIPO and its Intergovernmental Committee ('IGC') have been consistently engaged in efforts to establish a comprehensive agreement for the protection of traditional knowledge. The African Group within WIPO, proposed in 2009 that traditional knowledge should receive perpetual protection, a perspective that resonates with China's stance on the issue.[295] To China, traditional knowledge, especially TMK, extends beyond IP rights. Instead, it represents a crucial component of its cultural and historical identity that warrants perpetual preservation.

It is essential to understand that TMK in China, particularly within its diverse ethnic and local communities, is not merely a standalone set of medicinal practices. It is a knowledge system deeply ingrained within the social fabric of the communities.[296] This rich knowledge base encapsulates the cumulative wisdom that has been accrued over centuries.[297] Each aspect of TMK is a manifestation of experiences, observations, and insights handed down through countless generations, serving as a testament to the enduring and adaptive nature of these communities.[298] It is a living embodiment of cultural heritage, linking the past, present, and future in a continuous thread of shared knowledge and tradition.[299] Therefore, the preservation of TMK in China, especially that of its ethnic and local communities, represents more than just safeguarding a form of medical knowledge. It involves the maintenance of different

[293] Patent Law (n 175) art 42.

[294] 苗丽 [Miao Li],《浅议云南民族医药文化的内涵及其特征》[Brief Discussion on the Connotation and Characteristics of Yunnan Ethnic Medicine Culture] (2015) 24 (16) 中国民族民间医药 *Chinese Ethnic Folk Medicine* 1, 1.

[295] World Intellectual Property Organization, 'African Group Submission on Document WIPO/GRTKF/IC/13/9 14' WIPO Doc. WIPO/GRTKF/IC/14/9 (2009); World Intellectual Property Organization, 'The Protection of Traditional Knowledge, Draft Gap Analysis: Revision 28', WIPO Doc. WIPO/GRTKF/IC/13/5(b) Rev (2008).

[296] 苗丽 [Miao Li] (n 287) 1–2.

[297] 邓明峰 [Deng Mingfeng],《我国民族中医药传统知识专利保护研究》[Research on Patent Protection for TMK of China's Ethnic Groups] (2018) 12 贵州民族研究 *Guizhou Ethnic Studies* 96, 98.

[298] 鄢良 [Yan Liang],《世界传统医药体系及其在当代的法律地位形态》[World Traditional Medical Systems and Their Contemporary Legal Status and Forms] (2013) 9(5) 亚太传统医药 *Asia–Pacific Traditional Medicine* 7, 7–9.

[299] Ibid.

worldviews, rich cultural traditions, and historical lineages that have been cultivated and enriched over centuries necessitating perpetual protection, contrary to the finite periods of protection provided by IP systems.

China's cultural heritage, deeply rooted in communal knowledge sharing, presented a unique opportunity for the country to lead a distinctive path in the realm of IP, diverging from the prevailing Western-centric framework. This alternate path could have reflected the practices and values of China's ethnic and local communities, resonating with the communal traditions of Indigenous peoples and other societies in the Global South. Such an approach would have prioritised the sharing of knowledge for the public good, emphasising collective well-being over individualistic, commercial interests.

However, China's shift towards a Western-driven IP regime suggests a missed opportunity. This alignment with Western standards, characterised by a focus on individual ownership, novel disclosures, and rigid protection mechanisms, risks undermining the rich tapestry of TMK inherent in China's ethnic and local communities. This Western model, often insufficiently flexible to accommodate the oral, evolving, and communal nature of TMK, potentially jeopardises the cultural roots and interests of ethnic minority knowledge holders. This has vicarious consequences for Indigenous peoples and local communities in the Global South, as it sets a precedent that could influence global IP norms, potentially sidelining communal and collective knowledge systems.

In light of this, there's a critical need for China to reconsider its approach to IP, aiming for a framework that better aligns with the unique attributes of TMK. Such a framework would ideally offer perpetual protection, acknowledging the fluid and evolving character of TMK and its deep interconnection with the cultural heritage and identity of various communities. This approach would recognise the intrinsic value of TMK beyond its commercial utility, honouring its role in the fabric of community life and its significance in preserving cultural diversity.

A reimagined IP strategy in China should focus on the communal transmission and holistic nature of TMK. It should facilitate equitable sharing of benefits derived from TMK, ensuring that the communities that have nurtured this knowledge for generations are recognised and compensated fairly. This strategy would also involve a more inclusive policy-making process, actively engaging with the knowledge holders and ensuring their perspectives and needs are central to the formulation of IP laws and practices.

Moreover, China's approach could have set a precedent for a more inclusive global IP regime, one that respects and protects the knowledge systems of Indigenous peoples and local communities worldwide. By fostering an IP model that emphasises inclusivity, communal benefit, and cultural preservation, China could have contributed significantly to a more equitable and diverse global knowledge economy.

3.4.3 *The Barriers Imposed by the Western Requirements for IP Protection on TMK in China*

3.4.3.1 Evidentiary Obstacles

The rigorous evidentiary standards posed by the Western patent system represent a primary external obstacle for the TMK in China. A significant evidentiary barrier arises from the concept of prior art embedded in patent law, which refers to any documentation and materials published before a patent application.[300] In China, diverse forms of TMK are subjected to various levels of public exposure and dissemination.[301] Some TMK, such as Hani-Akha medicine, has been passed down through oral tradition within local communities for thousands of years and is mostly undocumented.[302] This poses challenges in using such undocumented knowledge as prior art according to the criteria required by most countries' patent regimes.

Moreover, when TMK has been documented, it is often recorded in secret terms that may be incomprehensible to patent examiners.[303] As a result, it fails to be recognised as prior art evidence to prevent third parties from patenting the same TMK. A typical example is the medical knowledge documented by the fifteenth-century Tibetan medical practitioner, Desi Sanggyé Gyatso, related to the healing of life-wind illnesses.[304] His medical texts contain 'secret' terms, making most of his manuscripts puzzling for those lacking the decrypting key.[305]

Considering the diverse nature of China's TMK, evidentiary challenges impede its protection through IP rights. These barriers arise when attempting to prove that a specific form of TMK satisfies the patentability requirements for a patent application or when asserting that a particular type of TMK qualifies as prior art evidence to defend against a third party's patent application.

[300] M Ruiz, 'The international Debate on Traditional Knowledge as Prior Art in the Patent System: Issues and Options for Developing Countries' (2006) *Centre for International Environmental Law* 1, 5.

[301] Tianbao Qin, 'Common Pools of Traditional Chinese Medical Knowledge in China' in Evanson Chege Kamau and Gerd Winter (eds), *Common Pools of Genetic Resources* (2013) 150, 150–164.

[302] Tsutomu Inamura, 'Traditional Knowledge and Chinese Traditional Medicine concerning ABS: Political Mistranslation by Chinese Government and Japanese Government' (17th Conference of the Science Council of Asia, 2017) 1, 2–6.

[303] 姚峥嵘[Yao Zhengrong],《中药老字号专有技术的法律特征及保护对策》[Legal Features and Protection Strategies for Exclusive Technologies of Traditional Chinese Medicine Time-honoured Brands] (2018) 38中国医院药学杂志 *Chin Hosp Pharm J* 1971, 1972.

[304] Tony Chui, '"Secret Medicine" in the Writings of Sanggyé Gyatso: the Encoded Esoteric Material of Therapeutics' in William A. McGrath (ed), *Knowledge and Context in Tibetan Medicine* (Brill Academic Publishers, 2019) 85, 85–110.

[305] Ibid.

3.4.3.2 Substantive Obstacles

TMK in China faces substantive obstacles under the existing patent system due to its vast diversity and unique characteristics. This is mainly because the patentability requirements in Chinese patent law do not recognise the wide variety and distinctions that exist in the development and use of TMK in China. Thus, this creates obstacles in providing a blanket solution for protecting all forms of TMK in China.

In modern Chinese patent law, a fundamental principle is that an innovation must be novel, meaning it is not anticipated by prior art immediately before the filing date of a patent application.[306] As one of the conditions for patentability, the novelty requirement serves as a substantive barrier for TMK holders seeking patent protection. This is due to the fact that a wide range of TMK practices in China are fixed through codification or recording, which is enough to negate novelty and, consequently, the patentability required for patenting TMK.[307] A prime example of this type of TMK in China is Chinese herbal medicine, specifically Han ethnic medicine (汉族中医),[308] which has been the most influential form of traditional medicine in the country.[309] It is usually documented in written form in renowned medical classics and has been widely circulated among the Chinese population.[310] As a result, it is challenging for such herbal medicine to meet the patentability criteria of novelty required by Chinese patent law.

Aside from the novelty requirement, another substantive barrier arises from the inventiveness threshold for patentability.[311] In the Chinese jurisdiction, an invention is considered to have inventiveness if, having regard to the State of the art, it is not 'obvious' to a person skilled in the art.[312] In assessing this lack of obviousness, differences must be first identified between the claimed invention and the closest prior

---

306 赵顺 [Zhao Shun],《中外专利审查中新颖性的判定比较研究》[A Comparative Study of Novelty Assessment in Chinese and Foreign Patent Examination] (2022) 24 河南科技 *Henan Science and Technology* 151, 151–154; Patent Law (n 175) art 22;《专利审查指南》[Chinese Patent Examination Guidelines] (People's Republic of China) National Intellectual Property Administration, Order No.391, 2020 (*Chinese Patent Examination Guidelines*) 153.

307 陈一孚[ChenYifu], 《中药发明的新颖性问题探究:兼论建立适合中药的新颖性审查规则》[Exploration of Novelty Issues in Traditional Chinese Medicine Inventions: Discussing the Establishment of Novelty Examination Rules Suitable for Traditional Chinese Medicine] (2013) 24 新疆社会科学 Xinjiang Social Sciences 151, 153.

308 Sijia Liu, 'New Law Sparks the Expectation over the Future of Traditional Chinese Medicine: Can TCM Law Effectively Promote the Development of TCM Industry in China?' (2018) 37(1) *Medicine and Law* 193, 202.

309 毕经正 [Bi Jingzheng],《现代中医概念的形成》[Formation of the Modern Concept of 'Traditional Chinese Medicine'] (2022) 37(2) 中华中医药杂志 *Chinese Journal of Traditional Chinese Medicine and Pharmacy* 975, 975–977.

310 Siyuan Pan et al, 'Traditional Medicines in the World: Where to Go Next?' (2014) *Evidence-Based Complementary and Alternative Medicine* 1, 2.

311 何隽 [He Juan],《中药领域发明的创造性判断》[Assessment of Inventiveness in Traditional Chinese Medicine Inventions] [2022)]人民司法 *People's Judiciary* 90, 90–93.

312 Ibid.

art.[313] However, this requirement poses a challenge when applying these inventiveness standards to TMK. This is because TMK in China often consists of a mix of a dozen or more herbs or ingredients.[314] Even a single herb or ingredient may contain hundreds of unknown compounds, making it exceedingly difficult to pinpoint the differences between the claimed innovation and the prior art.[315]

Furthermore, patent law requires that, after the differences are identified, the problem to be solved, the solution to the problem, and the advantageous effect, if any, of the claimed invention relative to the closest prior art, should be considered (the problem, solution, and effect test).[316] When applying these tests to China's TMK, the incremental characteristics of a substantial amount of TMK might preclude it from accessing patent protection. 'The problem, solution, and effect tests' adopted by the Chinese patent office suggest that inventiveness can be satisfied if and only if the claimed invention can address an unexpected and prominent solution to the problem, rather than an incremental or predictable solution.[317] On this basis, the threshold of inventiveness in Chinese patent law leaves no room for any TMK characterised as an incremental improvement on the existing knowledge that aims to meet the fundamental health needs of communities.

Another patentability criterion required by Chinese patent law provides that a claimed invention must be disclosed in sufficient detail to enable a person skilled in the art to understand and carry out the content of the invention.[318] Such disclosure requirements could present another insurmountable obstacle to patenting TMK in China. This is because some forms of TMK have a secret or sacred significance under the customary law of the respective ethnic and local communities.[319] Typical examples include the above-mentioned 'secret' medicine found across the writings of the Tibetan medical tradition, especially 'secret medicine' (*gsang sman*) in the text of *Sangs Rgyas Rgya Mtsho's Extended Commentary*.[320] The secret or sacred nature of such communities' TMK represents their cultural and spiritual values and is closely tied to their dignity and self-worth,[321] which inevitably makes them less likely to disclose sufficient information about their knowledge to meet the disclosure requirements of the Chinese patent law.

---

313 Xuan Li and Weiwei Li, 'Inadequacy of Patent Regime on Traditional Medicinal Knowledge—A Diagnosis of 13-year Traditional Medicinal Knowledge Patent Experience in China' (2007) 10 *The Journal of World Intellectual Property* 125, 136–137.

314 何隽 [He Juan] (n 304) 91–92.

315 Ibid.

316 《专利审查指南》 [Chinese Patent Examination Guidelines] (People's Republic of China) National Intellectual Property Administration, Order No 91, 2020 (*Chinese Patent Examination Guidelines*) 172.

317 Xuan Li and Weiwei Li (n 306) 142.

318 Patent Law (n 175) art 26.

319 Tianbao Qin (n 294) 151.

320 Chui (n 297) 85–110.

321 Ibid.

3.4.3.3 Administrative Obstacles

The patent system in China also poses administrative challenges that might prove to be daunting for the holders of TMK to overcome in order to obtain patents. Firstly, Article 26 of the Chinese patent law provides that the patent application must include the specific name and address of the applicant and the inventor. Identifying a specific inventor of Chinese TMK is typically challenging due to the fact that the 'ownership' of most types of TMK is not individualistic. Instead, it is traditionally vested in a collective entity such as a family group, clan group, or a broader community group.[322] It is therefore hard to prove that one member of the community is the first to invent the knowledge. More significantly, TMK in China is knowledge invented in an incremental fashion from generation to generation.[323] This incremental development adds more difficulties in identifying TMK creators in the community; thus, it fails to meet the administrative requirements under the law.

Secondly, the lack of financial aid and resources is another administrative obstacle in the process of patent application and litigation. The ethnic and local communities that hold TMK account for a disproportionate percentage of the poor.[324] According to Mackerras, 36.5% of the Chinese population suffering from absolute poverty come from the ethnic and local communities living in the western part of the State, even though China's ethnic and local communities only make up 8.5% of China's total population.[325] The communities holding TMK in China may thus not normally possess the appropriate financial resources to prepare and prosecute the patent applications.

Moreover, patent applications are often written in a complex manner, filled with scientific jargon, and typically required to be in Mandarin or another dominant language.[326] Given the prevalence of illiteracy and low educational attainment rates in China's local communities,[327] the complexity of patent applications creates significant administrative difficulties for these communities and holders of the TMK when seeking to acquire a patent. The language requirement further limits access for ethnic communities whose traditional knowledge may not be easily translatable into the mandated language.

---

322 Tianbao Qin (n 294) 151.

323 Li and Li (n 306) 142–145.

324 戴俊 [Dai Jun],《少数民族地区精准脱贫研究: 基于广西 DHYZ 自治县 QBN 乡的个案分析和现实思考》[Precision Poverty Alleviation Research in Minority Areas: A Case Study and Realistic Reflection Based on QBN Village in DHYZ Autonomous County, Guangxi] (2015) 1 广西民族研究*Guangxi Ethnic Studies* 149, 151–155; Samuel L Myers et al, 'Ethnic Minorities, Race, and Inequality in China: A New Perspective on Racial Dynamics' (2013) 40(3) *Rev Black Polit Econ* 231, 237.

325 Colin Mackerras, China's Ethnic Minorities and Globalisation (Routledge, 2003) 66.

326 Sumathi Subbiah, 'Reaping What They Sow: the Basmati Rice Controversy and Strategies for Protecting Traditional Knowledge' (2004) 27(2) *Boston College International and Comparative Law Review* 529, 546.

327 Lanrong Xue and Tianjian Shi, 'Inequality in Chinese Education' (2001) 10(26) *Journal of Contemporary China* 107, 115.

3.4.4 Protection of TMK via Tiered or Differentiated Approaches

The analysis above demonstrates that using an IP system to protect TMK in the Chinese context is a challenging task. To address this, this section proposes a tiered approach to the protection, utilisation, and dissemination of Chinese TMK. The approach takes into consideration the various forms of TMK subjected to different levels of public exposure, depending on how these forms are traditionally held, shared, and diffused.

Acknowledging that the concept of a tiered approach to TMK protection is not new and has been discussed in various forums, including the World Intellectual Property Organization-Intergovernmental Committee (WIPO-IGC),[328] this section proposes a customised application of this approach tailored to Chinese TMK. This proposal is informed by the insights of earlier discussions and studies, notably Chidi Oguamanam's work on the evolution of the tiered approach concept.[329]

This innovative approach aims to classify diverse types of TMK and identify corresponding rights, serving two purposes: to assess the types of rights applicable to specific forms of TMK in China; and to determine how IP structures can be reconciled with this mechanism.

In this proposed system, the level of protection corresponds to different tiers and their extent of diffusion. The tiers can be categorised based on how the TMK is held: secret TMK; TMK closely held by ethnic and local communities; TMK collectively held by national communities; and widely diffused TMK that becomes part of the global stock of knowledge. Consequently, different kinds of TMK are subject to varying levels of rights and obligations according to their degree of diffusion. Stronger exclusive rights should be granted for secret TMK, while TMK closely held by ethnic and local communities, and TMK collectively held by national communities, receive comparatively weaker rights. TMK that has been widely diffused as part of the global stock of knowledge typically attracts the weakest rights claim, as it is situated at the periphery of the public domain.

This tiered approach can be customised in accordance with specific TMK, the State, and communities' customary protocols, as well as the unique national contexts and circumstances. It aims to provide appropriate levels of protection to various forms of TMK and its knowledge holders while offering users certainty and legal confidence, and increasing their awareness of, and sensitivity to, different rules concerning different forms of TMK.

In conclusion, the tiered approach proposed for the protection of TMK in China takes into account the country's historical, cultural, and contextual nuances. By

---

328 World Intellectual Property Organization (WIPO), '*The Protection of Traditional Knowledge: Draft Articles*', WIPO Doc, WIPO/GRTKF/IC/27/REF/FACILITATORS DOCUMENT REV. 2 (2014) at paras 97, 226.

329 Chidi Oguamanam, 'Tiered or Differentiated Approach to Traditional Knowledge and Traditional Cultural Expressions: The Evolution of a Concept' (CIGI Papers No. 185, Centre for International Governance Innovation, August 2018).

tailoring protection levels to various forms of TMK and their degrees of diffusion, this approach addresses the difficulties in applying a conventional IP system to TMK in China. It also ensures that the rights and obligations are appropriately assigned to different TMK holders.

This approach directly addresses the research question of this book by offering a customised solution that accommodates the unique characteristics of China's TMK, bridging the gap between traditional knowledge and IP structures. By implementing this tiered system, China can better protect its rich cultural heritage and the interests of TMK holders, while fostering innovation and encouraging the respectful use of TMK. Future research should focus on providing more detailed guidance on the specific duties of different stakeholders associated with the various tiers, ensuring that the system remains adaptable to the evolving landscape of TMK in China.

3.5 Conclusion

This chapter has revealed the complex interplay between the TMK in China, IP rights, and the unique cultural and historical context that shapes their relationship. The significance of this book's problem lies in the necessity of prioritising the comprehensive protection, responsible utilisation, and suitable dissemination of Chinese TMK. This chapter emphasised that recognising the fine balance between these aspects is crucial, especially within the context of China's distinctive cultural heritage and legal framework, which are intricately woven into its historical tapestry.

By examining the historical roots of IP rights, the legal history of imperial China, and the time-honoured cultural traditions of China, this chapter highlighted the deep-seated conflict between the Western concept of IP rights and the characteristics of TMK that represent China's unique cultural identity, traditional values, and perspectives. This book sought to address the complexities and challenges in governing TMK within the Chinese context, and to answer the question of how to adapt the Western-style IP framework to effectively protect TMK and promote its appropriate use while taking into account China's unique cultural and historical background.

The historical analysis conducted in this chapter is crucial for understanding the present-day challenges in regulating Chinese TMK. It has provided valuable insights into the deeply rooted conflicts between the Western concept of IP rights and China's prevailing social norms and cultural values. These conflicts have been fuelled by several factors, including China's cultural traditions that prioritise collective over individual rights, which hinder the adoption of a Western-style IP system in the country. This chapter also explored China's involvement with international IP agreements, revealing that those external pressures from Western nations have driven the country's progress in meeting its international IP obligations, but that these pressures alone cannot overcome the historical and sociocultural challenges that impede China's acceptance of Western-style IP laws.

This chapter demonstrated the fundamental incompatibility between the Western-style IP system and China's TMK system, stemming from their distinct cultural and philosophical foundations. Through an in-depth examination of the historical and cultural aspects of TMK, it posited that a nuanced understanding of these perspectives can pave the way for identifying alternative IP protection methods better suited to the Chinese context. It proposed that by embracing a historically and culturally sensitive approach to IP, it is possible to bridge the gap between the two systems.

To address the unique challenges in regulating TMK within the IP system, particularly patent law, this chapter proposed a comprehensive tiered approach that offers a more flexible and tailored solution. This approach takes into account the specific national contexts and circumstances of China, as well as the customary protocols of State and local communities. Although it necessitates further research for broad acceptance and effectiveness verification, this strategy holds significant potential. It stands as a meaningful advancement in addressing this complex issue, aiming to create a harmonious balance between safeguarding TMK, respecting knowledge holders' rights, and facilitating the responsible use of TMK within China's unique context.

This chapter concluded by emphasising the need for continued exploration of more nuanced and culturally sensitive approaches to IP protection that honour the intrinsic value of TMK, prioritise the interests and perspectives of TMK holders, and promote the appropriate use and dissemination of TMK within its sociocultural contexts. By fostering a greater understanding of the historical and cultural perspectives underlying TMK, it is possible to bridge the gap between the Western IP systems and the Chinese TMK system, ultimately encouraging innovation, collaboration, and the preservation of invaluable traditional knowledge for generations to come.

References

《专利审查指南》[Chinese Patent Examination Guidelines] (People's Republic of China) National Intellectual Property Administration, Order No 391, 2020 (*Chinese Patent Examination Guidelines*) 153.

《专利审查指南》[Chinese Patent Examination Guidelines] (People's Republic of China) National Intellectual Property Administration, Order No 91, 2020 (*Chinese Patent Examination Guidelines*) 172.

《中华人民共和国专利法 (1992年修订)》[The Patent Law of the People's Republic of China (Revised in 1992)] (People's Republic of China) National People's Congress Standing Committee, Order No 3, September 1992.

《中华人民共和国专利法 (2000年修订)》[The Patent Law of the People's Republic of China (Revised in 2000)] (People's Republic of China) National People's Congress Standing Committee, Order No 36, August 2000.

《中华人民共和国专利法 (2008年修订)》[The Patent Law of the People's Republic of China (Revised in 2008)] (People's Republic of China) National People's Congress Standing Committee, Order No 8, December 2008.

《中华人民共和国专利法 (2020年修订)》[The Patent Law of the People's Republic of China (Revised in 2020)] (People's Republic of China) National People's Congress Standing Committee, Order No 55, August 2020.

《中华人民共和国专利法》[Patent Law of the People's Republic of China] (People's Republic of China) National People's Congress Standing Committee, Order No 11, March 1984.

《发明奖励条例》 [Regulation on Invention Reward] (People's Republic of China) State Council, November 1963.

A Eckstein, J K Fairbank and LS Yang, 'Economic Change in Early Modern China: An Analytical Framework' (1960) 9 *Economic Development and Cultural Change* 1, 1.

Agreement on Trade-Related Aspects of Intellectual Property Rights, April. 15, 1994, Marrakesh Agreement Establishing the World Trade Organization, Annex 1C, Legal Instrument Result of The Uruguay Round, 33 I.L.M. 81 (1994) (*'the TRIPS Agreement'*).

Akalemwa Ngenda, 'The Nature of the International Intellectual Property System: Universal Norms and Values or Western Chauvinism?' (2005) 14(1) *Information & Communications Technology Law* 59, 59–79.

Alexander Hendrie, 'China's commitment to Intellectual Property Rights More Rhetoric than Reality' *Property Rights Alliance* (Web Page, October 2014)

A Pang-White, 'Caring in Confucian Philosophy (2011) 6 *Philosophy Compass* 374, 377–378.

Alison Duxbury, 'The Role of WIPO as An International Organization' in Sam Ricketson (ed), *Research Handbook on the World Intellectual Property Organization: The First 50 Years and Beyond* (Edward Elgar Publishing, 2020) 1, 26.

Andrew Evans, 'Taming the Counterfeit Dragon: The WTO, TRIPS and Chinese Amendments to Intellectual Property Laws' (2003) 31(3) *Georgia Journal of International and Comparative Law* 587, 589.

Andrew TW Hung, 'Atomism, Communitarianism, and Confucian Familism' (2022) 15 *Fudan Journal of the Humanities and Social Sciences* 259, 268.

Anne D Birdwhistell, 'Medicine and History as Theoretical Tools in a Confucian Pragmatism' (1995) 45(1) *Philosophy East and Wes*t 1, 1–28.

Antony Taubman and Matthias Leister, 'Analysis of Different Areas of Indigenous Resources: Traditional Knowledge' in Silke von Lewinski (ed), *Indigenous Heritage and Intellectual Property: Genetic Resources, Traditional Knowledge and Folklore* (Kluwer Lae International, 2008) 59, 59–60.

Anwen Zheng, 'Ren (仁), the Benevolent Thought of Traditional Chinese Medicine' (2019) 2(3) *Chinese Medicine and Culture* 137, 138.

Article 27.3(B), Relationship between the TRIPS Agreement and the CBD, and Protection of Traditional Knowledge and Folklore WTO Doc IP/C/W/469 (13 March 2006) (Communication from the United States).

Berne Convention for the Protection of Literary and Artistic Works, signed 9 September 1886, 828 UNTS 221 (entered into force 5 December 1887).

Brad Sherman et al, *The Making of Modern Intellectual Property Law: The British Experience, 1760–1911* (Cambridge University Press 1999) 161–162.

Bryan Mercurio, 'TRIPS-Plus Provisions in FTAs: Recent Trends' in Lorand Bartels and Federico Ortino' (eds), *Regional Trade Agreement and the WTO Legal System* (Oxford University Press, 2006) 215.

C Bell and C Schier 'Control of Information Originating from Aboriginal Communities: Legal and Ethical Contexts' (2011) 35 *Études Inuit Studies* 36, 36–49.

C Saez, 'WIPO Talks on Future of TK, Genetic Resources, Folklore Intensify', IP Watch (Web Page, 2013) <https://www.ip-watch.org/2013/07/24/wipo-talks-on-future-of-tk-genetic-resources-folklore-intensify/> accessed 9 October 2022/

Cai Jingfeng, 'Integration of Traditional Chinese Medicine with Western Medicine—Right or Wrong?' (1988) 27(5) *Social Science & Medicine* 521, 521–529.

Catherine Seville, 'The Emergence and Development of Intellectual Property Law in Western Europe' in Rochelle Dreyfuss and Justine Pila (eds), *The Oxford Handbook of Intellectual Property Law* (Oxford University Press, 2017) 171, 192.

Certain Decision of the Seventh Conference of the Parties to the Convention on Biological Diversity, WIPO/GRTKF/IC/6/13 (15 March 2004).

Chan Hok-Lam, *Control of Publication in China, Past and Present* (The Chinese University of Hong Kong Press, 1983) 5.

Charles R Stone, 'What Plagiarism Was Not: Some Preliminary Observations on Classical Chinese Attitudes toward What the West Calls Intellectual Property' (2008) 92(1) *Marquette Law Review* 199, 223;

Cheng Wenting, 'The Protection of Genetic Resources in Chinese Patent Law' (2021) 43(4) *European Intellectual Property Review* 248, 251.

Chidi Oguamanam, International Law and Indigenous Knowledge: Intellectual Property, Plant Biodiversity, and Traditional Medicine (University of Toronto Press 2006) 158.

Chidi Oguamanam, 'Patents and Traditional Medicine: Digital Capture, Creative Legal Interventions and the Dialectics of Knowledge Transformation' (2008) 15 *Indiana Journal of Global Legal Studies* 505, 505–511.

Chidi Oguamanam, 'Tiered or Differentiated Approach to Traditional Knowledge and Traditional Cultural Expressions: The Evolution of a Concept' (CIGI Papers No. 185, Centre for International Governance Innovation, August 2018).

China—Certain Measures Concerning the Protection of Intellectual Property Rights, WTO Doc WT/DS542/1, IP/D/38 (26 March 2018) (Request for Consultation by the United States).

Chinese State Council, 'Several Opinions on Supporting and Promoting the Development of TMK' (2009).

Chris Noonan and Victoria Plekhanova, 'Digital Services Tax: Lessons from the Section 301 Investigation' (2021) *The British Tax Review* 83, 83–84.

Christopher Ford, The Mind of Empire: China's History and Modern Foreign Relations (University Press of Kentucky, 2010) 11.

Christopher May, 'The Hypocrisy of Forgetfulness: The Contemporary Significance of Early Innovations in Intellectual Property' (2007) 14 *Review of International Political Economy* 1, 1–25.

Christopher May, 'The Venetian Moment: New Technologies, Legal Innovation and the Institutional Origins of Intellectual Property' (2002) 20 *Prometheus* 159, 167.

CN Ciocoiu, 'Considerations about Intellectual Property Rights, Innovation and Economic Growth in the Digital Economy' (2011) 14(2) *Economia. Seria Management* 310, 310.

Colin Mackerras, China's Ethnic Minorities and Globalisation (Routledge, 2003) 66.

D Gareth Jones and Jing-Bao Nie, 'Does Confucianism Allow for Body Donation?' (2018) 11(5) *Anatomical Sciences Education* 525, 527.

D Greasley and L Oxley, 'Patenting, Intellectual Property Rights and Sectoral Outputs in Industrial Revolution Britain, 1780–1851' (2007) 139 (2) *Journal of Econometrics* 340, 340–352.

Dan Wielsch, 'Private Governance of Knowledge: Societally-crafted Intellectual Properties Regimes' (2013) 20(2) *Indian Journal of Global Legal Studies* 907, 911–912.

Daniel F Robinson, Pedro Roffe and Ahmed Abdel Latif, 'Introduction' in Ahmed Abdel-Latif, Pedro Roffe and Daniel F. Robinson (eds), *Protecting Traditional Knowledge: The WIPO Intergovernmental Committee on Intellectual Property and Genetic Resources, Traditional Knowledge and Folklore* (Routledge, 2017) 1, 3–8.

Deepa Varadarajan, 'A Trade Secret Approach to Protecting Traditional Knowledge' (2011) 36 *The Yale Journal of International Law* 371, 384.

Dexin Tian 'The USTR Special 301 Reports: An Analysis of the US Hegemonic Pressure upon the Organizational Change in China's IPR Regime' (2008) 1 *Chinese Journal of Communication* 224, 225.

Doha WTO Ministerial 2001: Ministerial Declaration, WTO Doc WT/MIN (01)/DEC/1 (14 Nov 2001).

Donald P Harris, 'The Honeymoon Is Over: the U.S.-China WTO Intellectual Property Complaint' in Perry Keller (ed), *Law and the Market Economy in China* (2011) 96, 97.

Draft Modalities for TRIPS Related Issues, WTO Doc TN/C/W/52 (19 July 2008); Daniel Robinson and Margraet Raven, 'Identifying and Preventing Biopiracy in Australia: Patent Landscapes and Legal Geographies for Plants with Indigenous Australian Uses' (2017) 48(3) *Australian Geographer* 311, 325.

Draft Report Prepared by the Secretariat, WIPO Doc WIPO/GRTKF/IC/23/8 (26 April 2013) <https://www.wipo.int/meetings/en/doc_details.jsp?doc_id=241343> accessed 15 October 2022.

EJ Buenz, 'The Ethno-pharmacologic Contribution to Bioprospecting Natural Products' (2018) 58 *Annual Review of Pharmacology and Toxicology* 509, 509–530.

Estelle Derclaye and Tim Taylor, 'Happy IP: Replacing the Law and Economics Justification for Intellectual Property Rights with a Well-being Approach' (2015) 37(4) *European Intellectual Property Review* 197, 199.

Frank D Prager, 'A History of Intellectual Property from 1545 to 1787' (1944) 26 (11) *Journal of the Patent Office Society* 711, 711–749.

Fuming Lee, 'The Legal Protection of Tibetan Intangible Cultural Heritage in China: From the Perspective of Tibetan Customary Law and Intellectual Property Law' (2019) 7(1) *China Legal Science* 91, 106–107.

GB Samuel, 'Tibetan Medicine and Biomedicine: Epistemological Conflicts, Practical Solutions' (2006) 2(1) *Asian Medicine* 72, 73.

Geoffrey T Willard, 'An Examination of China's Emerging Intellectual Property Regime: Historical Underpinnings, the Current System and Prospect for the Future' (1995) 6(2) *International and Comparative Law Review* 411, 421.

Geoffroy Fauchet, 'Dai Medicine: Preservation of and Changes in Ancient Healing Practices' (2006) 621 *Independent Study Project (ISP) Collection* 1, 5.

Guangzhou Hu and Gary H Jefferson, 'A Great Wall of Patents: What Is behind China's Recent Patent Explosion?' (2006) 90(1) *Journal of Development Economics* 1, 7.

Harilal Madhavan, 'Below the Radar Innovations and Emerging Property Right Approaches in Tibetan Medicine' (2017) 20 *The Journal of World Intellectual Property* 239, 252.

Henrietta Harrison, 'The Qianlong Emperor's Letter to George III and the Early-twentieth-century Origins of Ideas about Traditional China's Foreign Relations' (2017) 122(3) *American Journal of Ophthalmology* 680, 680.

黄渊琦 [Huang Yuanqi],《古代社会阻碍知识产权发展的负面因素》[Negative Factors that Hindered the Development of Intellectual Property Rights in Ancient Societies] (2016) 4,大东方 *Great East* 1, 1–3.

Institute of Information on Traditional Chinese Medicine (IITCM), 'TCM Database System' (Website, 2014) <http://www.cintcm.ac.cn> accessed 14 October 2022.

Ishan Parashar, 'Philosophical Foundation of Intellectual Property' (2020) 21 *Supremo Amicus* 484, 484–490.

J Sundaram, 'Brazil's Implementation of TRIPS Flexibilities: Ambitious Missions, Early Implementation, and the Plans for Reform' (2014) 23(2) *Information & Communications Technology Law* 81, 81.

J Weeks, 'Chinese TCM Renaissance and the Global Movement for Integrative Health and Medicine' (2017) 23(2) *The Journal of Alternative and Complementary Medicine* 79, 79–81.

Jane Anderson, 'Indigenous/ Traditional Knowledge Intellectual Property' (Issue Paper, 2010)<https://web.law.duke.edu/cspd/pdf/ip_Indigenous-traditionalknowledge.pdf> accessed 11 October 2022.

Jane E Anderson, *Law, Knowledge, Culture: The Production of Indigenous Knowledge in Intellectual Property Law* (Edward Elgar Publishing, 2009) 181.

Janiece Marshall, 'Current Developments in the People's Republic of China: Has China Changed?' (1988) 1(2) *Global Business & Development Law Journal* 505, 521.

Jay Erstling, 'Using Patent to Protect Traditional Knowledge' (2009) 15 *Texas Wesleyan Law Review* 295, 315.

Jean-Frederic Morin, 'Multilateralizing TRIPs-Plus Agreements: Is the US Strategy a Failure?' (2009) 12(3) *The Journal of World Intellectual Property* 175, 176.

Jeanne C Fromer, 'Expressive Incentives in Intellectual Property' (2012) 98(8) *Virginia Law Review* 1745, 1751.

Jeanne C Fromer, 'Patent Disclosure' (2009) 94 *Iowa Law Review* 539, 541.

Jia Li, 'Intangible Assets are More Valuable than the Tangible: Study on the Innovation and Development of the Traditional Time-Honored Brands' (Conference Paper, International Conference on Social Science and Education Research, 2018) 242, 242.

Jian Xu, 'The History of China's Patent System and Legislation', *China IP Blog* (Web Page, 2016) <https://niuyie.com/the-history-of-chinas-patent-system-and-legislation/>

JK Fairbank, 'Tributary Trade and China's Relations with the West' (1942) 1(2) *The Far Eastern Quarterly* 129, 133.

Joan Trullén and Rafael Boix, 'Knowledge Externalities and Networks of Cities in the Creative Metropolis' in Philip Cooke and Luciana Lazzeretti (eds), *Knowledge Externalities and Networks of Cities in the Creative Metropolis* (Edward Elgar Publishing, 2007) 211.

Joanna H Raven et al, 'Traditional Beliefs and Practices in the Postpartum Period in Fujian province, China: A Qualitative Study' (2007) 7 *BMC Pregnancy and Childbirth* 1, 2.

Joanna Kostylo, 'From Gunpowder to Print: The Common Origins of Copyright and Patent' in Ronan Deazley et al (eds), *Privilege and Property Essays on the History of Copyright* (Cambridge OpenBook Publishers 2010) 1.

Johanna Gibson, *Community Resources: Intellectual Property, International Trade and Protection of Traditional Knowledge* (Routledge, 2005) 115.

Jonathan R Sills, 'China's Copyright Crisis: How the Internet Has Exacerbated China's Already Weak Copyright Laws and How the U.S. Can Combat the Pirating of Its Software' *Connecticut Intellectual Property Notes* (Web Page, 2006) <http://www.law.uconn.edu/journals/ cipn/browse.html>.

Jyh-An Lee, 'Shifting IP Battlegrounds in the U.S.–China Trade War' (2020) 43(2) *Columbia Journal of Law & the Arts* 147, 147–194.

Shao and 'What May Validate Intellectual Property in a Traditional Chinese Mind? Examining the U.S.-China IP Disputes through An Historical Inquiry', , 2006. Ke Shao, 'What May Validate Intellectual Property in a Traditional Chinese Mind? Examining the U.S.-China IP Disputes through An Historical Inquiry' (2006) 1 *Journal of Information, Law & Technology* 1, 1.

Kwon Ivo, 'Confucianism Perspectives on Abortion' in Alireza Bagheri (ed), *Abortion: Global Positions and Practices, Religious and Legal Perspectives* (Springer, 2021) 217, 225.

Konstantina K Athanasakou, 'China IPR Enforcement: Hard as Steel or Soft as TOFU—Bringing the Question to the WTO under TRIPS (2007) 39(1) *Georgetown Journal of International Law* 217, 222–223.

Krishna Ravi Srinivas, 'Traditional knowledge and Intellectual Property Rights: A Note on Issues, Some Solutions and Some Suggestions' (2008) 3 *Asian Journal of WTO & International Health Law and Policy* 81, 82.

Kristie Thomas, Assessing Intellectual Property Compliance in Contemporary China (2017) 85, 89.

Krzysztof J Pelc, 'Constraining Coercion? Legitimacy and Its Role in U.S. Trade Policy, 1975–2000' (2010) 64 *International Organization* 65, 66.

Lanrong Xue and Tianjian Shi, 'Inequality in Chinese Education' (2001) 10(26) *Journal of Contemporary China* 107, 113.

Laurence Jacobs et al, 'Confucian Roots in China: A Force for Today's Business' (1995) 33 *Management Decision* 29, 31–32.

Laurence P Harrington, 'Recent Amendments to China's Patent Law: The Emperor's New Clothes '(1994) 17(2) *Boston College International and Comparative Law Review* 337, 337–370.

Laurence R Heifer, 'Regime shifting: The TRIPs Agreement and New Dynamics of International Intellectual Property Lawmaking' (2004) 29(1) *Yale Journal of International Law* 1, 2.

Laurence R Helfer, 'Regime Shifting in the International Intellectual Property System' (2009) 7(1) *Perspectives on Politics* 39, 39.

Li, Chenyang, 'Confucian Perspectives on Science and Technology', *Ethics, Science, Technology, and Engineering: An International Resource* (2013) 1, 1–7.

Liangnian Jin, *Annotated Translation of the Analects of Confucius* (Shanghai Ancient Books Publishing House 2004) 36.

Liguo Zhang and Niklas Bruun, 'Legal Transplantation of Intellectual Property Rights in China: Resistance, Adaptation and Reconciliation' (2017) 48 *International Review of Intellectual Property and Competition Law* 4, 12–14.

Linyi Zheng and Xinying Hu, 'Inventing the Barbarians: The Changing Contexts of Yi in the Late Qing Dynasty' (2022) 12(4) *Psychology Research* 183, 186–188.

Lisa Forman et al, 'Addressing Legal and Political Barriers to Global Pharmaceutical Access: Options for Remedying the Impact of the Agreement on Trade-Related Aspects of Intellectual Property Rights (TRIPS) and the Imposition of TRIPS-plus Standards' (2008) 3 *Health Economics, Policy and Law* 229, 244.

Lisa P Ramsey, 'Intellectual Property Rights in Advertising' (2006) 12(2) *Michigan Telecommunications and Technology Law Review* 189, 190.

Liwei Wang, 'Chinese Traditions Inimical to the Patent Law, The Symposium: Doing Business in China' (1993) 14(1) *Northwestern Journal of International Law & Business* 15, 40.

Liwei Wang, 'The Chinese Traditions Inimical to the Patent Law' (1993) 14 *Northwestern Journal of International Law & Business* 15, 15–65.

Linhua Zhang, 'China's Traditional Cultural Values and National Identity' (Carnegie Endowment for International Peace, 2013) <https://carnegieendowment.org/2013/11/21/china-s-traditional-cultural-values-and-national-identity-pub-53613> accessed 9 October 2022.

Louis S Sorell, 'A Comparative Analysis of Selected Aspects of Patent Law in China and the United States' (2002) 11(2) *Washington International Law Journal* 319, 321.

Luciana Lazzeretti et al, 'Do Creative Industries Cluster? Mapping Creative Local Production Systems in Italy and Spain' (2008) 15(5) *Industry and Innovation* 549, 549–567.

M Ruiz, 'The International Debate on Traditional Knowledge as Prior Art in the Patent System: Issues and Options for Developing Countries' (2006) *Centre for International Environmental Law* 1, 5.

MA Bagley, 'The Fallacy of Defensive Protection for Traditional Knowledge' (2019) 58(2) *Washburn L.J.* 323, 323–327.

Marci Hamilton, 'The TRIPS Agreement: Imperialistic, Outdated, and Overprotective' (1996) *Vand. J. Transnat'l L* 613, 617.

Margo A Bagley, 'The Fallacy of Defensive Protection for Traditional Knowledge' (2019) 58 *Washburn Law Journal* 323, 328.

Margo Bagley, 'Of Disclosure Straws and IP System Camels' in Daniel F Robinson et al (eds), Protecting Traditional Knowledge: The WIPO Intergovernmental Committee on Intellectual Property and Genetic Resources, Traditional Knowledge and Folklore (Routledge, 2017) 86, 89.

Martin A Girsberg, 'Transparency Measures under Patent Law regarding Genetic Resources and Traditional Knowledge:Disclosure of Source and Evidence of Prior Informed Consent and Benefit-sharing' (2004) 7(4) *The Journal of World Intellectual Property* 451, 454–456.

Martin Brink and Theo van Hintum, 'Practical Consequences of Digital Sequence Information (DSI) Definitions and Access and Benefit-Sharing Scenarios from a Plant Genebank's Perspective' (2021) *Plants, People, Planet*, 23, 23–32.

Matthew E Silverman, 'The Case for Flexible Intellectual Property Protections in the Trans-pacific Partnership' (2014) 27(2) *Journal of Law and Health* 215,219.

Matthew Kennedy, 'When Will the Protocol Amending the TRIPS Agreement Enter into Force?' (2010) 13(2) *Journal of International Economic Law* 1, 11.

Margrit Seckelmann, 'From the Paris Convention (1883) to the TRIPS Agreement (1994): The History of the International Patent Agreements as a History of Propertisation?' (2011) 21 *Jahrbuch der Juristischen Zeitgeschichte* 46, 54.

Memorandum of Understanding Between the Government of the People's Republic of China and the Government of the United States of America on the Protection of Intellectual Property (MOU) (China—United States) (Jan 17, 1992) 34 ILM 676.

Michael A Kanning, 'A Philosophical Analysis of Intellectual Property: In Defense of Instrumentalism' (2008) 8 *Scholars Commons University of Florida* 1, 16.

Mohammd Ushur, 'On Restructuring the Chinese IPR Regime from Ethnic Group Prospect' (2015) 10(4) *Frontiers of Law in China* 732, 742–744.

Mohammed Rafiquzzaman, 'The Optimal Patent Term under Uncertainty' (1987) 5 *International Journal of Industrial Organization* 233, 233.

MS Ansari, 'Evaluation of Role of Traditional Knowledge Digital Library and Traditional Chinese Medicine Database in Preservation of Traditional Medicinal Knowledge' (2016) 36 (2) *Journal of Library & Information Technology* 73, 73–78.

MS Gupta, 'Sufficiency of Disclosure in Patent Specification' (2009) 14 *Journal of Intellectual Property Rights* 307, 307–316; Jason Rantanen, 'The Doctrinal Structure of Patent Law's Enablement Requirement' (2016) 69(6) *Vanderbilt Law Review* 1679, 1679–1714.

Naomi A Bass, 'Implications of the TRIPs Agreement for Developing Countries: Pharmaceutical Patent Laws in Brazil and South Africa in the 21st Century' (2002) 34(1) *The George Washington International Law Review* 191, 195.

Natalie Stoianoff, 'The Development of Intellectual Property Law in China' in Chan Lai-Ha et al (eds), *China At 60: Global-Local Interactions* (World Scientific, 2011) 183, 183–184.

Neil Wilkof, 'Theories of Intellectual Property: Is It Worth the Effort?' (2014) 9(4) *Journal of Intellectual Property Law & Practice* 257, 257.

Niklas Bruun and Liguo Zhang, 'Legal Transplant of Intellectual Property Rights in China: Norm Taker or Norm Maker?' in Niklas Bruun et al (eds), *Governance of Intellectual Property Rights in China and Europe* (Edward Elgar Publishing 2016) 43, 48.

Ning Xin and Jingjing Liao, 'History of the Silk Road' (2018) 36 *Chronos* 167, 189–190.

Office of the United States Trade Representative, '2018 Special 301 Report' (Web Page, 2018) <https://ustr.gov/sites/default/files/files/Press/Reports/2018%20Special%20301.pdf> accessed 14 October 2022.

Pablo Miguez, 'Intellectual Property and the Forced Commodification of Knowledge' (2018) 29 *Universitas, Revista de Ciencias Sociales* 42, 44.

Pamela O Long, 'Invention, Authorship, Intellectual Property, and the Origin of Patents: Notes Toward a Conceptual History' (1991) 32 *Technology and Culture* 846, 869.

'Paper becomes expensive in Luoyang—Good Writings Make People Copy Them' *Chinlingo* (Web Page, 2016) <https://www.chinlingo.com/articles/800106/>.

Paris Convention for the Protection of Industrial Property, opened for signature 14 July 1967, 828 UNTS 305 (entered into force 26 April 1970).

Peter K Yu, 'Two Decades of TRIPS in China' (Research Paper, Texas A&M University School of Law Legal Studies Research, 2021) 1, 1–12.

Paul Kuruk, *Traditional Knowledge, Genetic Resources, Customary Law and Intellectual Property* (Edward Elgar Publishing, 2020) 33.

Peter K Yu, 'Intellectual Property and Confucianism' in Irene Calboli and Srividhya Ragavan (eds), *Diversity in Intellectual Property: Identities, Interests, and Intersections* (Cambridge University Press 2015) 1.

Paul Salmon, 'Cooperation Between the World Intellectual Property Organization (WIPO) and the World Trade Organization (WTO)' (2003) 17 *Journal of Civil Rights and Economic Development* 429, 433.

PE Campbell and M Pecht, 'The Emperor's New Clothes: Intellectual Property Protections in China' (2012) 7(1) *Journal of Business and Technology Law* 69, 73.

Peter Drahos, 'Bits and Bips: Bilateralism in Intellectual Property' (2001) 4(6) *The Journal of World Intellectual Property* 791, 791.

Peter Feng, *Intellectual Property in China* (Sweet & Maxwell Asia, 2003) 3.

Peter K Yu, 'Intellectual Property and Confucianism' in Irene Calboli and Srividhya Ragavan (eds), *Diversity in Intellectual Property: Identities, Interests, and Intersections* (Cambridge University Press, 2015) 1, 5.

Peter K Yu, 'Intellectual Property, Economic Development, and the China Puzzle' in Daniel J. Gervais (ed), *Intellectual Property, Trade and Development: Strategies to Optimize Economic Development in a TRIPS Plus Era* (Oxford University Press 2007) 173, 185–188.

Phil Chan, 'China's Approaches to International Law since the Opium War' (2014) 27 *Leiden Journal of International Law* 859, 860–861.

R Keith Sawyer, 'The Western Cultural Model of Creativity: Its Influence on Intellectual Property Law' (2011) 86(5) *Notre Dame Law Review* 2029, 2042.

R Lakshmi Poorna and Others, 'Preservation and Protection of Traditional Knowledge—Diverse Documentation Initiatives across the Globe' (2014) 107(8) Current Science 1240, 1242–1244.

Renzong Qiu, 'Confucianism, Traditional and Contemporary China' in Robert M Veatch (ed), *Cross-cultural Perspectives in Medical Ethics* (Jones & Bartlett Publishers, 2000) 292, 292–308.

Report Adopted by the Committee, WIPO Doc WTO Doc IP/C/W/469 (13 March 2006).

Reto M Hilty et al, 'Traditional Knowledge, Databases and Prior Art –Options for an Effective Defensive Use of TK against Undue Patent Granting' in Irini Stamatoudi (ed), *Research Handbook on Intellectual Property and Cultural Heritage* (Elgaronline, 2022) 132, 132–133.

Robert B Frost Jr, 'Intellectual Property Rights Disputes in the 1990s between the People's Republic of China and the United States' (1995) 4(1) *Tulane Journal of International and Comparative Law* 119, 134.

Ruth Lopert and Deborah Gleeson, 'The High Price of "Free" Trade: U.S. Trade Agreements and Access to Medicines' (2013) 41(1) *Journal of Law, Medicine & Ethics* 199, 199.

S Bannerman, 'The World Intellectual Property Organization and the Sustainable Development Agenda' (2020) 122 *Futures* 3, 6.

S Suzuki, 'China's Perceptions of International Society in the Nineteenth Century: Learning More about Power Politics?' (2004) 28 *Asian Perspectives* 115, 132.

Samuel L Myers et al, 'Ethnic Minorities, Race, and Inequality in China: A New Perspective on Racial Dynamics' (2013) 40(3) *Rev Black Polit Econ* 231, 237.

Sanqiang Qu, 'A Dilemma for Feudal China: To Launch a Copyright Scheme in the Late 19th Century' (2010) 5(3) *Frontiers of Law in China* 319, 328–329.

Scott J Palmer, 'An Identity Crisis: Regime Legitimacy and the Politics of Intellectual Property Rights in China' (2001) 8(2) *Indiana Journal of Global Legal Studies* 449, 449.

Servaas Storm, 'Why the West Grew Rich and the Rest did not, or How the Present Shapes Our Views of the Past' (2013) 44(5) *Development and Change* 1181, 1194.

Setsuo Miyazawa, 'Legal Transplants in Contemporary Asia: Foreword' (2021) 8(2) *Asian Journal of Law and Society* 348, 349.

Shao Ke, 'What May Validate Intellectual Property in the Traditional Chinese Mind? Examining the US-China IP Disputes through an Historical Inquiry' [2006] *Journal of Information, Law & Technology* 1, 3.

Shaohua Hu, 'Confucianism and Contemporary Chinese Politics' (2007) 35(1) *Politics & Policy* 136, 145.

Shi Wei, 'Cultural Perplexity in Intellectual Property: Is Stealing a Book an Elegant Offense?' (2006) 32(1) *North Carolina Journal of International Law* 1, 26.

Shoukang Guo, 'Some Remarks on the Third Revision Draft of the Chinese Patent Law' in Martin J Adelman et al (eds), *Patents and Technological Progress in a Globalized World* (Springer Berlin 2009) 713, 716–717.

Sijia Liu, 'New Law Sparks the Expectation over the Future of Traditional Chinese Medicine: Can TCM Law Effectively Promote the Development of TCM Industry in China?' (2018) 37(1) *Medicine and Law* 193, 202.

Simiao Sun, 'Prescriptions for Emergency Worth a Thousand Pieces of Gold (in Chinese)' in Chinese Medical Association (ed), *A Hundred Must Read Chinese Medicine Classics (in Chinese)* (Hua Xia Press 2008) 9–11.

Siyuan Pan et al, 'Traditional Medicines in the World: Where to Go Next?' (2014) *Evidence-Based Complementary and Alternative Medicine* 1, 2.

Stefan Szymanski and Tommaso Valletti, 'Parallel Trade Price Discrimination, Investment and Price Caps' (2005) 20(44) *Economic Policy* 705, 714.

Stephanie Peatman, 'Moving toward Uniform International Trademark Protection: How Amending the TRIPS Agreement will Make Parallel Importing of Gray Goods Less Gray' (2014) 20(2) *Southwestern Journal of International Law* 445, 458.

Sumathi Subbiah, 'Reaping What They Sow: the Basmati Rice Controversy and Strategies for Protecting Traditional Knowledge' (2004) 27(2) *Boston College International and Comparative Law Review* 529, 546.

Sunny Chang, 'Combating Trademark Squatting in China: New Developments in Chinese Trademark Law and Suggestions for the Future' (2014) 34(2) *Northwestern Journal of International Law & Business* 337, 342.

T Scassa and F Taylor, 'Legal and Ethical Issues around Traditional Knowledge in Polar Data Infrastructures' (2017) 16(3) *Data Science Journal* 1, 7.

Taking Forward the Review of Article 27.3(b) of the TRIPS Agreement WTO Doc IP/C/W/404 (26 June 2003) (Joint Communication from the African Group).

The European Patent Office ('EPO') and The Ministry of Commerce ('MOFCOM'), *Third Revision of China's Patent Law: Legal Texts and Documents on the Drafting Process 2006–2008* (EU-China IPR2, 2009)1, 5.

The Protection of Traditional Cultural Expressions: Draft Gap Analysis, WIPO Doc WIPO/GRTKF/IC/13/4(b) (26 March 2008); *The Protection of Traditional Cultural Expressions: Updated Draft Gap Analysis*, WIPO Doc WIPO/GRTKF/IC/37/6 (20 July 2018).

Thomas A Haag, 'TRIPS since Doha: How Far will the WTO Go toward Modifying the Terms for Compulsory Licensing' (2002) 84 (12) *Journal of the Patent and Trademark Office Society* 945, 947–981.

Thomas Kristie, 'The Fight against Piracy: Working within the Administrative Enforcement System in China' in Hailing Shan, Johan Erauw and Paul Torremans (eds), *Intellectual property and TRIPS compliance in China* (2007) 85, 85–106.

Tianbao Qin, 'Common Pools of Traditional Chinese Medical Knowledge in China' in Gerd Winter and Evanson Chege Kamau (eds), *Common Pools of Genetic Resources : Equity and Innovation in International Biodiversity Law* (2013) 150, 150–164.

Tianbao Qin, 'Common Pools of Traditional Chinese Medical Knowledge in China' in Evanson Chege Kamau and Gerd Winter (eds), *Common Pools of Genetic Resources* (2013) 150, 150–164.

Tony Chui, '"Secret Medicine" in the Writings of Sanggyé Gyatso: the Encoded Esoteric Material of Therapeutics' in William A. McGrath (ed), *Knowledge and Context in Tibetan Medicine* (Brill Academic Publishers, 2019) 85, 85–110.

'Trade Agreement', *Office of United States Trade Representative* (Web Page) <https://ustr.gov/trade-agreements>.

Tsutomu Inamura, 'Traditional Knowledge and Chinese Traditional Medicine concerning ABS: Political Mistranslation by Chinese Government and Japanese Government' (17th Conference of the Science Council of Asia, 2017) 1, 2–6.

Van Dongen, 'Confucianism, Community, Capitalism' in Tze-ki Hon and Kristin Stapleton (eds), *Confucianism for the Contemporary World: Global Order, Political Plurality, and Social Action* (SUNY Press, 2017) 19, 29.

Veronic Weinstein and Dennis Fernandez, 'Recent Development in China's Intellectual Property Laws' (2004) 3(1) *Chinese Journal of International Law* 227, 232.

Wang Heng, 'How to Assess Regional Trade Agreements? Deep FTAs v. China's Trade Agreements' (2021) 54 *International Lawyer* 1, 9–10.

Wang Juan, 'National Language Movement—An Indispensable Perspective of Literary Revolution' (2018) 17(2) *Studies in Literature and Language* 114, 115.

Wei Shi, 'Cultural Perplexity in Intellectual Property: Is Stealing a Book an Elegant Offense?' (2006) 32(1) *North Carolina Journal of International Law* 1, 26.

Weiming Tu, 'Implications of the Rise of Confucian East Asia in Shmuel N Eisenstadt (ed), *Multiple Modernities* (MIT Press 2019) 195.

White House, 'How China's Economic Aggression Threatens the Technologies and Intellectual Property of the United States and the World', *White House Office of Trade and Manufacturing Policy* (Web Page, June 2018) https://www.whitehouse.gov/wp-content/uploads/2018/06/FINAL-China-Technology-Report-6.18.18-PDF

William E Beaumont, 'The New Patent Law of the People's Republic of China (PRC): Evidence of a Second Chinese "Renaissance"?' (1988) 39 *IDEA* 1, 50.

William P Alford, To Steal a Book Is an Elegant Offense: Intellectual Property Law in Chinese Civilization (Stanford University Press, 1995) 9–29.

WIPO Treaty on Intellectual Property, Genetic Resources and Associated Traditional Knowledge, Diplomatic Conference to Conclude an International Legal Instrument Relating to Intellectual Property, Genetic Resources and Traditional Knowledge Associated with Genetic Resources, WIPO Doc GRATK/DC/7 (adopted 24 May 2024).

World Intellectual Property Organization (WIPO), *'The Protection of Traditional Knowledge: Draft Articles'*, WIPO Doc, WIPO/GRTKF/IC/27/REF/FACILITATORS DOCUMENT REV. 2 (2014) at paras 97, 226.

World Intellectual Property Organization (WIPO), *The Protection of Traditional Knowledge: Updated Draft Gap Analysis*, WIPO/GRTKF/IC/37/6 (20 July 2018).

World Intellectual Property Organization (WIPO), *The Protection of Traditional Knowledge*, WIPO/GRTKF/IC/40 (19 June 2019); World Intellectual Property Organization (WIPO), *The Protection of Traditional Cultural Expression,* WIPO/GRTKF/IC/40 (19 June 2019).

World Intellectual Property Organization, 'African Group Submission on Document WIPO/GRTKF/IC/13/9 14' WIPO Doc. WIPO/GRTKF/IC/14/9 (2009); World Intellectual Property Organization, 'The Protection of Traditional Knowledge, Draft Gap Analysis: Revision 28', WIPO Doc. WIPO/GRTKF/IC/13/5(b) Rev (2008).

Xi Yuhua, 'Shu: Naxi Nature Goddess Archetype' (2002) 6(3) *Gender, Technology and Development* 409, 414–422.

Xiangyu Hu, 'Drawing the Line Between the Civil and the Criminal: A Study of Civil Cases Handled by the Board of Punishment in Qing China' (2014) 40(1) *Modem China* 74, 75.

Xiaotong Fei, 'The Formation and Development of the Chinese Nation with Multi-ethnic Groups' (2017) 1(1) *International Journal of Anthropology and Ethnology* 1, 1–31.

Xiulan Zuo, 'Transnational Curriculum Inquiry' (2007) 4(1) *Journal of the International Association for the Advancement of Curriculum Studies* 80, 84.

Xuan Li and Weiwei Li, 'Inadequacy of Patent Regime on Traditional Medicinal Knowledge—A Diagnosis of 13-year Traditional Medicinal Knowledge Patent Experience in China' (2007) 10(2) *The Journal of World Intellectual Property* 125, 136–137.

Xuan Li and Weiwei Li, 'Inadequacy of Patent Regime on Traditional Medicinal Knowledge—A Diagnosis of 13-year Traditional Medicinal Knowledge Patent Experience in China' (2007) 10 *The Journal of World Intellectual Property* 125, 136–137.

Ye Dehui, *Quiet Talks among the Bookstacks* (Shanghai Classics Publishing House 1957) 143.

Yang Xue, 'The Confucianization of Law and the Lenient Punishments in China' (2015) 10(1) *International Journal of Criminal Justice Sciences* 32, 35.

Yanhuai Liu and Yanling Sun, 'China Traditional Chinese Medicine (TCM) Patent Database' (2004) 26(1) *World Patent Information* 91, 91–96.

YC Chen, 'Chinese Values, Health and Nursing' (2001) 36 *Journal of Advanced Nursing* 270, 270–275.

Yuet-Wah Cheung et al, 'Missionary doctors vs Chinese patients: Credibility of Missionary Health Care in Early Twentieth Century China' (1985) 21 *Social Science & Medicine* 309, 310–312.

Zewei Yang, 'Western International Law and China's Confucianism in the 19th century: Collision and Integration' (2011) 13 *Journal of the History of International Law* 285, 287–294.

Zhaoyun Zhu et al, 'Innovative Development Path of Ehnomedicines: An Overview of Ethnomedicines in China' (2016) 10 *Front Med* 166, 173.

Zhiyong Li et al, 'Policies and Problems of Modernizing Ethnomedicine in China: A Focus on the Yi and Dai Traditional Medicines of Yunnan Province' [2020] *Evidence-Based Complementary and Alternative Medicine* 1, 1.

伯雨鸿 [Bo Yuhong],《我国专利法第四次修正之评析》[An Analysis of the Fourth Amendment to China's Patent Law] (2021) 3 电子知识产权 Electronic Intellectual Property 39, 41–42.

何俗非 [He Sufei],《中医药传统知识保护现状与思考》(2019) 21(6) [Current Situation and Considerations on the Protection of Traditional Chinese Medicine Knowledge] 世界科学技术 *World Science and Technology* 1147, 1149.

何隽 [He Juan],《中药领域发明的创造性判断》[Assessment of Inventiveness in Traditional Chinese Medicine Inventions] [2022)] 人民司法 *People's Judiciary* 90, 90–93.

冯念华 [Feng Nianhua],《盗版对宋代版权保护现象的影响》[The Impact of Piracy on Copyright Protection in the Song Dynasty] (2006) 3 (133) 图书馆工作与研究*Library Work and Research* 63, 64–65.

凌金铸 [Ling Jinzhu],《中美知识产权关系的发生、发展与影响》[The Emergence, Development, and Impact of Sino-American Intellectual Property Relations] (2007) 14(5) 当代中国史研究 *Contemporary China History Studies* 108, 108–115.

刘钢 [Liu Gang],《对中国古代有无知识产权制度争议的思考》[A Reflection on the Controversy over the Existence of Intellectual Property Rights System in Ancient China] (2011) 24(6), 十堰职业技术学院学报 *Journal of Shiyan Technical Institute,* 36, 36–37.

吴立坤 钟赣生 [Wu Likun] and [Zhong Gansheng],《近代时期西方药学传入后对中药学发展的影响》(2009)9(4) [The Impact of the Introduction of Western Pharmacology on the Development of Traditional Chinese Medicine during the Modern Dra] (2009) 9(4) 中药与临床 *Pharmacy and Clinics of Chinese Materia Medica* 235, 235.

喻小航 [Yu Xiaohang],《重农与轻商的中西比较》[Comparison of the Emphasis on Agriculture and the Neglect of Commerce in China and the West] (2012) 38(4) 西南大学学报*Journal of Southwest University* 162, 169.

夏辰旭 [Xia Chenxu],《中国知识产权法律制度的历史发展与变革》[The Historical Development and Transformation of China's Intellectual Property Legal System] [2022] 法制视点 *The Rule of Law Perspectives* 128, 128–129

姚峥嵘[Yao Zhengrong],《中药老字号专有技术的法律特征及保护对策》[Legal Features and Protection Strategies for Exclusive Technologies of Traditional Chinese Medicine Time-honoured Brands] (2018) 38中国医院药学杂志 *Chin Hosp Pharm J* 1971, 1972.

孙丽伟 [Sun Liwei] (n 82) 1034; Natalie P Stoianoff, 'The Influence of the WTO over China's Intellectual Property Regime' (2012) 34 (1) *Sydney Law Review* 65, 69.

孙丽伟 [Sun Liwei],《新中国专利制度的历史回顾和现实思考》[Review of the History of China's Patent System and Practical Considerations] [2016] 科技与法律 *Journal of Science, Technology and Law* 1032, 1033.

孙相娜 [Sun Xiangna],《儒家仁爱思想与中医药文化》[Confucian Benevolence Thought and Traditional Chinese Medicine Culture] (2015) 1 林区教学 *Teaching of Forestry Region* 63, 63–64.

孙羽[Sun Yu],《我国知识产权法落后的文化原因》[The Cultural Reasons behind the Backwardness of Intellectual Property Laws in China] [2018] 法制博览 *Legality Vision* , 99, 99.

屈威,鲁楠 [Qu Wei] and [Lu Nan],《从专利法修改看中国知识产权制度的发展》[Examining the Development of China's Intellectual Property System through Patent Law Revisions] (2022) 1 法制博览 *Legal System Panorama* 4, 4–6.

崔立红 [Cui Lihong],《先秦儒家文化与知识产权法律》[Pre-Qin Confucian Culture and Intellectual Property Law] (2002) 15(1) 烟台大学学报 *Journal of Yantai University* 26, 26–31.

张甜甜[Zhang Tiantian],《论少数民族文化在中华文化形成与发展中的贡献》[On the Contributions of Ethnic Minority Cultures to the Formation and Development of Chinese Culture] (2018) 38(1) 中南民族大学学报 *Journal of South-Central University for Nationalities* 74, 74–78.

戴俊 [Dai Jun],《少数民族地区精准脱贫研究: 基于广西 DHYZ 自治县 QBN 乡的个案分析和现实思考》[Precision Poverty Alleviation Research in Minority Areas: A Case Study and

Realistic Reflection Based on QBN Village in DHYZ Autonomous County, Guangxi] (2015) 1 广西民族研究*Guangxi Ethnic Studies* 149, 151–155.

景威栋 [Jiang Weidong],《中华民族共同体意识视域下民族医药文化遗产保护探析》[Analysis on the Protection of Ethnic Medical Cultural Heritage in the Perspective of Chinese National Community Consciousness] (2023) 19(1) 亚太传统医药 *Asian Pacific Traditional Medicine* 4, 5.

曲三强 [Qu Sanqiang],《被动立法的百年轮回:谈中国知识产权保护的发展历程》[A Century of Passive Legislation: Discussing the Development of Intellectual Property Protection in China] (1999) 2 中外法学*Peking University Law Journal* 119, 120.

曹晟旻 [Cao Shengmin],《中西方视域下的群己权界论:基于对儒家与社群主义的比较解读》[The Discussion of Collective and Individual Rights from Chinese and Western Perspectives: A Comparative Interpretation of Confucianism and Communitarianism] (2020) 26(3) 中南大学学报*Journal of Central South University* 50, 50–55.

李建国 [Li Jianguo],《儒家文化对中国现代化发韧的负面影响》[The Negative Impact of Confucian Culture on the Modernization of China] [2006] 文化研究 *Cultural Research* 183, 183.

李强 [Li Qiang],《论知识产权制度的恶名》[On the Notoriety of the Intellectual Property System] (2007) 9(1) 西南政法大学学报*Journal of SWUPL* 42, 43.

李志明 [Li Zhiming],《中国知识产权文化发展中的文化冲突及解决方法:以知识产权文化的历史演变为视角》[2013] [Cultural Conflicts and Solutions in the Development of Chinese Intellectual Property Culture: An Historical Perspective on the Evolution of Intellectual Property Culture] 江汉论坛*The Yangtze-Han Forum*, 133, 133–134.

李江涛 [Li Jiangtao]《西学东渐以来中医药自信的质疑与重塑》[Since the Spread of Western Learning to the East: The Questioning and Reshaping of Confidence in Traditional Chinese Medicine] (2022) 1中国高等医学教育*Chinese Higher Medical Education* 6, 6–7.

李立峰 [Li Lifeng],《儒家价值观与当代中国核心价值文化》[Confucian Values and Contemporary China's Core Value Culture] (2015) 1 江苏省社会主义学院学报*Journal of Jiangsu Provincial Academy of Socialism* 72, 72–74.

杜赫 [Du He],《从天下到国家: 近代中国国家观念在文明碰撞中的确立》[From Sinocentrism to Nationhood: The Formation of Modern Chinese National Consciousness in the Clash of Civilizations] [2022] 公关世界*Public Relations World,*143, 143–144.

樊凯芳 [Fan Kaifang],《儒家思想对中医学的作用和影响》[The Influence and Impact of Confucianism on Traditional Chinese Medicine] (2011) 12(6) 山西中医学院学报 *Journal of Shanxi University of Traditional Chinese Medicine* 2, 2–3.

毕经正[Bi Jingzheng],《现代中医概念的形成》[Formation of the Modern Concept of 'Traditional Chinese Medicine'] (2022) 37(2) 中华中医药杂志 *Chinese Journal of Traditional Chinese Medicine and Pharmacy* 975, 975–977.

毛昊 [Mao Hao],《美国对华知识产权产权压力焦点变迁与趋势预见》[The Focus and Trend of US Pressure on China's Intellectual Property Rights and the Outlook for the Future] [2022] 科学学研究 *Studies in Science in Science* 1, 7.

沈浩蓝 [Shen Haolan],《从TRIPS到RCEP:加入WTO以来中国参与和完善知识产权国际规则研究》[From TRIPS to RCEP: A Study of China's Participation and Improvement of International Intellectual Property Rules Since Joining WTO] (2022) 7 广西社会科学 *Guangxi Social Sciences* 79, 79–80.

滕建卓 [Teng Jianzhuo],《论土家族医药学的整体观》[Discussion on the Holistic Characters of Tujia Medicine] (2007) 2中国民族民间医药 *Chinese Journal of Ethnomedicine and Ethnopharmacy* 6, 6–7.

王兆丁 [Wang Zhaoding],《加入WTO与我国的专利工作》(2003) 17(3) [Joining the WTO and Its Impact on China's Patent Work] 软科学 *Soft Science* 32, 32.

王华 [Wang Hua],《中医药知识产权客体主体研究》[A Study on the Subject and Object of Intellectual Property in Traditional Chinese Medicine] (2020) 1安徽广播电视大学学报*Anhui Radio & Television University Journal* 19, 22.

王居 [Wang Ju],《中国民族医药的保护与发展》[Protection and Development of Chinese Ethnic Medicine] [2006] 中国民族 *China's Ethnic Group* 52, 53.

盛辉 [Sheng Hui],《在我国传统文化中知识产权产生与发展的不利因素分析》[Analysis of the Adverse Factors in the Generation and Development of Intellectual Property Rights in China's Traditional Culture] (2014) 9 科技管理研究 *Science and Technology Management Research* 240, 240–243.

石硕 [Shi Shuo]《从汉族与少数民族的历史关系认识"中华民族共同体"的共同性》[Understanding the Commonality of the "Chinese National Community" from the Historical Relationship between the Han Ethnic Group and Minority Ethnic Groups] (2021) 3 中华民族共同体研究 *Research on the Chinese National Community* 73, 78–86.

祝尚书 [Zhu Shangshu],《论宋代的图书盗版与版权保护》[On Book Piracy and Copyright Protection in the Song Dynasty] (2000) 1 (1) 文献季刊 *Wen Xian Quarterly* 77, 83–86.

管荣齐 刘少华 [Guan Rongqi] and [Liu Shaohua],《药品专利挑战的机制和策略》[Mechanisms and Strategies for Pharmaceutical Patent Challenges] (2022) 15(2) 沈阳工业大学学报 *Journal of Shenyang University of Technology* 97, 98.

翟华强 [Zhai Huaqing],《基于师承与家传的古代中医药学人才培养模式》[Ancient Chinese Medicine Talent Cultivation Model Based on Inheritance and Family Tradition] (2014) 20(1) 中国中医基础医学杂志 *Chinese Journal of Basic Medicine in Traditional Chinese Medicine* 37, 38–39.

胡键 [Hu Jian],《中美竞合关系:从零和博弈到正和博弈,何以可能?》[The China-US Competitive Cooperation Relationship: From Zero-Sum Game to Positive-Sum Game—How Is It Possible?] (2022) 1国际观察*International Observation* 54, 67.

苗丽 [Miao Li],《浅议云南民族医药文化的内涵及其特征》[A Brief Discussion on the Connotation and Characteristics of Yunnan Ethnic Medicine Culture] (2015) 24(16) 中国民族民间医药 *Chinese Journal of Ethnomedicine and Ethnopharmacy* 1, 1–2.

滕建卓 [Teng Jianzhuo],《论土家族医药学的整体观》[Discussion on the Holistic Characters of Tujia Medicine] (2015) 24(16)中国民族民间医药 *Chinese Journal of Ethnomedicine and Ethnopharmacy* 6, 6–7.

袁南生 [Yuan Nansheng],《中国千年外交与主流价值观念》[Chinese Millennium Diplomacy and Mainstream Values] [2018] 同舟共进*Tóng Zhōu Gòng Jìn* 49, 49.

要然 [Yao Ran],《浅析传统知识数据库及其应用》[Analyzing Traditional Knowledge Databases and Their Applications] (2013) 6中国发明与专利*China Invention and Patent* 50, 50–53.

许子昀 [Xu Ziyun],《中美第一阶段经贸协议:推动知识产权保护全方位升级》[China-US Phase One Trade Agreement: Promoting a Comprehensive Upgrade in Intellectual Property Protection] (2023) 5中国外资 *Foreign Investment in China* 54, 54–57.

许纪霖 [Xu Jilin],《天下主义/夷夏之辨及其在近代的变异》[Distinction between 'All Under "Heaven" 'Ideology and 'Yi-Xia' Dichotomy and Their Transformations in Modern Times] (2012) 6 华东师范大学学报 *Journal of East China Normal University* 66, 66–71.

赵顺 [Zhao Shun],《中外专利审查中新颖性的判定比较研究》[A Comparative Study of Novelty Assessment in Chinese and Foreign Patent Examination] (2022) 24 河南科技 *Henan Science and Technology* 151, 151–154.

邓明峰 [Deng Mingfeng],《我国民族中医药传统知识专利保护研究》[Research on Patent Protection for TMK of China's Ethnic Groups] (2018) 12 贵州民族研究 *Guizhou Ethnic Studies* 96, 98.

邱冬梅 [Qiu Dongmei]《多元一体民族观视阈下的清代满医药文化》[The Manchu Medical Culture in the Qing Dynasty from the Perspective of a 'Multi-element Integrated' Ethnic View] (2019) 6 黑龙江民族丛刊 *Heilongjiang Ethnic Series* 101, 107.

郭晴 [Guo Qing],《中美贸易摩擦对中国经济贸易的中长期影响研究》[Study on the Medium and Long-Term Impact of China-US Trade Friction on China's Economy and Trade] (2019) 6 求索 *Quest* 55, 55–64.

郭雪军 [Guo Xuejun],《我国知识产权法律移植的不适应, 原因及转型》[The Inadaptability of Transplanted Intellectual Property Laws in Our Country, Reasons and Transformation] (2014)

31(1) 山东农业工程学院学报 *Journal of Shandong Agricultural Engineering College* 90, 90–92.

鄢良 [Yan Liang],《世界传统医药体系及其在当代的法律地位形态》[World Traditional Medical Systems and Their Contemporary Legal Status and Forms] (2013) 9(5) 亚太传统医药 *Asia-Pacific Traditional Medicine* 7, 7–9.

金春丽 [Jin Chunli],《中医药在日本传播与发展状况调查研究》[Investigating the Spread and Development of Traditional Chinese Medicine in Japan] (2022) 2 国际公关 *International Public Relations* 23.

陈一孚 [Chen Yifu],《中药发明的新颖性问题探究:兼论建立适合中药的新颖性审查规则》[Exploration of Novelty Issues in Traditional Chinese Medicine Inventions: Discussing the Establishment of Novelty Examination Rules Suitable for Traditional Chinese Medicine] (2013) 24 新疆社会科学 *Xinjiang Social Sciences* 151.

陈卫文[Chen Weiwen]《鸦片战争对中国近代化的影响》[The Impact of the Opium War on Modernization in China] (2009) 20 大众文艺 *Popular Culture* 235.

陈名涛 [Chen Mingtao],《中国知识产权移植问题探析》[An Analysis of Intellectual Property Transplant Issues in China] [2012] 社科纵横 *Social Science Review* 113.

陈染 [Chen Ran],《中医药传统知识特别权利保护模式探讨》[Discussion on the Protection Model of Special Rights for Traditional Chinese Medicine Knowledge] (2022) 36(4) 湖北第二师范学院学报*Journal of Hubei University of Education* 51.

靳凤林 [Jin Fenglin],《先秦儒家文化与知识产权法律》[On the Ethical Parallax between China's Worldview and Western International Perspective] (2018) 4, 伦理学研究 *Studies in Ethics* 121.

马得汶 [Ma DeWen],《基于师承与家传的古代中医药学人才培养模式》[Ancient Chinese Medicine Talent Cultivation Model Based on Inheritance and Family Tradition] (2014) 20 (1) 西北师大学报 *Journal of Northwest Normal University* 71.

马海生 [Ma Haisheng],《遗传资源保护与专利申请中遗传资源披露:兼评专利法修订草案中的相关条款》[Protection of Genetic Resources and Disclosure of Genetic Resources in Patent Applications: A Review of the Relevant Provisions in the Draft Amendment to the Patent Law] (2007) 17 知识产权 *Intellectual Property* 37.

黄丽萍 [Huang Liping],《论我国现行药品专利强制许可立法的不足与完善》(2012) 5 [On the Shortcomings and Improvements of China's Current Pharmaceutical Patent Compulsory Licensing Legislation] 法学杂志 *Legal Studies Journal* 92.

Chapter 4
Pharmaceutical Industry Influence, Traditional Medical Knowledge, and the Evolution of IP Governance in China

4.1 Introduction

In the rapidly evolving global landscape of IP rights, China faces the challenge of navigating the competing interests and needs of various stakeholders in the use and protection of TMK.[1] This chapter offers a comprehensive exploration of the intricacies of China's IP system as it relates to TMK, aiming to illuminate the complexities that define the contemporary Chinese IP framework and assess its impact on TMK, and the various stakeholders involved.

A central concern arising from this examination is the possibility of imbalances or inequities within China's IP system. These may grant an unfair advantage to corporate actors, posing a threat to the preservation of TMK within the Chinese IP framework. When the significant influence of China's unique historical and cultural context on its contemporary IP laws and policies is recognised, it becomes essential to investigate how these factors interplay in shaping the equity and fairness experienced by all stakeholders involved in the realm of TMK.

Thus, this chapter presents an examination of the distinctive features of China's IP system as it pertains to TMK. The analysis places a strong emphasis on domestic dynamics, aiming to unravel the intricate web of interconnected historical and socioeconomic factors that influence the balance of competing interests among TMK stakeholders such as knowledge holders and their communities, and corporate actors.

A vital aspect of the analysis lies in acknowledging the profound influence of China's historical and cultural context on the formation of its contemporary IP system. This context is particularly relevant when considering the comprehensive protection, responsible utilisation, and suitable dissemination of Chinese TMK, as these processes involve various stakeholders with diverse interests. To explore this, this chapter examines the extensive history and evolution of China's significant

[1] See discussion in Chapter 2.

N. Xia, *Medicinal Mandates*, https://doi.org/10.1007/978-981-96-4108-6_4

achievements in the pharmaceutical domain, tracing the evolution of its accomplishments from the roots of traditional Chinese medicine during the Warring States Period up to the present day. This exploration aids in understanding the distinct challenges China confronts in managing the comprehensive protection, responsible utilisation, and suitable dissemination of its TMK amidst diverse stakeholders' interests.

The findings of this book aim to provide a more in-depth and nuanced comprehension of China's IP laws and policies, taking into account the nation's historical and cultural context. By doing so, it seeks to inform the development of well-rounded reform proposals that consider the unique circumstances and challenges faced by China. Furthermore, it endeavours to offer insights into the intricate interplay between China's IP system, the guardians of TMK, the communities they belong to, and the role of corporations within this context, thereby contributing to a more comprehensive understanding of the dynamic relationships and the potential avenues for fostering balance, equity, and fairness within the IP landscape.

China's rich history and cultural traditions have played a significant role in shaping the country's contemporary legal and policy frameworks, particularly in the field of IP.[2] Scholars argue that China's historical and cultural heritage, characterised by inward-looking perspectives, strong nationalism, and a deep connection to the past, has shaped the evolution of its IP laws and policies.[3] As a result, these often promote imitation and enable the exploitation and appropriation of traditional knowledge, including TMK. However, the effects of these practices on TMK, knowledge holders, and their communities remain uncertain and warrant further examination.

This chapter provides an in-depth critique of China's IP system, positing that its functionality is significantly shaped by the country's historical and socioeconomic contexts. This influence has engendered a dialectical operation within the system, underpinned by the objectives of managing and balancing coexisting and dialectical interests among a diverse range of stakeholders including the State, foreign multinational enterprises, and domestic industries. Despite these intentions, the IP system may inadvertently foster a biased regulatory and policy environment that enables the exploitation of TMK, ultimately causing harm to this invaluable knowledge. This argument is presented in three sections.

Section 4.2 examines China's remarkable accomplishments and advancements within the pharmaceutical sphere, encompassing its early achievements since ancient times and the government's efforts to modernise the industry through recent policies. It brings to light the pivotal role of Chinese TMK in shaping the pharmaceutical sector. The section also sheds light on the IP system's challenges in promoting a balanced approach, focusing on ensuring the comprehensive protection, responsible utilisation,

[2] 邓琦 [Deng Qi],《中国传统法文化对现代法治建设的影响》[Influence of Chinese Traditional Legal Culture on Modern Rule of Law Construction] (2011) 2(1) 黑河学院学报 *Journal of Heihe University* 20, 20–22; Jonathan Ocko, 'Copying, Culture, and Control: Chinese Intellectual Property Law in Historical Context' (2013) 8 *Yale Journal of Law & the Humanities* 559, 559–578.

[3] Barry Buzan and Michael Cox, 'China and the US: Comparable Cases of 'Peaceful Rise'?' (2013) 6 *The Chinese Journal of International Politics* 109, 121–122; Yanchun Zhou and Yanhong Fan, 'A Contrastive Study of Temporal-spatial Metaphor between Chinese and Americans' (2015) 5(1) *Theory and Practice in Language Studies* 119, 120.

and suitable dissemination of TMK It accentuates the government's prioritisation of corporate interests over the inherent worth of TMK, culminating in a systemic bias within China's IP system.

Section 4.3 explores how China's corporate actors in the pharmaceutical field are affecting domestic IP affairs, which may have implications for TMK and give rise to concerns about misappropriation and exploitation. It highlights the increased political influence these corporations have gained due to their growth and profitability, allowing them to shape legal regulations and policy-making processes in their favour. The section emphasises the presence of a clear bias in China's IP system that supports corporate interests. This poses a threat to the TMK and its knowledge holders as it can lead to the exploitation of their knowledge by corporations claiming exclusive IP rights.

Section 4.4 critically analyses the complex nature of China's IP system which has been shaped by historical, cultural, and legal factors, resulting in a unique approach that combines Western-inspired IP standards with traditional Chinese legal thought and philosophy. The section highlights the need for China's IP system to adapt and reshape its norms in order to accommodate the interests and preferences of a broad range of actors, to promote fairness and equity across the entire IP regime.

Using China's patent system and its effects on TMK and associated genetic resources as a case study, this section builds on the analysis presented in Chapter 3 to further examine how the system's current design allows for the corporate exploitation of TMK. It argues that the patent system's structural bias favours industrial and corporate interests, leaving TMK vulnerable to exploitation and abuse, which can be detrimental to local communities and knowledge holders. To address these challenges, it suggests leveraging the flexibilities afforded by the *TRIPS Agreement* to create a more balanced and inclusive patent system that accommodates the interests of all stakeholders while taking into account China's historical and cultural particularities.

4.2 Evolution of China's Pharmaceutical Landscape

China boasts an extensive and rich history in the realm of pharmaceutical advancements. Since the Warring States Period of Chinese history (475–221 BC), the country has developed medical theories and methods to prevent epidemic diseases.[4] The Han dynasty (206 BC to 220) saw the development of medical therapies for the diagnosis,

[4] 骆志煌 [Luo Zhihuang], 《中国古代文化之中医药与中医学》[Influence of Chinese Traditional Legal Culture on Modern Rule of Law Construction] [2020] 海峡教育研究 *Strait Education Research* 65, 67–68; Liang Huigang et al, 'A Brief History of the Development of Infectious Disease Prevention, Control, and Biosafety Programs in China' (2020) (2) *Journal of Biosafety and Biosecurity* 1,1.

treatment, and prevention of mental disorders such as 'insomnia' and 'hysteria'.[5] During the Sui Dynasty (581–618), vaccination methods against smallpox were developed and later popularised and disseminated nationally throughout the Ming and Qing Dynasties.[6]

Building on this foundation, Chinese pharmaceutical innovations made their way to the West through various channels, impacting the development of Western medicine. As noted by Diao, they moved Westwards along the Silk Roads and eventually reached Europe through messengers such as Arab Emissaries and traders, thus significantly contributing to laying the foundations of Western pharmacy practice (before the arrival of the European Renaissance).[7] Chinese practices, such as inoculation to prevent smallpox, caught the attention of the Western countries in the seventeenth century and provided the essential groundwork for modern pharmaceutical science and technology, such as immunology and immunopathology.[8] During the seventeenth and eighteenth centuries, the adoption of ancient Chinese pharmaceutical insights, such as pulse diagnostics, by Europe marked a significant milestone in international knowledge exchange.[9] This transfer of medical wisdom was pivotal in the evolution of present-day diagnostic pathology and iridology. Some scholars, such as Finlay, have argued that, although China did not directly give rise to the modern scientific revolution (particularly in modern medicine), it had a distant influence on the conception of Western pharmaceutical and scientific establishments.[10]

While there is a belief that the advent of modern pharmaceutical science and technology was inspired, to some extent, by the TMK developed in China's historical environment, a comprehensive analysis of this claim is beyond the scope of this study. Nonetheless, it is important to recognise that China's rich history of pharmaceutical advancements and the resulting influence on Western practices demonstrates the value of TMK in contemporary times in terms of corporate use and pharmaceutical research.

This historical background offers valuable context for understanding the origins and importance of TMK in China. By emphasising China's substantial accomplishments in the pharmaceutical sphere, it lays the groundwork for understanding the

---

[5] Xiansu Chi et al, 'Research progress on Classical Traditional Chinese Medicine Formula Lily Bulb and Rehmannia Decoction in the Treatment of Depression' (2019) 112 *Biomedicine & Pharmacotherapy* 1, 1–5.

[6] 陈忠海 [Chen Zhonghai],《古代的防疫与疫苗》[Ancient Epidemic Prevention and Vaccines] [2019] 中国发展观察 *China Development Observation* 63, 63–64; K Wang et al, 'Evolution and Governance of the Biotechnology and Pharmaceutical Industry of China' (2009) 79(9) *Mathematics and Computers in Simulation* 2947, 2948.

[7] Junli Diao, 'The Influence of China/Asia on the West' in Suzanne M Stauffer (ed), *Libraries, Archives, and Museums: An Introduction to Cultural Heritage Institutions through the Ages* (Rowman & Littlefield, 2021) 81, 87.

[8] 谢蜀生 [Xie Shusheng],《中国人痘接种术向西方的传播及影响》[The Spread and Impact of Chinese Vaccination Techniques on the West] (2000) 30 (3) 中华医史杂志*Chinese Journal of Medical History* 133, 133–134.

[9] Boleslaw Szczesniak, 'John Floyer and Chinese Medicine' (1954) 11 *Osiris* 127, 155–156.

[10] R Finlay, 'China, the West, and World History in Joseph Needham's Science and Civilisation in China' (2000) 11 *Journal of World History* 265, 269.

value assigned to TMK in modern times. This historical perspective clarifies the reasons behind China's laws and policies being crafted with a deep understanding and keen awareness of the nation's unique history and cultural context. In order to safeguard the invaluable contributions of TMK and sustain its relevance in modern pharmaceutical advancements, a targeted regulatory and policy environment has been established. This environment encourages the protection of both tangible and intangible assets related to TMK for corporate actors, while promoting its integration into contemporary pharmaceutical innovations.[11] As a result, this tailored approach ultimately enables the strategic utilisation of TMK, ensuring its enduring influence on the development of modern pharmaceutical solutions.

Despite the remarkable early achievements and innovation efforts in China, there appears to be a shortfall in recognition from many scholars towards the historical significance of Chinese science and medicine. They often overlook the pivotal role that China has played in shaping pharmaceutical knowledge, both in theory and practice.

Indeed, some critics have characterised China's historical scientific and pharmaceutical contributions as merely 'proto-scientific'.[12] Yet, this view fails to acknowledge the profound legacy of China's ancient texts and traditional wisdom. These historical treasures have been instrumental in shaping Chinese ideologies and methodologies for centuries and continue to significantly influence contemporary Chinese approaches to pharmaceutical and scientific pursuits.[13] The enduring impact of these traditions demonstrates the rich depth of China's scientific heritage and its ongoing influence on modern advancements.

In July 1950, the National Health Work Conference in China marked a pivotal moment in this legacy, establishing principles for health work that included the integration of scientific and traditional medicine.[14] Initially, patients could consult both traditional Chinese and Western-style doctors, although the systems remained separate. By 1954, under Mao Zedong's directive, the integration of traditional Chinese and Western medicines became more pronounced.[15] This integration was characterised by Western medicine doctors studying Chinese medicine, medical graduates learning from traditional Chinese doctors, the promotion of medicinal herbs, and the modernisation of traditional Chinese medicine texts.[16]

---

[11] 程兆盛 [Cheng Zhaosheng],《中医药政策概述》[Overview of Traditional Chinese Medicine Policy] (2013) 21(11) 中医药管理杂志 *Journal of Traditional Chinese Medicine Management* 1139, 1139–1140.

[12] Carla Nappi and McKenzie Wark, 'Reading Needham Now' (2019) 110(1) *Isis*,100, 100–108.

[13] 王虎 [Wang Hu],《中国传统文化对科学技术发展影响初探》[A Preliminary Exploration of the Impact of Chinese Traditional Culture on the Development of Science and Technology] (2016) 云南省第 4–5 届科学技术哲学与科学技术史研究生论坛优秀论文集 *Collection of Outstanding Papers from the 4th–5th Graduate Forum on Philosophy of Science and Technology and History of Science and Technology in Yunnan Province* 269, 270–271.

[14] Li, En-chang, 'MAO Ze-dong's View on Traditional Chinese Medicine and Its Modern Significance' (2020) 26(6) *Chinese journal of integrative medicine* 469, 470

[15] Li (n 14) 470.

[16] Li (n 14) 471–472.

Significant efforts were made to integrate these medical practices, such as enrolling Western-style doctors in traditional Chinese medicine programmes, establishing colleges of traditional Chinese medicine, and incorporating traditional Chinese medicine courses into Western medical school curricula.[17] The Academy of Traditional Chinese Medicine, founded in December 1955, played a crucial role in this integration by researching traditional Chinese medicine.[18] Hospitals started establishing traditional Chinese medicine wards and clinics, integrating traditional Chinese doctors into their staff.[19] This period of integration, although experiencing fluctuations during the Great Leap Forward and the Cultural Revolution, marked a shift towards modernisation in China's medical practices, influencing all aspects of life.

The end of the Cultural Revolution heralded a new era in China, with the Minister of Public Health in 1980, Qian Xinzhong, outlining goals for elevating China's medical science and technology.[20] This included an emphasis on modern methods while also acknowledging the importance of integrating traditional Chinese medicine with Western medicine.[21] The integration aimed to create a new type of medical science that was both modernised and retained national characteristics, considering traditional Chinese medicine as a valuable resource for contemporary medicine.[22] The process involved clinical, experimental, and theoretical levels, with progress being made in each area.[23]

The evolution of China's modern pharmaceutical industry, however, was initially sluggish, with the nation grappling with a stark shortage of pharmaceutical products.[24] The tumultuous social and political context, accompanied by the destruction caused by wars, further hindered pharmaceutical production and trade.[25] The founding of the 'new China' in 1949 marked the beginning of the government's efforts to rebuild the nation's pharmaceutical sector and related supply chains.[26] In this context, the exploitation of TMK became a key strategy for developing the local pharmaceutical industry and generating technological breakthroughs.[27]

---

[17] Ralph C Croizier, Traditional Medicine in Modern China: Science, Nationalism, and the Tensions of Cultural Change (Harvard University Press, 1968) 180.

[18] Kwok, Pui-Yan. "Integration of Traditional Chinese Medicine and Western Medicine in Contemporary China" (Master of Science thesis, University of Chicago, 1981) 13–14.

[19] Ibid.

[20] Kwok (n 18) 16.

[21] Yu Lin, 'Medical and Health Service' (1980) 23(25) Beijing Review 1, 17.

[22] Kwok (n 18) 17.

[23] Kwok (n 18) 19.

[24] Liz PY Chee, Mao's Bestiary: Medicinal Animals and Modern China (Duke University Press, 1977) 38.

[25] Ibid.

[26] The Chinese Pharmaceutical Association, 'Pharmaceuticals in New China' (1960) 80 *Chinese Medical Journal* 208, 208.

[27] 张正 [Zhang Zheng],《百年征程和文化传承双视角下: 民族医药发展历程回望》[Under the Dual Perspectives of a Century-long Journey and Cultural Heritage: A Retrospective on the Development of Ethnic Medicine] (2021) 4 四川省社会主义学院学报 *Journal of Sichuan Socialist*

State-sponsored efforts to capitalise on TMK began in the late 1950s with the establishment of a network of State-owned pharmaceutical factories and TMK collection stations across China.[28] Many of these factories were located in southwest regions such as Sichuan, Yunnan, and Guizhou provinces to facilitate direct access to TMK and associated resources.[29] For example, Daxin Pharmaceutical Factory, established in the southwest region, produced pharmaceutical products like glucose, based on TMK and local herbs instead of using Western scientific knowledge.[30]

During China's State-planned economy period from the 1950s to the 1980s, efforts were made to utilise TMK to benefit the State economy. The Chinese government laid particular emphasis on mass participation, self-reliance, and Indigenous development in science and pharmaceuticals[31] and TMK became an example of China's contributions to the world of pharmaceutical science—one area where the enormous scientific borrowing from the West could be repaid. However, this resulted in extensive exploitation and recomposition of TMK, which favoured biomedical epistemology while disregarding its cultural and community origins and epistemic underpinnings.[32] As a result, TMK lost its distinctive values and did not require a particular cultural and spiritual context to be effective. This historical context may have contributed to a regulatory and policy environment that was less strict, permitting the exploitation of TMK, and potentially shaping the current legal and policy framework governing TMK in China. This environment likely played a role in creating an in-built bias in China's IP systems that substantially protects the tangible and intangible assets of corporate actors, facilitating their appropriation and utilisation of TMK.

In 1978, the Chinese government initiated a series of reforms aimed at restructuring its economy. This period was known as the 'Spring of Sciences' as it witnessed the establishment of China's modern pharmaceutical sector and a range of scientific research programmes.[33] The modernisation and development of China's pharmaceutical sector were first highlighted as a top priority in the nation's Science and Technology Development Program.[34]

Academy 61, 62; Lantian Li, 'Deconstructing and Historicizing Access to Medicines: The Changing Priority of Pharmaceutical Governance in China' (2021) 5 *Frontiers in Sociology* 1, 4; Chee, (n 24), 37–41.

[28] Chee (n 24) 38; 段资睿[Duan Zirui], 《20世纪60年代中央试办医药托拉斯的回顾及启示》[Review and Enlightenment of the Central Pilot Pharmaceutical Trust in the 1960s] (2022) 43 (18) 医学与哲学 *Medicine and Philosophy* 74, 74–79.

[29] Chee (n 24) 39.

[30] Ibid.

[31] Merle Goldman and Denis Fred Simon, 'The Onset of China's New Technological Revolution' in Denis Fred Simon and Merle Goldman (eds), *Science and Technology in Post-Mao China* (Brill, 1989) 3, 8.

[32] Chee (n 24) 31; Rhonda Chang, Chinese Medicine Masquerading as Yi: a Case of Chinese Self-Colonisation (Mani River Press, 2015) 1–271.

[33] K Wang et al, 'Evolution and Governance of the Biotechnology and Pharmaceutical Industry of China' (2009) 79(9) *Mathematics and Computers in Simulation* 1, 3.

[34] Ibid.

In 1986, China's State Council released a document known as the '863 Program'[35] that emphasised the development of the pharmaceutical sector based on advanced technologies as a key priority.[36] The following year, China's State Science and Technology Commission ('SSTC') issued a White Paper that reiterated the role of science and technology in China's ongoing modernisation efforts,[37] with the development of the pharmaceutical sector based on advanced biotechnology being identified as the country's top priority for high-tech development.[38]

The national government's strategic policies were instrumental in shaping the modern pharmaceutical industry in China, significantly fostering innovation within this sector.[39] These policies demonstrate the government's steadfast commitment to the industry, nurturing an environment that propels its growth and development. They underscore the importance of innovation as a key driver of the industry's sustained growth and future success.[40]

One of the key State-driven initiatives that significantly contributed to the growth of the pharmaceutical sector was the selective industrial policy introduced in 1989.[41] This policy was designed to stimulate a range of industries crucial for China's future development, including the pharmaceutical industry.[42] Leveraging tools such as government subsidies, tax incentives, and additional support measures, the policy strategically directed resources towards the domestic pharmaceutical industry.[43] This not only facilitated its growth but also fostered a climate of innovation, encouraging pharmaceutical companies to invest in research and development, ultimately driving the advancement of this sector in China.[44]

---

[35] Tong Shi et al, 'Driving force from authorities: the evolution of innovation system for biomedical industry in China' (2014) 28(10) *Technology Analysis & Strategic Management* 1210, 1212; See: http://www.863.gov.cn.

[36] 张军亮 [Zhang Junliang],《生物和医药技术领域知识生产分析: 基于 "863 计划" 科技报告》[Analysis of Knowledge Production in the Field of Biotechnology and Medicine: Based on the '863 Program' Scientific Reports] (2015) 34(1) 情报杂志*Journal of Intelligence* 67, 67–68.

[37]《国务院办公厅关于印发信息技术发展政策要点和生物技术发展政策要点的通知》[Notice of the General Office of the State Council on Printing and Distributing the Key Points of Information Technology Development Policies and Biotechnology Development Policies] (People's Republic of China) State Science and Technology Commission, Order No 18, 1988.

[38] Ibid.

[39] 柴慧婷 [Chai Huiting],《浅析药物创新体系初步建立和中国医药企业创新进展》[Preliminary Analysis of the Establishment of Drug Innovation System and Progress of Innovation in Chinese Pharmaceutical Enterprises] (2018) 33 (3) 华西医药 *Huaxi Pharmaceutical* 359, 360.

[40] Ibid.

[41] 唐永业 [Tang Yongye],《我国生化制药工业及其发展》[China's Biochemical Pharmaceutical Industry and Its Development] [1991] 商业科技*Commercial Technology* 13, 13–14; Baohui Zhang, 'Resource Centralization and Industrial Policies: State Capacity in Structural Adjustment in South Korea and China' (1998) 25(3) *Asian Affairs: An American Review* 165, 165.

[42] Ibid.

[43] Bole Zhou and Shouguo Zhao, 'Industrial Policy and Corporate Investment Efficiency' (2022) 78 *Journal of Asian Economics* 1, 1.

[44] Ibid.

However, while the government's policies have been effective in promoting the pharmaceutical industry and innovation, there have been unintended consequences for TMK. Over time, China's government support and policies have consistently prioritised corporate interests in the exploitation of TMK and associated resources.[45] These policies, by incentivising the accumulation and acquisition of IP, often overlook the inherent value of TMK and neglect the welfare of its holders and local communities.[46]

Consequently, China's IP system has evolved to advance corporate interests, securing their tangible and intangible assets while enabling the appropriation and utilisation of TMK at the expense of TMK holders and local communities. This lopsided emphasis on advancing corporate interests may have inadvertently created a systemic bias within China's IP systems, potentially disregarding the intrinsic values of TMK and the interests of TMK holders and local communities.

A clear example of this issue can be seen in the case of a State-funded pharmaceutical corporation in Qinghai province, China, called Arura.[47] According to Madhavan, Arura obtained exclusive IP rights during the 1990s to produce the three most renowned Tibetan 'precious pills': Ratna Samphel, Rinchen Mangjor, and Rinchen Drangjor.[48] This move excluded knowledge holders and associated communities from practising their monastery-taught medical knowledge. Despite the intense efforts of knowledge holders and community members to defend their customary rights to control and practise their TMK, they were unsuccessful in their legal endeavours and subsequently faced fines and prohibitions from continuing their practices.[49]

This example highlights the Chinese IP-related system's bias, which primarily serves to protect corporate assets and facilitate the appropriation and utilisation of TMK. By granting corporate actors extensive control over both the tangible and intangible assets associated with the TMK, the system neglects its intrinsic value, as well as the interests of the knowledge holders and local communities who have preserved and practised it for generations.

Furthermore, the Chinese IP system's inherent bias is emphasised by the unsuccessful attempts of knowledge holders and community members to legally defend

---

45 Shufan Sung,, 'The New Path of Green GDP in China' in Nurcan Kilinc-Ata (ed), *The Effects of Environmental Policies on Sustainability: Theory and Methods* (OMICS Group, 2017) 17,17–18; Qiu, Wanfei, 'Challenges in Developing China's Marine Protected Area System' (2009) 33(4) *Marine Policy* 599, 601; Shen, Jinyu et al, 'The Relationship between Marine Biodiversity Conservation and Poverty Alleviation in the Strategies of Rural Development in China' (2015) SI(73) *Journal of Coastal Research* 1, 2–4.

46 Haijun Jin etal, 'Government-backed Patent Funds in China: Their Roles as Policy Tools to Promote Innovation by SMEs' (2013) 30(4) *Tech Monitor* 24, 24–30.

47 高建美 [Gao Jianmei],《中药品种保护制度之法律职能》[The Legal Function of the Traditional Chinese Medicine Species Protection System] [2016] 科技与法律 *Scientific Technology and Law* 1044, 1050–1051.

48 Harilal Madhavan, 'Below the Radar Innovations and Emerging Property Right Approaches in Tibetan Medicine' (2017) 20 *The Journal of World Intellectual Property* 239, 247–248.

49 Ibid.

their customary rights to control and practise their TMK. Rather than providing a fair and balanced platform for all stakeholders, the IP system perpetuates a power dynamic that consistently favours corporate entities. This dynamic further underscores the system's built-in bias towards the protection of corporate assets and the appropriation and utilisation of TMK.

4.3 Corporate Influence on Chinese IP Laws and the Risk to Chinese TMK

In light of the aforementioned issues with the Chinese IP system and its bias towards corporate entities, the growing influence of these corporations further exacerbates the situation. The rapid growth and notable profitability of the modern pharmaceutical corporations in China have also brought them the ever-increasing political influences to intervene in the policy-making process fashioned in their interests.[50] Previously, many Chinese scholars only associated the concept of 'lobbying' (*youshui* 游说) with the tactics employed by businesses in developed capitalist countries. However, it is now also associated with China's national companies' behaviours at home.[51]

Crookes in his study concerning the IP regime evolution in China highlighted the significant roles that Chinese industrial actors have played in advancing the debate about IP regulation and influencing the relevant policy outcomes.[52] Among these industrial actors, China's pharmaceutical sector was identified as one of the most active stakeholders. As Yuan observed, pharmaceutical corporations in China at the national level seem to be taking on a role comparable to that of Western industrial lobby groups, advocating for increased awareness of IP issues, stronger law enforcement, and updates to existing legislation and policies.[53] This resemblance is further emphasised by the fact that Chinese pharmaceutical companies engage in lobbying efforts through business associations, rather than attempting to individually influence the government and the policy-making process.[54]

This strategy is considered an effective way to aggregate their voices through 'a common front and resource pooling',[55] thereby strengthening the power of their lobby efforts in negotiations with the government. Given the large scale of China's pharmaceutical sector (which has over 4,600 manufacturers, 13,000 distributors,

---

[50] Yoel Kornreich et al, 'Consultation and Deliberation in China: The Making of China's Health-Care Reform' (2012) 68 *The China Journal* 176, 176–203.

[51] Guosheng Deng and Scott Kennedy, 'Big Business and Industry Association Lobbying in China: the Paradox of Contrasting Styles' (2010) 63 *The China Journal* 101, 101; 张耀杰[Zhang Yaojie],《民间游说与立法之互动》[Interaction Between Popular Lobbying and Lawmaking] (2004) 11(3), 当代中国研究*Modern China Studies* 73, 73–80.

[52] Paul Crookes, Intellectual Property Regime Evolution in China and India (Brill, 2010) 141–182.

[53] Yuan Yuan, 'Intellectual Property Policy. Domestic Constraints on the International Negotiating Positions' (Master's Thesis, University of Cambridge, 2006).

[54] Kornreich et al (n 50) 194.

[55] Scott Kennedy, *The Business of Lobbying in China* (Harvard University Press, 2005).

and 32,900 retailers), pharmaceutical business associations representing China's domestic companies have grown rapidly, matching pace with the industry.[56]

In general, the system of China's pharmaceutical trade associations has three tiers, including the China Pharmaceutical Enterprises Association ('CPEA') which represents the top executives of China's large pharmaceutical companies; the China Association of Pharmaceutical Commerce ('CAPC'), which represents the domestic pharmaceutical distributors; and many local pharmaceutical associations.[57] These associations have a strong membership base, which includes previous national government officials and law-makers.[58] Many of China's high-ranking government officials have transitioned back and forth between roles in the pharmaceutical industry and positions within the national government. For instance, both CPEA and CAPC hired Qi Moujia, former Director of China's National Medical Products Administration as their Honorary President.[59] CPEA's Executive Chairman Yu Mingde, who was the former Deputy Director of China's National Development and Reform Commission, now publicly champions the pharmaceutical industry's position in negotiations with the national government.[60] Arguably, through such practices, the pharmaceutical business associations have been acting in roles much like the branch of a government ministry or commission. In this way, Member Companies gain privileged access to the sections of the government they serve, thereby enhancing their power to influence domestic public policy and law reform processes.

On the policy side, the business associations and their Member Companies have actively organised or engaged in meetings or public consultation processes with the various ministries and government agencies that are responsible for nationwide policy-making and implementation.[61] These ministries and government agencies may include the National Intellectual Property Administration ('NIPA'), the National

---

[56] Youdi, Zhu, *Big Country's Medical Reform* (World Book Publishing Company, 2011) 203; Kornreich et al (n 50) 194–195.

[57] Kornreich et al (n 50) 194.

[58] Ibid.

[59] 《中国医药企业管理协会》 *Baidu Encyclopedia* (Web Page, 2021) < https://baike.baidu.com/item/中国医药企业管理协会/964310?fr=aladdin > ; '中国医药商业协' *Baidu Encyclopedia* (Web Page, 2021) < https://baike.baidu.com/item/中国医药商业/6668263?fr=aladdin > .

[60] Yu Mingde, 'There Are Six Major Differences in the New Medical Reform Plan', *NetEase Finance* (Web Page, 2009) < http://news.163.com/08/1103/02/4PPS9UFH0001124J.html > ; Yu Mingde, 'Pharmaceutical Preparations Should Be Unswervingly Driven by Internationalized Biomedicine' *21 Finance* (Web Page, 2018).
< https://m.21jingji.com/article/20181024/5571b97328627ef4f6fbcc252d06f331.html > .

[61] 'The 2021 China Pharmaceutical Innovation 100 Summit was successfully opened, witnessing the rise of Chinese medicine and bringing together China's innovative strength', *Economic Situation Report Network* (Web Page, 2021) < http://www.china-cer.com.cn/guwen/2021041312112.html > ; 'The 6th China Pharmaceutical Intellectual Property Summit ended successfully', *Sohu.com* (Web Page, 2021) < https://www.sohu.com/a/491596717_221481 > ; 'Overhaul of China's Implementation Regulations of the Drug Administration Law: New Drugs for Rare diseases and Pediatric Drugs will Embrace Policy Dividends', *Sohu.com* (Web Page, 2022) < https://www.sohu.com/a/546435217_114988 > ; Scott Kennedy, *The Business of Lobbying in China* (Harvard University Press, 2005).

Medical Products Administration ('NMPA'), the State Council, and the National People's Congress. Through public consultations, meetings, and media campaigns, the associations and member companies have pushed for revisions to IP-related laws, policies, and other relevant regulations.[62]

For instance, the industry, by lobbying through media campaigns and consultation workshops with governments, has certainly affected the introduction of pharmaceutical-related TRIPS-plus rules in *China's Patent Law* (2020)[63] and its rules for implementation.[64] According to industry sources directly involved in the drafting and consultation process, despite the recent increase in the innovation capabilities of some Chinese national pharmaceutical companies, many local Chinese pharmaceutical firms are still producing patented drugs under licence from foreign companies while those companies rely on local counterparts to adapt their products for Chinese customers.[65] Therefore, the consistencies between the interests of Chinese domestic pharmaceutical corporations and those of their Western counterparts (mostly American and Western European) have led both groups to actively advocate for data exclusivity, pharmaceutical patent term extension, and other TRIPS-Plus provisions in China's Patent Law.[66]

Although the interests of China's domestic corporations often converge with those of foreign multinational enterprises, the market-oriented transformation of the Chinese pharmaceutical sector has led to intense competition among domestic small and medium-sized enterprises and foreign multinational enterprises.[67] When local pharmaceutical entities face a threat to their interests, interest groups often launch aggressive lobbying campaigns, persuading governments to adjust their stance or amend their enforcement of unfavourable laws or regulations.[68] As a result, the Chinese judicial and administrative authorities at all levels often provide the support that domestic small and medium-sized enterprises need.

---

62 'The Fourth Patent Law Amendment of China: Corporations Call for More Punishment According to Law', *China National Intellectual Property Administration* (Web Page, 2017) < http://www.cnipa.gov.cn/art/2017/7/28/art_317_134063.html > .

63 《中华人民共和国专利法》[Patent Law of the People's Republic of China] (People's Republic of China) National People's Congress, Order No.55, 2020.

64 'The Fourth Patent Law Amendment of China: Corporations Call for More Punishment According to Law' (Web Page, 2017) < http://www.cnipa.gov.cn/art/2017/7/28/art_317_134063.html > .

65 'National People's Congress Representative and Chairman of Hengrui Medicine, Sun Piaoyang: Extend the Effectiveness and Grant Conditions of Drug Patent Term Compensation to Promote Pharmaceutical Innovation', *China Times* (Web Page, 2022) https://baijiahao.baidu.com/s?id=1726909378742602282&wfr=spider&for=pc.

66 Ibid; 'Mr Sun suggested the cooperation between China's domestic and foreign pharmaceutical companies should be fully considered while amending China's patent laws and patent examination guidelines'.

67 赖丽娟 [Lai Lijuan],《中国医药市场走进新竞争时代》[China's Pharmaceutical Market Enters a New Era of Competition] [2004] 医药经济报*Pharmaceutical Economy News* 1, 1–4.

68 Guosheng Deng and Scott Kennedy, 'Big Business and Industry Association Lobbying in China: the Paradox of Contrasting Styles' (2010) 63 *The China Journal* 101, 101–125; Kornreich et al (n 40) 176–203.

One typical example is the controversial decision from the review board in China's State Intellectual Property Office ('SIPO'), made in response to an aggressive high-profile petition from twelve Chinese domestic pharmaceutical corporations.[69] The interest groups and member companies sought to persuade the SIPO that it was in China's interest to invalidate the Chinese patent granted to Pfizer for the drug sildenafil which was actually patented all over the world at that time.[70] In the end, SIPO's Patent Re-examination Board ruled in favour of the local companies and decided that the patent granted to Pfizer should be revoked because of its failure to satisfy certain patentability requirements.[71] As noted by Andrews, the strategy of challenging the patent in the Patent Re-examination Board, instead of simply counterfeiting the pharmaceutical product, has since emerged as a unique approach in competing against foreign corporations.[72]

The sildenafil decision also created a precedent that has since led to a series of systematic revocations and invalidations of foreign pharmaceutical patents by Chinese local stakeholders. For instance, due to the sildenafil decision, GlaxoSmithKline (GSK) made a decision to abandon its patent for rosiglitazone, an important ingredient of its widely used diabetes drug Avandia, which was similarly disputed by China's local pharmaceutical companies.[73] These incidents, along with others, expose a clear bias in China's IP system that has allowed corporate actors and their associations to use domestic IP regimes to further their interests and expand their influence. The result is that they have been able to expand and protect their interests by influencing public officials and government agencies to adopt higher levels of IP protection in their favour. Their influence extends beyond lobbying, as their corporate power can also persuade government agencies and judicial organs to 'bend the law' to support the development of local economies, resulting in unfair treatment of foreign companies and other stakeholders in the Chinese administrative and judicial system.

The domestic pharmaceutical industry in China has played a significant role in affecting the course of negotiations and the domestic rule-making process in the

---

69 肖玮 [Zhou Hubin],《12家中国药企铁心告辉瑞：伟哥知识产权案胜负一线间》[Twelve Chinese Pharmaceutical Companies Determined to Sue Pfizer: Victory or Defeat in Viagra Intellectual Property Case Hangs by a Thread] [2006] 北京现代商报 *Beijing Modern Business News* 1, 1; Jeffrey A Andrews, 'Pfizer's Viagra Patent and the Promise of Patent Protection in China' (2006) 28(1) *Loyola of Los Angeles International and Comparative Law Review* 11, 11–15; Anonymous, 'TRIPS: With a Painful Birth, Uncertain Health, and a Host of Issues in China, Where Lies Its Future?' (2006) 7(523) *San Diego International Law Journal* 523, 537.

70 Andrews (n 69) 11–15; 谷禾 [Gu He],《博弈伟哥》[Battling Viagra] [2004] 中国医药指南 *China Medicine Guide* 9, 9.

71 Ibid.

72 Andrews (n 69) 12.

73 周胡斌 [Zhou Hubin],《专利审查中公众的角色：由"罗格列酮"专利无效案说起》[The Role of the Public in Patent Examination: Starting from the 'Rosiglitazone' Patent Invalidity Case] (2004)14(3) 中国医药导刊 *Chinese Journal of Medical Guide* 548, 548–549; Jane Parry, 'Drug Company Pulls Out of Chinese Lawsuit Over Diabetes Drug' (2004) 329 (7474) *BMJ* 476, 476; Hepeng Jia, 'Drugmakers Wrestle over Medicine Patents', *China Business Weekly* (Web Page, 2004). < http://www.chinadaily.com.cn/english/doc/2004-08/17/content_366249.htm >.

field of IP protection. They have sought to enhance their authority and legitimacy on controversial IP issues through lobbying activities and the creation of various business associations. As a result, many of the existing Chinese IP laws and enforcement policies have been created to protect 'entrenched IP commoditization interests'[74] and to enhance corporate rights and monopolies. This has resulted in an inherent bias in China's IP systems, which heavily favours corporate interests, provides them with significant protection for their tangible and intangible assets, and facilitates their appropriation and utilisation of TMK.

Nevertheless, such 'corporate protectionism[75] in terms of IP rights (particularly patents) poses an imminent threat to the protection of TMK and its knowledge holders. Most of the local communities in China are highly dependent upon the conservation and utilisation of TMK and genetic resources for their health care.[76] These are mostly passed on from generation to generation, usually through the medium of oral tradition and practice.[77] The communities' rights to assert their legitimate ownership over TMK are often customary and not codified into law, while the corporate practices can utilise the IP system to claim ownership over TMK and exploit it for corporate gain. The situation is highly damaging for TMK and the communities in China because it makes them susceptible to the exploitation of their knowledge by corporations who claim exclusive IP rights.

[74] Steven D Jamar and Lateef Mtima, 'The Centrality of Social Justice for an Academic Intellectual Property Institute' (2011) 64(3) *SMU Law Review* 101, 113.

[75] C Chaufan and F Mohamed, 'Unfortunate Distinction or Corporate Protectionism by Design?' (2020) 395(10,235) *Lancet* 1486, 1486.

[76] Huang Ji et al, 'An Ethnobotanical Study of Medicinal Plants Used by the Lisu people in Nujiang, Northwest Yunnan, China' (2004) 58 *Journal of Ethnobiology and Ethnomedicine* 253, 253–263; X Zhang, 'Traditional Medicine: Its Importance and Protection' in Sophia Twarog and Promila Kapoor (eds), *Protecting and Promoting Traditional Knowledge: System, National Experience and International Dimensions* (United Nations, 2004) 3, 3–6.

[77] 黄旭东 [Huang Xudong],《贵州民族民间医药知识产权保护研究》[Research on Intellectual Property Protection of Guizhou Ethnic Folk Medicine] (2006) 2(2) 贵州社会科学*Guizhou Social Sciences* 63, 63–69; 陈海玉 [Chen Haiyu],《云南少数民族口述医药文献的档案式保护研究》[Research on Archival Protection of Oral Medical Documents of Ethnic Minorities in Yunnan] (2011) 11(3), 兰台论坛 *Lantai Forum* 1, 3–4.

4.4 The Complex Nature of the Chinese IP System and Structural Bias Towards Industrial and Corporate Entities

4.4.1 The Two Faces of China's IP System

The history of IP indicates that when countries transform into innovative and creative economies, they normally become supporters of Western-style IP protection, as Japanese, South Korean, and Singaporean experiences indicate.[78] China is no exception to this trend as there have been strong sentiments and expectations among the Chinese people for the expansion of Western IP protection standards in China to attract advanced foreign technology and investment and to vitalise its domestic industries.[79] Nevertheless, instead of emulating and following the manner in which Western countries (such as the US) establish their IP systems, China has been charting its own path in designing, enforcing, and interpreting its IP-related laws (in particular, patent law), drawing inspiration extensively from its historical sources and cultural traditions.[80]

If there is anything specifically characteristic of the Chinese tradition in legal thought and philosophy, it is the Chinese dialectical epistemology, reasoning in ways that are entirely different from the formal logic paradigm in the Western tradition.[81] Chinese dialectical epistemology has a cognitive tendency to embrace inconsistencies, contradictions, and vagueness as the catalysts through which positive change and development occur.[82] It involves observing and understanding the interactions of contradictory relations in the social world, as well as the underlying principles and patterns that govern them.[83]

This approach to thinking has influenced China's IP law-making and law-implementation processes, resulting in two faces of IP-related laws and policies. On the one hand, the major themes of the very Western-inspired IP standards have been

---

78 PK Yu, 'Building Intellectual Property Coalitions for Development' in Jeremy de Beer (ed), *Implementing WIPO's Development Agenda* (Wilfrid Laurier University Press, 2008) 79, 94.

79 Mikhaelle Schiappacasse, 'Intellectual Property Rights in China: Technology Transfers and Economic Development ' (2004) 2(2) *Buffalo Intellectual Property Law Journal* 164, 164–185.

80 Mo Zhang, 'The Socialist Legal System with Chinese Characteristics: China's Discourse for the Rule of Law and a Bitter Experience' (2010) 39 *Temple International & Comparative Law Journal* 1, 5.

81 David YF Ho, 'Dialectical Thinking: Neither Eastern nor Western' (2000) 55(9) *The American Psychologist* 1064, 1064–1065.

82 左亚文 [Zuo Yawen],《中华和谐辩证思维的智慧特色与理性回归》[The Wisdom Characteristics and Rational Return of Chinese Harmonious Dialectical Thinking] [2019] 2 新时代马克思主义论丛 *New Era Marxist Theory Series* 199, 202–203.

83 郭方园 [Guo Fangyuan],《中华优秀传统文化中的和谐辩证思维方法意蕴探析》[An Analysis of the Implications of Harmonious Dialectical Thinking Methods in the Excellent Traditional Chinese Culture] [2021] 4 福建省社会主义学院学报 *Journal of Fujian Province Socialist College* 42, 44–46.

strongly embedded in China's IP legislation rhetoric: concepts such as individualism, exclusivity, and just reward are clear goals that the Chinese IP legislation adheres to, even though some are occasionally defined in contradictory and ambiguous ways. This situation projects the country's aspirations of becoming a more responsible great power in the global system.[84] Thus, China holds quite a tolerant attitude when foreign companies expand their businesses to China and create a market monopoly through their IP rights within the Chinese jurisdiction.

On the other hand, China's historical experience with a Western-centric international legal system has led to the practice of traditional wisdom acting conservatively and selectively, prioritising its self-interest. This includes imposing limits on the interpretation of international IP norms and the reach of international IP institutions.[85] As a result, China's national IP-related laws and policies have been created in an 'evolutionary way[86] to safeguard the economic contributions of small and medium-sized enterprises and aggressively safeguard against Western corporate powers.

Despite the apparent contradictions in China's approach to IP protection, these two aspects of China's IP system do not form a dichotomy; instead they interact in complicated and dialectical ways which build on one another, operate in both directions simultaneously, and respond to dissatisfactions with one another while then raising new problems.

The dialectical process that conjoins the two faces of China's IP system does not end when the two aspects are 'reconciled to form a new proposition'.[87] In contrast, they can later become new dialectical struggles which can then be integrated into a new cycle of dialectical thinking. To be specific, in the changing political, economic, and social context, China gradually changes its mindset and continuously embraces the Western-style IP norms.[88] However, in the characteristic Chinese manner of assimilating each contradiction, this is not an indication of passive acceptance. After decades of adapting to the Western imposition of IP, many in China have become convinced that, as most foreign technologies have some combination of patents, copyrights, and trademarks, the adoption of Western IP protection mechanisms is

[84] Björn Ahl, 'China's Perspectives on Public International Law: Selective Adaptation of International Treaties and the Community of Common Destiny Concept' (2022) *German Yearbook of International Law* 1,3.

[85] Lina Benabdallah, 'Contesting the International Order by Integrating It: The Case of China's Belt and Road Initiative' (2019) 40 *Third World Quarterly* 92, 92–108; Pitman B Potter, 'Globalization and Economic Regulation in China: Selective Adaptation of Globalized Norms and Practices' (2003) 2(1) *Washington University Global Studies Law Review* 119, 119–150.

[86] Thomas J Horton, 'Confucianism and Antitrust: China Confucianism and Antitrust: China's Emerging Evolutionary Approach to Anti-Monopoly Law' (2013) 47(2) *International Lawyer* 193, 216.

[87] Robert Emmons and Sarah Schnitker, 'Hegel's Thesis-Antithesis-Synthesis Model' in Anne Runehov and Lluis Oviedo (eds), *Encyclopedia of Sciences and Religions* (Springer, 2013) 978, 978.

[88] 吴珏[Wu Jue],《中国在知识产权问题上的立场与路径选择》[China's Stance and Path Selection on Intellectual Property Issues] [2015], 人民论坛 *People's Forum* 250, 252.

essential for, and instrumental in, attracting external technology and investment.[89] Nevertheless, by strictly complying with the Western-style IP system, the Chinese government has to address the detrimental effects that foreign activities and IP protection might have on local entities' interests if the foreign entities operating within China are unchecked.[90] To address these new dialectical struggles, the provisions of China's IP-related laws and policies must be carefully phrased and formulated to strike a balance between the country's desire to establish robust IP rights protection (to promote foreign investment and technology transfer) and its desire to impose greater limitations and exceptions to IP laws (to protect the interests of its domestic companies).

Article 56 of China's Patent Law (2020) is a typical existing provision that reflects the concept of the balance between the above-mentioned tensions and interplays, and which provides a detailed exception in the form of compulsory licensing: Patentees who hold patents to advanced versions of original patented invention and technologies can request a compulsory licence to exploit the original patented invention and technology where the creation of the subsequent invention depends upon the utilisation of the original patented invention. Similarly, the original patentee who holds patents to the original patented invention can request a compulsory licence of the subsequent patented invention that depends upon the exploitation of the original patented invention.[91]

The overall aim of this provision is the proper handling of the interactive relationship among the State, foreign multinational enterprises, and domestic industries in China. Its aim is to aid the State government in balancing the interests of foreign multinational corporations (typically holders of basic patents), while maintaining control over the invention for China's domestic corporations. It also strives to ensure reasonable flexibility in utilising the basic invention, and to curtail the monopoly position of the original patentee. China's existing approach to structuring the IP system (particularly the patent system) demonstrates its distinctive way of coping with disagreements and conflicts: retaining and strengthening the fundamental elements of opposing perspectives by seeking a 'middle way' between competing propositions.[92] This approach represents the complicated and dialectical interactions between modern legal norms and the traditional folk wisdom that stems from historical continuity,

---

[89] BM Hoekman, KE Maskus and K Saggi, 'Transfer of Technology to Developing Countries: Unilateral and Multilateral Policy Options' (2005) 33 *World Development* 1, 8; Maskus Keith, 'The New Globalisation of Intellectual Property Rights: What's New This Time?' (2014) 54(3) *Australian Economic History Review* 262.

[90] Richard Student, 'China's New Anti-Monopoly Law: Addressing Foreign Competitors and Commentators' (2008) 243 *Minnesota Journal of International Law* 503, 503.

[91] Patent Law (n 63) art 56.

[92] Dan Zhang and Emiliano T Hudtohan, 'Ecological Civilization: Creativity and Innovation in the New Normal Era' (2021) 1(3) *International Journal of Management and Education in Human Development* 85, 88.

and that has its roots in Confucius' golden mean theory. This theory seeks to cultivate the moderation, balance, and harmony within the change of circumstances.[93]

Arguably, the two dimensions of China's IP system have a dialectic relationship in that neither should replace the other, nor function without the other. The potential contribution of dialectical thinking and processes that conjoin the two faces of China's IP system is 'a state of permanent questioning, of transformation, change, an endless probing of appearances',[94] through which a dynamic balance can be sustained in the system. Nevertheless, these two faces are mere projections of the powerful corporate interests that remain centred on the competing propositions between foreign multinational enterprises and domestic small and medium-sized enterprises. Therefore, since the development of China's IP system is a dialectical process with an endless array of possibilities, attempts should be made to modify and reshape existing norms to accommodate and absorb the diverse interests and preferences of all groups of people. Ensuring that the vulnerable actors (such as China's local communities) are properly represented and their TMK adequately protected, is one of the most necessary steps for doing this, as well as for remedying broader shortcomings in terms of fairness and equity embedded within the regime as a whole.

4.4.2 The Roles of China's IP System in Assisting the Corporate Plunder of TMK and Associated Genetic Resources: The Example of Chinese Patent Law

The development, interpretation, and implementation of China's IP laws are not solely driven by the global expansion and harmonisation of Western legal culture, principles, and institutions. They are also significantly influenced by China's unique historical context and cultural values.[95] This hybrid system, blending Western legal doctrine with Chinese historical traditions, arguably forms a 'unique humanistic legal system'[96] that balances the interests of various stakeholders, including foreign multinational corporations and domestic industries.

However, it can be argued that this system tends to favour the interests of industrial players, particularly in the pharmaceutical sector, often at the expense of local communities who bear the brunt of the current IP system. This bias is evident in

[93] Y Fu, 'The Golden Mean of Confucianism and Intercultural Communication' (2005) 3 *The Northern Forum* 75, 75–78; 衣仁翠 [Yi Rencui]《中庸文化思想与司法正义研究》[Research on the Doctrine of the Mean (Zhongyong) Culture and Judicial Justice] (2013) 23(5) 梧州学院学报 *Journal of Wuzhou University*, 52, 52–55.

[94] L Stone, 'Julie Kristeva's "Mystery" of the Subject-in-Process' in JD Marshall (ed), *Poststructuralism, Philosophy, Pedagogy* (Kluwer Academic Publishers, 2004) 119, 133.

[95] 邱洪华 [Qiu Honghua],《文化视阈下的知识产权保护研究》[Research on Intellectual Property Protection under the Perspective of Cultural View] (2013) 28(5) 广西政法管理干部学院 *Journal of Guangxi Administration Institute for Political and Legal Cadres*, 65, 65–68.

[96] Thomas J Horton, 'Confucianism and Antitrust: China's Emerging Evolutionary Approach to Anti-Monopoly Law' (2013) 47(2) *International Lawyer* 193, 214.

the ease with which slight modifications or superficial changes to existing TMK and related genetic resources can be patented.[97]

Currently, China is witnessing an uptick in situations where research institutions and commercial entities exploit Chinese TMK, medicinal plants, and genetic resources.[98] This exploitation, typically facilitated by the national patent system,[99] has been likened to a 'contemporary gold rush', often with detrimental consequences for local communities.[100] This practice heightens the risks to the livelihoods of local communities and potentially undermines their capacity to sustain themselves, and has led to accusations of misappropriation or corporate hijacking of TMK.

Although the patent system is an area of IP law where considerable international harmonisations have occurred, the registration and enforcement of patent rights are peculiarly nationalistic.[101] In particular, under TRIPS, the Member States are required to comply with certain minimum standards for patent protection.[102] Nevertheless, they have a wide margin of discretion to fashion patent systems to fit their national conditions and satisfy local needs.[103]

Over the past few decades, China has made progresses in industry and technology, which has influenced its choices when designing its patent system.[104] Its reform agenda, aimed at industrial restructuring and advancing innovation and technology, has played a significant role in shaping its patent system.[105] On the one hand, strengthened patent protection is needed to attract investment and the most advanced

---

[97] Tesh W Dagne, 'The Protection of Traditional Knowledge in the Knowledge Economy: Cross-Cutting Challenges in International Intellectual Property Law' (2012) 14(2) *International Community Law Review* 1, 29.

[98] Pei Sheng-Ji, 'Ethnobotanical Approaches of Traditional Medicine Studies: Some Experiences from Asia' (2001) 39 *Pharmaceutical Biology* 74, 78; Weijuan Huang et al, 'Ethnobotanical Study on Medicinal Plants Used by Li People in Ledong, Hainan Island, China' (2016) 85(1) *Acta Societatis Botanicorum Poloniae* 1, 2.

[99] Ibid.

[100] Ikechi Mgbeoji, 'Patents and Traditional Knowledge of the Uses of Plants: Is a Communal Patent Regime Part of the Solution to the Scourge of Bio Piracy' (2001) 9(1) *Indiana Journal of Global Legal Studies* 163, 185.

[101] Studies have proved beyond a shadow of doubt that States, especially in the 'global North', Latin America, and Asia, prefer to have patent laws that serve their respective national agendas, particularly in terms of social, cultural, and economic priorities, and sovereignty: See generally Ikechi Mgbeoji, 'Patents and Traditional Knowledge of the Uses of Plants: Is a Communal Patent Regime Part of the Solution to the Scourge of Bio Piracy' (2001) 9(1) *Indian Journal of Global Legal Studies* 163, 174.

[102] *The Agreement on Trade-Related Aspects of Intellectual Property Rights 1995*, art 1.1.

[103] 黄凤达 [Huang Fengda],《国际投资仲裁对TRIPS协议灵活性的挑战及其应对》[The Challenge of International Investment Arbitration to the Flexibility of the TRIPS Agreement and Its Response] [2020] 西部学刊 *Western Academic Journal* 73, 73–76; Patricia L Judd, 'Retooling TRIPS' (2014) 55 *Virginia Journal of International Law* 117, 120.

[104] Ping Li, 'The Outlook for China's Innovation-Driven development Beyond COVID-19' (2020) 3(4) *Cultures of Science* 232, 235.

[105] 赵元果 [Zhao Yuanguo],《中国专利法的孕育与诞生》[The Nurturing and Birth of Chinese Patent Law] (Intellectual Property Press, 2016) 33–41.

technologies from foreign countries, thus fostering economic advancement.[106] On the other hand, the country also has the willingness to create greater limitations and exceptions to patent-related laws and regulations so that the development of its domestic industries and their need to practice the transferred technologies are not disadvantaged.[107] On this basis, China's contemporary regime on patents has been deliberately created to manage these dialectical tension. Nevertheless, there is arguably a structural bias in the Chinese patent regime—a bias conferring privileges on more powerful industrial and corporate actors. Its particular standards for patentability have tilted sharply in favour of the industrial and corporate interests while more vulnerable actors such as China's local communities may see their TMK and associated genetic resources whittled away by corporate privatisation through the patent process.

4.4.2.1 Patent-Eligible Subject Matter

At the time of writing, the Chinese patent system is operating under the *Patent Law of the People's Republic of China* as amended in 2020. This legislation, as described in Chapter 2, outlines the parameters of patentability.[108] Chief among the requirements is whether the claimed invention is patentable subject matter. This requirement becomes especially controversial when dealing with inventions derived from TMK and genetic resources.

Article 25 of the *Chinese Patent Law (2020)* sets out exceptions to patentable subject matter, stating that mere discoveries of nature are not inherently patentable, no matter how perfectly worded and comprehensively drafted the claims might be.[109] Nevertheless, the *Chinese Patent Examination Guidelines (2020)* provide a counterpoint,[110] suggesting that naturally occurring materials isolated or purified through 'a human manufacturing process' could be patentable subject matter, provided they meet all other patentability criteria.[111] This suggests the necessity for human interventions or activities to justify patent protection for inventions linked to TMK and genetic resources in China.

This broader understanding of patentable subject matter (stretching to include the idea of human intervention in traditional knowledge and genetic resources) has led to unprecedented increases in audacious human tampering with TMK and associated genetic resources in China. As a result, the Chinese patent offices have

---

[106] Ibid.

[107] Ibid.

[108] China's Patent Law (n 63) ch 2.

[109] China's Patent Law, (n 63) art 25.

[110] 《专利审查指南》 [Chinese Patent Examination Guidelines] (People's Republic of China) National Intellectual Property Administration, Order No.391, 2020 (*Chinese Patent Examination Guidelines*).

[111] *Chinese Patent Examination Guidelines*, (n 110) 284 [6.1].

started granting patents on living organisms and on TMK embodied in products and processes.

Given this context, pharmaceutical companies in China are arguably incentivised to secure broadly scoped patents pertaining to 'invention' closely related to TMK and genetic resources through the proper construction of patent claims. For instance, they often seek to patent bioactive compounds and medicinal products consisting of active ingredients purified from genetic resources and informed by TMK. This approach is justifiable as isolating, purifying, and concentrating compounds and active ingredients from natural substances that necessitates significant human intervention and innovation, potentially constituting patentable subject matter as per the Chinese Patent Examination Guidelines (2020). Typically, the language in patent claims for such purified compounds includes statements like 'the compounds are essentially pure and free from contaminants encountered when such compounds are isolated from natural resources'.

Additionally, there may be situations where it is not feasible to purify a bioactive compound from its natural source using existing TMK in combination with modern pharmaceutical techniques. In these cases, patentable claims related to TMK and associated genetic resources can be derived from a description of their unique 'fingerprint'.[112] For example, rather than defining a purified compound by its formal chemical structure, China frequently employs 'product-by-process claims'.[113] This approach aligns more closely with the nature of China's TMK.[114] "It is utilised to characterise inventions arising from TMK and associated genetic resources which cannot be identified by physical attributes'; instead it focuses on their manufacturing process".[115]

China's traditional medicinal products contain a wide range of unknown bioactive compounds with various unknown concentrations.[116] These complex mixtures have synergistic effects and must be used as an interrelated entity to treat illnesses.[117] The single bioactive compound is difficult to purify and not as effective as the original medicinal mixtures. In this situation, the product-by-process claim format arguably provides a desirable option for constructing the patent claims for China's TMK-based inventions and products. In general, these claims can be drafted as 'X obtained by process Y' or 'X obtainable by process Y', and 'X of process Y comprising the steps of'. Since the claimed product is defined by the process, such a product patent

---

[112] Rochelle K Seide and Janet M MacLeod, 'Drafting Claims for Biotechnology Inventions' (2000) 4 *International Intellectual Property Law & Policy* 52–53.

[113] 田晓玲 [Tian Xiaoling],《中药复方专利保护研究》[Research on the patent protection of traditional Chinese medicine compound prescriptions] (2007) 2 江西社会科学 *Journal of Southwest University for Nationalities* 122, 122–123; Xuan Li and Weiwei Li, 'Inadequacy of Patent Regime on Traditional Medicinal Knowledge' 10(2) *The Journal of World Intellectual Property* 125, 140.

[114] Ibid.

[115] Ibid.

[116] Xiaojie Xu, 'New Concepts and Approaches for Drug Discovery based on Traditional Chinese Medicine' (2006) 3(3) *Drug Discov Today Technol* 247, 250.

[117] Yinghong Liu et al, 'Synergistic Effect of Traditional Chinese Medicine' (2007) 19(2) *Asian Journal of Chemistry* 867, 868–869.

avoids the exclusion of patentability on the condition that the process is ‘a human manufacturing process’.

Based on the above analysis, China is arguably moving towards a more encompassing patent system by expanding its patent-eligible subject matter. The system has largely been developed to suit China’s national goals of driving pharmaceutical innovation and seizing advanced technology. Nevertheless, despite this noticeable progress, the extension of patent-eligible subject matter in Chinese jurisdiction largely favours corporate privatisation through the patent of TMK and associated genetic resources. This can possibly result in social and economic conditions that are detrimental to TMK holders and their communities, for example, undermining knowledge holders and their communities’ control over TMK. The argument here is not advocating against a more encompassing patent system in China, but simply that, if it is necessary to expand the patent-eligible subject matter, it has to be done in a considered and balanced way. Such an approach should make sure that the boundary of the invention is reasoned and framed in a way that involves appropriate consideration of the TMK of communities, for instance, taking into account the needs and interests of knowledge holders and their communities.

4.4.2.2 Novelty

The element of novelty is one of the basic requirements for an invention to be patentable in China.[118] The novelty criteria in China’s patent system restrict patents for all inventions that are part of any prior art, which includes everything made available to the public through published documentation, public use, or any other means before the filing date (priority date).[119]

Despite China’s very strict novelty standard, in practice, meeting the requirements for novelty is not as difficult as might be expected. For example, while the properties and uses of TMK and associated genetic resources—ultimately leading to the commercial development of pharmaceutical products—may be publicly known or even well documented by the State and local communities, the novelty of the pharmaceutical invention derived from TMK and associated genetic resources can still be acknowledged.

This acknowledgement is possible because patent claims usually define the subject matter as the active ingredients or compounds derived from genetic resources or inspired by TMK.[120] In this context, the mere publication of genetic resources used in China’s traditional medical systems, or even describing their specific uses, activities, and effects are, in many cases, not sufficient to destroy the novelty of patent claims that include the active ingredients, the structure of the compounds, and the methods for isolating them.

---

[118] China’s Patent Law (n 63) art 22[1].

[119] *Chinese Patent Examination Guidelines* (n 110) 153 [22.2].

[120] Li and Li (n 113) 133–134.

In other instances, there are patent applications claiming to contain herbal compositions and formulations (obtained from a mixture of Indigenous herbs and genetic materials), which are usually acquired based on the TMK of China.[121] In this situation, it is common practice in China's pharmaceutical field to claim the whole class of herbal composition and the formulae with a myriad of possible variants by using 'Markush patent claims'—a patent claim style, introduced by Eugene Markush in 1924, allowing the applicant to claim an extensive range of related chemical compounds in one single claim by identifying their variable components.[122]

Thus, even if the novelty of one class of compositions and formulations may be destroyed by prior publication or disclosure, the novelty of a myriad of other alternative compositions and formulations may not be as easily undermined.

Most notably, unlike many other jurisdictions, China's Patent Law requires an almost 'photographic' disclosure of the invention (disclosing all features and elements of the relevant claims) in a single prior publication to destroy novelty.[123] This is despite the fact that a skilled person in the art may be able to derive the invention without effort from a combination of various prior publications.[124] Arguably, this 'single prior publication' rule narrows the reservoir of prior art for novelty purposes, thus having the effect of further lowering the actual novelty threshold in China.

Moreover, China's patent system may also confer rights over new medical use or second medical use of known genetic resources and TMK, as long as such new uses are based on a technical effect that is unknown previously.[125] On this basis, so-called 'Swiss-type' claims are often used in China as a common way to obtain a patent right for new medical use or second medical use of TMK and associated genetic resources.[126] The claims are usually drafted as 'use of X for manufacturing a medicament for the treatment of disease Y' or the like.[127] Arguably, the merit of conferring patents upon new uses and second uses (typically relevant to the uses of known genetic resources or TMK for therapeutic aims) is that the corporate actors could exploit this legal possibility to circumvent the novelty requirements under China's patent systems. This is because the use of the invention is an invention of the method of application. Its novelty largely resides in the specific use of the claimed subject matter, and the substance of the invention lies in how to use the product rather than the product per se.[128] More significantly, the new uses of patent and Swiss-type claims arguably remove the barriers to the commercial exploitation of the TMK and associated genetic resources. For example, without these, the established knowledge

[121] Li and Li (n 113) 134.

[122] Xinsheng Wang and Albert Wai-Kit Chan, 'Commentary Challenges and Patenting Strategies for Chinese Herbal Medicine' (2010) 5 *Chinese Medicine* 1, 2.

[123] *Chinese Patent Examination Guidelines* (n 110) 157 [3.1.2].

[124] Ibid.

[125] *Chinese Patent Examination Guidelines* (n 110) 179 [4.5], 284[5.4].

[126] Ouyang Shiwen and Zhang Lihua, 'China's Developing Approach to Swiss-type Claims' (2014) 241 *Managing Intellectual Property* 34.

[127] *Chinese Patent Examination Guidelines* (n 110) 282 [4.5.2].

[128] *Chinese Patent Examination Guidelines* (n 110) 284 [5.4].

of *Artemisia annua*'s antimalarial properties or its acknowledged use as traditional medicine in China might fail to meet the novelty requirements for patentability. This, in turn, somewhat limits the commercial exploitation of TMK and genetic resources.

Nonetheless, the presence of new uses patents and Swiss-type claims allows continued exploitation of *Artemisia annua*'s antimalarial properties, given that novel applications continue to be discovered. This scenario could conceivably equip corporations with the motivation to broaden their exploitation into new applications of TMK and recognised resources, held by generations of local communities in China, for industrial or commercial gains.

4.4.2.3 Inventiveness

Another patentability requirement in China is the existence of inventiveness or non-obviousness. This is usually examined after the novelty has been affirmed, as something might be novel but might not involve a substantial contribution to the existing art.[129] The Chinese patent system allows for two different categories of patents—the invention patent and the utility model.[130] These two types of patents are subject to different standards of inventiveness. An invention patent is required to have 'prominent substantive features and to represent notable progress when compared with prior art.[131] The threshold of inventiveness for the utility model is lower, requiring merely 'substantive features' and 'improvement' over existing art (compared with that expected of the invention patent).[132] However, these requirements for analysing the inventiveness of patent claims in China do not adopt the term 'non-obviousness' as often used in other jurisdictions; instead they adopt broad and descriptive terms such as 'prominent', 'notable', and 'substantive' in defining inventiveness. Arguably, these elusive standards in defining inventiveness reflect the country's imperatives to develop a patent system that is, in principle, as 'fluid and changeable as the economy and society which it is supposed to regulate',[133] thus allowing some room for harbouring a major tension, or a paradox, within the changing dynamics of the enterprises and economy in China. This principle represents the 'extension of the tenets and qualities of Confucianism'[134] rooted in Chinese traditional culture, which emphasises the context-dependent and flexible relationships among things in changing fields of focus, and the possibilities of using this flexibility to accommodate

[129] China's Patent Law (n 63) art 22[2].

[130] China's Patent Law (n 63) art 2.

[131] China's Patent Law (n 63) art 22[2]; *Chinese Patent Examination Guidelines* (n 110) 170 [2.2]–[2.3].

[132] China's Patent Law, (n 63) art 22[2]; *Chinese Patent Examination Guidelines* (n 110) 411[22.3].

[133] PH Corne, 'Creation and Application of Law in the PRC' (2002) 50(2) *The American Journal of Comparative Law* 369, 375.

[134] Micaela Tucker, '"Guanxi!"—"Gesundheit!" An Alternative View on the "Rule of Law" Panacea in China' (2011) 35 *Vermont Law Review* 689, 711.

tensions and potential conflicts.[135] On this basis, the vagueness and excessive generality embedded in the inventiveness standards reflect China's unique legal reform experience, during which it was able to mix foreign imports with Chinese historical traditions, and to recast many imported foreign ideas to be in line with the ideological aims and policy goals of the State.

On the one hand, China's leadership and law-makers possess a profound desire to enhance the country's global standing, to cultivate its reputation as a responsible major world power, and to advance its international interests, all of which, in part, rely on the inflow of foreign technology and investments.[136] In this regard, the ostensible adoption of Western standards for patentability and the strict compliance with the fundamental legal obligations of the WTO's TRIPS is arguably the prerequisite for addressing foreign corporations' anxiety about the lack of IP protection in China, thus attracting technology transfer and investments.[137] On the other hand, China has 'preserved the most cherished aspects of their traditional culture' to carefully analyse all sides of an issue and be ready to selectively and flexibly adapt elements of international legal rules. As one of many 'historical artifacts', such domestic legal flexibility and 'selective adaptation' (embedded in the inventiveness standards of China's Patent Law) provide the authorities with an opportunity to construe the law's broad language to reduce the risks of overpaying for foreign patents and to create opportunities for domestic innovators and firms to engage those flexibilities to their own ends.[138] Arguably, the ideological commitment to both adaptability and compliance with international legal obligations, as manifested in the inventiveness standards, presents a viable and effective combination. This combination not only mirrors the historical continuity of dialectic traditions found in China but, more importantly, this commitment has been instrumental in enabling the standards of inventiveness in China's Patent Law to address a variety of modern policy objectives. These include fostering domestic innovation and promoting the economic advancement of entire societies.

Despite attempts to balance the interests of various stakeholders in China, the threshold level of inventiveness required for patentability leans heavily in favour of industrial actors, particularly those in the pharmaceutical sector. This is arguably due to China's relative lack of maturity in the pharmaceutical field, where radical innovation is rare and research activities are typically incremental.[139] This scenario complicates the evaluation of the scope of prior art, the combination of prior art, and the determination of knowledge of a person with ordinary skill in the art.

---

[135] Ibid 702.

[136] Justin W Evans, 'Explaining China's Legal Flexibility: History and the Institutional Imperative' (2018) 31 *Pace International Law Review* 173, 238.

[137] Ada Yue Wang, 'The Test Of Inventiveness In Chinese Patent Jurisprudence: Recent History, Cases, And Analysis' (2019) 265 *Journal Of Law, Technology & Policy* 265, 277.

[138] 赵元果[Zhao Yuanguo],《中国专利法的孕育与诞生》[The Nurturing and Birth of Chinese Patent Law] (Intellectual Property Press, 2016) 253.

[139] 徐惟 [Xu Wei],《我国医药制造业创新不足原因探究: 以江苏省为例》[Investigating the Lack of Innovation in China's Pharmaceutical Manufacturing Industry: A Case Study of Jiangsu Province] [2022]中国医疗保险 Chinese Health Insurance 113, 114–115.

As a result, China has developed industry-specific standards for obviousness in the pharmaceutical context to cater to corporate interests.[140] For instance, the *Chinese Patent Examination Guidelines (2020)* state that the inventiveness of a pharmaceutical compound for disease treatment should not be denied solely based on structural similarity unless it lacks any unexpected effects.[141] Likewise, the inventiveness of the medical use of already known pharmaceutical products should not be denied simply based on similarities of structure, composition, and physicochemical properties unless they do not provide any unexpected effects or new uses.[142]

These guidelines arguably lower the bar for pharmaceutical patents, accounting for the complexity, uncertainty, and expensive nature of pharmaceutical innovations. Additionally, the utility model patent regime in China serves as another policy lever favouring pharmaceutical corporations and their innovations. As already discussed, the inventiveness standards for utility model patents under China's patent law are easier to meet than those for invention patents.

More significantly, the *Chinese Patent Examination Guidelines (2020)* state that the utility model patent application only undergoes a formality examination without substantive examination. This policy arguably dilutes, and even waives, the inventiveness requirements for utility models in practice. This could provide an overly easy pathway for less innovative pharmaceutical patents to be granted.

Given that TMK and associated genetic resources can provide valuable inputs for developing useful compounds and pharmaceutical products, the low inventiveness bar, heavily favouring corporations, could offer an advantageous platform for companies that thrive on innovations derived from TMK and associated resources within local Chinese communities.

However, the inventiveness standards under China's Patent law do not account for potential unfairness towards other stakeholders or pre-existing providers of TMK and associated genetic resources, such as China's local communities, who fall outside of the corporate-consumer nexus. This situation could legitimise corporate exploitation of TMK and associated genetic resources and facilitate corporate profiteering at the expense of China's local communities.

4.4.2.4 'Practical Applicability' or 'Utility'

The requirements that an invention must have 'utility' or 'practical applicability' constitute another fundamental patentability criterion in China.[143] Based on Article 22 of *Chinese Patent Law* (2020), the utility or practical applicability' requires that an invention or utility model must be 'capable of being made or used', in such a way

---

[140] Yi-Chen Su, 'What About Know-How: Heightened Obviousness and Lowered Disclosure is Not a Panacea to the Patent System for Biotechnology Medication and Pharmaceutical Inventions in the Post-KSR Era' (2010) 14(2) *Marquette Intellectual Property Law Review* 322, 346.

[141] *Chinese Patent Examination Guidelines* (n 110) 284 [6.1].

[142] Ibid [6.2].

[143] China's Patent Law (n 63) art 22.

as to 'create effective results'.[144] 'Capable of being made or used' is further defined and explained in the *Chinese Patent Examination Guidelines* as 'being susceptible to industrial manufacturing or application'.[145] The Guidelines outline specific conditions under which inventions may be deemed lacking in utility or practical applicability.[146] This encompasses inventions that cannot be reliably reproduced, among other criteria.[147] Arguably, such requirements for patentability provide narrow and relaxed thresholds that are primarily intended to encourage the transformation of resources, knowledge, and locally generated information to industrial applications or mass-produced products, thus advancing corporate and industrial interests.

These thresholds are narrow because they are merely aiming to maximise industrial and commercial utility.[148] The simple processes of isolation, purification, and adding a few technical elements and improvements that are suitable for industrial mass-production and for certain useful purposes are sufficient to meet these criteria.[149] Nevertheless, unlike some other jurisdictions (such as the US) where the utility requirements are focused on being capable of 'some beneficial use to society',[150]

Moreover, the utility or practical applicability requirements under China's Patent Law are arguably relaxed because they allow almost all the inventions that are susceptible to industrial manufacturing or application to pass the requirements.[151] This situation demonstrates why these requirements are recognised as a relatively low bar to patentability,[152] thus receiving very little consideration in China. Nevertheless, some exceptional cases do occur in which the relaxed requirements have not been given sufficient consideration. For instance, the developments of many pharmaceutical inventions are based on access to endangered TMK and jeopardised species held by local communities. These cannot be acquired on a large scale, thus making industrial mass production unfeasible.[153] However, the requirements of utility or practical

[144] Ibid.

[145] *Chinese Patent Examination Guidelines* (n 110) 186 [3.2].

[146] Ibid [3.2.1]–[3.2.6].

[147] Ibid.

[148] 陈一孚[Chen Yifu],《论中药和专利制度之间的兼容性：以中药发明的实用性审查为视角》[Compatibility between Traditional Chinese Medicine and Patent System—From the Perspective of "Practical Applicability" of Chinese Medicine Inventions] (2016) 2理论与改革*Theory and Reform* 122, 124.

[149] 谢立安娜[Xie Lianna],《浅述中国制药业的专利权保护》[Discussion about Patent Protection in Chinese Pharmaceutical Industry] (2015) 2法制博览*Legality Vision* 228, 228.

[150] Timothy A Worrall, 'The 2001 PTO Utility Examination Guidelines and DNA Patents' (2001) 16 *Berkeley Technology Law Journal* 123, 129; Dev A Ghose, 'A Proposal to Modify the Utility Standard for Patenting Biotechnology Research Tools' (2007) 56 *Emory Law Journal* 1662, 1666.

[151] 管荣齐[Guan Rongqi],《我国专利实质条件的改进建议》[Suggestions for Improvement of the Patentability Requirements in China] (2013) 2知识产权*Intellectual Property* 71, 73; 李昭[Guan Rongqi],《基因专利申请与审查问题研究》[Research on Gene Patent Application and Examination] (2020) 11黑龙江科学*Helongjiang Science* 145, 146.

[152] Ibid.

[153] 陈一孚[Chen Yifu] (n 148) 125.

applicability under China's Patent Law do not bar the patentability of inventions that are based on limited access to the endangered TMK and associated species, as long as the knowledge and associated species are accessible to the public.

Therefore, arguably, these narrow and relaxed standards may make it easier for industrial and corporate actors in the pharmaceutical field to appropriate the TMK and associated genetic resources by patenting them for their own use. On this basis, pharmaceutical corporations in China could simply justify their patents (related to TMK, associated genetic resources, and locally generated information) on the basis that they have invested money to put the invention into industrial-scale production for pharmaceutical use (despite not much being added to transform the TMK and associated raw material into a new product). This would then meet the utility or practical applicability standards of patentability. This situation challenges the overall fairness of the current patent regime in China, which adds to the assets of pharmaceutical corporations at the expense of the economic enhancement of local communities (upon whose TMK and associated genetic resources the patented pharmaceutical inventions are based).

4.4.2.5 Disclosure of Origin Requirements in Patent Applications

Disclosure of origin requirements exists in the domestic laws of many countries, including China. These have the intention of promoting transparency and accountability in the use of genetic resources and traditional knowledge during the invention process.[154] These requirements are particularly relevant when IP rights, such as patents, are sought. Despite the lack of a universally accepted model for formulating these requirements, their overarching goal is to prevent the granting of patents based on knowledge or resources that have been improperly acquired by third parties.[155]

In this context, it is important to note that discussions and critical analyses around disclosure of origin requirements are ongoing at both the international and national levels, with countries adopting various approaches to address this issue. For instance, Article 26 (5) of the *Chinese Patent Law (2020)* mandates patent applicants to disclose the origin of genetic resources used in their inventions: An applicant who files a patent application for an invention-creation completed on the basis of genetic resources shall in the patent application document indicate the direct and indirect source of the genetic resources; the applicant unable to indicate the original source of the genetic resource must provide an explanation.[156]Arguably, the language used in this

[154] M Rahmah, N Barizah and S Blay, 'Ensuring Disclosure of Origin of Genetic Resources in Patent Applications: Indonesia's efforts to Combat Biopiracy' (2020) 25(1–2) *Journal of Intellectual Property Rights* 40, 40–54; Margo A Bagley, 'Designing Disclosure: Disclosure Of Cultural And Genetic Resource Utilisation In Design Protection Regimes' in Susy Frankel (ed), *The Object and Purpose of Intellectual Property* (Elgaronline, 2019) 110, 110–153.

[155] 黎舒婷 [Li Shuting],《浅析专利申请中如何对遗传资源来源进行披露》[A Brief Analysis of How to Disclose the Source of Genetic Resources in Patent Applications] (2014) 21(4) 药物生物技术*Pharmaceutical Biotechnology* 355, 355; Bagley (n 154) 148.

[156] China's Patent Law (n 63) art 26(5).

provision suggests that the requirement for disclosing the origin in Chinese patent applications is perceived more as a formality than as a critical part of substantive patentability requirements. In other words, the emphasis on disclosure of origin seems to be more of a procedural step, rather than a strict requirement that could impact the success or failure of the patent application. For example, the provision implies that if an applicant, such as a corporation, can provide an explanation, any failure or even wrongful disclosure of the genetic resources' origin will not hinder the acceptance or granting of the patent application. This could potentially create a significant loophole in the patent application process, with the risk that some entities might exploit this gap to their advantage. More significantly, SIPO does not monitor the applications in which disclosure of origin has been made.[157] If an applicant submits misleading information regarding the origin, it may go undetected by the patent examiners.[158] On this basis, while corporations and other interested parties may voluntarily subscribe to the requirements on disclosure of origin, there are significant gaps to allow them to circumvent the requirements.

Furthermore, it is worth noting that the disclosure of origin obligation is not required for inventions involving traditional knowledge (including TMK).[159] This approach can be seen as consistent with the perspectives of some scholars who argue that China's legal and policy options prioritise the utilisation of TMK for innovation over its protection as a standalone entity.[160] This approach may disproportionately favour pharmaceutical corporations' motivations and interests in exploiting TMK for profit over the collective interests of knowledge holders and their communities who seek to protect TMK and their traditional health practices.

By excluding traditional knowledge from the disclosure of origin requirement, its value and significance may be undermined. This could indirectly encourage corporations to exploit, research, and test TMK, potentially leading to its development into commercial pharmaceutical products and the granting of patents that favour corporate interests. As a result, TMK, knowledge holders, and their communities may experience more harm than good.

Moreover, the lack of disclosure of origin requirements for traditional knowledge in national patent law may inadvertently relegate it to the public domain, treating it as 'the property of nobody'.[161] This situation could further diminish the ability of knowledge holders and their communities to control their traditional knowledge,

---

[157] Wenting Cheng, 'The Protection of Genetic Resources in Chinese Patent Law' (2021) 43(4) *European Intellectual Property Review* 248, 251.

[158] Ibid.

[159] 严永和 [Yan Yonghe],《中国专利法传统资源来源披露的制度构建: 以中医药传统知识为对象》[The Construction of A Disclosure System for Traditional Resource Sources in China's Patent Law: With Traditional Chinese Medicine Knowledge as the Object] (2020) 33(10)中国医学伦理学*Chinese Medical Ethics* 1167, 1170.

[160] C Schulz, 'Money or Pride? On the Why and How of Traditional Knowledge Protection in India and China' (2011) 1(1) *Konstanzer Journal für Politik und Verwaltung* 52, 55.

[161] Suchita Shah, 'Plants, Patents and Biopiracy: The Globalization of Intellectual Property Rights and Traditional Medicine' (2014) 8(1) *Global Health Governance* 57, 65.

while also obstructing the recognition of the value of their long-term and incremental management efforts.

4.5 Beyond the Present: A Cultural and Historical Approach to Reforming Patent Law

The above analysis demonstrates that China's IP-related laws, particularly patent laws, are arguably oppressive as they stand, and have 'neither intellectual nor moral support'.[162] Instead, they operate as a justification for the unfair exploitation of TMK and reinforce structural inequalities where corporate interests are prioritised over protecting the TMK of knowledge holders and their communities. Recognising these shortcomings necessitates urgent reform. The aim of such an overhaul should be to realign China's patent laws, pivoting away from a system that encourages corporate monopolisation, towards one that appreciates and upholds the historical and cultural essence deeply rooted within the nation.

4.5.1 Reforming China's Patentability Requirements: A Historical and Cultural Approach

China's current patent system emphasises key requirements like novelty, inventiveness, and industrial applicability. As highlighted above, this approach fosters a technological innovation perspective, often favouring large corporations equipped with extensive resources for research and development. To create a more equitable patent system, China could consider reforming the existing patentability criteria by integrating traditional values that have deep roots in the country's culture and history. Central to this reform could be principles deeply rooted in Confucianism, such as enhancing social welfare, encouraging environmental sustainability, and fostering societal harmony.[163]

Implementing these changes would necessitate a thorough re-evaluation and overhaul of the existing patent application guidelines and the current patent laws. The goal would be to incorporate these specific areas—social welfare, environmental sustainability, and societal harmony—as crucial factors in the patentability assessment. This is not just an addition of new criteria, but rather, a profound reorientation of the system that could fundamentally change the nature of patents granted.

There could be a unique, forward-thinking system established to assign preferential bonus points to specific patent applications—a model that not only evaluates the

---

[162] E Moglen, 'The Melting of Patent Law' (2009) 5 *Indian JL & Tech* 33, 33.

[163] Ying Li et al, 'Sustainability from a Chinese Cultural Perspective: The Implications of Harmonious Development in Environmental Management' (2016) 18 *Environment, Development and Sustainability* 679, 682–688.

novelty, inventiveness, and utility of the invention, but also its potential social impact. This system would encourage inventions that are profoundly aligned with Chinese traditional values, primarily drawing from Confucian tenets. The emphasis could be placed on advancing social welfare, advocating for environmental sustainability, and cultivating societal harmony. All these aspects are pillars of Confucian philosophy, indicating that the system would not only stimulate innovation but would also ensure that such innovation respects societal and environmental considerations, guiding all involved towards a harmoniously balanced future.

For instance, an invention that puts forward a solution to a pressing social issue could be awarded additional points, facilitating its progress through the patent examination process. Similarly, innovations that are eco-friendly could be recognised and prioritised, as they resonate with the Confucian respect for nature and environmental preservation. Furthermore, patent applications that embody principles of societal harmony, such as technologies that bridge social inequalities or enhance community engagement, could be expedited.

In addition to the proposed revisions, there is the potential for the establishment of an independent, dedicated panel consisting of experts within these specialised areas. The primary function of these specialists would be to meticulously evaluate the compatibility of the proposed innovations with the underlying Confucian principles, the potential societal and environmental benefits, as well as their economic viability. This could ensure that the inventions not only meet technical patenting requirements but also align with the strategic objectives underlined by these traditional values.

Such an approach could transform the patenting process from being purely corporate and innovation-focused to a holistic one, aligning technological progress with societal needs, while also upholding key cultural values and respecting historical legacy and wisdom. By assigning value to the societal benefits and environmental impacts of an invention, alongside its novelty and inventiveness, China could usher in a paradigm shift, paving the way for patents that contribute positively to society and the environment, echoing the historical and cultural essence deeply rooted within the nation.

4.5.2 *Enhancing Disclosure of Origin Requirements in the Chinese Patents Regime*

Confucianism places significant emphasis on tradition, historical precedent, and a deep reverence for ancestors and the recognition of their contributions. China could undertake a reform of its patent system based on the principles of Confucianism to introduce a more robust and explicit acknowledgement of traditional knowledge and associated genetic resources, fostering an environment of respect and reverence for past wisdom within the realm of modern innovation. The key to achieving this lies in refining the disclosure of origin requirements in China's patent system, whereby a deeper connection is forged between the wisdom of the past and the innovation of the present.

As previously discussed in this chapter, the current Chinese patent system, while it requires the disclosure of origin in patent applications, has certain limitations. These shortcomings can inadvertently contribute to structural inequalities, thus necessitating careful scrutiny and potential reform. These insights form the basis for the proposed reform, where enhancing the disclosure of origin requirements in patent applications stands as a critical strategy to address these inequalities. The envisaged reform could manifest as a strengthened requirement for patent applicants to fully disclose the origin of the traditional knowledge (including TMK) incorporated in their invention. A crucial element of this reform would be the stipulation for applicants to prove that they have obtained Prior Informed Consent (PIC) from the Indigenous and local communities who have traditionally been the guardians of this knowledge.

To further streamline and support the reform, the creation of a centralised national entity is proposed. This body would shoulder the responsibility of the comprehensive protection, preservation, and promotion of traditional knowledge, including TMK. By dedicating its representation to TMK holders and their communities, this organisation would function as a collective voice for these stakeholders, bolstering their rights and contributing to a more equitable patent system. The establishment of this organisation would act as a direct response to the strengthened disclosure requirements, further fostering a harmonious interface between traditional knowledge and contemporary patent practices.

Within this revamped structure, patent applicants in China would be required to affirm whether their invention was developed utilising Chinese traditional knowledge, including TMK. In situations where this connection is disputed, the centralised authority, as the representative of traditional knowledge holders, would have the right to challenge the claim. This authoritative role of the central entity would further safeguard the interests of these knowledge holders. It would reinforce the need for disclosure and respect for traditional knowledge, including TMK, in the innovation process, creating an environment that honours both scientific advancement and cultural heritage.

Building upon this context, the reform in China's patent laws can be interpreted not only as a practical adjustment but also as a philosophical realignment that reflects the country's profound intellectual traditions. The proposed reinforcement of the origin disclosure requirement coherently aligns with the distinct ethos and historical wisdom inherent in Chinese dialectical philosophy, a system emphasising balance, change, and interconnectedness.[164] This enhancement seeks to strike a balance between technological advancements led by corporate innovation and the preservation of traditional knowledge, including TMK. This harmonious balance embodies the fundamental Chinese dialectical concept of unifying opposites. The proposal acknowledges the dynamic relationship between new inventions and traditional knowledge, reflecting the acceptance of continual transformation that is a

[164] 左亚文[Zuo Yawen] (n 82) 202–203.

cornerstone of Chinese cultural thought.[165] Additionally, by fostering transparency about the sources from which patented inventions or innovations arise, it underscores the philosophy's tenet of interconnectedness among system stakeholders. Therefore, this enhanced origin disclosure requirement demonstrates a real-world implementation of Chinese dialectical philosophy, bringing to life its key tenets of balance, transformation, and interdependence within the IP landscape.

4.5.3 A Statutory Exclusion to Patentability

A more audacious strategy to address the systemic bias in China's patent system is to enact a statutory exclusion for patentability of inventions predicated on traditional knowledge, with a focus on TMK, paired with other modifications to China's prevailing patent law. Central to these exclusions are notions of 'ordre public' and 'morality'.[166] The underlying aim is to protect TMK from exploitation, while ensuring that the patent law remains flexible enough to adapt to changing ethical and moral standards, and to harmonise the differing needs of stakeholders within the IP field.

It is worth acknowledging that the proposed modifications reflect a sophisticated approach that embeds a cultural-historical context into legal enhancements. They resonate deeply with the Confucian ethos, a philosophy renowned for its emphasis on social harmony, respect for tradition, and the crucial role of morality and customs in maintaining societal cohesion.[167] In essence, these adjustments are firmly rooted in Confucian philosophy, integrating the cultural-historical narrative of China into its legal framework.

The heart of these modifications is the establishment of statutory exclusions focusing on public order and morality, signalling a profound respect for the societal structure inherent in Confucianism. This action underscores the importance of morality and ethical customs in fostering societal harmony, effectively reflecting the core tenets of Confucian philosophy in a tangible legal context. Indeed, these amendments go beyond being simple adjustments to the law; they represent a purposeful blend of China's ancient wisdom with its modern legal system. These changes highlight China's ongoing commitment to align its legal system with its deep-rooted Confucian values, contextualising these legal transitions within the broader cultural and historical narrative of China. In this light, the proposed modifications to the patent laws are much more than mere legal refinements; they represent a manifestation of the application of a cultural-historical approach in legal reform, ensuring

---

[165] Ibid.

[166] This terminology comes from the international *Agreement on Trade Related Aspects of Intellectual Property Rights 1995*, article 27.

[167] Alejo José G Sison, 'Some Virtue Ethics Implications from Aristotelian and Confucian Perspectives on Family and Business' (2020) 165 *Journal of Business Ethics* 241, 241–254.

that, as China's legal system evolves, it continues to align with, and reflect, its rich cultural and philosophical heritage.

To implement this proposal effectively, it is recommended that a centralised national authority is established. This entity would act as a trusted custodian for traditional knowledge, including TMK, standing as a testament to the nation's commitment to preserve and oversee such invaluable cultural assets. This national authority would bear a substantial responsibility for examining and assessing patent applications that are based on traditional knowledge, including TMK. Its mandate would include determining whether the invention's application aligns with the statutory exclusions to patentability. Should the utilisation be determined to fall within statutory exclusions, the patent application would then be considered unfit for patent protection.

This is not a hypothetical concept, but rather an approach that has been successfully adopted elsewhere. A case in point is the *New Zealand Patents Act 2013*, which saw the establishment of the Māori Advisory Committee to assist the Commissioner in determining whether the commercial exploitation of an invention would be contrary to Māori values.[168] According to Lai, this move has significantly expanded the scope of the existing patent functions, blending *te ao Māori* (the Māori worldview) with the Western legal framework.[169] This integration has impacted the granting of exclusive rights, leading to a more inclusive and representative patent system.[170]

Moreover, implementing statutory exclusions for patentability, like the principles of ordre public and morality, can be made more effective by crafting more specific and unambiguous guidelines. As it stands, Article 5 of the *Chinese Patent Law 2020* states that 'patents should not be granted for inventions that contravene laws, societal ethics, or public interest'. However, the broad wording of this provision often makes it subject to varied interpretations, leading to difficulties in its consistent application and enforcement. Addressing this ambiguity calls for a harmonious integration with China's culturally and historically significant philosophical systems, notably Confucianism. In particular, the notions of 'social ethics' and 'public interest', as referenced in the patent law, necessitate further clarification, particularly when addressing issues of traditional knowledge, including TMK.

Confucianism, with its emphasis on social harmony, deference to hierarchical structures, and adherence to designated roles and duties, offers a compelling lens through which these concepts can be examined. From a Confucian perspective, traditional knowledge, including TMK, is a collective asset to be treated with deep respect and preserved for future generations.[171] It's not merely a collection of facts or practices; it represents the cumulative intellectual and creative contributions of

---

[168] *New Zealand Patents Act 2013*, Section 225–228.

[169] Jessica C Lai., 'A Successful Recalibration of Patent Law vis-à-vis Mātauranga Māori? A Case Study of Mānuka (Leptospermum scoparium)' in Susy Frankel (ed), *The Object and Purpose of Intellectual Property* (Edward Elgar Publishing, 2019) 30, 32.

[170] Ibid.

[171] Snejina Michailova and Kate Hutchings, 'National Cultural Influences on Knowledge Sharing: A Comparison of China and Russia' (2006) 43(3) *Journal of Management Studies* 383, 396–398.

a community. Consequently, social ethics within patent law, seen through this lens, would advocate for the protection and respectful utilisation of such shared intellectual resources.

Moreover, Confucianism's emphasis on societal harmony and public welfare offers valuable insights into the understanding of public interest within patent law. This philosophy sees the ultimate goal of any policy or law as serving the public good, maintaining harmony, and promoting societal well-being.[172] From this standpoint, public interest is not just about the advancement of science or economics, but also about ensuring fairness, justice, and respect for all societal members. Therefore, any misuse or inappropriate commercialisation of traditional knowledge, particularly TMK, would be seen as a disruption in the societal order and an infringement of the public interest.

One practical approach to realising this alignment involves the inclusion of explicit references to the wrongful use or inappropriate commercialisation of traditional knowledge, particularly TMK, within the patent laws. Such misappropriation could be considered as a direct contradiction to public interest and social ethics. This perspective can find resonance with the principles of Confucian philosophy, which values communal cohesion, societal morality, and reverence for ancestral wisdom.[173] In line with this, unauthorised use of traditional knowledge, including TMK, could be interpreted as a disruption of societal balance and a breach of the respect owed to the predecessors and related communities who have preserved and passed down this knowledge through generations.

Moreover, it could be advantageous to include knowledge holders and their communities in the evaluation of patent applications, ensuring that their unique perspectives and cultural values are adequately respected. This cooperative approach is not just about fairness; it would also facilitate a more culturally sensitive interpretation of innovation, which is traditionally viewed from a predominantly Western perspective. This cultural sensitivity would help to address issues of biopiracy, where entities patent TMK without acknowledging the source or sharing benefits with the community.

In a general context, some potential reforms could include:

1. adding a new clause to clarify that the text of patent law, including the provision on morality and ordre public, must be understood and interpreted in line with China's historical experience, cultural values, and the customary laws of various traditional knowledge-holding communities;
2. rewriting the morality and ordre public exclusion in Chinese patent law to specifically exclude patentable inventions that exploit traditional knowledge or are offensive to knowledge holders and related local communities;
3. modifying the opposition and invalidation grounds to include offensiveness to traditional knowledge holders and related local communities, or contravention of Chinese traditional cultural norms on morality as conditions for refusing a patent application; and

[172] Sison (n 167) 241–254.

[173] Sison (n 167) 241–254.

4. mandating compulsory consultation with various traditional knowledge holders and knowledge-holding communities through the establishment of advisory committees. These committees could advise patent examiners on traditional knowledge, China's cultural values, and the customary laws of various traditional knowledge-holding communities.

4.6 Conclusion

This chapter focused on the complex and dialectical IP system in China, highlighting the interplay of historical, socioeconomic, and other domestic factors that contribute to the development of China's domestic IP system. It presented an analysis that showed that this unique system has significant implications for the protection and utilisation of TMK. These domestic factors heavily influence the balance of competing interests among TMK stakeholders. The historical context and socioeconomic forces have significantly influenced China's approach to IP protection for TMK. This has led to a unique system characterised by inherent biases, which has resulted in imbalances in power dynamics and structural inequalities among various stakeholders involved in TMK.

This chapter first critically examined China's historical accomplishments and challenges in the pharmaceutical sphere, revealing the significant impact of TMK on domestic practices and innovations. It then presented an exploration of various historical periods, policies, and case studies, and an analysis that demonstrated that the Chinese government's pursuit of modernising the pharmaceutical sector and fostering economic growth has unintentionally resulted in an imbalanced legal and policy landscape, especially in the domain of IP. It also highlighted that this environment has disproportionately benefited corporate actors in TMK exploitation, prioritising their interests and facilitating the appropriation and utilisation of TMK, often at the expense of TMK holders and local communities. Moreover, the increasing influence of corporations in domestic IP affairs has enabled them to actively shape legal and policy-making processes to suit their interests. This corporate-centric approach has led to the overshadowing of TMK's intrinsic value, which encompasses its cultural, historical, and community-based importance. With these challenges in mind, this chapter concluded that understanding China's complex socioeconomic and historical landscape surrounding TMK was crucial for effectively preserving and protecting its valuable knowledge within the IP framework.

The critical analysis presented in this chapter showed the complex nature of China's IP system, shaped by a combination of historical, cultural, and legal factors. It revealed that this unique framework exemplified a dialectical process influenced by China's distinct historical and socioeconomic context, enabling the country to adopt Western-style IP standards while prioritising national self-interest.

While the dialectical approach facilitated the adaptation and evolution of China's IP system, it was argued that a reformation of existing norms was crucial for effectively safeguarding TMK and addressing the diverse interests of stakeholders. Consequently, it was concluded that, by reforming the current IP system, China can foster a more inclusive, equitable, and just IP regime that would benefit all stakeholders, ensuring the preservation and sustainable utilisation of TMK.

Building on this, this chapter then offered a critical examination of the impact of China's patent system on TMK and its associated genetic resources. It revealed an inherent bias within the system that tended to favour the patentability of TMK and associated genetic resources, potentially paving the way for corporate misuse and exploitation of this knowledge. By exposing the inherent biases embedded in the existing Chinese patent system, it was argued that there was a pressing need for comprehensive reforms within China's patent system.

This chapter presented key recommendations that included a shift in patentability criteria to align with traditional Chinese values; the introduction of more robust disclosure of origin obligations; and advocacy for statutory exclusions that would deter the patentability of inventions based on TMK. In essence, the reforms proposed represent a distinctive fusion of law and culture, drawing upon China's rich cultural and historical legacy to shape its contemporary legal landscape. They mark a transition towards an approach to patent law in China that is more integrative and culturally contextualised. The aim was to weave China's vast cultural tapestry and profound historical narrative into its present-day legal structures, thereby crafting a patent system that is globally competitive while maintaining its unique cultural nuances. This was a delicate balancing act—one that aimed to advance innovation and economic competitiveness, while preserving and promoting the country's rich cultural heritage and historical wisdom.

However, this chapter highlighted that it was crucial to recognise that relying exclusively on IP laws and policies may not be entirely adequate to ensure the full-scale protection and preservation of TMK. These laws, while essential, may not encompass all aspects or nuances inherent to Chinese TMK, potentially leaving gaps in regulating these valuable resources. Given this constraint, it became necessary to explore other mechanisms and strategies that extended beyond the scope of IP frameworks.

References

Ada Yue Wang, 'The Test Of Inventiveness In Chinese Patent Jurisprudence: Recent History, Cases, And Analysis' (2019) 265 *Journal Of Law, Technology & Policy* 265.

Alejo José G Sison, 'Some Virtue Ethics Implications from Aristotelian and Confucian Perspectives on Family and Business' (2020) 165 *Journal of Business Ethics* 241.

Anonymous, 'TRIPS: With a Painful Birth, Uncertain Health, and a Host of Issues in China, Where Lies Its Future?' (2006) 7(523) *San Diego International Law Journal* 523.

Baohui Zhang, 'Resource Centralization and Industrial Policies: State Capacity in Structural Adjustment in South Korea and China' (1998) 25(3) *Asian Affairs: An American Review* 165.

Barry Buzan and Michael Cox, 'China and the US: Comparable Cases of 'Peaceful Rise'?' (2013) 6 *The Chinese Journal of International Politics* 109.
Björn Ahl, 'China's Perspectives on Public International Law: Selective Adaptation of International Treaties and the Community of Common Destiny Concept' (2022) *German Yearbook of International Law* 1.
BM Hoekman, KE Maskus and K Saggi, 'Transfer of Technology to Developing Countries: Unilateral and Multilateral Policy Options' (2005) 33 *World Development* 1.
Bole Zhou and Shouguo Zhao, 'Industrial Policy and Corporate Investment Efficiency' (2022) 78 *Journal of Asian Economics* 1.
Boleslaw Szczesniak, 'John Floyer and Chinese Medicine' (1954) 11 *Osiris* 127.
C Chaufan and F Mohamed, 'Unfortunate Distinction or Corporate Protectionism by Design?' (2020) 395(10235) *Lancet* 1486.
C Schulz, 'Money or Pride? On the Why and How of Traditional Knowledge Protection in India and China' (2011) 1(1) *Konstanzer Journal für Politik und Verwaltung* 52.
Carla Nappi and McKenzie Wark, 'Reading Needham Now' (2019) 110(1) *Isis,*100.
Dan Zhang and Emiliano T Hudtohan, 'Ecological Civilization: Creativity and Innovation in the New Normal Era' (2021) 1(3) *International Journal of Management and Education in Human Development* 85
David YF Ho, 'Dialectical Thinking: Neither Eastern nor Western' (2000) 55(9) *The American Psychologist* 1064.
Dev A Ghose, 'A Proposal to Modify the Utility Standard for Patenting Biotechnology Research Tools' (2007) 56 *Emory Law Journal* 1662.
E Moglen, 'The Melting of Patent Law' (2009) 5 *Indian JL & Tech* 33.
Guosheng Deng and Scott Kennedy, 'Big Business and Industry Association Lobbying in China: the Paradox of Contrasting Styles' (2010) 63 *The China Journal* 101.
Haijun Jin etal, 'Government-backed Patent Funds in China: Their Roles as Policy Tools to Promote Innovation by SMEs' (2013) 30(4) *Tech Monitor* 24.
Harilal Madhavan, 'Below the Radar Innovations and Emerging Property Right Approaches in Tibetan Medicine' (2017) 20 *The Journal of World Intellectual Property* 239.
Hepeng Jia, 'Drugmakers Wrestle over Medicine Patents', *China Business Weekly* (Web Page, 2004). <http://www.chinadaily.com.cn/english/doc/2004-08/17/content_366249.htm>.
Huang Ji et al, 'An Ethnobotanical Study of Medicinal Plants Used by the Lisu people in Nujiang, Northwest Yunnan, China' (2004) 58 *Journal of Ethnobiology and Ethnomedicine* 253.
Ikechi Mgbeoji, 'Patents and Traditional Knowledge of the Uses of Plants: Is a Communal Patent Regime Part of the Solution to the Scourge of Bio Piracy' (2001) 9(1) *Indiana Journal of Global Legal Studies* 163.
Jane Parry, 'Drug Company Pulls Out of Chinese Lawsuit Over Diabetes Drug' (2004) 329 (7474) *BMJ* 476.
Jeffrey A Andrews, 'Pfizer's Viagra Patent and the Promise of Patent Protection in China' (2006) 28(1) *Loyola of Los Angeles International and Comparative Law Review* 11.
Jessica C Lai., 'A Successful Recalibration of Patent Law vis-à-vis Mātauranga Māori? A Case Study of Mānuka (Leptospermum scoparium)' in Susy Frankel (ed), *The Object and Purpose of Intellectual Property* (Edward Elgar Publishing, 2019) 30.
Junli Diao, 'The Influence of China/Asia on the West' in Suzanne M Stauffer (ed), *Libraries, Archives, and Museums: An Introduction to Cultural Heritage Institutions through the Ages* (Rowman & Littlefield, 2021) 81.
Justin W Evans, 'Explaining China's Legal Flexibility: History and the Institutional Imperative' (2018) 31 *Pace International Law Review* 173.
Jonathan Ocko, 'Copying, Culture, and Control: Chinese Intellectual Property Law in Historical Context' (2013) 8 *Yale Journal of Law & the Humanities* 559.
K Wang et al, 'Evolution and Governance of the Biotechnology and Pharmaceutical Industry of China' (2009) 79(9) *Mathematics and Computers in Simulation* 2947.

Kwok, Pui-Yan. "Integration of Traditional Chinese Medicine and Western Medicine in Contemporary China" (Master of Science thesis, University of Chicago, 1981) 13–14.

L Stone, 'Julie Kristeva's "Mystery" of the Subject-in-Process' in JD Marshall (ed), *Poststructuralism, Philosophy, Pedagogy* (Kluwer Academic Publishers, 2004) 119.

Lantian Li, , 'Deconstructing and Historicizing Access to Medicines: The Changing Priority of Pharmaceutical Governance in China' (2021) 5 *Frontiers in Sociology* 1.

Li, En-chang, 'MAO Ze-dong's View on Traditional Chinese Medicine and Its Modern Significance' (2020) 26(6) *Chinese journal of integrative medicine* 469.

Liang Huigang et al, 'A Brief History of the Development of Infectious Disease Prevention, Control, and Biosafety Programs in China' (2020) (2) *Journal of Biosafety and Biosecurity* 1.

Lina Benabdallah, 'Contesting the International Order by Integrating It: The Case of China's Belt and Road Initiative' (2019) 40 *Third World Quarterly* 92.

Liz PY Chee, Mao's Bestiary: Medicinal Animals and Modern China (Duke University Press, 1977) 38.

M Rahmah, N Barizah and S Blay, 'Ensuring Disclosure of Origin of Genetic Resources in Patent Applications: Indonesia's efforts to Combat Biopiracy' (2020) 25(1–2) *Journal of Intellectual Property Rights* 40.

Margo A Bagley, 'Designing Disclosure: Disclosure Of Cultural And Genetic Resource Utilisation In Design Protection Regimes' in Susy Frankel (ed), *The Object and Purpose of Intellectual Property* (Elgaronline, 2019) 110

Maskus Keith, 'The New Globalisation of Intellectual Property Rights: What's New This Time? '(2014) 54(3) *Australian Economic History Review* 262.

Merle Goldman and Denis Fred Simon, 'The Onset of China's New Technological Revolution' in Denis Fred Simon and Merle Goldman (eds), *Science and Technology in Post-Mao China* (Brill, 1989) 3.

Micaela Tucker, '"Guanxi!"—"Gesundheit!" An Alternative View on the "Rule of Law" Panacea in China' (2011) 35 *Vermont Law Review* 689.

Mikhaelle Schiappacasse, 'Intellectual Property Rights in China: Technology Transfers and Economic Development '(2004) 2(2) *Buffalo Intellectual Property Law Journal 164.*

Mo Zhang, 'The Socialist Legal System with Chinese Characteristics: China's Discourse for the Rule of Law and a Bitter Experience' (2010) 39 *Temple International & Comparative Law Journal* 1.

Ouyang Shiwen and Zhang Lihua, 'China's Developing Approach to Swiss-type Claims' (2014) 241 *Managing Intellectual Property* 34.

Patricia L Judd, 'Retooling TRIPS' (2014) 55 *Virginia Journal of International Law* 117.

Paul Crookes, Intellectual Property Regime Evolution in China and India (Brill, 2010) 141–182.

Pei Sheng-Ji, 'Ethnobotanical Approaches of Traditional Medicine Studies: Some Experiences from Asia' (2001) 39 *Pharmaceutical Biology* 74.

PH Corne, 'Creation and Application of Law in the PRC' (2002) 50(2) *The American Journal of Comparative Law* 369.

Ping Li , 'The Outlook for China's Innovation-Driven Development Beyond COVID-19' (2020) 3(4) *Cultures of Science* 232.

Pitman B Potter, 'Globalization and Economic Regulation in China: Selective Adaptation of Globalized Norms and Practices' (2003) 2(1) *Washington University Global Studies Law Review* 119.

PK Yu, 'Building Intellectual Property Coalitions for Development' in Jeremy de Beer (ed), *Implementing WIPO's Development Agenda* (Wilfrid Laurier University Press, 2008) 79.

Qiu, Wanfei, 'Challenges in Developing China's Marine Protected Area System' (2009) 33(4) *Marine Policy* 599.

R Finlay, 'China, the West, and World History in Joseph Needham's Science and Civilisation in China' (2000) 11 *Journal of World History* 265.

Ralph C Croizier, *Traditional Medicine in Modern China: Science, Nationalism, and the Tensions of Cultural Change* (Harvard University Press, 1968) 180.

Rhonda Chang, *Chinese Medicine Masquerading as Yi: a Case of Chinese Self-Colonisation* (Mani River Press, 2015) 1–271.

Richard Student, 'China's New Anti-Monopoly Law: Addressing Foreign Competitors and Commentators' (2008) 243 *Minnesota Journal of International Law* 503.

Robert Emmons and Sarah Schnitker, 'Hegel's Thesis-Antithesis-Synthesis Model' in Anne Runehov and Lluis Oviedo (eds), *Encyclopedia of Sciences and Religions* (Springer, 2013) 978.

Rochelle K Seide and Janet M MacLeod, 'Drafting Claims for Biotechnology Inventions' (2000) 4 *International Intellectual Property Law & Policy* 52–53.

Scott Kennedy, *The Business of Lobbying in China* (Harvard University Press, 2005).

Shen, Jinyu et al, 'The Relationship Between Marine Biodiversity Conservation and Poverty Alleviation in the Strategies of Rural Development in China' (2015) SI(73) *Journal of Coastal Research* 1.

Shufan Sung, , 'The New Path of Green GDP in China' in Nurcan Kilinc-Ata (ed), *The Effects of Environmental Policies on Sustainability: Theory and Methods* (OMICS Group, 2017) 17.

Snejina Michailova and Kate Hutchings, 'National Cultural Influences on Knowledge Sharing: A Comparison of China and Russia' (2006) 43(3) *Journal of Management Studies* 383.

Steven D Jamar and Lateef Mtima, 'The Centrality of Social Justice for an Academic Intellectual Property Institute' (2011) 64(3) *SMU Law Review* 101.

Suchita Shah, 'Plants, Patents and Biopiracy: The Globalization of Intellectual Property Rights and Traditional Medicine' (2014) 8(1) *Global Health Governance* 57.

Tesh W Dagne, 'The Protection of Traditional Knowledge in the Knowledge Economy: Cross-Cutting Challenges in International Intellectual Property Law' (2012) 14(2) *International Community Law Review* 1.

The Chinese Pharmaceutical Association, 'Pharmaceuticals in New China' (1960) 80 *Chinese Medical Journal* 208.

Thomas J Horton, 'Confucianism and Antitrust: China Confucianism and Antitrust: China's Emerging Evolutionary Approach to Anti-Monopoly Law' (2013) 47(2) *International Lawyer* 193.

Timothy A Worrall, 'The 2001 PTO Utility Examination Guidelines and DNA Patents' (2001) 16 *Berkeley Technology Law Journal* 123.

Tong Shi et al, 'Driving force from Authorities: the Evolution of Innovation System for Biomedical Industry in China' (2014) 28(10) *Technology Analysis & Strategic Management* 1210.

Weijuan Huang et al, 'Ethnobotanical Study on Medicinal Plants Used by Li People in Ledong, Hainan Island, China' (2016) 85(1) *Acta Societatis Botanicorum Poloniae* 1.

Wenting Cheng, 'The Protection of Genetic Resources in Chinese Patent Law' (2021) 43(4) *European Intellectual Property Review* 248.

X Zhang, 'Traditional Medicine: Its Importance and Protection' in Sophia Twarog and Promila Kapoor (eds), *Protecting and Promoting Traditional Knowledge: System, National Experience and International Dimensions* (United Nations, 2004) 3.

Xiansu Chi et al, 'Research Progress on Classical Traditional Chinese Medicine Formula Lily Bulb and Rehmannia Decoction in the Treatment of Depression' (2019) 112 *Biomedicine & Pharmacotherapy* 1.

Xiaojie Xu, 'New Concepts and Approaches for Drug Discovery Based on Traditional Chinese Medicine' (2006) 3(3) *Drug Discov Today Technol* 247.

Xinsheng Wang and Albert Wai-Kit Chan, 'Commentary Challenges and Patenting Strategies for Chinese Herbal Medicine' (2010) 5 *Chinese Medicine* 1.

Xuan Li and Weiwei Li, 'Inadequacy of Patent Regime on Traditional Medicinal Knowledge' 10(2) *The Journal of World Intellectual Property* 125.

Y Fu, 'The Golden Mean of Confucianism and Intercultural Communication' (2005) 3 *The Northern Forum* 75.

Yanchun Zhou and Yanhong Fan, 'A Contrastive Study of Temporal-spatial Metaphor Between Chinese and Americans' (2015) 5(1) *Theory and Practice in Language Studies* 119.

Yi-Chen Su, 'What About Know-How: Heightened Obviousness and Lowered Disclosure is Not a Panacea to the Patent System for Biotechnology Medication and Pharmaceutical Inventions in the Post-KSR Era' (2010) 14(2) *Marquette Intellectual Property Law Review* 322.

Ying Li et al, 'Sustainability from a Chinese Cultural Perspective: The Implications of Harmonious Development in Environmental Management' (2016) 18 *Environment, Development and Sustainability* 679.

Yinghong Liu et al, 'Synergistic Effect of Traditional Chinese Medicine' (2007) 19(2) *Asian Journal of Chemistry* 867.

Yoel Kornreich et al, 'Consultation and Deliberation in China: The Making of China's Health-Care Reform' (2012) 68 *The China Journal* 176.

Youdi, Zhu, *Big Country's Medical Reform* (World Book Publishing Company, 2011) 203.

Yu Lin, 'Medical and Health Service' (1980) 23(25) Beijing Review 1.

Yu Mingde, 'Pharmaceutical Preparations Should Be Unswervingly Driven by Internationalized Biomedicine' *21 Finance* (Web Page, 2018) <https://m.21jingji.com/article/20181024/5571b97328627ef4f6fbcc252d06f331.html>.

Yu Mingde, 'There are Six Major Differences in the New Medical Reform Plan', *NetEase Finance* (Web Page, 2009) <http://news.163.com/08/1103/02/4PPS9UFH0001124J.html>.

Yuan Yuan, 'Intellectual Property Policy. Domestic Constraints on the International Negotiating Positions' (Master's Thesis, University of Cambridge, 2006).

柴慧婷 [Chai Huiting],《浅析药物创新体系初步建立和中国医药企业创新进展》[Preliminary Analysis of the Establishment of Drug Innovation System and Progress of Innovation in Chinese Pharmaceutical Enterprises] (2018) 33 (3)华西医药*Huaxi Pharmaceutical* 359.

陈海玉[Chen Haiyu],《云南少数民族口述医药文献的档案式保护研究》[Research on Archival Protection of Oral Medical Documents of Ethnic Minorities in Yunnan] (2011) 11(3), 兰台论坛*Lantai Forum* 1.

陈一孚[Chen Yifu], 《论中药和专利制度之间的兼容性: 以中药发明的实用性审查为视角》[Compatibility between Traditional Chinese Medicine and Patent System—From the Perspective of "Practical Applicability" of Chinese Medicine Inventions] (2016) 2理论与改革*Theory and Reform* 122.

陈忠海 [Chen Zhonghai],《古代的防疫与疫苗》[Ancient Epidemic Prevention and Vaccines] [2019] 中国发展观察 *China Development Observation* 63.

程兆盛 [Cheng Zhaosheng],《中医药政策概述》[Overview of Traditional Chinese Medicine Policy] (2013) 21(11) 中医药管理杂志*Journal of Traditional Chinese Medicine Management* 1139.

邓琦 [Deng Qi],《中国传统法文化对现代法治建设的影响》[Influence of Chinese Traditional Legal Culture on Modern Rule of Law Construction] (2011) 2(1) 黑河学院学报*Journal of Heihe University* 20.

段资睿[Duan Zirui],《20世纪60年代中央试办医药托拉斯的回顾及启示》[Review and Enlightenment of the Central Pilot Pharmaceutical Trust in the 1960s] (2022) 43 (18) 医学与哲学*Medicine and Philosophy* 74.

高建美 [Gao Jianmei],《中药品种保护制度之法律职能》[The Legal Function of the Traditional Chinese Medicine Species Protection System] [2016] 科技与法律*Scientific Technology and Law* 1044.

谷禾 [Gu He],《博弈伟哥》[Battling Viagra] [2004] 中国医药指南*China Medicine Guide* 9.

管荣齐[Guan Rongqi],《我国专利实质条件的改进建议》[Suggestions for Improvement of the Patentability Requirements in China] (2013) 2知识产权*Intellectual Property* 71.

郭方园 [Guo Fangyuan],《中华优秀传统文化中的和谐辩证思维方法意蕴探析》[An Analysis of the Implications of Harmonious Dialectical Thinking Methods in the Excellent Traditional Chinese Culture] [2021] 4 福建省社会主义学院学报*Journal of Fujian Province Socialist College* 42.

黄凤达 [Huang Fengda],《国际投资仲裁对TRIPS协议灵活性的挑战及其应对》[The Challenge of International Investment Arbitration to the Flexibility of the TRIPS Agreement and Its Response] [2020] 西部学刊 *Western Academic Journal* 73.

黄旭东[Huang Xudong],《贵州民族民间医药知识产权保护研究》[Research on Intellectual Property Protection of Guizhou Ethnic Folk Medicine] (2006) 2(2) 贵州社会科学*Guizhou Social Sciences* 63.
赖丽娟 [Lai Lijuan],《中国医药市场走进新竞争时代》[China's Pharmaceutical Market Enters a New Era of Competition] [2004] 医药经济报*Pharmaceutical Economy News* 1.
黎舒婷 [Li Shuting],《浅析专利申请中如何对遗传资源来源进行披露》[A Brief Analysis of How to Disclose the Source of Genetic Resources in Patent Applications] (2014) 21(4) 药物生物技术*Pharmaceutical Biotechnology* 355.
李昭 [Guan Rongqi],《基因专利申请与审查问题研究》[Research on Gene Patent Application and Examination] (2020) 11黑龙江科学*Helongjiang Science* 145.
骆志煌 [Luo Zhihuang],《中国古代文化之中医药与中医学》[Influence of Chinese Traditional Legal Culture on Modern Rule of Law Construction] [2020] 海峡教育研究*Strait Education Research* 65.
邱洪华 [Qiu Honghua],《文化视阈下的知识产权保护研究》[Research on Intellectual Property Protection under the Perspective of Cultural View] (2013) 28(5) 广西政法管理干部学院*Journal of Guangxi Administration Institute for Political and Legal Cadres*, 65.
唐永业 [Tang Yongye],《我国生化制药工业及其发展》[China's Biochemical Pharmaceutical Industry and Its Development] [1991] 商业科技*Commercial Technology* 13.
田晓玲 [Tian Xiaoling],《中药复方专利保护研究》[Research on the Patent Protection of Traditional Chinese Medicine Compound Prescriptions] (2007) 2 江西社会科学 *Journal of Southwest University for Nationalities* 122.
王虎 [Wang Hu],《中国传统文化对科学技术发展影响初探》[A Preliminary Exploration of the Impact of Chinese Traditional Culture on the Development of Science and Technology] (2016) 云南省第4–5届科学技术哲学与科学技术史研究生论坛优秀论文集*Collection of Outstanding Papers from the 4th-5th Graduate Forum on Philosophy of Science and Technology and History of Science and Technology in Yunnan Province* 269.
吴珏[Wu Jue],《中国在知识产权问题上的立场与路径选择》[China's Stance and Path Selection on Intellectual Property Issues] [2015], 人民论坛 *People's Forum* 250.
肖玮 [Zhou Hubin],《12家中国药企铁心告辉瑞:伟哥知识产权案胜负一线间》[Twelve Chinese Pharmaceutical Companies Determined to Sue Pfizer: Victory or Defeat in Viagra Intellectual Property Case Hangs by a Thread] [2006] 北京现代商报*Beijing Modern Business News* 1.
谢立安娜[Xie Lianna],《浅述中国制药业的专利权保护》[Discussion about Patent Protection in Chinese Pharmaceutical Industry] (2015) 2法制博览*Legality Vision* 228.
谢蜀生[Xie Shusheng],《中国人痘接种术向西方的传播及影响》[The Spread and Impact of Chinese Vaccination Techniques on the West] (2000) 30 (3) 中华医史杂志*Chinese Journal of Medical History* 133.
徐惟 [Xu Wei],《我国医药制造业创新不足原因探究: 以江苏省为例》[Investigating the Lack of Innovation in China's Pharmaceutical Manufacturing Industry: A Case Study of Jiangsu Province] [2022]中国医疗保险 Chinese Health Insurance 113.
严永和 [Yan Yonghe],《中国专利法传统资源来源披露的制度构建: 以中医药传统知识为对象》[The Construction of A Disclosure System for Traditional Resource Sources in China's Patent Law: With Traditional Chinese Medicine Knowledge as the Object] (2020) 33(10)中国医学伦理学*Chinese Medical Ethics* 1167.
衣仁翠 [Yi Rencui]《中庸文化思想与司法正义研究》[Research on the Doctrine of the Mean (Zhongyong) Culture and Judicial Justice] (2013) 23(5) 梧州学院学报 *Journal of Wuzhou University*, 52.
张军亮 [Zhang Junliang],《生物和医药技术领域知识生产分析: 基于"863 计划" 科技报告》[Analysis of Knowledge Production in the Field of Biotechnology and Medicine: Based on the '863 Program' Scientific Reports] (2015) 34(1) 情报杂志*Journal of Intelligence* 67.
张耀杰[Zhang Yaojie],《民间游说与立法之互动》[Interaction Between Popular Lobbying and Lawmaking] (2004) 11(3), 当代中国研究*Modern China Studies* 73.
张正 [Zhang Zheng],《百年征程和文化传承双视角下: 民族医药发展历程回望》[Under the Dual Perspectives of a Century-long Journey and Cultural Heritage: A Retrospective on the

Development of Ethnic Medicine] (2021) 4 四川省社会主义学院学报*Journal of Sichuan Socialist Academy* 61.
赵元果[Zhao Yuanguo],《中国专利法的孕育与诞生》[The Nurturing and Birth of Chinese Patent Law] (Intellectual Property Press, 2016) 253.
周胡斌 [Zhou Hubin],《专利审查中公众的角色:由 ”罗格列酮“专利无效案说起》[The Role of the Public in Patent Examination: Starting from the 'Rosiglitazone' Patent Invalidity Case] (2004)14(3) 中国医药导刊*Chinese Journal of Medical Guide* 548.
左亚文[Zuo Yawen],《中华和谐辩证思维的智慧特色与理性回归》[The Wisdom Characteristics and Rational Return of Chinese Harmonious Dialectical Thinking] [2019] 2 新时代马克思主义论丛*New Era Marxist Theory Series* 199.
《国务院办公厅关于印发信息技术发展政策要点和生物技术发展政策要点的通知》 [Notice of the General Office of the State Council on Printing and Distributing the Key Points of Information Technology Development Policies and Biotechnology Development Policies] (People's Republic of China) State Science and Technology Commission, Order No 18, 1988.
《中国医药企业管理协会》*Baidu Encyclopedia* (Web Page, 2021) <https://baike.baidu.com/item/中国医药企业管理协会/964310?fr=aladdin>; '中国医药商业协' *Baidu Encyclopedia* (Web Page, 2021) <https://baike.baidu.com/item/中国医药商业/6668263?fr=aladdin>.
《中华人民共和国专利法》[Patent Law of the People's Republic of China] (People's Republic of China) National People's Congress, Order No.55, 2020.
《专利审查指南》[Chinese Patent Examination Guidelines] (People's Republic of China) National Intellectual Property Administration, Order No.391, 2020 (*Chinese Patent Examination Guidelines*).

Chapter 5
Establishing an Access and Benefit-Sharing Mechanism for Traditional Medical Knowledge Management: A Novel Approach in China

5.1 Introduction

The international ABS system, through a robust mechanism, serves to preserve and enable responsible use of traditional knowledge linked with genetic resources.[1] This system is founded on principles of equity, promoting mutual respect and understanding between knowledge holders and potential users. It assures that access to traditional knowledge is obtained legally and ethically, thus encouraging transparency and accountability.[2] At the same time, it guarantees the fair distribution of benefits arising from its usage, acknowledging and rewarding the invaluable contribution of Indigenous Peoples and Local Communities ('IPLCs') in their role as custodians and conveyors of traditional knowledge.[3]

ABS principles, as they pertain to the access and benefit-sharing of genetic resources and traditional knowledge (including TMK), have been elaborated in a series of multilateral environmental agreements.[4] As previously discussed, these agreements include the *Convention on Biological Diversity* ('CBD'),[5] the *Nagoya*

---

[1] 李保平 [Li Baoping],《遗传资源相关传统知识获取与惠益分享制度研究 以青蒿衍生物的开发利用为例》[Study on the Acquisition and Benefit-sharing System of Traditional Knowledge Related to Genetic Resources—A Case Study of the Development and Utilization of Artemisia Annua Derivatives] (2023) 31(4)中央民族大学学报*Journal of MUC* 24, 24–25.

[2] Ibid.

[3] Ibid.

[4] Claudio Chiarolla, 'The Role of Private International Law under the Nagoya Protocol' in Elisa Morgera et al. (eds), The 2010 Nagoya Protocol on Access and Benefit-sharing in perspective: implications for international law and implementation challenges (Martinus Nijhoff, 2013) 423, 426.

[5] *Convention on Biological Diversity*, opened for signature 5 June 1992,1760 UNTS 79 (entered into force 29 December 1993) ('CBD').

N. Xia, *Medicinal Mandates*, https://doi.org/10.1007/978-981-96-4108-6_5

Protocol,[6] and other complementary legal instruments, with the *Nagoya Protocol* representing the pinnacle of normative development of ABS rules.[7] Specialised ABS instruments, such as the *International Treaty on Plant Genetic Resources for Food and Agriculture* ('ITPGRFA'), govern ABS for plant genetic resources essential to agriculture.[8] Other specialised instruments include the World Health Organization *Pandemic Influenza Preparedness Framework (PIP Framework)*, which facilitates the sharing of pandemic-potential influenza viruses, access to vaccines, and the distribution of other benefits.[9]

Nevertheless, this intricate array of international frameworks on ABS, akin to other international legal instruments, largely represents a 'Western construct', inherently highlighting the tenets of exchange, profit, and capital accumulation that are intrinsic to capitalism.[10] In this sense, the intrinsic characteristics of these frameworks can be seen as emblematic of a Eurocentric world view, tacitly setting a universal standard that draws heavily from Western philosophies and systems. In this scenario, the inherent Western-centric bias in the implementation of ABS frameworks might inadvertently diminish or overlook the unique social, economic, and cultural contexts of developing countries. This could lead to a disproportionate prioritisation and representation of Western viewpoints and economic interests, risking the marginalisation of developing nations' distinct realities and challenges. Among these unique contexts are Indigenous rights, traditional knowledge, and diverse interpretations of what is considered fair and equitable benefit-sharing.

Despite the substantial body of existing literature,[11] a noticeable gap persists when it comes to analysing the practicalities of implementing ABS frameworks and assessing their potential impacts on governing the protection, dissemination, and utilisation of TMK, particularly within the unique sociocultural and historical contexts of China. Understanding these contexts is important as China's TMK forms an integral

[6] *Nagoya Protocol on Access to Genetic Resources and the Fair and Equitable Sharing of Benefits Arising from their Utilization to the Convention on Biological Diversity*, UN Doc UNEP/CBD/COP/DEC/X/1(2010) (Nagoya Protocol).

[7] Elisa Morgera, Elsa Tsioumani and Matthias Buck, Unraveling the Nagoya Protocol: A Commentary on the Nagoya Protocol on Access and Benefit-sharing to the Convention on Biological Diversity (Brill, 2014) 1, 32.

[8] *International Treaty on Plant Genetic Resources for Food and Agriculture*, opened for signature, 3 November 2001, 2400 UNTS 303 (entered into force 26 June 2004).

[9] World Health Assembly Resolution 64, Pandemic Influenza Preparedness: Sharing of Influenza Viruses and Access to Vaccines and Other Benefits, 2011 (Sixty-fourth World Health Assembly, WHA64/5, 2011).

[10] DQ Hodnett, 'Legitimising Biopiracy? Fairness and Efficacy of the Nagoya Protocol' (2021) 2 *York Law Review* 75, 86.

[11] 尹伦 [Ying Lun],《中法两国遗传资源相关传统知识获取与惠益分享法律制度比较研究》[Comparative Study on the Legal Systems of Genetic Resource-Related Traditional Knowledge Acquisition and Benefit Sharing between China and France] [2021] 法国研究 *French Study* 55, 55–65; 宋健 [Song Jian],《建立中医药传统知识利益分享机制初探》[Preliminary exploration on establishing a benefit-sharing mechanism for traditional knowledge of Chinese medicine] [2021] 世界科学技术-中医药现代化 *World Science and Technology—Modernization of Traditional Chinese Medicine* 1, 1–6.

part of its rich, millennial civilisation. This invaluable body of wisdom and practices, deeply rooted in the nation's past, is intricately interwoven with China's extensive historical experiences, societal frameworks, and cultural traditions.[12] The essence of TMK transcends beyond pure knowledge, reflecting the unique tapestry of China's past and present, making it an integral part of the country's identity.[13] To bridge this gap, this chapter seeks to critically analyse the practicality of implementing the international ABS regimes in governing Chinese TMK, emphasising the reconciliation of China's unique sociocultural and historical contexts with this internationally accepted framework.

It also employs a cultural-historical methodology to gain a deeper understanding of the legal, cultural, and social contexts influencing these implementations. The resulting cultural and historical analysis lays a solid foundation for proposing contextually grounded reforms that are not only pertinent and viable, but also deeply sensitive to China's unique sociocultural fabric and historical nuances.

Despite China's adoption of a patchwork of laws and regulations governing access to genetic resources and traditional knowledge since the 1990s,[14] it is clear that these domestic ABS regimes still require improvement.[15] With the signing of the *Nagoya Protocol* in 2016, China initiated the drafting of a comprehensive ABS framework.[16] However, this chapter argues that, for a successful implementation of this ABS system, it is imperative for law-makers and policymakers to recognise and adhere to international ABS obligations, while addressing the State's localised concerns that stem from its unique historical and sociocultural context.

This chapter has three main sections: Sect. 5.2 examines the context and progress leading to the establishment of the international ABS Regime and explores the conceptual controversies concerning the regulation of traditional knowledge (including TMK) within major ABS legal instruments at the international level.

Section 5.3 examines some key conceptual differences under the ABS system from a Chinese-Western comparative perspective to explore the reasons why implementing ABS for governing the protection and utilisation of Chinese TMK is a controversial practice in China's unique context.

Section 5.4 seeks to examine recent Chinese policy and legal measures to implement ABS frameworks for governing the protection and utilisation of Chinese TMK

---

[12] 傅义第 [Fu Wendi],《关于传统中医药文化历史局限的现实思考》[Realistic Reflections on the Historical Limitations of Traditional Chinese Medicine Culture] (2017) 38 (10) 医学与哲学 *Medicine and Philosophy* 83, 83.

[13] Ibid.

[14] Article 16 of 'China's Husbandry Law (2006)', Article 11 of the revised *China's Seed Law (2015)* and Article 43 of *China's Traditional Chinese Medicine Law (2017).*

[15] Nan Xia, 'Access and benefit-sharing in China: Exploring the Extent to Which China Fulfils the Obligations of the Nagoya Protocol' (2023) 13(1) *Queen Mary Journal of Intellectual Property* 97, 97–120.

[16]《生物遗传资源获取与惠益分享管理条例(草案)》[The Draft Regulation on Access and Benefit-Sharing for Genetic Resources and Associated Traditional Knowledge] (People's Republic of China) Ministry of Environmental Protection (23 March 2017) ('the Draft Regulation').

and provides recommendations for how international obligations could be married with China's historical-cultural particularities and settings in which the TMK system is created, preserved, and regenerated.

5.2 Legal Framework for ABS and Conceptual Controversies

5.2.1 The Rationale of ABS in International Law

The calls for the establishment of the international regime on ABS emerged out of the objectives of inhibiting biopiracy.[17] This term refers to 'the unauthorised extraction of biological resources and/or associated traditional knowledge from developing countries, or to the patenting of spurious "inventions" based on such knowledge or resources without compensation'.[18] As noted by Robinson, contemporary history is rife with instances of biopiracy and the exploitation of traditional knowledge.[19]

This occurrence is arguably a result of the asymmetrical worldwide distribution of biological resources and traditional knowledge, and the scientific and technological capacities between the global North and South.[20] A practice coined by Whit as 'bio-colonialism' describes how developed nations in the global North historically sought out traditional practices in developing countries in their search for substances of commercial value.[21]

By the early 1990s, a discourse on biopiracy emerged to critique how Northern companies exploited the genetic resources and traditional knowledge (which had been discovered or used by Southern local communities for centuries) without providing adequate compensation to the developing nations or their communities.[22] Concurrently, IP rights and trade agreements were problematised as a threat

---

[17] K Jospeh Reji, 'International Regime on Access and Benefit Sharing: Where Are We Now?' (2010) 12(3) *Asian Biotechnology and Development Review* 77, 78.

[18] G Dutfield, Intellectual Property, *Biogenetic Resources and Traditional Knowledge* (Routledge, 2004) 52,52.

[19] Daniel Robinson, *Confronting Biopiracy Challenges, Cases and International Debates* (Routledge, 2010) 1,9.

[20] Lisanne Groen, 'Explaining European Union Effectiveness (Goal Achievement) In the Convention On Biological Diversity: The Importance Of Diplomatic Engagement' (2019) 19 *Int Environ Agreements* 69, 78.

[21] LA Whitt, 'Biocolonialism and the commodification of knowledge' (1998) 7(1) *Science as Culture* 33, 33–67.

[22] Martin Fredriksson, 'Dilemmas of Protection: Decolonising the Regulation of Genetic Resources as Cultural Heritage' [2021] *International Journal of Heritage Studies* 720, 722.

to developing countries and their local communities because they facilitated the misappropriation and privatisation of traditional knowledge.[23]

In this context, the developing countries in the global South, which had a rich endowment in biological resources and traditional knowledge, bargained with developed countries in the global North, offering access to their genetic resources and traditional knowledge in exchange for 'debt relief, royalties, technology transfers, and research data'.[24]

Simultaneously, the CBD was developed and adopted for conserving biodiversity and promoting its sustainable use. It also aimed to establish the legal framework for ABS and commit Member States to facilitate 'the equitable exchange, on Mutually Agreed Terms ('MAT'), of access to genetic resources, and associated knowledge in return for finance, technology, and the opportunity to participate in research'.[25]

One of the critical and compelling advantages of the CBD is that it provides broad recognition for the value of traditional knowledge and addresses the biopiracy in a way that facilitates the countries in the global South to better benefit from their abundant repository of traditional knowledge.[26] Under its rules, a biodiversity-rich country could expect that the use of traditional knowledge for bioprospecting activities would be with the approval and involvement of the knowledge holders, who would receive a reasonable share of benefits from the use of the knowledge.[27]

Nevertheless, the CBD was described as ushering in 'a new era concerning access to genetic resources and the sharing of benefits arising from these resources'.[28] Despite this, the global issue of misappropriation of traditional knowledge and exploitation of genetic resources continues to be a widespread problem, seemingly without effective constraint.[29] This failure to address the problem effectively is largely attributable to the vague nature of the CBD's ABS provisions. These provisions leave considerable ambiguity regarding the concrete obligations of Member States, rendering the provisions inadequate to regulate the intricate and multifaceted issues surrounding ABS.[30] Many developed countries in the global North did little

---

[23] Martin Fredriksson, 'From Biopiracy to Bioprospecting: Negotiating the Limits of Propertization' in Martin Fredriksson and James Arvanitakis (eds), *Property, Place and Piracy* (Routledge, 2018) 174,175.

[24] Claudio Chiarolla, *Intellectual Property, Agriculture and Global Food Security: The Privatization of Crop Diversity* (Edward Elgar Publishing, 2011) 135.

[25] KT Kate and Sarah A Laird, *The Commercial Use of Biodiversity: Access to Genetic Resources and Benefit-Sharing* (Routledge, 2000) 4.

[26] Jasmine Biba et al., 'Traditional Knowledge System in India for Biodiversity Conservation' (216) 15(2) *Indian Journal of Traditional Knowledge* 304, 305.

[27] The CBD (n 5) arts 15.4, 15.5, and 15.7.

[28] Statement from the CBD's COP to the Commission on Sustainable Development at its Third Session, Annex to Decision I/8, para 10.

[29] Reji (n 17) 78.

[30] John Tustin, 'Traditional Knowledge and Intellectual Property in Brazilian Biodiversity Law' [2006] *Texas Intellectual Property Law Journal* 132, 137.

to fulfil their obligations under the CBD, thus nullifying its ABS objective.[31] Therefore, being increasingly discontented with the inaction of developed countries, the developing countries in the global South began to advocate for the adoption of a comprehensive international ABS regime through joining forces and lobbying groups, in particular the Like-Minded Megadiverse Countries ('LMMC').[32] They expressed their concerns over the limited applicability of the existing international regime to protect the interests of developing countries (with their rich bioresources and traditional knowledge),[33] thus seeking the creation of an international regime to 'effectively promote and safeguard the fair and equitable sharing of benefits arising from the use of biodiversity and its components'.[34] After various Expert Group meetings, ad hoc committee sessions, along with a thorough review of diverse frameworks, guidelines, and agreements adopted at the Conferences of Parties ('COP') for the CBD,[35] the *Nagoya Protocol*—the international regime on ABS—was finally adopted at the 10th meeting of COP in Nagoya, Japan, in 2010.[36] Arguably, the *Nagoya Protocol* and its various innovative provisions greatly strengthen and expand upon the CBD's ABS provisions.[37] One typical instance is that it, for the first time, spelled out in its legally binding provisions, the ABS obligations concerning the traditional knowledge of IPLCs (that the CBD had done very little with), thus explicitly acknowledging the interests and rights of IPLCs in relation to their traditional knowledge and other intangible cultural heritage.[38]

---

[31] M Lewis, 'Access and Benefit-sharing in the Wake of CBD COP10: the Nagoya Protocol and Its Potential Implications for South Africa' (2010) 17 *South African Journal of Environmental Law and Policy* 69, 69–76.

[32] Carmen Richerzhagen, 'The Nagoya Protocol: Fragmentation or Consolidation?' (2014) 3 *Resources* 135,136.

[33] Ibid.

[34] The Cancún Declaration recognised the need for the 'creation of an international regime to effectively promote and safeguard the fair and equitable sharing of benefits arising from the use of biodiversity and its components'.

See http://www.megadiverse.org/armado_ingles/PDF/three/three1.pdf. for the Cancun Declaration of Like-Minded Megadiverse Countries.

[35] See especially, the CBD website at www.cbd.int/abs/ background/#timeline.

[36] Morgera et al. (n 7) 32.

[37] Lyle Glowka and Valérie Normand, 'The Nagoya Protocol on Access and Benefit-sharing: Innovations in International Environmental Law' in Elisa Morgera et al. (eds), *The 2010 Nagoya Protocol on Access and Benefit-sharing in Perspective* (Brill, 2012) 21, 21.

[38] Morgera et al. (n 7) 24.

5.2.2 *TMK and ABS: The conceptual Controversies in the International Arena*

5.2.2.1 Navigating Challenges Surrounding TMK Within the CBD Framework

The preservation, protection, and promotion of the traditional knowledge (including TMK), of IPLCs, has begun to attract increasing international attention since the adoption of the CBD in 1992.[39] Through a number of significant provisions, the CBD has aimed to promote the protection of traditional knowledge. For instance, Article 10(c), requires the Member States to 'protect and encourage customary use of biological resources in accordance with traditional cultural practices'.[40] Its foremost provision for purposes of considering traditional knowledge is Article 8 (j), which provides that[41]:

> Subject to national legislation, respect, preserve and maintain knowledge, innovations, and practices of Indigenous and local communities embodying traditional lifestyles relevant for the conservation and sustainable use of biological diversity and promote their wider application with the approval and involvement of the holders of such knowledge, innovations, and practices and encourage the equitable sharing of the benefits arising from the utilization of such knowledge innovations and practices.

The inclusion of 'subject to national legislation' in Article 8(j) frames traditional knowledge within the context of 'state sovereignty', assigning control and ownership of this knowledge to the State. This approach dramatically shifts the conventional view of traditional knowledge as 'the common heritage of mankind'.[42] However, the universally applied concept of 'state sovereignty' under ABS is largely influenced by the historical experiences of European nations.[43]

Discussions and analyses on State sovereignty often refer to 'Westphalian sovereignty', which traces back to the 1648 Peace of Westphalia treaties.[44] The Westphalian model recognises each nation-state's sovereignty over its territory and domestic affairs, including Indigenous and local communities' traditional knowledge. This essentially means that the State has the right to own, use, and regulate this traditional knowledge.[45] However, as the world becomes more globalised and

---

[39] S Kannaiyan, 'Biological Diversity and Traditional Knowledge (Discussion Paper, National Consultation Workshop on Agro Biodiversity Hotspots and Access and Benefit sharing, 2007) 1, 9.

[40] The CBD (n 5) art 10(c).

[41] The CBD (5 2) art 8(j).

[42] Michael F Brown, 'Heritage Trouble: Recent Work on the Protection of Intangible Cultural Property' (2005) 12 *International Journal of Cultural Property* 40, 49.

[43] Sara Bannerman, *Canadian Communication Policy and Law* (Canadian Scholars, 2020) 43.

[44] BinXing Fang, *Cyberspace Sovereignty: Reflections on Building a Community of Common Future in Cyberspace* (Springer, 2018) 55–57; Gerard Prinsen and Severine Blaise, 'An Emerging "Islandian" Sovereignty of Non-self-governing Islands' (2017) 72(1) *International Journal* 56, 58.

[45] Jennifer Amiott, 'Investigating the Convention on Biological Diversity's Protections for Traditional Knowledge' (2003) 11(1) *Journal of Environmental and Sustainability Law* 3, 31–32.

interdependent, with increasing cross-border transfer of traditional knowledge and genetic materials,[46] the concept of 'national sovereignty' appears ill-suited.

Growing cross-border flows of traditional knowledge create stronger connections and dependencies between nations, limiting the autonomy and independence of States.[47] As global integration intensifies, the principle of sovereignty within the international ABS framework should be redefined to accommodate the surge in cross-border traditional knowledge exchanges and the demands for multilateral cooperation.

Article 8(j) of the CBD with a heavily qualified formulation requires the Member States to 'encourage the equitable sharing of the benefits derived from the use of traditional knowledge', which is in furtherance of the third objective of the CBD—the fair and equitable sharing of benefits. Despite fair and equitable in relation to benefit-sharing not being clearly defined in the international treaties, the inherent notion of 'the fair and equitable sharing of benefits' in the context of the CBD has been generally conceptualised by many scholars as 'the concerted and dialogic process aimed at building partnerships in identifying and allocating economic, socio-cultural and environmental benefits among state and non-state actors, with an emphasis on the vulnerable'.[48] On this basis, it becomes clear that under the CBD, the shared benefits include not only a sharing of the monetary profits of the processing and other uses of TMK but also a sharing of activities and methods such as a transfer of technology. These types of benefits have been underpinned by particular provisions of the CBD: transfer of relevant technologies (Article 16) and appropriate funding (discussed in Articles 20 and 21).

Although the concept of benefit-sharing has never been precisely defined under the CBD, its connection to commutative justice is frequently discussed within the broader CBD discourse.[49] At the 2002 World Summit on Sustainable Development in Johannesburg, South Africa, negotiators agreed that the destruction of biodiversity resources would continue to increase unless those who held this natural wealth could benefit from conservation efforts.[50] In other words, without equitable and fair benefit-sharing, the conservation and sustainable use of biodiversity resources are at risk.

The justification for benefit-sharing under the CBD aims to strike a fair and equitable balance between the interests of countries rich in traditional knowledge and biodiversity resources and those with the technical and technological capabilities to utilise these resources. This situation can be best understood as a compensation mechanism, requiring countries with abundant biodiversity to be compensated for their

---

[46] Susy Frankel, 'The challenge of Cross-Border Protection of Traditional Knowledge' in Daniel F Robinson et al. (eds), *Protecting Traditional Knowledge* (Routledge, 2017) 325, 325–331.

[47] Ibid.

[48] Elisa Morgera, 'The Need for an International Legal Concept of Fair and Equitable Benefit Sharing' (2016) 27(2) *The European Journal of International Law* 353, 382.

[49] Brad de Jonge and Michiel Korthals, 'Vicissitudes of Benefit Sharing of Crop Genetic Resources: Downstream and Upstream' (2006) 6(3) *Developing World Bioethics* 144, 150; D Schroeder, 'Benefit sharing: It's Time for a Definition' (2007) 33 *Journal of Medical Ethics* 205, 207.

[50] Schroeder (n 49) 207.

contributions.[51] In philosophical terms, this is best illustrated by Aristotelian theories of commutative justice, focusing on the equivalence of exchange, namely 'where each party gives one thing and receives another, with a focus on the equivalence of the exchange'.[52]

However, the narrow interpretation of benefit-sharing promoted through international ABS rules and agreements may not align with the historical and cultural particularities of specific countries. For example, in China, people value the principles of egalitarianism (均平) over commutative justice, rooted in ancient Chinese belief systems like Confucianism.[53] Confucius' theory of 'Bu Huan Gua Er Huan Bu Jun' (translated as 'we are not troubled with fears of poverty but are troubled with fears of a lack of equality of wealth') assumes that egalitarian wealth distribution ultimately benefits society as a whole.[54]

The Chinese perception of egalitarian wealth distribution is also closely linked to the country's traditional generation-based Confucian kinship hierarchies.[55] As noted by Zhang, within these hierarchies, age and generational seniority often play significant roles, enabling individuals with less wealth but greater seniority to hold a respected status that is independent of their wealthier counterparts.[56]

Therefore, it is crucial to recognise that the notion of fair and equitable benefit-sharing as outlined by the CBD, although globally applicable, stems from a concept of commutative justice that has its roots in Western philosophical traditions. This concept focuses on equity in transactions, meaning that all parties involved in an exchange should get what is rightly due to them.

However, the application of this ostensibly universal principle, which draws heavily upon Western philosophies and ideologies, may not align seamlessly across diverse cultural, social, and political contexts. Different nations have unique interpretations and ideologies that inform their understanding of what constitutes fair and equitable distribution of benefits. This discrepancy is particularly apparent when comparing Western ideals of commutative justice to China's egalitarian ideology.

In this light, it can be argued that directly transplanting the CBD's benefit-sharing frameworks into the local contexts of countries like China may not effectively address

---

[51] Bram De Jonge, 'What is Fair and Equitable Benefit-sharing?' (2011) 24 J *Agric Environ Ethics* 127,129.

[52] Bege Dauda et al., 'What Do the Various Principles of Justice Mean within the Concept of Benefit Sharing?' (2016) 13 *Bioethical Inquiry* 281, 287.

[53] 张自慧 [Zhang Zihui],《真相与启示：先秦儒家"均平"思想探微》[Truth and Revelation: A Detailed Exploration of the 'Equilibrium and Harmony' Concept in Pre-Qin Confucian Thought] (2017) 38 (10) 孔子研究 *Confucianism Study* 36, 36–41; Xiaogang Wu, 'Income Inequality and Distributive Justice: A Comparative Analysis of Mainland China and Hong Kong' (2009) 200 *The China Quarterly* 1033, 1038.

[54] Yang Bojun, *Annotated Translation of the Analects* (Zhonghua Book Company, 1980) 172–174.

[55] Taisu Zhang, *The Laws and Economics of Confucianism. Kinship and Property in Preindustrial China and England* (Cambridge University Press, 2017) 163.

[56] Taisu Zhang, 'Social Hierarchies and the Formation of Customary Property Law in Pre-Industrial China and England' (2014) 62 *The American Journal of Comparative Law* 171, 193–198.

justice issues. It is necessary to adapt these frameworks to respect and accommodate national and cultural differences in interpretations of justice and equity.

Therefore, while fair and equitable benefit-sharing is a principle grounded in Western philosophies and ideologies, universally asserting its value, its practical application requires sensitivity to local cultural, social, and political realities. Recognising this complexity can foster a more sophisticated approach to applying the CBD's principles. It encourages a form of global justice that both acknowledges the principle's universality and respects the multitude of its interpretations.

5.2.2.2 The Nagoya Protocol and TMK

Legal Obligations to Indigenous Peoples

After enduring a protracted and convoluted process with a series of significant milestones, the *Nagoya Protocol* was adopted during the COP's tenth session in Nagoya, Japan, in 2010. According to some commentators, one of the most important tasks of the *Nagoya Protocol* is to address the criticisms against the ABS provisions in the CBD.[57] The basic criticisms have been that it is largely concerned with ensuring access to, and the sharing of, the benefits of genetic resources, but little has been done to address the issues of protection for traditional knowledge and the rights of IPLCs.[58] Despite the *Nagoya Protocol* being a supplementary agreement to the CBD, its adoption has been seen as a significant milestone and an important step forward in terms of recognising Indigenous rights and developing mechanisms for protecting their traditional knowledge.[59] More significantly, it extends the obligation of State parties not only to Indigenous but also to local communities. The inclusion of local community along with Indigenous peoples in its ABS system, and the distinction made between them, is important for those States that claim that no Indigenous population exists within their borders.[60] According to its Preamble, there are seven paragraphs related to the traditional knowledge of IPLCs.[61] Specifically, these paragraphs refer to Article 8(j) of the CBD, highlighting its relevance to traditional knowledge and the benefit-sharing that arises from the utilisation of such knowledge. The preamble notes 'the interrelationship and inseparable nature between genetic resources and traditional knowledge', recognising the rights of IPLCs to identify the holders of traditional knowledge within their communities. The Preamble also acknowledges

---

[57] Saskia Vermeylen, 'The Nagoya Protocol and Customary Law: The Paradox of Narratives in the Law ' (2013) 9/2 *Law, Environment and Development Journal* 185,189.

[58] Vermeylen (n 57) 190.

[59] KR Srinivas, 'Protecting Traditional Knowledge Holders' Interests and Preventing Misappropriation—Traditional Knowledge Commons and Biocultural Protocols: Necessary but Not Sufficient?' (2012) 19 *International Journal of Cultural Property* 401, 403.

[60] Mohit Gupta, 'Right of Indigenous Communities to Prior Informed Consent under Article 7 of the Nagoya Protocol and a Comparative Analysis of Its Implementation by India and Bhutan' (2020) 28(1) *International Journal on Minority and Group Rights* 36, 43.

[61] Preamble of the *Nagoya Protocol* < https://www.cbd.int/abs/text/articles/?sec=abs-00 > .

the diverse and unique circumstances in which IPLCs, and their respective countries have safeguarded traditional knowledge.

Indigenous peoples and local communities, and the global understanding and recognition of their unique rights and knowledge systems have been subjects of ever-increasing importance, particularly after the adoption of the *Nagoya Protocol*. As noted by Tobin, the *Nagoya Protocol* has indeed affirmed the intimate connection between the customary law of IPLCs and the safeguarding of their traditional knowledge rights.[62] This recognition has been translated into legally binding obligations under Articles 7, 12, and 16.[63] These articles mandate Member States to adopt specific measures ensuring the protection of IPLCs' traditional knowledge, underscoring an enhanced global commitment to Indigenous rights through international legislation.

The term Indigenous people may often be perceived as a contemporary concept[64]; however, it has been in use since the Renaissance period.[65] The origins of acknowledging and granting specific rights to these communities trace back to Europe during the late Renaissance.[66] The writings of Michel de Montaigne (1533–1592) during this era can be considered one of the earliest popular portrayals of Indigenous peoples.[67] In his essay, 'Of Cannibals', he depicted Indigenous communities as dwelling in an Eden-like state—close to nature, typically unclothed, and living in simplistic harmony with their environment.[68]

Legal scholars have grappled with the issue of Indigenous peoples from the earliest Spanish expeditions and incursions into the Western hemisphere that for the first time brought European explorers into contact with the Indigenous peoples of the Americas.[69] Debates took place among Western scholars concerning the legality of the Spanish incursion into the Americas and the propriety of the treatment applied to its Indigenous people.[70] These debates have been closely linked with the development of international law over the centuries.[71] However, these debates (concerning

---

[62] Brendan Tobin, ' Why Customary Law Matters: The Role of Customary Law in the Protection of Indigenous Peoples' Human Rights. ' (PhD Thesis, National University of Ireland Galway, 2011) 245.

[63] Arts 7, 12 and 16 of the *Nagoya Protocol*.

[64] SJ Anaya, *Indigenous Peoples in International Law* (Oxford University Press, 2004) 9.

[65] Ibid.

[66] Ibid.

[67] Danielle Lorenz, 'Walking the Noble (Savage) Path: The Didactics of Indigenous Knowledge (Re)Presentation in the Toronto Zoo's Canadian Domain' (Master Thesis, Carleton University, 2012) 38.

[68] Michel de Montaigne, *'Of Cannibals'. The Longman Anthology of World Literature* (Pearson Longman, 2009) 335–43; C Cornelius, *Iroquois Corn in a Culture-Based Curriculum: A Framework for Respectfully Teaching About Cultures* (State University of New York Press, 1999) 3.

[69] Kealeboga N Bojosi and GM Wachira, 'Protecting Indigenous Peoples in Africa: An Analysis of the Approach of the African Commission on Human and Peoples' Rights' (2006) 6(2) *African Human Rights Law Journal* 382, 385.

[70] Ibid.

[71] Ibid.

Indigenous peoples) conducted within the framework of international law did not arise from the outcome of Indigenous assertions of rights but rather focused on 'the nature, scope and justification which others claimed over them'.[72] As noted by Bojosi, the position of Indigenous peoples within the international legal framework was assumed to have relevance to the rights that the European 'others' claimed over them.[73] Thus, the degree to which international law acknowledges and safeguards the rights of Indigenous peoples, and the capacity of the broadly Western notion of the Indigenous peoples category to be tailored to the unique characteristics of diverse nations and communities, continue to be subjects of considerable debate.

In light of the historical anticolonial significance of the term 'Indigenous peoples', it is essential to acknowledge its role as a symbol of resistance and empowerment for those communities who have faced and continue to face dispossession, racism, and in some cases, genocide. This term has not only been a banner under which these communities have rallied for their rights and recognition but has also provided them with a platform to voice their struggles on an international stage. The concept of 'Indigenous peoples', therefore, carries a weight beyond its academic or legal definitions, symbolising a fight against oppression and a quest for justice.

For groups like the Maori, the term 'Indigenous peoples' is intertwined with their identity and history of resistance against colonisation. It is more than a Western construct; it is part of their narrative of self-identification and struggle. Thus, while it is recognised that the term does have Western influences, it would be oversimplified to view it solely through this lens, especially when it holds such profound meaning for the communities it represents.

While the concept of Indigenous peoples and indigeneity are treated as a unified legal category under the international ABS framework, there are significant differences in how these terms are perceived worldwide.[74] For instance, in South American countries, the concept of indigeneity has gained wide acceptance.[75] Nevertheless, many who identify themselves as Indigenous peoples still struggle to realise their Indigenous rights. In Asian and African countries, many governments resist the term Indigenous peoples and negate the existence of such populations with their States' territory, thus refusing to recognise their distinct rights.[76]

In the context of China, the approach towards Indigenous peoples and traditional knowledge is framed differently, with the focus on recognising the diverse ethnic groups within the nation. China's perspective is rooted in its cultural and political

---

[72] Bojosi and Wachira (n 69) 385.

[73] Ibid.

[74] Charles R Hales, 'Comment ' (2009) 50(3) *Current Anthropology* 322, 322.

[75] Maria Luz Endere, 'Archaeological Heritage Legislation and Indigenous Rights in Latin America: Trends and Challenges' (2014) 21 *International Journal of Cultural Property* 319, 323–324.

[76] Mara Matta, 'The Novel and the North-East: Indigenous Narratives in Indian Literatures' in Rossella Ciocca and Neelam Srivastava (eds), *Indian Literature and the World: Multilingualism, Translation, and the Public Sphere* (2017) 199, 211; Dorothy L Hodgson, 'Introduction: Comparative Perspectives on the Indigenous Rights Movement in Africa and the Americas' (2002) 104(4) *American Anthropologist* 1037, 1037–1049.

ethos, emphasising the unity and equal rights of all ethnic groups under its constitution. This approach, while differing from the concept of indigeneity as understood in a Western context, demonstrates an alternative way of acknowledging and supporting traditional knowledge holders.

The concept of Indigenous people, while being universal, is deeply rooted in Western thought and understanding. This global concept does not always translate seamlessly into different national contexts due to varying cultural, social, and political constructs. For instance, China's official stance emphasises a unified State that encompasses diverse ethnic groups.[77] Under the Chinese Constitution, all ethnic groups are accorded equal rights.[78] The notion of indigeneity, as seen from a Western perspective, is not recognised by China.

As pointed out by Merlan, indigeneity is a social construct with multiple uses and outcomes, determined largely by the context in which it is used.[79] This construct presents a complex interplay between social, moral, and political dimensions, as different societies and cultures interpret and apply the concept based on their specific contexts and histories.[80] Consequently, despite the global acceptance of the term Indigenous people and the pressing need for a consistent definition to address the issues faced by these communities, the concept of indigeneity and the particular rights associated with it are still subjects of ongoing debate.

In essence, while the notion of Indigenous peoples is universal in its scope and recognition, it carries the imprint of Western thought and perspective. It encapsulates the challenge of defining a concept that is inherently diverse, multifaceted, and deeply influenced by cultural, social, and political contexts. This calls for ongoing dialogue and understanding, acknowledging the inherent diversities and unique experiences of Indigenous communities worldwide, while also recognising the commonalities that define their shared experiences.

Prior Informed Consent ('PIC') and Traditional Knowledge System

The discussions in relation to the rights of IPLCs to manage access to traditional knowledge have been active in the *Nagoya Protocol* negotiations.[81] To address this

---

[77] 罗静 [Luo Jing],《国民主体性的塑造与中华民族共同体秩序的建立》[The shaping of National Subjectivity and the Establishment of the Order of the Chinese National Community] [2023] 中南民族大学学报 *Journal of South-Central Minzu University* 1, 1–8; Stevan Harrell, *Ways of Being Ethnic in Southwest China* (University of Washington Press, 2001) 1, 25.

[78] 邵六益 [Shao Liuyi],《宪法如何铸牢中华民族共同体意识:现行宪法民族团结条款研究》[How Does the Constitution Strengthen the Sense of Community Among the Chinese Nation? A Study of the Existing Constitutional Provisions on Ethnic Unity] [2023] 西南民族大学学报 *Journal of Southwest University for Nationalities* 88, 89.

[79] Francesca Merlan, 'Indigeneity. Global and Local' (2009) 50(3) *Current Anthropology* 303, 306.

[80] Ibid.

[81] Maria Yolanda Teran, 'The Nagoya Protocol and Indigenous Peoples' (2016) 7(2) *The International Indigenous Policy Journal* 1, 6–8.

issue, it mandates the Member States to ensure that the PIC of the IPLCs is taken prior to their knowledge being accessed.[82] Article 7 provides that:

> In accordance with domestic law, each Party shall take measures, as appropriate, with the aim of ensuring that traditional knowledge associated with genetic resources that are held by Indigenous and local communities is accessed with the prior and informed consent or approval and involvement of these Indigenous and local communities and that mutually agreed terms have been established.

The concept of PIC has its origins in medical practice, where it constitutes one of the most fundamental tenets of bioethics.[83] In this context, PIC involves a dialogue between doctors and patients to ensure that doctors disclose adequate information, enabling patients to make informed decisions about their healthcare.[84] According to some commentators, the primary rationale for PIC is to uphold the patient's dignity and independence during decision-making and choice of medical options,[85] as well as to minimise risks and prevent unfairness and exploitation.[86] Therefore, in its original context, PIC relates to information exchange between individuals.

PIC emerged most prominently in international environmental law within the context of ABS, focusing on preventing the exploitation and movement of beneficial materials out of the country and ensuring that benefits arising from the use of these materials accrue to the provider country.[87] The actual expression of PIC used in the CBD (Article 15(5)) is: 'Access to genetic resources shall be subject to PIC of the Contracting Party providing such resources unless otherwise determined by that Party'. Clearly, the applications of PIC principles (required by the CBD) extend beyond the individual level and encompass the inter-state level.

Building upon the spirit of PIC enshrined in the CBD, which emphasises the State's sovereign rights as the basis for requiring PIC, the *Nagoya Protocol* goes further by mandating that access to traditional knowledge can only proceed with the PIC of IPLCs.[88] As noted by Rourke, the access obligations required by Article 7 of the

---

[82] *Nagoya Protocol* (n 6) Art 7.

[83] Maria Papamichail, 'The Patient's Right to Information and Consent in the Execution of Medical Procedures: The Legal and Sociological Dimension' (2010) 3(4) *Hellenic Journal of Nursing Science* 100, 103.

[84] Anne Perrault, 'Facilitating Prior Informed Consent in The Context of Genetic Resources And Traditional Knowledge' (2004) 4(2) *Sustainable Development Law & Policy* 21,21.

[85] V Mallardi, 'The Origin of Informed Consent' (2005) 25(5) *Acta Otorhinolaryngologica Italica: Organo Ufficiale Della Società Italiana Di Otorinolaringologia E Chirurgia Cervico-Faccial* 312, 313.

[86] KR Srinivas, 'Protecting Traditional Knowledge Holders' Interests and Preventing Misappropriation—Traditional Knowledge Commons and Biocultural Protocols: Necessary but Not Sufficient?' (2012) 19 *International Journal of Cultural Property* 401, 404.

[87] Kuei-Jung Ni, 'Legal Aspects of Prior Informed Consent on Access to Genetic Resources' (2009) 42(1) *Vanderbilt Journal of Transnational Law* 227, 232.

[88] Matthias Buck and Clare Hamilton, 'The Nagoya Protocol on Access to Genetic Resources and the Fair and Equitable Sharing of Benefits Arising from their Utilization to the Convention on Biological Diversity' (2011) 20(1) *Review of European Community & International Environmental Law* 47, 52.

Nagoya Protocol represent the first instance where specific procedural and substantive requirements are explicitly outlined for community PIC over the traditional knowledge held by IPLCs.[89]

However, despite the widespread acceptance of PIC principles established by international ABS rules as legally binding obligations on Member States, challenges remain. The common understandings of PIC across countries can lead to a paradoxical situation where it serves as a standard for corporate and state engagement with biodiversity-rich countries, Indigenous people, and local communities, but may not be sensitive to the unique social, cultural, and historical factors of different nations.[90] As a result, the rights and interests of IPLCs might not be adequately protected. This situation has been criticised as 'bureaucratic terrorism', where the PIC principle becomes a 'technocratic tool designed to meet corporate exigencies instead of genuinely safeguarding the rights and interests of the impacted communities'.[91]

The principles of PIC, originating from Western perspectives, frequently encounter challenges when adapted to diverse national and local contexts.[92] This happens because interpretations and applications of PIC differ across regions, moulded by their unique traditions, moral values, historical legacies, and cultural norms. Western societies, characterised by individualistic values and a viewpoint of human dominance over nature, tend to approach PIC from a standpoint of liberal individualism and self-determination.[93] These societies perceive PIC as a mechanism to ensure personal freedom and autonomy within decision-making processes.[94]

Conversely, societies like China, with traditions deeply rooted in sustainability, responsibility, and relationships, approach PIC from a unique perspective.[95] They emphasise spiritual needs, familial ties, and communal values, seeking harmony between humans and nature. PIC, in these contexts, extends beyond individual

---

[89] MF Rourke, 'Who Are "Indigenous and Local Communities" and What Is "Traditional Knowledge" for Virus Access' (2018) 25 *Journal of Law and Medicine* 707, 717.

[90] Cathal M Doyle, Indigenous Peoples, *Title to Territory, Rights and Resources: The Transformative Role of Free Prior and Informed Consent* (Routledge, 2017) 252.

[91] Ibid.

[92] Philippe Hanna and Frank Vanclay, 'Human Rights, Indigenous Peoples and the Concept of Free, Prior and Informed Consent' (2013) 31(2) *Impact Assessment and Project Appraisal* 146, 150–153; Ricarda Roesch, 'The Story of A Legal Transplant: The Right to Free, Prior and Informed Consent in Sub-Saharan Africa ' (2016) 16 *African Human Rights Law Journal* 505, 505–531; Joseph Tham et al., *Cross-Cultural and Religious Critiques of Informed Consent* (Routledge Focus, 2022).

[93] Mark J Cherry, 'Individually Directed Informed Consent and the Decline of the Family in the West' in Ruiping Fan (ed), *Family-Oriented Informed Consent: East Asian and American Perspectives* (Springer, 2015) 43, 43–58.

[94] Ibid.

[95] 刘月树 [Liu Yueshu],《知情同意原则的中国化：一种生命伦理学视角的转换》[Sinicization of the Principle of Informed Consent: A Transformation from the Perspective of Bioethics] (2013) 1 伦理学研究 *Studies in Ethics* 128, 129–130; Kam-Por Yu, 'The Confucian Alternative to the Individual-Oriented Model of Informed Consent: Family and Beyond' in Ruiping Fan (ed), *Family-Oriented Informed Consent: East Asian and American Perspectives* (Springer, 2015) 93, 93–106; JB Nie, 'Is Informed Consent Not Applicable to China?: Intellectual Flaws of the Cultural Difference Argument' (2000) 2 *Formos J Med Humanit* 67, 67–74.

rights, encompassing societal relationships and spiritual harmony.[96] Consequently, it is imperative to understand the cultural context when implementing PIC, as its interpretation and importance can vary significantly.

However, this perspective does not imply the impracticability of international ABS rules concerning PIC; rather, it stresses the importance of respecting and understanding historical and cultural specificities, as well as the roles of unique traditional practices. This approach, nuanced and considerate, promises a more responsible and contextualised application of PIC principles. Though these principles, rooted in Western thought, hold universal relevance that transcends geographical boundaries, their practical implementation demands a certain degree of flexibility and adaptability.

However, for these principles to be truly effective, it is imperative to adapt and refine them to better align with the unique cultural subtleties and traditional practices of various regions worldwide. This process involves much more than a mere transplant of Western ideas. It necessitates the recognition and integration of non-Western perceptions of consent, communal responsibility, and proprietary rights over resources. This could involve creating more inclusive negotiation methods that respect and incorporate traditional decision-making structures, or more comprehensive benefit-sharing arrangements that acknowledge traditional knowledge and its value in a more profound and equitable manner.

5.3 Exploring Opportunities and Challenges of ABS Implementation in China's Social Cultural Context

The implementation of ABS standards illuminates the inherent intricacies and diversity of global practices. This scenario becomes especially significant in the context of China, given its unique sociocultural landscape.

Implementing an international ABS framework within China's national structure is a multifaceted challenge, involving the navigation of various linguistic, interpretive, and technical obstacles. The complexities of its legal system, in tandem with existing ambiguities in ABS operationalisation, often lead to misinterpretations and misapplications.[97] Furthermore, cultural variances contribute an additional layer of complexity, creating less tangible challenges for the integration of international ABS norms, particularly those under the *Nagoya Protocol*.[98] In this regard, due to

[96] 董平平 [Dong Pingping],《论中国家庭文化对知情同意原则实践的影响》[Discussing the impact of Chinese family culture on the practice of informed consent principles] (2011) 24 (2) 中国医学伦理学 *Chinese Medical Ethic Nationalities* 262, 262–264.

[97] Nan Xia, 'Access and benefit-sharing in China: Exploring the Extent to Which China Fulfils the Obligations of the Nagoya Protocol' (2023) 13(1) *Queen Mary Journal of Intellectual Property* 97, 97–120.

[98] FM Birhanu, 'Challenges and Prospects of Implementing the Access and Benefit-Sharing Regime of the Convention on Biological Diversity in Africa: the Case of Ethiopia' (2010) 10 *International Environmental Agreements: Politics, Law and Economics* 249, 259.

China's unique cultural nuances, traditional practices, and historical legacies, the full implementation of ABS standards poses a distinct challenge.

Admittedly, the existing ABS system has demonstrated its capacity to strike a balance between safeguarding traditional knowledge through just access requirements and enabling the use of traditional knowledge through equitable benefit-sharing mechanisms.[99] In this way, ABS could enhance the value of traditional knowledge, for users as inputs for research and development, and for providers as sources of benefits that produce incentives for the protection of traditional knowledge. Nevertheless, as analysed above, it is crucial to consider that the foundations of the ABS mechanism are predominantly embedded in Western ideologies. Such ideologies, while potent and influential, may not necessarily align with the cultural, political, and economic realities of many countries. China is such a representative example, with its historical and sociocultural particularities.[100] This dichotomy prompts a profound exploration of the compatibility between these global norms and China's unique national context.

5.3.1 Access to the Knowledge

As analysed above, the CBD and the *Nagoya Protocol* have explicitly established provisions that grant IPLCs the right to manage and control access to their knowledge, recognising their traditional ownership. These provisions can be seen as efforts to support the claims of sovereignty and autonomy by IPLCs over the access to, and utilisation of, their knowledge. In Chinese culture, there is a prevailing notion that without State sovereignty, exclusive control over the access to and use of knowledge cannot be claimed by individuals.[101] Instead, this culture traditionally esteems the practice of copying and sharing knowledge and creative works, a sentiment which permeates and guides all aspects of life in China.[102]

The Compendium of Materia Medica, considered one of the most comprehensive traditional medical manuscripts in Chinese history, offers an illuminating example of traditional Chinese attitudes towards knowledge access. This revered work was

---

[99] Aysegul Sirakaya et al., 'Designing Regulatory Frameworks for Access to Genetic Resources: A Multi-Stakeholder Multi-Criteria Approach' (2020) 11 *Frontier in Genetics* 1, 2.

[100] Yuan-kang Wang, 'The Myth of Chinese Exceptionalism: An Historical Perspective on China's Rise' in Vinod K Aggarwal and Sara A Newland (eds), *Responding to China's Rise* (Springer, 2014) 51, 51–71.

[101] Shao Ken, 'The Promotion of Learning in Chinese History: Discovering the Lost Soul of Modern Copyright' (2010) 24(1) *Columbia Journal of Asian Law* 64, 79.

[102] 董火民 [Dong Huomin],《知识的复制: 古代传抄活动对知识传播的影响》[The Reproduction of Knowledge: The Impact of Ancient Copying Activities on Knowledge Dissemination] (2010) 31(11) 东岳论丛 *Dongyue Collected Essays* 102, 102–106; Wei Shi, ' The Paradox of Confucian Determinism: Tracking the Root Causes of Intellectual Property Rights Problem in China ' (2008) 7(3) *The John Marshall Review of Intellectual Property Law* 454, 455.

unexpectedly discovered by an ancient book collector, Hu Chenglong.[103] In a move that profoundly demonstrates the ethos of knowledge sharing embedded in traditional Chinese culture, Hu invested his own resources to carve and block-print the manuscript, then distributed it freely.[104] This edition, known as the Jinling edition, is the earliest known version.[105] Hu Chenglong's contribution, still celebrated today, ensured the survival and propagation of the Compendium into the modern era.[106] This seminal work, widely utilised by physicians, healers, and laypeople alike, continues to serve as an authoritative reference in traditional medicine.[107] Hu's actions echo the values encapsulated in a traditional Chinese proverb: 'He that shares are to be rewarded; he that does not, condemned'.[108] This historical episode illuminates a fundamental aspect of the Chinese viewpoint on knowledge accessibility. Rather than enforcing proprietary control, the traditional Chinese ethos has always emphasised the broad dissemination and open accessibility of knowledge.

Confucian philosophy and teachings also influence China's attitudes and perceptions towards access to traditional knowledge (including TMK). It was said that Confucius as a sage of profound greatness in China, spent most of his life learning and transmitting ancient knowledge and thought with his main attention and labours focused on gathering, storing, and disseminating the philosophy, values, and documents of his predecessors. His lifetime commitment and contribution is reflected in the Analects: 述而不作,信而好古, 'my function is to transmit, not to innovate; and I treat antiquity with trust and admiration'.[109] Such Confucian views (that have significantly influenced the Chinese for over 2000 years) reveal that, in order to access the wealth of traditional knowledge, that knowledge should be widely accessible, without too much control.[110] In other words, the TMK and other ancient knowledge are regarded as the common heritage of China's society and encouraged to be shared and placed in the social domain. The understanding of access to TMK and other ancient knowledge in China's contexts differs significantly from the well-defined

---

[103] 王剑 [Wang Jian],《对李时珍本草纲目编撰与初刻出版作出重要贡献的有关历史人物之探考》[Exploring the Historical Figures Who Made Significant Contributions to the Compilation and Initial Publication of Li Shizhen's 'Compendium of Materia Medica] (2019) 30(12) 时珍国医国药*Lishizhen Medicine and Materia Medica Research* 3012, 3014–3016;Kuan-chih Chen, 'A Study on the Book Market of Nanjing in Ming Dynasty' (2014) (2) *National Central Library Journal* 153, 160.

[104] 王剑 [Wang Jian] (n 103) 3014–3016.

[105] 周艳红 [Zhou Yanhong]《明代地方官刻医籍考略》[A Study on the Printing of Medical Books by Local Officials in the Ming Dynasty] (2021) 44 (2) 陕西中医药大学学报*Journal of Shaanxi University of Chinese Medicine* 40, 42.

[106] Chen (n 103) 160.

[107] Ibid.

[108] WR Swinyard et al., 'The Morality of Software Piracy: A Cross-Cultural Analysis' in Alex C Michalos and Deborah C Poff (eds), *Citation Classics from the Journal of Business Ethnics* (Springer, 2013) 565, 567.

[109]《论语》述而篇第七, The Analects 7.1.

[110] Brigitte Binkert, 'Why the Current Global Intellectual Property Framework Under TRIPS Is Not Working' (2006) 10 *Intell. Prop. L. Bull* 143, 147.

sovereignty that certain communities have over their knowledge, as established by the international ABS regime, particularly the *Nagoya Protocol*.

5.3.2 Fair and Equitable Benefit-Sharing

The concept of fair and equitable benefit-sharing is a critical objective in many fields of international environmental law and is a focus of many policy and regulation efforts.[111] This principle addresses the distribution of benefits that arise from the use of genetic resources and traditional knowledge, ensuring that all stakeholders involved, including local communities and Indigenous populations, receive their rightful share.[112] The recognition of this principle, however, demands a nuanced analysis to ensure its applicability and relevance in a broader context. It needs to align with a variety of cultural perspectives and societal structures, acknowledging the diversity that exists across the globe.

In the case of China, for instance, traditional systems of justice and governance have been shaped by distinctive cultural, historical, and philosophical factors.[113] This may pose a challenge when trying to adopt benefit-sharing principles that are based on Western-centric views of justice. In Chinese traditional values, justice is primarily concerned with promoting social harmony and balance, rather than prioritising the individual pursuit of fairness and equality with regard to the distribution of socioeconomic goods within the society.[114] This perspective on justice originates from the Confucian belief that all individuals have an obligation to uphold the moral and ethical standards of their community and that the well-being of the individual is closely tied to the well-being of society as a whole.[115] The Chinese notion of justice that prioritises social harmony and balance over individual gains can be traced back to Confucius' classic *Book of Rites*, which describes a time when people prioritised

[111] Elsa Tsioumani, *Fair and Equitable Benefit-Sharing in Agriculture: Reinventing Agrarian Justice* (Routledge, 2021) 1, 39.

[112] Elisa Morgera, Elsa Tsioumani and Matthias Buck, *Unraveling the Nagoya Protocol: A Commentary on the Nagoya Protocol on Access and Benefit-sharing to the Convention on Biological Diversity* (Brill, 2014) 110–135.

[113] 麻宝斌 [Ma Baobin],《中国传统的社群正义观念：主要特征与社会根源》[Chinese Traditional Notion of Community Justice: Key Characteristics and Social Roots] (2018) 4 理论探讨*Theoretical Investigation* 143, 143–149; Tim Murphy, 'Justice and the Common Good in Dispute Resolution Discourse in the United States and the People's Republic of China' (2017) 10(2) *Law Dev Rev* 305, 305–339; Tim Murphy and Ralph Weber, 'Ideas of Justice and Reconstructions of Confucian Justice' (2016) 26(2) *An International Journal of the Philosophical Traditions of the East* 99, 99–118.

[114] 陈科华 [Chen Kehua],《中重于正: 中国传统正义思想的理论构建》[Moderation Over Justice: The Theoretical Construction of Traditional Chinese Concepts of Justice] (2016) 40(4) 湘潭大学学报*Journal of Xiangtan University* 122, 126–128; Christophe Duvert, 'How is Justice Understood in Classic Confucianism?' (2018) 28(4) *Asian Philosophy* 295, 295.

[115] Uzma Khan et al., 'The Philosophical Thought of Confucius and Mencius, and the Concept of the Community of a Shared Future for Mankind' (2022) 14(9854) *Sustainability* 1, 2–5.

virtues such as compassion, respect, integrity, and communal well-being over individual goals and ambitions.[116] In this vision of society, leaders were chosen according to their talent and integrity, and their voices were respected and heeded in the interests of promoting harmony.[117] People treated each other's parents and children with care and compassion, and extended hospitality and support to those in need, such as the elderly, widows, orphans, and the sick.[118] There was a strong sense of community and shared responsibility, with everyone having their own role to play and contributing to the well-being of the group.[119] People worked hard and diligently, not for personal gain or ambition, but for the betterment of the community as a whole. Therefore, there was little room for individualistic pursuits or selfish motives.

The same idea can be found in the teachings of Mencius who was often referred to as the Second Sage of Confucianism.[120] He described a type of primitive agrarian communism where the fields were divided into nine parts, with eight lots going to families and the ninth cultivated commonly for the prince.[121] This was known as the 'field in the shape of a well', or *ching-t'ien*, where those who cultivated the same *ching* could work together, share the job of defence and keeping watch.[122] They could also share equal access to resources and provide mutual support in times of sickness or hardship, leading to a harmonious and cooperative society, regardless of their individual abilities or status.[123] Mencius' ideal society, as written in his work, reflects a commitment to the principles of egalitarianism, which focuses on the equitable distribution of resources and the satisfying of the needs of all people to ensure that everyone has access to the resources they need to live a decent life.[124] In addition to Mencius' teachings, the Taoist school that emerged during the fifth and sixth centuries BCE is particularly rich in promoting the principle of egalitarianism and is known for advocating a utopian vision of society that prioritises mutual support and cooperation.[125] Taoist teachings usually express a longing for a Golden Age that prioritises cooperation over individual acquisition and emphasises the commitment to a more egalitarian and cooperative society.[126]

Thus, the perspectives on justice presented in traditional Chinese thought—as embodied in Confucianism, Mencian philosophy, and Taoism—diverge from the notions of justice advanced by international ABS frameworks like the CBD and the *Nagoya Protocol*.

---

[116] Jean Chesneaux, 'Egalitarian and Utopian Traditions in the East' (1968) 16(62) *Diogenes* 76, 79.

[117] Ibid.

[118] Ibid.

[119] Ibid.

[120] Chesneaux (n 116) 79–80.

[121] Ibid.

[122] Ibid.

[123] Ibid.

[124] Ibid.

[125] Chesneaux (n 116) 80.

[126] Chesneaux (n 116) 82.

5.3.3 Recognising the Indigenous Rights to TMK

ABS in international environmental laws converges with human rights discourses on Indigenous people and their rights to traditional knowledge (including TMK).[127] The *Nagoya Protocol*, for example, promises to protect the traditional knowledge (including TMK) conforming to the Indigenous worldviews and rules of IPLCs.[128] Nevertheless, as noted by Smith, 'problematising the Indigenous is a Western obsession',[129] which largely ignores the system of values and practices of other great ancient civilisations in the world. As one of the world's oldest civilisations, China has divergent interpretations of the term Indigenous, and of Indigenous rights to traditional knowledge which is arguably based on factors in its local legal culture.[130] In this culture, the issues of Indigenous peoples are usually considered the product of Western countries' pursuit of colonial objectives and policies, which represents acute political and cultural humiliation for China.[131] This unique culture arises from China's negative experience concerning colonial aggression, the acquisition of territory, and commercial exploitation in the nineteenth century, which was known as 'the Century of Humiliation'.[132] On this basis, China has often resisted international supervision and recognition of Indigenous rights, arguing that it is the forcible imposition of Western legal order and an infringement of China's national sovereignty.[133]

In many international surveys and studies on global Indigenous populations, prominent international and intergovernmental organisations such as the United Nations often count China.[134] It is worth noting, however, that despite China being among the countries that initially endorsed the *United Nations Declaration on the Rights of Indigenous Peoples* in 2007, it has firmly maintained that the term Indigenous peoples is not applicable to any group within its borders.[135] In the discussions that took place during the Human Rights Council's drafting meetings, China

---

[127] Abebe Kebede Jalleta, 'Access and Benefit Sharing Effectiveness: International Environmental Law Implementation at the Domestic Ethiopian Level' (2021) 12 *Beijing Law Review* 485,485.

[128] S Vermeylen, 'The Nagoya Protocol and Customary Law: the Paradox of Narratives in the Law' (2013) 9(2) *Law, Environment and Development Journal* 187,187.

[129] Linda Tuhiwai Smith, *Decolonizing Methodologies: Research and Indigenous* (University of Otago Press, 2008) 91.

[130] Linzhu Wang, 'The Definition of Indigenous Peoples and its Applicability in China' (2015) 22 *International Journal on Minority and Group Rights* 232, 232–258.

[131] Ibid 242.

[132] Alison Adcock Kaufman, 'The "Century of Humiliation", Then and Now: Chinese Perceptions of the International Order' (2010) 25(1) *Pacific Focus* 1, 1–28.

[133] Ben Saul, 'China, Natural Resources, Sovereignty and International Law' (2013) 37(2) *Asian Studies Review* 196, 198.

[134] Michael J Hathaway, 'China's Indigenous Peoples? How Global Environmentalism Unintentionally Smuggled the Notion of Indigeneity into China' (2016) 5 *Humanities* 1,2.

[135] Embassy of the People's Republic of China in Switzerland, China Concerned with Protection of Indigenous Peoples' Rights (1 Apr. 1997), available at < http://ch.China-embassy.org/eng/ztnr/rqwt/t138829.htm >.

leveraged historical narratives, asserting that its fifty-six recognised nationalities and ethnic minorities have harmoniously intertwined and coexisted for over 5,000 years.[136] Yet, identifying who is truly Indigenous to the area is a daunting task. It is a challenge steeped in historical, anthropological, and political complexities due to centuries of migration, assimilation, and intermarriage among these groups.

Adding to this complexity is China's historic *gaito kuiliu* policy, aimed at assimilating ethnic minorities into the dominant Han Chinese culture and centralising administrative control.[137] The term, meaning 'changing local customs to conform to the mainstream', underscores the government's agenda of fostering a more uniform society.[138] This policy significantly impacts the recognition of Indigenous peoples within China. By promoting the blending of ethnic minorities into the mainstream Han culture, the policy blurs the distinctive attributes of different ethnic groups.[139] It drives towards a singular, unified Chinese identity, effectively watering down the distinctiveness intrinsic to the global understanding of Indigenous peoples.[140]

Likewise, in the ABS context, Chinese Government officials have reported to the CBD's ABS Clearing House that China does not have Indigenous people.[141] Instead, China positions itself as home to the ethnic minority population[142] which should not be conceptualised as Indigenous. From China's perspective, Indigenous peoples are more likely to seek a separate political unit from the present State while the recognition of minorities' rights is to integrate ethnic communities into the Chinese nation and allow them to have their own separate identities.[143] This recognition of minority rights rather than Indigenous rights in China corresponds with what Wang has noted, recognising one group of the population as Indigenous in China may indicate the rest are not,[144] which could be significantly at odds with China's pursuit of pluralistic integration or unity of diversity of the Chinese nation.[145]

Moreover, China's commitment to ethnic minorities rather than Indigenous peoples is largely determined by its history and particular legal circumstances.[146] During a century of revolution in China which transformed the Chinese empire

---

[136] Ibid; Michael C Davis, 'China & the UN Declaration on the Rights of Indigenous Peoples: The Tibetan Case' (Research Paper No. 2014/044, Faculty of Law, University of Hong Kong, May 2014) 1, 4.

[137] Baogang He, 'The Contested Politics of Asian Responses to Indigenous Rights' (2011) 18 *International Journal on Minority and Group Rights* 461, 471.

[138] 郭家翔 [Guo JiaXiang],《改土归流: 巩固统一多民族国家的重要举措》["Gaito kuiliu": An Important Measure to Consolidate A Unified Multi-ethnic Nation.] (2021) 4 中国民族报*China Ethnic Daily* 1, 1–2.

[139] He (n 137) 471.

[140] Ibid.

[141] *China's Interim National Report on The Implementation of The Nagoya Protocol* (Interim Report, 2017).

[142] Ibid.

[143] Wang (n 133) 244.

[144] Ibid.

[145] Jinzhou Song, 'Commentary and Discussion on Zhou Ping's Chinese Nation: Integration or Pluralism?' (2021) 11(3) *Journalism and Mass Communication* 112, 112–123.

[146] Wang (n 133) 244.

into a modern State, the Indigenous rights to self-determination were once recognised.[147] In particular, Article 14 of the 1931 Communist State constitution, officially recognised 'the right of self-determination of the national minorities in China, their right to complete separation from China, and to the formulation of an independent state for each national minority'. Nevertheless, upon inheriting the territory from the Qing Empire and the founding of the new China, the Indigenous right to self-determination was replaced by the minority right to regional autonomy to prevent the separateness of the communities from the nation-state.[148] This is because as noted by Wang, the exercise of the minority right to regional autonomy needs to be authorised under China's national law, in which democratic secessionism and self-determination are not allowed.[149] Indigenous peoples, instead, are entitled to the right to self-determination upheld by international law, which is superior to domestic law in China; in any contradictions between the two, international law prevails.[150] Therefore, China's commitment to ethnic minorities is shaped by its legal and historical context, and this approach may differ from other countries' approaches to Indigenous peoples. When it comes to the ABS obligations required by the *Nagoya Protocol*, China's commitment to ethnic minorities and its rejection of the concept of Indigenous peoples may impact its ability to fully comply with its international obligations. The *Nagyoa Protocol* aims to facilitate the assertion of Indigenous rights over traditional knowledge and genetic resources. However, China's position may not fully align with these obligations, especially when doing so conflicts with its own cultural and political identity.

5.4 China's ABS Measures Related to TMK Governance

China's efforts in regulating ABS have a lengthy history and trajectory, which commenced since the adoption of the CBD in 1992, and continued thereafter.[151] These efforts can be generalised into two broad categories.[152] The first category involves policy frameworks and guidelines that are expected to inspire law-making, administrative decisions, and all other ABS activities.[153] The relevant policy

[147] Anonymous, 'China and the Principle of Self-Determination of Peoples' (2010) 6(1) *St Antony's International Review* 79, 81.

[148] Ibid; Upon the establishment of the PRC, the right of minorities to self-determination was tailored into ethnic regional autonomy.

[149] Wang (n 133) 244.

[150] Ibid.

[151] Dayuan Xue and Lijie Cai, 'China's Legal and Policy Frameworks for Access to Genetic Resources and Benefit-Sharing from their Use' (2009) 18(1) *The Review of European Comparative & International Environmental Law* 91, 92.

[152] Yu Wen-xuan and Mu Tong, 'Legal Framework of Access and Benefit-Sharing for Genetic Resources and Local Practice in China' (2021) (4) *China Food & Drug Administration Magazine* 100, 100–105.

[153] Ibid 101–102.

documents include the 'National Biodiversity Conservation Strategy and Action Plan (2011–2030)', the 'Major Project Implementation Plan for Biodiversity Conservation', and 'The 13th Five-Year Plan for Ecological Environment Protection'. In these documents, the clear priorities include the need to establish a comprehensive ABS system by incorporating international rules at the national level and bringing traditional knowledge into the policy deliberations.[154] The second category is a series of legislative and regulatory measures pertaining to the ABS.[155] To be specific, China's first legislative effort addressing ABS-related issues is the *Husbandry Law* adopted in 2005, which included specific provisions focusing on the access to livestock genetic resources and sharing of benefits arising from the utilisation of livestock genetic resources. Other laws and regulations that have also incorporated specific provisions addressing ABS issues include *China's Seed Law* adopted in 2015, the *Biosecurity Law* adopted in 2020, and the *Traditional Chinese Medicine Law* adopted in 2017. Nevertheless, arguably, the language used in these adopted law and policies was particularly vague and loosely written, which made implementation efforts almost impossible. For example, the *Traditional Chinese Medicine Law (2017)* addressing ABS issues pertaining to TMK, simply 'exhorted' the TMK holders to uphold their rights to benefit-sharing upon the utilisation of their TMK.[156] Beyond this, however, these adopted laws and policies did not provide any concrete and practical measures under which the rights of TMK holders can be realised. This situation reinforced the impression that China does not seem to be serious about adopting and enforcing effective ABS measures at its national level.

This situation is expected to change dramatically with the upcoming development and adoption of the *Draft Regulation* (for the purpose of implementing *the Nagoya Protocol*).[157] This has a total of seven Sections and forty-eight Provisions with the objectives of promoting the ABS principles of the CBD, contributing to the conservation and sustainable use of biodiversity, and fulfilling the obligations of the *Nagoya Protocol*.[158] It breaks new ground by establishing the most comprehensive piece of legislation for ABS in China and spelling out for the first time legally binding

---

[154] 《"十三五"生态环境保护规划》[The 13th Five-Year Plan for Ecological Environment Protection] (People's Republic of China) the State Council, Order No 65, 2016 ('the Plan'),Art 7; 《加强生物遗传资源管理国家工作方案》[National work programme on strengthening the management of biological genetic resources] (People's Republic of China) the Department of Environmental Protection, Order No 193, 2014, Art 2 and Art 3.

[155] Yu and Mu (n152) 103–104.

[156] 《中华人民共和国中医药法》[Law of the People's Republic of China on Traditional Chinese Medicine] (People's Republic of China) Standing Committee of the National People's Congress 2016, Art 43.

[157] 《生物遗传资源获取与惠益分享管理条例(草案)》[the Draft Regulation on Access and Benefit-Sharing for Genetic Resources and Associated Traditional Knowledge] (People's Republic of China) Ministry of Environmental Protection (23 March 2017) ('the Draft Regulation').

[158] Ibid; The *Draft Regulation* on ABS was released on 23 July 2017 and it is currently under public consultation. For it to be adopted, it must be submitted to the State Council for examination and approvals, further revised by the State Council's Legislative Affairs Office and then submitted to the Premier for signature and promulgation. If there are any controversies during the progress, the

rules on the ABS obligations arising from the utilisation of the traditional knowledge (including TMK) in China.[159] Moreover, in October 2021, the General Office of the Central Committee of the Communist Party of China along with the PRC State Council General Office issued 'Opinions on Further Strengthening the Protection of Biodiversity'. One significant point highlighted is to accelerate the revision and adoption of the *Draft Regulation.* As this policy document has been issued by both the highest governing body of China and the Communist Party of China, it shows the serious attitude of the Chinese government to developing the ABS framework to ensure the protection, preservation, and sustainable use of traditional knowledge (and genetic resources) in China.

5.4.1 Traditional Knowledge (Including TMK) Defined by the Draft Regulation

In the *Draft Regulation,* the traditional knowledge is only that 'associated with genetic resources', which is defined as 'the knowledge, innovations and practices that are created, inherited and developed by the people of all ethnic groups and local communities in their long-term practice of traditional lifestyles relevant for the conservation and sustainable use of genetic resources'.[160] Notably, rather than adopt the politically contentious term of Indigenous peoples used in the CBD and *Nagoya Protocol,* China's *Draft Regulation* adopts the term of ethnic groups to divert the attention away from historically and politically controversial issues of Indigenous identity and transnational claims for recognising Indigenous rights.[161] This situation reflects China's consistent commitment to the historical rights of China's minority nationalities or ethnic groups while denying the very existence of Indigenous peoples or Indigenous rights. However, in addition to the use of distinct term of ethnic groups to eschew the effects produced by the politically controversial term of Indigenous (fostered by the international environmental organisations), the *Draft Regulation*'s definition for traditional knowledge almost mechanically mirrors the definition in the CBD regardless of whether these definitions match China's local needs, interests or priorities. China's adherence to international obligations regarding traditional knowledge (including TMK) and ABS is commendable, but it is important to consider the local cultural and historical context in which these regulations are being implemented.

representatives from various departments will be convened to resolve them. see < http://www.npc.gov.cn/npc/sjb/2013-02/19/content_1755104.htm > .

[159] Nan Xia, 'Access and Benefit-sharing in China: Exploring the Extent to Which China Fulfils the Obligations of the Nagoya Protocol ' (2023) 13(1) *Queen Mary Journal of Intellectual Property* 97, 112.

[160] The *Draft Regulation,* art 2.

[161] Ibid.

The one-size-fits-all definition of traditional knowledge used in international agreements may not align with China's unique traditions and values and transplanting this definition mechanically could lead to a clash with local distinctiveness.

Arguably, the definitions of traditional knowledge (including TMK) provided in the *Draft Regulation* that mirror the definitions in the CBD and other international environmental treaties, in effect reflect the Western visions that seek to describe traditional knowledge as something old, primitive, or antithetical to modernity, and treat the traditional knowledge holders as peripheral members of society that are required to shed their own traditions.[162] Nevertheless, traditional knowledge, specifically TMK in China, is contingent upon its complicated historical, cultural, and social dynamics, which are continually evolving against the ever-changing forms of China's health and environmental risks.[163] Therefore, a more nuanced definition of traditional knowledge, specifically TMK, is necessary. This should be framed by both an outward interaction with global trends and obligations, and an inward exploration of its local uniqueness and traditions and how its national and local communities have historically defined, validated, and managed their traditional knowledge. Adopting a more nuanced approach to developing ABS measures in China involves taking into account the country's unique historical, cultural, and social dynamics. By doing so, policymakers and stakeholders can ensure that any ABS measures implemented are equitable, effective, and respectful of the country's unique perspective and traditions.

As pointed out by Luo, a good example of the nuanced approach to developing ABS measures in China is the use of the concept of *Yuan shengtai* to describe the unique form of local knowledge and traditional wisdom in Guizhou province.[164] It carries the dual meanings of traditional knowledge and grassroots wisdom. It emphasises the historic continuity, cultural purity, and local distinctiveness of traditional knowledge, reflecting the essence of China's local traditional cultural values such as the Confucian tradition of 'harmonious yet different' and the idea of 'the oneness of Heaven and humankind'.[165] This highlights the significant spiritual and cultural connections to traditional knowledge and grassroots wisdom in the region.

At the same time, the conceptual emphasis of the term *Yuan shengtai* also provides a romanticised portrayal of local folkloric practices, which is similar to the representation of Indigenous peoples developed in Western culture. This resonates with the international legal concept of indigeneity, which emphasises the cultural distinctiveness of Indigenous communities and their connection to their lands and resources.

Arguably, a similar approach should be adopted in the *Draft Regulation*, with definitions and phrases that capture the cultural distinctiveness of China's national

---

[162] K Matsui, 'Problems of Defining and Validating Traditional Knowledge: An Historical Approach' (2015) 6(2) *The International Indigenous Policy Journal* 1, 4.

[163] Shuo Gu and Jianfeng Pei, 'Innovating Chinese Herbal Medicine: From Traditional Health Practice to Scientific Drug Discovery' (2017) 8 *Frontier in Pharmacology* 1, 1–2.

[164] Yu Luo, 'An Alternative to the "Indigenous" in Early Twenty-First-Century China: Guizhou's Branding of Yuanshengtai' (2018) 44(1) *Modern China* 68, 68–102.

[165] Ibid 70.

and local communities. This can involve interrelating the advanced Western environmental concepts and global environmental value systems with China's nationalistic flavour. By doing so, ABS measures in China can better reflect the country's unique historical, cultural, and social dynamics, while also meeting international standards and expectations. This approach could ensure that any ABS measures implemented are equitable, effective, and respectful of the country's unique perspective and traditions.

5.4.2 The Complexity of Traditional Knowledge Access in China

Chapter 3 of China's Draft Regulation is the main chapter dealing with access to traditional knowledge (including TMK).[166] It develops a series of domestic access measures required by Articles 6 and 7 of the *Nagoya Protocol* to ensure that access to traditional knowledge can only proceed with some regulatory burdens borne by the potential users of traditional knowledge. The text includes the following critical elements: Article 18 provides that the access to traditional knowledge should be subjected to the PIC of the holders of traditional knowledge and other registration or approval procedures, based on mutually agreed terms ('MAT')[167]; Articles 19 and 20 make an important distinction between domestic and foreign users with regards to the access to traditional knowledge.[168] To be specific, in order to access traditional knowledge in China, foreign users are required to partner with China's domestic institutions, obtain PIC, and negotiate benefit-sharing arrangements (known as mutually agreed terms or 'MAT') with the holders of the traditional knowledge at all times, regardless of the commercial or non-commercial nature of the use.[169] As stressed by Article 20, 'any foreign users applications and acts relating to the genetic resources and associated TK in China must be conducted in China and with the substantial participation of Chinese personnel'.[170] In comparison, domestic users who seek access to traditional knowledge would be subject to PIC and other regulatory burdens only when their accesses are for commercial purposes. As suggested by Article 19, 'Access to genetic resources and associated traditional knowledge by domestic entities or individuals for commercial purposes shall be subjected to the PIC of the holders and based on MAT'. Additional bureaucratic burdens provided by the Draft Regulation include obtaining Internationally Recognized Certificates of Compliance (IRCC) and meeting the disclosure of origin requirements.[171]

166 The *Draft Regulation* arts 18–30.

167 The *Draft Regulation* art 18.

168 The *Draft Regulation* arts 19 and 20.

169 The *Draft Regulation* art 3(20).

170 The *Draft Regulation* art 20.

171 The *Draft Regulation* arts 25 and 29.

Arguably, China's proposed ABS measures provide overly restrictive or burdensome impediments such as uncertainty and complexity for the potential users to access traditional knowledge (including TMK). This situation is inconsistent with China's traditional attitudes towards access to knowledge, which sees intellectual attainment and knowledge as a part of the larger society and recognises that access to knowledge should not be restricted if it is beneficial to the collective well-being.[172]

Moreover, although various new principles with regard to access to traditional knowledge, such as PIC, have functioned as formal concepts in China's proposed ABS measures, they are often hard to implement and give a practical form in China's context. This is because, from a Chinese perspective, these concepts and requirements arguably contradict Chinese understandings of ownership and fundamental rights over traditional knowledge.

For instance, the PIC born as a Western idea (that has an individual basis) usually assumes, in all standard cases, that the holders of traditional knowledge giving consent can be straightforwardly identified.[173] However, in China's context, the individuals are considered as being 'embedded in a network of relations and are identified in terms of their connections with others',[174] and the larger community (such as family) is at the centre of decision-making.

More significantly, traditional knowledge, specifically TMK in China is likely shared broadly across various communities and groups, where the claims to traditional knowledge are from various sources.[175] On this basis, it can be difficult to identify a legitimate consentee within or across the communities to provide PIC access to traditional knowledge. Therefore, arguably, there are responsibilities for China to adapt its legislative, policy, or practical system to its international ABS obligations, particularly in order to implement the legal standards and fundamental principles for dealing with access to its traditional knowledge.[176]

However, the proposed legislative, policy, or practical measures established are not based on a comprehensive understanding of its socio-legal culture and the needs of its local inhabitants. This situation may lead to what Grief has called a 'contaminant'[177] in its local context. To avoid introducing such a contaminant, its proposed ABS measures might require reinterpretation or modification to be combined with

---

[172] Daniel E Martin, 'Culture and unethical conduct: Understanding the impact of individualism and collectivism on actual plagiarism' (2011) *Management Learning* 1,4.

[173] Doris Schroeder, 'Informed Consent: From Medical Research to Traditional Knowledge' in Doris Schroeder, Roger Chennells and Rachel Wynberg (eds), *Indigenous Peoples, Consent and Benefit Sharing: Lessons from the San-Hoodia Case* (Springer, 2009) 1, 38.

[174] Vera Lúcia Raposo, 'Lost in 'Culturation': medical informed consent in China (from a Western perspective)' (2018) 22 *Medicine, Health Care and Philosophy* 17, 24.

[175] Zhang Jian Shan et al., 'Assessing Conservation Priorities of Threatened Medicinal Plants in China: A New Comprehensive Phylogenetic Scoring System' (2022) 61 *Journal of Systematics and Evolution* 709.

[176] China ratified the CBD in 1993 and ratified the *Nagoya Protocol* in 2016.

[177] Nicholas Grief, 'The Pervasive Influence of European Community Law in the United Kingdom' in PBH Birks (ed), *What are Law Schools For? Pressing Problems in the Law* (Bournemouth University, 1996) 1, 1–138.

a comprehensive understanding of its social-legal context, instead of minimising its competing cultural perspectives.

5.4.3 Sharing of Benefits Arising from Utilisations of TMK in China

China has adopted a series of domestic legislative, policy, and practical measures for benefit-sharing with IPLCs and the role that traditional knowledge plays within these benefit-sharing arrangements. On the policy side, China's 13th Five-Year Plan for the Protection of Ecological Environment sets the target of establishing compensation mechanisms that aim to enable the benefit-sharing arising from traditional knowledge associated with genetic resources.[178] On this basis, the legislative measures as exemplified by the Draft Regulation were subsequently proposed to provide a series of concrete and practical benefit-sharing arrangements. Firstly, a National Fund for Benefit-sharing has been proposed, into which equitable shares of monetary payments are made and from which the monetary benefit-sharing would be operated in a fair and constructive manner[179]; Secondly, collective management organisations ('CMOs') would be established to be responsible for licensing, tracking, and collecting the benefits arising from the utilisation of the traditional knowledge and paying them out to the respective registered traditional knowledge holders.[180] Thirdly, to support the collective management system of traditional knowledge and organise equitable sharing of benefits arising from the utilisation of traditional knowledge, a traditional knowledge register would be established, which provides that 'the relevant competent departments of the provincial people's governments shall register the openly accessible traditional knowledge within the district and in the public domain, and periodically upload the registration information to the national database of genetic resources'.[181]

Despite these efforts made so far, the proposed benefit-sharing measures (for traditional knowledge) in China are arguably based on the compensatory model. There are two schools of thoughts that have been put forward to justify this compensatory-based benefit-sharing scheme.[182] The first is that traditional knowledge is subject to proprietary claims and can be protected (an opinion not so different from common defences of IP protection for traditional knowledge); the second is that the use of traditional knowledge by third parties is inherently unjust and deserves redress. On this basis,

178 《"十三五"生态环境保护规划》[The 13th Five-Year Plan for Ecological Environment Protection] (People's Republic of China) the State Council, Order No 65, 2016 ('the Plan').

179 The *Draft Regulation* art 33.

180 The *Draft Regulation* art 7 and art 35.

181 The *Draft Regulation* art 6.

182 David Castle and Richard Gold, 'Traditional Knowledge and Benefit Sharing: From Compensation to Transaction' (Conference Paper, 8 th ICABR International Conference on Agricultural Biotechnology: International Trade and Domestic Production, 2004)1, 3–4.

the benefit-sharing mechanisms established by China's legislative, policy, and practical measures amount to a compensatory activity for redressing the wrongful use of that traditional knowledge and the harm done to the alleged holders of traditional knowledge. Nevertheless, the Chinese culture and value systems do not conceive of traditional knowledge as proprietary, nor as something that should be subject to restrictive protection.[183] On this basis, a benefit-sharing mechanism in China should not aim to remedy others' use of traditional knowledge since traditional knowledge (including TMK) in the Chinese value system is not considered something that gives direct rise to a proprietary claim; thus, there can be no harm caused to the alleged holders of traditional knowledge. More significantly, as analysed in Sect. 2.3.1.2, China's long tradition of egalitarianism leads to the belief that a compensatory-based benefit-sharing mechanism may not be suitable for the Chinese context and more effective benefit-sharing models need to be explored further.

Arguably, the effective benefit-sharing model in China's context must go well beyond the sovereignty paradigm, and beyond the assessment of how traditional knowledge was exploited and how the past harms could be compensated. On this basis, it is suggested to break the links made between traditional knowledge (including TMK) and benefit-sharing and build the benefit-sharing system as a mechanism to distribute the benefit and resources that are beneficial for the public interest and society as a whole. The principle on which to base the benefit-sharing model in China should also be consistent with the Chinese traditional conceptual framework such as Confucius' conception of justice, which advocates that 'one should obtain merely what he deserves, and the distribution of the benefits should be implemented under rules that take into considerations of the fundamental interests of all members in a society to achieve the ultimate goal of harmony of social and economic order'.[184]

Moreover, the traditional Chinese conceptual framework believes that justice is the 'harmony' of disparate interests, which can normally be achieved through the instillation of a sense of shame.[185] On this basis, the legal measures are considered a last resort because resorting to legal remedies represents a 'shameful failure to settle matters amicably'.[186] This strong preference for non-judicial mechanisms makes the policy and legislative benefit-sharing option unviable. In addition, according to Confucius' notion of justice, the just State is the humane State, in which every member of the community contributes their unique talents to the realisation of the

---

[183] Binkert (n 110) 147.

[184] Jin Hui, 'Rawlsian and Confucian Distributive Justice and the Worst Off' (2022) *Philosophia* 1,10.
< https://doi.org/10.1007/s11406-022-00486-z > .

[185] 刘宇 [Liu Yu],《论中国儒家文化中的耻感伦理及其现代性转化》[On the Ethics of Shame in Chinese Confucian Culture and Its Modern Transformation] (2022) 6 南开学报 *Nankai Journal* 89, 89–98; Sophia Wilson, 'A Review of "Authoritarian Rule of Law: Legislation, Discourse and Legitimate in Singapore," by Jothie Rajah ' (2014) 21(1) *Indian Journal of Global Legal Studies* 297, 299.

[186] William Heye, 'Forum Selection for International Dispute Resolution in China—Chinese Courts vs. CIETAC' (2004) 27(3) *Hastings International and Comparative Law Review* 535, 553.

highest quality of the just State.[187] To achieve such a just State in the wider community, the options are not that of 'honouring the right' or 'remedying the wrong'. Rather the options are between what is more appropriate and what is qualitatively better, the criteria for which are open-textured, flexible, and normally determined by the participants themselves.[188] Therefore, equitable benefit-sharing is more likely to be achieved through negotiated bilateral agreements than by means of simple retroactive compensation.

A multilateral framework at the national and community level could provide a promising route in negotiating a benefit-sharing framework, to define and craft the benefit-sharing model that is consistent with Chinese cultural values, norms, and policy preferences. In this context, it is vital to consider the guidance provided by Article 10 of the Nagoya Protocol, which emphasises a global multilateral benefit-sharing mechanism. This article is particularly relevant as it advocates for a more inclusive and holistic approach to ABS, especially in scenarios where individual prior informed consent might not be practical. Incorporating the principles of Article 10 into the Chinese framework would align it with international standards, ensuring a comprehensive and globally resonant approach to benefit-sharing.

The innovative benefit-sharing system created through the *International Treaty for Plant Genetic Resources for Food and Agriculture* (Plant Treaty) and the ongoing reform of the *Pandemic Influenza Preparedness (PIP) Framework* could be a source of inspiration for creating a multilateral system of ABS in China, which could serve the purpose of the common benefit of humanity, and contribute to adequate protection, proper utilisation, and suitable dissemination of Chinese TMK. For example, a multilateral benefit-sharing framework could be developed to create a collective pool for TMK, governed by standardised agreements. This approach aligns with Article 10's emphasis on creating flexible mechanisms for benefit-sharing, especially when dealing with widespread and diffuse traditional knowledge relevant to multiple stakeholders.

This model would foster harmonious collaboration among various stakeholders, including TMK guardians, researchers, and commercial entities. By adopting this approach, benefit-sharing could be effectively transformed into a mechanism that ensures the equitable distribution of benefits among various stakeholders. This would allow all parties to access and utilise the shared TMK, fostering collaboration and mutual respect, while upholding Chinese values and Confucian principles of harmony, collective welfare, and egalitarianism.

The implementation of this framework would enable the availability of necessary resources and benefits within the multilateral mechanism for all interested parties, following standardised agreements such as a Material Transfer Agreement ('MTA'). The benefits comprising training, infrastructure, IP rights, and financial support can be distributed among the communities in need and society at large. The primary objective is to promote social welfare rather than solely compensating specific TMK

[187] Erin Cline, *Confucius, Rawls, and the Sense of Justice* (Fordham University Press, 2013) 16.

[188] RP Peerenboom, 'Confucian Justice-Achieving A Humane Society' (1990) 30(1) *International Philosophical Quarterly* 17, 31.

holders for any potential harm. In doing so, the framework would be fully in line with the spirit of Article 10 of the Nagoya Protocol, fostering an environment of shared responsibility and mutual benefit, central to the ethos of ABS agreements. This approach is consistent with Chinese values and Confucian principles that foster social welfare and harmony within the larger community, placing emphasis on the collective good over individual interests.

5.4.4 Considerations for Renaming the ABS Framework in China

Following the detailed discussions above, it becomes evident that the current nomenclature of the ABS framework in China, particularly in the context of TMK, necessitates reconsideration. The renaming should reflect a more culturally congruent, contextually relevant, and philosophically aligned approach to the management of genetic resources and traditional knowledge. The proposed renaming is not merely a semantic change but a substantive realignment that recognises the unique historical, cultural, and social intricacies of China. It acknowledges the evolving nature of traditional knowledge and its integration with modern socioeconomic and legal systems. Moreover, the proposed name should encapsulate core Confucian principles such as harmony, collective prosperity, and equitable sharing, which are foundational to the Chinese worldview. By choosing a name that resonates with these values, the framework would not only engage domestic stakeholders but also harmonise with international standards, bridging local traditions with global commitments.

A proposed renaming could be the 'Harmonious Resource and Knowledge Integration Framework' (HRKIF). This name encapsulates several key elements:

Harmonious: Emphasising the Confucian ideal of harmony, this term signifies the desired balance between various interests—be it environmental, cultural, or commercial.

Resource and Knowledge Integration: This reflects the dual focus on integrating both the physical aspects of biodiversity (genetic resources) and the intangible aspects (traditional knowledge and wisdom).

Framework: Suggesting a structured yet flexible approach, accommodating the dynamic and evolving nature of traditional knowledge and its interaction with modern legal and economic systems.

The HRKIF would thus provide a more culturally resonant and contextually appropriate nomenclature. It would also encourage a broader interpretation of ABS, one that goes beyond mere legal compliance to encompass a holistic understanding of traditional knowledge's role in societal development, environmental stewardship, and cultural preservation. This renaming initiative should be accompanied by a comprehensive communication strategy to inform and engage all relevant stakeholders, ensuring that the new terminology is understood, accepted, and effectively implemented across various levels of governance and community engagement.

5.5 Conclusion

The critical analysis presented in this chapter identified that the implementation of an international ABS framework for governing the protection, utilisation, and dissemination of TMK in China presents both opportunities and challenges due to the country's complex social, cultural, historical, and legal contexts. This chapter highlighted that China's historical legacy, traditional practices, and sociocultural particularities inherently affect the implementation of ABS principles. Its understanding of, and perspectives on, access to traditional knowledge, fair and equitable benefit-sharing, and recognition of Indigenous rights could differ considerably from those outlined in international ABS frameworks.

This chapter underscored that the Chinese approach to traditional knowledge access and benefit-sharing reflects a distinct cultural ethos that values communal benefit and open access over exclusive rights and individual control. This perspective, deeply rooted in historical traditions and Confucian teachings, diverges from the global ABS norms, which advocate for the sovereignty and autonomy of Indigenous and local communities over their traditional knowledge. This cultural divergence could present significant challenges in harmonising the Chinese approach with the international ABS framework.

Similarly, the Chinese understanding of justice, heavily influenced by Confucian and Taoist philosophies, primarily emphasises social harmony and balance, potentially conflicting with the ABS principle of fair and equitable benefit-sharing, which is more individualistic in nature. These distinctive ethical and cultural nuances could complicate China's implementation of the international ABS benefit-sharing obligations.

China's unique approach to the concept of Indigenous rights, preferring to recognise ethnic minorities rather than Indigenous communities, also poses a potential challenge to the ABS implementation. This view is historically and politically influenced, notably by China's past experience of colonial aggression and its subsequent emphasis on national sovereignty. Such a stance may inhibit China's complete compliance with the principles and stipulations of ABS, which are aimed at asserting Indigenous rights over traditional knowledge and genetic resources.

Despite these challenges, the implementation of ABS principles in China, through the introduction of the *Draft Regulation*, opens up considerable possibilities. This regulatory initiative could pave the way for a fresh paradigm in protecting China's TMK. It possesses the potential to serve as a driving force for safeguarding it, fostering its sustainable utilisation, and facilitating equitable sharing of benefits. However, the potential success of this framework would largely depend on careful contextual adaptation to China's unique context, incorporating considerations of its distinctive historical, cultural, and socio-political dynamics.

China's unique historical, cultural, and social dynamics demand a nuanced approach to defining traditional knowledge and formulating ABS measures. This is underscored by its preference for the term ethnic groups over Indigenous peoples, which diverges from the contentious terms used in international agreements, and which reflect China's own complexities in dealing with Indigenous identity and rights.

Concepts like *Yuan shengtai*, which encapsulates the continuity, cultural purity, and local distinctiveness of traditional knowledge, reflect China's own cultural values and should be considered in defining traditional knowledge in the *Draft Regulation*. By doing so, it could maintain a harmonious balance between aligning with international expectations and preserving its national and local uniqueness.

In examining the provisions that regulate access to traditional knowledge (including TMK) in China, the book underscored the potential difficulties and inconsistencies posed by the Draft Regulation, particularly relating to the PIC and MAT requirements. It was argued that these Western concepts may not align with traditional Chinese perceptions of knowledge ownership and the communal nature of decision-making.

The analysis suggested that China needs a careful and nuanced approach to the access of traditional knowledge, one that respects its distinctive cultural, social, and legal context. Adherence to international rules is essential, but it should not lead to undue restrictions on traditional knowledge users or conflict with Chinese norms regarding knowledge access. Implementing principles like PIC and MAT requires thoughtful navigation, given the complexities within China's historical and socio-cultural landscape. Therefore, proposed ABS measures might necessitate tailored modifications or reinterpretations, which factor in China's local socio-legal circumstances and its inhabitants' needs. These findings emphasised the importance of formulating culturally sensitive, locally relevant regulations that align with global ABS standards without undermining the local cultural context.

The benefit-sharing mechanisms proposed by China's *Draft Regulation* have been criticised for being compensatory-based, which might not align with traditional Chinese values that conceive traditional knowledge as non-proprietary and its use as not necessarily causing harm. A departure from this compensatory model was recommended, whereby a benefit-sharing system is created to distribute benefits beneficial for public interest and societal harmony.

Moreover, Confucius' conception of justice and harmony could serve as guiding principles for these mechanisms, favouring negotiated bilateral agreements over legal remedies, and preferring what was qualitatively better over merely remedying a wrong. This could lead to the establishment of a multilateral benefit-sharing framework that allows for harmonious collaboration among TMK guardians, researchers, and commercial entities, thus ensuring the equitable distribution of benefits while upholding China's values and the Confucian principles of harmony, collective welfare, and egalitarianism.

To this end, effective ABS implementation for governing the protection, utilisation, and dissemination of Chinese TMK may necessitate: combining international norms with local traditional practices and values; a better understanding and respect for China's unique perspectives on access, benefit-sharing, and the recognition of Indigenous rights; and constructive international dialogue and cooperation. Balancing these complex factors could enable a culturally sensitive approach, ensuring the ABS framework's success in China while also significantly contributing to the efforts towards the protection, utilisation, and dissemination of TMK.

References

Abebe Kebede Jalleta, 'Access and Benefit Sharing Effectiveness: International Environmental Law Implementation at the Domestic Ethiopian Level' (2021) 12 *Beijing Law Review* 485.

Alison Adcock Kaufman, 'The "Century of Humiliation", Then and Now: Chinese Perceptions of the International Order' (2010) 25(1) *Pacific Focus* 1.

Anne Perrault, 'Facilitating Prior Informed Consent in The Context of Genetic Resources And Traditional Knowledge' (2004) 4(2) *Sustainable Development Law & Policy* 21.

Anonymous, 'China and the Principle of Self-Determination of Peoples' (2010) 6(1) *St Antony's International Review* 79.

Aysegul Sirakaya et al, 'Designing Regulatory Frameworks for Access to Genetic Resources: A Multi-Stakeholder Multi-Criteria Approach' (2020) 11 *Frontier in Genetics* 1.

Baogang He, 'The Contested Politics of Asian Responses to Indigenous Rights' (2011) 18 *International Journal on Minority and Group Rights* 461.

Bege Dauda et al, 'What Do the Various Principles of Justice Mean within the Concept of Benefit Sharing?' (2016) 13 *Bioethical Inquiry* 281.

Ben Saul, 'China, Natural Resources, Sovereignty and International Law' (2013) 37(2) *Asian Studies Review* 196.

BinXing Fang, *Cyberspace Sovereignty: Reflections on Building a Community of Common Future in Cyberspace* (Springer, 2018) 55–57.

Brad de Jonge and Michiel Korthals, 'Vicissitudes of Benefit Sharing of Crop Genetic Resources: Downstream and Upstream' (2006) 6(3) *Developing World Bioethics* 144.

Bram De Jonge, 'What is Fair and Equitable Benefit-sharing?' (2011) 24 *J Agric Environ Ethics* 127.

Brendan Tobin, 'Why Customary Law Matters: The Role of Customary Law in the Protection of Indigenous Peoples' Human Rights.' (PhD Thesis, National University of Ireland Galway, 2011) 245.

Brigitte Binkert, 'Why the Current Global Intellectual Property Framework Under TRIPS Is Not Working' (2006) 10 *Intell. Prop. L. Bull* 143.

Carmen Richerzhagen, 'The Nagoya Protocol: Fragmentation or Consolidation?' (2014) 3 *Resources* 135.

Cathal M Doyle, Indigenous Peoples, *Title to Territory, Rights and Resources: The Transformative Role of Free Prior and Informed Consent* (Routledge, 2017) 252.

Charles R Hales, 'Comment' (2009) 50(3) *Current Anthropology* 322.

China's Interim National Report on The Implementation of The Nagoya Protocol (Interim Report, 2017).

Christophe Duvert, 'How is Justice Understood in Classic Confucianism?' (2018) 28(4) *Asian Philosophy* 295.

Claudio Chiarolla, *Intellectual Property, Agriculture and Global Food Security: The Privatization of Crop Diversity* (Edward Elgar Publishing, 2011) 135.

Claudio Chiarolla, 'The Role of Private International Law under the Nagoya Protocol' in Elisa Morgera et al (eds), The 2010 Nagoya Protocol on Access and Benefit-sharing in perspective: Implications for international law and implementation challenges (Martinus Nijhoff, 2013) 423.

C Cornelius, *Iroquois Corn in a Culture-Based Curriculum: A Framework for Respectfully Teaching About Cultures* (State University of New York Press, 1999) 3.

Convention on Biological Diversity, opened for signature 5 June 1992, 1760 UNTS 79 (entered into force 29 December 1993) ('CBD').

D Schroeder, 'Benefit sharing: It's Time for a Definition' (2007) 33 *Journal of Medical Ethics* 205.

Daniel E Martin, 'Culture and unethical conduct: Understanding the impact of individualism and collectivism on actual plagiarism' (2011) *Management Learning* 1.

Daniel Robinson, *Confronting Biopiracy Challenges, Cases and International Debates* (Routledge, 2010) 1.

Danielle Lorenz, 'Walking the Noble (Savage) Path: The Didactics of Indigenous Knowledge (Re)Presentation in the Toronto Zoo's Canadian Domain' (Master Thesis, Carleton University, 2012) 38.

David Castle and Richard Gold, 'Traditional Knowledge and Benefit Sharing: From Compensation to Transaction' (Conference Paper, 8th ICABR International Conference on Agricultural Biotechnology: International Trade and Domestic Production, 2004)1.

Dayuan Xue and Lijie Cai, 'China's Legal and Policy Frameworks for Access to Genetic Resources and Benefit-Sharing from their Use' (2009) 18(1) *The Review of European Comparative & International Environmental Law* 91.

Doris Schroeder, 'Informed Consent: From Medical Research to Traditional Knowledge' in Doris Schroeder, Roger Chennells and Rachel Wynberg (eds), *Indigenous Peoples, Consent and Benefit Sharing: Lessons from the San-Hoodia Case* (Springer, 2009) 1.

Dorothy L Hodgson, 'Introduction: Comparative Perspectives on the Indigenous Rights Movement in Africa and the Americas' (2002) 104(4) *American Anthropologist* 1037.

DQ Hodnett, 'Legitimising Biopiracy? Fairness and Efficacy of the Nagoya Protocol' (2021) 2 *York Law Review* 75.

Elisa Morgera, Elsa Tsioumani and Matthias Buck, *Unraveling the Nagoya Protocol: A Commentary on the Nagoya Protocol on Access and Benefit-sharing to the Convention on Biological Diversity* (Brill, 2014) 110–135.

Elisa Morgera, 'The Need for an International Legal Concept of Fair and Equitable Benefit Sharing' (2016) 27(2) *The European Journal of International Law* 353.

Elsa Tsioumani, *Fair and Equitable Benefit-Sharing in Agriculture: Reinventing Agrarian Justice* (Routledge, 2021) 39.

Embassy of the People's Republic of China in Switzerland, China Concerned with Protection of Indigenous Peoples' Rights (1 Apr. 1997), available at <http://ch.China-embassy.org/eng/ztnr/rqwt/t138829.htm>.

Erin Cline, *Confucius, Rawls, and the Sense of Justice* (Fordham University Press, 2013) 16.

FM Birhanu, 'Challenges and Prospects of Implementing the Access and Benefit-Sharing Regime of the Convention on Biological Diversity in Africa: The Case of Ethiopia' (2010) 10 *International Environmental Agreements: Politics, Law and Economics* 249

Francesca Merlan, 'Indigeneity. Global and Local' (2009) 50(3) *Current Anthropology* 303.

G Dutfield, Intellectual Property, *Biogenetic Resources and Traditional Knowledge* (Routledge, 2004) 52.

Gerard Prinsen and Severine Blaise, 'An Emerging "Islandian" Sovereignty of Non-self-governing Islands' (2017) 72(1) *International Journal* 56.

International Treaty on Plant Genetic Resources for Food and Agriculture, opened for signature, 3 November 2001, 2400 UNTS 303 (entered into force 26 June 2004).

Jasmine Biba et al, 'Traditional Knowledge System in India for Biodiversity Conservation' (216) 15(2) *Indian Journal of Traditional Knowledge* 304.

JB Nie, 'Is Informed Consent Not Applicable to China?: Intellectual Flaws of the Cultural Difference Argument' (2000) 2 *Formos J Med Humanit* 67.

Jean Chesneaux, 'Egalitarian and Utopian Traditions in the East' (1968) 16(62) *Diogenes* 76.

Jennifer Amiott, 'Investigating the Convention on Biological Diversity's Protections for Traditional Knowledge' (2003) 11(1) *Journal of Environmental and Sustainability Law* 3.

Jin Hui, 'Rawlsian and Confucian Distributive Justice and the Worst Off' (2022) *Philosophia* 1

Jinzhou Song, 'Commentary and Discussion on Zhou Ping's Chinese Nation: Integration or Pluralism?' (2021) 11(3) *Journalism and Mass Communication* 112.

John Tustin, 'Traditional Knowledge and Intellectual Property in Brazilian Biodiversity Law' [2006] *Texas Intellectual Property Law Journal* 132.

Joseph Tham et al, *Cross-Cultural and Religious Critiques of Informed Consent* (Routledge Focus, 2022).

K Jospeh Reji, 'International Regime on Access and Benefit Sharing: Where Are We Now?' (2010) 12(3) *Asian Biotechnology and Development Review* 77.

K Matsui, 'Problems of Defining and Validating Traditional Knowledge: An Historical Approach' (2015) 6(2) *The International Indigenous Policy Journal* 1.

Kam-Por Yu, 'The Confucian Alternative to the Individual-Oriented Model of Informed Consent: Family and Beyond' in Ruiping Fan (ed), *Family-Oriented Informed Consent: East Asian and American Perspectives* (Springer, 2015) 93.

Kealeboga N Bojosi and GM Wachira, 'Protecting Indigenous Peoples in Africa: An Analysis of the Approach of the African Commission on Human and Peoples' Rights' (2006) 6(2) *African Human Rights Law Journal* 382.

KR Srinivas, 'Protecting Traditional Knowledge Holders' Interests and Preventing Misappropriation—Traditional Knowledge Commons and Biocultural Protocols: Necessary but Not Sufficient?' (2012) 19 *International Journal of Cultural Property* 401.

KT Kate and Sarah A Laird, *The Commercial Use of Biodiversity: Access to Genetic Resources and Benefit-Sharing* (Routledge, 2000) 4.

Kuan-chih Chen, 'A Study on the Book Market of Nanjing in Ming Dynasty' (2014) (2) *National Central Library Journal* 153.

Kuei-Jung Ni, 'Legal Aspects of Prior Informed Consent on Access to Genetic Resources' (2009) 42(1) *Vanderbilt Journal of Transnational Law* 227

LA Whitt, 'Biocolonialism and the commodification of knowledge' (1998) 7(1) *Science as Culture* 33.

Linda Tuhiwai Smith, *Decolonizing Methodologies: Research and Indigenous* (University of Otago Press, 2008) 91.

Linzhu Wang, 'The Definition of Indigenous Peoples and its Applicability in China' (2015) 22 *International Journal on Minority and Group Rights* 232.

Lisanne Groen, 'Explaining European Union Effectiveness (Goal Achievement) In the Convention On Biological Diversity: The Importance Of Diplomatic Engagement' (2019) 19 *Int Environ Agreements* 69.

Lyle Glowka and Valérie Normand, 'The Nagoya Protocol on Access and Benefit-sharing: Innovations in International Environmental Law' in Elisa Morgera et al (eds), *The 2010 Nagoya Protocol on Access and Benefit-sharing in Perspective* (Brill, 2012) 21.

M Lewis, 'Access and Benefit-sharing in the Wake of CBD COP10: The Nagoya Protocol and Its Potential Implications for South Africa' (2010) 17 *South African Journal of Environmental Law and Policy* 69.

Mara Matta, 'The Novel and the North-East: Indigenous Narratives in Indian Literatures' in Rossella Ciocca and Neelam Srivastava (eds), *Indian Literature and the World: Multilingualism, Translation, and the Public Sphere* (2017) 199.

Maria Luz Endere, 'Archaeological Heritage Legislation and Indigenous Rights in Latin America: Trends and Challenges' (2014) 21 *International Journal of Cultural Property* 319.

Maria Papamichail, 'The Patient's Right to Information and Consent in the Execution of Medical Procedures: The Legal and Sociological Dimension' (2010) 3(4) *Hellenic Journal of Nursing Science* 100.

Maria Yolanda Teran, 'The Nagoya Protocol and Indigenous Peoples' (2016) 7(2) *The International Indigenous Policy Journal* 1.

Mark J Cherry, 'Individually Directed Informed Consent and the Decline of the Family in the West' in Ruiping Fan (ed), *Family-Oriented Informed Consent: East Asian and American Perspectives* (Springer, 2015) 43.

Martin Fredriksson, 'Dilemmas of Protection: Decolonising the Regulation of Genetic Resources as Cultural Heritage' [2021] *International Journal of Heritage Studies* 720.

Martin Fredriksson, 'From Biopiracy to Bioprospecting: Negotiating the Limits of Propertization' in Martin Fredriksson and James Arvanitakis (eds), *Property, Place and Piracy* (Routledge, 2018) 174.

Matthias Buck and Clare Hamilton, 'The Nagoya Protocol on Access to Genetic Resources and the Fair and Equitable Sharing of Benefits Arising from their Utilization to the Convention on Biological Diversity' (2011) 20(1) *Review of European Community & International Environmental Law* 47.

MF Rourke, 'Who Are "Indigenous and Local Communities" and What Is "Traditional Knowledge" for Virus Access' (2018) 25 *Journal of Law and Medicine* 707.

Michael C Davis, 'China & the UN Declaration on the Rights of Indigenous Peoples: The Tibetan Case' (Research Paper No. 2014/044, Faculty of Law, University of Hong Kong, May 2014) 1.

Michael F Brown, 'Heritage Trouble: Recent Work on the Protection of Intangible Cultural Property' (2005) 12 *International Journal of Cultural Property* 40.

Michael J Hathaway, 'China's Indigenous Peoples? How Global Environmentalism Unintentionally Smuggled the Notion of Indigeneity into China' (2016) 5 *Humanities* 1.

Michel de Montaigne, *'Of Cannibals'. The Longman Anthology of World Literature* (Pearson Longman, 2009) 335–343.

Mohit Gupta, 'Right of Indigenous Communities to Prior Informed Consent under Article 7 of the Nagoya Protocol and a Comparative Analysis of Its Implementation by India and Bhutan' (2020) 28(1) *International Journal on Minority and Group Rights* 36.

Nagoya Protocol on Access to Genetic Resources and the Fair and Equitable Sharing of Benefits Arising from their Utilization to the Convention on Biological Diversity, UN Doc UNEP/CBD/COP/DEC/X/1(2010) (Nagoya Protocol).

Nan Xia, 'Access and benefit-sharing in China: Exploring the Extent to Which China Fulfils the Obligations of the Nagoya Protocol' (2023) 13(1) *Queen Mary Journal of Intellectual Property* 97.

Nicholas Grief, 'The Pervasive Influence of European Community Law in the United Kingdom' in PBH Birks (ed), *What are Law Schools For? Pressing Problems in the Law* (Bournemouth University, 1996) 1.

Philippe Hanna and Frank Vanclay, 'Human Rights, Indigenous Peoples and the Concept of Free, Prior and Informed Consent' (2013) 31(2) *Impact Assessment and Project Appraisal* 146;

Ricarda Roesch, 'The Story of A Legal Transplant: The Right to Free, Prior and Informed Consent in Sub-Saharan Africa' (2016) 16 *African Human Rights Law Journal* 505.

RP Peerenboom, 'Confucian Justice-Achieving A Humane Society' (1990) 30(1) *International Philosophical Quarterly* 17.

S Kannaiyan, 'Biological Diversity and Traditional Knowledge (Discussion Paper, National Consultation Workshop on Agro Biodiversity Hotspots and Access and Benefit sharing, 2007) 1.

S Vermeylen, 'The Nagoya Protocol and Customary Law: the Paradox of Narratives in the Law' (2013) 9(2) *Law, Environment and Development Journal* 187.

Sara Bannerman, *Canadian Communication Policy and Law* (Canadian Scholars, 2020) 43.

Saskia Vermeylen, 'The Nagoya Protocol and Customary Law: The Paradox of Narratives in the Law' (2013) 9/2 *Law, Environment and Development Journal* 185.

Shao Ken, 'The Promotion of Learning in Chinese History: Discovering the Lost Soul of Modern Copyright' (2010) 24(1) *Columbia Journal of Asian Law* 64.

Shuo Gu and Jianfeng Pei, 'Innovating Chinese Herbal Medicine: From Traditional Health Practice to Scientific Drug Discovery' (2017) 8 *Frontier in Pharmacology* 1.

SJ Anaya, *Indigenous Peoples in International Law* (Oxford University Press, 2004) 9.

Sophia Wilson, 'A Review of "Authoritarian Rule of Law: Legislation, Discourse and Legitimate in Singapore," by Jothie Rajah' (2014) 21(1) *Indian Journal of Global Legal Studies* 297.

Stevan Harrell, *Ways of Being Ethnic in Southwest China* (University of Washington Press, 2001) 1.

Susy Frankel, 'The challenge of Cross-Border Protection of Traditional Knowledge' in Daniel F Robinson et al (eds), *Protecting Traditional Knowledge* (Routledge, 2017) 325.
Taisu Zhang, 'Social Hierarchies and the Formation of Customary Property Law in Pre-Industrial China and England' (2014) 62 *The American Journal of Comparative Law* 171.
Taisu Zhang, *The Laws and Economics of Confucianism. Kinship and Property in Preindustrial China and England* (Cambridge University Press, 2017) 163.
Tim Murphy and Ralph Weber, 'Ideas of Justice and Reconstructions of Confucian Justice' (2016) 26(2) *An International Journal of the Philosophical Traditions of the East* 99.
Tim Murphy, 'Justice and the Common Good in Dispute Resolution Discourse in the United States and the People's Republic of China' (2017) 10(2) *Law Dev Rev* 305.
Uzma Khan et al, 'The Philosophical Thought of Confucius and Mencius, and the Concept of the Community of a Shared Future for Mankind' (2022) 14(9854) *Sustainability* 1.
V Mallardi, 'The Origin of Informed Consent' (2005) 25(5) *Acta Otorhinolaryngologica Italica: Organo Ufficiale Della Società Italiana Di Otorinolaringologia E Chirurgia Cervico-Faccial* 312.
Vera Lúcia Raposo, 'Lost in 'Culturation': Medical informed consent in China (from a Western perspective)' (2018) 22 *Medicine, Health Care and Philosophy* 17.
Wei Shi, 'The Paradox of Confucian Determinism: Tracking the Root Causes of Intellectual Property Rights Problem in China' (2008) 7(3) *The John Marshall Review of Intellectual Property Law* 454.
William Heye, 'Forum Selection for International Dispute Resolution in China—Chinese Courts vs. CIETAC' (2004) 27(3) *Hastings International and Comparative Law Review* 535.
World Health Assembly Resolution 64, Pandemic Influenza Preparedness: Sharing of Influenza Viruses and Access to Vaccines and Other Benefits, 2011 (Sixty-fourth World Health Assembly, WHA64/5, 2011).
WR Swinyard et al, 'The Morality of Software Piracy: A Cross-Cultural Analysis' in Alex C Michalos and Deborah C Poff (eds), *Citation Classics from the Journal of Business Ethnics* (Springer, 2013) 565.
Xiaogang Wu, 'Income Inequality and Distributive Justice: A Comparative Analysis of Mainland China and Hong Kong' (2009) 200 *The China Quarterly* 1033.
Yang Bojun, *Annotated Translation of the Analects* (Zhonghua Book Company, 1980) 172–174.
Yu Luo, 'An Alternative to the "Indigenous" in Early Twenty-First-Century China: Guizhou's Branding of Yuanshengtai' (2018) 44(1) *Modern China* 68.
Yu Wen-xuan and Mu Tong, 'Legal Framework of Access and Benefit-Sharing for Genetic Resources and Local Practice in China' (2021) (4) *China Food & Drug Administration Magazine* 100.
Yuan-kang Wang, 'The Myth of Chinese Exceptionalism: An Historical Perspective on China's Rise' in Vinod K Aggarwal and Sara A Newland (eds), *Responding to China's Rise* (Springer, 2014) 51.
Zhang Jian Shan et al, 'Assessing Conservation Priorities of Threatened Medicinal Plants in China: A New Comprehensive Phylogenetic Scoring System' (2022) 61 *Journal of Systematics and Evolution* 709
陈科华 [Chen Kehua],《中重于正: 中国传统正义思想的理论构建》[Moderation Over Justice: The Theoretical Construction of Traditional Chinese Concepts of Justice] (2016) 40(4) 湘潭大学学报*Journal of Xiangtan University* 122.
董火民 [Dong Huomin],《知识的复制:古代传抄活动对知识传播的影响》[The Reproduction of Knowledge: The Impact of Ancient Copying Activities on Knowledge Dissemination] (2010) 31(11) 东岳论丛 *Dongyue Collected Essays* 102.
董平平 [Dong Pingping],《论中国家庭文化对知情同意原则实践的影响》[Discussing the impact of Chinese family culture on the practice of informed consent principles] (2011) 24 (2) 中国医学伦理学 *Chinese Medical Ethic Nationalities* 262.
傅文第 [Fu Wendi],《关于传统中医药文化历史局限的现实思考》[Realistic Reflections on the Historical Limitations of Traditional Chinese Medicine Culture] (2017) 38 (10) 医学与哲学 *Medicine and Philosophy* 83.

郭家翔 [Guo JiaXiang],《改土归流:巩固统一多民族国家的重要举措》["Gaito kuiliu": An Important Measure to Consolidate A Unified Multi-ethnic Nation.] (2021) 4 中国民族报*China Ethnic Daily* 1.
李保平 [Li Baoping],《遗传资源相关传统知识获取与惠益分享制度研究——以青蒿衍生物的开发利用为例》[Study on the Acquisition and Benefit-sharing System of Traditional Knowledge Related to Genetic Resources—A Case Study of the Development and Utilization of Artemisia Annua Derivatives] (2023) 31(4)中央民族大学学报*Journal of MUC* 245.
刘宇 [Liu Yu],《论中国儒家文化中的耻感伦理及其现代性转化》[On the Ethics of Shame in Chinese Confucian Culture and Its Modern Transformation] (2022) 6 南开学报 *Nankai Journal* 89.
刘月树 [Liu Yueshu],《知情同意原则的中国化: 一种生命伦理学视角的转换》[Sinicization of the Principle of Informed Consent: A Transformation from the Perspective of Bioethics] (2013) 1 伦理学研究 *Studies in Ethics* 128.
罗静 [Luo Jing],《国民主体性的塑造与中华民族共同体秩序的建立》[The shaping of National Subjectivity and the Establishment of the Order of the Chinese National Community] [2023] 中南民族大学学报 *Journal of South-Central Minzu University* 1.
麻宝斌 [Ma Baobin],《中国传统的社群正义观念: 主要特征与社会根源》[Chinese Traditional Notion of Community Justice: Key Characteristics and Social Roots] (2018) 4 理论探讨*Theoretical Investigation* 143.
邵六益 [Shao Liuyi],《宪法如何铸牢中华民族共同体意识:现行宪法民族团结条款研究》[How Does the Constitution Strengthen the Sense of Community Among the Chinese Nation? A Study of the Existing Constitutional Provisions on Ethnic Unity] [2023] 西南民族大学学报 *Journal of Southwest University for Nationalities* 88.
宋健 [Song Jian],《建立中医药传统知识利益分享机制初探》[Preliminary exploration on establishing a benefit-sharing mechanism for traditional knowledge of Chinese medicine] [2021] 世界科学技术-中医药现代化 *World Science and Technology—Modernization of Traditional Chinese Medicine* 1.
王剑 [Wang Jian],《对李时珍本草纲目编撰与初刻出版作出重要贡献的有关历史人物之探考》[Exploring the Historical Figures Who Made Significant Contributions to the Compilation and Initial Publication of Li Shizhen's 'Compendium of Materia Medica] (2019) 30(12) 时珍国医国药*Lishizhen Medicine and Materia Medica Research* 3012.
尹伦 [Ying Lun],《中法两国遗传资源相关传统知识获取与惠益分享法律制度比较研究》[Comparative Study on the Legal Systems of Genetic Resource-Related Traditional Knowledge Acquisition and Benefit Sharing between China and France] [2021] 法国研究 *French Study* 55.
张自慧 [Zhang Zihui],《真相与启示: 先秦儒家"均平"思想探微》[Truth and Revelation: A Detailed Exploration of the 'Equilibrium and Harmony' Concept in Pre-Qin Confucian Thought] (2017) 38 (10) 孔子研究 *Confucianism Study* 36.
周艳红 [Zhou Yanhong]《明代地方官刻医籍考略》[A Study on the Printing of Medical Books by Local Officials in the Ming Dynasty] (2021) 44 (2) 陕西中医药大学学报*Journal of Shaanxi University of Chinese Medicine* 40.
《"十三五"生态环境保护规划》[The 13th Five-Year Plan for Ecological Environment Protection] (People's Republic of China) the State Council , Order No 65, 2016 ('the Plan').
《加强生物遗传资源管理国家工作方案》[National work programme on strengthening the management of biological genetic resources] (People's Republic of China) the Department of Environmental Protection , Order No 193, 2014.
《生物遗传资源获取与惠益分享管理条例(草案)》[the Draft Regulation on Access and Benefit-Sharing for Genetic Resources and Associated Traditional Knowledge] (People's Republic of China) Ministry of Environmental Protection (23 March 2017) ('the Draft Regulation').

Chapter 6
Challenges in Developing the TMK Information Systems in China: Exploring the Past, Illuminating the Present, and Implications for Future

6.1 Introduction

This chapter examines the complexities of reconciling Chinese TMK with a TMK information system for its adequate protection, responsible utilisation, and appropriate dissemination, while being mindful of the country's cultural-historical subtleties. It offers a critical analysis of the complex interplay between China's unique historical and cultural fabric, global dynamics, and the evolution of the TMK information systems within the nation. The focus is on illuminating how these multifaceted elements converge to shape the way TMK is managed and represented digitally, thereby offering insights for developing more responsive, culturally sensitive, and effective TMK information systems.

As a pivotal step in this investigation, this chapter identifies the limitations of current approaches and emphasises the need for a more inclusive and effective TMK information system. Through this analysis, it aims to provide valuable insights and recommendations for creating a system that is better suited to China's unique cultural, social, and historical context. The ultimate goal is to develop a TMK information system that is deeply rooted in China's rich history and cultural diversity, paving the way for a more inclusive and culturally sensitive approach to adequately protect, responsibly utilise, and properly disseminate Chinese TMK.

Against this backdrop, it is worth noting the emerging trends and challenges that are putting TMK at risk. Recent years have seen an alarming rise in the misappropriation of TMK, often without just recognition of, or compensation to, the traditional custodians of the knowledge.[1] This manifests in various forms, such as commercial enterprises profiteering from natural remedies discovered by the communities, or even broader societal trends that strip the context and history from TMK and commodify it.[2] Confronted with these challenges, it becomes a pressing obligation

[1] See discussion in Chapter 2.

[2] Ibid.

N. Xia, *Medicinal Mandates*, https://doi.org/10.1007/978-981-96-4108-6_6

to effectively protect, properly utilise, and appropriately disseminate this wealth of knowledge.

One burgeoning strategy in response to these issues involves the use of the information systems to store and share the traditional knowledge of IPLCs.[3] This mechanism can serve to preserve the knowledge, facilitate its appropriate use and dissemination, and potentially provide a means for recognising and respecting the rights of these knowledge holders.[4] This concept of information systems, as currently integrated into the work of the Intergovernmental Committee (IGC) and similar initiatives, plays a crucial role in the realm of traditional knowledge.

China holds a deep and extensive repository of TMK.[5] This treasure trove of knowledge has been recorded in various mediums throughout history, including oracle bones, silk, and bamboo strips, even before the invention of paper over two thousand years ago.[6] Archaeologists have traced the earliest organised collections of TMK in China back to the era of the oracle bone inscriptions, which range from the twenty-first century BC to the eleventh century BC.[7]

However, despite this rich history, there has been a pattern of rulers intentionally destroying the existing collections of manuscripts and documents from the previous dynasty.[8] As pointed out by Zhang, it was a common occurrence in Chinese history for archives and documented collections of knowledge, including TMK, to be burned as one dynasty was overthrown and replaced by another.[9]

This practice of erasing the documented knowledge of previous regimes seems to have been a strategic measure to establish and maintain State power. The suppression of any nonconforming thoughts and knowledge was integral to this strategy.[10] Concurrently, the State created and controlled systems for storing, retrieving, and disseminating knowledge. Thus, individuals seeking to acquire such knowledge had to do so under the supervision of government officials.[11]

---

3 Martin Fredriksson, 'Balancing Community Rights and National Interests in International Protection of Traditional Knowledge: A Study of India's Traditional Knowledge Digital Library' (2022) 43(2) *Third World Quarterly* 352, 357.

4 James O Young and Conrad G Brunk, *The Ethics of Cultural Appropriation* (2012)1, 151.

5 Brian H May et al, 'Chinese Herbs for Cognitive Decline: Historical and Contemporary Applications', *Diet and Nutrition in Dementia and Cognitive Decline* (2015) 1, 805.

6 Yongsheng Chen and Huanning Su, 'Disciplines Derived from the Discovery of Historical Archives' (2018) 5(2) *Proceedings from the Document Academy* 1, 1–6.

7 Kanwen Ma, 'Classic Chinese Medical Literature in Contemporary China: Texts Selected for Modern Editions, and Problems Associated with This Work' in Paul U Unschuld (ed), *Approaches to Traditional Chinese Medical Literature* (1989) 1, 7.

8 Wenxian Zhang, 'Dang An: A Brief History of the Chinese Imperial Archives and Its Administration' (2004) 2 *Journal of Archival Organization* 17, 18.

9 Ibid.

10 Xiangshu Fang, 'Burning Books and Burying Scholars: on the Policies of the Short-lived Qin Dynasty in Ancient China (221–207 BC' (2015) 3(7) *International Journal of Liberal Arts and Social Science* 54, 55.

11 Lois Mai Chan, 'The Burning of the Books in China, 213 B.C.' (1972) 7(2) *The Journal of Library History (1966–1972)* 101, 105.

The cultural and historical context of these practices underscores a crucial point: the efforts to record and compile knowledge, including TMK, in China were not driven primarily by a desire to protect and preserve this knowledge, but rather to serve the State's authority and interests. This cultural-historical context provides a distinctive perspective for understanding the complexities and obstacles encountered in the task of preserving and protecting Chinese TMK through the information systems, as explored in this chapter.

In today's digital age, the mediums for recording and compiling knowledge have undergone a transformative shift from physical to digital media such as the databases, the cloud storage solutions, and other information systems.[12] The driving rationale behind this transition is to enable universal access to information, ensuring its efficient preservation, retrieval, and distribution.[13]

In light of these developments, China embarked on the creation of the TMK information systems in the early 2000s.[14] This significant undertaking, facilitated by the widespread application of information technology and bolstered by the Chinese central government, revolutionised the protection, utilisation, and propagation of Chinese TMK.

The most advanced TMK information system in China is the CTCMPD. It uniquely operates within IP frameworks, particularly patents, aiming to ensure adequate protection, proper utilisation, and suitable dissemination of Chinese TMK. Its successful model acknowledges the codified TMK as prior art. This approach equips patent examiners with the necessary reference information to curtail inaccurate patent applications and potential infringements, bolstering the integrity of Chinese TMK and its applications.[15]

Despite the technological advancements in safeguarding Chinese TMK through the information systems, it is arguable that historical and contextual factors continue to shape the current practices of the TMK information systems in China. China's archival practices, imbued with a rich cultural history, have often been steered by political considerations, primarily safeguarding the imperial power's interests. Such historical experiences provide invaluable lessons for China's contemporary TMK information systems' usage, impacting the protection, utilisation, and dissemination of its TMK.

To date, the majority of scholarly work in the Chinese context has predominantly concentrated on a comparative analysis between China's TMK information systems and those of foreign countries.[16] The primary objective has been to discern

[12] PKJain and Parveen Babbar, 'Digital libraries initiatives in India' (2006) 38(3) *The International Information & Library Review* 161, 161.

[13] Ibid.

[14] Yanling Sun and Yanhuai Liu, 'China Traditional Chinese Medicine (TCM) Patent Database' (2004) 26(1) *World Patent Information* 91, 91.

[15] Ibid; Anindya Bhukta, 'Protecting Traditional Knowledge: Ways and Means' [2020] *Legal Protection for Traditional Knowledge* 73, 73–95.

[16] 李一丁 [Li Yiding],《印度传统知识数据库治理体系动态及启示》[Dynamics and Enlightenment of the Governance System of Indian Traditional Knowledge Database] [2020] 知识产权*Intellectual Property* 86, 86–96; 黄玉烨 [Huang Yuye],《我国传统知识数据库保护模式及其

lessons that could enhance China's TMK information systems for better protection and promotion of traditional knowledge.[17] However, there is a substantial gap in literature examining how China's unique cultural and historical backdrop shapes the role of information systems in overseeing the protection, utilisation, and dissemination of its TMK.

Addressing this book's void is critical. Appreciating China's historical context and the threads that connect its past to the present can offer valuable insights into the present-day role of information systems in the governance of TMK protection, utilisation, and dissemination. Therefore, this chapter aims to explore the extent to which China's historical context influences the regulatory roles of its existing TMK information systems.

The investigation also offers a potential route for ensuring historical continuity while addressing the limitations of China's current TMK information system. In essence, this chapter argues that China's TMK information systems, influenced by various historical factors, exemplify a delicate balance of local, subnational, and national interests. However, this intricate balance, rather than fostering a robust system for the protection of TMK, opens up a potential risk that the genuine regulatory roles of these information systems in guarding TMK against misappropriation and exploitation might be overshadowed or repurposed to serve disparate national agendas.

This chapter has three main sections: Sect. 6.2 traces the historical trajectory of traditional knowledge documentation practices in China, examining their roots and transformations across different eras of Chinese civilisation; Sect. 6.3 analyses the creation and usage of the information systems for TMK in present-day China, focusing on the historical and socio-political factors that have influenced its creation and utilisation; and Sect. 6.4 critically analyses the limitations of China's TMK information systems and proposes a possible avenue for upgrading this existing information systems, to ensure robust protection, appropriate utilisation, and suitable dissemination of diverse Chinese TMK forms, mindful of China's unique historical, social, and cultural contexts.

6.2 The Historical Origin of TMK Information Systems in China

Despite being a product of the modern digital age, today's TMK information systems in China, more specifically, the CTCMPD, inherently connects with China's magnificent history. It serves as a testament to the seamless continuity of Chinese history, effectively bridging the past with the present. Hence, to truly comprehend the

法律机制研究》(2020) 4 [Research on the Protection Mode and Legal Mechanism of the Traditional Knowledge Database in Our Country] 河南财经政法大学学报 *Journal of Henan University of Economics and Law* 55, 58–60.

[17] Ibid.

full extent of the current information systems in China, it is essential to appreciate its historical roots and context. The historical roots of today's TMK information systems in China, including CTCMPD are believed to extend back to the era of the Shang Dynasty (1600–1050 BCE).[18] Archaeological research shows that a vast body of knowledge inscribed on oracle bones or tortoise shells (excavated in the ruins of Yin) formed China's earliest collections of State archives.[19] Among these oracle bone messages, some were found to be related to medicine, diagnosis, and some basic methods of illness treatment, such as alcoholic wines for medical purposes and bronze knives for surgeries.[20] This valuable knowledge was preserved in the oracle bones storage pits,[21] which were comparable in function and usability to today's knowledge information systems. Arguably, from these earliest storehouses of knowledge and the documents found in them, it can be argued that, although the technologies and formats for preserving TMK have changed dramatically with the march of time, their key functions for collecting, organising, and preserving the knowledge have changed very little.

The process of collecting, organising, and preserving knowledge in China soon required the development of specialised techniques, including techniques for copying and recording knowledge. By the tenth century, the Chinese had invented an early form of printing and paper, which innovated the way they recorded and organised knowledge.[22] Since then, most of the crucial medical manuscripts that had appeared before the Song Dynasty could be collated, documented, and published in printed form.[23] To be specific, some emperors, notably *Renzong* (宋仁宗) (1023–1063) commissioned a series of projects for the collation, archiving, and printing of authoritative editions of classical medical literature to demonstrate their commitments to textual scholarship and the welfare of State and populace.[24] Such editions included many famous medical manuscripts that have been used up to modern times, such as the *Jin Gui Yao Lue* (金匮要略) [Synopsis of Prescriptions of the Golden Casket], *Huangdi Neijing* (黄帝内经) [The Yellow Emperor's Inner Canon of Medicine].[25]

After printing was invented and became widespread in the eighth and ninth centuries, there was a massive increase in archival records, which significantly

[18] Chen Keji and Xu Hao 'The Integration of Traditional Chinese Medicine and Western Medicine' (2003) 11(2) *European Review* 225, 226.

[19] Ibid.

[20] N Sivin, 'Science and Medicine in Imperial China—the State of the Field' (1988) 47(1) *The Journal of Asian Studies* 41, 70.

[21] Junli Diao, 'In Search of China's First Library: Materials, Housing and Arrangement' (2019) 35(1) *Library & Information History* 21, 28.

[22] Wung-seok Cha et al, 'Historical difference between Traditional Korean Medicine and Traditional Chinese Medicine' (2007) 29(1) *Neurological Research* 5, 6.

[23] Kanwen Ma, 'Classic Chinese Medical Literature in Contemporary China: Texts Selected for Modern Editions, and Problems Associated with This Work' in Paul U Unschuld (ed), *Approaches to Traditional Chinese Medical Literature* (Springer, 1989) 7, 7.

[24] Lucille Chia and Hilde De Weerdt, *Knowledge and Text Production in an Age of Print: China, 900–1400* (Brill, 2011) 219.

[25] Ma (n 25).

promoted the growth in the size and number of the collections or repositories of knowledge (including TMK) in China.[26] There is evidence showing that the collections of knowledge exceeded the past dynasties in quality and quantity since the advances in printing technology.[27] To organise the massive archival records and make them easy to retrieve, manage and store for future use, a comprehensive filing and index system (similar to a modern classification system and labelling process used in the TMK information systems) was developed during the Song Dynasty (960–1279).[28] To be specific, the collections of recorded knowledge were arranged by dates, categories, and regions.[29] The catalogues were compiled to record the author names, titles, and page numbers of files, and the column names and indexing notation were also added.[30] This series of developments in China's past historical periods dramatically increased the country's overall archival capacity and significantly influenced the way China organised the collections of historical knowledge (including TMK) or records in the modern age.

Nevertheless, although these State projects to archive, retrieve, and categorise TMK did contribute to the survival and preservation of China's medical knowledge, the fruition of these efforts had more to do with political concerns, which largely came to be associated with maintaining the supremacy of the State power.[31] In China's historical context (particularly since the Song Dynasty), the country had seen the increasing prevalence of the avoidance of the sick (for fear of contagion) and the preference for shamanism over medical remedies in the local communities, which gradually became integral to a broad network of local customs (in the Southern communities of China).[32] These local medical customs and exotic healing figures could have been a threat to State security, becoming critical nodes of resistant power, authority, and knowledge. This had the potential to cause harm to individuals and extend to more widespread disorder throughout the country.[33] In this regard, the compilation, recording, and deployment of TMK had become key weapons for the government to use to address these political concerns, extending the reach of the State's power and homogenising medical knowledge throughout the empire.

One typical example of this was that the Imperial Decree of 974 ordered to deploy prescriptions and distribute medical texts in Qiong (瓊) Prefecture, on Hainan (海南)

---

[26] Stuart AP Murray, *The Library: An Illustrated History* (Skyhorse Publishing Company, 2019) 49.

[27] David Wei Ze, 'Printing as an Agent of Social Stability: The Social Organization of Book Production in China During the Sung Dynasty' (Doctor of Philosophy Thesis, Simon Fraser University, 1995) 1, 150.

[28] Zhang (n 10) 29.

[29] Ibid 30.

[30] Ibid.

[31] TJ Hinrichs, 'Governance Through Medical Texts and The Role of Print' in Sinica Leidensia (ed), *Knowledge and Text Production in an Age of Print: China, 900–1400* (Brill, 2011) 217, 217–238.

[32] 袁倩[Yuan Qian],《宋代巫医及政府禁巫对医学的影响》[Government' Prohibition of Witch Doctor Impact on Development of Medicine in the Song Dynasty] [2021] 中国中医基础医学杂志*Journal of Basic Chinese Medicine* 1, 1–7.

[33] Ibid.

Island.[34] The complaints of local medical customs there stated that 'when people get sick, they just seek out the incantations of shamans'.[35] To transform the local customs, the Imperial State commissioned the collection of medical prescriptions and the compilation of medical texts such as *Taiping shenghui fang* (太平聖惠方) [Taiping Era Prescriptions of Sagely Grace] for dissemination in Qiong (瓊) Prefecture.[36] In response, the districts and communities engraved these prescriptions and medical texts on wooden blocks and posted them at the district gates (which were comparable in usability to today's TMK information systems) so that they could be known by, and accessible to, the clerks and common people without their having to submit applications through various authorities.[37]

Arguably, the custody of the medical texts or the use of printing blocks as vehicles of TMK was actually a sacred trust, which went beyond the conveyance of medical knowledge.[38] In this regard, as told in the official *History of the Song Dynasty of China*, 'the people were affected (*gan* 感) [by the distribution and engraving of the prescriptions and medical text] and transformed'. The local populace was 'edified and transformed' (*Jiaohua*), as Hinrichs put it, through awe.[39] Considering the local populace of China was largely illiterate at that time, it was unclear whether or not it was truly edified 'through the trickle down of medical knowledge'.[40] Nevertheless, by archiving, engraving, and distributing these definitive medical works, the Imperial State had identified itself with this medical knowledge. This created possibilities for determining which knowledge was State-recognised orthodox medical knowledge and which was heterodox medical practices and thus should be circumscribed in the State's best interests.[41] Therefore, it could be argued that the historical precedents of today's TMK information systems in China primarily evolved from, and should be viewed through the lens of, the Imperial State's interest in preserving its power. This perspective underscores that the purpose of these information systems extends beyond merely protecting and providing accessibility to TMK; it significantly intersects with the dynamics of imperial control and influence.

Throughout Chinese history, as long as knowledge (including TMK) has been generated and documented, in whatever form, format, or arrangement, it has also

---

[34] Hinrichs (n 33) 222.

[35] Ibid.

[36] 冯翔[Feng Xiang],《关于宋代至明代南方的瘴病及其历史的研究》[Miasma and its history research from the Southern Song Dynasty to the Ming Dynasty] [2007] 广西民族大学学报 *Journal of Guangxi University for Nationalities* 28, 28–33; 韩毅[Han Yi],《太平圣惠方与宋代社会》[Taiping Shenghui Fang and Song Dynasty Society] [2021] 中华医史杂志*Chinese Medical History Journal* 198, 198–205.

[37] TJ Hinrichs, *The Medical Transforming of Governance and Southern Customs in Song Dynasty China (960–1279 CE)* (Harvard University, 2003) 92.

[38] Ibid 105.

[39] Hinrichs (n 39) 108.

[40] Ibid.

[41] 韩毅[Han Yi],《国家, 医学与社会:太平圣惠方在宋代的应用与传播》[State, Medicine and Society: The Application and Dissemination of Taiping Shenghui Fang in Song Dynasty] [2010] 宋史研究论丛*Collection of Studies on Song Dynasty History* 499, 499–500.

been destroyed as part of the process of conquest or by malicious acts of erasure.[42] A persistent pattern is observed: 'no sooner was a collection of knowledge built up than it was partly destroyed or scattered, only to be recovered and restored in the succeeding dynasties'.[43] The Ruler of the Qin dynasty (221–206 BC), also referred to as the First Emperor of China, for the first time in Chinese history, ordered the horrendous actions of 'burning the knowledge and burying the scholars' (焚書坑儒) in order to eradicate all earlier teachings and silence the prevailing culture of the previous dynasty.[44] As noted by Ouellette, the aim of the deliberate destruction of knowledge in the Qin dynasty was not to eliminate knowledge per se, but to keep knowledge in the hands of a selected privileged few, thus sustaining the imperial power.[45] Since then, the legend of burning of the knowledge and burying the scholars became a substantial part of historical tradition in Chinese chronicles, which the following dynasties usually imitated and added their own experiences to.

The repository of traditional knowledge (including TMK) has been attacked since ancient times but has been especially threatened in the modern era, through various socio-political movements, especially where ethnic and cultural issues have prompted or justified such acts. During the Cultural Revolution (1966–1976), Chairman Mao Zedong took the ruler of the Qin dynasty as his guiding light, thus also encouraging the destruction and purification of traditional knowledge (including TMK).[46] The iconoclastic campaign that was launched and morphed into the cultural revolution was labelled as 'eradicating the four olds' (破四旧). TMK was considered one of the 'four olds': old knowledge, culture, customs, and habits. In this regard, a vast collection of traditional medical treatises was destroyed.[47] Therefore, throughout China's history, despite the fact that Chinese society has entrusted the preservation of TMK to various forms of repositories, these organised collections of knowledge have been subject to spectacular acts of destruction.

Moreover, the evolution of the TMK system and the means of documenting TMK in China has also involved the continued interactions between the dominant traditional knowledge (embodied in classic Han literary texts and the lives of Han Chinese) and the localised place-bound traditional knowledge (linked to various ethnic and local communities), as a result of a historical process of millennia.[48] These interactions constituted the context and dynamics that led to today's TMK system in

[42] Zhang (n 10) 18.

[43] Lucien X Polastron, *Books on Fire: the Destruction of Libraries throughout History* (Inner Traditions, 2007) 80, 88.

[44] Hongyi Harry Lai, 'The Life Span of Unified Regimes in China' (2002) 2(2) *The China Review* 93, 112.

[45] P Ouellette, *Power in the Qin Dynasty: Legalism and External Influence over the Decisions and Legacy of the First Emperor of China* (Haverford College, 2010) 20. < http://thesis.haverford.edu/dspace/bitstream/handle/10066/5251/2010OuelletteP.pdf?sequence=1 > .

[46] Volker Scheid and Eric I Karchmer, 'History of Chinese Medicine, 1890–2010' in TJ Hinrichs and Linda L Barnes (eds), *Modern Chinese Religion II: 1850–2015* (2016) 1, 258.

[47] Ibid.

[48] Zhen Gao et al, 'Emergence and development of Uyghur medicine from the perspective of Chinese traditional medicine' (2019) 2(4) *Traditional Medicine and Modern Medicine* 139, 141–151.

China, which is characterised by the confluence of multiple traditions of observation, philosophical exploration, and lived experience practised by both Han Chinese and the surrounding ethnic minority communities.[49] Nevertheless, many Chinese and Western scholars have painted such interactions between the majority and minority traditions and TMK systems in China as a one-way assimilation and hierarchisation process in which ethnic outsiders proactively embraced 'more advanced Han civilisation in terms of language, customs and knowledge'.[50] In China's historical context, the nucleus of the TMK system was arguably built on 'the higher' culture and civilisation of Han people arising from the fertile Yellow River Valley and espousing Confucianism.[51] On this basis, the bearers of the Han civilisation and traditional knowledge (including TMK) historically considered themselves and their knowledge system to be superior, thus retaining an oppositional or dichotomic relationship with the surrounding ethnic minorities (that were traditionally assumed to be barbaric inferiors).[52] Thus, their TMK systems were incompatible with those belonging to significant populations of other ethnic origins in China.

In his classical discourse on Han civilisation, Confucius was even more blunt about the inferiority of surrounding ethnic minorities and their knowledge systems.[53] He further said it was necessary to ensure that Han civilisation and the ethnic minorities formed an enduring dichotomy of civilised/barbarian and superior/inferior.[54] Such a distinction between Han civilisations and those of the ethnic minorities asserted Han superiority, thus creating a hierarchy where knowledge systems in close proximity to Han civilisation were considered as being more valid than those belonging to populations of other ethnic origins.[55]

Despite being confident in the superiority of their civilisations and knowledge systems, the bearers of Han civilisation and knowledge systems explored all the options throughout China's long history, including both coercive

---

[49] 罗婕[Luo Jie], 中华民族共同体视野下的民族医药传承创新 [Inheritance and Innovation of Ethnic Medicine under the Vision of Chinese National Community] (2021) 15, 世界中医药 *World Traditional Chinese Medicine* 2211, 2211.

[50] Ang, Jennifer, 'Sinicizing the Uyghurs' (2016) 28(4) *Journal of Social Justice* 399, 399; Helen Rees, *Echoes of History: Naxi Music in Modern China* (Oxford University Press, 2000) 1, 30.

[51] L Cooper, 'The International Relations of the 'Imagined Community': Explaining the Late Nineteenth-Century Genesis of the Chinese Nation.' (2015) 41(3) *Review of International Studies* 477, 498.

[52] Tom Grunfeld, 'In Search of Equality: Relations Between China's Ethnic Minorities and the Majority Han' (1985) 17(1) *Bulletin of Concerned Asian Scholars* 54, 57.

[53] DC Lau, *Confucius: the Analects* (Penguin Books, 1979) 5.

[54] Y Shao-Yun, 'Becoming Zhongguo, Becoming Han: Tracing and Reconceptualizing Ethnicity in Ancient North China, 770 BC-AD 581' (Master of Arts Thesis, National University of Singapore, 2007) 29.

[55] Edward Wang, 'History, Space, and Ethnicity: The Chinese Worldview' (1999) 10(2) *Journal of World History* 285, 292.

and complaisant tactics, to spread their knowledge among the surrounding ethnic minorities.[56] The underlying hope was to facilitate the assimilation of these groups.[57]

As explained by Fairbank, these tactics included indoctrinating the ethnic minorities in the Chinese worldview by using cultural-ideological strategies, for instance, setting one ethnic community against another through diplomatic means, or adopting bribery policies by promising marriage, honours or material inducements.[58] For instance, the Northern Song (960–1127) is particularly notable in Chinese history for medical knowledge and healing practice reforms that extended the reach of the bureaucracy into ethnic and local communities.[59] These reform initiatives included the distribution of Han medicines and medical texts, establishing Han medical schools, pharmacies, and hospices in the local communities, and arresting local shamans or coercing them into practising Han medicine.[60] Nevertheless, these approaches to TMK governance were vigorously contested as being invasive and coercive.[61] During the Southern Song (1127–1279), the invasive and coercive intervention into local medical knowledge and healing practices was changed into many milder and more persuasive modes.[62] The Emperor of the Southern Song instructed his senior clerks to implement guidance to the local populace moderately, not harshly, in order to minimise disturbances.[63] The approaches varied from caring for the sick in person, issuing rewards, and distributing medicine, to actively challenging and debating the traditional local understanding of the nature and causes of illnesses.[64] This 'concrete charity' was said to be the instrument of the Southern Song for educating and transforming TMK in ethnic and local communities.[65] Such a strategy for education and transformation' arguably contributed to the blending of the dominant Han TMK with its various tiers and discrete forms into the ethnic and local communities.

There had been narratives that Chinese history and the development of its knowledge systems were a continuing process of 'sinicization'—namely the barbarian ethnic minorities were assimilated into the higher-dimensional Han civilisation.[66] Nevertheless, many recognised the ethnic heterogeneity and diversity that had long

---

[56] Ibid.

[57] Ibid.

[58] John King Fairbank, *The Chinese World Order: Traditional China's Foreign Relations* (Harvard University Press, 1968) 11–12.

[59] Hinrichs (n 39) 20.

[60] Ibid 20–60.

[61] Ibid 20.

[62] Ibid 228.

[63] Ibid 77.

[64] Ibid 54.

[65] Ibid.

[66] D O'Brien and MS Brown 'Becoming Chinese: Sinicization, Nation, and Race in Xinjiang, China', *Oxford Research Encyclopedias* (Web Page, 15 September 2022) < https://oxfordre.com/communication/view/10.1093/acrefore/9780190228613.001.0001/acrefore-9780190228613-e-1333?rskey=ImhBnB&result=1 > .

been a defining characteristic of China's cultural landscape.[67] According to this view, ethnic differences were not a challenge to be overcome, but rather a destiny to be embraced.

As a result, the bearers of Han civilisation changed their expectations.[68] Rather than attempting to culturally assimilate every knowledge system outside Han civilisation, they conceded a wide spectrum of internal autonomy to ethnic and local communities.[69] This occurred during a time of accelerating State encroachment, and this has usually been referred to as 'using barbarians to rule barbarians' (以夷治夷).[70] Another strategy involved a hierarchical approach, that involved reclassifying the traditions and associated knowledge systems while, at the same time, emphasising common identities and mutual benefits. The knowledge was ranked by distance from, or proximity to, a paradigmatic criterion of superior civilisation set by the Han culture.[71] Due to these strategies, the TMK system arising from the peripheral ethnic communities has survived to today and could be passed on to those willing to take on the custodians' roles. Arguably, such processes occurring in China's history have had profound influences on the way that different types of TMK have been documented and shared (for example, some in oral forms and some in written forms). The historical context analysed above provides important insights into the origins and development of the TMK system in China and, as the next section will argue, this context has continued to shape the regulatory roles of the TMK information systems in modern times.

---

[67] Richard J Smith, *Chinese Maps: Images of All Under Heaven* (Oxford University Press, 1996) 8–9.

[68] Wang (n 57) 292.

[69] Ibid.

[70] J Friedrichs, 'Sino-Muslim relations: the Han, the Hui, and the Uyghurs' (2017) 37(1) *Journal of Muslim Minority Affairs* 55, 56.

[71] Ibid.

6.3 Information Systems Development for TMK: Chinese Approach

6.3.1 *An Overview of TMK Information Systems Discussions in the International and Institutional Context*

The TMK information systems were developed against the background of continuing ecological and political imperatives (surrounding the protection of TMK and the recognition of Indigenous rights) and involved a range of organisations and institutions.[72] In this global context, India's experience with TK databases, particularly the Traditional Knowledge Digital Library (TKDL) and biodiversity registers under the 2002 Biodiversity Act, stands out as a proactive approach in preserving traditional knowledge. The TKDL, a comprehensive database, translates and documents traditional Indian medical knowledge in several international languages, effectively preventing the misappropriation of this knowledge by creating a bridge between traditional systems and modern intellectual property regimes. This initiative underscores India's commitment to protecting its Indigenous knowledge heritage while engaging constructively with global patent systems. In parallel, the biodiversity registers, established under the 2002 Biodiversity Act, reflect India's efforts to document and protect the rich biodiversity and associated traditional knowledge at a local level. This grassroots approach empowers local communities, enabling them to play a crucial role in managing and preserving their knowledge. This is in contrast to the centralised TMK systems observed in other countries, such as China, where the China Traditional Chinese Medicine Patent Database (CTCMPD) has raised concerns over state-centric control and potential marginalisation of local and ethnic TMK.

While much of the TMK system arising from peripheral ethnic communities has survived today due to certain strategies, there is still a risk of irreversible loss of Indigenous knowledge and a breakdown of the social and ecological systems that maintain it, making it imperative to take on the custodians' roles and continue to preserve and pass on this valuable knowledge.[73] Another major issue is that the rampant misappropriation of TMK without consent of, or benefit-sharing agreements with, the country of origin is threatening and hampering the livelihoods of the communities who have invested their time, efforts, and costs to sustain the TMK and related cultural practices (see Chapter 5).

---

[72] Sudhir Krishnaswamy, 'Access to Knowledge and Traditional Knowledge Protection: The Indian experience' in Ed Ramesh Subramanian and Lea Shaver (eds), *Access to Knowledge in India: New Research on Intellectual Property, Innovation & Development* (Bloomsbury Academic, 2011) 14, 24.

[73] D Shankar and PM Unnikrishnan, *Challenging the Indian Medical Heritage* (Foundation Books, 2004) 10–12.

On this basis, a large number of international institutions and development agencies have actively embraced the idea of creating the information systems as an effective strategy to preserve and spread traditional knowledge (including TMK).[74] For instance, at the WTO's Committee on Trade and the Environment and the TRIPS Council, proposals concerning the main features of the international information systems on traditional knowledge were made in the context of the mandated review of Article 27.3(b) of the *TRIPS Agreement*. In the proposals, Member States emphasised the need for the information systems to be international in scope and to act as a gateway to existing regional and national databases and information networks.[75] There are also forums and institutions working on the creation of information systems relating specifically to TMK. For example, in December 2000, the WHO held an Inter-regional Workshop on IP Rights in the Context of Traditional Medicine, where the Member States were recommended to document TMK in the public domain in the form of various information systems and exchange this knowledge through systems related to IP rights.[76] In addition, the strategy of creating information systems for traditional knowledge (including TMK) protection has received great support from a vast array of donor agencies and researchers, including the World Bank, the United Nations Educational, Scientific and Cultural Organization ('UNESCO'), and also many networks of researchers and policy activists. For instance, UNESCO has adopted specific provisions in the 2003 *Convention for the Safeguarding of the Intangible Cultural Heritage* to encourage the establishment of various information systems of traditional knowledge.[77]

The most extensive work on issues concerning the development of TMK information systems has taken place in WIPO, in the form of texts that have the potential to become the new international legal standards. The significant consolidation of ideas surrounding the construction of information systems for traditional knowledge was first proposed at the Third Plenary Session of the WIPO Standing Committee on Information Technology ('SCIT'), which adopted a Strategic Information Technology Plan that emphasised the need to create information systems for traditional knowledge.[78] At the intergovernmental level, WIPO set up an Inter-Governmental Committee on IP and Genetic Resources, Traditional Knowledge, and Folklore ('IGC'). The aim of the IGC was to provide a forum for discussion among the

[74] Arun Agrawal, 'Indigenous Knowledge and the Politics of Classification' (2002) 54(173) *International Social Science Journal* 287, 288.

[75] *Review of Article 27.3(b): the View of Switzerland*, WTO Docs IP/C/W/284 (15 June 2001).

[76] *Report of the Inter-Regional Workshop on Intellectual Property Rights in the Context of Traditional Medicine*, WHO Doc WHO/EDM/TRM/2001.1 (6–8 December 2000).

[77] *Convention for the Safeguarding of the Intangible Cultural Heritage*, open for signature 17 October 2003, 2368 UNTS 3 (entered into force 20 April 2006) art 12.

[78] *SCIT Strategic Information Technology Plan into the Twenty-First Century, WIPO Docs SCIT/3/4 (15 June 1999); Information Technology Strategic Implementation Plan*, WIPO Docs SCIT/4/2 (24 September 1999) annex 2.

Member States on cross-cutting IP issues (such as protection of traditional knowledge), that do not fit into existing bodies such as the SCIT.[79] At the first session of the IGC held from April 30 to May 3, 2001, the Member States expressed that they wished to consider the current criteria and the need for new criteria to support more effective integration of documented traditional knowledge into searchable prior art.[80] These practical issues that the Member States wished to address have been expressed under Task B.3, which is tasked to evaluate how best to make sure that the International Searching Authority can implement international searches and discover relevant traditional knowledge when it constitutes prior art relevant to the invention.[81] During the Second Session, held from December 10 to 14, 2001, the IGC debated extensively concerning the implementation of this task.[82] The activities required for the development of information systems were considered in order to implement Task B.3, including the assessment of the viability of the electronic exchange of traditional knowledge documentation data through the establishment of the information systems, and the assessment of the means of assisting Indigenous peoples and their traditional knowledge documentation initiatives.[83]

Nevertheless, despite these efforts in the international and institutional context, Robinson and Chiarolla noted that the goal of information systems for traditional knowledge is limited to addressing the critical issue of the erroneous grant of patents, but has no value in ensuring compliance with other legal requirements exogenous to the patent system.[84] Some Member States even feared that an exclusive focus on information systems might divert attention away from the goal of creating effective legal protection for traditional knowledge (such as ABS measures).[85] Therefore, arguably, this situation provides countries that do not show real interest in protecting TMK with a high degree of leeway to avoid the obligations of creating a primary legal mechanism to protect it at the national level. Even worse is that the creation of the information systems at the national level could present an alternative means for the national authorities to reinforce the historical practice rationale—that is, that the recognised need to protect TMK could be co-opted to benefit the State when it is enforced through documenting the TMK in whatever form, forma, or arrangement.

[79] M Ruiz, 'The International Debate on Traditional Knowledge as Prior Art in the Patent System: Issues and Options for Developing Countries' (Occasional Paper No 9, Center for International Environmental Law, October 2002) 1, 14.

[80] *Report*, WIPO Doc. WIPO/GRTKF/IC/1/13 (May 23, 2001).

[81] Ibid.

[82] *Progress Report on the Status of Traditional Knowledge as Prior Art*, WIPO Doc. WIPO/GRTKF/IC/2/6 (1 July 2001).

[83] Ibid 29–32.

[84] Daniel F Robinson and Claudio Chiarolla, 'The Role of Databases, Contracts and Codes of Conduct' in Ahmed Abdel-Latif, Daniel F Robinson, and Pedro Roffe (eds), *Protecting Traditional Knowledge: The WIPO Intergovernmental Committee on Intellectual Property and Genetic Resources, Traditional Knowledge and Folklore* (Routledge, 2017) 108, 108–121.

[85] *Inventory of Existing Online Database Containing Traditional Knowledge Documentation Data*, WIPO Doc. WIPO/GRTKF/IC/3/6 (June 13 to 21, 2002) §3.

6.3.2 National Interest vs. Global Cooperation: China's Complex Dynamics with the TMK Information Systems

The protection of TMK has been a major concern for biodiverse-rich countries in general, and China in particular.[86] To address this concern, many biodiverse-rich countries (led by India) have been able to use international organisations such as WIPO as a platform to promote the creation of the information systems to the global community.[87] China has been a proactive and visible participant in various negotiations of intergovernmental organisations, often acting in concert with biodiversity countries. There are several examples of China making proposals in concert with major biodiversity countries within WIPO. For instance, in the second session of the IGC in December 2001, the Chinese delegation, together with other Asian groups, submitted a position paper suggesting information systems for the protection of traditional knowledge.[88] The position paper suggested that Member Parties should, 'as appropriate, compile databases of traditional knowledge which is in the public domain and make these databases available to patent-granting authorities for the purposes of prior art searches, in order to prevent the grant of any IP rights over such public domain knowledge'.[89] During the third session in June 2002, China, along with India and Venezuela, shared their practical experiences in the compilation of traditional knowledge information systems to facilitate the study of the issues stemming from their development, management, and use.[90]

Nevertheless, despite China's efforts to grasp every opportunity to advance the proposals and draft resolutions for developing the TMK information systems, the country did not seem to be very convinced of the proposals that it fervently supported in international conferences and meetings.[91] In fact, as noted by Cui, Chinese leaders, policymakers, and academics expressed significant scepticism concerning the proposals put forth by the biodiverse-rich countries' group. These proposals, aimed at creating the information systems for the protection of TMK, raised questions about their compatibility with China's interests.[92] China's integration of TMK with Western medicine has made the creation of the information systems to protect

---

[86] R Lakshmi Poorna, M Mymoon and A Hariharan, 'Preservation and Protection of Traditional Knowledge—Diverse Documentation Initiatives Across the Globe' (2014) 107(8) *Current Science* 1240, 1240–1246.

[87] Chidi Oguamanam, 'Documentation and Digitization of Traditional Knowledge and Intangible Cultural Heritage: Challenges and Prospects' in Toshiyuki Kono (ed), *Intangible Cultural Heritage and Intellectual Property: Cultural Diversity and Sustainable Development* (Intersentia, 2009).

[88] *Progress Report on the Status of Traditional Knowledge as Prior Art*, WIPO Doc. WIPO/GRTKF/IC/2/6 (1 July 2001).

[89] Ibid.

[90] *Inventory of Existing Online Database Containing Traditional Knowledge Documentation Data*, WIPO Doc. WIPO/GRTKF/IC/2/6 (13 to 21 July 2001).

[91] C Schulz, 'Money or Pride? On the Why and How of Traditional Knowledge Protection in India and China' (2011) 1(1) *Konstanzer Journal für Politik und Verwaltung* 52, 58.

[92] Guobin Cui, 'A Review of the Status Quo of Genetic Resources and Traditional Knowledge Protection in China' (Working Paper, Tsinghua University School of Law, August 2009) 2.

TMK against misappropriation unattractive to China.[93] In other words, the integration of TMK with Western medicine has changed its priorities. Instead of focusing on protecting TMK on its own terms, China has prioritised facilitating the use of TMK for commercial purposes and encouraging research and development in this area. For example, it has implemented various legal, policy, and practical measures since the 1990s to promote the use of TMK in modern healthcare systems and support the growth of the TMK industry.[94] These measures aim to benefit China's economy and scientific development rather than solely focusing on protecting TMK from being misappropriated.[95] However, it is important to note that these measures primarily protect recently invented TMK and do not necessarily address the protection of local-scale TMK expertise that is exclusive to certain communities and not readily available to the general public.

In 1992, the substantive *Regulations on the Protection of Varieties of Chinese Traditional Medicine* were established to protect innovation, and research and development ('R&D') in the field of TMK,[96] and adopted language suggestive of a Western scientific standard for validating TMK.[97] Nevertheless, the Regulations did not contain any provision that introduced measures to prevent the undue appropriation of TMK as local knowledge of communities and recognise the meaning and values of TMK embodied in the traditional lifeways of the communities. As noted by Oguamanam, the Chinese protection of TMK focuses on protecting innovations on TMK as a prelude to bolstering its integration into the Western scientific system, which is considered essential, as it not only fuels China's ongoing economic growth but also serves high-priority national objectives and interests.[98] China's TMK information systems were established in the early 2000s, a period when the nation's interests were keenly focused on integrating innovations within China's TMK fields. This historical context is important to understand the creation and purpose of the information systems. With the TMK information systems, China's vast traditional knowledge becomes readily accessible, making the innovation process easier for those seeking to develop new drugs from this knowledge. As a result, the need to consult traditional textual sources or engage with local communities for information could be substantially lessened.

In this context, one could argue that China has cleverly used the discourse of TMK protection to justify the establishment of the TMK information systems. By maintaining one narrative internationally and another domestically, China has crafted a strategy that allows the state authorities to harness generations of TMK—from

---

[93] Chidi Oguamanam, 'Patents and Traditional Medicine: Digital Capture, Creative Legal Interventions and the Dialectics of Knowledge Transformation' (2008) 15(2) *Indiana Journal of Global Legal Studies* 489, 507.

[94] Oguamanam (n 95) 506.

[95] Ibid.

[96]《中药品种保护条例》[China's Regulation on the Protection of Traditional Chinese Medicine] (People's Republic of China) State Council, Order No 106, 1992 ('Regulations').

[97] In Article 3, the regulation makes reference to the protection of 'stable' forms of TCM which is suggestive of 'scientific replicability'.

[98] Ibid.

national, subnational, and local communities—for the State's benefit. This approach aligns with China's historical tendency to document its wealth of knowledge, which often prioritises the elevation of State interests, social order, harmony, and authority over the concerns of individuals, private entities, or marginalised communities.

6.3.3 TMK Information Systems in China's Context

With the dawn of the modern age, many traditional approaches for collecting, documenting, and accessing knowledge and information have experienced a massive transformation because of the development of digital technology and computer networks.[99] Against this backdrop, in China, a number of government agencies and bureaucratic institutions have initiated projects to digitise ancient books and manuscripts, handwritten notes, and darkened photocopies to preserve its TMK.[100] One typical example is the China Traditional Chinese Medicine Patent Database ('CTCMPD').[101] Upon the promulgation of the *Medicine Administration Law* at the 20th Meeting of the Chinese National People's Congress Standing Committee in early 2001, the CTCMPD was compiled by the State Intellectual Property Office ('SIPO') of the People's Republic of China with the objective of preventing the erroneous grant of patents over TMK.[102] It should be noted that the creation of the CTCMPD in 2002 followed closely after WIPO's decision to establish the IGC in 2001. At the time when the IGC was founded, the development of the CTCMPD was already well underway.

The CTCMPD contains more than 20,000 bibliographic records and over 40,000 TMK formulas (published from 1985 to the present).[103] It is important to note that accessing the CTCMPD in Chinese may require permission, but the entries in the CTCMPD that have been translated into English and made available through the WIPO Web gate are open access.[104] According to many scholars in China, the creation of the information systems of this scale has been associated with the need to safeguard China's sovereignty over TMK and protect it from being misused in patenting.[105] More significantly, the underlying assumption is that patent examiners of the SIPO in China may mistakenly grant patents utilising existing TMK due to the

[99] N Varatharajan and M Chandrashekara, 'Digital Library Initiatives at Higher Education and Research Institutions in India' [2007] *Library Philosophy and Practice* 1.

[100] Poorna et al, (n 88)1242–1244; A Bhukta, Legal Protection for Traditional Knowledge: Towards A New Law for Indigenous Intellectual Property (Emerald Publishing, 2020) 73, 92.

[101] Bhukta (n 102) 92–93; Poorna et al (n 88) 1243–1244.

[102] Bhukta (n 102) 93.

[103] Yanhuai Liu and Yanling Sun, 'China Traditional Chinese Medicine (TCM) Patent Database' (2004) 26(1) *World Patent Information* 91, 91.

[104] Ibid.

[105] 吴弈天[Wu Yitian],《中医药传统知识数据库构建思路初探》[A preliminary study on the construction of traditional Chinese medicine knowledge database](2022)30(5) 中国卫生法制 *China Health Law* 6, 8.

lack of easily accessible information on this knowledge.[106] This concern catalysed the creation of the CTCMPD, backed by the dedication of the Chinese State and relevant agencies, with a goal to preserve national sovereignty over TMK and to streamline bureaucratic procedures. Nevertheless, while the CTCMPD is fundamentally an information system, it operates under bureaucratic control and is associated with 'national interest'. As such, its role in safeguarding TMK and protecting TMK holder's rights could be compromised by potential political interference, misuse, and manipulation. These potential challenges should be understood in light of China's historical context.

The institutionalisation process of China's TMK culminated with the establishment of the National Administration of Traditional Chinese Medicine, which can be traced back to the 1950s when the Chinese Central Ministry of Health established a special office affiliated with the Medical Affairs Department.[107] The National Administration of Traditional Chinese Medicine has been transformed into the National Health Commission directly under the State Council, which played a significant role, along with SIPO, in the creation and promotion of the CTCMPD.[108] The newly founded National Health Commission was given extended mandates and means to promote TMK activities in China's national interest.[109] The TMK information systems, including the CTCMPD, are part of a broader effort promoted by the National Health Commission, SIPO and other government agencies to support innovation and deployment of the domestic pharmaceutical sector, building on China's TMK.[110] Within this framework, the primary goal of the CTCMPD initiative is to align with China's overarching national interests related to economic benefits, development, and fostering a thriving and competitive industrial sector. This focus is particularly evident in the pharmaceutical field, where creativity and innovation are of paramount importance. In this context, the significance of the CTCMPD extends beyond being merely a database or information system—it serves as a strategic tool for the country's industrial growth and competitiveness in the pharmaceutical industry.

In China, the creativity and innovation based on TMK do not merely mean adapting the traditional medical practices into an industrial context, but also including

---

[106] Ibid.

[107] Lau Kin Chi and Sit Tsui, 'The Need for Recovering the Subjugated Knowledge of Traditional Chinese Medicine' (2020) 63 *Development* 249, 253.

[108] 商 宇 [Shang Yu],《新中国成立后中央中医管理组织变迁研究》[Research on the Changes of the Central Management Organization of Traditional Chinese Medicine after the Founding of New China] (2016) 29(6), 医学与社会, *Medicine and Society* 28, 29.

[109] 刘海英 [Liu Haiying],《中国中医药政策变迁的阶段历程与演进逻辑-基于1949-2020政策文本的实证研究》[The different stages and evolutionary logic of Traditional Chinese medicine policy: an empirical study based on the policy texts from 1949 to 2020] (2021) 17(12) 亚太传统医药, *Asia–Pacific Traditional Medicine* 3, 8–11.

[110]《十三五中医药科技创新专项规划》[The 13th Five-Year Special Plan for Scientific and Technological Innovation of Traditional Chinese Medicine] (People's Republic of China) National Health Commission and Ministry of Science and Technology, Order No 146, 2017, art 4.2.1.

innovation through exploiting and reinventing TMK.[111] Such a model consists of reinventing and mining the properties of the existing TMK to produce novel compositions of medical herbs based on distinctive knowledge-prospecting mechanisms, borrowing the thoughts from various TMK systems in China.[112] For this reason, the industrialists and public administrations (both national and regional) naturally consider China's TMK as resources to be exploited for inventing, industrialising, and other commercial purposes, thus organising the inventory and codifying China's various TMK systems within the framework of the TMK information systems (e.g. the CTCMPD).

In addition, there have been a series of policies and initiatives that suggest that the TMK should be extended and put to more active use in R&D. For instance, in the *Law of the People's Republic of China on Traditional Chinese Medicine*, enacted on December 25, 2016 to promote scientific research and technological innovation in the field of TMK, contains a section on the high priority for law enforcement.[113] This was followed in 2019 by *Opinions of the CPC Central Committee and the State Council on Promoting the Preservation, Innovation, and Development of Traditional Chinese Medicine*, and in 2022 by China's *New Five-Year Plan for the Development of Traditional Chinese Medicine*. These were dedicated to promoting local innovation arising from TMK, and encouraging the use of TMK and related information systems (such as the CTCMPD) as a source of scientific innovations for the economic and social benefit of the country. The establishment of the CTCMPD and other types of TMK information systems in China fit in well with this series of policies and legislative imperatives to innovate and monetise TMK, working with China's existing patent system to optimise the information systems' operations. According to statistics, SIPO has granted thousands of patents related to TMK in the past decade.[114] Most of these have been documented in the CTCMPD for domestic use only.[115] On this basis, arguably, China's initiatives of creating the TMK information systems such as the CTCMPD should be viewed as yet another State-sponsored project related systematically to China's past historical practices, which serve as sources to uplift the economic, social, and political benefits of the State. However, whether or not the disempowered and marginalised knowledge holders and communities who hold the TMK are able to benefit from such an exercise may not have received sufficient attention. Likely skewed by China's 'historical vicissitudes' and hierarchical

[111] 杨义芳 [Yang Yifang],《中药创新药物研究开发的回顾、策略与实践》[Review, Strategy and Practice of Research and Development of Innovative Traditional Chinese Medicine] (2009) 40(10), 中草药, *Chinese Traditional and Herbal Drugs* 1513, 1517.

[112] Ibid.

[113]《中华人民共和国中医药法》[Law of the People's Republic of China on Traditional Chinese Medicine] (People's Republic of China) Standing Committee of the National People's Congress, Order No. 59, 2017, art 3, art 8, arts 38–41, art 52.

[114] 秦宇 [Qin Yu],《我国中药专利申请现状分析及建议》[Analysis of the current situation of the Chinese traditional medicine patent application in China and the corresponding suggestions] (2016) 25(8), 中国新药杂志, *Chinese Journal of New Drugs* 841, 841–844.

[115] Ibid.

practices that centred on the Han superiority over other ethnic minorities,[116] the creation of the CTCMPD and other types of TMK information systems reinforce this well-known ethnocentric hierarchy of Han TMK (in written form) and other ethnic minorities' TMK (in oral form). To be specific, the CTCMPD (and other types of TMK information systems) appear to be based on the expectation that all forms of TMK in China can be represented in written form, which therefore provides relatively advantaged frameworks of recognition for the classical and elite form of TMK that is grounded in textual canons. This is particularly relevant to Han TMK, which is grounded in China's millennial long history of highly formalised bodies of textual writing, and thus is often promoted as the only homegrown and authentically Chinese TMK.[117] As the most socially elite medical system, 'TMK has had absolute dominance throughout China's history'.[118] Its historical links with mainstream Chinese nationalism and ethnic and cultural superiority have further given it the most privileged position within the hierarchy.[119] Han medicine is regarded as the national heritage of China, while more marginalised TMK remains undocumented, creating a distinction between the localised, place-bound TMK and the socially elite TMK.[120]

Throughout the twentieth century in China, the gradual institutionalisation of socially elite Han medicine, in the form of medical schools, print culture, and bureaucratic techniques (such as integrating with Western medicine within China's national health policies), has been closely linked to a nationalistic movement founded on Han-centric ideology.[121] This movement, led by Han nationalists, emphasises the association of Chinese identity with Han heritage, leading to a situation where Han TMK is often considered more Chinese than other forms.[122]

The influence of Han-centric nationalism can be found in much Chinese literature and is also reflected in the development and functioning of the CTCMPD and other TMK information systems.[123] These information systems align with the nationalistic agenda to protect socially elite and textually grounded forms of Han TMK against foreign misappropriation and to promote it as the primary Chinese national heritage.

---

[116] Grunfeld (n 54) 57.

[117] 芦 笛[Lu Di],《中国近代医药史研究及相关问题评论》[Research on the History of Traditional Chinese Medicine and Comments on Related Issues] (2016) 1, 史林, *Journal of History* 195, 200–201.

[118] 李佛基 [Li Foji],《中医中药概念探析》[Analysis on the Concept of Traditional Chinese Medicine] (1999) 11(5), 安徽中医临床杂志, *Clinical Journal of Anhui Traditional Chinese Medicine* 346, 347.

[119] Ibid.

[120] Ibid.

[121] Elisabeth Hsu, 'The History of Chinese Medicine in the People's Republic of China and Its Globalization' (2008) 2(4) *East Asian Science, Technology and Society: An International Journal* 465, 467–468; RalphCroizier, 'Traditional Medicine in Communist China: Science, Communism and Cultural Nationalism' (1965)23 *The China Quarterly* 1, 27.

[122] Liang Yongjia, 'Developmentalism, Secularism, Nationalism and Essentialism: Current Situation and Challenges of the Ethnic Issue in China' in Litao Zhao (ed), *China's Social Development and Policy: Into the Next Stage?* (Taylor & Francis Group, 2013) 186, 195.

[123] John M Friend and Bradley A Thayer, 'The Rise of Han-Centrism and What It Means for International Politics (2017) 17(1) *Studies in Ethnicity and Nationalism* 91, 104–106.

In particular, TMK stored in the CTCMPD, and other information systems is often managed and maintained using the Mandarin language (commonly referred to as the language of the Han people), using documentation and classification systems that are familiar to well-educated urban Han Chinese.[124] This approach tends to ignore the local language ideologies, ontologies, and epistemologies of diverse knowledge-holder communities.[125]

As a result, the CTCMPD and similar information systems may inadvertently perpetuate a hierarchy where TMK systems associated with Han TMK that satisfy the criteria set by Han Chinese elites receive greater recognition and protection as the national heritage of China. This situation underscores the interplay among local, subnational, and national interests in the TMK information systems and how the protection of TMK against misappropriation and exploitation risks being co-opted to serve national purposes, often at the expense of other marginalised communities and knowledge systems.

More significantly, the creators of the CTCMPD and other TMK information systems in China may have positive intentions of aligning the distinctly local and place-bound TMK system to the socially elite and textually grounded forms of TMK (of Han ethnic origin). Nevertheless, they arguably participate in the one-way assimilation process (similar to the historical practice) that contributes to fixing the TMK (held by ethnic and local communities) as static knowledge, and decontextualising it from the local context when in fact these forms of TMK exist in oral-aural form and are dynamic in the light of the lived experiences of the communities. As noted by Thomas, this situation is a hugely complicated quandary, which is reflected in the tendencies to shape TMK 'in the image of modern, abstracted, scientific knowledge amenable to translation into forms of rent-seeking property'.[126] On this basis, powerful as the decontextualisation and abstractions produced by the CTCMPD and other TMK information systems can be, their aims are not—nor have they ever been—to represent 'subaltern'[127] TMK held by the local and ethnic communities.

Other critical researchers argue that the persistent tendency of information systems like the CTCMPD is to alienate the TMK from its original communities and strip from it all the meanings that are incompatible with the logic and purpose of the information system, typically to serve the agenda of the State.[128] Arguably, the implication derived from Chinese history (as discussed in the previous sections) indicates that there must be underlying political reasons why today's strategies for documenting TMK in China have often served the interests of the States, while not representing

---

[124] Poorna et al (n 88) 1242–1243.

[125] Ibid.

[126] Pradip N Thomas., 'Traditional Knowledge and the Traditional Knowledge Digital Library: Digital Quandaries and Other Concerns' (2010) 72(8) *The International Communication Gazette* 659, 667.

[127] Projit Bihari Mukharji, 'Subaltern Surgeries: Colonial Law and the Regulation of Traditional Medicines in the British Raj and Beyond' (2021) 36 *Osiris* 89, 89–112.

[128] Sita Reddy, 'Making Heritage Legible: Who Owns Traditional Medical Knowledge?' (2006) 13 *International Journal of Cultural Property* 161, 175.

TMK and its local community holders on their own terms. Simply put, the preservation and protection of TMK and its local community holders' rights could threaten the stability of conventional power structures rooted in modern China's industrial and social system. The motivations and rationale behind this system are the industrial development (particularly pharmaceutical industrial growth), and its positive impacts on the economic and social benefit of the nation and the welfare of its populace. Empowering TMK and its local community holders on their own terms essentially means giving voice to a system of understanding that may challenge the priority and interests of the State.[129] Therefore, despite being frequently promoted as social justice tools, TMK information systems and various documenting initiatives in China have often served to limit the real protection and genuine empowerment of TMK (and its local community holders), via assimilating the living TMK system into existing schemes developed to 'treat collections as fragmented and static materials preserving "frozen" knowledge'.[130]

As analysed above, China's TMK information systems (such as the CTCMPD) embody its historical, social, and political legacy—for example, representing a destructive mechanism that has made China's TMK system 'forever rickety',[131] and homogenising or repressing the plurality and multiplicity of TMK that the agenda of the State motivates and political action postulates. China's TMK system discounts, rather than embraces, the complex, dynamic nature of the discrete forms of TMK that exist in various communities. The causes for this situation are partly due to the system's constant and unbroken links with China's distantly past historical values, beliefs, and attitudes towards TMK that emphasise the centrality of the State and the pervasive Han supremacism, while routinely limiting the real protection of TMK and its community holders' interests. Given this perspective, it can be argued that, despite the best intentions to establish an inclusive space for documenting various categories of TMK with diverse types of rights, the TMK information systems in China may inevitably become intertwined with the nation's historical values, practices, and institutions. To effectively address this problem, a fundamental restructuring of the TMK information system is essential.

6.3.4 The Rise of Biopharmaceutical Sectors in China

The systemic challenges within China's TMK information systems reflect the historical and political influences shaping their structure while also intersecting with

[129] SC Ellis, 'Meaningful Consideration? A Review of Traditional Knowledge in Environmental Decision Making' (2005) 58(1) *Arctic* 66, 75.

[130] María Montenegro, 'Subverting the Universality of Metadata Standards: The TK Labels as a Tool to Promote Indigenous Data Sovereignty' (2019) 75(4) *Journal of Documentation* 731, 734.

[131] Lucien X Polastron, *Books on Fire: The Destruction of Libraries Throughout History* (Inner Traditions, 2007) 80, 97.

contemporary economic and industrial imperatives. The rise of China's biopharmaceutical sector has added complexity to this dynamic. Biopharmaceutical innovation increasingly relies on genetic resources and the rich traditional knowledge embedded within TMK, highlighting the limitations of existing information systems. This growing reliance underscores both the immense potential of TMK and the urgent need for its equitable and effective management. Biopharmaceuticals, which are medicinal products derived from biological resources, depend heavily on genetic information and traditional knowledge for drug discovery and development.[132] TMK plays a critical role in this process by providing leads for diagnosing, preventing, and treating diseases. Studies show that around 75% of the modern biopharmaceutical products derived from genetic resources in one year are developed through the research based on their traditional medicinal uses.[133] Through the use of TMK for biopharmaceutical innovation, the success rate of producing at least one commercial drug product derived from a thousand medicinal species increases from 22 to 78%.[134] Moreover, TMK's role in screening genetic resources for medicinal properties is thought to increase the efficiency by more than 400%.[135] The success rate of drug development at the lead discovery phase is known to increase as much as 50 per cent.[136]

In this context, TMK information systems, such as the China Traditional Chinese Medicine Patent Database (CTCMPD), play an increasingly pivotal role. These systems serve as repositories of valuable knowledge that not only prevent the misappropriation of TMK but also facilitate its appropriate use in biopharmaceutical research and development. By providing accessible, well-organised data on TMK formulations and their traditional applications, these systems allow biopharmaceutical researchers to efficiently identify potential leads for new drug development. However, despite their utility, the limitations of these systems—such as biases towards written, Han-dominated TMK and the decontextualisation of local knowledge—may restrict their ability to fully support the biopharmaceutical sector's needs.

The pressures faced by China's local pharmaceutical industry vary significantly based on whether the focus is on traditional or non-traditional (Western) medicine. For the industry focused on TMK, challenges include the need to safeguard traditional knowledge from misappropriation, ensure equitable benefit-sharing with local

---

132 Bhupinder Singh Sekhon 'Biopharmaceuticals: an overview' (2010) 34 *Thai J. Pharm. Sci.* 2.

133 Kuruk, Paul, 'Exploitation of traditional knowledge of Indigenous and local communities' in Paul Kuruk (ed), *Traditional Knowledge, Genetic Resources, Customary Law and Intellectual Property* (2020) 17; Kanehe, Debra Harry and Le'a Malia, 'Asserting Tribal Sovereignty over Cultural Property: Moving Towards Protection of Genetic Material and Indigenous Knowledge' (2006) 5(1) *Seattle Journal for Social Justice* 33–34.

134 Curtis M. Horton, 'Protecting Biological Diversity and Cultural Diversity Under Intellectual Property Law' (1995) 10(1) *Journal of Environmental Law and Litigation* 1, 5.

135 Nijar, Singh, 'Incorporating Traditional Knowledge in an International Regime on Access to Genetic Resources and Benefit Sharing: Problems and Prospects' (2010) 21(2) *The European Journal of International Law* 458.

136 Ibid.

communities, and integrate TMK into modern drug development while maintaining its cultural and ethical significance. TMK-based firms must also navigate intellectual property frameworks that are often unsuited to the collective and community-based nature of traditional knowledge. Conversely, the non-traditional or Western biopharmaceutical industry operates within a global framework emphasising molecular innovation, advanced clinical trials, and compliance with international drug approval standards. This sector faces pressures to achieve cutting-edge scientific breakthroughs and maintain competitiveness in a rapidly evolving global market. While both sectors share overarching challenges, such as regulatory compliance and access to capital, the traditional sector uniquely balances cultural preservation with commercial viability, while the non-traditional sector emphasises high-tech innovation and global scalability. These differences highlight the importance of tailoring policy and support frameworks to address the distinct pressures of each sector, rather than treating them as a unified pharmaceutical industry.

China's biopharmaceutical sector has grown rapidly in recent years.[137] It has been estimated that China's biopharmaceutical market has a total value of around US$130 billion, which makes China the second-largest biopharmaceutical market in the entire world.[138] By the end of October 2021, the number of China's biopharmaceutical patent applications accounts for 52.37% of total biopharmaceutical patent applications worldwide.[139] Nevertheless, China's rise in biopharmaceuticals may appear inevitable. If for no other reasons, its enormous population, abundant biodiversity resources, and especially the significant TMK associated with the use of genetic resources provide timely benefits for industry and research sectors involved in biopharmaceutical research and development. The use of TMK is important for biopharmaceutical innovation in a variety of ways. First, the progress in biopharmaceutical innovation usually goes backwards and forwards with winding complex pathways and often with no obvious starting point.[140] TMK is, therefore, a reasonable starting point as a source of original leads, which could significantly save the cost and time of pharmaceutical research and development.[141] Second, TMK could also provide a source of leads for 'new' uses and undiscovered properties for old drugs, which was described by Graham Dutfield as 'renew the old'.[142] The typical renewing case is Qinghao. The ancient Chinese pharmacopoeia provides a direct lead

---

[137] Liu, Kerong Zhang and Wuyi, 'The Current Status, Trend, and Development Strategies of Chinese Biopharmaceutical Industry with a Challenging Perspective' (2020) *Sage Journals* 1–16; Kiki Han, 'The Dawn of China Biopharma Innovation' (2021) *McKinsey & Company* 1–9.

[138] Bill Beeson, 'Weighing the Opportunities & Risks Within China's Biopharmaceutical Industry' (2021) *The China Guys;* QianXun Consultation, 2021 *China Biopharmaceutical Market Analysis Report: Analysis of Market Scale, Status and Development Trend* (Report, 2021).

[139] Qianzhan Industry Institute (前瞻産業研究院), *Technology Landscape of the Global Biopharmaceutical industry in 2022* (Report, 2021).

[140] Graham Dutfield, 'Why Traditional Knowledge Is Important in Drug Discovery' (2010) 2(9) *Future Med. Chem,* 1406–1407.

[141] D.Syiem and M.B.Syiem, 'Medicinal Plants and Conservation: Some Issues and Concerns' in P.Tandon and Y.P.A.Suman (ed), *Biodiversity and Its Significance* (2007) 150.

[142] Ibid 1407–1408.

for Chinese scientists to investigate the potential new use of Qinghao as a treatment for malaria.[143] Third, the biopharmaceutical sector is one of the major beneficiaries of use of TMK. This is because it relies heavily on bioresources such as raw genetic and biological samples, extractions, and compounds from wild resources to develop new biopharmaceuticals.[144] Where the pharmaceutical products have flora and fauna origin, TMK has a good chance of being relevant. Therefore, as the biopharmaceutical sectors rise in China, the rates of the use of TMK and genetic resources for biopharmaceutical innovation and development are likely to increase in the coming years.

There are several factors that have contributed to the rise of China's domestic biopharmaceutical sector. First, in recent years, China has introduced a series of national plans and policies explicitly to improve market access and foster biopharmaceutical innovation. For instance, China announced its 13th Five-Year plan in March 2016, which outlines several major tasks and measures aiming to encourage the innovation and use of China's domestically produced pharmaceutical products and lessen reliance on foreign imports for pharmaceutical products.[145] These measures include the establishment of Good Clinical Practice international standards, fast-track approval for new drugs, and so on.[146] As detailed in the national strategic plan 'Made in China 2025', Chinese central government has set targets to streamline the process of pharmaceutical product approval, encourage innovation of Chinese domestic pharmaceutical sector, and reduce the reliance on foreign imports for pharmaceutical products.[147] Additionally, China's National People's Congress passed the amendments to the Drug Administration Law ('DAL') in August 2019.[148] It came into effect in December 2019 with the objectives of encouraging the pharmaceutical innovation and streamlining the procedure for drugs examination and

[143] Elisabeth Hsu, 'Reflections on the 'discovery' of the antimalarial qinghao' (2006) 61(6) *British Journal of Clinical Pharmacology* 667.

[144] Jozala AF, Geraldes DC, Tundisi LL, et al, 'Biopharmaceuticals from microorganisms: from production to purification' (2016) 47 *Braz J Microbiol* 51–63; Surendra Sarsaiya et al, 'Bioengineering Tools for the Production of Pharmaceuticals: Current Perspective and Future Outlook' (2019) 10(1) *Bioengineering* 469–470.

[145]《中华人民共和国国民经济和社会发展第十三个五年规划纲要》[Outline of the 13th Five-Year Plan for the National Economic and Social Development of the People's Republic of China] (People's Republic of China) National People's Congress, March 2016; Mackenzie Mills, Anwen Zhang and Panos Kanavos (2019) 'Pharmaceutical Policy in China' *London School of Economics* 24, https://doi.org/10.21953/lse.fg2t522b8r1x

[146] Ibid.

[147]《中国制造2025》[Made in China 2025] (People's Republic of China) State Council, May 2016 http://www.dahe.com/standard/standard%20folder/made%20in%20China%202025.pdf; Robert D. Atkinson, 'China's Biopharmaceutical Strategy: Challenge or Complement to U.S. Industry Competitiveness?' *Information Technology and Innovation Foundation* (2019).

[148]《中华人民共和国药品管理法》[The Drug Administration Law of the People's Republic of China] (People's Republic of China) National People's Congress, 2019. https://gkml.samr.gov.cn/nsjg/fgs/201909/t20190917_306828.html

approvals.[149] Besides the Law, there are a number of Opinions and Notices which also regulate the Chinese Pharmaceutical jurisdiction.[150] For instance, an *Opinion on Deepening the Reform of Review and Approval System to Encourage Innovation on Drugs and Medical Devices* was issued by the General Office of the State Council in 2017.Notably, these policies have facilitated the development and utilisation of TMK information systems, such as the China Traditional Chinese Medicine Patent Database (CTCMPD), which are increasingly integral to the biopharmaceutical sector. These systems provide structured repositories of TMK, enabling more efficient identification of promising leads for drug development. By aligning TMK information systems with broader pharmaceutical reforms, China has ensured that traditional knowledge is systematically cataloged, safeguarded, and made accessible for responsible industrial application.

Additionally, several pilot programmes have been launched under these regulatory frameworks to further integrate TMK information systems into the R&D ecosystem.[151] For example, TMK databases allow pharmaceutical researchers to navigate complex traditional medicinal formulations, facilitating their transformation into modern biopharmaceutical products. These systems also help prevent the misappropriation of traditional knowledge by documenting it in a form that patent examiners and industry professionals can access, ensuring that innovations derived from TMK are appropriately recognised and protected.

These combined policies, guidelines, and regulations—while fostering innovation and market growth—have made TMK information systems a cornerstone of China's biopharmaceutical strategy. By improving the interface between traditional knowledge and modern drug development, these systems contribute significantly to the rise of China's domestic biopharmaceutical sector, enhancing both innovation capacity and the equitable utilisation of TMK.

Second, while the government policy and law reforms within China have largely improved the prospects for biopharmaceutical sector, it is the increased access to larger capital flows that have provided a catalyst for transformation and innovation of China's biopharmaceutical sector.[152] For instance, because most of the biopharmaceutical corporations have legitimate capital flow needs ahead of having a profitable pharmaceutical product, Hong Kong's stock exchange has changed its listing rules to allow for early-stage biopharmaceuticals, even pre-revenue firms, to access public capitals since 2018.[153] The Shanghai's STAR Market (the Science and Technology

---

[149] Ibid; Yueqiang Wang et al, 'A brief introduction to China's new Drug Administration Law and its impact on medications for rare diseases' (2019) 8(4) *Intractable Rare Dis Res.* 226–227.

[150] Andrea Sorgato, 'New Drug Administration Law—New Rules and Liabilities' *ICLG* (2020).

[151] Ibid.

[152] Robert D. Atkinson, 'Healthy Funding: The Critical Role of Investing in NIH to Boost Health and Lower Costs' *Information Technology and Innovation Foundation* (2019); James McBride and Andrew Chatzky, 'Is 'Made in China 2025' a Threat to Global Trade?' (2019) Backgrounder; L.E.K. Consulting, 'Innovation in China, "Made in China 2025" and Implications for Healthcare MNCs' (2018) *GPS Healthcare Quarterly.*

[153] Ellis, Shannon, 'Hong Kong stock exchange opens to biotechs' (2018) 36 *nature Biotechnology* 482.

Innovation Board) launched in late 2019 and Beijing Stock Exchange launched in 2021 are both targeting 'innovative companies', in which the biopharmaceutical sector is a major focus.[154] In addition to the increased access to the public capital markets, there is also an increasing number of available private capitals through venture and private equity (PE) funds to invest in biopharmaceutical research and development in China.[155] National and local government's grants and institutional fundings are also poured into venture capitals and PE firms to invest in biopharmaceutical innovation and development.[156] Nowadays, China has the second-highest funding in the world, preceded only by the US.[157] This influx of funding has significantly enhanced the prospects for biopharmaceutical innovation, providing resources to develop advanced technologies and tap into underexplored knowledge resources such as TMK.

Amid these developments, TMK information systems, such as the China Traditional Chinese Medicine Patent Database (CTCMPD), play a pivotal role in bridging traditional knowledge and biopharmaceutical innovation. These systems serve as centralised repositories that document and classify TMK, enabling researchers and innovators to identify valuable leads for drug development. By cataloging traditional remedies, formulations, and associated genetic resources, TMK information systems reduce the barriers to accessing this knowledge and allow firms to integrate TMK into the biopharmaceutical innovation process more efficiently.

Moreover, the enhanced availability of capital has prompted greater utilisation of TMK information systems in biopharmaceutical R&D. For example, venture capital and PE firms often look for projects with a clear pathway from traditional knowledge to commercially viable products. TMK information systems provide this critical linkage by offering a structured and scientifically validated database of traditional remedies, increasing the likelihood of success in drug discovery and reducing R&D costs.

As innovation and technology continue to advance, the integration of TMK information systems into the biopharmaceutical sector will only deepen. These systems not only facilitate the extraction of value from TMK but also serve as safeguards against its misappropriation, ensuring equitable benefit-sharing with traditional knowledge holders. TMK that may currently lack obvious applications could gain significant

---

[154] Lu, Lerong, 'Promoting High-Tech Innovations through Capital Markets Law Reform: Deciphering the Sci-Tech Innovation Board of the Shanghai Stock Exchange' (2020) 35 *Journal of International Banking and Financial Law* 140–143; Li, Jane, 'China's newest stock exchange follows Xi Jinping's cues for the economy', Quartz (2017) < https://qz.com/2089277/beijings-new-stock-exchange-shows-chinas-focus-on-the-real-economy/ >

[155] Lan Qiu, et al, 'Public Funding and Private Investment for R&D: a Survey in China's Pharmaceutical Industry' (2014) 12(27) *Health Research Policy and Systems* 1-11; Vicky Qing Xia, 'China Looks Inward and Outward: Investments in US and EU Biopharmaceutical Companies Are on the Rise', *Bioprocess International* (2019); John Wong et al, 'Competing in China's Booming Biopharma Market', *BCG* (2020). https://www.bcg.com/publications/2020/competing-in-chinas-biopharma-market.

[156] Ibid.

[157] John Wong et al, above 59, 2.

biopharmaceutical and commercial value through the systematic exploration and innovation supported by these information systems. This dual role of TMK information systems—catalysing innovation while ensuring ethical and sustainable utilisation—positions them as indispensable tools in the growth and evolution of China's biopharmaceutical sector.

6.3.5 Revival and Modernisation of TMK Practice

The growing integration of TMK information systems into the biopharmaceutical sector reflects a broader transformation in how traditional medicinal knowledge is perceived, utilised, and preserved in modern China. This shift is not limited to the industrial and technological realms but extends to the revival and modernisation of TMK practices within healthcare systems and everyday life. Many Chinese people grew up being exposed to traditional Chinese medicine. In their memories, the use of TMK is usually linked with elderly traditional healers practising in dusty old corners and stinky concoctions boiling up for hours.[158] While the potent potions and concoctions are still in use today, the outdated image has changed significantly. For instance, the requirements for becoming a traditional medicine practitioner have changed dramatically. The practitioners are currently required to be registered with a license to practice as Western doctors do.[159] Additionally, the medical environment has also made remarkable advances. According to official statistics, by 2019, there are 5232 hospitals designated as TMK specialty hospitals to provide traditional medicine services across China.[160] Most of these TMK specialty hospitals are equipped with high-end facilities, advanced equipment and top medical, scientific, and nursing staff.[161]

The modernisation of these services has been supported by the establishment of TMK information systems, such as the China Traditional Chinese Medicine Patent Database (CTCMPD). These systems ensure that traditional practices are documented, preserved, and accessible for research, thus providing practitioners with a robust foundation for maintaining traditional medical standards while incorporating modern technology. By offering comprehensive databases that categorise traditional

[158] Zanzanaini, Gabriella, 'Forgotten Hong Kong Icon: The Revival of Traditional Chinese Medicine', *Zolima City Mag* < https://zolimacitymag.com/forgotten-hong-kong-icon-the-revival-of-traditional-chinese-medicine/ > .

[159] Zhang Z.B and Yang J.S. 'Comparative Analysis of Jinxian dai licensing procedure and rules for TCM doctors' (2004) 23(6) *Education of Chinese Medicine (ECM)* 55–59; Judy Xu and Yue Yang, 'Traditional Chinese medicine in the Chinese health care system' (2009) 90(2) *Health Policy* 135.

[160] 《2019 年中医药事业发展统计提要报告》 [Statistical Summary Report on the Development of Traditional Chinese Medicine in 2019] (People's Republic of China) National Administration of Traditional Chinese Medicine, 2021 http://gcs.satcm.gov.cn/zhengcewenjian/2021-01-15/

[161] Ruiping Fan and Ian Holliday, 'Policies for Traditional Medicine in Peripheral China' (2006) 12(5) *Policies for Traditional Medicine in Peripheral China* 485.

knowledge into searchable formats, these systems have helped elevate the credibility and applicability of TMK in modern medical contexts.

As noted by Gabriella Zanzanaini, the application of China's TMK as a health care strategy has become 'the new trendy kid on the alternative medicine block'.[162] In recent years, there has been a global and national resurgence in the use of China's TMK for health care needs.[163] According to the statistics, from 2011 to 2019, the total number of consultations with TMK practitioners in China increased by 72%.[164] This dramatic increase over past eight years shows how TMK practice is gaining new strength as a serious option for health care needs in China. In addition, there is also an increasing use of TMK products as complementary and alternative medicine within Western nations. For instance, government surveys show that complementary and alternative medicines are used by more than half the people in Australia.[165] Almost 75% of healthy Australians over 70 years utilise complementary medicines either daily or occasionally.[166] Examples include acupuncture, aromatherapy, and traditional Chinese medicine. Similar findings have also been released in the US[167] and Great Britain.[168]

The challenges encountered by China's local pharmaceutical industry vary greatly depending on whether the emphasis is placed on traditional medicine or Western medicine. For TMK-oriented pharmaceutical companies, the primary challenge is balancing heritage preservation with industrialisation and modern scientific validation. These firms must invest heavily in documenting traditional practices, ensuring regulatory compliance, and safeguarding intellectual property associated with TMK. The market expects traditional medicine to retain its cultural authenticity while meeting the efficiency and safety standards of modern pharmaceuticals. Moreover, TMK firms must navigate public and governmental scrutiny regarding benefit-sharing

162 Zanzanaini, Gabriella, above n 100.

163 C.-T. Che et al, 'Traditional Medicine' in Rupika Delgoda (ed), *Pharmacognosy: Fundamentals, Applications and Strategies* (2017) 15, 19.

164 《2019 年中医药事业发展统计提要报告》[Statistical Summary Report on the Development of Traditional Chinese Medicine in 2019] (People's Republic of China) National Administration of Traditional Chinese Medicine, 2021 http://gcs.satcm.gov.cn/zhengcewenjian/2021-01-15/; 《中国卫生和计划生育统计年鉴》2017[China Health and Family Planning Statistical Yearbook 2017] (People's Republic of China) China Health and Family Planning Commission, 2017;《中国卫生健康统计年鉴》[China Health Statistics Yearbook 2019] (People's Republic of China) National Health Commission of the PRC, 2019; 《中国卫生统计年鉴》[China Health Statistics Yearbook 2011] (People's Republic of China) The Ministry of Health of the PRC, 2011.

165 Complementary Medicines Australia. Australia's Complementary Medicines Industry Audit 2019. http://www.cmaustralia.org.au/resources/CMA-INDUSTRY_AUDIT-V4.pdf.

166 Aimee Lefevre et al, 'Complementary medicine use by community-dwelling older Australians' (2021) 214(3) *The Medical Journal of Australia* 140–141.

167 Sissi Wachtel-Galor and Iris F. F. Benzie, 'Herbal Medicine: An Introduction to Its History, Usage, Regulation, Current Trends, and Research Needs' in Benzie IFF and Wachtel-Galor S (ed), *Herbal Medicine: Biomolecular and Clinical Aspects* (2011); Barnes P. M, et al, 'Complementary and alternative medicine use among adults and children: United States' (2008) 10 CDC National Health Statistics Report 12. http://www.cdc.gov/nchs/data/nhsr/nhsr012.pdf.

168 'CAM research in Britain: The last 10 years', (2005) 11 *Complement Ther Clin Pract* 17–20.

and ethical sourcing of traditional knowledge, especially given the role of local communities in preserving this heritage.

In contrast, pharmaceutical companies focused on Western medicine face pressures to continuously innovate in molecular and genetic research, maintain high R&D expenditures, and adhere to global regulatory frameworks such as Good Manufacturing Practices (GMP) and FDA-equivalent standards. These firms often face intense competition from multinational corporations, requiring them to integrate advanced technologies like artificial intelligence for drug discovery and comply with international intellectual property norms. Additionally, the competition between traditional and Western pharmaceutical sectors creates overlapping pressures, as TMK-based companies increasingly adopt modern technologies and Western firms look to traditional knowledge for bioactive compound discovery. These contrasting priorities have resulted in distinct operational models, resource allocations, and market strategies within China's pharmaceutical landscape.

Foreign pharmaceutical companies operating in China face additional challenges, primarily stemming from regulatory hurdles, market localisation, and competition from rapidly advancing local firms. As China transitions from being a manufacturer of APIs to an R&D hub, foreign companies are under pressure to adapt to the domestic market's needs, regulatory landscape, and technological developments. This includes navigating compliance with the National Medical Products Administration (NMPA), China's drug approval agency, and adapting to China's increasingly complex regulatory framework. Moreover, foreign companies often face local competition from Chinese firms that are rapidly advancing in both R&D and market penetration, particularly in sectors like biotechnology and artificial intelligence-driven drug discovery.

Foreign pharmaceutical giants, however, often collaborate with local companies to ease market entry and leverage local expertise. For example, multinationals such as Pfizer, AstraZeneca, and Novartis have formed partnerships with Chinese pharmaceutical firms to co-develop drugs and conduct clinical trials locally. These collaborations allow foreign firms to benefit from China's robust healthcare market and its increasing investment in R&D. These partnerships also enable foreign firms to navigate regulatory processes more smoothly, gain insights into local healthcare needs, and foster goodwill with local communities and governments.

Yet, competition remains fierce, particularly in the intellectual property space, as foreign companies must contend with local companies that are now more adept at protecting and leveraging their own innovations. Notably, China's increasing push for IP protection, especially in biopharmaceuticals, has prompted both local and foreign companies to engage in patent filings at unprecedented rates. Local companies such as Yunnan Baiyao and CR Sanjiu, for instance, have successfully modernised traditional medicine and expanded their global footprint, creating significant competition for foreign players.

These collaborations and competitive dynamics influence China's IP policies and the development of both TMK and Western pharmaceuticals. The Chinese government has taken steps to strengthen IP protections, which has created a more favourable environment for R&D collaborations. However, there are also concerns regarding technology transfers, particularly with respect to traditional knowledge. The commercialisation of bioactive compounds from Chinese herbal medicine, for instance, has sparked debates over the ethical use of traditional knowledge and the equitable distribution of benefits, especially when foreign firms are involved.

The interaction between local and foreign pharmaceutical companies in China has thus created a dynamic environment, where the pressures and strategies vary widely depending on whether companies are focused on traditional medicine or non-traditional pharmaceuticals. Local companies engaged in TMK must navigate the delicate balance between modernisation and cultural preservation, while Western pharmaceutical firms face regulatory and competitive pressures in a rapidly evolving market. These dynamics are reshaping China's pharmaceutical landscape, influencing both the development of TMK and Western pharmaceuticals and driving a more competitive and innovative sector.

The revival of TMK practice in contemporary societies is inextricably associated with the question of how to understand the juxtaposition of tradition and modernity. In former times, it was a custom for the Chinese people living within the extended families or local communities to use the medicinal items and herbal remedies in their households.[169] With bare hands and nails, the medicinal plants were collected, the undesirable parts were singled out and separated and herbs were grinded, crushed, and rubbed to make a fine powder.[170] After the medicinal materials have been collected, separated, and cut, the substances need to be prepared before use. This traditional preparation technique is known as, *pao zhi* in Chinese, which includes various production processes with basic tools and that are based on manual skills such as dry-frying (*chao*), steaming (*shu*), calcining (*duan*), roasting (*wei*), scorching (*jiao*), and charring (*tan*).[171]

The introduction of TMK information systems has further enhanced these traditional practices. By documenting and standardising the **pao zhi** techniques and their corresponding empirical rules, these systems ensure that the heritage of TMK preparation methods is preserved while being adapted for modern healthcare and pharmaceutical production. The inclusion of detailed, scientifically validated records within these databases also enables the seamless integration of these techniques into industrial-scale methods.

With the advancement of technology, these traditional processes have been replaced by mass production and industrial-scale methods such as the use of modern machines. For instance, the extraction process for making fluid and solid extracts

[169] 'Healing and Medicine: Healing and Medicine in China' *Encyclopedia.com,* (Web Page) https://www.encyclopedia.com/environment/encyclopedias-almanacs-transcripts-and-maps/healing-and-medicine-healing-and-medicine.

[170] Ong, Jean Ho and Poh Hong, 'Traditional Chinese Medicine in Dermatology' in Nanette B. Silverberg et al (ed), *Pediatric Skin of Color* (2015) 430; John D. Keys, *Chinese Herbs: Their Botany, Chemistry and Pharmacodynamics* (1989)12.

[171] Brand, Eric, 'The Clinical Importance of 'Pao Zhi'- Medicinal Processing ' (2016) *The Register of Chinese Herbal Medicine Journal* 22-25; 'What Is Herbal Processing and Why Is It Important?' *Urban Herbs*, (Web Page) https://urbanherbsco.com/pages/herbal-processing-pao-zhi.

of herbal plants has been technologically upgraded.[172] Both ultrasonic extraction devices and microwave-assisted extraction devices have now been used to enhance extraction efficiency.[173] The production line, designed to ensure a steady supply and effective utilisation of raw materials and generate continuous output, is now furnished with an automatic control system and monitoring devices to carry out online monitoring of the key processes.[174] The packaging process normally includes the use of seals and labelling information relating to the name of the active ingredients, dosages, quantities, and batch numbers.[175] To ensure quality control, more sophisticated producers usually use the tools such as pH meters and various spectrometers.[176] Some traditional therapy clinics also use modern diagnostic technologies. Nevertheless, despite all the modern technologies available, many elements discernible as 'traditional' are still retained. For instance, the so-called 'combinatorial formula rules' following empirical rules of the traditions are still fundamental for medicine production and innovation.[177] As is well known, most of the traditional use of TMK in China is based on mono- and multi-herbal combinations.[178] The 'combinatorial formula rules' presuppose that each herb plays a different role during treatment and multi-herbal combinations could exhibit synergistic efficiency based on multi-target mechanisms of action.[179]

TMK information systems are instrumental in maintaining the integrity of these traditional empirical rules while enabling their refinement and adaptation. By systematically categorising and documenting the traditional combinatorial formula rules, these systems support researchers and practitioners in applying these methods to contemporary treatment protocols and new drug development.

[172] Handa, Sukhdev Swami, 'Extraction Technologies for Medicinal and Aromatic Plants' in SS Handa et al (ed), Extraction Technologies for Medicinal and Aromatic Plants (2008) 21–54; Fermeglia, M., 'Role of Process Simulation in Extraction Technologies for Medicinal and Aromatic Plants' in SS Handa et al (ed), Extraction Technologies for Medicinal and Aromatic Plants (2008) 55–66.

[173] Qing-Wen Zhang et al, 'Techniques for extraction and isolation of natural products: a comprehensive review' (2018) 13(30) *Chinese Medicine* 8–9; LI Gong-ke et al, 'Application of Microwave-assisted Extraction in the Modernization of Chinese Traditional Medicine' (2007) *Fine Chemicals*.

[174] Zhang Huimei, 'Present Situation and Ways of Technical Upgrading of Traditional Chinese Medicine Pharmaceutical Equipment' (Conference Paper, International Conference on Biology, Chemistry and Medical Engineering, 2019)110–111.

[175] 'Requirements for the name of the active ingredients' *Chinese Medicine Council of Hong Kong*, (Web Page) https://www.cmchk.org.hk/pcm/eng/main_faq05l.htm.

[176] Xiangwei ma, et al, 'A Bioassay-Based Approach for the Batch-To-Batch Consistency Evaluation of Xuesaitong Injection on a Zebrafish Thrombosis Model' (2021) 12 *Frontiers in Pharmacology* 1–10.

[177] Dinis, S, 'Integrative Pharmacology–Interconnecting the World of Ayurveda (Traditional Indian Medicine-TIM), Traditional Chinese Medicine (TCM), and Conventional Medicine (CM)' in Anne et al George (ed), *Holistic healthcare: possibilities and challenges* (2017) 74.

[178] Xian Zhou et al, 'Synergistic Effects of Chinese Herbal Medicine: A Comprehensive Review of Methodology and Current Research' (2016) 7 *Frontiers in Pharmacology* 1–2.

[179] Dinis, S, above 74.

This intermingling of modern technology and tradition has now become a common occurrence in China.[180] Nevertheless, this situation will unavoidably increase the use of TMK outside the confines of traditional cultures as well as beyond the traditional geographical regions.

Over the past decades, China has purposively made efforts to develop its traditional medicine industry with the intention of promoting its TMK heritage and optimising the cost-efficacy in health care delivery to its people.[181] The development of China's traditional medicine industry is a typical example of a mix of modernity and tradition. This is because, despite its traditional nature, China's traditional medicine industry is increasingly regarded as one with modern industrial features and high technology content.[182] According to the industrial classification by *the China Pharmaceutical Yearbook*, China's traditional medicine industry encompasses various sectors including harvesting, cultivating, processing, production, research, and other economic activities based on traditional medical theories and with the assistance of modern technology.[183] This situation indicates that both tradition and modernity form the basis of the industry.

In this context, TMK information systems, such as the CTCMPD, have played a critical role in bridging traditional knowledge and industrial practices. By providing comprehensive documentation of traditional medical theories and their applications, these systems enable traditional medicine companies to remain competitive in a market that increasingly values both scientific validation and cultural authenticity.

Most of the small and medium-sized traditional medicine companies in China have to compete, not only with the companies within the traditional pharmaceutical category but also with the emerging modern biopharmaceuticals. Unlike biopharmaceutical innovation relying on molecular research, China's traditional medicine industry adheres to its traditional trajectory and extensive empirical observations.[184] It predominantly focuses on the production of classical and traditional medical products (based on traditional herbal formulations) and other novel proprietary products despite not rejecting the modern technology. Its innovative strategies include creative

---

[180] Wang Wen-jian and Zhang Teng, 'Integration of traditional Chinese medicine and Western medicine in the era of precision medicine' (2017) 15(1) *Journal of integrative medicine* 1–7; Xu Hao and Chen ke-ji, 'Integrating traditional Medicine with Biomedicine towards a Patient-Centered Healthcare System' (2011) 17(2) *Chin J Integr Med* 83–84; Weeks, John, 'Chinese TCM Renaissance and the Global Movement for Integrative Health and Medicine' (2017) 23(2) THE JOURNAL OF ALTERNATIVE AND COMPLEMENTARY MEDICINE 79–81.

[181] Payyappallimana, Unnikrishnan, 'Role of Traditional Medicine in Primary Health Care: An Overview of Perspectives and Challenges' 14(6) *Yokohama Journal of Social Sciences* 62.

[182] Su,Yi et al, Research on Industrial Organization of Chinese Medicine Based on SCP Paradgm' (Conference Paper, International Conference on Management Science & Engineering 21th Annual Conference Proceedings, June 2018)751–758.

[183] 彭司勋[Peng sixun], 2017年中国药学年鉴 [the China Pharmaceutical Yearbook in 2017] (2017) (33); Marco R. Tommaso et al, 'The Chinese TCM Industry: Growth, Changes, and Policies' in Attilio Mucelli and Francesca Spigarelli (ed), *Healthcare Policies and Systems in Europe And China: Comparisons And Synergies* (2018) 38–40.

[184] Yu Huatao and Zhang Yang, 'The Yin and Yang of traditional Chinese and Western medicine' (2021) 41(6) *Medicinal Research Reviews* 2–3.

reformulations through additive and accumulative innovations that may give rise to new products or novel processes or entirely new forms of the old product, which may serve as a substitute to the old ones.[185] This situation makes China's traditional medicine industry vastly different from biopharmaceuticals in terms of innovation and access to knowledge and resources.

Moreover, the innovation and development of China's traditional medicine industry are to a great extent anchored on the increased use of TMK held or owned by the local communities.[186] The increasing use of TMK can be further fuelled by a global and national resurgence in the use of China's TMK for health care needs. Such knowledge might be oral, codified, or in other forms.

TMK information systems ensure that codified knowledge is preserved and accessible while addressing the challenge of documenting and protecting orally transmitted knowledge. These systems play a vital role in ensuring that the rights and contributions of local communities are recognised, thereby supporting ethical and equitable utilisation practices.

Nevertheless, there are concerns that the increased use of TMK may increase the risks relevant to the misappropriation of that knowledge, threats to the livelihood of the local communities, and an undermining of cultural belief.[187] For instance, some type of TMK inherent to a local community is generally used without an understanding of values and ethical principles attached to it and, more critically, without due recognition to their customs, tradition, legal rights, and benefits of varied kinds.[188] This situation may lead to the possible tension between the forces in favour of the protection of TMK as collective heritages held by the local communities and the forces which are interested in the use and appropriation of TMK for commercial purposes.

TMK information systems, if designed with inclusive and community-centric frameworks, have the potential to mediate these tensions. By incorporating mechanisms for benefit-sharing, ethical use, and community participation, these systems can act as safeguards against the exploitation of TMK while promoting its sustainable integration into modern industries.

---

185 李文红[Li Wenhong], 以莲花清瘟方为例探讨中药复方的创新及专利布局策略[Taking Lianhua Qingwen Recipe as an Example to Discuss the Innovation and Patent Layout Strategy of Traditional Chinese Medicine Formulations](2021)46(5), 中国中药杂志Chinese Journal of Traditional Chinese Medicine 1293–1300.

186 Zhiyong Li et al,'Policies and Problems of Modernizing Ethnomedicine in China: A Focus on the Yi and Dai Traditional Medicines of Yunnan Province' (2020) *Evidence-Based Complementary and Alternative Medicine* 7; D. shaw, 'Toxicological risks of Chinese herbs' (2010) 76(17) *Planta Medica* 2012–2018, 2010; Zhaoyun Zhu et al, 'Innovative development path of ethnomedicines: an overview of ethnomedicines in China' (2016) 10 *Frontiers of Medicine* 166–177.

187 Krystyna Swiderska, *Protecting Community Rights over Traditional Knowledge: Implications of Customary Laws and Practices* (Report, 2021) 9–10.

188 Ibid.

6.4 Towards a New Strategy for the TMK Information Systems

As argued in this chapter, influenced by China's historical constraints, the country's existing TMK information systems (such as the CTCMPD) are largely a political body, predominantly concerned with social, economic, and political aims. Typically, what van der Velden calls a 'cognitive injustice'[189] is embedded in China's TMK information system that primarily serves the interests of the State, and this bias is further strengthened by its selective emphasis on the socially elite type of TMK practice at the expense of others. On this basis, although China's TMK information systems (particularly, the CTCMPD) are often articulated as a protection of China's national heritage against foreign exploitation, they are fundamentally dictated by the motivation to limit the protection of 'subaltern TMK' and its knowledge holders, and to help the Chinese authorities utilise generations of TMK from various ethnic and local communities to serve the national purpose.

Against this situation, the underlying issue is how China should devise a new strategy for not only constructing, but also implementing, managing, and utilising information systems that support the protection of various tiers and discrete forms of TMK and its knowledge holders. This strategy should simultaneously promote the dynamic and culturally embedded utilisation of this knowledge, acknowledging its deep social and cultural significance. Before addressing this question, it is necessary to first investigate the role of technology. The analysis in the former section has created the impression that China's TMK information systems could contribute to preserving and protecting TMK and related knowledge holders, even if the protection may risk being co-opted to serve other purposes. While some of the characteristics can be preserved by current information systems, the existing technology design is arguably rooted in a different epistemology and value system than the ones from which China's TMK originates. As noted by Agrawal, the currently available TMK information systems in the world (including China's CTCMPD) are primarily based on an instrumentalist logic of technological development,[190] which normally considers technology and information systems as 'a narrow technical rationality, uncreative and devoid of values'.[191] This approach typically demonstrates less interest in the broader social, cultural, and historical factors that affect the production of knowledge. Instead, it promotes homogenising processes where knowledge is particularised (separated into types and fixed in time), validated (abstracted from context), and generalised (catalogued, documented, and circulated).[192]

[189] Maja van der Velden, 'Programming for Cognitive Justice: Towards an Ethical Framework for Democratic Code' (2005) 17 *Interacting with Computers* 105, 105–120.

[190] Arun Agrawal, 'Indigenous Knowledge and the Politics of Classification' (2002) 54 *International Social Science Journal* 173, 287–297.

[191] Jon Agar, 'What is Technology?' (2020) 77(3) *Annals of Science* 377, 380.

[192] Ibid 137.

It is also worth noting that this instrumentalist and homogenising logic on which the TMK information systems are based corresponds to China's distantly past historical practices of homogenising or assimilating the plurality and multiplicity of TMK for national interests.[193] On this basis, China's TMK information systems in itself include a sense of belonging to a historical continuum, which has been historically faulty, assimilating and even stripping away the detailed, contextual, and cultural aspects of TMK that are significant characteristics for its traditional custodians. To overcome these limitations, it is necessary to design new information systems in China that consciously focus on historical context, processes, and environmental variables that affect the use of new technologies. More significantly, in order to 'keep the relational, performative, and dynamic characteristics of TMK'[194] alive in the new design, the new system should reject the 'divorce of technology from the essence of art',[195] and should view the adoption of technology as an outgrowth of a broad spectrum of social and historical trends, and human factors.

To tackle the cognitive injustice, present in China's current TMK information systems and better protect and preserve the diverse forms of TMK, a new approach that emphasises historical context, cultural significance, and knowledge locality is necessary. This involves differentiating between two crucial aspects: knowledge dissemination and protection. In terms of the protection of TMK, Suchman introduced an approach called 'design-from-somewhere' in technology design for knowledge management[196] that is based on Haraway's proposals for grounding knowledge by accounting for how it is locally and historically contingent.[197] Suchman specifically argued that the design practices for knowledge management should be situated, located somewhere, and connected with social and historical conditions.[198] This means that the design processes should no longer be considered as set procedures simply to be implemented but as guidelines that can be continually adjusted according to the context and situation at hand.[199] The far-reaching implication of this proposal is that the designers should not only see themselves as actors in practices with a broad range of experiences and knowledge but should also be aware that their own ideas are created from 'somewhere'. Accordingly, the design process for constructing the TMK information systems in China should focus on how designers construct and interpret the context to make designs fit into, or stretch, the concrete situations.

---

[193] See discussion in Sect. 3.3.

[194] Maja Van der Velden, 'Design for the Contact Zone: Knowledge Management Software and the Structures of Indigenous Knowledges' in F Sudweeks (ed), *Cultural Attitudes Towards Technology and Communication* (Murdoch University, 2010) 1.

[195] Sarah Menin, 'Fragments from the Forest: Aalto's Requisitioning of Forest Place and Matter' (2001) 6(3) *The Journal of Architecture* 279, 279.

[196] L Suchman, 'Located Accountabilities in Technology Production' (2002) 14(2) *Scandinavian Journal of Information Systems*, 91, 91–105.

[197] Donna Haraway, 'Situated Knowledges: The Science Question in Feminism and the Privilege of Partial Perspective' (1988) 14(3) *Feminist Studies* 575, 575–599.

[198] Suchman (n 141) 91–105.

[199] Jesper Simonsen et al, *Situated Methods in Design* (MIT Press, 2014) 1, 5.

Suchman's 'design-from-somewhere' approach can be applied to the design process of constructing TMK information systems in China.[200] By examining the country's historical context, this study seeks to find an archetype for this approach in the Confucius academies.[201] These academies served as repositories of knowledge and sources of literature, with their unique characteristics deeply embedded in the local context. For instance, the Yuelu Academy was established through cooperation between the local prefect and the local elite, integrating itself into the lives of both academic elites and commoners.[202]

In this historical context, Confucius academies can be seen as examples of situated and located knowledge management systems, where intellectual discourses and talented scholars interacted with the unique local environment and culture. They offer a broad spectrum of possibilities to document and access knowledge, not as isolated entities, but as dynamic organisms in their multiple intellectual, cultural, and social interactions.

This historical example can serve as inspiration for reforming the design process of the TMK information systems in China. By incorporating the 'design-from-somewhere' approach, designers can ensure that the design of knowledge management systems is grounded in the local and historical context, just as Confucius academies were. This means that designers should not only consider set procedures but also continually adjust their design strategies according to the specific context and situation at hand. By doing so, they will create knowledge management systems that are more attuned to the unique needs, traditions, and customs of the communities they serve.

To establish the historical continuities connecting the present with an ancient past, the information systems design and development process should first make it possible to create a system where various types of traditional, contextual, and situated medical knowledge can be well managed without being decontextualised from their original contexts. One typical measure is to inscribe the communities' own cultural terms and local protocols into the information systems design. In any and all cases, the key to this measure is to make the cultural and communities' protocols within the information system adaptable, flexible, and changeable over time, according to the needs of the various knowledge holders and related communities. If a community has traditional access requirements that restrict access to certain types of TMK to one gender or to individuals having a particular status within the community, or if some form of TMK should only be utilised in particular festivals or seasons, cultural, and communities' protocols could be customised to determine various levels of access to, and circulation of, their TMK within the information system. For instance, a first-time user of the information systems normally uploads a login-based profile to create an account. Based on the nature of the profile, the cultural and communities' protocol functions associated with gender, community status, and a person's individual status

200 Suchman (n 141) 91–105.

201 Hoyt Cleveland Tillman, 'Some Reflections on Confucian Academies in China' in Vladimir Glomb et al (eds), *Confucian Academies in East Asia* (Brill, 2020) 21, 25.

202 Ibid.

could be applied in practice to allow the knowledge holders to 'lock' their TMK or to apply a 'request access function' to suit their own cultural tradition and guidelines.

Another measure in a 'design-from-somewhere' context is to develop a TMK classification scheme in the information systems that can better reflect various knowledge holders' and communities' ways of knowing the world. The current classification system adopted in China's CTCMPD (and other TMK information systems) is based on international standard classification schemes such as the *International Patent Classification* ('IPC') system,[203] which has arguably documented cultural biases towards the scientific classification of knowledge. These biases typically concern the ways in which knowledge holders and communities are represented within the classification scheme. However, it particularly lacks concepts and subject terms concerning the knowledge holders' and communities' worldviews, epistemology, and realities.[204]

In addition, the typical imposition of universality on the language (Mandarin Chinese) used within China's TMK information systems and its classification schemes could further lead to unfavourable representations of the epistemic complexity and diverse ways of knowing the world, particularly knowledge holders' and communities' ways of thought. On this basis, it is necessary to design a new classification system within China's TMK information systems that represents 'cognitive justice', where the TMK is not decontextualised from living and everyday culture but represents an ecosystem where diverse forms of TMK have their places. For instance, since the classification scheme is supposed to be applied in various cultural and community contexts reflecting diverse ways of knowing the world, the default settings of the classification system can be adapted to meet the particular needs of the knowledge holders, their local communities, and organisations. Closely related to this is the need for the classification schemes to correctly incorporate various local and communities' languages because language inherently carries the worldview and epistemology of different linguistic groups and cultures and varies from place to place.

In response to these potential limitations, Chapter 3 of this book offered an innovative resolution through the proposition of a tiered approach to protect Chinese TMK. This approach thoughtfully creates a culturally sensitive categorisation of TMK, effectively classifying it into four distinct classes: secret TMK; TMK closely held by ethnic and local communities; TMK collectively held by national communities; and 'widely diffused TMK that eventually becomes part of the global stock of knowledge'.

---

[203] *Special Union for the International Patent Classification (IPC Union),* WIPO Doc. IPC/CE/31/6 (18 February 2002) 2: 'Chinese delegates describes in detail an internal classification scheme for traditional medicine elaborated by the Chinese Intellectual Property Office (SIPO). An extract of this scheme, representing further extension of the IPC and based on taxonomic names, is shown in Appendix III to this report. In order to facilitate the use of botanical classification, an IPC Classification Database for TCM has been established by SIPO and made available through the Patent Literature Database'.

[204] CK Maina, 'Traditional Knowledge Management and Preservation: Intersections with Library and Information Science' (2012) 44 *The International Information & Library Review* 13, 19.

Each category is based on the way the knowledge is traditionally held, shared, and diffused and, accordingly, is assigned a distinct level of protection and rights. This setup presents a more refined and culturally sensitive stratification of TMK, challenging the existing uniformity of the IPC-based system.

This novel framework could enrich the current TMK classification system used within information systems. It focuses on integrating a comprehensive collection of diverse knowledge-sharing traditions and practices. Such an integration markedly amplifies the depth and breadth of these systems, transitioning them into more sophisticated, culturally resonant hubs of information. This evolution represents a 'design-from-context' approach, enabling information systems to be exceptionally adaptive and responsive. Consequently, these systems become adept at reflecting the dynamic and evolving nature of Chinese TMK, effectively mirroring its rich, multifaceted character.

In addition, the design of the new TMK information systems in China should not merely emphasise the protection of TMK and its knowledge holders; it also needs to be re-oriented simultaneously to facilitate the communication, dissemination, and utilisation of the TMK. To promote this objective, the design process should make it possible to create a space which enables the continuous communication and negotiation of differences and, in the end, best expresses the visions, intentions, and needs of both users and providers. Pratt described this space as the 'contact zone', in which different ontologies, expectations, needs, and understandings of autonomy and privacy could collide and mix in a cognitively just manner.[205] On this basis, to allow China's TMK information systems to perform as a contact zone, a new framework is required for creating sociotechnical spaces that enable collaborations on, and exchanges of, ideas for protecting and sharing TMK. One potential approach is to transform the TMK information systems from a static knowledge container into an open and flexible authoring tool. By doing so, users could engage with others in generating, organising, and sharing diverse forms of content related to TMK through the use of social computing tools, such as commenting systems and tagging services.[206] This approach would allow for more dynamic and interactive engagement with the information systems, promoting the free flow of ideas while providing a platform for cooperative learning and knowledge creation.

This authoring tool approach would offer numerous benefits, allowing every aspect of the information system to be open for discussion, contribution, and change. Users, including knowledge holders and communities, as well as knowledge-collecting institutions, could jointly determine access parameters, customise cultural and sharing protocols, and upload TMK-related content and metadata to the information systems. As a result, this new information systems design would become closer to Pratt's concept of a contact zone, allowing information systems users to create

[205] Mary Louise Pratt, 'Arts of the Contact Zone' in Vivian Zamel and Ruth Spack (eds), *Negotiating Academic Literacies* (Routledge, 1998) 316–341.

[206] Maja Van der Velden, 'When Knowledge Meet Wikipedia and Other Stories from the Contact Zone' in Geert Lovink and Nathaniel Tkacz (eds), *Critical Point of View: A Wikipedia Reader* (Institute of Network Cultures, 2011) 236, 254.

their own interfaces and trajectories and enabling collaborative design to take place among individual and community users.[207] In essence, this approach would facilitate a more inclusive and participatory process of knowledge creation and sharing, while promoting mutual respect and understanding among different stakeholders. What this essentially implies is that it would mitigate the potential for inadvertent misappropriation of knowledge by those external to the context, who might lack the cultural understanding inherent to that knowledge. By leveraging social computing tools and collaborative design, this authoring tool approach would enable the TMK information systems to evolve into a living and growing repository of knowledge, benefiting not only its users but also the wider community.

To take a step further, envisioning the TMK information systems as a contact zone prompts consideration of transforming the information systems into a nationally distributed system. Within this system, diverse forms of TMK, even those seemingly incompatible, could coexist and remain active. This structure would allow both users and providers of TMK to engage in dialogues concerning knowledge management, fostering a dynamic and collaborative environment for TMK's preservation and utilisation.

In this system, TMK would be shared and disseminated across communities, organisations, and networks independently, without a centralised information system. In contrast, the national distributed system would consist of various small information systems and independent hubs (including various local communities, organisations, and individuals with or without internet access) that aim to provide the knowledge holders and seekers with a decentralised national structure to share TMK through the existing or newly established, locally based organisations and networks. Through this system, the users and providers of TMK could not only publish or access it via the Internet but also through a variety of other technologies and media to communicate with each other.

In applying this system, the PIC and MAT principles must also be well accounted for. To incorporate them into this decentralised system, each system or hub would need to have robust mechanisms for obtaining and recording consent. For instance, digital consent forms could be adopted as a standardised method of recording consent. This format could offer advantages such as clear, easy-to-understand language and the ability to reach remote contributors. In cases where digital forms may not be viable or culturally appropriate, alternatives like recorded verbal consents could be employed. These could be especially valuable for communities where oral traditions dominate. In enhancing the reliability of the existing consent capture methods, it might be beneficial to incorporate a secondary confirmation during data entry. This could necessitate the involvement of either a designated community representative or an authorised legal entity, tasked with the responsibility of validating the consent. This additional check would aim to bolster the robustness of the consent process, further ensuring its integrity and accuracy.

The implementation of rigorous measures for the verification, documentation, and acknowledgement of the original sources of TMK in publications would also be

[207] Ibid.

crucial in this distributed system. This would ensure the precise documentation and rightful crediting of knowledge to its original custodians, thereby maintaining the integrity and authenticity of the TMK shared within the information system. These measures could include adopting digital tools for authentication, such as blockchain technologies which can provide a secure and transparent means for tracking the trajectory of knowledge from its source to its end-users. Additionally, the adoption of culturally sensitive validation methods, such as direct engagement with the knowledge holders or community leaders, could also enhance the accuracy and reliability of source documentation.

As this information systems design is concerned with context and interconnections, it is beneficial to perceive the TMK information systems as perpetually adaptable and 'never completed once and for all'.[208] On this basis, one would expect to make several cycles of design (together with the knowledge holders and users) to make this system open to adaptation and capable of responding to evolving technology and evolution in the knowledge holders' and communities' own cultural practices.

Of utmost significance is the consistent application of the PIC and MAT principles in this evolving process. Each design iteration should engage knowledge holders, not just as informants, but as active participants and decision-makers, ensuring that they give their informed consent before any use or publication of the knowledge they hold.

Moreover, the associated legal and policy frameworks should evolve correspondingly to uphold various types of TMK safeguarded within the system. These frameworks should foster transparency for knowledge users, while implementing robust access control measures. A cornerstone of these frameworks should be the commitment to consistently and appropriately recognise the origins of the TMK and the significant contributions of the knowledge holders in all publications within the information systems. This would involve not only acknowledging these sources but also respecting the traditions and cultural contexts from which they originate.

By incorporating these enhancements, China's TMK information systems have the potential to transform into a pioneering standard for the management of TMK. This transition could provide substantial benefits in terms of safeguarding, preserving, and disseminating this unique body of knowledge. Embracing a model that is more inclusive, collaborative, and culturally sensitive can further heighten understanding, appreciation, and application of TMK, fostering its influence and significance, not just within China's boundaries, but also on a global scale.

One of the key aspects of this transformation involves acknowledging historical continuities, integrating local protocols, embedding cultural practices, and accommodating community-specific needs within the TMK information systems. This would

[208] Bjorg Elsa Pettersen, 'Mind the Digital Gap: Questions and Possible Solutions for Design of Databases and Information Systems for Sami Traditional Knowledge' in J Porsanger and G Guttorm (eds), *Working with Traditional Knowledge: Communities, Institutions, Information Systems, Law and Ethics* (Sami University College, 2011) 163, 185.

allow the system to be more responsive to the myriad ways in which TMK is interpreted, practised, and transmitted. By increasing the cultural sensitivity of the system, the TMK information systems would better represent the diverse medical practices and knowledge systems across China. This representation could consequently guide more precise policy-making and efficient resource allocation within the TMK sphere.

Another significant change includes evolving the TMK information systems into an open, adaptive authoring tool, capable of facilitating broader communication, dissemination, and application of TMK. By harnessing social computing tools and collaborative design principles, the information systems could transform into a dynamic knowledge repository, encouraging cooperative learning, knowledge creation, and exchange. This would not only be advantageous for its direct users, but also for the wider community by creating an interactive platform for engaging with, and endorsing, traditional medicine.

Lastly, the proposition of a national distributed system suggests a decentralised, adaptable framework for sharing and managing TMK across a range of local communities, organisations, and networks. This approach respects the sovereignty and diversity of knowledge holders and communities, while simultaneously promoting dialogue around knowledge management. By focusing on context and interconnections, the information systems would remain agile, able to respond to changing technologies and cultural practices, ensuring its sustainable development and relevance.

In essence, the restructuring of the TMK information systems could lead to a transformative overhaul of the existing system. By addressing current limitations and fostering an environment that is more inclusive, collaborative, and culturally attuned, this transformative approach could serve as a promising paradigm in linking IP rights and ABS frameworks. For instance, by consistently applying the principles of PIC and MAT, the TMK information systems would ensure that IP rights are safeguarded, and ABS mechanisms are transparently and effectively implemented. In this context, the TMK information systems would not merely be a repository of knowledge but would serve as an evolving bridge between IP and ABS frameworks.

6.5 Conclusion

This chapter examined the complexities of reconciling Chinese TMK with the existing TMK information systems. It evaluated approaches for sufficient protection, proper use, and suitable distribution of Chinese TMK, while carefully considering the cultural and historical nuances.

This chapter navigated the intricate interconnections between China's unique TMK repository and the evolution of TMK information systems within the nation. This exploration revealed an undeniable intertwining of these elements with the historical fabric of China, embodying both the imposing force of State control and the tenacious resilience of TMK, which has managed to persist even in the face of systematic efforts aimed at its erasure. The narrative brought to light the complex and multifaceted factors that have influenced, and continue to influence, the management and representation of TMK in China's digital age.

The analysis highlighted the strategic use and documentation of Chinese TMK throughout history for political purposes, reinforcing State power and fostering ideological alignment. However, despite these dynamics, the richness and adaptability of TMK have been sustained by the ethnic diversity of the Chinese nation. This chapter particularly underscored the complex interactions between Han-dominated TMK and diverse localised knowledge systems. This interplay, which has evolved from coercion to persuasion over time, contributes to the richness and complexity of China's TMK information systems.

This chapter examined the establishment and development of the China Traditional Chinese Medicine Patent Database ('CTCMPD') and other TMK information systems that represent significant strides towards digitising, preserving, and protecting Chinese TMK. However, it found that this development is not without its shortcomings. Potential political interference, misuse, ethnocentric bias, and decontextualisation of TMK all pose substantial challenges. It was suggested that these issues necessitate future initiatives to address biases, political influences, and the potential alienation of TMK from its original holders, to ensure that the information systems evolve to become more inclusive, representative, culturally aware, and respectful towards the original contexts and custodians of TMK.

The transformative potential of reconceptualising the TMK information system could offer a compelling vision for the future. By transforming the TMK information systems into an open, adaptive authoring tool and a contact zone for dynamic engagement, this new approach would respect the sovereignty and diversity of knowledge holders and support localised knowledge sharing.

By striving to overcome current limitations, the new approach would support a more inclusive, collaborative, and culturally sensitive environment. The proposed changes could connect IP frameworks and ABS systems in an unprecedented way, positioning the TMK information system as a promising paradigm shift.

For instance, the consistent application of the principles of PIC and MAT would ensure robust IP rights protection and the effective, transparent implementation of ABS mechanisms. In this revamped context, the TMK information systems would become more than a mere knowledge repository; it would evolve into an active intermediary between IP and ABS frameworks. This would position the information systems as an evolving bridge, facilitating a better understanding and stronger connection between these two critical areas.

In conclusion, this book illuminated the importance of recognising the historical, cultural, and political complexities inherent in TMK information systems development. It proposed a future direction that is rooted in inclusivity, diversity, and respect for TMK holders. This transformative approach to TMK information systems design holds promise for setting a new global standard, increasing the appreciation and application of Chinese TMK, in China and beyond, and ensuring that the TMK system evolves in line with technological and cultural shifts.

This chapter emphasised that the preservation, utilisation, and dissemination of TMK via the TMK information systems is not a static endeavour but a dynamic process. This insight underscored the significance of continuous adaptation and revision in the regulation and governance of Chinese TMK through TMK information systems, reinforcing the fact that the understanding and application of this knowledge is 'never completed once and for all'.

References

A Bhukta, *Legal Protection for Traditional Knowledge: Towards A New Law for Indigenous Intellectual Property* (Emerald Publishing, 2020) 73.

Aimee Lefevre et al, 'Complementary Medicine use by Community-Dwelling Older Australians' (2021) 214(3) *The Medical Journal of Australia* 140.

Andrea Sorgato, 'New Drug Administration Law—New Rules and Liabilities' *ICLG* (2020)5

Ang, Jennifer, 'Sinicizing the Uyghurs' (2016) 28(4) *Journal of Social Justice* 399, 399; Helen Rees, *Echoes of History: Naxi Music in Modern China* (Oxford University Press, 2000) 1.

Anindya Bhukta, 'Protecting Traditional Knowledge: Ways and Means' (2020) *Legal Protection for Traditional Knowledge* 73.

Arun Agrawal, 'Indigenous Knowledge and the Politics of Classification' (2002) 54(173) *International Social Science Journal* 287.

Arun Agrawal, 'Indigenous Knowledge and the Politics of Classification' (2002) 54 *International Social Science Journal* 173.

Barnes P. M, et al, 'Complementary and Alternative Medicine use Among Adults and Children: United States' (2008) 10 CDC National Health Statistics Report 12.

Bhupinder Singh Sekhon 'Biopharmaceuticals: an overview' (2010) 34 *Thai J. Pharm. Sci.* 2.

Bill Beeson, 'Weighing the Opportunities & Risks Within China's Biopharmaceutical Industry' (2021) *The China Guys* 21.

QianXun Consultation, *2021 China Biopharmaceutical Market Analysis Report: Analysis of Market Scale, Status and Development Trend* (Report, 2021).

Bjorg Elsa Pettersen, 'Mind the Digital Gap: Questions and Possible Solutions for Design of Databases and Information Systems for Sami Traditional Knowledge' in J Porsanger and G Guttorm (eds), *Working with Traditional Knowledge: Communities, Institutions, Information Systems, Law and Ethics* (Sami University College, 2011) 163.

Brand, Eric, 'The Clinical Importance of 'Pao Zhi'- Medicinal Processing' (2016) *The Register of Chinese Herbal Medicine Journal* 22.

Brian H May et al, 'Chinese Herbs for Cognitive Decline: Historical and Contemporary Applications', *Diet and Nutrition in Dementia and Cognitive Decline* (2015) 1.

C Schulz, 'Money or Pride? On the Why and How of Traditional Knowledge Protection in India and China' (2011) 1(1) *Konstanzer Journal für Politik und Verwaltung* 52.

C.-T. Che et al, 'Traditional Medicine' in Rupika Delgoda (ed), *Pharmacognosy: Fundamentals, Applications and Strategies* (2017) 15.

'CAM Research in Britain: The Last 10 Years', (2005) 11 *Complement Ther Clin Pract* 17.

Chen Keji and Xu Hao 'The Integration of Traditional Chinese Medicine and Western Medicine' (2003) 11(2) *European Review* 225.

Chidi Oguamanam, 'Documentation and Digitization of Traditional Knowledge and Intangible Cultural Heritage: Challenges and Prospects' in Toshiyuki Kono (ed), *Intangible Cultural Heritage and Intellectual Property: Cultural Diversity and Sustainable Development* (Intersentia, 2009).

Chidi Oguamanam, 'Patents and Traditional Medicine: Digital Capture, Creative Legal Interventions and the Dialectics of Knowledge Transformation' (2008) 15(2) *Indiana Journal of Global Legal Studies* 489.

CK Maina, 'Traditional Knowledge Management and Preservation: Intersections with Library and Information Science' (2012) 44 *The International Information & Library Review* 13.

Convention for the Safeguarding of the Intangible Cultural Heritage, Open for Signature 17 October 2003, 2368 UNTS 3 (Entered into Force 20 April 2006) Art 12.

Curtis M. Horton, 'Protecting Biological Diversity and Cultural Diversity Under Intellectual Property Law' (1995) 10(1) *Journal of Environmental Law and Litigation* 1.

D O'Brien and MS Brown 'Becoming Chinese: Sinicization, Nation, and Race in Xinjiang, China', *Oxford Research Encyclopedias* (Web Page, 15 September 2022)

D Shankar and PM Unnikrishnan, *Challenging the Indian Medical Heritage* (Foundation Books, 2004) 10–12.

D. shaw, 'Toxicological Risks of Chinese herbs' (2010) 76(17) *Planta Medica* 2012.

D.Syiem and M.B.Syiem, 'Medicinal Plants and Conservation: Some Issues and Concerns' in P.Tandon and Y.P.A.Suman (ed), *Biodiversity and Its Significance* (2007) 150.

Daniel F Robinson and Claudio Chiarolla, 'The Role of Databases, Contracts and Codes of Conduct' in Ahmed Abdel-Latif, Daniel F Robinson, and Pedro Roffe (eds), *Protecting Traditional Knowledge: The WIPO Intergovernmental Committee on Intellectual Property and Genetic Resources, Traditional Knowledge and Folklore* (Routledge, 2017) 108.

David Wei Ze, 'Printing as an Agent of Social Stability: The Social Organization of Book Production in China During the Sung Dynasty' (Doctor of Philosophy Thesis, Simon Fraser University, 1995) 1.

DC Lau, *Confucius: The Analects* (Penguin Books, 1979) 5.

Dinis, S, 'Integrative Pharmacology–Interconnecting the World of Ayurveda (Traditional Indian Medicine-TIM), Traditional Chinese Medicine (TCM), and Conventional Medicine (CM)' in Anne et al George (ed), *Holistic healthcare: possibilities and challenges* (2017) 74.

Donna Haraway, 'Situated Knowledges: The Science Question in Feminism and the Privilege of Partial Perspective' (1988) 14(3) *Feminist Studies* 575.

Edward Wang, 'History, Space, and Ethnicity: The Chinese Worldview' (1999) 10(2) *Journal of World History* 285, 292.

Elisabeth Hsu, 'Reflections on the 'discovery' of the Antimalarial Qinghao' (2006) 61(6) *British Journal of Clinical Pharmacology* 667.

Elisabeth Hsu, 'The History of Chinese Medicine in the People's Republic of China and Its Globalization' (2008) 2(4) *East Asian Science, Technology and Society: An International Journal* 465.

Ellis, Shannon, 'Hong Kong Stock Exchange Opens to Biotechs' (2018) 36 *Nature Biotechnology* 482.

Fermeglia, M., 'Role of Process Simulation in Extraction Technologies for Medicinal and Aromatic Plants' in SS Handa et al (ed), Extraction Technologies for Medicinal and Aromatic Plants (2008) 55

Graham Dutfield, 'Why Traditional Knowledge is Important in Drug Discovery' (2010) 2(9) *Future Med. Chem,* 1406.

Guobin Cui, 'A Review of the Status Quo of Genetic Resources and Traditional Knowledge Protection in China' (Working Paper, Tsinghua University School of Law, August 2009) 2.

Handa, Sukhdev Swami, 'Extraction Technologies for Medicinal and Aromatic Plants' in SS Handa et al (ed), Extraction Technologies for Medicinal and Aromatic Plants (2008) 21.

Hongyi Harry Lai, 'The Life Span of Unified Regimes in China' (2002) 2(2) *The China Review* 93.

Hoyt Cleveland Tillman, 'Some Reflections on Confucian Academies in China' in Vladimir Glomb et al (eds), *Confucian Academies in East Asia* (Brill, 2020) 21.

Inventory of Existing Online Database Containing Traditional Knowledge Documentation Data, WIPO Doc. WIPO/GRTKF/IC/2/6 (13 to 21 July 2001).

J Friedrichs, 'Sino-Muslim Relations: The Han, the Hui, and the Uyghurs' (2017) 37(1) *Journal of Muslim Minority Affairs* 55.

James O Young and Conrad G Brunk, *The Ethics of Cultural Appropriation* (2012)1.

Jesper Simonsen et al, *Situated Methods in Design* (MIT Press, 2014) 1.

John D. Keys, *Chinese Herbs: Their Botany, Chemistry and Pharmacodynamics* (1989)12.

John King Fairbank, *The Chinese World Order: Traditional China's Foreign Relations* (Harvard University Press, 1968) 11–12.

John M Friend and Bradley A Thayer, 'The Rise of Han-Centrism and What It Means for International Politics (2017) 17(1) *Studies in Ethnicity and Nationalism* 91.

Jon Agar, 'What is Technology?' (2020) 77(3) *Annals of Science* 377.

Jozala AF, Geraldes DC, Tundisi LL, et al, 'Biopharmaceuticals from Microorganisms: From Production to Purification' (2016) 47 *Braz J Microbiol* 51.

Judy Xu and Yue Yang, 'Traditional Chinese medicine in the Chinese Health Care System' (2009) 90(2) *Health Policy* 135.

Junli Diao, 'In Search of China's First Library: Materials, Housing and Arrangement' (2019) 35(1) *Library & Information History* 21.

Kanehe, Debra Harry and Le'a Malia, 'Asserting Tribal Sovereignty over Cultural Property: Moving Towards Protection of Genetic Material and Indigenous Knowledge' (2006) 5(1) *Seattle Journal for Social Justice* 33.

Kanwen Ma, 'Classic Chinese Medical Literature in Contemporary China: Texts Selected for Modern Editions, and Problems Associated with This Work' in Paul U Unschuld (ed), *Approaches to Traditional Chinese Medical Literature* (Springer, 1989) 7

Kiki Han, 'The Dawn of China Biopharma Innovation' (2021) *McKinsey & Company* 1.

Krystyna Swiderska, *Protecting Community Rights over Traditional Knowledge: Implications of Customary Laws and Practices* (Report, 2021) 9–10.

Kuruk, Paul, 'Exploitation of Traditional Knowledge of Indigenous and Local Communities' in Paul Kuruk (ed), *Traditional Knowledge, Genetic Resources, Customary Law and Intellectual Property* (2020) 17.

L Cooper, 'The International Relations of the 'Imagined Community': Explaining the Late Nineteenth-Century Genesis of the Chinese Nation.' (2015) 41(3) *Review of International Studies* 477.

L Suchman, 'Located Accountabilities in Technology Production' (2002) 14(2) *Scandinavian Journal of Information Systems,* 91.

Lan Qiu, et al, 'Public Funding and Private Investment for R&D: A Survey in China's Pharmaceutical Industry' (2014) 12(27) *Health Research Policy and Systems* 1.

Lau Kin Chi and Sit Tsui, 'The Need for Recovering the Subjugated Knowledge of Traditional Chinese Medicine' (2020) 63 *Development* 249.

Li Gong-ke et al, 'Application of Microwave-assisted Extraction in the Modernization of Chinese Traditional Medicine' (2007) *Fine Chemicals* 8.

Li, Jane, 'China's Newest Stock Exchange Follows Xi Jinping's Cues for the Economy', *Quartz* (2017) 4 <https://qz.com/2089277/beijings-new-stock-exchange-shows-chinas-focus-on-the-real-economy/>

Liang Yongjia, 'Developmentalism, Secularism, Nationalism and Essentialism: Current Situation and Challenges of the Ethnic Issue in China' in Litao Zhao (ed), *China's Social Development and Policy: Into the Next Stage?* (Taylor & Francis Group, 2013) 186.

Liu, Kerong Zhang and Wuyi, 'The Current Status, Trend, and Development Strategies of Chinese Biopharmaceutical Industry with a Challenging Perspective' (2020) *Sage Journals* 1.

Lois Mai Chan, 'The Burning of the Books in China, 213 B.C. ' (1972) 7(2) *The Journal of Library History (1966–1972)* 101.

Lu, Lerong, 'Promoting High-Tech Innovations Through Capital Markets Law Reform: Deciphering the Sci-Tech Innovation Board of the Shanghai Stock Exchange' (2020) 35 *Journal of International Banking and Financial Law* 140–143.

Lucien X Polastron, *Books on Fire: The Destruction of Libraries Throughout History* (Inner Traditions, 2007) 80.

Lucille Chia and Hilde De Weerdt, Knowledge and Text Production in an Age of Print: China, 900–1400 (Brill, 2011) 219.

M Ruiz, 'The International Debate on Traditional Knowledge as Prior Art in the Patent System: Issues and Options for Developing Countries' (Occasional Paper No 9, Center for International Environmental Law, October 2002) 1.

Maja Van der Velden, 'Design for the Contact Zone: Knowledge Management Software and the Structures of Indigenous Knowledges' in F Sudweeks (ed), *Cultural Attitudes Towards Technology and Communication* (Murdoch University, 2010) 1.

Maja van der Velden, 'Programming for Cognitive Justice: Towards an Ethical Framework for Democratic Code' (2005) 17 *Interacting with Computers* 105.

Maja Van der Velden, 'When Knowledge Meet Wikipedia and Other Stories from the Contact Zone' in Geert Lovink and Nathaniel Tkacz (eds), *Critical Point of View: A Wikipedia Reader* (Institute of Network Cultures, 2011) 236.

Marco R. Tommaso et al, 'The Chinese TCM Industry: Growth, Changes, and Policies' in Attilio Mucelli and Francesca Spigarelli (ed), *Healthcare Policies and Systems in Europe And China: Comparisons And Synergies* (2018) 38.

María Montenegro, 'Subverting the Universality of Metadata Standards: The TK Labels as a Tool to Promote Indigenous Data Sovereignty' (2019) 75(4) *Journal of Documentation* 731.

Martin Fredriksson, 'Balancing Community Rights and National Interests in International Protection of Traditional Knowledge: A Study of India's Traditional Knowledge Digital Library' (2022) 43(2) *Third World Quarterly* 352.

Mary Louise Pratt, 'Arts of the Contact Zone' in Vivian Zamel and Ruth Spack (eds), *Negotiating Academic Literacies* (Routledge, 1998) 316.

N Sivin, 'Science and Medicine in Imperial China—The State of the Field' (1988) 47(1) *The Journal of Asian Studies* 41.

N Varatharajan and M Chandrashekara, 'Digital Library Initiatives at Higher Education and Research Institutions in India' (2007) *Library Philosophy and Practice* 1.

Nijar, Singh, 'Incorporating Traditional Knowledge in an International Regime on Access to Genetic Resources and Benefit Sharing: Problems and Prospects' (2010) 21(2) *The European Journal of International Law* 458.

Ong, Jean Ho and Poh Hong, 'Traditional Chinese Medicine in Dermatology' in Nanette B. Silverberg et al (ed), *Pediatric Skin of Color* (2015) 430.

P Ouellette, *Power in the Qin Dynasty: Legalism and External Influence Over the Decisions and Legacy of the First Emperor of China* (Haverford College, 2010) 20.

Payyappallimana, Unnikrishnan, 'Role of Traditional Medicine in Primary Health Care: An Overview of Perspectives and Challenges' 14(6) *Yokohama Journal of Social Sciences* 62.

PKJain and Parveen Babbar, 'Digital Libraries Initiatives in India' (2006) 38(3) *The International Information & Library Review* 161.

Pradip N Thomas., 'Traditional Knowledge and the Traditional Knowledge Digital Library: Digital Quandaries and Other Concerns' (2010) 72(8) *The International Communication Gazette* 659.

Progress Report on the Status of Traditional Knowledge as Prior Art, WIPO Doc. WIPO/GRTKF/IC/2/6 (1 July 2001).

Projit Bihari Mukharji, 'Subaltern Surgeries: Colonial Law and the Regulation of Traditional Medicines in the British Raj and Beyond' (2021) 36 *Osiris* 89.

Qianzhan Industry Institute (前瞻產業研究院), *Technology Landscape of the Global Biopharmaceutical industry in 2022* (Report, 2021).

Qing-Wen Zhang et al, 'Techniques for Extraction and Isolation of Natural Products: A Comprehensive Review' (2018) 13(30) *Chinese Medicine* 8.

R Lakshmi Poorna, M Mymoon and A Hariharan, 'Preservation and Protection of Traditional Knowledge—Diverse Documentation Initiatives Across the Globe' (2014) 107(8) *Current Science* 1240.

RalphCroizier, 'Traditional Medicine in Communist China: Science, Communism and Cultural Nationalism' (1965)23 *The China Quarterly* 1.

Report of the Inter-Regional Workshop on Intellectual Property Rights in the Context of Traditional Medicine, WHO Doc WHO/EDM/TRM/2001.1 (6–8 December 2000).

Review of Article 27.3(b): The View of Switzerland, WTO Docs IP/C/W/284 (15 June 2001).
Richard J Smith, *Chinese Maps: Images of All Under Heaven* (Oxford University Press, 1996) 8–9.
Robert D. Atkinson, 'China's Biopharmaceutical Strategy: Challenge or Complement to U.S. Industry Competitiveness?' *Information Technology and Innovation Foundation* (2019)1.
Robert D. Atkinson, 'Healthy Funding: The Critical Role of Investing in NIH to Boost Health and Lower Costs' *Information Technology and Innovation Foundation* (2019)5.
Ruiping Fan and Ian Holliday, 'Policies for Traditional Medicine in Peripheral China' (2006) 12(5) *Policies for Traditional Medicine in Peripheral China* 485.
Sarah Menin, 'Fragments from the Forest: Aalto's Requisitioning of Forest Place and Matter' (2001) 6(3) *The Journal of Architecture* 279.
SC Ellis, 'Meaningful Consideration? A Review of Traditional Knowledge in Environmental Decision Making' (2005) 58(1) *Arctic* 66.
SCIT Strategic Information Technology Plan into the Twenty-First Century, WIPO Docs SCIT/3/4 (15 June 1999); Information Technology Strategic Implementation Plan, WIPO Docs SCIT/4/2 (24 September 1999) annex 2.
Sissi Wachtel-Galor and Iris F. F. Benzie, 'Herbal Medicine: An Introduction to its History, Usage, Regulation, Current Trends, and Research Needs' in Benzie IFF and Wachtel-Galor S (ed), *Herbal Medicine: Biomolecular and Clinical Aspects* (2011).
Sita Reddy, 'Making Heritage Legible: Who Owns Traditional Medical Knowledge?' (2006) 13 *International Journal of Cultural Property* 161.
Stuart AP Murray, *The Library: An Illustrated History* (Skyhorse Publishing Company, 2019) 49.
Su, Yi et al, 'Research on Industrial Organization of Chinese Medicine Based on SCP Paradgm' (Conference Paper, International Conference on Management Science & Engineering 21th Annual Conference Proceedings, June 2018) 751–758.
Sudhir Krishnaswamy, 'Access to Knowledge and Traditional Knowledge Protection: The Indian experience' in Ed Ramesh Subramanian and Lea Shaver (eds), *Access to Knowledge in India: New Research on Intellectual Property, Innovation & Development* (Bloomsbury Academic, 2011) 14.
Surendra Sarsaiya et al, 'Bioengineering Tools for the Production of Pharmaceuticals: Current Perspective and Future Outlook' (2019) 10(1) *Bioengineering* 469.
TJ Hinrichs, 'Governance Through Medical Texts and The Role of Print' in Sinica Leidensia (ed), *Knowledge and Text Production in an Age of Print: China, 900–1400* (Brill, 2011) 217.
TJ Hinrichs, *The Medical Transforming of Governance and Southern Customs in Song Dynasty China (960–1279 CE)* (Harvard University, 2003) 92.
Tom Grunfeld, 'In Search of Equality: Relations Between China's Ethnic Minorities and the Majority Han' (1985) 17(1) *Bulletin of Concerned Asian Scholars* 54.
Vicky Qing Xia, 'China Looks Inward and Outward: Investments in US and EU Biopharmaceutical Companies Are on the Rise', *Bioprocess International* (2019)3(1)5.
Volker Scheid and Eric I Karchmer, 'History of Chinese Medicine, 1890–2010' in TJ Hinrichs and Linda L Barnes (eds), *Modern Chinese Religion II: 1850–2015* (2016) 1.
Wang Wen-jian and Zhang Teng, 'Integration of traditional Chinese medicine and Western medicine in the era of precision medicine' (2017) 15(1) *Journal of integrative medicine* 1.
Weeks, John, 'Chinese TCM Renaissance and the Global Movement for Integrative Health and Medicine' (2017) 23(2) *The Journal of Alternative and Complementary Medicine* 79.
Wenxian Zhang, 'Dang An: A Brief History of the Chinese Imperial Archives and its Administration' (2004) 2 *Journal of Archival Organization* 17.
Wung-seok Cha et al, 'Historical Difference between Traditional Korean Medicine and Traditional Chinese Medicine' (2007) 29(1) *Neurological Research* 5.
Xian Zhou et al, 'Synergistic Effects of Chinese Herbal Medicine: A Comprehensive Review of Methodology and Current Research' (2016) 7 *Frontiers in Pharmacology* 1.
Xiangshu Fang, 'Burning Books and Burying Scholars: On the Policies of the Short-lived Qin Dynasty in Ancient China (221–207 BC' (2015) 3(7) *International Journal of Liberal Arts and Social Science* 54.

Xiangwei ma, et al, 'A Bioassay-Based Approach for the Batch-To-Batch Consistency Evaluation of Xuesaitong Injection on a Zebrafish Thrombosis Model' (2021) 12 *Frontiers in Pharmacology* 1.

Xu Hao and Chen ke-ji, 'Integrating traditional Medicine with Biomedicine Towards a Patient-Centered Healthcare System' (2011) 17(2) *Chin J Integr Med* 83.

Y Shao-Yun, 'Becoming Zhongguo, Becoming Han: Tracing and Reconceptualizing Ethnicity in Ancient North China, 770 BC-AD 581' (Master of Arts Thesis, National University of Singapore, 2007) 29.

Yanling Sun and Yanhuai Liu, 'China Traditional Chinese Medicine (TCM) Patent Database' (2004) 26(1) *World Patent Information* 91.

Yongsheng Chen and Huanning Su, 'Disciplines Derived from the Discovery of Historical Archives' (2018) 5(2) *Proceedings from the Document Academy* 1.

Yu Huatao and Zhang Yang, 'The Yin and Yang of Traditional Chinese and Western medicine' (2021) 41(6) *Medicinal Research Reviews* 2.

Yueqiang Wang et al, 'A Brief Introduction to China's New Drug Administration Law and its Impact on Medications for Rare Diseases' (2019) 8(4) *Intractable Rare Dis Res.* 226.

Zanzanaini, Gabriella, 'Forgotten Hong Kong Icon: The Revival of Traditional Chinese Medicine', *Zolima City Mag* 1.

Zhang Huimei, 'Present Situation and Ways of Technical Upgrading of Traditional Chinese Medicine Pharmaceutical Equipment' (Conference Paper, International Conference on Biology, Chemistry and Medical Engineering, 2019)110.

Zhang Z.B and Yang J.S. 'Comparative Analysis of Jinxian Dai Licensing Procedure and Rules for TCM Doctors' (2004) 23(6) *Education of Chinese Medicine (ECM)* 55.

Zhaoyun Zhu et al, 'Innovative Development Path of Ethnomedicines: An Overview of Ethnomedicines in China' (2016) 10 *Frontiers of Medicine* 166.

Zhen Gao et al, 'Emergence and Development of Uyghur Medicine from the Perspective of Chinese Traditional Medicine' (2019) 2(4) *Traditional Medicine and Modern Medicine* 139.

Zhiyong Li et al, 'Policies and Problems of Modernizing Ethnomedicine in China: A Focus on the Yi and Dai Traditional Medicines of Yunnan Province' (2020) *Evidence-Based Complementary and Alternative Medicine* 7.

冯翔[Feng Xiang],《关于宋代至明代南方的 瘴病及其历史的研究》[Miasma and its History Research from the Southern Song Dynasty to the Ming Dynasty] (2007) 广西民族大学学报 *Journal of Guangxi University for Nationalities* 28.

韩毅[Han Yi],《国家，医学与社会:太平圣惠方在宋代的应用与传播》[State, Medicine and Society: The Application and Dissemination of Taiping Shenghui Fang in Song Dynasty] (2010) 宋史研究论丛*Collection of Studies on Song Dynasty History* 499.

韩毅[Han Yi],《太平圣惠方与宋代社会》[Taiping Shenghui Fang and Song Dynasty Society] (2021) 中华医史杂志*Chinese Medical History Journal* 198.

黄玉烨 [Huang Yuye],《我国传统知识数据库保护模式及其法律机制研究》(2020) 4 [Research on the Protection Mode and Legal Mechanism of the Traditional Knowledge Database in Our Country] 河南财经政法大学学报 *Journal of Henan University of Economics and Law* 55.

李佛基 [Li Foji],《中医中药概念探析》[Analysis on the Concept of Traditional Chinese Medicine] (1999) 11(5), 安徽中医临床杂志, *Clinical Journal of Anhui Traditional Chinese Medicine* 346.

李文红[Li Wenhong], 以莲花清瘟方为例探讨中药复方的创新及专利布局策略[Taking Lianhua Qingwen Recipe as an Example to Discuss the Innovation and Patent Layout Strategy of Traditional Chinese Medicine Formulations](2021)46(5), 中国中药杂志*Chinese Journal of Traditional Chinese Medicine* 1293.

李一丁 [Li Yiding],《印度传统知识数据库治理体系动态及启示》[Dynamics and Enlightenment of the Governance System of Indian Traditional Knowledge Database] (2020) 知识产权*Intellectual Property* 86;

刘海英 [Liu Haiying],《中国中医药政策变迁的阶段历程与演进逻辑-基于1949–2020政策文本的实证研究》[The Different Stages and Evolutionary Logic of Traditional Chinese Medicine

Policy: An Empirical Study Based on the Policy Texts from 1949 to 2020] (2021) 17(12) 亚太传统医药, *Asia-Pacific Traditional Medicine* 3.
芦 笛[Lu Di],《中国近代医药史研究及相关问题评论》[Research on the History of Traditional Chinese Medicine and Comments on Related Issues] (2016) 1, 史林, *Journal of History* 195.
罗婕[Luo Jie], 中华民族共同体视野下的民族医药传承创新 [Inheritance and Innovation of Ethnic Medicine under the Vision of Chinese National Community] (2021) 15, 世界中医药 *World Traditional Chinese Medicine* 2211.
彭司勋[Peng sixun], 2017年中国药学年鉴 [the China Pharmaceutical Yearbook in 2017] (2017) (33) 35.
秦宇 [Qin Yu],《我国中药专利申请现状分析及建议》[Analysis of the Current Situation of the Chinese Traditional Medicine Patent Application in China and the Corresponding Suggestions] (2016) 25(8), 中国新药杂志, *Chinese Journal of New Drugs* 841.
商 宇 [Shang Yu],《新中国成立后中央中医管理组织变迁研究》[Research on the Changes of the Central Management Organization of Traditional Chinese Medicine after the Founding of New China] (2016) 29(6), 医学与社会, *Medicine and Society* 28.
吴弈天[Wu Yitian],《中医药传统知识数据库构建思路初探》[A Preliminary Study on the Construction of Traditional Chinese Medicine Knowledge Database] (2022) 30(5) 中国卫生法制 *China Health Law* 6.
杨义芳 [Yang Yifang],《中药创新药物研究开发的回顾、策略与实践》[Review, Strategy and Practice of Research and Development of Innovative Traditional Chinese Medicine] (2009) 40(10), 中草药, *Chinese Traditional and Herbal Drugs* 1513.
袁倩[Yuan Qian],《宋代巫医及政府禁巫对医学的影响》[Government' Prohibition of Witch Doctor Impact on Development of Medicine in the Song Dynasty] (2021) 中国中医基础医学杂志*Journal of Basic Chinese Medicine* 1.
《2019年中医药事业发展统计提要报告》[Statistical Summary Report on the Development of Traditional Chinese Medicine in 2019] (People's Republic of China) National Administration of Traditional Chinese Medicine, 2021.
《十三五中医药科技创新专项规划》[The 13th Five-Year Special Plan for Scientific and Technological Innovation of Traditional Chinese Medicine] (People's Republic of China) National Health Commission and Ministry of Science and Technology, Order No 146, 2017.
《中华人民共和国国民经济和社会发展第十三个五年规划纲要》[Outline of the 13th Five-Year Plan for the National Economic and Social Development of the People's Republic of China] (People's Republic of China) National People's Congress, March 2016; Mackenzie Mills, Anwen Zhang and Panos Kanavos (2019) 'Pharmaceutical Policy in China' *London School of Economics* 24.
《中华人民共和国药品管理法》[The Drug Administration Law of the People's Republic of China] (People's Republic of China) National People's Congress, 2019.
《中华人民共和国中医药法》[Law of the People's Republic of China on Traditional Chinese Medicine] (People's Republic of China) Standing Committee of the National People's Congress, Order No. 59, 2017, art 3, art 8, arts 38–41, art 52.
《中药品种保护条例》[China's Regulation on the Protection of Traditional Chinese Medicine] (People's Republic of China) State Council, Order No 106, 1992 ('Regulations').

Chapter 7
Findings and Conclusion

7.1 Introduction

This book provided a thorough examination of the challenges and opportunities involved in ensuring the effective preservation, responsible use, and proper dissemination of traditional medical knowledge in China. This revealed that TMK in China is an invaluable asset that has been passed down through generations.[1] The knowledge is highly valued by knowledge holders and local communities for its healing properties and effectiveness and has played an integral role in China's healthcare system for centuries.[2] However, it is facing a growing threat due to increasing instances of unauthorised exploitation and commercialisation,[3] resulting in third parties using and claiming this knowledge without proper consent. These practices have had a profound impact on the traditional livelihoods of Chinese communities, especially those that are more vulnerable, by depriving them of the due recognition and rightful benefits associated with their knowledge.[4]

The escalating situation necessitated the immediate development of a comprehensive and robust framework that would ensure the protection and preservation of TMK. This framework, inherently multifaceted, must address the various intricacies of the issue, including advocating for respectful use of TMK by recognising the rights of knowledge holders to ensure its ethical and responsible usage. Furthermore, it should

---

[1] 邓明峰 [Deng Mingfeng], 《我国民族中医药传统知识专利保护研究》[Research on Patent Protection for TMK of China's Ethnic Groups] (2018) 12 贵州民族研究 *Guizhou Ethnic Studies* 96, 98.

[2] Ibid.

[3] Yi-Chia Ke and Jiun-Hong Chen, 'Interrelationship Between Genetic Resources and Traditional Knowledge: An Example from Earthworm Fibrinolytic Enzyme' (2020) 39(6) *Biotechnology Law Report* 440, 442; Zhiyong Li et al., 'Policies and Problems of Modernizing Ethnomedicine in China: A Focus on the Yi and Dai Traditional Medicines of Yunnan Province' [2020] *Evidence-Based Complementary and Alternative Medicine* 1, 1–12.

[4] Ibid.

N. Xia, *Medicinal Mandates*, https://doi.org/10.1007/978-981-96-4108-6_7

facilitate suitable dissemination by establishing mechanisms for sharing and utilising TMK that respect the rights and dignity of knowledge holders, while simultaneously promoting a wider understanding and appreciation of its inherent cultural value.

However, the discourse around TMK has transcended mere legal or economic dimensions. TMK is embedded within specific Chinese communities and is contextually bound to the historical and cultural context it developed from.[5] Its principles and practices have been shaped by the cultural-historical factors that define these communities, and it is vital to acknowledge this intricate relationship.

The preservation of TMK, thus, has transcended mere safeguarding of knowledge; it is about preserving a heritage, a way of life that has been nurtured over generations. Any endeavour to safeguard and leverage it, and harness its potential must, therefore, approach it from a holistic perspective. This means not only addressing its legal and economic dimensions but also taking into account the cultural, social, and historical contexts that have shaped its evolution.

The primary objective of this book was to foster a thorough understanding of how China's distinct historical and cultural nuances interact with and influence Chinese TMK, and how these factors can be reconciled with the globally recognised mechanisms intended to protect, disseminate, and utilise it. By investigating this dynamic, the research endeavoured to unearth strategies that could be seamlessly integrated with the internationally established frameworks to protect, disseminate and use TMK, while concurrently respecting and conserving Chinese TMK's inherent cultural and historical nuances.

The core objective of this exploration was to nurture a holistic understanding that would enable the development of contextually sensitive solutions. These solutions were designed to tackle the challenges associated with the preservation, utilisation, and dissemination of Chinese TMK. The insights gleaned from China's experience could encourage other nations to consider a similar methodology that is deeply rooted in their cultural and historical contexts. This would enable them to tailor their approaches to protecting, utilising, and disseminating their own TMK effectively, reflecting their unique circumstances and values.

This book focused on the intricate dynamics of three globally recognised mechanisms: IP frameworks, ABS systems, and TMK information systems. The findings revealed that these mechanisms, largely shaped by Western ideologies, present a fascinating interplay of opportunities and challenges when interfacing with Chinese TMK, a type of knowledge deeply entrenched in the sociocultural and historical tapestry of China.

In the face of this complex landscape, the study adopted the cultural-historical approach to scrutinise the effectiveness of these mechanisms and their alignment with the unique characteristics of Chinese TMK. It offered a critical analysis of the compatibility of these predominantly Western-influenced structures with China's unique sociocultural and historical landscape.

---

[5] S Liu, JJ Zhu and JC Li, 'The Interpretation of Human Body in Traditional Chinese Medicine and Its Influence on the Characteristics of TCM Theory' (2021) 304(11) *The Anatomical Record* 2559, 2560.

The goal was to illuminate potential discordances and investigate avenues for harmonisation and reconciliation, while acknowledging the inherent dynamism and cultural sensitivity of Chinese TMK. This cultural-historical approach facilitated the proposition of culturally sensitive adaptations or alternatives that honour the intrinsic characteristics of Chinese TMK.

The findings of this book proposed that, while IP law has demonstrated effectiveness in addressing certain aspects of Chinese TMK, particularly those with economic and technical implications, it might not be universally suitable for all facets. This was especially relevant to those aspects with profound cultural or historical significance, where the standard IP framework might not fully capture or protect the nuanced complexities inherent in them.

ABS regimes and TMK information systems were suggested to potentially serve as practical tools to effectively protect, responsibly utilise, and suitably disseminate TMK in China. Nevertheless, it was emphasised that the implementation of these tools should not be a mere transplant of Western systems. Instead, they must be thoroughly contextualised within China's unique historical and cultural landscape to ensure their effectiveness and relevance. This necessitated the careful consideration of China's distinct sociocultural norms, values, and legal practices when designing and implementing these systems.

Ultimately, this book underscored the necessity of a comprehensive approach in reconciling Chinese TMK with globally recognised frameworks. It advocated for the development and implementation of integrated, culturally attuned, and context-specific strategies. These strategies should not only address the economic and technical aspects of Chinese TMK but also honour and protect its rich cultural and historical significance.

Based on the findings discussed, this book put forth four pivotal contributions to the existing body of knowledge. Firstly, it introduced an innovative methodology for critical legal analysis, one that utilised a distinct historical and sociocultural lens. Considering the intricate nature of universally recognised structures—particularly the IP scheme, the ABS system, and TMK information systems—it invoked a cultural-historical methodology to meticulously analyse their application and effectiveness. In this context, the cultural-historical methodology played a two-fold role. On one hand, it aided in proposing culturally sensitive adaptations or alternatives that paid due respect to the inherent traits of Chinese TMK. On the other hand, it advocated for the suitable preservation, respectful application, and equitable dissemination of Chinese TMK, all in harmony with the unique cultural, historical, and legal nuances of China.

Secondly, the book presented a thorough critical analysis to develop a comprehensive understanding of how China's distinct historical and cultural nuances influence the use, protection, and dissemination of Chinese TMK, while simultaneously exploring the reconciliation of these factors with globally established frameworks. Going beyond the limitations of existing published analyses, which often imported Western perspectives and biases, the study conducted a critical analysis of the chosen globally established frameworks that integrate both Western international law perspectives and national cultural-historical perspectives. By adopting this dual approach, it effectively uncovered the tensions and legal challenges that emerged during the implementation of IP, ABS, and TMK information systems in China, providing a comprehensive understanding that bridged the gaps between these distinct viewpoints.

Thirdly, the study integrated a wide range of perspectives from both Western and Chinese literature, providing an academic contribution. This enabled a nuanced and contextually sensitive exploration of the historical and sociocultural factors influencing the regulatory frameworks that govern the protection, utilisation, and dissemination of Chinese TMK. This approach aimed to enhance understanding of these frameworks and contribute to a more comprehensive and culturally nuanced discourse in the field.

Fourthly, this book presented a proposed set of practical reform options that aligned China's unique cultural and historical nuances inherent in TMK with globally recognised mechanisms. Specifically, it suggested reforms to the existing IP frameworks, particularly patent systems, as well as to the development of the ABS framework and the implementation of TMK information systems. These proposals aimed to effectively protect TMK and its holders, promoted appropriate dissemination, ensured responsible utilisation of TMK, and concurrently supported China's objectives of developing its pharmaceutical sectors. Section 7.2 provides a comprehensive and nuanced analysis of the contributions of the study. The intention of this detailed examination is to underscore the academic merit and the wider implications of the research undertaken, thus illuminating its prospective influence within the field.

This concluding chapter summarises and synthesises the findings and conclusions of the study, providing a comprehensive overview of how the research questions outlined in Chapter 1 have been addressed. It examines the implications of this book for the broader field of legal scholarship, specifically in relation to the governance of traditional knowledge. It explores the potential contributions that the research could make to the ongoing dialogue around traditional knowledge governance, and the ways in which it can inform future research in this area. This chapter also acknowledges the limitations and constraints of the research, including the challenges associated with accessing and analysing historical and sociocultural data. It identifies opportunities for future research.

7.2 Navigating Tensions Surrounding Traditional Medical Knowledge Governance in China

This book effectively unveiled the intricacies and challenges faced when integrating globally recognised frameworks, namely IP frameworks, ABS mechanisms, and TMK information systems, into the protection, utilisation, and dissemination of Chinese TMK. It was argued that these challenges largely stem from the unique cultural-historical aspects embedded within Chinese TMK, which stand in stark contrast to the Western-oriented ideologies that form the foundation of these global mechanisms.

Building on this understanding, Chapter 2 explored the various challenges associated with the improper handling of Chinese TMK, which included the misappropriation, misuse, decontextualisation, and marginalisation of this significant cultural asset. This chapter particularly emphasised the potential risks of these issues transforming into more severe, multifaceted conflicts and tensions if they were not promptly and appropriately addressed. It advocated that an in-depth, nuanced comprehension of Chinese TMK and its cultural-historical context was crucial to resolving these challenges. The proposition championed a comprehensive, nuanced understanding of Chinese TMK, articulating the need for a rigorous, detailed examination of the prevailing globally established mechanisms such as IP frameworks, ABS systems, and TMK information systems, all examined through a cultural-historical lens.

Moving into the specifics of Chinese TMK, Chapter 2 explored the rich diversity and practices of Chinese TMK, its customary rules and practices, dynamic evolution, and the patterns of its preservation and dissemination within China's unique context. The primary findings highlighted the complex interrelationships and distinctions between the cohesive national community and the myriad of local communities within China. This exploration revealed how these relationships have influenced and shaped the overall structure and evolution of Chinese TMK, reinforcing the balance between uniformity and diversity within the national and local sociocultural context of China.

In this context, the 'unified national community' of China referred to the collective entity comprising all ethnic groups and local communities living within China's borders. This concept embodied the notion that these diverse groups are interconnected, mutually influencing each other's cultures and jointly shaping the development of a unified Chinese culture, with Confucianism as its cornerstone. This process included the proposal, establishment, and widespread acceptance of a national consciousness and identity across all ethnic groups, contributing to the unity and cohesiveness of the nation. Conversely, 'local communities' in China pertained to smaller, more specific groups of individuals who share a common geographic location, culture, language, and lifestyle. These communities are often composed of individuals who are related to one another by family ties and who have a shared history and cultural heritage, making them distinct entities within the larger tapestry of China's national community.

This chapter underscored that the interlocking relationship between the unified national community and local communities lies in the fact that local communities are an integral part of the unified national community. Their cultural and historical contributions have shaped and influenced Chinese culture and traditions which, in turn, contribute to the identity and cohesion of the unified national community. The relationship is also characterised by a symbiotic exchange, where the unified national community provides a sense of national identity and protection, while local communities contribute to the diversity and richness of Chinese culture. However, there are also differences between the unified national community and local communities in terms of their identities and interests. The unified national community emphasises the importance of a shared national identity and unity, while local communities prioritise their unique cultural heritage and traditions. This difference in perspective can sometimes lead to tensions between them. The relationship is complex and multifaceted, showcasing the intricacies and complexities of TMK in China. The dynamic between the two communities is marked by a delicate balance between unity and diversity. While they share a common cultural heritage and history, they also have unique identities and interests that need to be respected and protected.

The chapter also highlighted one of the major challenges facing Chinese TMK—the rising unauthorised exploitation within the swiftly expanding pharmaceutical sector in China. In response to this growing concern, the chapter emphasised the pressing need for effective protection of TMK, while concurrently advocating for a balanced approach towards its responsible use and appropriate dissemination. It argued that striking such a balance was critical to avoid deepening societal divisions or provoking potential political conflicts. It proposed that this balance can be achieved by aligning China's approach to TMK protection and utilisation with internationally recognised and accepted mechanisms. This harmonisation could provide a more comprehensive and integrated solution to protecting TMK, thereby enhancing its sustainable use and respectful dissemination within the dynamic context of China's rapid societal and economic development.

Utilising the case of antimalarial drugs extracted from the Chinese medicinal herb, Qing hao (*Artemisia annua*), the chapter uncovered the possible exploitation of TMK and instances of biopiracy within China. This situation exemplifies a challenging scenario where TMK, maintained by national and local communities, may be used without appropriately acknowledging its origins or the sociocultural context that fostered its creation and preservation. A comprehensive patent landscape analysis further revealed a concerning trend of TMK misappropriation or biopiracy within China's domestic landscape. The analysis pinpointed a substantial increase in patent applications linked to TMK and active ingredients sourced from Qinghao over the last three decades. Intriguingly, despite the mandates of China's patent law requiring disclosure of origin, these applications often lacked acknowledgement of Indigenous contributions or the community origins, signalling the possibility of biopiracy.

Following from these insights, the chapter presented an argument that China urgently requires appropriate legal, policy, and pragmatic solutions to address the distinctive nature of TMK within its borders. This need has become particularly pressing in the face of the potentially intensified use of TMK, spurred by China's rapidly burgeoning pharmaceutical sector and the revitalisation and modernisation of TMK. The chapter emphasised that, while IP laws should remain a priority, other governance tools, including ABS mechanisms and TMK information systems, warrant serious consideration. This multifaceted approach is crucial to achieving a fair balance between the comprehensive protection, suitable utilisation, and respectful dissemination of TMK, within the unique contours of China's sociocultural landscape.

7.2.1 *Fitting Square Pegs into Round Holes: The Challenges of Regulating Traditional Medical Knowledge Through IP Rights in China*

Chapter 3 critically analysed the compatibility of Chinese TMK with international and China's domestic IP laws, contextualised through historical and cultural perspectives. The discussion revealed a pronounced divergence between Western IP ideologies and China's cultural norms, underscoring that the distinctive Chinese values and identity encapsulated in Chinese TMK may not align with Western IP notions.

The chapter foregrounded several challenges standing in the way of embedding Chinese TMK into the Western-centric IP framework. It asserted that China has historically seen Western IP laws as imperialism instruments, thereby impeding their adoption. This perception, coupled with the clashing ideologies of individual property rights and China's collective and State ownership preference, presents difficulties. Additionally, Western scientific biases and cultural disparities pose barriers, given their potential discordance with Chinese TMK's traditional values. Despite the modernisation of China's IP laws, enforcing them effectively remains problematic. Therefore, the chapter posited that the integration of Chinese TMK into the existing IP framework, while vital, is a complex endeavour demanding a comprehensive, nuanced understanding of both the Western IP constructs and China's unique sociocultural fabric.

The chapter then presented a critical examination of the evolutionary trajectory of China's IP laws, assessing both its endeavours to comply with global IP norms and the intrinsic conflict it experiences when attempting to embed its own TMK in these global norms. The narrative unravelled a complex dynamic, characterised by the recurring cycle of China's IP law amendments, intertwined with profound external pressures. The influence exerted by global powers, most notably the US, emerged as a catalyst that led to significant changes to China's patent laws. A significant contention unveiled in the chapter is the intricate balance required between aligning with global IP norms that predominantly favour technologically advanced nations and safeguarding China's unique traditional knowledge in this uniform system. The chapter culminated in an argument suggesting that international IP agreement negotiations should embrace a more comprehensive understanding of each nation's societal contexts and unique characteristics. It advocated for a more nuanced and inclusive approach that recognises and respects the diversity of knowledge systems and traditions, thus underscoring the imperative to transcend rigid, universally applied IP frameworks.

The key argument in the chapter built on these insights and advanced the idea of reshaping the IP framework to better align with China's traditional cultural values and localised practices. This proposition acknowledged the inherent deficiencies of the current IP system, which primarily arose from the cultural characteristics, historical backgrounds, and societal implications intrinsic to Chinese TMK. This acknowledgement highlighted the issues with regulating Chinese TMK under a Western-centric IP approach.

In response to these identified shortcomings, the discussion subsequently introduced an innovative, culturally tailored strategy for regulating TMK in China—a tiered system. This system's innovation rests on classifying TMK according to the extent of its public exposure and dissemination, thus acknowledging the intricate nature of Chinese TMK. This proposed framework offers the prospect of enhanced protection, mindful usage, and equitable distribution of TMK, while simultaneously upholding its cultural importance and societal function.

In conclusion, the chapter argued for a fundamental transformation in the regulation of TMK, advocating a system that is culturally sensitive and adapted to local practices. This approach thereby uncovered a feasible path towards harmonising China's traditional cultural values with contemporary IP rights, presenting a solution with extensive implications for the preservation and sustainable use of TMK in China. It suggested a progressive approach that could serve as a model for other cultures facing similar challenges and contribute valuable insights to the global discourse on the intersection of traditional knowledge and IP rights.

7.2.2 *Unpacking the In-Built Bias in China's IP System: Implications for TMK Governance*

Chapter 4 provided a critical analysis of China's IP system, with a particular focus on the intricate interplay of the country's historical trajectory, cultural richness, and socioeconomic evolution with its IP frameworks. This examination particularly highlighted the influence of these factors on the preservation and utilisation of Chinese TMK. The main finding drawn from this analysis was that the nation's IP systems are not a standalone aspect of law, but a construct deeply interwoven with its rich history, cultural heritage, and socioeconomic progress. This interdependent relationship has engendered a uniquely Chinese approach to the preservation and utilisation of its TMK.

Building upon these foundational insights, the chapter then expanded its lens to critically examine China's significant historical milestones in the development and evolution of its pharmaceutical practices. The analysis placed a particular emphasis on the profound influence of Chinese TMK on these advancements, thereby outlining its instrumental role in shaping the nation's medical landscape. Subsequently, the chapter provided a detailed analysis of the evolving role of corporations, specifically pharmaceutical ones, within China's IP landscape. The analysis underscored how the burgeoning growth and profitability of modern pharmaceutical corporations in China has amplified their political influence, enabling them to mould policy-making processes to their advantage. Such influence, once thought to be exclusive to advanced capitalist societies, has now become a notable feature of corporate conduct within China.

Deeper analysis uncovered several critical insights. Among the most significant was the systemic bias present in China's IP framework that tends to disproportionately favour corporate entities. This bias has often led to a negative impact on Chinese TMK, as well as the original holders of this knowledge and the local communities that fostered it. The study also revealed a historical negligence that resulted in the exploitation of TMK, particularly during the era of China's centrally planned economy. This negligence was inextricably linked to the intricate nuances that have shaped China's advancements in medicine, drawing on a web of historical contexts, cultural influences, industrial developments, and legal regulations. The main contention underscored by these findings is that Chinese TMK, while being a pivotal element in the evolution of China's pharmaceutical landscape, has often been manipulated to cater to corporate agendas. This situation not only poses severe ethical issues but also raises critical cultural concerns.

Drawing from the insights of the previous discussion, Chapter 4 then highlighted the unique dichotomy inherent in China's IP system, which stems from the interplay between Western IP norms and China's deep-rooted cultural philosophies. While these two elements may seem antagonistic, the research suggested a more complex, dialectical relationship. On the one hand, part of China's IP system resonates with Western IP ideologies, primarily targeting the attraction of foreign technology and capital to boost domestic industrial development. On the other hand, another aspect of the system aims to defend China's national interests by protecting its small and medium-sized enterprises and curtailing the influence of Western corporations. This is achieved by placing restrictions on universally accepted IP standards, demonstrating a remarkable fusion of Western and unique Chinese approaches.

However, the study found that amidst this dichotomy, the system often exhibits a marked bias towards corporate interests, overlooking the inherent value of TMK in the process. This shortcoming has resulted in the unjust neglect of its custodians—local communities that have carefully preserved and enriched this knowledge through numerous generations. Accordingly, the chapter underscored the pressing necessity for constant revisions to existing norms, advocating for an IP regime that is more inclusive, protective, and equitable.

Expanding on the critique of the corporate bias inherent in China's IP regime, the chapter then turned to a more specific exploration of China's patent system and its interaction with TMK. The findings suggested that while the patent system bolsters innovation, it unintentionally paves the way for the commercial exploitation of TMK. Its lenient novelty standards foster patenting of pharmaceutical breakthroughs rooted in TMK and genetic resources. Additionally, the system's relaxed inventiveness standard, particularly pronounced in utility model patents, skews favouritism towards industrial players. This, coupled with a relaxed utility requirement, enables corporations to capitalise on TMK without significant value adding. Further exacerbating this issue is the weak enforcement of origin disclosure norms that leave China's TMK and its knowledge holders vulnerable to exploitation. Thus, the primary argument put forth was that China's patent system unfairly prioritises corporate interests, leading to the undue exploitation of China's TMK. This system-induced bias has left the knowledge holders shouldering the detrimental effects of exploitation without enjoying corresponding benefits, thereby exposing a fundamental imbalance within the patent system itself.

Recognising the outlined shortcomings and imbalances, this chapter proposed substantial reforms to China's current patent system, with a focus on embedding traditional values deeply ingrained in the Chinese cultural and historical tapestry. Key suggestions included revising patentability criteria to reward inventions reflecting societal benefits and traditional values; bolstering 'disclosure of origin' requirements to safeguard traditional knowledge and related genetic resources; and introducing statutory exclusions to protect inventions based on traditional knowledge from exploitation.

These reforms seek to balance technological innovation and societal needs while preserving China's historical legacy. They are designed to pivot the patent process from a purely corporate, innovation-centric model towards a holistic one, ensuring compatibility with strategic societal objectives and ethical standards. It was also proposed that a national authority be established to protect, preserve, and promote TMK, thus creating a balanced IP landscape. Centred on Confucian values of societal harmony, respect for tradition, and communal cohesion, these reforms envisage a patent system that blends China's modern legal practice with traditional philosophy. Essentially, they represent not only an evolution in China's legal system but also a continuous commitment to uphold its rich cultural and philosophical heritage.

7.2.3 Navigating TMK Governance and ABS: A Focus on China's Unique Context

Chapter 5 presented a critical analysis of the potential of ABS regimes as a viable mechanism for balancing the protection, utilisation, and dissemination of TMK in China. In this analysis, the distinctive historical and sociocultural context of China was emphasised as a crucial consideration for the implementation of ABS regimes geared towards TMK. This emphasis stemmed from the recognition that ingrained traditional values and philosophies of China can potentially pose conflicts with the foundational principles of ABS frameworks, necessitating an approach that is sensitive to China's distinctive cultural and societal fabric.

This chapter drew attention to the deep-seated Western ideologies in ABS principles and the difficulties they present when applied to China, where the sociocultural realities differ significantly. Historically, China has demonstrated openness in knowledge sharing. This is notably illustrated by the *Compendium of Materia Medica*, a pivotal work in Chinese medicine that has remained freely accessible to the public for several centuries. This openness contrasts sharply with the implications of restricted access to knowledge and resources inherent in ABS frameworks. China's philosophy is heavily influenced by Confucianism, Taoism, and Mencian ideologies, focusing on egalitarianism and communal harmony over individualistic gain. This collective emphasis diverges considerably from the Western notions of justice that underpin

ABS frameworks, which tend to focus on individual rights and monetary compensation. ABS principles, thus, might not resonate well with China's traditional views on benefit-sharing.

In the same vein, China's interpretation of Indigenous rights deviates from the commonly understood definitions within international ABS frameworks. This is because China's policy orientation and historical context have led it to focus on ethnic minority rights, as opposed to rights for Indigenous peoples. This is reflected in China's *Draft Regulation* that adopted the term ethnic groups instead of Indigenous peoples, reinforcing its national narrative and focus on the rights of ethnic minorities over recognition of Indigenous rights.

In essence, the chapter underscored the intricate task of marrying global ABS principles with distinctive national circumstances pertaining to TMK in China. It accentuated the necessity of a profound exploration of ABS mechanisms while stressing the importance of understanding cultural sensitivities, historical contexts, and socio-political realities. This chapter emphasised a mindful approach towards these challenges for the successful implementation of ABS standards in China. This consideration suggested adjustments to ABS principles to resonate more effectively with China's unique cultural-historical, political, and economic landscape.

Moving towards a solution, the chapter introduced an innovative model, which could serve as a viable alternative to the ABS principles traditionally shaped by Western-oriented ideals. This model underscored the need to build a multilateral system, a notion significantly diverging from conventional methodologies. It stands as challenges to the prevailing narrative by promoting collective interests and equitable benefits among all stakeholders. It advocates for the primacy of collective welfare over individualistic gains, effectively reframing the ABS framework. This proposal illuminates the possibility and indeed, the attractiveness of a new ABS model that is more inclusive and culturally sensitive, particularly beneficial in culturally diverse contexts like China.

7.2.4 TMK Information Systems Development in China: Navigating Historical Challenges and Current Realities

Chapter 6 provided a critical analysis of the nuanced dynamics of harmonising Chinese TMK with Western-centric information systems, unearthing key insights for policymakers striving to strike a balance between protection, utilisation, and dissemination of TMK within China's distinctive historical and sociocultural context. The study found that TMK information systems in China, rather than just being creations of contemporary technology, have their roots deeply entrenched in the country's rich history and culture. These information systems were seen as an evolving continuation of a historical legacy that encapsulates a multitude of recording methods, ranging from oracle bones and early printing forms to modern digital information systems.

By unravelling the dynamics of TMK documentation and sharing, the analysis spotlighted how the historical interaction between dominant Han traditional knowledge and the local wisdoms of various ethnic and community groups has shaped the nation's TMK landscape. At the heart of the discussion was the hierarchical approach historically used in China, which ranks knowledge systems based on their proximity to Han Chinese culture. This approach is evidenced in the current regulatory structure of the TMK information systems in contemporary China. Through this mechanism, Han TMK, in its dominant position, has assimilated the many layers and embodiments of TMK inherent in ethnic and local communities, allowing different types of TMK to survive and be passed on to those willing to take on the custodians' roles.

This analysis emphasised that China's unique cultural-historical milieu has significantly shaped the TMK information system's developmental trajectory and regulatory functions. Consequently, understanding these interplays is crucial for policymakers working to balance the preservation, utilisation, and dissemination of TMK.

By exploring China's intricate domestic landscape further, the chapter revealed the complicated interplay of cultural, economic, and political forces that have shaped the formation of information systems such as the China Traditional Chinese Medicine Patent Database ('CTCMPD'). Arguably, while the preservation and digitisation of TMK through an information system represents a significant step towards preserving these precious medical knowledge systems, it has inadvertently bolstered Han-centric nationalism, leading to further marginalisation of non-Han ethnic knowledge systems.

The system in place also runs the risk of alienating TMK from its original contexts, turning dynamic, local knowledge into static, decontextualised entities. Furthermore, this process could inadvertently enhance the State's central role, possibly infringing on the rights and interests of the local knowledge-holder communities, reflecting longstanding historical structures that favour Han supremacism and State centrality. Therefore, these historical, social, and political dynamic embedded in China's TMK information systems underscore the need for a fundamental restructuring of these systems to ensure a truly inclusive representation of diverse TMK and the real empowerment of its community holders.

Recognising these challenges, the chapter advocated for a transformative restructuring of TMK information systems in China. This innovative approach adopted a design-from-somewhere perspective, valuing the richness of local and historical contexts and drawing inspiration from time-honoured models such as Confucian academies. The aim was to evolve TMK information systems from mere static entities into dynamic, culturally sensitive repositories that accurately mirror the diversity of China's medical practices. By challenging the prevailing Han-centric model, this approach would foster inclusivity and empowerment across all TMK communities in China, paving the way for a more holistic, inclusive, and resilient TMK ecosystem that truly reflects the multifaceted medical landscape of China.

Further, the chapter suggested inscribing cultural terms, local protocols, and a classification scheme reflecting diverse ways of knowing into the information systems design. It also argued for a tiered approach for TMK protection, countering the uniformity of the current system and offering a more culturally sensitive stratification.

A key recommendation was the transformation of the TMK information systems into an authoring tool and a nationally distributed system that is not just a static repository, but a dynamic, evolving contact zone promoting dialogues and co-creation of knowledge. This novel system would foster mutual understanding, cultural sensitivity, and an adaptive, responsive approach to technological and cultural changes.

Ultimately, the proposed TMK information system could revolutionise the way TMK is managed, incorporating robust measures, such as PIC and MAT, for IP rights protection and fair benefit-sharing. By connecting the TMK information systems with IP and ABS frameworks, the proposed system has the potential to establish a global standard in TMK management, preserving and promoting TMK in a dynamic, culturally sensitive, and equitable manner.

7.3 Research Contribution to the Body of Knowledge on TMK Governance

Although China has diverse approaches to addressing the key challenge of regulating TMK, the existing literature is very limited, with key gaps in assessing the implications of various legal, policy, and practical measures for the protection and sustainable use of TMK in China. More significantly, there is a significant lack of analysis of the options for implementing various strategies and arrangements that may accommodate TMK's special characteristics in relation to China's distinctive cultural and historical context. These substantial gaps pose a potential hindrance to the successful development of legal, practical, and policy measures for regulating Chinese TMK. Due to a scarcity of published evidence and analysis, it is challenging to ascertain the effectiveness and efficiency of existing frameworks in managing the comprehensive protection, responsible utilisation and suitable dissemination of TMK within China's unique context. This book substantially enhances the comprehension of China's TMK and its associated regulatory infrastructure. It presented an in-depth exploration of a range of TMK-related laws and policies, including IP frameworks, ABS systems, and TMK information systems, along with their legal underpinnings and practical applications. Additionally, it articulated an extensive range of suggested reforms intended to optimise the implementation of these regulatory strategies.

The study critically analysed China's framework for TMK regulation and governance, such as IP and ABS frameworks, through a historical and sociocultural lens that drew its sources from both Chinese and Western literature that belonged to two entirely different sociocultural contexts. This book provided insight into how China's culture and history have influenced the regulation of TMK through legal, policy, and practical frameworks. It also suggested ways to reform existing frameworks in a manner that reflects China's historical and cultural values. These considerations are important because China's TMK is embedded in its sociocultural fabric and health practices through the ages. It represents the country's local culture, history, and Indigenous theories of health before the emergence of modern medicine; thus, reforming the existing TMK-related frameworks by taking these into account opens the way for making an important link between China's past and present, and helps to plan the future in a constructive manner.

This book embarked on a detailed investigation, specifically tailored for policy makers and other stakeholders, with the intention of cultivating a comprehensive understanding of the ways in which China's distinct historical and cultural nuances have shaped the interaction and influence of Chinese TMK, and how these factors are reconciled with three vital global mechanisms for TMK protection, dissemination, and utilisation—IP frameworks, ABS systems, and TMK information systems. Each of these mechanisms, predominantly guided by Western ideologies, presents opportunities and challenges when engaging with the multifaceted nature of Chinese TMK, together forming a robust strategy that contributes uniquely to the overall regulatory landscape in China.

In addition, this book offered valuable insights through a critical examination of these mechanisms. The aim was to identify potential inconsistencies, explore harmonisation and reconciliation pathways, and suggest culturally sensitive adaptations or alternatives that respected the intrinsic features of Chinese TMK. These adaptations and alternatives strived to ensure the effective preservation and respectful utilisation of Chinese TMK, while also promoting its rightful dissemination in alignment with the distinctive nuances of China's cultural, historical, and legal context.

Firstly, the book systematically analysed the adequacy and suitability of the existing IP system (particularly patent laws) for regulating and governing TMK in China's context. The legal analysis of the roles of China's IP system for regulating TMK in the existing literature has largely ignored the special characteristics of China's TMK that have been shaped by historical and cultural factors and comprise values and practices central to the identities of various communities. This book acknowledges the complexities involved in accommodating diverse types of TMK within China's conventional IP system. In light of this, it builds upon the ideas previously advocated by scholars such as Oguamanam and Okediji, who have suggested a tiered and differentiated approach. This approach is particularly relevant given TMK's historical and cultural connections to various communities in China. It aligns well with the policy goals of the IP system while safeguarding the distinctive characteristics of TMK systems.

By adapting this strategy, the book proposes a tailored solution that acknowledges the unique characteristics and needs of diverse TMK systems in China. This solution is designed to integrate seamlessly with the existing IP framework, reflecting the historical and cultural ties TMK has with different Chinese communities.

Additionally, the book contributes to the ongoing dialogue and development in TMK governance. By analysing and applying the tiered approach within the Chinese context, the book offers insights into how this model can be effectively utilised and further refined. It aims to establish practical and normative guidelines for future endeavours in TMK regulation, thereby supporting the continuous enhancement of the TMK regulatory framework.

Secondly, this book adds to an understanding of the impact of China's IP system on power relations and structural interactions (that are intrinsically tied to TMK) within China. It represents the first effort to illustrate the existence of an inherent bias within China's current IP system. This bias has resulted in uneven power dynamics and structural inequality, primarily revolving around Chinese TMK, among various stakeholders. The presence of this bias further challenges the effectiveness of current legal regulations in establishing a balanced framework for the comprehensive protection, responsible utilisation, and suitable dissemination of TMK in China's unique context.

This book provides novel insights for modifying Chinese IP-related laws, especially patent laws. These insights could be instrumental in rebalancing the unequal power relations centred around Chinese TMK and fostering an optimal balance between comprehensive protection, responsible utilisation, and suitable dissemination of TMK within China's unique sociocultural and legal context. For instance, it recommended that Chinese patent law includes consideration of denying otherwise patentable inventions (that benefit from the exploitation of TMK) through the exception to patentability on the grounds of ordre public and morality. A critical outcome of this book is the fresh approach to addressing legal problems by transforming the current approach that contains an in-built bias heavily in favour of the corporate actors to the exclusion of other stakeholders, towards approaches with in-built flexibility.

Thirdly, this was the first study of Chinese and English literature that analysed the Chinese practice of implementing international ABS rules from a cultural-historical lens, focusing on how these practices contributed to the protection, utilisation, and responsible dissemination of Chinese TMK. This book highlighted the worldview bias towards Western ideals and Eurocentric epistemologies contained in the international ABS norms, which makes the implementation of, or compliance with, international ABS obligations a controversial practice in China's social-cultural context. While critiquing the Eurocentric rhetoric created in international ABS frameworks, this book also contributes to the understanding of how historically different civilisational values of China have influenced its unique approaches to international legal commitments on ABS. For example, the Confucian paradigm, with its profound impact on Chinese history, has evolved the Chinese mindset, which in turn affects its modern practices. These modern practices influence the systematic application of international ABS rules for the regulation and governance of TMK. By examining the civilisational and historical influences that are intrinsically woven into Chinese society and that shape its legal thinking, this book offers novel recommendations on how international ABS obligations could be implemented and married with the sociocultural particularities of the Chinese TMK system. It indicates that successfully adapting international ABS rules in China's context involves at least two elements: outward interaction with global trends and obligations by paying particular attention to issues of cultural sensitivity when transmitting the concepts and ideas surrounding ABS; and inward searches for China's local uniqueness and traditions with a historical and cultural-contextual sensibility that is useful in interpreting and implementing the complicated obligations of ABS for TMK regulation and governance.

Fourthly, this book provides insights into the connection between today's regulatory roles of China's TMK information systems in TMK regulation and governance and the country's vibrant cultural history of archival and knowledge-keeping practices. It is the first to demonstrate that China's TMK information system, influenced by the country's unique historical context, reflects an interplay among local, subnational, and national interests, where the information systems' real regulatory roles for protecting and preserving the TMK against misappropriation and exploitation risk being co-opted to serve national purposes. To construct a reliable and knowledgeable system that aptly balances the requirements of comprehensive protection of Chinese TMK and its custodians with responsible utilisation of such knowledge, this book proposed a novel information system. This innovative mechanism is geared towards adequate protection, responsible utilisation, and suitable dissemination of TMK, aligning with the unique sociocultural and legal framework of China.

The overall approach proposed for the design of a novel TMK information system is context and practice-based, relates to the historical context of China, and is consistent with the country's cultural and social goals. This book noted that, in China, there are various forms of TMK held by many different communities across the country, which show broad variations in cultural forms and knowledge. Responding to this diversity, it is the first to suggest that new TMK information system should be open to adaptation and capable of responding to developments in technology and evolution in the communities' contexts and cultural practices. This approach is dramatically different from the way that existing TMK information systems in China have been implemented, where the approach has centred on the end product: the knowledge system itself. Rather, by adopting context and practice-based approaches to develop the TMK information system, the practical effects are that the TMK information system could therefore become a contact zone or an authoring tool that provides the participants and users of the information systems the possibility for self-representation and self-organisation. For instance, participants of the information systems (particularly TMK holders and their communities) could gain control of the development process and construct their own systems that reflect their particular culture and community's needs and are suited to cultural traditions and protocols. Additionally, the study advocated for the parallel expansion of the associated legal and policy frameworks to support these information systems. This would enhance transparency for both the contributors and users of the TMK information systems, thereby ensuring a balanced approach for the comprehensive protection, responsible utilisation, and suitable dissemination of TMK within the unique sociocultural and legal context of China.

7.4 Future Research Directions

Although there are several draft policies and regulations concerning the protection of TMK in China,[6] accessing these documents could be difficult from outside the country. Furthermore, since they are in draft form, they are not yet fully implemented and might not reflect the actual implementation of TMK regulation and governance in China. Therefore, while acknowledging their existence, this study did not explore these measures in depth, as they were beyond its scope.[7] However, the limited accessibility and potential impact of these policies open up opportunities for future research. A historical and cultural lens might provide new options for better protection of TMK in China, and the methodology adopted in this study could be applied to analyse the impacts of these new measures on TMK regulation and governance. Therefore, future research could examine these policies and their implementation to better understand how TMK protection could be improved in China. Moreover, the methodology adopted in this study, which involved a historical analysis of TMK governance in China, could provide a unique perspective to investigate the potential impact of these new measures on TMK regulation and governance. By contextualising current TMK protection measures within their historical and cultural background, researchers could identify gaps and areas for improvement in the existing policies. Therefore, future research could use this approach to explore the impact of the draft policies and regulations on TMK regulation and governance, as well as to propose ways to improve TMK protection in China that take into account the historical and cultural factors shaping this issue. By integrating this historical and cultural perspective, researchers could contribute to the development of more effective TMK protection measures that are grounded in local contexts.

There is a growing body of research and literature investigating the significance and usefulness of IPLCs' customary laws for TMK regulation and governance.[8] This book has suggested that solutions to TMK issues drawn from the customary

---

[6] Over the course of this research, the Chinese government has reviewed the existing legal, policy and practical frameworks, and introduced new measures for TMK regulation and governance, which include the release of the *Draft Regulations on Chinese Traditional Medical Knowledge Protection* (October 2021), and the releases of many specialized ABS rules related to TMK across various autonomous prefectures and provincial jurisdictions such as "Xiangxi Tujia and Miao Autonomous Prefecture Biodiversity Protection Regulations" (June 2020) and the *Draft ABS Administrative Measures for Biogenetic Resources and Related Traditional Knowledge in Guangxi Zhuang Autonomous Region* (September 2021). These new measures represent the most recent policy, administrative and legislative efforts to address the limitations of the existing frameworks for TMK regulation and governance in China.

[7] For a more in-depth analysis, please refer to my article examining the draft regulations: Nan Xia, 'Access and Benefit-sharing in China: Exploring the Extent to Which China Fulfils the Obligations of the Nagoya Protocol ' (2023) 13(1) *Queen Mary Journal of Intellectual Property* 97, 97–120.

[8] Kent Nnadozie, 'Old Wine in New Skin: Traditional Knowledge and Customary Law Under the Evolving Normative Environment in Kenya' in Tania Bubela and E Richard Gold (eds), *Genetic Resources and Traditional Knowledge* (Edward Elgar, 2012) 183, 183–204; Carlos Potiara Castro and Roberta Ramos, 'The Brazilian Experience with Community Protocols and the Building of Prior Informed Consent to Protect Traditional Knowledge' (2016) 1 *Policy Brief OELA* 1, 1–6.

law of the concerned communities were more likely to be successful than the top-down approaches reflected in the existing international instruments on traditional knowledge (including TMK).[9] Nevertheless, there is a significant gap in the existing literature analysing the potential impacts of customary rules and practices on TMK in China. These laws and rules, that have governed the protection and use of TMK in China for centuries, could provide insights to practically improve the existing frameworks related to TMK regulation and governance. Therefore, future research could be conducted to verify the relevance of the analysis and methodology presented in this book for understanding the impacts of customary laws and norms on TMK regulation and governance in China. More importantly, since these laws and practices reflect, directly or indirectly, particular States' or communities' historical traditions and cultural identities, expressing the distinctive interplay of these aspects of their lives and livelihoods, future research could proceed in the same direction as this book, by adopting the cultural-historical methodology it developed to understand the extent to which China's customary laws and practices could help effectively regulate TMK in China.

Further research adopting the methodology presented in this book could aid in examining the degree to which existing frameworks in China might support or impede the effective management of other types of traditional knowledge, such as Traditional Agricultural Knowledge ('TAK') and Traditional Ecological Knowledge ('TEK'). The reform proposals suggested could also offer practical guidance and implications on how to refine and enhance existing regulatory frameworks to manage other categories of traditional knowledge in a culturally relevant and appropriate manner.

Rather than propose a completely new system, this book focused on proposing some priority areas for changes in the mechanisms that have actually taken place in China. It identified areas where change would be most beneficial and impactful, based on extensive analysis of existing conditions. This book has the potential to act as a stepping-stone for future studies, facilitating further exploration and critical examination of other potential areas that could benefit from reforms in China's existing legal and non-legal frameworks. It also has the potential to pave the way for more transformative reform in the future.

Moreover, as novel technologies and modalities emerge and develop in China, TMK shapes and is shaped by them. While Chapter 6 analysed the benefits of information and digital technologies for regulating TMK in China through various information systems, there remains a gap focusing on the emerging challenges and opportunities of the new digital environment. Digital technologies such as Big Data, software coding, the Internet of Things, personal computing, and increased communication speeds have dramatically facilitated the use, modification, and distribution of traditional knowledge (including TMK).[10] This has led to legislative and policy

[9] Paul Kuruk, *Traditional Knowledge, Genetic Resources, Customary Law and IP* (Edward Elgar Publishing, 2020) 346.

[10] Murray E Jennex, 'Big Data, the Internet of Things, and the Revised Knowledge Pyramid' (2017) 48(4) *ACM SIGMIS Database: the DATABASE for Advances in Information Systems* 69, 70–76; Y

difficulties for establishing a more balanced and sustainable approach to the comprehensive protection, responsible utilisation, and suitable dissemination of Chinese TMK within the unique fabric of China's sociocultural milieu. Yet, apart from the general threat that increased distribution and uncontrolled access in digital contexts may pose to TMK, certain norms and rules inherent in the digital technologies and environment may present additional, more specific challenges to TMK and bolster the threat of its misappropriation. Thus, a potential avenue for further research could involve investigating the most appropriate strategies, whether legal or otherwise, to achieve a balance between the comprehensive protection and responsible utilisation of Chinese TMK within China's digital contexts.

7.5 Concluding Remarks

This book explores how China's unique history and culture shape its approach to preserving and sharing traditional medical knowledge. The findings have confirmed that these unique aspects could indeed be reconciled with internationally recognised mechanisms within IP frameworks, ABS systems, and TMK information systems. This harmonisation, however, necessitates a cooperative undertaking that involves all stakeholders, such as local communities, holders of TMK, policymakers, and industry professionals.

A significant factor in this harmonisation and reconciliation process is achieving a profound understanding of the unique traits and specificities of Chinese TMK systems. It is equally important to respect the unique historical and sociocultural contexts that underlie these systems. These factors are indispensable for attaining a full understanding of the multifaceted characteristics of Chinese TMK and its integral role within Chinese society.

As a global influencer, China is in an ideal position to set a worldwide precedent. To do this, it must consistently prioritise the preservation and regulation of TMK in its policies and actions. Additionally, it should actively engage in shaping international frameworks. This approach would ensure that the benefits of Chinese TMK are utilised globally, while still preserving its distinctiveness.

In conclusion, overcoming the challenges of reconciling the distinct cultural and historical subtleties of Chinese TMK with globally recognised mechanisms for its protection, dissemination, and utilisation calls for a transition. This transition necessitates a move away from a strict legalistic approach, advocating instead for a more nuanced approach that is attuned to cultural sensitivities and promotes inclusivity. This requires recognising the intricate and complicated nature of TMK as a product of sociocultural and historical contexts. Through a comprehensive and culturally

---

Yingping et al., 'Knowledge Management Process, Technical Tools, Models and Strategies in the Period of the Big Data' (2019) 63(5) *Library and Information Service* 5, 5–11.

sensitive approach, China could set a precedent for the world, showcasing the possibilities of effective protection, respectful utilisation, and rightful dissemination of TMK on a global scale, and contribute to maintaining global health and well-being.

References

Carlos Potiara Castro and Roberta Ramos, 'The Brazilian Experience with Community Protocols and the Building of Prior Informed Consent to Protect Traditional Knowledge' (2016) 1 *Policy Brief OELA* 1.

Kent Nnadozie, 'Old Wine in New Skin: Traditional Knowledge and Customary Law Under the Evolving Normative Environment in Kenya' in Tania Bubela and E Richard Gold (eds), *Genetic Resources and Traditional Knowledge* (Edward Elgar, 2012) 183.

Murray E Jennex, 'Big Data, the Internet of Things, and the Revised Knowledge Pyramid' (2017) 48(4) *ACM SIGMIS Database: the DATABASE for Advances in Information Systems* 69.

Nan Xia, 'Access and Benefit-sharing in China: Exploring the Extent to Which China Fulfils the Obligations of the Nagoya Protocol' (2023) 13(1) *Queen Mary Journal of Intellectual Property* 97

Paul Kuruk, *Traditional Knowledge, Genetic Resources, Customary Law and IP* (Edward Elgar Publishing, 2020) 346.

S Liu, JJ Zhu and JC Li, 'The Interpretation of Human Body in Traditional Chinese Medicine and Its Influence on the Characteristics of TCM Theory' (2021) 304(11) *The Anatomical Record* 2559.

Yi-Chia Ke and Jiun-Hong Chen, 'Interrelationship Between Genetic Resources and Traditional Knowledge: An Example from Earthworm Fibrinolytic Enzyme' (2020) 39(6) *Biotechnology Law Report* 440.

Y Yingping et al, 'Knowledge Management Process, Technical Tools, Models and Strategies in the Period of the Big Data' (2019) 63(5) *Library and Information Service* 5.

Zhiyong Li et al, 'Policies and Problems of Modernizing Ethnomedicine in China: A Focus on the Yi and Dai Traditional Medicines of Yunnan Province' [2020] *Evidence-Based Complementary and Alternative Medicine* 1.

邓明峰 [Deng Mingfeng], 《我国民族中医药传统知识专利保护研究》[Research on Patent Protection for TMK of China's Ethnic Groups] (2018) 12贵州民族研究 *Guizhou Ethnic Studies* 96.

The manufacturer's authorised representative in the EU is Springer Nature Customer Service Centre GmbH, Europaplatz 3, 69115 Heidelberg, Germany. If you have any concerns regarding our products, please contact ProductSafety@springernature.com

Printed and bound by CPI Group (UK) Ltd, Croydon, CR0 4YY
01/10/2026
02225928-0006